أهلاً وسهلاً

أهلاً وسهلاً

العربية الوظيفية للمبتدئين
الطبعة الثالثة

مهدي العش   ألن كلارك

دار جامعة ييل للنشر
نيو هيڤن ولندن

Ahlan wa Sahlan

Functional Modern Standard Arabic for Beginners
Third Edition

Mahdi Alosh   Allen Clark

Yale UNIVERSITY PRESS
New Haven and London

Project Editor:	Ashley Lago
Development Editor:	Karen Hohner
Production Editor:	Ann-Marie Imbornoni
Production Controller:	Katie Golden
Designer:	Mary Valencia
Typesetter:	Allen Clark

Printed in China.

Library of Congress Control Number 2019956860

ISBN 978-0-300-23371-1 (hardcover : alk. paper)

A catalogue record for this book is available from the British Library.

This paper meets the requirements of ANSI/NISO Z39.48-1992 (Permanence of Paper).

10 9 8 7 6 5 4 3 2 1

To my wife

Ibtissam

and to the memory of my parents

Falak and Abulfaraj

To my son

Noah Burkette

To access the video, audio, and interactive exercises programs, go to
yalebooks.com/ahlan

المحتويات

Introduction xxi

Acknowledgments xxxii

الدَرْسُ الأوّل 2

1. School Surroundings........ 3

2. Prepositions 4

3. Enumerating: The Coordinating Particle وَ 6

4. Demonstratives: Gender Agreement........ 7

5. Contrasting: The Particles لكِنَّ and لكِنْ 9

A. The Strong Version لكِنَّ 9

B. The Weak Version لكِنْ 10

6. Nominal Sentences 10

7. Negating with لَيْسَ "is not" / "are not" 12

8. Use of لكِنَّ and لكِنْ........ 14

9. The Definite Article الـ: Assimilating and Non-Assimilating Sounds. 15

10. Definite and Indefinite Nouns 18

المُفرَدات 21

الدَرْسُ الثاني 24

1. School Surroundings and Facilities: جامِعتي 25

غُرْفةُ مَكتَبي 26

2. *Nisba* Revisited 29

3. The *Iḍāfa* Structure: الإضافة 30

A. Cases of the Nouns in الإضافة structure........ 32

B. Definiteness of an إضافة structure........ 32

4. Identifying Objects: Demonstratives: “this” and “that” 36

5. Colloquial Arabic 37

المُفرَدات 40

الدَّرْسُ الثالث 42

1. Seeking and Providing Information أنا من جَبلة 44

2. Question Words... 45

A. Yes /No Questions 45

B. Content Questions 45

3. The Arabic Verb 48

A. Verb Stem and Root.. 48

B. Negating the Present-Tense Verb Using لا.................................... 49

4. Cardinal Numbers 1 – 10 50

5. Learning How to Say “I know” and “I don’t know” 53

6. Eliciting Information 54

7. Expressing Admiration Using ما شاءَ الله 55

8. The Particle يا 55

9. The Question Particle كَم: “how many”... 55

المُفرَدات 62

الدَّرْسُ الرابع 64

1. Describing Background طالبتان في جامِعة حَلَب 65

2. Forming Dual Nouns 68

3. Number-Noun Agreement 69

A. The Numbers *one* and *two* (1, 2) 69

B. The Numbers *three* through *ten* (3–10) 70
4. Plurals of Non-Rational Nouns 73
المُفرَدات 78

الدَرْسُ الخامِس 80
1. Describing Family Members عائِلة مازِن نَجّار 81
2. Describing School Subjects طُلاّب عَرَب في أمريكا 82
3. Arabic Last Names 87
4. Objects of Verbs المَفعول بِه 88
A. A *fatḥa* فتحة 89
B. تَنوين فَتحة 89
C. The Suffix ـيَن 89
5. Objects of Prepositions 89
A. A *kasra* كَسرة 90
B. تَنوين كَسرة 90
C. The Suffix ـيَن 90
6. Ordinal Numbers الأعْداد التَرْتيبيّة 91
7. Pronouns of Separation ضَمائِر الفَصل 93
المُفرَدات 98

الدَرْسُ السادِس 100
1. Terms of Address !يا آنِسة 104
2. Expressing Regret or Apology Using آسِف 108
3. Expressing Lack of Knowledge Using الله أعلَم 109
4. Expressing Degree 110
5. The Present Tense: Negation and Conjugation 112
A. Negation 112

B. Conjugation 113
6. Secrets of the Language: Prefixes and Suffixes 113
A. Overall 113
B. First Person.......... 114
C. Second Person 114
D. Third Person 115
7. Cardinal Numbers 11–999 الأعداد الأَصْليّة 116
A. Cardinal Numbers 11 and 12 116
B. Cardinal Numbers 13–19 116
C. Cardinal Numbers 20–90 117
D. Inside the Numbers 119
E. The Number 100 (مِئة) 119
المُفرَدات 122

الدَرْسُ السابِع 124
جَرائد ومَجلاّت عَرَبيّة 127
مَن يَقرَأ هذِه الجَرائِد والمَجلاّت ؟ 128
ماذا يَقرَأون ؟ 128
1. Using أي "which" 129
2. Making Polite Requests with مِن فَضلِك and Using تَفَضَّل.......... 130
A. The Imperative 130
B. Forming the Imperative 131
C. Doubly Transitive Verbs 133
D. Pronunciation of the Attached Pronoun هُ 133
3. Cases of the Noun 136
A. The Nominative Case الرَفْع 136

B. The Genitive Case الجَرّ 137
C. The Accusative Case النَّصْب 137
4. Expressing Possession with the Prepositions لِـ and مَعَ 139
5. Attached Pronouns Suffixed to Verbs 140
6. More on Arabic Names 142
المُفرَدات 145

الدَرْسُ الثامِن 146
شاي مِن فَضلِك! 149
1. Requesting and Declining Things Politely 149
2. Describing Daily Activities 151
3. Expressing Likes and Dislikes 153
4. Adverbials of Time 154
5. The Imperative 159
6. Food and Drink 159
7. Prepositions and Attached Pronouns 160
8. Plurals of Nouns 160
A. Sound Masculine Plurals جَمْع مُذَكَّر سالِم 160
B. Sound Feminine Plurals جَمْع مُؤنَّث سالِم 161
C. Broken Plurals جَمْع تكسير 161
9. المُضاف والمُضاف إليه Structures Revisited 163
المُفرَدات 166

الدَرْسُ التاسِع 170
1. قِراءةُ الساعة 171
A. Grammatical Structure 172
B. تَقسيم الساعة 173

سَحَر في جامِعة حَلَب 177
مايكِل براون في القاهِرة 178
2. Telling Time Informally 184
3. Suppressing the Initial Sound of the Article 186
4. Mass and Count Nouns 186
5. Numbers: Reading Hundreds and Thousands 187
المُفرَدات 190

الدَرْسُ العاشِر 192
لُؤلُؤة القَطامي فَتاة عَرَبيّة مِن قَطَر 194
العائلة 198
المرأة العَرَبيّة 198
أسماء الشَخْصيّات الوارِدة في الدَرس وعلاقَتُها بِالتاريخ الحَديث 200
اللُغة في الخَليج 200
الغُتْرة أو الكوفيّة 200
1. The Past-Tense Verb الفِعْل الماضي 201
أ. الفِعْل دَرَسَ في صيغة الماضي 201
ب. Negating the Past-Tense نَفي الفِعْل الماضي 202
2. The Gerund, or the Verbal Noun المَصْدَر 204
3. Noun-Adjective Agreement Revisited مُراجَعة مُطابَقة الصِفة لِلمَوصوف 206
آ. Number: Singular, Dual, and Plural الإفراد والتَثنية والجَمع 206
ب. Gender التَذْكير والتأنيث 207
ج. Case حالة الإعراب 208
د. Definiteness النَكِرة والمَعرِفة 210
المُفرَدات 214

الدَرْسُ الحادي عشر 216
يَوْميّات طالِب عَرَبيّ في أمريكا 220
عُطلة نِهاية الأسبوع في البِلادِ العَرَبيّة 222
1. Describing Activities in Past, Present, and Future 223
2. اِستِخدام قَبْلَ وبَعْدَ 224
3. اِستِخدام ظَنَّ أنَّ 226
آ. اِستِخدام الحَرف أنّ 226
ب. Verbs with Doubled Consonants الفِعْل المُشَدَّد 227
4. Using "to say that" in Reported Speech اِستِخدام قالَ إنَّ 230
5. Comparative and Superlative اِسم التَفضيل 231
6. مُراجَعة الإضافة 236
7. كانَ وأخواتُها 237
8. Calendars in the Arab World التَقويم في العالَم العَرَبيّ 239
آ. التَقويم الهِجْريّ 240
ب. التَقويم الغَربيّ 241
9. حَرف الجَرّ الباء 242
10. Of the Five Special Nouns مِن الأسماء الخَمسة الخاصّة 243
المُفرَدات 246

الدَرْسُ الثاني عشر 250
الفُصول الأربَعة والطَقْس 253
1. Partitive Nouns بَعْض / كُلّ / مُعْظَم 259
2. Converting Temperature Scales تَحويل دَرَجة الحَرارة 261
المُفرَدات 263

الدَرْسُ الثالِث عشر 266
ماذا تَفعَل هالة بُستاني كُلَّ يَوْم ؟ 269

يَوميّات عَدنان مارتيني 270
1. Partitive Nouns كَلِمات مِثل بَعض 276
2. Negating Imperative Verbs نَفي فِعْل الأمْر 277
3. Weak Verbs الفِعْل المُعْتَلّ 278
4. اِستِخدام لأنَّ 280
5. Verb Position in Arabic Sentences تَركيب الجُملة العَرَبيّة: الفِعْل 281
6. Giving an Oath اِستِخدام واو القَسَم 283
المُفرَدات 285

الدَرْسُ الرابِع عشر 288
يَوميّات مايكل براون 291
يَوميّات عَدنان مارتيني 292
1. اِستِخدام حَرف الشَرط أمّا . . . فَـ 294
2. اِستِخدام لِذلِكَ 296
3. اِستِخدام حَرف الجَرّ لِـ بَعد الفِعْل قالَ 297
4. مَحلّ اِسم الإشارة في الجُملة العَرَبيّة 298
5. مُراجَعة اِسم النِسبة مئويّ 300
المُفرَدات 303

الدَرْسُ الخامِس عشر 306
أعياد عَرَبيّة وإسلاميّة ومَسيحيّة وأمريكيّة 309
عيدان إسلاميّان 310
عيدان مَسيحيّان 311
أعياد أمريكيّة 311
سُعاد ريماوي 312
1. الأسماء الخَمسة 315
2. Diptotes المَمْنوع مِن الصَرف 319

3. The Passive Voice الفِعْل المَبْني لِلمَجهول 321

آ. Past Tense Passive الفِعْل المَبْني لِلمَجهول: الفِعْل الماضي 321

ب. Present Tense Passive الفِعْل المَبْني لِلمَجهول: الفِعْل المُضارِع 322

ج. الفاعِل ونائِب الفاعِل 323

4. الفِعْل الناقِص: صار 326

المُفرَدات 328

الدَرْسُ السادِس عشر 330

شَخصيّات أمريكيّة وعَرَبيّة 334

1. Secrets of the Language: Forms of the Arabic Verb:

أسرار اللُغة العَرَبيّة: أوزان الفِعْل المَزيد 340

2. Patterns and the Root System أوزان الفِعْل المَزيد: معانيها ودلالاتُها 342

3. Review of Ordinal Numbers مُراجَعة العَدَد التَرتيبيّ 347

المُفرَدات 351

الدَرْسُ السابِع عشر 354

عيدُ الفِطْر 357

عام دِراسيّ جَديد 359

1. الإضافة: نون المُثنّي ونون الجَمْع المُذكَّر السالِم 365

2. اِستِخدام كُلّ ومَرّة 366

3. اِستِخدام ما عَدا 367

4. اِستِخدام لِـ + الجُملة الاسميّة 367

آ. التَذَكُّر 367

ب. Because of بِسَبَب 368

ج. لِـ + المُضارِع المَنصوب 368

5. اِستِخدام اِسم الفاعِل واسم المَفعول 369

6. اِستِخدام لَمْ + المُضارِع المَجزوم 373

7. مُراجَعة الفِعْل المُعتَلّ 374
المُفرَدات 381

الدَرْسُ الثامِن عشر 384
شَقّة مايكل الجَديدة 388
مُخَطَّط شَقّة مايكل 388
1. اِستِخدام: أراد أنْ + المُضارِع المَنصوب 396
2. The Noun of Instrument اِستِخدام: اِسم الآلة 400
3. اِستِخدام: حُروف الجَرّ 401
آ. حُروف الجَرّ في فِئتَين (two categories) 402
ب. ظَرف المَكان 403
المُفرَدات 411

الدَرْسُ التاسِع عشر 416
مايكِل براون في القاهِرة والإسكَندَريّة 420
عَدنان مارتيني في نيويورك وكَنَدا وفلوريدا 422
1. كِتابة الرِسالة والبِطاقة البَريديّة 432
2. ظَرفا الزَمان والمَكان 433
3. حَرف نَفي المُستَقبَل: لَنْ 435
4. "which" or "who" الأسماء المَوصولة: الّذي والّتي 437
آ. الأسماء المَوصولة الخاصّة 438
ب. الأسماء المَوصولة العامّة: ما ومَن 440
ج. إدغام (assimilation) حَرف الجَرّ والاسم المَوصول 441
د. الاسم المَوصوف في حالة النَكِرة 441
ي. الضَمير العائِد في صِلة المَوصول 442
5. مُراجَعة حُروف الجَرّ 445

الإضافة .6 446
المُفرَدات 448

الدَّرْسُ العشرون 452
رياضات وأطعِمة مُفَضَّلة 455
من يوميّات مايكل براون 457
الخُضَر 458
الفَواكِه 459
اِستِخدام كانَ + المُضارِع المَرفوع .1 465
اللَون .2 467
اِستِخدام اسم التَفضيل الّذي لَه حَرف مُضعَّف .3 468
مُراجَعة الفِعْل المُعتَلّ .4 469
المُفرَدات 473

الدَّرْسُ الحادي والعِشرون 478
جُغرافيّة الوَطَن العَرَبيّ والوِلايات المُتّحِدة الأمريكيّة 483
الوِلايات المُتّحِدة الأمريكيّة 485
سوريا 486
وِلاية أوهايو 488
الجِهات الأربَع .1 496
الظُروف .آ 496
الجِهات الأربَع: الجارّ والمَجرور .ب 497
2. “both of” الاسم: كِلا وكِلتا 498
3. المُستَثنى بِاستِخدام ما عَدا وإلاّ وغَير 499
أداة الاستِثناء ما عَدا .آ 499
أداة الاستِثناء إلاّ .ب 499
أداة الاستِثناء غَير .ج 500

المُفرَدات 502

الدَرْسُ الثاني والعِشرون 506

الإذاعة والتِلفاز في الوِلايات المُتَّحِدة والوَطَن العَرَبيّ 510

من يوميّات مايكل براون 512

بَرامَج إذاعة وتَلفزيون 514

1. "have to" التَعبير عن الضَرورة باستِخدام على + أنْ 521

2. "to be possible" التَعبير عن الاِحتِمال باستِخدام أمكَنَ 523

3. "no longer" اِستِخدام لَمْ يَعُد 524

4. مُراجَعة الاسم المَوصول العامّ ما 525

5. الحَرف أنْ بَعدَ ظَرف الزَمان 526

6. "a few" الاسم بِضْع 527

المُفرَدات 529

الدَرْسُ الثالث والعِشرون 532

عَدنان في مَدينة دِنْـفَر 535

لاليَنيا تَزور المِنيا 538

1. اِستِخدام الحَرف الفاء 543

آ. الفاء المُلحَقة بالاسم 543

ب. الفاء المُلحَقة بالفِعْل 543

2. وَظيفة الحَرف قَد 544

آ. قَد + الفِعْل الماضي 544

ب. قَد + الفِعْل المُضارِع 545

3. Substitution or the Permutative البَدَل 546

4. مُراجَعة الإضافة 548

5. وَظيفة حَرف الشَرط إنْ 548

المُفرَدات 551

الدَرْسُ الرابِع والعِشرون	554
أسرة عَدنان مارتيني	558
رِسالة ياسِر مارتيني إلى ابنِه عَدنان	560
1. مُراجَعة اسم التَفضيل	567
2. "in order to" حَرفا لِـ و كَي	568
3. مُراجَعة المَصدَر	570
المُفرَدات	572

Appendix A: Arabic Alphabet and Diacritical Marks 577
Appendix B: A Key to the Arabic Sound and Transliteration System 580
Appendix C: Verb Conjugations 582
Appendix D: Postcards 596
Cumulative Vocabulary المُعجَمُ 600
English Index 640
فِهرس عربيّ 646
Credits 652

Introduction

Welcome to the third edition of ***Ahlan wa Sahlan***—a complete educational package that presents the learner with multiple avenues to explore the Arabic language: a workbook for sound and script, a two-volume set of textbooks for beginner and intermediate learners, video files, audio files, an updated online interactive computer program, and an updated website. We provide the instructor with an Annotated Instructor's Edition of this textbook and online language resources that include: lesson plans, detailed homework schedules for regular and intensive (beginning-advanced) Arabic programs for both the summer and the regular academic year, ancillary audio and video exercises, PPT presentations for every lesson, handouts, exercises, texts, and examinations to facilitate the use of this educational package in a classroom setting.

Predicated on the success of immersive language learning through functional usage of Arabic, we present to you the first Arabic textbook that gradually transitions from English instruction to all Arabic instruction. Starting in lesson eight of *Ahlan wa Sahlan* for beginners we begin the three-lesson journey into learning Arabic in Arabic; avoiding learning concepts in English that are then transferred into Arabic. We accomplish this feat by using simple, unencumbered Arabic to explain complex concepts replete with intuitive examples, illustrative images, and audio/video scenes.

It was our intention that the overall feel of the third edition would be to convey the voice of a master teacher directly to the learner. A secondary goal in the development of these materials was to produce a textbook that not only engaged the student but was visually appealing as well. The concept of producing an attractive learning/teaching environment was the driving force behind publishing a full-color workbook and textbook, in order to stimulate the learner's desire to spend additional hours engrossed in the materials and pique the learner's curiosity about Arabic. We have replaced all vector-line drawings and illustrations with real pictures; the use of colors allowed us not only to highlight grammatical points, but also to open our lessons with full-color images representative of the Arab world, giving the learner a peek into its culture, heritage and history.

We have increased the number of communicative exercises per lesson. On average, there are three communicative exercises per lesson, all of which are the result of over seventeen years of teaching with the functional approach to language learning. Only those communicative exercises that have been tested and revised, and have received a warm welcome in the classroom have been blended into the textbook to reinforce lesson themes as well as vocabulary and grammatical items. The grammatical explanations throughout the third edition have been edited and, starting in lesson eight, are written in Arabic, with additional examples and a generous number of tables that cleanly summarize many grammatical points in an easily digestible visual format, resulting in enhanced retention and recall. The grammatical explanations in the third edition have been shortened, simplified, and come with more examples and concise bulleted explanations. The vocabulary lists in each lesson and the cumulative vocabulary glossary at the end of the book have been greatly expanded to include more vocabulary from the main reading passages as well as those vocabulary items that are introduced in the video dialogues and scenes. Most of the video scenes are now introduced with short vocabulary lists that introduce new words and phrases specific to them, particularly words commonly used in the Syrian dialect. The video dialogues set up the context for the language functions shown in the non-dramatic scenes, while the video scenes offer a glimpse into Syrian culture through natural interaction between and among Arabs and Westerners.

To the Student

What is the key to learning a foreign language well? Before you embark on your journey in learning Arabic using ***Ahlan wa Sahlan***, Third Edition, you may wish to take some time to reflect on this question. Over the past seventeen years, students have offered nearly every conceivable answer after I pose it on the first day of my Arabic classes. The answer that I have become convinced is "correct" is: to think in the language. No matter what your original answer may have been, thinking in the language is central to learning a language well by practicing it on a minute-by-minute basis. This is possible even at the very beginning of your Arabic studies by containing your thoughts in Arabic, using an internal banter as practice, and gradually widening the scope of language use by introducing new words to your idiolect. Make this language your own by actively seeking out those vocabulary words that you use in your mother tongue. These are the words with which you will be expressing yourself and that, in turn, will create an Arabic persona. The more you practice the more permanent your learning becomes and the stronger your individuality will become in Arabic. We encourage you to actively surround yourself with the language as much as possible, and we have made this quite easy for you in fact. ***Ahlan wa Sahlan***'s audio and video materials can be accessed on our website at **yalebooks.com/ahlan** from mobile devices so that you may listen to or watch them wherever you are and whenever you wish.

Much has been said about the difficulty of learning Arabic. In fact, the United States government lists Arabic as a category four language—among the most difficult for an American to learn. You may view the notion of difficulty in one of two ways: as an obstacle or as a challenge. We tend to think that Arabic is not so much difficult for the Western learner as it is different. According to studies completed in 2006 in which Arabic grammar was compared to other word languages, it was found that verb conjugation in Arabic is logical (less complex than Spanish), its tense system is easier than English, and given that Arabic is a root-based derivational language, it is quite mathematical and elegant in its dexterity—meaning that it is able to accommodate new concepts using its derivational qualities. What this means for you is that you can not only learn Arabic, but learn it well.

The instructional package before you includes:

- The textbook
- *The Letters and Sounds of the Arabic Language* workbook
- The videos (available at yalebooks.com/ahlan)
- The audio program (available at yalebooks.com/ahlan)
- The online interactive exercise program available at www.yalebooks.com/ahlan

All of these components are designed to work in concert, offering you a variety of sources that address and enhance the different skill sets of reading, writing, listening, speaking, and culture. We designed ***Ahlan wa Sahlan*** to guide you along on the most direct learning path to achieve functional language goals and proficiency. We also address known pitfalls and, in a section termed Error prevention, offer solutions before these problems become fossilized. It is our hope that this textbook will not only serve to anticipate pitfalls but will also allow you to experience the joy of learning one of the oldest living languages on the planet and the riches that it has to offer.

The images found in ***Ahlan wa Sahlan,*** in particular those images depicting Palmyra, Aleppo, and other Syrian cities and towns, were taken and chosen before the war and are to be considered historical images of places that may have been destroyed during the conflict.

To the Instructor

Purpose and Approach

Ahlan wa Sahlan, Third Edition, provides learners with basic structural and lexical knowledge that will enable them to function completely in Arabic. The ability to perform language functions such as greeting others, thanking someone, introducing oneself, describing one's background, seeking and providing information, etc., in real life or lifelike situations is developed by engaging the learner in structured, practical activities and grammatical exercises. In every lesson, a variety of such activities is designed to build up overall language proficiency systematically. In this fashion, learners will be able to take part in communicating with their classmates and their instructor by employing all five language skills in Arabic (including culture). The focus, therefore, is on performing language functions by using the language forms learned, not on analyzing them grammatically. This does not mean, however, that grammar is not important. On the contrary, grammar enables learners to use language forms appropriately and correctly—read "enables" here to mean "puts grammatical structures and explanations in the service of language use." For example, presenting, explaining, and practicing the subjunctive mood in Arabic should, in our view, always be related to a language function or functions through use in context. In this textbook, the subjunctive mood is dealt with in the contexts of expressing obligation, intention, and reason. As the learner tries to acquire the ability to express these functions, they will internalize accurate usage of the subjunctive, not for its own sake, but in order to express a given meaning.

In addition, presenting and practicing the Arabic language from functional as well as structural perspectives accommodates the needs and learning styles of most learners. Students learn differently; some benefit primarily from a functional presentation and practice, others find structural information useful. A functional presentation normally activates inductive cognitive processes, while structural presentations activate deductive processes. Research tells us that the human mind, regardless of how it acquires knowledge, assimilates, modifies, and reconstructs this knowledge and then uses it in appropriate, yet specific ways. The aim, in both modes of presentation, is to develop overall proficiency and competency in using Arabic.

Audience

This textbook is designed to take learners from the absolute beginner stage to the intermediate range. At the university level, this can be translated into a first-year program providing approximately 150 contact hours, the equivalent of three academic quarters or two semesters.

The Ahlan wa Sahlan Instructional Package

The Annotated Instructor's Edition

The Annotated Instructor's Edition provides a guided tour of how we have successfully taught from the first and second editions of this textbook for a combined total of more than twenty-five years at the university level. The comments and suggestions on how an instructor may wish to introduce certain complex ideas and concepts constitute a pedagogically sound and systematic process of teaching known as the instructional cycle: Review, Present, Practice, Apply, and Evaluate. Within the cycle, we leave the review and evaluation up to the discretion of the instructor and break exercises down into the present, practice, and application phases. Furthermore, the annotations offer additional communicative activities for every lesson, answers to certain questions that students seem to pose almost every year, and some cultural notes. It is our intention to provide every available means to set you—the instructor—up for success in implementing the functional approach to language learning.

The Student Textbook

Lesson Format: All of the twenty-four lessons have a similar format. They start with a list of learning objectives (both functional and structural) to introduce the user to the content, topics, and grammatical points that are covered. The objectives are followed by vocabulary presentations and reading passages accompanied by comprehension and communicative activities. These reading exercises are followed by a list of words used in video scenes that, in turn, introduces the learner to the video exercises. Grammatical points presented in the lesson are tied to the functions used in the main reading passages and video scenes. Cultural notes are peppered throughout the book and expand on key points of the reading, listening, and video passages. Most lessons conclude with a listening passage and a comprehension exercise, followed by a list of the vocabulary presented in the lesson.

Learning Objectives: The objectives listed at the beginning of each lesson are of two types: (1) functional objectives that describe what learners will be able to do in Arabic at the end of the lesson, and (2) structural objectives that specify exactly which language forms need to be practiced and used in order to perform the functional objectives correctly.

Activities: Each lesson contains activities associated with each type of objective. There are two major types of activities: (1) classroom activities designed to develop interactive aural/oral communicative competence, and (2) out-of-class activities, which primarily focus on enhancing the listening/reading skill set through reading passages of varying lengths, recorded materials, and computer-assisted and written exercises. Written exercises follow the reading passages and are subdivided into five types: vocabulary, reading comprehension, writing, listening comprehension, and grammar exercises. There are also integrative exercises that combine two types, such as reading comprehension and writing. Each exercise is made up of one or more sections. For example, a vocabulary exercise may contain several sections, such as matching, categorization, odd word out, and multiple choice. Some vocabulary exercises precede the main reading passages, acting as advance organizers in establishing context and introducing key vocabulary words used in the passage. Reading comprehension and writing exercises immediately follow each reading passage to encourage immediate review and recall of the reading material. Grammar exercises have one or two sections each, since each grammar exercise deals with a specific point. They are structured and proceed from simple to complex.

Listening exercises (marked by the listening icon) provide practice in pronunciation, word recognition, and dictation, which, in turn, develops the ability to communicate orally by systematically guiding learners through communicative exchanges. Each dialogue or set of communicative phrases is presented at the beginning of each lesson, followed by oral practice of its component parts. Listening comprehension exercises usually comprise three types: content questions, multiple choice, and true-false. Content questions should be read before listening to the passage in order to guide learners to what they should listen for. Learners are expected to deal with true-false exercises at a level higher than mere recognition or simply labeling items true or false. They should elaborate on each item, amplify it, or correct it in order to reflect their understanding of the text.

It is recommended that the listening and reading exercises be done after the vocabulary has been covered, since the purpose of written vocabulary exercises is to reinforce the learning of the new words. The same thing applies to reading comprehension exercises, which must be done during or immediately after reading. Most of the written activities are expected to be done outside of the classroom. The instructor may provide feedback, though, in class or on paper.

Reading Passages: The reading material consists of simple communicative phrases, dialogues, expository prose, or personal journals written by the two main characters, Michael Brown and Adnān Martīnī. The reading passages are usually accompanied with illustrations, graphics, or maps. They are designed to provide the necessary contexts for the language functions listed in the objectives and constitute a source for the vocabulary and language forms needed to realize these functions. The reading passages also provide cultural glimpses of both the target and local culture. The content of these passages is expected to promote general cultural knowledge through the Arabic language. At an intermediate level, such as the one served by part of this textbook and by its sequel, ***Ahlan wa Sahlan***: *Intermediate Arabic*, the amount of knowledge that is imparted to the learner through Arabic makes it partially content-based. In most foreign-language courses, content-based materials represent the first step toward discipline-based materials, where the learner is prepared to embark on dealing with original texts within a particular field of study.

Most of the passages here have been developed specifically for ***Ahlan wa Sahlan***. Thus, the language is rather controlled, that is, it is not "authentic" in the traditional sense of the term, although it has been written by a native speaker. Authenticity is interpreted here, however, in a functional sense, where the language used by teacher and learner is considered authentic if it serves some genuine functional or communicative purpose, regardless of whether or not native speakers use the same forms orally to accomplish the same or similar linguistic goal (see the following section on the language situation in the Arab world). The written passages, on the other hand, can be considered both authentic in function and sociolinguistically appropriate, since the majority of them are expository passages, written communication (e.g., messages, postcards, letters), or personal diaries.

Arab Culture: The content of the reading passages offers cultural insights into the target and local (American) cultures. Since the two main characters are students at universities (Michael Brown is studying Arabic in Cairo, Egypt, while Adnān Martīnī studies computer science in Columbus, Ohio), heritage learners using this textbook might be able to identify with the activities and interests the characters describe. Students should take into account the fact that there is no single Arab culture, but rather a multiplicity of cultures. In fact, diversity rather than homogeneity characterizes the cultures of the Arab world. No one textbook can provide a comprehensive look at culture. Instead, the reading passages and the story line maintained through the lessons in ***Ahlan wa Sahlan*** attempt to show selected aspects of Arab culture. These include food and drink, clothing, customs, family, entertainment, sports, homes, schools, geography of the Arab world, significant Arab personalities, and festivities. The presentation of the cultural and language items proceeds from the immediate to the wider environment.

Grammatical Explanations and Exercises: The grammatical notes in this textbook are by no means comprehensive, nor do they constitute a reference grammar for the student. However, they are adequate for the tasks at hand, providing the necessary knowledge about structures that occur in the reading passages and the practice needed to internalize this knowledge. Grammar acquisition is not the goal of instruction, but rather a facilitating element to achieve the goal, which is to develop the ability to use the Arabic language (Modern Standard Arabic) as native speakers would use it in formal and semi-formal situations. The ultimate test of this success is the students' ability to perform tasks specified in the functional exercises following the reading passages. Students are expected, for example, to provide a biographical sketch of themselves or of people they know, describe possessions and activities, express preferences and opinions, and be able to read and understand simple passages.

We suggest that the vast majority of grammatical explanations and exercises be read and done outside of the classroom, thus preserving valuable class time for conducting lifelike interactive activities with classmates and the instructor. Students can even read the grammar sections before working with the reading selection because this information is about the language and does not require special language skills. Grammatical explanations basically provide information or knowledge that can be learned without external help, whereas language abilities are skills that must be developed physically as well as cognitively with the assistance of an instructor and interaction with classmates. Instructors can, of course, provide brief feedback on their students' work on grammar exercises in class.

Glossaries: An Arabic-English vocabulary list containing the new words introduced in the lesson is found at the end of each lesson. At the end of the book, there is a cumulative glossary, or dictionary, containing all the words found in the individual vocabulary lists as well as key words from the listening and video passages. The vocabulary in the cumulative glossary is marked with the lesson number where each word first appears.

Appendices: Appendix A contains the Arabic alphabet with the different forms of the letters according to their positions in the word and the Roman symbol representing each letter. Appendix B contains a key to the sound system of Arabic and the transliteration system used in this textbook (that is, the Roman symbols used to represent Arabic letters). Appendix C has a representative sample of thirteen verb conjugation paradigms, showing tense, mood, imperative, verbal nouns, and active and passive participles. Appendix D contains the texts of the handwritten postcards and letters that appear in lesson 19 and 24.

Answer Key: The answer key is available for download (to instructors, TAs, and independent learners only) at **yalebooks.com/ahlan** and includes all the discrete-answer exercises in the book, including listening and video exercises.

The Arabic Language

Modern Standard Arabic: The Arabic variety used in this textbook is known in the West as Modern Standard Arabic (MSA) and as *al-fuṣḥā* (meaning "most elegant," "most eloquent," or "purest") in the Arab world. It is more or less invariable throughout the Arab world and is used for specialized functions, including classroom instruction, the electronic and print media, and formal situations. MSA is generally not used at home or on the street for interpersonal communication.

Colloquial Arabic (The Dialects): The previously described features of MSA differentiate it from the various spoken regional and local dialects, which vary considerably from place to place. Arabic dialects are oral for the most part, rarely being written. Variation among the dialects takes place at all linguistic levels: phonological, morphological, syntactic, and lexical. The dialects are numerous, but for convenience they may be grouped roughly into five categories: (1) Levantine (Syria, Lebanon, Palestine, and Jordan), (2) Iraqi, (3) Arabian (the Arabian Peninsula), (4) Egyptian (Egypt and Sudan), and (5) North African (Libya, Tunisia, Algeria, and Morocco). Somalia and Djibouti are not normally included in these classifications because, although they are members of the Arab League, the Arabic in these regions is used mostly as a liturgical language and in some areas as a second language where it is learned formally. Therefore, this variety of Arabic is classifiable as MSA, or even classical Arabic, rather than as a dialect or colloquial variety.

The dialects are known collectively as colloquial Arabic (CA), which is distinct from MSA at all linguistic levels. Learning MSA before any colloquial variety provides learners

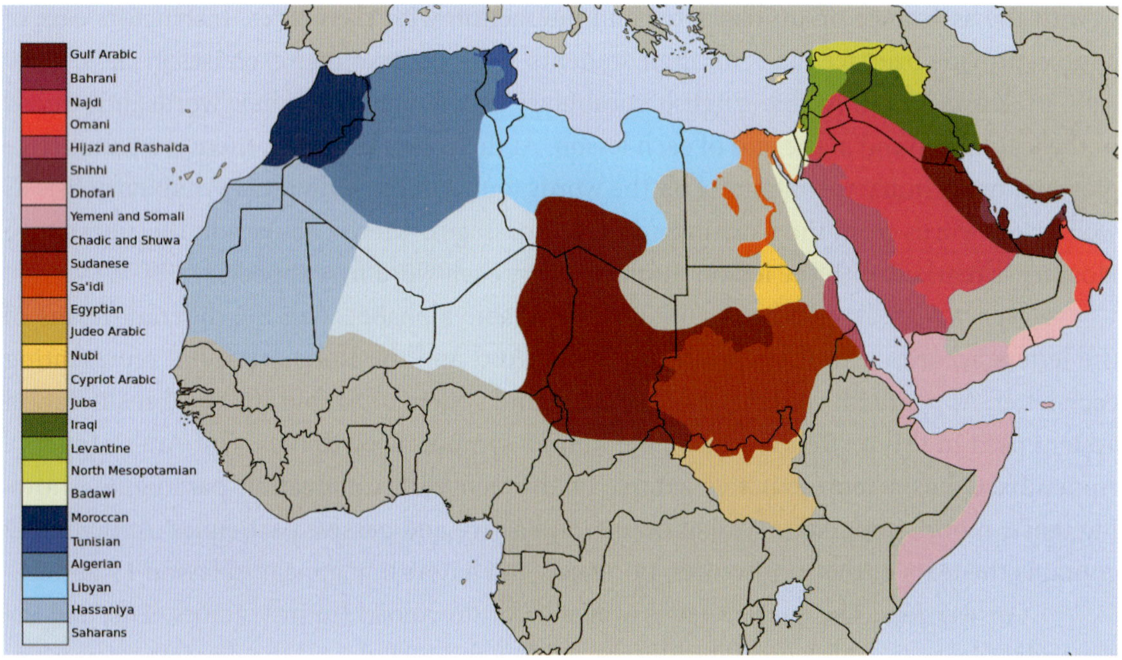

with two advantages. First, a good foundation in MSA facilitates the acquisition of any dialect a learner might wish to learn later, for generally dialects are structurally less complex than MSA. Therefore, it may be easier for learners to acquire a colloquial variety after they have learned MSA because learning colloquial utterances involves applying deletion rather than augmentation rules. Secondly, and unlike local dialects, MSA is readily understood anywhere in the Arab world. In addition, by learning MSA, learners will be literate and have access to a vast heritage of ancient and modern literature, scholarly work, and the media.

Given this situation, some Arabists might object to using MSA as a vehicle for oral communication in situations normally reserved for colloquial Arabic. We recognize this sociolinguistic discrepancy and find that the response to that view may rest on educational and pedagogical grounds. First of all, for most Arabic programs reading is the primary goal, especially at institutions where there is a graduate program. Secondly, in order to avoid confusing learners with two varieties at the beginning stage, MSA may be used to fulfill both its own linguistic function (primarily reading and writing) as well as that of CA (speaking). In addition to the expected reading skills, learners will develop oral skills in MSA, which are, at any rate, required for proficiency in MSA; these skills can be transferred later to any dialect when the opportunity to learn it arises. Most of those involved in Arabic pedagogy agree that the ideal situation would be one that can replicate native-speaker performance in the classroom, but they also acknowledge the restricted nature of the classroom, which cannot accommodate this ambitious goal. Nevertheless, students should be made aware of this linguistic situation even if CA is not the target of instruction and should be presented, when appropriate, with CA equivalents of MSA communicative utterances in contexts in which they are used.

The Ahlan wa Sahlan Learning Package

Arabic Script: The Arabic writing system is presented gradually over the six units of the *Letters and Sounds of the Arabic Language* workbook, along with communicative phrases and new vocabulary. During this initial phase (at least the first five units), learners are of course unable to read. Instead, they should depend on recorded material and classroom communicative activities to learn the language content. Although Arabic script might seem exotic and undecipherable at first, it is in fact quite consistent and, to the pleasant surprise of most learners, can be acquired quickly and easily. Unlike the English system, there is a high degree of correspondence between sound and symbol (each symbol represents one sound). Phonetic explanations are immediately followed by a writing practice exercise that is based on visual information, which is followed by two or more exercises that combine visual and aural cues for word recognition. Practice of the script culminates in a dictation exercise.

Digitally-Recorded Material: ***Ahlan wa Sahlan*** is accompanied by digital sound files that contain a rendition of dialogues or communicative phrases, new vocabulary, reading passages, listening passages, and oral drills recorded by native speakers at a near-normal speed. The audio material is signaled by a listening icon and includes sound-discrimination exercises as well as exercises for word recognition and listening comprehension. All the audio material for a given lesson is recorded in the sequence in which it appears in the textbook: new vocabulary, dialogues, and reading passages are followed by listening exercises and finally by a listening comprehension passage. In the first few lessons, learners are guided word-by-word and phrase-by-phrase on how to communicate orally and to recognize and produce the language forms correctly.

Video Dialogues and Scenes: The audio-visual materials that were developed for ***Ahlan wa Sahlan*** are intended to reinforce the main reading passages not only by establishing context, but also by bringing the subject matter to life. These video materials are divided into two separate learning tracks: non-dramatic language functions and dramatic scenes (indicated by this symbol). The non-dramatic language functions establish context for the various language components covered in the lessons, expanding the learner's knowledge of the register and appropriateness of language use in different situations.

The dramatic scenes reiterate and multiply the main reading passage themes, story line, and grammatical structures while offering a different source from which learners gather information. The dramatic story line takes Michael Brown, who studies at the American University in Cairo, to Damascus, Syria, where he visits his friend Steve who is studying at the University of Damascus. Because Michael Brown does not know the Syrian dialect on this short vacation, he poses questions to his Syrian interlocutors about the meanings of certain Syrian expressions. It is through these interactions that the learner is systematically exposed to new colloquial phrases that are translated for Michael from Syrian colloquial to Modern Standard Arabic (MSA). Additionally, the learner benefits from exposure to two different cultures, as the Egyptian culture is presented and described in the reading passages, while the Syrian culture is experienced through the video scenes. Video comprehension questions get progressively more difficult with each lesson to continually present a challenge to the learners.

Online Interactive Exercise Program: Available with this textbook is an online computer-assisted language learning program. It provides drill and practice in the sound and writing systems of Arabic and contains a large number of vocabulary, grammar, and listening comprehension exercises. Much of the language material contained in the online exercise program mirrors the objectives found in the textbook.

The online exercise program contains drills and exercises designed to help in learning the sound and writing systems of Arabic quickly and easily. It combines the printed word, digitized voice, and pictures for an interactive and effective learning experience. The exercises include word construction, word recognition, matching, multiple choice, fill-in-the-blank, scrambled sentences and paragraphs, and much more. Each exercise format is intended to activate a different cognitive skill and sub-skill. Multiple-choice items make learners view a word in a linguistic context, matching lets them look lexical items as pairs that share at least one semantic trait, and categorization makes them view words as collocations that have some common function in the language. Such cognitive exercises improve learning by re-organizing lexical items in the learners' cognitive structures.

To access the audio, video, and interactive exercises programs, go to
yalebooks.com/ahlan

Ahlan wa Sahlan, Third Edition, along with the supplementary materials that accompany it, attempts to provide a learning environment conducive to effective acquisition of specific language abilities. These abilities, in their totality, create a measure of proficiency in Arabic. Upon completing this course, the average learner may achieve a proficiency level within the Intermediate Mid-range established by the American Council on the Teaching of Foreign Languages (ACTFL). Naturally, results vary with respect to individual learner differences and may range between higher or lower proficiency levels.

Mahdi Alosh
Visiting Professor of Arabic and Applied Linguistics
San Diego State University and Damascus University
mahdi.alosh@gmail.com

Allen Clark
Associate Professor of Arabic
Co-Director of the Arabic Flagship Language Program
The University of Mississippi
University, MS 38677

Acknowledgments

I am indebted to so many individuals whose contributions improved the quality of this work, including students of Arabic at various institutions inside and outside the United States as well as colleagues who used the first edition and took time out of their busy schedules to provide me with feedback. I am especially indebted to my wife, Ibtissam, for putting up with the endless hours I spent on developing the material and for her designing and programming the computer-assisted program that accompanied the first edition. I would like to acknowledge the opportunity to work initially on the project and the administrative support provided by Professor Frederick Cadora, Chair of the Department of Near Eastern Languages and Cultures at The Ohio State University. I am indebted to the extraordinary assistance and input by Allen Clark, who serves as a co-author of the third edition. He brings with him extensive experience in teaching the first two editions as well as the perspectives of learner and specialist. I also appreciate the expert assistance of Fayez Al-Ghalayini, whose meticulous editing of the Arabic portion of this textbook and assiduous input and profuse comments on the grammatical aspect improved the quality of this work and made it more accurate. I thank Lalainya Goldsberry, Hiba Abdallah, and Nevine Demian for providing factual and cultural information about Egypt. The peripheral materials associated with the textbook have received much assistance from several individuals. The online program has gone through several phases to which Abdulkafi Albirini, Allen Clark, Hanan Kashou, Rick Trinkle, Farah Combs, and J. C. Raymond contributed, each one in his or her area of expertise. I am also indebted to Khaled Huthaily, whose meticulous work on the program has made it more user friendly and effective. I thank Nonie Williams and Lana Khodary for the many hours they devoted to the recording of the audio material. I recognize the quality work by Dima Barakat and a special thanks to Karen Hohner for her meticulous editing, keen and discerning eye, and extraordinary patience to provide us with extremely helpful suggestions and insight.

Finally, I thank the outside reviewers, whose comments on the manuscript and suggestions for improvements are gratefully appreciated:

Abdulkafi Albirini, University of Illinois, Urbana-Champaign
Carl Sharif El-Tobgui, Brandeis University
David J. Mehall, University of Maryland
Elizabeth Bergman, Georgetown University
Ellen McLarney, Stanford University
Eric Lewis
Fadia Hamid, Chagrin Falls Schools, Ohio
Ghazi Abu-Hakema, Middlebury College
Harry Neale, University of California, Berkeley
Liljana Elverskog, University of North Texas
Mirena Christoff, Brown University
Muhammad Aziz, Yale University
Oraib Mango, Arizona State University
Roger Allen, University of Pennsylvania

Shukri Abed, Middle East Institute
Summer Loomis, University of Washington, Seattle
The late Waheed Samy, University of Michigan

أهلاً وسهلاً

الدرس الأول

Objectives

- Identifying objects in the school environment
- Describing location, using prepositions
- Enumerating items using the coordinating particle وَ
- Introduction to demonstrative pronouns هذا هذِه هُنا هُناكَ
- Showing contrasts with لكِنْ and لكِنَّ
- Introduction to the nominal sentence and cases of its nouns
- Negating with لَيْسَ
- Introduction to the definite article الـ: Assimilating and non-assimilating sounds
- Introduction to definite and indefinite nouns

«صباح» في الخط العربي

Overall comment on having students read aloud: Ask content questions while students are looking at the reading passages. Do not require them to read the entire passage aloud, only the part relevant to the question. This will help them to develop efficient reading strategies.
Reading aloud may be used as a measure of the students' ability to pronounce Arabic, or rather to convert the printed words to spoken utterances. In the beginning, the majority of a student's cognitive resources are allocated to the decoding-recoding process, so reading comprehension may take a secondary seat at this point.

1. School Surroundings

غُرْفَة صَفّ في فاس المَغرِب

اِسْمي هالَة بُسْتاني. أنا طالِبَة هُنا في جامِعَة حَلَب. لكِنّني مِن مَدينة دِمَشْق. هذِهِ غُرفة صَفّي. وَهذا أُسْتاذي. اِسْمُهُ الياس زِيادَة. هُوَ أُسْتاذ رِياضيّات.

هالَة بُسْتاني

هُناكَ طاوِلَة وَكُرْسيّ في غُرْفَةِ الصَفّ. على الجِدارِ لَوْح وَصورَة وَساعَة. في الغُرفَة أيْضاً باب وَنافِذَة. هُناكَ صورة على الجِدار بِجانِبِ الباب.

2. Prepositions

Look at the pictures below to determine what preposition they refer to.

على

أمامَ

خَلْفَ

في

بِجانِب

تَحْتَ

فَوْقَ

بَيْنَ

Presentation: The "أين game." Take a pencil and place it on a book and say

القَلَمُ على الكِتابِ

Have the class echo the sentence. Afterward, move the pencil around the book, in the book, between two books, etc., utilizing all of the prepositions in sentences.

Practice: Now, take the pencil and place it wherever you wish with relation to the book and then ask where the pencil is. The class will answer in chorus. The learners tend to find it amusing if you ask where the instructor is as you move around the classroom as well.

Application I: Pass out pictures of various objects that the students are certain to have in their house or on their person: computer, calculator, table, TV, etc. Break the class down into pairs and have partners ask each other whether they have a particular item and where the item is.

Application II: Have the students record the items in writing and then ask them to report their findings. This allows the students to use third-person possessive pronouns in their responses.

تمرين ١

In groups of two and three, take turns describing the picture below in as much detail as you can using the prepositions on the previous page. Once you have finished, write your description down on a separate sheet of paper.

تمرين ٢

Fill in the blanks in the following sentences with information from the reading passage.

١- هالَة مِنْ مَدينَة ______________________.

٢- هِيَ طالِبَة في ______________________ حَلَب.

٣- في غُرْفَةِ الصَفِّ لَوْح وَ ______________________ وَ ______________________ عَلى الجِدار.

٤- هُناكَ طاوِلَة وَ ______________________ عَلى الأَرْض.

٥- هُناكَ ______________________ بِجانِبِ الباب.

٦- الياس زِيادَة أُسْتاذ ______________________.

تمرين ٣

Match words from the right-hand column with words in the left-hand column. Take the time to practice writing Arabic by writing both words in the middle column.

صورَة		لَوْح	١-
لكِنْ		غُرفَة	٢-
صَفّ		أُسْتاذ	٣-
في		جِدار	٤-
باب		هُنا	٥-
هُناكَ		عَلى	٦-
طالِب			

3. Enumerating: The Coordinating Particle وَ

Enumerating involves stringing a number of words together (e.g., "She speaks Italian, French, German, and Russian"). Unlike English, where the conjunction "and" is used only before the last enumerated item, Arabic requires the use of the conjunction وَ before every enumerated item, as in the example:

١ في غُرْفَتي طاوِلَة وَكُرسِيّ وَحاسوب وَمُسَجِّلَة.

Important: The coordinating particle in Arabic is a prefix rather than an independent word. It should never be separated from the word it modifies (i.e., the word it precedes).

تمرين ٤

Conversation: Ask your classmates what they have in terms of those objects that we have studied thus far and then write a list using the conjunction وَ as in the examples below. Once you have gathered information on three of your classmates, report your findings to your teacher. As a follow-up exercise at home, try listing several objects that you own, that are in your room, or that are in your classroom.

١- عِندي سَيّارَة وَ ____________ وَ ____________.

٢- في غُرْفَتي طاوِلَة و ____________ وَ ____________.

You may wish to make 3. Enumerating: The Coordingating Particle وَ a bit more sophisticated by giving the students a list of items and asking them to go around the room to find out who has these particular items, as well as who does not.

Practice: Conduct a chain drill in which each person states at least two objects that he/she has. The next person relates what the previous student has and then states his/her objects.

A chain drill is one in which students are seated in a circle or in a single row. The instructor begins the drill acting as a model with the first student. Once the Q&A has concluded between the instructor and the student, that student asks the next student the questions. The drill continues as such until the last student is conducting the Q&A with the instructor to complete the loop.

4. Demonstratives: Gender Agreement

Demonstratives demonstrate things, like "this" or "that" as in:

This is a boy (m.s.)	هذا وَلَد	٢
This is a girl (f.s.)	هذِه بِنْت	٣

In Arabic, demonstratives agree with the nouns they modify in number as well as in gender. We use هذا for masculine nouns (example 2) and هذه for the feminine nouns (example 3). Here, we shall limit our discussion to singular masculine and feminine nouns.

Two other demonstratives are used in the main text: هُنا "here" and هُناكَ "there."

The demonstrative هُناكَ can also be used in the sense of "there is/are" to indicate the existence of an entity. It is used with singular (example 4), dual (5), and plural nouns (6).

There is a book on the table.	هُناكَ كِتاب عَلى الطاوِلة	٤
There are two books on the table.	هُناكَ كِتابان عَلى الطاوِلة	٥
There are books on the table.	هُناكَ كُتُب عَلى الطاوِلة	٦

تمرين ٥

Conversation: In groups of two or three, ask your classmates if they have some items in the picture, and, if so, where they are. When answering, please try to use all the prepositions that we have learned, as well as using هناك and في as in the examples:

١- هَناكَ كِتاب عَلى الطاوِلَة.

٢- في حَقيبتي وَرَقة وقَلَم.

تمرين ٦

A. Identifying when to use هذا or هذه: Indicate objects by using هذا or هذه, as in the example. You will need to check the gender of each noun.

مِثال:  هذا كِتاب

 هذِهِ صورة

١-  ______ ______

٢-  ______ ______

٣- ______ ______

٤-  ______ ______

٥-  ______ ______

٦-  ______ ______

٧-  ______ ______

٨-  ______ ______

Presentation: Establish context and model carefully. It is important to call the students' attention to the pronunciation of words ending with a *tā' marbūṭa*. The *tā'* must be pronounced when a suffix is attached or when the word is the first word of an *iḍāfa* structure. Use words such as غُرفة، سيّارة، درّاجة with personal possessive pronouns:

أنا	سيّارتي
أنْتَ	سَيّارتُكَ
أنْتِ	سَيّارتُكِ
هُوَ	سَيّارتُه
هِيَ	سَيّارتُها

Practice: Drill: Bring in some objects that are masculine and feminine to class such as a calculator, a book bag, a ruler, or an eraser. Tell the class that the calculator (or other object) is yours

هذِه حاسبتي

and then ask a student if the calculator is his/hers.

هَل هذِه حاسبتُك؟

The student will then answer

لا. هذِه ليست حاسبتي، لكنّها حاسبتُك.

It is possible to use multiple items here that are not even in the room through the use of pictures of items such as your car or bicycle.

B. Watch the video in which Fādī talks about what is in his office. Write down what he lists under the appropriate category.

هُناكَ	هُنا	هذِه	هذا

5. Contrasting: The Particles لكِنَّ and لكِنْ

Showing contrasts between objects, people, states of affairs, and so forth can be done by using the word لكِنْ, which is used similarly to the English "but" or "however." There are two versions of this particle: (1) the weak version لكِنْ (pronounced *lākin*) and (2) the strong version لكِنَّ (pronounced *lākinna*).

A. The Strong Version لكِنَّ

noun	or	pronoun	+	لكِنَّ

The strong version, as used in the main reading passage, must be followed by a nominal sentence, meaning it must have either an attached pronoun suffixed to it or a noun that follows it.

This noun or pronoun is considered the subject of لكِنَّ, which places it in the accusative case. Example 7 below is a sentence taken from our reading passage that contains the strong version لكِنَّ.

٧ أنا طالِبة في جامِعةِ حَلَب لكِنَّني مِن دِمَشق.

The word لكِنَّني in the above example is a combination of لكِنَّ and the suffix ني, which is the attached counterpart of the separate pronoun أنا, serving as the subject.

رَنا

ساندي

B. The Weak Version لكِنْ

You may also use the weak version لكِنْ in order to make contrasts, as in examples 8 and 9 below. The part contrasted after لكِنْ is a nominal sentence (e.g., عِندي دَرّاجة) whose preposed predicate is a phrase made up of the adverb عِندَ and the attached pronoun ي. A sentence beginning with such a phrase may be contrasted with a similar sentence using the weak version لكِنْ. Consider the following example:

٨ عِندي سيّارَة لكِنْ لَيسَ عِندي دَرّاجَة.

However, a more acceptable and simpler style is to begin with the negative part:

٩ لَيسَ عِندي دَرّاجَة لكِنْ سيّارَة.

Note: No changes occur in the forms of the constituents of the contrasted sentences as a consequence to the use of لكِنْ.

6. Nominal Sentences

Arabic sentences that do not start with a verb are called nominal sentences. The first noun is the "subject" or is sometimes called the "topic," and the second is the "predicate" or the "comment." Both nouns are in the nominative case.

Definite nouns in the nominative case are marked by a *ḍamma* (see ex. 10: الطالِبَةُ) on the end. If the noun is indefinite, the marker is double *ḍamma* (see ex. 10: عَرَبِيَّةٌ).

١٠ الطالِبَةُ عَرَبِيَّةٌ.

When the particle لكِنَّ is used with a nominal sentence, it causes the subject to change its grammatical case from nominative to accusative—meaning the word that follows لكِنَّ will take a *fatḥa*.

Nouns in the accusative case are marked by a *fatḥa* for definite nouns and double *fatḥa* for indefinite nouns:

١١ الطالِبَةُ تونسِيَّةٌ لكِنَّ الطالِبَ مَغرِبِيٌّ ولَيسَ تونسيّاً.

تمرين ٧

On a separate sheet of paper, combine each pair of sentences using لكِنَّ to contrast them. Remember that the noun that follows لكِنَّ must be in the accusative case and must be marked with a *fatḥa*. Consider the example:

مثال: سَيّارَتُكَ يابانيّةٌ. سَيّارَتُها أمريكيّةٌ. سَيّارَتُكَ يابانيّةٌ لكِنَّ سَيّارَتَها أمريكيّةٌ.

١- صورَةُ هالَة عَلى الجِدار. صورَتُكِ عَلى الباب.

٢- دِمَشقُ في سورية. عَمّانُ في الأُرْدُن.

٣- أنتِ مِصريَّةٌ. أنا سودانيٌّ.

٤- حاسوبُ الأستاذِ أمريكيٌّ. حاسوبُ الطالِبِ يابانيٌّ.

٥- جامِعتي في وِلايَةِ تكْساس. جامِعتُكِ في وِلايةِ فلوريدا.

٦- ساعَةُ الأسْتاذِ سُويسْريَّةٌ. ساعَةُ الطالِبِ أمريكيَّةٌ.

٧- جَريدَةُ نيو يورك تايمز أمريكيّةٌ. جَريدَةُ الأهْرام مِصريَّةٌ.

٨- مِفْتاحي عَلى الكِتاب. مِفْتاحُكَ بِجانِب التِلْفاز.

٩- صورَةُ مونا ليزا إيطاليّةٌ. صورَةُ بابلو بيكاسو إسْبانيّةٌ.

١٠- قَلَمُ الأسْتاذِ عَلى الطاوِلَةِ. حَقيبَةُ الأسْتاذِ عَلى الأرض.

7. Negating with لَيسَ "is not" / "are not"

The statements in the captions below are negated by لَيسَ, which is used to negate nominal sentences. In nominal sentences, such as those said by the professor below, the predicate (which appears in blue) acquires the accusative case (which appears in red) with the use of لَيسَ (see also examples 12–14).

Note: When the man said the word كِتابي, it did not take an accusative marker (i.e., *fatḥa* or double *fatḥa*). This is because the pronominal suffix ي (= my) was attached in the place of the marker preventing the *fatḥa* from appearing.

Feminine singular	لَيسَتْ نادِيَةُ طالِبَةً.	⟸	نادِيَةُ طالِبَةٌ.	١٢
Masculine singular	لَيسَ الأُسْتاذُ لُبْنانِيّاً.	⟸	الأُسْتاذُ لُبْنانيٌّ.	١٣

The use of لَيسَ makes the predicate accusative (لُبْنانِيّاً، طالِبَةً in examples 12 and 13). Accusative nouns are marked by *fatḥa* or double *fatḥa*.

Regular rational (human) plurals that end with ونَ in the nominative case take the ending ينَ in the accusative case. When لَيسَ follows the noun or pronoun, which is permitted, it should agree with it in number and in gender, as in the following example:

They are Canadians.	هُمْ كَنَديّون.	١٤
They aren't Canadians.	هُمْ لَيسوا كَنَديّين.	

Presentation: Use names and pictures of celebrities with typical hand gestures to illustrate the meaning and use of ليسَ. The following examples may prove to be beneficial:

مارتِن لوثَر كِنغ أمريكيّ. هُوَ ليسَ كَنَدِيّا.
مادونا ليسَتْ من أتلانتا.

Practice: Have the students guess where their neighbors are from:

هل أنت من مدينة . . .
لا، أنا لستُ من تلك المدينة لكني من مدينة . . .

Then have them report their findings:

هَوَ ليس من مدينة . . . لكنّه من مدينة . . .

In example 14, لَيْسَ agrees with the pronoun هُم in gender and number (m., pl.). The predicate in 14, a plural noun, takes the plural accusative marker ينَ instead of ونَ as a result of the use of لَيْسَ.

If the predicate, however, is a prepositional phrase (مِن فِلَسطين in 15), no change takes place in the form of words:

١٥	محمود مِن فِلَسطين.	محمود لَيْسَ مِن فِلَسطين.

هؤلاءِ الشَبابُ لَيْسوا مِصْريّينَ لكِنْ لُبنانيّينَ.

هُم لَيْسوا مِن مِصر لكِنّهُم مِن لُبنان.

Conjugations of لَيْسَ				
Conjugation	**Pronoun**	**Number**	**Gender**	**Person**
لَسْتُ	أنا	singular	-----	1st
لَسْنا	نَحْنُ	plural	-----	
لَسْتَ	أنْتَ	singular	masculine	2nd
لَسْتِ	أنْتِ	dual		
لَسْتما	أنْتُما	plural		
لَسْتما	أنْتما	singular	feminine	
لَسْتُم	أنْتُم	dual		
لَسْتُنَّ	أنْتُنَ	plural		
لَيسَ	هُوَ	singular	masculine	3rd
لَيْسَت	هِيَ	dual		
لَيسا	هُما	plural		
لَيستا	هُما	singular	feminine	
لَيسوا	هُم	dual		
لَسْنَ	هُنَّ	plural		

تمرين ٨

Using لَيسَ: Underline the predicate, which may be a word or a phrase, in each sentence. Then negate these sentences and phrases, using appropriate forms of لَيسَ. Make changes to the predicate if necessary, according to the rules stated above. Consider the example:

مِثال: هذِه الطالِبَةُ مِن الأردُن. ← هذِه الطالِبَةُ مِن الأردُن. ←
هذِه الطالِبَةُ لَيسَتْ مِن الأردُن.

١- أُستاذُنا مِصْريٌّ. ______________________.

٢- الحَقيبةُ عَلى الطاوِلَةِ. ______________________.

٣- نَحْنُ سوريّون. ______________________.

٤- أنا أُستاذٌ. ______________________.

٥- هذه السَيّارَةُ أمريكيَّةٌ. ______________________.

٦- جامِعةُ هارفرد في وِلايةِ مِشيغان ______________________.

٧- أنا في الصَفِّ. ______________________.

٨- سوزانُ أوسْتَراليّةٌ ______________________.

٩- الدَفْتَرُ بِجانِبِ الهاتِفِ. ______________________.

8. Use of لكِنَّ and لكِنْ

Contrasts are expressed in Arabic using لكِنْ and لكِنَّ. Remember that لكِنْ has no effect on the structure of the sentence, but with لكِنَّ the subject is in the accusative case:

١٦	لَيسَ عِنْدي حاسِبة لكِنْ حاسوب.	I don't have a calculator, but I have a computer.
١٧	أُستاذُكَ مِنَ القاهِرة لكِنَّ أُستاذَها مِن تونِس.	Your teacher is from Cairo, but her teacher is from Tunis (note the two endings on أستاذ).

تمرين ٩

Translation: Use the following sentences as guides to form your Arabic sentences. Remember to provide the appropriate endings.

1. His school is in Damascus, but his house is in Cairo.
2. She doesn't have a car, but she has a bike.
3. There's no newspaper on the table, but there is a book. (هُناكَ)
4. This is a book bag, but that is a book.
5. There's no picture in the classroom, but there's a teacher and a chalkboard.
6. He has an American car, but a Japanese computer.

9. The Definite Article الـ: Assimilating and Non-Assimilating Sounds

The definite article in Arabic (the prefix equivalent to "the") is made up of the letters *alif* and *lām* (الـ) and is prefixed to nouns and adjectives. It is pronounced *al* when prefixed to words beginning with a sound that belongs to a group of sounds known as "moon" letters. They are thus called because long ago Arab grammarians used the word *qamar* قَمَر 'moon' to exemplify this group of sounds. If you prefix the definite article to this word, you have القَمَر, which is pronounced *al-qamar*.

- The sound represented by the letter ق and those in its class does not assimilate the ل of the definite article. In other words, the *lām* is pronounced as an *l* sound when prefixed to a word starting with one of these sounds. The sounds of this group are known as أحرُف قَمَرية "moon or lunar letters."

Moon Letters (Non-Assimilating)

ء ب ج ح خ ع غ ف ق ك م هـ و ي

In contrast, there are words which start with sounds that do assimilate the *lām* of the article; that is, a sound of this group causes the *lām* to be pronounced just like the letter following it. These are the "sun" letters, which were so named for the reason cited above: Arab grammarians have used the word *ŝams* شَمس "sun" to exemplify this class of sounds. If you prefix the article to this word, you have الشَمس, which is pronounced *aŝ-ŝams* (*ŝ* = *sh* as in *shoe*). As you can see, the *l* sound changes to *ŝ*, thus resulting in two *ŝ* sounds: one is the result of assimilating the *lām* of the article and the other is the original initial sound of the word. The sounds of this group are known as أحْرُف شَمسيّة "sun or solar letters," and are listed on the following page.

Sun Letters (Assimilating)

ت ث د ذ ر ز س ش ص ض ط ظ ل ن

Up until now, you have been using the process of assimilation unconsciously. The morning greeting صَباحُ الخَيْر, for example, contains the article in the second word followed by a "moon" letter خ, which allows the *lām* of the article to be pronounced as *l*. Its response صَباحُ النور, on the other hand, contains the word النور, which starts with the "sun" letter ن that causes the *lām* of the article to assimilate to ن, thus resulting in *an-nūr*.

The article, whether or not it has an assimilated *l*, starts with an initial *a-* sound, which is basically a *hamza*. Thus, the word السودان "the Sudan" is pronounced *as-sūdān* and البَيْت "the house" is pronounced *al-bayt*. This particular pronunciation occurs only when these words are pronounced independently, that is, when they are not preceded by a word or a prefix. The definite article, however, loses the *hamza*, or the initial *a-* sound, if a word precedes it, such as the coordinating particle *wa* وَ "and" or a preposition. This type of hamza is call *hamzatu-l-waṣl* هَمزَةُ الوَصْل. Consider the following examples:

(the Sudan)	*as-sūdān*	السودان	١٨
(from the Sudan)	*mina s-sūdān*	مِنَ السودان	
(the house)	*al-bayt*	البَيْت	١٩
(and the house)	*wal-bayt*	وَالبَيْت	

Important: These processes only affect the pronunciation of the article, not its spelling.

Pronunciation tip: One way of thinking about when to assimilate the *lām* and when not to is to compare the point of articulation of the sound that follows the *lām* with that of the *lām* itself. If the sound of the letter shares nearly the same point of articulation as the *lām*, then it is assimilated. In other words, "backed" consonants (those whose points of articulation are in the back of the mouth like the pharyngealized letters) are not assimilated, whereas the fronted letters, excluding the labials (those that occur on the lips like the *mīm* and the *bā'*), are assimilated.

تمرين ١٠

Listen and recognize: Listen to each word and mark the appropriate box. If the *l* of the article is pronounced *l*, then mark the box under the phrase حَرْفٌ قَمَرِيّ "moon letter." If the *l* is not pronounced as an *l* and you hear a doubled consonant, then mark the box under حَرْفٌ شَمْسِيّ "sun letter". If you are experiencing any difficulty in differentiating the sun and moon letters, it might be a good idea to write the word down on a piece of paper and then refer to the sun and moon letter tables on the previous two pages.

		حَرْفٌ قَمَرِيّ	حَرْفٌ شَمْسِيّ
مِثال:	القَلْب	☑	☐
١-		☐	☐
٢-		☐	☐
٣-		☐	☐
٤-		☐	☐
٥-		☐	☐
٦-		☐	☐
٧-		☐	☐
٨-		☐	☐

تمرين ١١

Spelling Contest: Add the letters together to make a word, and then in the left column write the meaning of the word.

١- جَ + ر + ي + دَ + ة + ي = ______ ______

٢- نَ + ظَّ + ا + ر + ةُ + ه = ______ ______

٣- ح + ا + س + و + بُ + كِ = ______ ______

٤- عِ + نْ + دَ + ه + ا = ______ ______

٥- ط + ا + وِ + ل + ة = ______ ______

٦- صَ + فُّ + كُ + م = ______ ______

٧- كُ + رْ + س + يٌّ = ______ ______

10. Definite and Indefinite Nouns

Obviously, nouns marked with the definite article are definite and those that are not marked are indefinite. For example, the word كِتابٌ is indefinite and الكِتابُ is definite. There are other ways of making a noun definite, such as a suffixed possessive pronoun, e.g., كِتابي "my book."

Unlike English, which has indefinite articles (*a* and *an*), there is no indefinite article in Arabic, though, as you have seen, the three *tanwīn* markers (double *fatḥa*, double *ḍamma*, and double *kasra*) on the end of a noun indicate an indefinite status.

تمرين ١٢

Listen and recognize: Listen as each word is pronounced and indicate whether it is a definite or indefinite noun by marking the appropriate box. A definite noun either contains the definite article **ال** (whether or not it is assimilated to the following sound) or has a possessive pronoun suffixed to it (e.g., **كِتابي**). An indefinite noun ends with a *tanwīn*.

Definite	Indefinite	
☐	☐	١-
☐	☐	٢-
☐	☐	٣-
☐	☐	٤-
☐	☐	٥-
☐	☐	٦-
☐	☐	٧-
☐	☐	٨-
☐	☐	٩-
☐	☐	١٠-

غُرفة صَفّ في مَدينة فاس في المَغرِب

تمرين ١٣

In groups of two or three, ask your speaking partner the following questions and fill in the blanks with their responses.

صَباحُ الخَيْر!

________________________!

كَيْف الحال؟

________________________.

هل عِندَك بَيْت؟

__________، __________ __________.

بَيْتُكَ في دِمشَق ؟

__________ ، ______________________.

أينَ هُوَ (= بَيْتُك) ؟

________________________.

في بَيْتِكَ حاسوب؟

__________، ______________________.

أين هُوَ؟

________________________.

ماذا أيضاً في بَيْتك؟

________________________.

هل عندك سيارة؟

________________________.

أين هي؟

________________________.

يللاّ، مَعَ السَّلامة!

_____ __________!

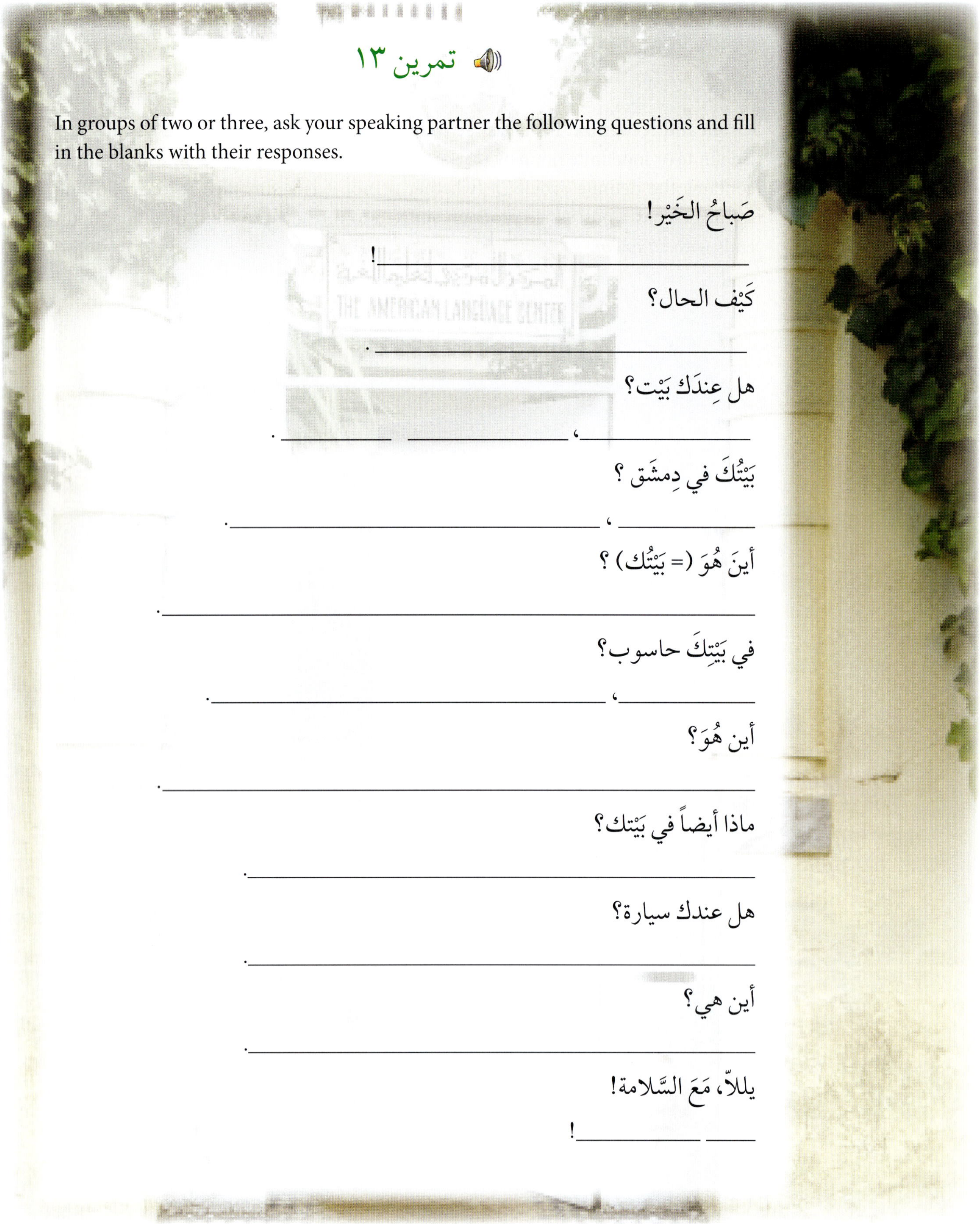

مدخل معهد في فاس

Vocabulary المُفْرَدات

Listen to the vocabulary items on the audio file and practice their pronunciation.

professor, teacher . . . . (n., m.) أُسْتاذ ج أساتِذَة

too, also . . . . (adv.) أَيْضاً

on, in, by, with, for . . . . (prep.) بِـ

to learn . . . . (v.) تَعَلَّمَ

university . . . . (n., f.) جامِعَة ج جامِعات

side . . . . (n., m.) جانِب

wall . . . . (n., m.) جِدار ج جُدْران

Aleppo . . . . (n., f.) حَلَب

mathematics, calculus . . . . (n., f.) رياضِيّات

of the sun; solar . . . . (adj.) شَمْسِيّ

thing . . . . (n., m.) شَيء ج أشْياء

class . . . . (n., m.) صَفّ ج صُفوف

male student . . . . (n., m.) طالِب ج طُلّاب

female student . . . . (n., f.) طالِبَة ج طالِبات

you're welcome . . . . عَفْواً

on . . . . (prep.) عَلى

room . . . . (n., f.) غُرْفَة ج غُرَف

of the moon; lunar . . . . (adj.) قَمَرِيّ

but . . . . (particle, weak version) لٰكِنْ

but . . . . (particle, strong version) لٰكِنَّ

if you would; please. . . . . لَو سَمَحْت

not . . . . (particle) لَيْسَ

place; store . . . . (n., m.) مَحَلّ

with . . . . (prep.) مَعَ

found. . . . . (n., m.) مَوْجود

there, there is/are . . . . (demonstrative) هُناكَ

and . . . . (conj.) وَ

مدرسة بن يوسف في مراكش

مسجد الحَسَن الثاني في دار البيضاء

الدرس الثاني

مدرسة علي ابن يوسف المغرب

Objectives

- Describing school surroundings and facilities
- Revisiting the *nisba*
- Introduction to an element of the *iḍāfa* structure
- Identifying objects by using demonstratives
- Introduction to an element of colloquial Arabic

كُلّيّةُ الطِبّ جامعة دمشق

كُلّيّةُ الهَنْدَسةِ المَعلوماتيّة
جامعة دمشق

1. School Surroundings and Facilities:

جامِعتي

اِسْمي هَيْثم نَجّار. أنا طالِب في كُلِّيَّةِ العُلوم في جامِعَة دِمَشْق.
في جامِعَتي عِدّة كُلِّيّات. هُناكَ كُلِّيَّةُ الهَنْدَسة وَكُلِّيَّةُ الآداب وَكُلِّيَّةُ العُلوم وَكُلِّيَّةُ الطِبّ وَكُلِّيَّةُ التِجارة وَكُلِّيَّةُ الحُقوق.
هُناكَ مَلْعَب رِياضِيّ وَمَسْبَح بِجانِبِ كُلِّيَّتي. في كُلِّيَّتي مَخْبَر عِلْميّ وَهُناكَ مَخْبَر لُغَوِيّ في كُلِّيَّةِ الآداب. المَكْتَبة بِجانِبِ كُلِّيَّةِ الحُقوق.

غُرْفَةُ مَكْتَبي

اِسْمي راغِب طَبّاع. أنا أسْتاذ رِياضِيّات في الجامِعَةِ الأُرْدُنِيَّة. في غُرفَة مَكْتَبي طاوِلة وَكُرسيّ وَلَوْح وَمَكْتَبَة. عِندي هاتِف في مَكْتَبي. هاتِفي عَلى الطاوِلَة، لكِنْ لَيْسَ عِندي حاسوب في المَكْتَب لكِنْ في البَيت. هذِه حَقيبَتي عَلى الأرْض بِجانِبِ الطاوِلَة. مَكْتَبي في كُلِّيَّةِ العُلوم في الجامِعَةِ الأُرْدُنِيَّة.

تمرين ١

Identity cards: Fill out these identification cards for the persons described in the previous passages. Then fill in the blanks with information found in the main passage.

Presentation: Using pictures, present the following items one by one, always recycling previously presented words. كلية، مكتبة، مسبح، مكتب، ملعب، مخبر، أرض Recycling in this manner will also serve as practice if you involve students in repeating the items after you model them. Note that أرض is feminine.

العام الجامعي: ٢٠٢٠/ ٢٠٢١

اسم الطالب: ____________

الكلية: ____________

الجامعة: ____________

١- هُناكَ ___________ كُلِّيّات في جامِعَة دِمَشْق.
٢- هُناكَ ___________ وَ___________ بِجانِب كُلِّيَّةِ العُلوم.
٣- هُناكَ ___________ في كُلِّيَّةِ الآداب.
٤- راغِب طَبّاع ___________ في الجامِعَةِ الأُرْدُنيَّة.
٥- هُوَ أُسْتاذ ___________.
٦- مَكْتَبُ الأُسْتاذ راغِب في ___________.
٧- هُناكَ ___________ عَلى طاوِلَةِ الأُسْتاذ راغِب.
٨- حَقيبَةُ الأُسْتاذ راغِب عَلى ___________.

تمرين ٢

Read and emulate:

A. Study the first passage in this lesson about هَيْثَم نَجّار and replicate it in writing, providing information about yourself and your school. You may provide actual names of buildings, colleges, and streets as applicable to your own situation.

B. Study the second passage in this lesson about راغِب طَبّاع and compose another passage similar to it, but in the third person, describing a professor you know. Make necessary changes in content and form to fit the new situation.

مُدَرَّج الحسن بن طلال الجامِعة الأردنيّة

تمرين ٣

Conversation: In groups of two, have one person describe their university or college to the other in Arabic. The other person should draw a picture of what they understand from the description on a separate sheet of paper. Once you are finished, compare how closely the drawing resembles reality. Now switch roles. Try to use as much of the language as possible, and if you cannot figure out how to say something directly, try to work around it.

جامعة دمشق

تمرين ٤

Match words from the right-hand column with words in the left-hand column. Take the time to practice writing Arabic by writing both words in the middle column.

١-	رِياضَة		طِبّ
٢-	مَخبَر		مَلعَب
٣-	ذلِكَ		سَكَن
٤-	كُلِّيَّة		لُغَوِيّ
٥-	كِتاب		تِلكَ
			مَكتَبَة

تمرين ٥

Odd word out: Underline the word that does not belong to each set and explain your choice if needed.

١-	جانِب	جامِعَة	كُلِّيَّة	طِبّ
٢-	مَلعَب	مَسْبَح	هَندَسَة	مَخبَر
٣-	مَكتَب	غُرْفَة	صَفّ	عِدَّة
٤-	هذا	ذلِكَ	رِياضِيّ	تِلكَ

Presentation: Show some pictures depicting things like a sport and then one that depicts an athlete; America and then an American; France and then a Frenchwoman; Japan and a person with a callout written in Japanese, etc.

2. *Nisba* Revisited

In Unit 5 of the Workbook, we derived relative nouns called *nisba* اِسْمُ نِسْبَة (which function like adjectives in English) from names of countries. The process involves adding a doubled يّ to a noun and can be applied to just about any Arabic noun. In the main reading passage, three *nisba* nouns are derived from the words رِياضَة "sport," عِلْم "science," and لُغَة "language."

١	رِياضَة	*sport*	←	رِياضيّ	*athlete; sporty*
٢	عِلم	*science*	←	عِلميّ	*scientific*
٣	لُغة	*language*	←	لُغَويّ	*linguistic*

If you recall, deriving a *nisba* from some nouns requires the addition of the letter و before suffixing يّ, as in example 3 لُغَويّ.

In addition to the rules of derivation specified in Unit 5, note that if a noun is plural, it is generally changed to the singular before a *nisba* is derived. For example, the plural noun عُلوم "sciences" must be changed to the singular عِلْم "science" before deriving the word عِلميّ.

Word Order and Gender Agreement

Adjectives in Arabic follow nouns and agree with them in gender, number, and case. For example, the noun مَخبَر may be modified by the adjective-like *nisba* عِلميّ (مَخبَر عِلميٌّ), which follows the noun and agrees with it in number (both being singular), gender (both being masculine), and case (both being nominative). If the noun is feminine (e.g., كُلِّيَّة), the adjective must also be feminine (e.g., كُلِّيَّةٌ عِلمِيَّة), where the *tā' marbūṭa* on the end of عِلمِيَّة marks the *nisba* as feminine.

مَنظَر جامِعة دِمَشق
من الداخِل

تمرين ٦

Construct the *nisba*: Construct the *nisba* (adjective) from the pairs of words below. Derive a *nisba* from the second noun of each pair. The *nisba* must agree with the first noun in number and gender as in the examples. You may wish to review the derivation rules explained in Unit Five.

مِثال:	مَخبَرٌ	لُغَةٌ	مَخبَرٌ لُغَوِيٌّ
	كُلِّيَّةٌ	عِلْمٌ	كُلِّيَّةٌ عِلْمِيَّةٌ
١-	جَريدَةٌ	رِياضَةٌ	
٢-	كِتابٌ	طِبٌّ	
٣-	غُرْفَةٌ	مَدْرَسَةٌ	
٤-	صَفٌّ	صَباحٌ	
٥-	طالِبَةٌ	جامِعَةٌ	
٦-	سَيّارَةٌ	اليابانُ	
٧-	الجامِعَةُ	الأُرْدُنّ	
٨-	اللُّغَةُ	عَرَبٌ	
٩-	كُلِّيَّةٌ	أمريكا	
١٠-	كِتابٌ	عِلْمٌ	

3. The *Iḍāfa* Structure: الإضافة

The phrases مَدينَةُ دِمَشق "city of Damascus" and جامِعَةُ حَلَب "University of Aleppo" may be familiar to you by now. They represent a structure in Arabic called *iḍāfa*. The term إضافة literally means "addition." It denotes "adding" one noun to another to form a relationship of possession or belonging. The *iḍāfa* structure binds the two (or more) nouns together, forming one entity. The main referent of this entity is represented by the first word of the structure.

جامِعة حَلَب

The *iḍāfa* structure is equivalent to three English structures:

(1) The *of*-structure (e.g., City of New York, top of the hill, college of medicine)
(2) The apostrophe 's used on the end of nouns (e.g., Sandy's room, the instructor's car)
(3) Compound nouns (e.g., a car key, stock market, The Ohio State University)

City of New York	مَدينَةُ نيويورك	٤
Sandy's room (literally, *room of Sandy*)	غُرفَةُ ساندي	٥
a car key (literally, *a key of a car*)	مِفتاحُ سَيّارَةٍ	٦

So far, you have used a number of *iḍāfa* phrases, including the following:

the classroom (literally, *the room of the class*)	غُرفَةُ الصَفِّ	٧
University of Aleppo	جامِعَةُ حَلَبَ	٨
City of Damascus	مَدينَةُ دِمَشقَ	٩

Pronunciation tip: When the first word(s) of the *iḍāfa* structure are feminine, as in examples 4, 5, 7, 8, and 9, the *tā' marbūṭa* must be pronounced like a *t* (= a regular ت). It parallels the phonetic rule in English of the possessive apostrophe -*s* in that when we say "Sandy's room," we must hear the *z* sound or we cannot tell that a possession is taking place. It is the same in Arabic; if we do not hear the ت sound at the end of feminine nouns in the structure, we cannot tell that a possession is taking place.

As you can see in the six examples above, the final noun of the *iḍāfa* structure does the possessing and the nouns that precede it are what is possessed. The first noun is the focus of the phrase. When reference is made to Sandy's room, for example, the reference is to the room (غُرفَةُ) rather than to Sandy.

A. Cases of the Nouns in the إضافة Structure

An إضافة structure is made up of two or more nouns. The first noun in an إضافة structure can be one of the three grammatical cases in Arabic, depending on its position in the sentence. All nouns following that first noun will always be in genitive case (known as حالَةُ الجَرِّ). Nouns in the genitive are marked in a variety of ways. One of them is appending the short vowel *kasra* to the end of a definite noun (see examples 10 and 11).

the professor's car (the car of the professor)	سَيّارَةُ الأستاذِ	١٠
the classroom (the room of the class)	غُرفَةُ الصَفِّ	١١

B. Definiteness of an إضافة Structure

An إضافة structure is definite if:

(1)	the definite article الـ is prefixed to the last noun of the structure	جَريدَةُ الطالِبِ
(2)	an attached possessive pronoun is suffixed to it	جَريدَتُه
(3)	it is a proper noun	جَريدَةُ مُحَمَّدٍ

Note: The first noun of an إضافة <u>*never*</u> takes a definite article or an attached pronoun. The first noun is, however, considered definite if the last noun of the structure is definite.

Now let's examine example 12, which is an indefinite إضافة phrase:

a car key (a key of a car)	مِفتاحُ سيّارَةٍ	١٢

Notice that the last noun is marked with تَنوين كَسرة. This marker denotes both a genitive case and an indefinite state (double فَتْحة and double ضُمّة also denote an indefinite state).

Remember, if the last noun of an إضافة structure is indefinite, the whole structure is indefinite. And if the last noun is definite, the whole structure is definite.

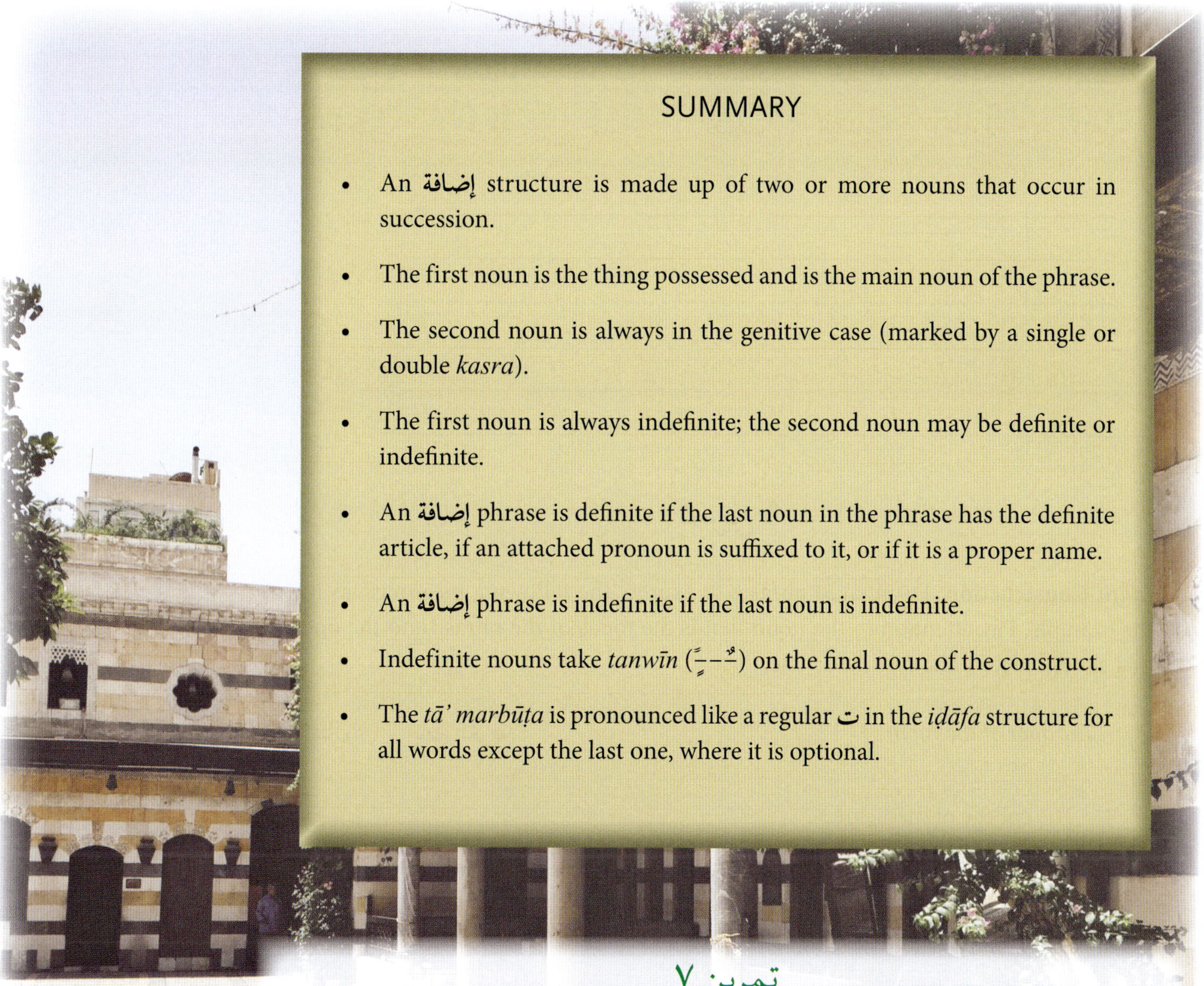

SUMMARY

- An إضافة structure is made up of two or more nouns that occur in succession.
- The first noun is the thing possessed and is the main noun of the phrase.
- The second noun is always in the genitive case (marked by a single or double *kasra*).
- The first noun is always indefinite; the second noun may be definite or indefinite.
- An إضافة phrase is definite if the last noun in the phrase has the definite article, if an attached pronoun is suffixed to it, or if it is a proper name.
- An إضافة phrase is indefinite if the last noun is indefinite.
- Indefinite nouns take *tanwīn* (ـٍ-ـً-ـٌ) on the final noun of the construct.
- The *tā' marbūṭa* is pronounced like a regular ت in the *iḍāfa* structure for all words except the last one, where it is optional.

تمرين ٧

إضافة Identification: Identify the إضافة phrases in the two passages at the beginning of this lesson and copy them down on a separate sheet of paper to turn in. There are 16 phrases altogether, including repeated phrases.

تمرين ٨

Form the إضافة: Form at least six إضافة structures from the following bank of nouns. After that, form three sentences using some of the إضافة structures that you have formed (you may use more than one إضافة per sentence). Pay close attention to the definiteness and the cases of these nouns to form the إضافة correctly.

صورةٌ	العُلوم	غُرْفَة	الأسْتاذِ	حَلَب	جامِعَةُ	الطِبِّ
مَكتَبُ	غُرفَةُ	كُلِّيَّةٌ	الصَفِّ	المَدينَةِ	طاوِلَةُ	كِتابُ

________________ ________________

________________ ________________

________________ ________________

١- ________________________________.

٢- ________________________________.

٣- ________________________________.

تمرين ٩

***Iḍāfa* Construction:** Form إضافة phrases to express the following meanings, as in the example. Pay attention to the noun that is the focus of the phrase and the one that should receive the definite article.

مِثال: بابُ الغُرفَةِ — *The door of the room*

1. The college of medicine ________________
2. The window of my room ________________
3. The car key ________________
4. Eyeglasses of a female student ________________
5. Sandy's female professor ________________
6. A bicycle of a male student ________________
7. A picture of Aleppo ________________
8. The classroom's door ________________
9. Ahmed's newspaper ________________
10. The Ohio State University ________________

تمرين ١٠

إضافة or نِسْبَة? Write the word نِسْبَة next to the نِسْبَة constructions and the word إضافَة next to the إضافة structures.

١- سَيّارَةٌ يابانِيَّةٌ ____________

٢- أسْتاذُ رِياضيّات ____________

٣- غُرفَةُ الصَفِّ ____________

٤- حَقيبَةُ طالِبَةٍ ____________

٥- الطُلاّبُ الكُويتيّون ____________

٦- صورَةُ مِصْرَ ____________

٧- صورَةٌ مِصْرِيَّةٌ ____________

٨- كُلّيّة العُلوم ____________

٩- كِتابُ الطِبِّ ____________

١٠- الكِتابُ الطِبيّ ____________

تمرين ١١

Form the نِسبة: Match the words from the right-hand column with the words in the left-hand column to form النِسبة correctly:

ألمانيّة		صورة
الهَندَسيّة		سيّارة
صينيّ		صفّ
عِلميّ		جامِعة
تاريخيّة		شاب
لُغويّ		هاتف
عَرَبيّة		الكُلّيّة
دِمشقيّ		كِتاب
عالميّ		

4. Identifying Objects: Demonstratives: "this" and "that"

That	This	
ذلكَ	هذا	masculine
تِلْكَ	هذِه	feminine

The woman in the picture is identifying her car (سَيّارة), which is feminine, by using the demonstrative هذِه and her house (بَيت), which is masculine, by the demonstrative ذلِكَ. The سَيّارة is near her while the بَيْت is far from her.

تمرين ١٢

Using هذا or هذِه: Identify the people and objects in the following pictures, using appropriate demonstratives (تلك ,ذلك ,هذه ,هذا). Use هذا and هذه for objects close to the hand and ذلِكَ and تِلْكَ for objects far away from the hand. Be sure to pay close attention to the gender of the object. Consider the examples:

مِثال: هذا حاسوب 

تِلكَ طالِبَة 

١- ________________ 

٢- ________________ 

٣- ________________ 

٤- ________________ 

٥- ________________

٦- ________________ 

٧- ________________ 

٨- ________________ 

Presentation: Identify objects previously presented using these demonstratives:

هذا، هذه، ذلك، تلك

Demonstrate the difference in usage between the two sets on the basis of proximity to the object. Have students respond individually and in chorus.

Practice: Pair Activity. Have students ask each other questions posed in this manner to ensure use of ذلك:

مدينة . . . هل أنت من تلك المدينة؟

شارع . . . هل بيتك في ذلك الشارع ؟

By contrast, هذا وهذه should be treated as regular questions:

هل هذا كتابك؟

هل هذه ورقتك؟

5. Colloquial Arabic

A. Suppression of Short Vowels

A distinct aspect of phonological variation in colloquial Arabic is the suppression of one or more internal short vowels. For example, the word كِتاب is pronounced *kitāb* in Standard Arabic, but in urban areas in the Levant it is pronounced *ktāb*, where the *i* sound is dropped. The same process applies to جامِعة (*jāmi'a*), which is pronounced *jām'a* in colloquial speech, where the short vowel *i* is deleted.

B. Quality of the Vowel Preceding ة:

The word (مُسَجِّلَة) exemplifies another phonological process in Levantine colloquial Arabic: the change of the *a* sound preceding the *tā' marbūṭa* into an *e* sound (as in *net*) after certain consonants in feminine nouns. For example, no change in the final vowel occurs in صورة, but the word طاولة (*ṭāwila*) is pronounced *ṭāwle* in Syrian colloquial speech, where the *a* sound changes into an *e* sound. Below is a classification of consonants in final word positions that are followed by the sound *a* in feminine nouns and adjectives in Syrian colloquial speech as well as those followed by the *e* sound. Please note that this is a general rule and that variations do exist.

Consonants preceding the ة followed by an *a* sound:

ح خ ع غ ق هـ و ر ص ض ط ظ ل

Consonants preceding the ة followed by an *e* sound:

ب ج ف ك م ي ت ث د ذ س ش

Pronunciation note: The letter ق is usually pronounced as a glottal stop (i.e., *hamza*) in Arabic dialects in some urban centers, such as Damascus, Jerusalem, Beirut, Amman, and Cairo. In some other areas, it is pronounced [g] or [q].

تمرين ١٣

A. Listen and answer: Select the alternative that best represents the information from the listening passage.

١- اِسمُ الأُسْتاذ نَديم . . .

☐ ساحوري ☐ ساهوري ☐ سَمْهوري

٢- الأُسْتاذ نَديم مِن جامِعَة . . .

☐ القُدْس ☐ الآداب ☐ بير زَيْت

٣- مَكتَبُ الأُسْتاذ نَديم في كُلِّيَّةِ . . .

☐ الآداب ☐ العُلوم ☐ الطِبّ

٤- في مَكتَبِ الأُسْتاذ نَديم صورَة مَدينَة . . .

☐ بير زَيْت ☐ القُدس ☐ فِلَسطين

B. Mark the following statement صَواب (true) or خَطَأ (false) based on the information in the listening passage and correct any false statements.

٥- لَيسَ عِندَ الأُسْتاذ نَديم حاسوب. ______________

٦- هُناكَ هاتِف عَلى طاوِلَةِ الأُسْتاذ نَديم. ______________

٧- صورَة مَدينَةِ القُدس عَلى جِدارِ المَكتَب. ______________

صَواب = 

خَطأ = 

تمرين ١٤

Online: Video for Lesson 2. When you are watching the dialogues, become an active participant by repeating what you hear, trying to imitate the sounds and inflections used in the scenes.

Answer the following questions:

١ - في جامِعة فادي عيسى عِدّة كُلّيّات، ما هي؟

________________ ________________

________________ ________________

________________ ________________

٢ - ماذا يُوجَد في مَكْتَب سامر نصر؟

________________ ________________

________________ ________________

________________ ________________

جامِعة القاهِرة في مِصر

Vocabulary المُفْرَدات

Listen to the vocabulary items on the audio and practice their pronunciation.

literature . . . . (n., m.) أَدَب ج آداب

ground . . . . (n., f.) أَرْض ج أَراضٍ

those . . . . (pl., demonstrative) أولائِكَ

house, home . . . .(n., m.) بَيْت ج بُيوت

those . . . . (dual, nom.; *rare*) تانِكَ

trade, business, commerce . . . . (n., f.) تِجارة

that . . . . (n., f., sg.) تِلكَ

those . . . . (dual, acc., gen.; *rare*) تَيْنِكَ

right, law. (n., m.) حَقّ ج حُقوق

that . . . . (n., m., s.) ذلِكَ

sport . . . . (n., f.) رِياضَة ج رِياضات

of sports . . . .(adj.) رياضيّ

medicine. . . . . (m.) طِبّ

a number of, several . . . . (n., f.) عِدَّةُ

science, discipline. . . . . (n., m.) عِلْم ج عُلوم

of science, scientific. . . . . (adj.) عِلميّ

college . . . . (n., f.) كُلِّيَّة ج كُلِّيات

language . . . . (n., f.) لُغَة ج لُغات

of language, linguistic . . . . (adj.) لُغَويّ

laboratory . . . . (n., m.) مَخْبَر ج مَخابِر

swimming pool . . . . (n., m.) مَسْبَح ج مَسابِح

office . . . . (n., m.) مَكْتَب ج مَكاتِب

library, bookstore, bookcase . . . . (n., f.) مَكْتَبة ج مَكْتَبات

playground, sports field . . . . (n., m.) مَلْعَب ج مَلاعِب

these . . . . (dual, f., nom.) هاتانِ

these . . . . (dual, f., acc., gen.) هاتَيْنِ

these . . . . (dual, m., nom.) هذانِ

these . . . . (dual, m., acc., gen.) هذَيْنِ

engineering . . . . (n., f.) هَنْدَسَة

these . . . . (pl., m.) هؤُلاءِ

مِن مَخطوطات طِبيّة يَرجِع تاريخُها إلى عام ١٢٢٤ م

الدرس الثالث

مُقابَلة صَحافيّة

Objectives

- Seeking and providing information
- Asking yes/no and content questions
- Introduction to the Arabic verb
- Introduction to the cardinal numbers 1–10
- Learning how to say "I know" أعْرِف and "I don't know" لا أعْرِف
- Eliciting information using ما مَعنى
- Expressing admiration using ما شاء الله
- Introduction to the particle يا
- Introduction to the question particle كَم

تمرين ١

Matching: Match words from the right-hand column with words in the left-hand column. Take the time to practice writing Arabic by writing both words in the middle column.

تِجارَة		بَلْدَة	١-
ثَلاثَة		عُنوان	٢-
عَفْواً		العَرَبِيَّة	٣-
مَدينَة		رَقْم	٤-
شارِع		بِطاقَة	٥-
لُغَة		شُكْراً	٦-
هُوِيَّة			

1. Seeking and Providing Information

Presentation: The context in this lesson is that of a job interview, which involves eliciting and providing personal information. In the classroom, build on what the students already know. First ask their names, where they come from, where they live, and where their hometowns are located.
Delay teaching phone numbers, home addresses, and number of languages they know until after the numbers are adequately practiced.

أنا مِنْ جَبْلة

المَرأة: مَرحباً!

الرَّجُل: أهلاً!

المَرأة: ما اسْمُكَ؟

الرَّجُل: اِسْمي نِزار حَدّاد.

المَرأة: مِن أينَ أنْتَ؟

الرَّجُل: أنا مِنْ جَبْلة.

المَرأة: أينَ جَبلة؟

الرَّجُل: هذِه بَلْدَة في سورِيَة.

المَرأة: ما عُنوانُكَ؟

الرَّجُل: ٥ شارِع ابن خَلدون.

المَرأة: أتَسْكُن في شَقَّة أم في بَيْت؟

الرَّجُل: أسْكُن في شَقَّة.

المَرأة: عِندَكَ سَيّارَة؟

الرَّجُل: نَعَم، عِندي سَيّارَة.

المَرأة: هَل عِندَكَ هاتِف في شَقَّتِكَ؟

الرَّجُل: نَعَم، عِندي هاتِف.

المَرأة: ما رَقْم هاتِفِكَ؟

الرَّجُل: رَقْم هاتِفي سِتّة صِفْر واحِد خَمْسَة سَبْعَة تِسْعَة أرْبعَة.

المَرأة: هَل عِندَكَ حاسوب؟

الرَّجُل: لا. لَيسَ عِندي حاسوب.

المَرأة: شُكْراً.

الرَّجُل: عَفْواً.

مدينة جبلة في سوريا

بعض الشقق في جبلة

مدرج روماني في جبلة

Reflecting on our reading: In the above passage we were introduced to our first verb. From context, can you guess the meaning of أَسْكُنُ and تَسْكُنُ in this present tense verb?

أنا أَسْكُن في شَقَّة وأنْتَ تَسْكُن في بَيْت.

2. Question Words

The main reading/listening passage included a variety of different ways to pose questions in Arabic. Let's take a look at some Arabic question particles and how they are used:

A. Yes/No Questions

Yes/no questions may be posed either by rising intonation on the last word of the question, or by using the question particles هَلْ and أَ. These question particles can be inserted at the beginning of a sentence without causing any changes in word order or in the forms of the words.

Note: The particle أَمْ "or" is used in questions (e.g., عِندَك سَيّارة أم دَرّاجة؟), its counterpart أَوْ "or" is used in statements (e.g., اليوم أو غداً).

B. Content Questions

Questions that seek information concerning time, place, manner, or reason use other question particles or words.

Yes/No Questions	أَ		هَلْ		
Content Questions	أَيْنَ *where*	ما *what*	ماذا *what (verbs)*	مَنْ *who*	كَيْفَ *how*

In this interview أَيْنَ "where" and ما "what" are used. أين is used to inquire about the location of someone or something and ما inquires about the identity of something. The particle ما is followed by a noun or a pronoun (e.g., ما اسْمُك؟ "What's your name?" ما هُو؟ "What is it?").

Notice that أينَ "where" and مَنْ "who" may be followed by either a noun, a pronoun, or a verb:

	أينَ	مَن
١	أينَ جَبْلَة؟	مَنْ هُناكَ؟
٢	أينَ هِيَ؟	مَن هُوَ؟
٣	أينَ تَسْكُن؟	مَنْ يَسْكُن في الشَقَّة؟

The particle ماذا "what" is usually used before verbs:

٤	ماذا يَدْرُس زياد؟

The question word كَيْفَ "how" is used to inquire about a state of affairs, that is, the process or manner of doing something:

٥	كَيفَ الحال؟
٦	كَيفَ تَعْرِف عُنوانه؟

Note: These question words cause no change either in the form or order of the words in a sentence.

SUMMARY

- The particles هَلْ and أ are used for forming yes/no questions. They are placed at the beginning of a sentence, but they do not cause any structural changes.
- Question particles cause no change either in word form or order.

Presentation: Using pictures of your family, show where you live and state:

أنا أسكن في بيت/ شقّة.

followed by pictures of your family:

هذه نانسي وهي تسكن في فلوريدا

هذا سامي وهو يسكن في ولاية . . . في بيت كبير.

هذه مريم وهي تسكن في . . .

Now ask students individually, "أين تسكن\تسكنين؟" The students may conjugate the verb incorrectly. Just gently repeat the sentence the student said, but correctly emphasizing the words:

أنا أسكن

while pointing to yourself. Some students will catch on to the conjugations here and start helping the other students understand. Rarely will you have to break out of Arabic to explain something.

Practice: Directly after asking one student (e.g., Marie) where she lives, ask another student where Marie lives to check student comprehension as well as to make sure the class is paying attention to the content of what is being said. Students usually respond in first-person (I live in . . .). Simply indicate that you are now talking about Marie and that the exercise has just gotten a little more sophisticated.

Application: Pair Activity. Pass out some pictures of celebrities, political personalities, and well-known characters (cartoon, fictional, or real) and have the students talk about where these people are (geographical location, house/apartment) and record their answers. Upon completion of the task, have the students show the class their pictures and describe the character and where he/she lives.

تمرين ٢

Ask your classmate: Use the question particles presented in this lesson to pose questions to your classmates. Write your answers down on a separate sheet of paper and be prepared to report this information to your instructor. Find out . . .

1. where the library is and whether it is a city or university library
2. whether or not your classmate has a car and if so, where it is
3. if they have a morning class and if so, what it is
4. where the language laboratory is and what is in it
5. who the professor of Arabic is

تمرين ٣

What's the Question? Read the answers to come up with the proper questions, then write the questions in the blanks:

١	.............................؟	٥	.............................؟
	اسمي ماهِر فَتْحي.		عُمري خَمس وعِشرون سَنة.
٢	.............................؟	٦	.............................؟
	أسكن في مصر الجديدة.		عُنواني مِصر الجَديدة، شارِع النيل، بِناية رَقم ٥.
٣	.............................؟	٧	.............................؟
	أدرس التاريخ في جامعة عين شمس.		لا، لَستُ مُتَزَوِّجاً.
٤	.............................؟	٨	.............................؟
	نَعم، أعرِف اللُغة العربية والإنكليزيّة.		أنا الآن أذهَب إلى مَكتَبة الجامِعة.

تمرين ٤

Conversation: Interview a classmate or pretend to interview your favorite personality using the question particles from this lesson to elicit information. Then write a short paragraph about that person in terms of name, address, origin, school, possessions, and place of residence. The example paragraph on the following page gives information about هالَة بُسْتاني, the student who was described in Lesson 1.

هالَة بُسْتاني طالِبَة مِن مَدينَة دِمَشق. عُنْوانُها ٨ شارِع الكَواكِبيّ في مَدينَة حَلَب. هِيَ طالِبَة في جامِعَة حَلَب. لَيْسَ عِندَ هالَة سَيّارة، لكِنْ دَرّاجة. تَسْكُن هالَة في شَقّة. هِيَ لا تَسْكُن في سَكَنِ الطالِبات.

3. The Arabic Verb

A. Verb Stem and Root

The dialogue at the beginning of this lesson introduces the first verb in this textbook. There are two instances of the verb "to live": the first time it was used in second-person masculine singular (تَسْكُنُ "you live") and the second time it was used in first-person singular (أَسْكُنُ "I live"). In English, both instances have the same form: "live." In Arabic, however, verbs vary in form because, unlike English, person is indicated in verbs as a prefix, suffix, or both. In addition, the form of a verb is affected by tense, number, and gender. At this point, we will consider the present tense, or the imperfect, which indicates an uncompleted or unfinished action. The conjugation table on the following page illustrates six forms which correspond to six personal pronouns. As we learned in Unit 4 of the Workbook, there are a total of 14 Arabic pronouns.

If you look closely, you will find that the initial letter of the verb forms changes because a prefix is added to the stem of the verb (سْكُن). In the second-person feminine, the Arabic verb always takes a prefix as well as a suffix. As a rule, all present-tense conjugations must contain prefixes, but some have both prefixes and suffixes, and these attached suffixes indicate gender (ين 2nd f.sg. as in our example), or number (= ان for dual, ون for m.pl., ـنَ for f.pl.). We have highlighted in blue the prefix and suffix for second-person feminine singular to make the stem (سْكُن) apparent.

تَسْكُنينَ	←	أَنْتِ تَسْكُنينَ

Dictionary Use: Arabic verbs (and almost all derivatives) are generally organized in the dictionary according to their root, which is the minimal form of a word. Like most Arabic verbs, the root of the verb in our example is made up of the three letters (س ك ن).

Unlike English, verbs are cited in the third-person masculine singular past tense (e.g., سَكَنَ "he lived"). In other words, no true infinitive exists in Arabic (= to live; to reside); third-person past tense is used instead.

Present-Tense Conjugations of the Verb سَكَنَ		
English	**Arabic Verb Form**	**Separate Pronoun**
I live	أَسْكُن	أنا
we live	نَسْكُن	نَحْنُ
you (m.) live	تَسْكُن	أَنْتَ
you (f.) live	تَسْكُنينَ	أَنْتِ
he lives	يَسْكُن	هُوَ
she lives	تَسْكُن	هِيَ

B. Negating the Present-Tense Verb using لا

Negating the present is done simply by using the negative particle لا (which as we have learned also means "no") before the verb. The use of لا does not affect the form of the verb in any way. Consider the following examples:

I live in a house.	أَسْكُن في بَيْت.	٨
I don't live in an apartment.	لا أَسْكُن في شَقَّة.	٩

تمرين ٥

Asking/answering questions: Now that we have learned how to form questions and the present-tense verb, let's put this knowledge to use. Answer the following questions about yourself on a separate sheet of paper.

١- ما اسْمُك؟

٢- ما عُنوانُك؟

٣- مِنْ أَيْنَ أَنْت؟

٤- ما اسْم جامِعَتِك؟

٥- هَل عِندَكَ / عِندَكِ دَرّاجة أو سَيّارة أو حاسوب أو هاتِف؟

٦- هَل تَسْكُن / تَسْكُنينَ في شَقَّة أَمْ في بَيْت؟

4. Cardinal Numbers 1–10

ما رَقْم هاتِفِكِ؟

رَقْم هاتِفي ٤٦٨٢٣٧٥.

Cardinal numbers may be used for counting and labeling things. Let's consider counting first. The numbers in exercise 6 below represent the typed/printed form which is very similar to the handwritten form, except for number two which is written as follows: ٢. It starts from the top right-hand side, moves to the left and then down.

At this point, you may say telephone numbers one digit at a time from left to right, as in English. Thus, the woman on the telephone might say her telephone number in the following manner:

أرْبَعَة - سِتَّة - ثَمانِيَة - اِثْنان - ثَلاثَة - سَبْعَة - خَمْسَة

تمرين ٦

The Arabic numbers: Listen and repeat after the recording. Read the numbers (and words) below from right to left. Copy them several times, paying attention to the handwritten form of the number "two."

10	9	8	7	6	5	4	3	2	1	0
عَشَرَة	تِسْعَة	ثَمانِيَة	سَبْعَة	سِتَّة	خَمْسَة	أرْبَعَة	ثَلاثَة	اِثْنان	واحِد	صِفْر
١٠	٩	٨	٧	٦	٥	٤	٣	٢	١	٠

Presentation: Write the numbers 0–10 on the board in Arabic. Point to the first number (صِفْر) and say it aloud clearly. Have the class repeat in chorus. Work through the introduction of the new numbers while always recycling the old numbers.

Practice: Point to صِفْر on the board, but do not say anything. The class will respond in chorus (almost in unison amazingly enough, as long as you point definitively). Now, slowly point in sequence to the numbers you have presented in increasing and decreasing order. The students always start laughing if you gradually build up speed in your pointing to the extent that they cannot keep up. Once they have built up mastery in sequence, challenge them by pointing to the numbers randomly.

As well, you may simply use your fingers to identify numbers from 1–10. Both techniques are effective and seem to work better if you use both of them to add a bit of variety into the exercise. Note that the finger gestures used in Arab culture differ from those used in America.

Application on page 51.

Application: Conduct a communicative activity in which every student inquires about his or her partner's telephone number (the students can make up imaginary numbers for privacy purposes). Ensure that students know the question they should ask and how to respond.

١ – عندك هاتف؟
٢ – نعم/ لا.
١ – ما رقم هاتفك؟
٢ – رقم هاتفي . . .
١ – شكراً.
٢ – عفوا.

Conduct the same exercise to elicit house and license plate numbers.

The numbers we are learning here are known as **cardinal numbers**, which are also used for labeling things (telephone numbers, car numbers, house numbers, etc.).

How do you think the man below might say his ID number?

ما رَقْم هُوِيَّتِك؟

رَقْم هُوِيَّتي ١٠٣٢٦

تمرين ٧

Do the following calculations:

١)	٣ + ٥ =	________	
٢)	١ + ٧ =	________	
٣)	٩ – ٤ =	________	
٤)	١٠ – ٥ =	________	
٥)	٢ + ٨ =	________	
٦)	٦ + ٤ =	________	
٧)	٨ – ١ =	________	
٨)	٧ – ٣ =	________	

NOTE ملاحظة

The word for the plus sign is زائِد, for the minus sign is ناقِص, and for the word "equals" is يُساوي.

تمرين ٨

Translation: You have just found the following identification card on the ground and wish to return it to its owner. Carefully translate this card into English on a separate sheet of paper. Be sure to include the institution that issued the card, to whom it was issued, the address, telephone number, and card number.

جامِعَة حَلَب

بِطاقَة هُوِيَّة

الإِسم: هالَة بُستاني

إِسمُ الأب: وَحيد

العُنوان: ٥٢ شارِع المَنصور – دِمَشق

رَقْمُ الهاتِف: ٢٨٤٨٥٦٩

رَقْمُ الهُوِيَّة: ٩٧١٤٠٢

تمرين ٩

A. Fill in the blanks: Listen to the following three passages and fill in the blanks:

١- إِسمي عَدنان مَحمود، رَقم هُوِيّتي __________، أسكُن في مَدينة دِمَشق، البِناية رَقم __________، رَقم شَقّتي __________ .

٢- إِسمي أمير سالِم، أنا طالِب في كُلّيّة الهَندَسة، عِندي سَيّارة، رَقم سَيّارتي __________ .

٣- إِسمي مُحَمَّد مُحَمَّد، أنا أُستاذ في الجامِعةِ الأُردُنيّة، أسكُن في مَدينة إربد، الشارِع رَقم __________، البَيت رَقم __________، رَقم هاتِفي __________ .

Presentation: One means of introducing أعرف is by using your ID card. Say that you know your name, student ID number, etc., by pointing to them and then saying them aloud.

The same procedure may be used to introduce لا أعرف. For instance say, "I know Arabic, but I don't know language x" (you may wish to seize this opportunity to teach the names of the more common languages since they are cognates in the Arabic-English language pair).

Practice: Group Activity. Scavenger hunt. Find out who in class knows or does not know (Japanese, French, Spanish, Italian, Russian, etc.). Have students record their answers and call upon some of them to list their findings of who does and does not know certain languages.

B. Read and select: Listen to and read the main text at the beginning of this lesson. Based on that information, select the best choice:

١- اِسْمُ الرَجُل . . .

☐ نِزار ☐ جَبْلَة ☐ ابنُ خَلدون

٢- يَسْكُنُ الرَجُل في . . .

☐ بَيْت ☐ شَقّة ☐ الجامِعَة

٣- عِندَ الرَجُل . . .

☐ سَيّارَة ☐ حاسوب ☐ دَرّاجَة

٤- رَقْم هاتِفِ الرَجُل . . .

☐ ٠١٥٧٩٤ ☐ ٤٩٧٥١٠٦ ☐ ١٠٦٤٩٧٥

C. Read and respond: Respond in Arabic or English to these questions with reference to the dialogue:

5. What does the word جَبْلَة refer to? ________________________.
6. What is the woman's name? ________________________.
7. What is the man's address? ________________________.

5. Learning How to Say "I know" and "I don't know"

رانيا: كَمْ لُغَةً تَعرِفينَ يا سَناء؟
سَناء: أعْرِف أربَع لُغات.
رانيا: ما هِيَ؟
سَناء: العَرَبيّة والإنكليزيَّة والفَرَنسيَّة واليابانيّة.
رايا: ما شاءَ الله!! ما مَعْنى كَلِمَةِ "لُغَة" بِاليابانِيَّة؟
سَناء: آسِفَة. لا أعْرِف.

The verb عَرَفَ "to know" in the dialogue above expresses knowledge about something. The phrase لا أعرف "I don't know" expresses lack of knowledge of something. It is made up of the negative particle لا and the verb أعرف. Like English, this phrase is used very frequently and can come in handy, especially when you do not know the answer to a question.

تمرين ١٠

Translation: On a separate sheet of paper, translate the following sentences. Provide answers for those sentences that are questions.

1. سارة where do you live?
2. I do not live on Lincoln Street.
3. خالد do you live in an apartment or a house?
4. My teacher (f.) lives in (name of a town).
5. I (do not) know (Chinese, Russian, Japanese).
6. I do not know your teacher's (m.) address.
7. بَدْر what is your telephone number?
8. لينا what is your address?

6. Eliciting Information

In order to inquire about the meaning of a word you do not know in Arabic, you may use the phrase ما مَعْنى كَلِمَة . . .؟ "What is the meaning of the word . . . ?" followed by the English word you wish to know. For example, to find out the word for "police," you may ask:

١٠   ما مَعْنى كَلِمَةِ "police" بِالعَرَبِيَّة؟

Note that the words مَعْنى and كَلِمَة are both nouns and together they form an إضافة structure. Notice also the preposition بِـ "in" prefixed to the noun العَرَبِيَّة (بالعَرَبِيَّة).

Presentation: Write a list of English words on the board that the students know and some that they don't know. The list should be about ten words long. Then ask:
ما معنى هذه الكلمة؟
The students respond by stating:
لا أعرفُ معنى هذه الكلمة. / معنى هذه الكلمة . . .
You may also wish to conduct this exercise using Arabic words, but this time, have a student play the role of the teacher in asking whether or not the class knows the words.

تمرين ١١

Ask your teacher about the meanings of at least six words in Arabic that you would like to know, using the phrase ما مَعنى كَلِمَة . . . ؟. Give this exercise some thought in terms of asking about those words that you would like to add to your personal vocabulary but that have not been introduced thus far.

Presentation: Model and practice the pronunciation of the phrase ما شاء الله. Indicate that it is used to express admiration. For relatively long phrases such as this, use backward buildup, a pronunciation technique in which you start with the last word or syllable and build up the entire phrase gradually. This phrase can be built up as follows:
الله . . . الله شاء . . . شاءَ، شاءَ الله، ما . . .
ما شاء الله . . . ما شاء الله.

7. Expressing Admiration Using ما شاءَ اللّه

One way of expressing admiration is by using the phrase ما شاءَ اللّه (literally "God has willed it"). If you see a beautiful baby or hear that someone has won a million dollars, this would be the appropriate response. It connotes joy for someone else's good fortunes devoid of any envy.

8. The Particle يا

This particle is called **vocative** because it is used to call the attention of someone (e.g., يا سَناء! يا أُسْتاذ!). It is used before names, terms of address, and titles, but never by itself. Possibly the closest meaning in English is "Yo," although the particles "Hey" and "Oh" are close in meaning. Consider this sentence:

١١	كَيْفَ الحال يا أحْمَد؟	*Yo/Hey Ahmed, how are you?*

9. The Question Particle كَم : "how many"

كَم + singular + ـاً

In the dialogue in section 5, عادِل asks about the number of languages سَناء knows by using the question particle كَم "how many?".

١٢ كَمْ كِتاباً عِنْدَك؟

Note: *This particle should be followed by a singular indefinite noun. Contrast this with English in which the noun after* "how many" is *plural—"how many books do you have?"*

The word that follows كَمْ is in the accusative case نَصْب, meaning that the last consonant of the word takes a double *fatḥa*. Consider the following examples:

١٣	كَمْ سَيّارةً عِندَ عَمْرو دياب؟
١٤	كَمْ جامِعَةً في هذِه المَدينَة؟
١٥	كَمْ دَفْتَراً عَلى الطاوِلَة؟

Remember: The *alif* above which the double *fatḥa* is written كِتاباً in example 12 and دَفْتَراً in example 15, but serves only as a seat for this marker. It has no phonetic value.

SUMMARY خلاصة

- The particle كَمْ is followed by a singular, indefinite noun in the accusative case = كَمْ ______اً
- The noun following كَمْ thus has a double *fatḥa* (ً) on its end كِتاباً.

تمرين ١٢

Complete the following questions with the appropriate form of the noun in parentheses as in the example. Remember that كَمْ must be followed by an accusative, singular, indefinite noun, and that the ة, ى, and ء do not require an *alif* to seat a double *fatḥa*.

مِثال: كَمْ (حاسوب) ______حاسوباً______ عِندَكِ؟

١- كَمْ (دَرّاجَة) ____________ عِندَكَ؟

٢- كَمْ (مِفْتاح) ____________ على الطاوِلة؟

٣- كَمْ (قَلَم) ____________ في حَقيبَتِكَ؟

٤- كَمْ (مُسَجِّلَة) ____________ عِندَكِ؟

٥- كَمْ (هاتِف) ____________ في بَيتِكَ؟

٦- كَمْ (جامِعَة) ____________ في هذِه المَدينَة؟

٧- كَمْ (كَلِمَة) ____________ في هذا التَمْرين؟

٨- كَمْ (أسْتاذ) ____________ في هذِه الجامِعَة؟

تمرين ١٣

Ask your classmate: Find out from your classmate how many . . . (Remember to use the singular accusative Arabic noun.) Write your answers down on a separate sheet of paper and be prepared to share your answers with your classmates.

1. languages they know
2. televisions they have
3. computers they have
4. bikes they own
5. cars they have
6. classes they have
7. instructors they have
8. keys they have

داخِل قَصر العظم في دمشق

تمرين ١٤

Odd word out: Underline the word that does not belong to each set and explain your choice if needed.

١-	سَكَنَ	شَقَّة	تِسْعة	بَيْت
٢-	هَلْ	لَيْسَ	ماذا	كَمْ
٣-	عِلْمِيّ	يابانِيّ	عَرَبِيّ	إنْكليزِيّ
٤-	هاتِف	رَقْم	عُنوان	طاوِلَة

تمرين ١٥

Numbers: Provide the numbers that have been requested in the following items. If the information is not available, indicate the reason in Arabic.

١- رَقْم غُرْفَة صَفّ اللُغَةِ العَرَبِيّة ____________

٢- رَقْم هاتِفك ____________

٣- رَقْم سَيّارَتك ____________

٤- رَقْم شَقَّتِك ____________

٥- رَقْم هُوِيّتِك ____________

٦- رَقْم بَيْتِك ____________

تمرين ١٦

Listen and respond: Read the following dialogue and fill in the blanks with appropriate responses. After you have filled in the blanks, listen to the recording and respond during the pauses. Practice pronouncing *tā' marbūṭa* when it occurs in the *iḍāfa* structure.

السَلامُ عليكُم!

__________ __________!

كَيْفَ الحال؟

__________ __________. __________؟

الحَمْدُ للهِ بِخَير. أينَ سيّارة أسْتاذَتِك ؟

__________ .

هَلْ عِنْدَها حَقيبة في سَيّارتِها؟

نَعَم، ________ ________ في ________.

ماذا هُناكَ في حَقيبَتِها ؟

في ________، هُناكَ ________ و________ و________ ؟

طَيّب، ما اسْم أسْتاذَتِك ؟

________ ريم.

هل هي أسْتاذة في هذه الجامِعَة؟

نَعَم، ________ ________ في ________ ________.

مَعَ السَّلامة!

_____ __________!

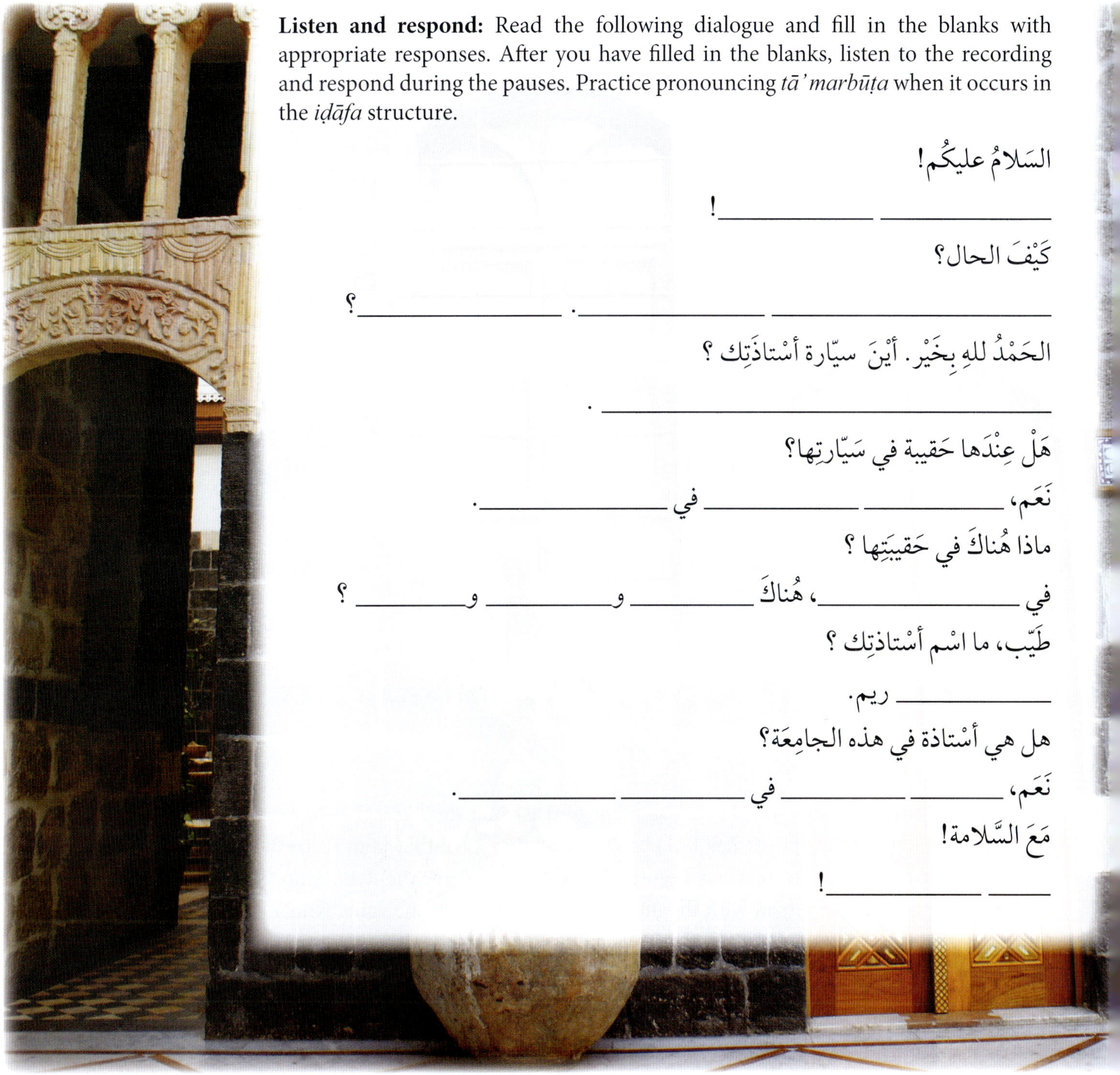

فُندُق الباشا في دِمَشق

تمرين ١٧

A. Listen and select: Check the box that matches the information as expressed in the listening passages for this lesson.

١- وَفاء مِن . . .

☐ مَدينَة دِمَشق ☐ بَلْدَةِ الباب ☐ مَدينَة حَلَب

٢- عِندَ وَفاء صَفّ في . . .

☐ اللُغَةِ العَرَبيَّة ☐ اللُغَةِ الإنكليزيَّة ☐ التِجارَة

٣- عِندَ وَفاء . . .

☐ هاتِف ☐ حاسوب ☐ حاسِبة

B. صواب أم خطأ: Mark the following sentences صواب (true) or خَطأ (false) according to the information in the listening passage and correct any false statements in Arabic.

٤- تَسْكُنُ وَفاءُ في شَقَّة.

٥- وَفاءُ طالِبَةٌ في جامِعَةِ دِمَشق.

٦- تَعرِفُ وَفاءُ ثَلاثَ لُغات.

تمرين ١٨

Scavenger Hunt: Have everyone in class stand up and ask one another if they have the following items. If a student has the item, they have to give that item to the person who asked. Once an item has been obtained by a student, the item is no longer up for grabs. The person with the most items at the end of the game wins. Once the game is over, the teacher asks who has item x and how many they were able to get. Each student relates how many of which items they have until the game is over.

1. sunglasses they have
2. backpacks they have
3. pencils they have
4. books they have
5. notebooks they have
6. phones they have
7. newspapers they have

تمرين ١٩

Online: Watch Lesson 3. When you are watching the dialogues, become an active participant by repeating what you hear, trying to imitate the sounds and inflections used in the scenes.

Scene One: Practice your numbers by counting with John. How high does John count? ___________

Scene Two: Answer the following questions:

١- ما جِنْسيَّة نبيل السَيِّد؟

أ - أمريكيَّة

ب- لُبنانيَّة

ج- سوريَّة

٢- هَل يَسْكُن نبيل السَيِّد في بَيْت أم شَقَّة؟

____

٣- ما رَقْم هاتِفِ نبيل السَيِّد؟

أ- ٦٦٢١٠٦

ب- ٦٦٢١٣٤

ج- ٦٦٢١٥

٤- ما رَقْم هاتِف بِلال السُلطان؟

أ- ٦٦٢٧٠٠٣

ب- ٦٦٢٧٠٥٦

ج- ٦٦٢١٥٣٠

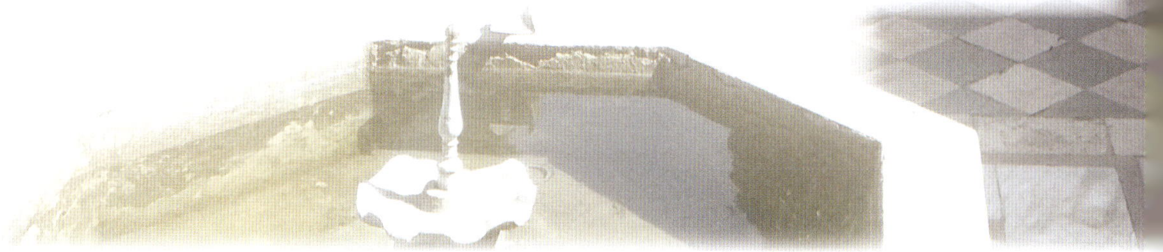

داخِل بَيت تَقليديّ في دِمَشق

المُفْرَدات

Verbs are shown (third person past tense / third person present tense / verbal noun). For example: (he resided / he resides / residing). This is the conventional method for introducing verb conjugations in Arabic.

Nouns are shown in their singular followed by a ج standing for (جَمْع = plural), and then their plural.

a question particle to form yes/no questions	أ
a 14th-century Arab historian and sociologist	(proper noun) ابْنُ خَلْدون
two	(n., m.) اِثنان
four	(n., f.) أَرْبَعة
sorry	(n., f.) آسِفة / (n., m.) آسِف
now	(n.) الآنَ
God	(n., m.) الله
or (particle used in questions)	(conj.) أَمْ
woman	(n., f.) اِمرأة ج نِساء
English (language)	(adj., f.) الإنكليزية
or (used with statements)	(conj.) أو
in, with, by	(prep.) بِـ
card	(n., f.) بِطاقة ج بِطاقات
small town	(n., f.) بَلْدة ج بَلْدات
nine	(n., f.) تِسْعة
three	(n., f.) ثَلاثة
eight	(n., f.) ثَمانِية
name of a town in Syria	(n., f.) جَبْلة
five	(n., f.) خَمْسة
man	(n., m.) رَجُل ج رِجال
number	(n., m.) رَقْم ج أَرْقام
plus	(n., m.) زائِد

to equal . . . . (v.) ساوى (يُساوي) مُساواة

seven . . . . (n., f.) سَبْعة

six . . . . (n., f.) سِتّة

to live, to reside . . . . (v.) سَكَنَ (يَسْكُنُ) سَكَن

(student) living, residence, dormitory . . . . (verbal noun, m.) سَكَنُ (الطُلاّبِ)

street . . . . (n., m.) شارِع ج شَوارِع

want, will . . . . (v.) شاءَ (يَشاءُ) مَشيئة

apartment . . . . (n., f.) شَقّة ج شُقَق

thank you . . . . شُكْراً

zero. . . . . (n., m.) صِفْر ج أصْفار

Arabic (language). . . . . (adj., f.) العَرَبيّة

to know . . . . (v.) عَرَفَ (يَعرِفُ) مَعْرِفة

ten . . . . (n., f.) عَشَرة

you're welcome (response to "thank you") . . . . عَفْواً

address. (n., m.) عُنوان ج عَناوين

French (language) . . . . (adj., f.) الفَرَنْسيَّة

word . . . . (n., f.) كَلِمَة ج كَلِمات

how many/much . . . . (interrogative particle) كَمْ

what (question particle used in front of nouns). . . . . ما

what (used with verbs). . . . . ماذا

married . . . . (n., m.) مُتَزَوِّج ج مُتَزَوِّجون

meaning . . . . (n., m.) مَعْنى ج مَعانٍ / المعاني

minus . . . . (n., m.) ناقِص

question particle for yes/no questions . . . . هَلْ

identity. . . . . (n., f.) هُويّة ج هُويّات

one . . . . (n., m.) واحِد

vocative particle used to call the attention of the addressee . . . يا

Japanese (language). . . . . (adj., f.) اليابانِيَّة

الدرس الرابع

حلب القديمة

Objectives

- Describing background
- Learning how to form dual nouns
- Learning about number-noun agreement
- Introduction to the concept of non-rational noun plurals

1. Describing Background

طالِبتان في جامِعة حَلَب

Presentation: Ask students,
أنت طالب في أيّ جامعة؟
في أيّ جامعةٍ تدرُس/ تَدرُسينَ؟
The answer should be:
أدرُس في جامعة كذا.
Show pictures of a house and an apartment. Practice the pronunciation of شقّة (especially with attached pronouns). Ask individual students where they live, expecting to elicit one of three answers:
أسكن في شقّة، بيت، سكن الطلاب.

Practice: Conduct a chain drill as follows:
١- أسكن في شقّة. أين تسكن/ تسكنين؟
٢- أسكن في بيت. أين تسكن/ تسكنين؟
٣- أسكن في سكن الطلاّب. أين تسكن/ تسكنين؟

هالَة بُسْتاني وسَحَر حَلاّق طالِبَتان في جامِعَة حَلَب. هالَة مِن دِمَشق وسَحَر مِن دِمَشق أيْضاً. تَسكُن هالَة في شَقَّة مَعَ سَحَر حَلاّق، والشَقَّة في البِنايَة رَقْم خَمسَة في شارِعِ الحَمَداني. رَقْم شَقَّتِهِما ٩. في شَقَّة هالَة وسَحَر غُرفَتان وسَريران وطاوِلَتان وكُرسيّان. هالَة وسَحَر لا تَدرُسان في مَكتَبَةِ الجامِعَة بَلْ في شَقَّتِهِما.

تَدرُس هالَة الطِبّ وعِندَها الآن ثَلاث موادّ وهِيَ الأَحْياء والكيمْياء واللُغَةُ الإنكِليزيَّة. تَدرُس سَحَر التِجارَة وهِيَ تَعرِف ثَلاثَ لُغات هِيَ العَرَبيَّة والفَرَنسيَّة والإنكِليزيَّة.

سَرير

سَريران

بِناية

بِنايتان

Upon completion of this exercise, you may wish to ask individual students where one of their classmates lives. If, as is likely, they do not remember, have them direct the question to their classmate, listen to the answer, and then report back to the class.

الأستاذ: أين يسكن مارك؟
ستيف: لا أعرف. يا مارك، أين تسكن؟
مارك: أسكن في سكن الطلاّب في شارع كذا.
ستيف: يسكن مارك في سكن الطلاّب في شارع كذا.

Reflecting on our reading: What rule can we make concerning the creation of the dual form in Arabic?

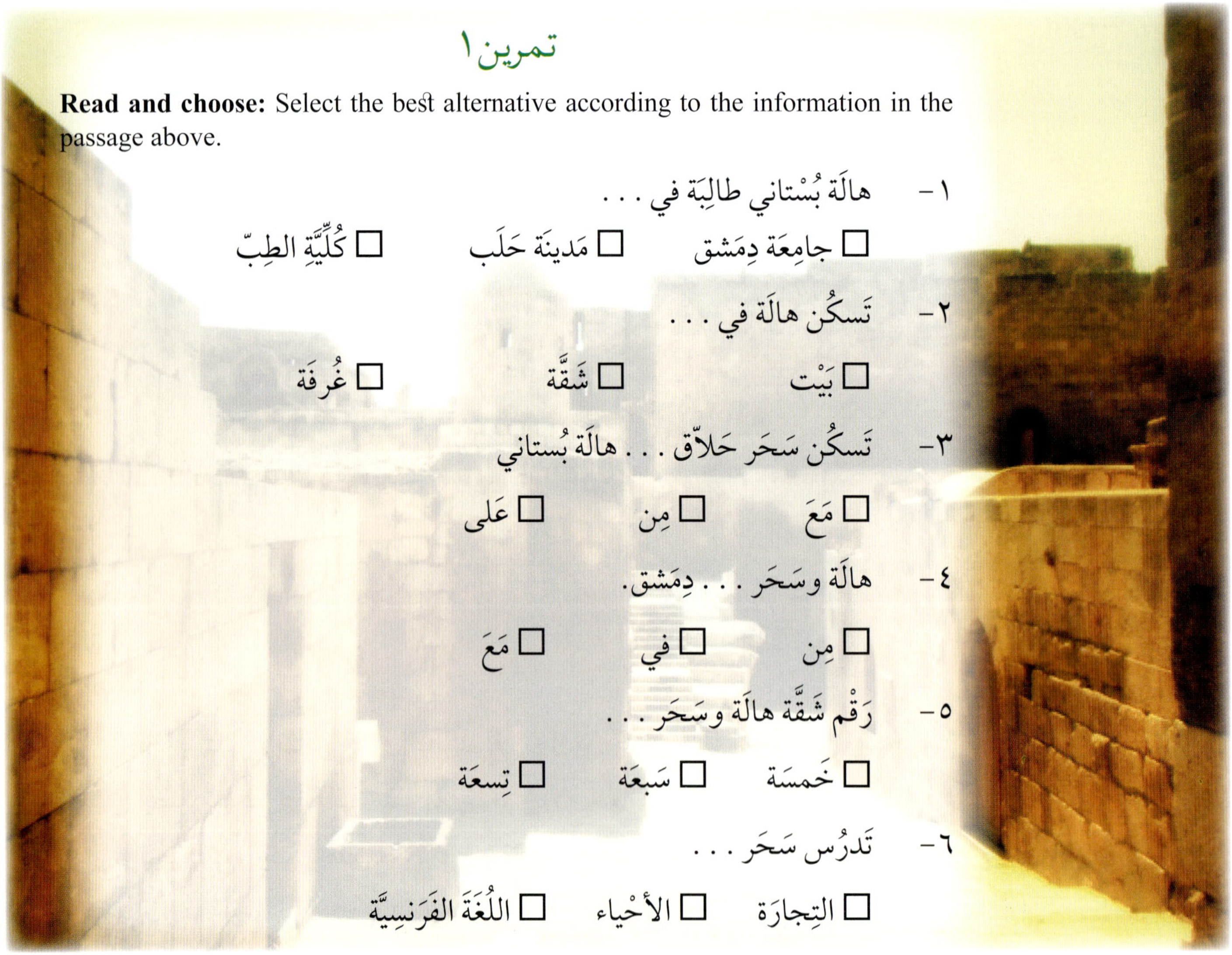

تمرين ١

Read and choose: Select the best alternative according to the information in the passage above.

١- هالَة بُسْتاني طالِبَة في . . .

☐ جامِعَة دِمَشق ☐ مَدينَة حَلَب ☐ كُلِّيَّة الطِبّ

٢- تَسكُن هالَة في . . .

☐ بَيْت ☐ شَقَّة ☐ غُرفَة

٣- تَسكُن سَحَر حَلاّق . . . هالَة بُستاني

☐ مَعَ ☐ مِن ☐ عَلى

٤- هالَة وسَحَر . . . دِمَشق.

☐ مِن ☐ في ☐ مَعَ

٥- رَقْم شَقَّة هالَة وسَحَر . . .

☐ خَمسَة ☐ سَبعَة ☐ تِسعَة

٦- تَدرُس سَحَر . . .

☐ التِجارَة ☐ الأَحْياء ☐ اللُغَة الفَرَنسيَّة

داخِل قَلعة حَلَب

تمرين ٢

صَواب أم خَطأ: Mark the following statement **صَواب** (true) or **خَطأ** (false) based on the information in the passage and correct any false statements in Arabic.

١- سَحَر أستاذة هالَة. ______________________.

٢- تدرُس سَحَر حَلاّق ثَلاث مواد. ______________________.

٣- تَسكُن هالَة مَعَ طالِبَة مِن دِمَشق. ______________________.

٤- تَدرُس هالَة الطِبّ في جامِعَة دِمَشق. ______________________.

٥- في غُرفَة هالَة سَريران. ______________________.

تمرين ٣

Matching: Match words from the right-hand column with words in the left-hand column. Take the time to practice writing Arabic by writing both words in the middle column.

١-	مادَّة		سَرير
٢-	اللُغَة		أيْضاً
٣-	كُرسيّ		تَسكُن
٤-	بِنايَة		مَعَ
٥-	تَعرِف		الإنكليزيَّة
٦-	في		أحْياء
			شَقَّة

تمرين ٤

Odd word out: Underline the word that does not belong to each set and explain your choice if needed.

١-	الرِياضِيّات	الفَرَنسيَّة	الأحْياء	الكيمياء
٢-	شَقَّة	بِنايّة	بَيْت	كُلِّيَّة
٣-	دَرّاجَة	طاوِلَة	كُرسيّ	سَرير

2. Forming Dual Nouns

As you may have noticed, nouns (and adjectives) in Arabic are either singular, dual (two), or plural (more than two). The dual has two endings, depending on the case of the noun (or adjective):

A. Dual	*-āni*		
Nominative subject of the sentence	انِ	+	**word**

dual		singular	
هذانِ كِتابانِ	←	هذا كِتابٌ	١

In the dual, both the demonstrative هذا and كتابٌ acquire the suffix *-āni* انِ. This suffix is used for both definite and indefinite nouns. Normally the *kasra* on the end of the suffix is not pronounced in casual speech (e.g., the word كِتابانِ is pronounced *kitābān*).

B. Dual	*-āni*		
Accusative and Genitive	يْنِ	+	**word**

		Feminine word	**Masculine word**	
Accusative case	*object of the verb*	أدرُس مادّتَيْنِ	أقرأُ كِتابَيْنِ	٢
Genitive case	*object of the preposition*	في جامِعتَيْنِ	في كِتابَيْنِ	٣

Notice the change of the ة to a regular *tā'* ت when the suffix ـَيْنِ is attached to it. Just like انِ, the suffix *-ayni* ـَيْنِ is used with definite and indefinite nouns.

Memory Device: Examine the word "two" in Arabic: اِثنان (nominative) اِثنين (genitive; accusative). Notice that when we form the dual forms in nouns, all we are doing is taking the final two letters from the word "two" اِثنان and adding that ending to the noun. In fact, the use of اِثنانِ and اِثنَيْنِ with dual nouns is redundant because duality is already expressed by *-ān* and *-ayni*. However, they are used for emphasis in this context.

Presentation: Show pictures of a furnished room in a house or an apartment. Describe the room's furnishings, the number of specific objects in the room, and their location relative to one another. Now question students on the location of the furnishings.
Practice: Show a picture similar to presentation on page 66 and ask questions like:
كم كرسيًا في هذه الغرفة؟
هل هناك طاولة في هذه الصورة؟
Immediately after the yes/no question, follow up with content questions:
ماذا في الصورة أيضا؟

Application: Pair Activity. Have students take turns in questioning one another about what is in the rooms in their house, apartment, or dorm room. Have one student describe in detail their room while the other listens and draws a picture of what they understand from the description. The listener should be encouraged to ask questions for clarification. The speaker will then take a look at the drawing and verbally correct any mistakes in comprehension. Upon completion of the exercise, have students switch roles.

3. Number-Noun Agreement

In order to express quantity, a number is combined with a noun. In the dialogue in Lesson 3, section 5, the woman specifies the number of languages she knows by saying: أعرِفُ أربَعَ لُغات. In Arabic, numbers are gendered—that is to say that they are either feminine (end with a ة) or masculine (do not end with a ة). You may be wondering why the number أربَع is masculine when the word for language لُغَة is feminine. Let's examine some rules that govern numbers in Arabic.

A. The Numbers *one* and *two* (1, 2)

The numbers **1** and **2** follow their modified noun, because they act as adjectives and, like adjectives, agree with their modified nouns in gender, number, and case. They are usually used for emphasis, since the suffixes انِ and ـَيْنِ denote dual number, as we discussed in section 2 in this lesson.

	Dual	Singular
Nominative (m.)	كِتابانِ اِثنانِ	كِتابٌ واحِدٌ
Nominative (f.)	سَيّارتانِ اِثنَتانِ	سَيّارَةٌ واحِدَةٌ
Accusative/Genitive (m.)	كِتابَيْنِ اِثنَيْنِ	
Accusative/Genitive (f.)	سيّارَتَيْنِ اِثنَتَيْنِ	

B. The Numbers *three* through *ten* (3–10)

1. The numbers **3–10** precede the noun they modify.
2. They have a reverse gender agreement with the singular counted noun; that is, if the counted noun is masculine, the number is feminine (by suffixing ـة to it) and vice versa. Consider the following example:

masculine noun		*feminine noun*	
أربَعَةُ كُتُبٍ		أربَعُ سَيَّاراتٍ	٤

The singular of سيارات is سَيّارَة, which is feminine; therefore the number modifying it أربَع is in the masculine form. Similarly, the singular of كُتُب "books" is كِتاب, which is masculine; therefore, the number modifying it is in the feminine form in that it ends with a تاء مربوطة.

3. The specified noun being counted must be indefinite (no الـ), hence the تَنْوين on the end of the words.

4. The numbers **3–10** form an إضافة structure with the following noun, because these numbers are nouns. The plural counted nouns are thus marked with a تنوين كسرة, being *genitive* جَرّ and *indefinite.*

Note that the feminine form of the number **10** is pronounced عَشَرَة (e.g., عَشَرَةُ كُتُبٍ) and the masculine form is pronounced عَشْر (e.g., عَشْرُ سَيّاراتٍ).

SUMMARY

- **The Numbers 1, 2**

  Numbers **1** and **2** follow the noun they modify. These numbers function as adjectives and therefore agree with the preceding noun in gender, number, and case.

- **The Numbers 3–10**

  These numbers precede the noun they modify and have a reverse gender agreement with the noun in the singular. They form an إضافة structure with their noun, which is indefinite, genitive, and plural.

Numbers 1–10 with Nouns	
Feminine مُؤنَّث	**Masculine مُذَكَّر**
سَيّارَةٌ واحِدَةٌ	كِتابٌ واحِدٌ
سَيّارَتانِ اِثْنَتانِ	كِتابانِ اِثْنانِ
ثَلاثُ سَيّاراتٍ	ثَلاثَةُ كُتُبٍ
أربَعُ سَيّاراتٍ	أربَعَةُ كُتُبٍ
خَمسُ سَيّاراتٍ	خَمسَةُ كُتُبٍ
سِتُّ سَيّاراتٍ	سِتّةُ كُتُبٍ
سَبعُ سَيّاراتٍ	سَبعَةُ كُتُبٍ
ثَماني سَيّاراتٍ	ثَمانيةُ كُتُبٍ
تِسعُ سَيّاراتٍ	تِسعَةُ كُتُبٍ
عَشْرُ سَيّاراتٍ	عَشَرَةُ كُتُبٍ

تمرين ٥

A. Using numbers: Hāla Bustānī is writing a journal entry about what she has in her apartment. On a separate sheet of paper, let's help her translate her list into English.

في بَيْتي ثَلاثُ طاوِلاتٍ وبِجانِبِ واحِدةٍ مِنها أربَعَةُ كَراسٍ ولَيْسَ هُناكَ حاسوبٌ عَلى الطاوِلَةِ بَلْ ثَلاثَةُ حَواسيب وأيضاً على الطاوِلَة تِلفازانِ اِثنانِ وفي غُرفتي ثَلاثةُ هواتِفَ وعَشَرَةُ كُتُبٍ وسَبعةُ دَفاتِرَ وسِتُّ نَظّارات.

B. Michael Brown thinks that he may have left his keys at home. Let's help him translate his thoughts into Arabic as he takes stock of what is in his book bag. Remember to use the appropriate form of the number and remember to pay attention to the word order. Refer to section 3 as well as the word bank of plurals on the left.

In my bookbag there are three pencils, four books, two telephones, three identity cards, a computer, and five keys.

بِطاقَة ج بِطاقات	
تِلْفاز ج تِلْفازات	
طاوِلَة ج طاوِلات	
نَظّارَة ج نَظّارات	
دَفْتَر ج دَفاتِر	
هاتِف ج هَواتِف	
حَقيبَة ج حَقائب	
مِفْتاح ج مَفاتيح	
حاسوب ج حَواسيب	
كِتاب ج كُتُب	
كُرسيّ ج كَراسٍ	

تمرين ٦

Conversation: Negating Numbers: Ask your neighbor some questions about the number of objects that they own. For the person answering, if you have that number, then simply answer "I have x objects." But if you do not have that number, then answer, "I do not have two cars; rather, I have three cars."

مِثال: هَلْ عِندَكَ سَيّارَتانِ؟

لا، لَيْسَ عِندي سَيّارَتانِ بَل سَيّارة. ______.

هَلْ عِندَكَ . . .

١- ساعة واحِدَة ______.

٢- أربَعَة كُتُب ______.

٣- ثَلاث دَرّاجات ______.

٤- حاسوبان ______.

٥- نَظّارَتان ______.

٦- خَمسَة هَواتِف ______.

٧- ثَلاث جَرائد ______.

٨- أربَع حَقائب ______.

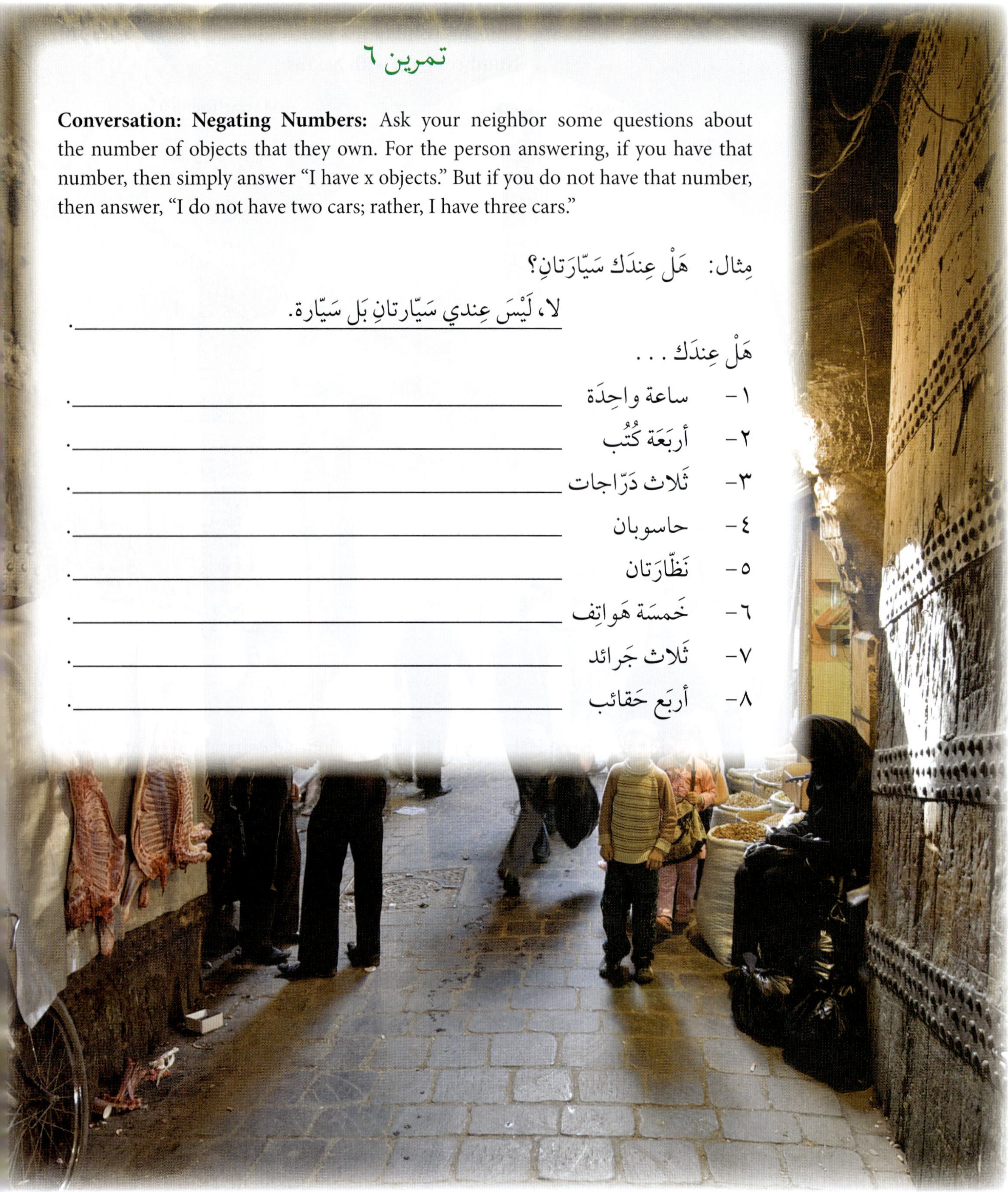

حَلَب سوريا

Presentation: Using pictures of various objects that you have, state where they are.

الصورة الأولى: عندي ثلاثة حواسيب وهي في بيتي.

الصورة الثانية: وأيضاً عندي سبعة مَفاتيح وهي معي هنا.

الصورة الثالثة: وفي حقيبتي أربعة أقلام وهي جديدة.

Practice: Ask students how many of certain objects they have.

أ – كم نظارةً عندك؟

ط – عندي ثلاث نظارات.

أ – أين هي؟

ط – هي في البيت

أ – كم كتاباً في حقيبتك؟

ط – أربعة كتب.

أ – هل هي جديدة؟

ط – نعم هي جديدة/ لا، هي ليست جديدة.

Application: Group work. Have students ask each other what they have in their book bag or room. Have them ask if those objects are new. Once the exercise has run its course, ask some students to relate their findings.

تمرين ٧

Numbers in conversation: Ask your classmate the following questions and then record the answers on a separate sheet of paper. Be prepared to share this information with the rest of the class.

مِثال: كَمْ قَلَماً مَعك؟

كَمْ مِفْتاحاً عِندَكَ وأينَ هي؟

Find out how many ...

1. languages they know and what they are
2. Arab cities they can name and which ones
3. students they know in this Arabic course and their names
4. classes they have and which ones
5. computers they own and where they are
6. phones they have and where they are

4. Plurals of Non-Rational Nouns

Read this section closely and carefully: In the dialogue in Lesson 3, section 5, the man refers to the four languages the woman knows, using the separate pronoun هِيَ "she," which is feminine singular. He asks, **ما هِيَ؟**. The reason for using هِيَ is that all non-rational (or non-human) nouns are usually referred to in the feminine singular, regardless of gender.

That is to say that plural nouns, even those that are masculine when singular such as كِتاب ج كُتُب, are treated as feminine singular by using **هي** , **هذه** and **تِلك**. The same pronouns (**هِيَ، هذِه، تِلك**) are also used to refer to both feminine singular nouns such as **ساعة** as well as non-rational (non-human) plurals. Thus, the man's question **ما هِيَ؟** may be translated in this context, "what are they?" rather than "what is it?" or "what is she?":

٥	هٰذِه الكُتُب	*these books*	هٰذِه السَّيّارات	*these cars*
٦	تِلْكَ الكُتُب	*those books*	تِلْكَ السَّيّارات	*those cars*

By contrast, rational plurals (those referring to people) are referred to by pronouns and demonstratives that agree with them in gender and number, for example:

these instructors (m.pl.)	هؤلاءِ الأساتِذة	٧
they are students (m. pl.)	هُم طُلاّب	٨
these women	هؤلاءِ النِساء	٩
they are students (f. pl.)	هُنَّ طالِبات	١٠

SUMMARY

- Non-rational plurals are referred to by feminine singular pronouns and demonstratives, regardless of the noun's gender in the singular.
- **Non-rational plurals are treated as feminine singular.** *Memorize this rule.*

الجَمع **Plural**				المُفْرَد **Singular**	
تِلْكَ كُتُب	هذِه كُتُب	هِيَ كُتُب	كُتُب	كِتاب	مُذَكَّر (masculine)
تِلْكَ سَيّارات	هذِه سَيّارات	هِيَ سَيّارات	سَيّارات	سَيّارَة	مُؤَنَّث (feminine)

قَلعة حَلَب بِاللَيل

تمرين ٨

Use of demonstrative pronouns: Use the appropriate pronoun and demonstrative to refer to each of the following nouns. Note that the nouns listed may be singular, plural, masculine, or feminine. Also, use the proper demonstrative based on its proximity from the pointing hand.

هذا	هذِه	هؤلاءِ	ذلِكَ	تِلْكَ	هُوَ	هِيَ	هُمْ	هُنَّ

مِثال: قَلَم  هُوَ قَلَمٌ / هذا قَلَمٌ

١- حَقيبَة  ____________________

٢- كَراسٍ  ____________________

٣- ساعَة  ____________________

٤- بُيوت  ____________________

٥- طُلّاب  ____________________

٦- حاوسب  ____________________

٧- مَفاتيح  ____________________

٨- طالِبَة  ____________________

٩- نَظّارَة  ____________________

١٠- سَيّارات  ____________________

تمرين ٩

A. Listen and select: Check the box that matches the information as expressed in the listening passage for this lesson.

١- اِسمُ الطالِبِ المَغرِبيِّ . . .

☐ عَبدُ الرَحمن ☐ عَبدُ الرَحيم ☐ عَبدُ الله

٢- يَدرُسُ الطالِبُ المَغرِبيّ . . .

☐ الأدبَ العَرَبيَّ ☐ اللُغَةَ الإنكليزية ☐ الطِبّ

٣- الطالِبُ المَغربيّ مِن مَدينَةِ . . .

☐ القاهِرة ☐ وُجدة ☐ عَيْن شَمْس

٤- في شَقَّة هذا الطالِب . . .

☐ حاسوبان ☐ تِلفازان ☐ سَريران

أسْواق حَلَب القَديمة

B. صواب أم خطأ: Mark the following sentences صواب (true) or خَطأ (false) according to the information in the listening passage and correct any false statements.

٥- يَدرُس عَبدُ الرَحمنِ الأدَبَ العَرَبيّ.

٦- يَسكُن عَبدُ الرَحمنِ في شَقَّة.

٧- يَسكُن مَعَ عَبدِ الرَحمن طالِب مَغرِبيّ.

٨- يَعرِف عَبدُ الرَحمن اللُغَة الفَرَنسيَّة.

تمرين ١٠

Video: Watch Lesson 4. When you are watching the dialogues, become an active participant by repeating what you hear, trying to imitate the sounds and inflections used in the scenes.

Answer the following questions:

١- ماذا يُوجَد في غُرْفة سارة؟

________________ ________________

________________ ________________

____

٢- كَم بِنْتاً وكَم وَلَداً في عائلة سارة؟ ________________

____

٣- أَيْنَ يَدْرُسُ الأولاد؟ ________________

____

____

____

المُفْرَدات

Listen to the vocabulary items on the audio and practice their pronunciation.

biology . . . . (f., pl.) أحْياء

rather, but . . . . (particle) بَلْ

building . . . . (n., f.) بِناية ج بِنايات

bag; briefcase . . . . (n., f.) حَقيبة ج حقائب

closet, cupboard. . . . . (n., f.) خِزانة ج خَزائِن / خِزانات

study . . . . (v.) دَرَسَ (يَدرُسُ) دِراسة / دَرْس

bed . . . . (n., m.) سَرير ج أسِرّة

small; young. . . . . (adj., f.) صَغيرة

school subject, course . . . . (n., f.) مادّة ج مَوادّ

with (someone; not thing) . . . . (prep.) مَعَ

middle . . . . (adj., f.) وُسْطى

قَلْعة حَلَب

داخِل قَلْعة حَلَب

الدرس الخامس

Objectives

- Describing family members
- Describing school subjects
- Learning about Arabic last names
- Introduction to objects of verbs
- Introduction to objects of prepositions
- Introduction to ordinal numbers
- Introduction to pronouns of separation

Presentation: It is beneficial if you have photographs that clearly depict family relationships. Authentic photographs (especially yours) tend to have a positive impact on students. If you use a family tree with pictures, make sure the relations are not confusing.

Practice: Repeat the pronunciation of each relationship in a clear voice and many times. Relate the relationships to the students' personal backgrounds:

أ – عندك أخ/ أخت/ زوج/ زوجة؟
ط – نعم/ لا. عندي/ ليس عندي ...
أ – كم أخا/ أختاً عندك؟
ط – عندي أَخوان/ أختان . . .
أ – ما اسم أخيك/ أختك؟
ط – اسم أخي/ أختي كذا.

As with every exercise, after mastering this Q&A session, have students relate answers from other students. If they do not remember the answers given by their peers, have them ask, listen to the answer, and report that information.

Application: Group Activity. Take a survey of who in class has a sister or brother. Have the students record their answers and report their findings.

1. Describing Family Members

عائِلة مازِن نَجّار

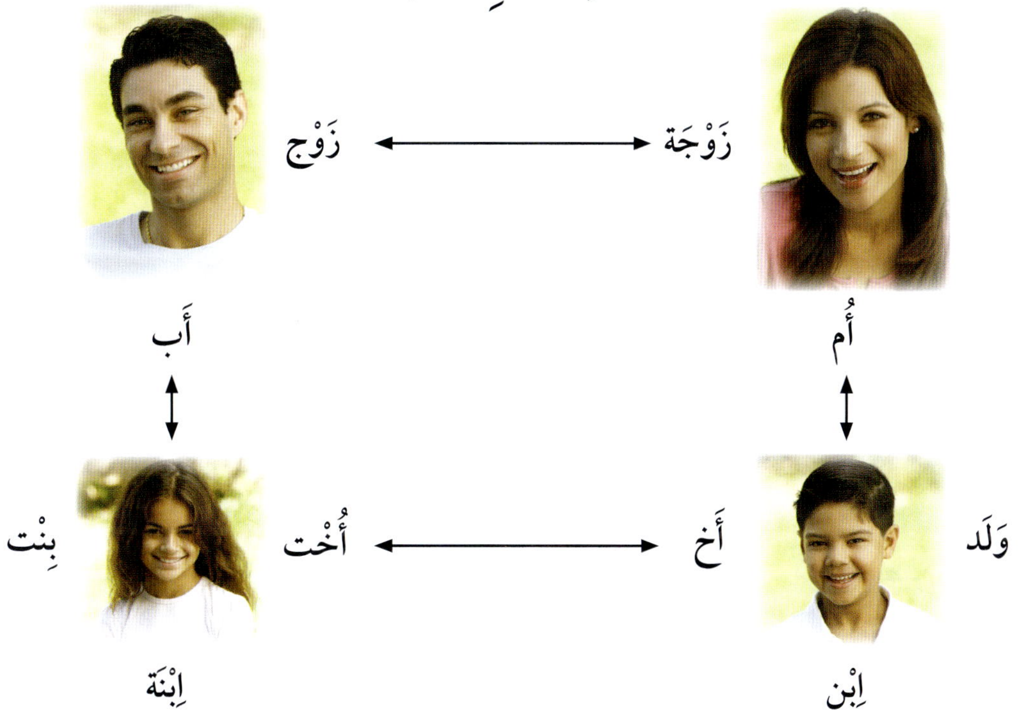

هذِه عائِلة مازِن نَجّار. اِسم زَوْجتِهِ ناديا الخولي. عِندَهُ ابن واحِد اسمُهُ أحمَد وَابنَتان: واحِدَة اسمُها رانِيَة وواحِدَة اسمُها رِحاب.

أي نَعم، عِندي ابنَتان وَابن واحِد.

أحمَد في المَدرَسَة في الصَفّ الثالِث الابتِدائيّ وأختُهُ رانِيَة في الصَفّ الرابع وَرِحاب في الصَفّ السادِس. أحمَدُ الوَلَدُ الوَحيد في عائِلَة مازِن وَناديا.

Note: Women in most Arab countries (e.g., Syria, Egypt) retain their maiden names after marriage.

2. Describing School Subjects

طُلّاب عَرَب في أمريكا

هذا عَدْنان مارتيني. يَدرُس عدنان عِلمَ الحاسوب في جامِعَة وِلايَة أوهايو. هُوَ طالِب عَرَبيّ مِن سوريَّة. يَدرُس عدنان الآن مادَّةَ الرِياضِيّات ومادَّةَ اللُغَةِ الإنكليزيَّة.

أبو عَدنان وأمّ عَدنان يَسكُنان في مَدينَة حَلَب في سوريَّة ويَسكُن مَعَهُما في البَيت إخوَة عَدنانَ الثَلاثَة وأختاهُ. لكِنَّ عَدنان يَسكُن في شَقَّة في مَدينَة كَلَمبُس مَعَ طالِبَيْن عَرَبِيَّيْن، واحِد مِن فِلَسطين اِسمُهُ زِياد نابُلسي وَواحِد مِن لُبنان اِسمُهُ وَليد صايغ. يَدرُس زِياد مادَّةَ الهَندَسة ويَدرُس وَليد مادَّةَ الكيمْياء.

Presentation: Present some of the school subjects that students are currently taking in your class, using a picture or an illustrative prop. Cycle through the school subjects (no more than seven) using choral and individual repetition. Focus on using the word مادّة before every subject to elucidate its meaning.

Practice: Model the questions that the students will be asking in the application portion of this functional exercise.

الأستاذ: كم مادّةً تدرس/ تدرسين؟
الطالب: أدرس ثلاث موادّ.
الأستاذ: ما هي؟
الطالب: أدرس العربية والرياضيات والتاريخ.

Once the students start catching on, then call on a student to relate what subjects another is taking. If the student does not remember, have him/her ask, listen to the answer, and then report the information. Repeat a couple of times, and then allow this exercise to flow into the application.

Application: Group Activity. Have students ask and record what subjects they are studying this quarter or semester. Once the exercise has reached its conclusion, allow students to work in groups of two for a couple of minutes to compile a list of who is studying what subjects and then call on some groups to relate the information.

الأحْياء

الهَنْدَسَة

الكيمْياء

في هذا الفَصْلِ الدِراسيّ يَدرُس زِياد هذِهِ المَوادّ: اللُغَةُ الإنكليزيَّة والفيزياء والتَفاضُل. ويَدرُس وَليد في هذا الفَصْل مادَّتَيْن فَقَط هُما اللُغَةُ الإنكليزيَّة والأحْياء.

Reflecting on our reading: Can you deduce the meaning of **مادّة ج مَوادّ** from context? Do you see a pattern? Does it occur before or after certain nouns?

تمرين ١

A. **Read and select:** Check the box that matches the information as expressed in the reading passages in sections 1 and 2.

١- عائِلَةُ النَجّار فيها . . .

☐ اِبن واحِد ☐ اِبنان ☐ ثَلاثَة أبْناء

٢- رانية في الصَفّ . . . الابتِدائيّ.

☐ الثالِث ☐ الرابع ☐ السادِس

٣- وَليد صايغ طالِب . . .

☐ سوريّ ☐ لُبنانيّ ☐ فِلَسطينيّ

٤- يَدرُس عَدنان مارتيني . . .

☐ مادّة واحِدَة ☐ مادَّتَيْن ☐ ثَلاث مَوادّ

٥- يَدرُس عَدنان مارتيني . . .

☐ عِلمَ الحاسوب ☐ الهَندَسة ☐ الكيمْياء

٦- يَسكُن عَدنان مارتيني في . . .

☐ سَكَنِ الطُلّاب ☐ بَيت ☐ شَقَّة

٧- يَسكُن عَدنان مارتيني في . . .

☐ كاليفورنيا ☐ أوهايو ☐ تكساس

B. Answer these questions with reference to the reading passages.

٨- ما اسم أبي رانية؟ ________________________.

٩- مَنْ يَدرُس مادَّةَ التَفاضُل؟ ________________________.

١٠- مَعَ مَنْ يَسكُن عَدنان مارتيني؟ ________________________.

١١- كَمْ مادَّة يَدرُس عَدنان في هذا الفَصْل؟ ________________________.

١٢- ماذا يَدرُس زياد نابُلسي في جامِعَة أوهايو؟ ____________________.

تمرين ٢

صواب أم خطأ: Mark the following statement صَواب (true) or خَطَأ (false) based on the information in the passage and <u>correct</u> any false statements.

١- رانِيَة أخت رِحاب. ________________________.

٢- مازِن ابن ناديا. ________________________.

٣- أحمَد أخو رانِية. ________________________.

٤- رِحاب ابنَة أحمَد. ________________________.

٥- ناديا زَوْجَة مازِن. ________________________.

٦- أحمَد أبو مازِن. ________________________.

٧- أحمَد زَوْج ناديا. ________________________.

تمرين ٣

Family roles: Check the appropriate box to indicate the family role of the people specified below. Each one may have more than one role.

		أب	أم	زَوْج	زَوجَة	اِبن	اِبنَة	أخ	أُخْت
١-	أنا	☐	☐	☐	☐	☐	☐	☐	☐
٢-	أبي	☐	☐	☐	☐	☐	☐	☐	☐
٣-	أُمي	☐	☐	☐	☐	☐	☐	☐	☐
٤-	أَخي	☐	☐	☐	☐	☐	☐	☐	☐
٥-	أُختي	☐	☐	☐	☐	☐	☐	☐	☐

تمرين ٤

Odd word out: Underline the word that does not belong to each set and explain your choice if needed.

١-	تَفاضُل	أحْياء	أُخْت	كيمْياء
٢-	وَحيد	فَصْل	مادَّة	فيزْياء
٣-	زَوْج	اِبْن	وَلَد	أوَّل
٤-	اِبنَة	عَلى	مَنْ	في

تمرين ٥

Ask your classmates: On a separate sheet of paper, write down your classmates' responses. Find out . . .

1. how many of your classmates study biology or engineering this term
2. who has a brother or sister and how many
3. who has a brother or sister in elementary school and if so, what grade
4. where your classmate's family is from
5. where your classmate's family lives now

Be prepared to report your findings to your class.

تمرين ٦

Writing a personal sketch: On a separate sheet of paper, compose a paragraph about yourself modeled after our reading passage. Describe who you are, where you are from, what courses you are currently taking (studying), where you live, where your parents live, and whether you live with others. Use as much of the vocabulary as you can that we have learned so far—past-tense verbs as well as the possessive "have" and the particle "but." Be as creative as possible with your paragraph, displaying what you have learned so far. Use this writing exercise to focus on the words that you want to establish in your own vocabulary.

As a follow-up exercise, give a brief biographical sketch of at least one of your family members.

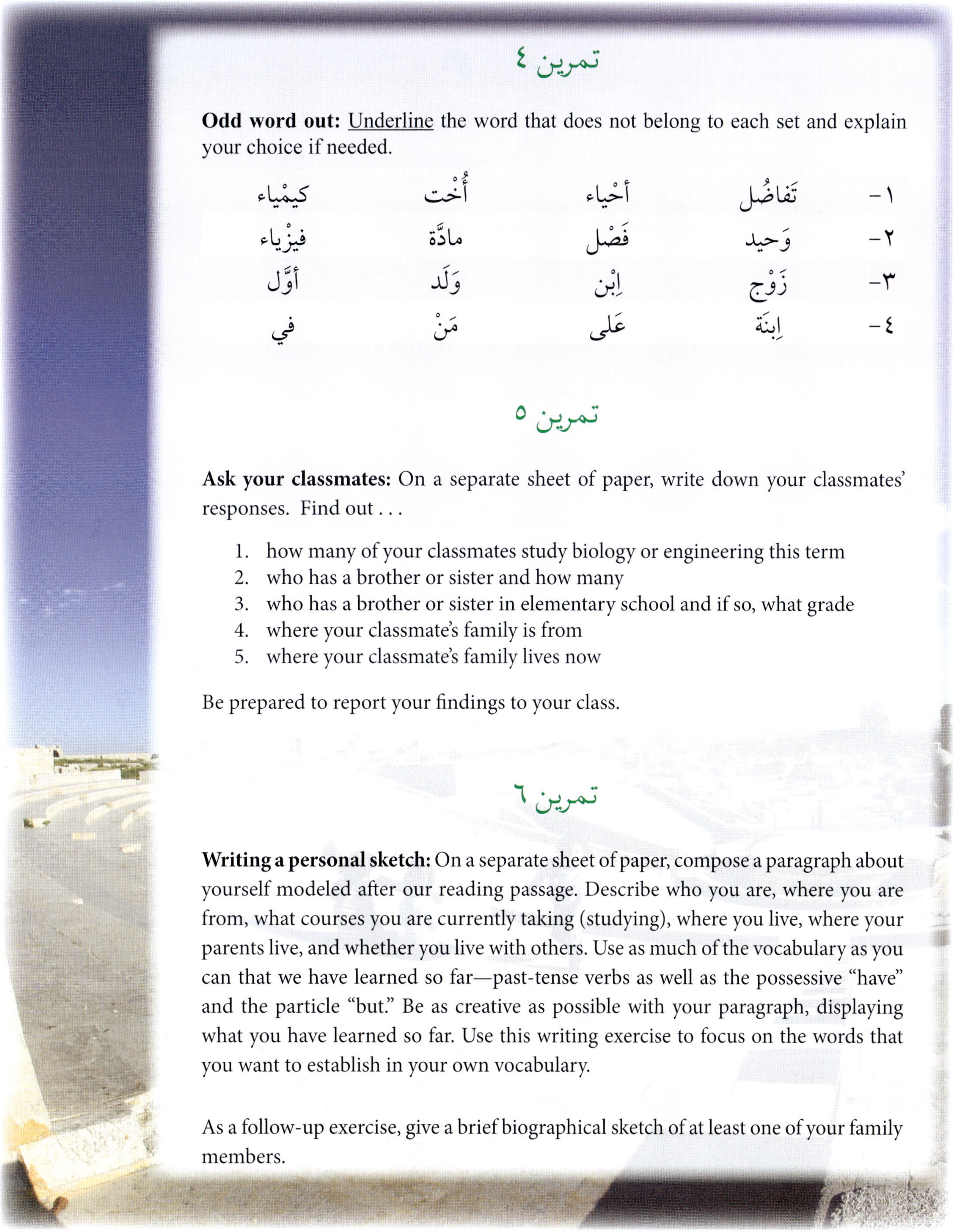

قلعة حلب

تمرين ٧

تَمرينُ المُشاهَدة: شاهِدوا الدَرْسَ الخامِس على الشابِكة.

١- مَع مَن يَسكُن هاني مُحَمَّد؟ ________________________________
____

٢- ماذا يَدْرُس هاني؟ ________________________________
____

٣- أَيْنَ يَسكُن أخو هاني؟ ________________________________
____

٤- ماذا تَدرُس أُخْت هاني؟ ________________________________
____

٥- مَع مَن يَسكُن عِماد حَسَن؟ ________________________________
____

٦- في أيَّة كُلّيّة يَدرُسُ الطالِبان من مِصر؟ ________________________________

تمرين ٨

Conversation: In groups of two, one person reads the prompts while the other pretends that they are Hani Muhammad from the video and fills in the blanks with appropriate answers. Switch roles upon completion. For part two, redo the exercise, but this time fill in the blanks with your own personal information.

السلامُ علَيْكم!

__________ __________!

كَيْف الحال؟

__________________ . __________؟

الحَمْدُ لله بِخَيْر. من أَيْنَ أنت ؟

______ ______ مَدينة ______ . وأنتَ؟

أنا من مَدينة اللاذقية في سوريا. ماذا يَعمَل أبوكَ وأُمُّكَ؟

أبي ________ في ________ . لِلحاسوب وأمي

__________ في __________.

وأخوكَ الكَبير، هل هوَ طالِب في الجامِعة؟

______، هو______ ويَسكُن ______ ______.

أمّا أُختي فَهي ______ في كُلّيّة ______.

وماذا تَدرُس أنتَ ؟

______ ______.

تَشَرَّفنا.

______.

طَيِّب، شُكْراً ! مَعَ السَّلامة!

____ ______!

3. Arabic Last Names

Arabic last names generally refer either to place of origin, profession, an attribute acquired by one of the forebears of the family, or the person's father's and/or grandfather's names. For example, the surname **مارتيني** in the main reading passage is derived from the name of a small town in northern Syria near the city of **إدْلِب** called **مارتين**. As you can see, the name **مارتيني** is a **نِسبَة**, or adjective, derived from the name of the town itself **مارتين**.

Similarly, the surname **نابُلسي** refers to **نابُلُس**, a town on the West Bank of the Jordan River. The surname **صايغ** is the word for a profession (goldsmith). Some names are composed of two or more proper names. The second name is usually the father's first name and the third one is the grandfather's first name (e.g., the boy's name **نِزار أحْمَد صالِح** pictured below). In regions like the Arabian Peninsula and North Africa, some names may have the word **بِن** for **ابْن** "son of" inserted after the first name, which explicitly shows the relationship (e.g., **عَبّاس بِن مَسعود** ʿAbbas bin masʿūd).

نِزار أحمَد صالِح

تمرين ٩

A. The following is the cover of a book. On a separate sheet of paper, give the first author's last or family name, and then explain the author's name in terms of the description above.

B. Take a look at these excerpts from Arabic magazines. Identify the last names of the persons mentioned.

4. Objects of Verbs المَفْعول بِه

Direct objects of verbs answer the question, "what" did the verb do.

"I saw a man." What did I see? "A man."   "I bought a car." What did I buy? "A car."

In English, nouns that are *direct objects* are not marked for case (i.e., whether they are the subject or object), though pronouns are. Notice that the word "apples" remains unchanged in both positions in examples 1 and 2 in the table below. However, if a pronoun is used instead of "apples" in example 1, the pronoun "them" would be used (not "they").

	Subject	Verb	Direct Object
1	I	like	apples (them).
2	Apples (They)	are	good food.

In Arabic, nouns that are direct objects are in the *accusative case*, known as نَصْب. There are different markers or endings that indicate this case:

A. A *fatḥa* فتحة appears at the end of the direct object if it is definite:

Direct Object	Subject	Verb	
الأحْياءَ	وَليدُ	يَدرُسُ	٣

In this instance, يَدْرُسُ is the verb (= the action), وَليدُ the subject, which answers 'who' did the action, and الأحْياءَ , which answers "what" did the subject do?

B. تَنوين فَتحة appears at the end of a direct object if it is indefinite:

Direct Object	Subject	Verb	
مادَّةً واحِدَةً	وَليدُ	يَدرُسُ	٤

In example 4, مادّةً is the direct object (answering the question "what does Walid study?"), which is indefinite; hence the use of تَنوين.

Sound masculine plurals are discussed in Lesson 8, section 8.

C. The suffix *-ayni* ـَيْنِ is attached to dual nouns in the accusative case (as in example 5) and the suffix *-īna* ـينَ to some sound masculine plural nouns (as in example 6 and discussed in detail in Lesson 8 on page 160). Both of these suffixes are used with definite and indefinite nouns.

dual	يَدرُسُ وَليدُ مادَّتَيْنِ.	٥
plural	أعرِفُ ثَلاثَةَ أمريكيينَ.	٦

5. Objects of Prepositions

A prepositional phrase, that is, a preposition followed by a noun, is in the *genitive case* or حالة الجَرّ. An Arabic noun is marked in the genitive in four ways, three of which will be discussed at this point:

A. A كَسْرة appears at the end of an object of a preposition if it is **definite**:

٧	يَدرُسُ عَدنانُ في الجامِعَةِ.

B. تَنوين كَسْرة appears at the end of an **indefinite** noun:

٨	يَدرُسُ عَدنانُ في جامِعَةٍ أمريكيَّةٍ.

C. The suffix *-ayni* ـَيْنِ is attached to **dual** nouns and the suffix *-īna* ينَ to some plural nouns:

	Dual	Plural
٩	في جامِعَتَيْنِ	أعْرِفُ المِصْريّينَ

SUMMARY

- The direct object of a verb is marked by a single فَتحة if it is definite, a double فَتحة if it is indefinite, and by suffixing ـَيْنِ to both definite and indefinite dual nouns and ينَ to some sound masculine plurals.
- The object of a preposition is marked by a *kasra* if it is a definite noun, a double *kasra* if it is indefinite, and by suffixing ـَيْنِ to both definite and indefinite dual nouns and ينَ to sound masculine plurals.

تمرين ١٠

Recognizing grammar: Underline the direct objects of verbs and draw a rectangle around the objects of prepositions. Provide the case markers where necessary. Some sentences contain both the object of a verb and the object of a preposition.

١- تَعرِفُ سَناء أربَعَ لُغاتٍ.
٢- أدرُسُ مادَّتَيْنِ في هذا الفَصْلِ.
٣- لا تَعرِفُ سامية عُنوانَ هالَة.
٤- تَدرُسُ هالَة مادَّةَ الأحْياءِ في جامِعَةِ القاهِرة.
٥- أسكُنُ في بَيْتٍ في هذِه المَدينةِ.

Presentation: First list cardinal numbers 1–10 on the board (or using flash cards, or your fingers) for review. Then show an overhead (or PowerPoint presentation) of the list of ordinal numbers both masculine and feminine listed next to their cardinal counterpart. Gradually introduce each ordinal number. Practice their pronunciation and memorization in a manner similar to that of Lesson 4.

Practice: Chain drill (student 1 says الأوَّل, student 2 الثاني, and so forth).

Application: Group Activity. Take a survey to find out who is the first/second/third sibling in his/her family. Then have them produce the forms by asking them similar questions with numbers that do not fit their situation.

هل أنت الابن الأوّل في عائلتك؟

هل أنت الابنة الأولى في عائلتك؟

6. Ordinal Numbers الأعْداد التَّرْتيبيّة

Ordinal numbers are used to *order* items, hence their name (e.g., first, second, etc.). Arabic ordinal numbers are derived from cardinal numbers (e.g., one, two, etc.). Ordinal numbers *follow* the modified noun and function as an *adjective*. Look at the examples below:

Cardinal number	*five lessons*	خَمْسَةُ دُروس	١٠
Ordinal number	*the fifth lesson*	الدَّرْسُ الخامِسُ	١١

Cardinal and Ordinal Numbers

Root	Ordinal (f.)	Ordinal (m.)	Cardinal	Digit
وَحَد	أُولى	أوَّل	واحِد	١
ثَني	ثانِية	ثاني	اِثْنان	٢
ثَلَث	ثالِثة	ثالِث	ثَلاثة	٣
رَبَع	رابِعة	رابِع	أربَعة	٤
خَمَس	خامِسة	خامِس	خَمسة	٥
سَدَس	سادِسة	سادِس	سِتّة	٦
سَبَع	سابِعة	سابِع	سَبعة	٧
ثَمَن	ثامِنة	ثامِن	ثمانِية	٨
تَسَع	تاسِعة	تاسِع	تِسعة	٩
عَشَر	عاشِرة	عاشِر	عَشرة	١٠
	حادِيَةَ عَشْرَةَ	حادِيَ عَشَرَ	أَحَدَ عَشَرَ	١١
	ثانِيَةَ عَشْرَةَ	ثانِيَ عَشَرَ	اثنا عَشَرَ	١٢

Note that the cardinal number واحِد and its ordinal counterpart أوّل have different forms. Ordinal numbers 11 and 12 are indeclinable (i.e., they do not vary in case and only a فتحة can occur after the final letter).

Ordinal numbers are either feminine or masculine. As adjectives they agree with a preceding noun in gender, number, case, and definiteness and appear in blue below.

this is the eleventh lesson	هذا الدَّرْسُ الحادي عَشَر	١٢
a third book	كِتابٌ ثالِثٌ	١٣
in the first two lessons	في الدَّرْسَيْنِ الأَوَّلَيْنِ	١٤

Note that the ordinal forms for numbers 2–10 follow the **فاعِل** pattern. This means that if you know the root letters of the number, you can just substitute them for the **ف ع ل** and add a **تاء مربوطة** when necessary. Be aware that when an ordinal number is definite, it will take the definite article **الـ** as a prefix, as can be seen in examples 12 and 14.

Ordinal Pattern	
فاعِل (ة)	١٥

تمرين ١١

التطابق: اكتب الكلمات المتطابقة في العمود الأوسط:

الثاني		واحِد	١-
ثامِن		رابع	٢-
خَمسة		سَبعة	٣-
أربَعة		سِتَّة	٤-
سادِس		الاِثنان	٥-
سابع		ثَماني	٦-
عائِلَة		خامِس	٧-
أوَّل			
المَكتَبة			

تمرين ١٢

أملأ الفراغات الآتية بكلمات مناسبة من المربّعات .

الثاني	زَوْجَة	مادّةً	الابتِدائيّ	تَدرُس

١- ______________ هالَة مادّةَ الرِياضِيّات في هذا الفَصل.

٢- كَمْ ______________ عِندَكَ يا سالِم؟

٣- هَلْ أنتَ الابن ______________ في أُسرَتِك؟

٤- أخي في الصَفّ الرابِع ______________.

تمرين ١٣

Conversation: Police investigation: A theft has occurred in our classroom. The thief has stolen a حَقيبة. We need some background information that will help catch this criminal. Find out who . . .

1. has Arabic as their first course today
2. has a book bag with two books in it and one notebook
3. lives in the dormitory
4. lives with two students
5. studies computer science
6. sits in the second row of the classroom

Have we caught our thief?

7. Pronouns of Separation ضَمائِر الفَصل

The independent personal pronouns (e.g., هُوَ، هِيَ) may be used to separate subjects from their predicates and also to distinguish sentences from phrases. When used as pronouns of separation, personal pronouns are comparable to the verb "is" in English, as you can see in these examples from the passage:

This is Mazen's family.	هذِهِ هِيَ عائِلَةُ مازِن.	١٦
Ahmed is the only child.	أحمَدُ هُوَ الوَلَدُ الوَحيد.	١٧

Pronouns of separation are especially called for when the predicate is a single noun defined by the article, as in:

This book . . .	هذا الكِتابُ . . .	١٨

The use of هُوَ in this context spells the difference between a noun phrase (18) and a sentence (19).

This is the book.	هذا هُوَ الكِتابُ.	١٩

SUMMARY

- Pronouns of separation are independent personal pronouns.
- They are used to separate subjects and predicates.
- They distinguish a noun phrase from a sentence.
- The predicate must be definite.
- Pronouns of separation agree in number and gender with subjects.

تمرين ١٤

Pronouns of separation in use: Change the following phrases into sentences by using the appropriate pronoun in the proper place.

١- هذِه كُلّيّةُ الآداب. ________________________.

٢- الأستاذ راغِب طَبّاع. ________________________.

٣- أخي نِزار. ________________________.

٤- هذا دَفتَرُ العائلَة. ________________________.

٥- هذانِ الطالِبان. ________________________.

٦- هؤلاءِ إخوَتي. ________________________.

تمرين ١٥

Filling out the دَفْتَرُ العائِلة: In some Arab countries there is what is called a "family identification card," known in Arabic as **دَفْتَرُ العائِلة**. Fill out the first page of this document according to the information about the **نَجّار** family in the main reading passage.

دَفْتَرُ العائِلَة

اِسمُ الأب: ______________________

اِسمُ الأم: ______________________

الوَلَدُ الأوَّل: ______________________

الوَلَدُ الثانِي: ______________________

البِنْتُ الأُولى: ______________________

البِنْتُ الثانِية: ______________________

تمرين ١٦

Conversation: Ask your classmates questions concerning their family.

Find out from your classmate . . .

1. if they have a brother or sister and if so, what their name is
2. where they live (country, state, city, street) and whether they live in a house or an apartment
3. what is in the house or apartment
4. what they study, and where
5. if they are the only child

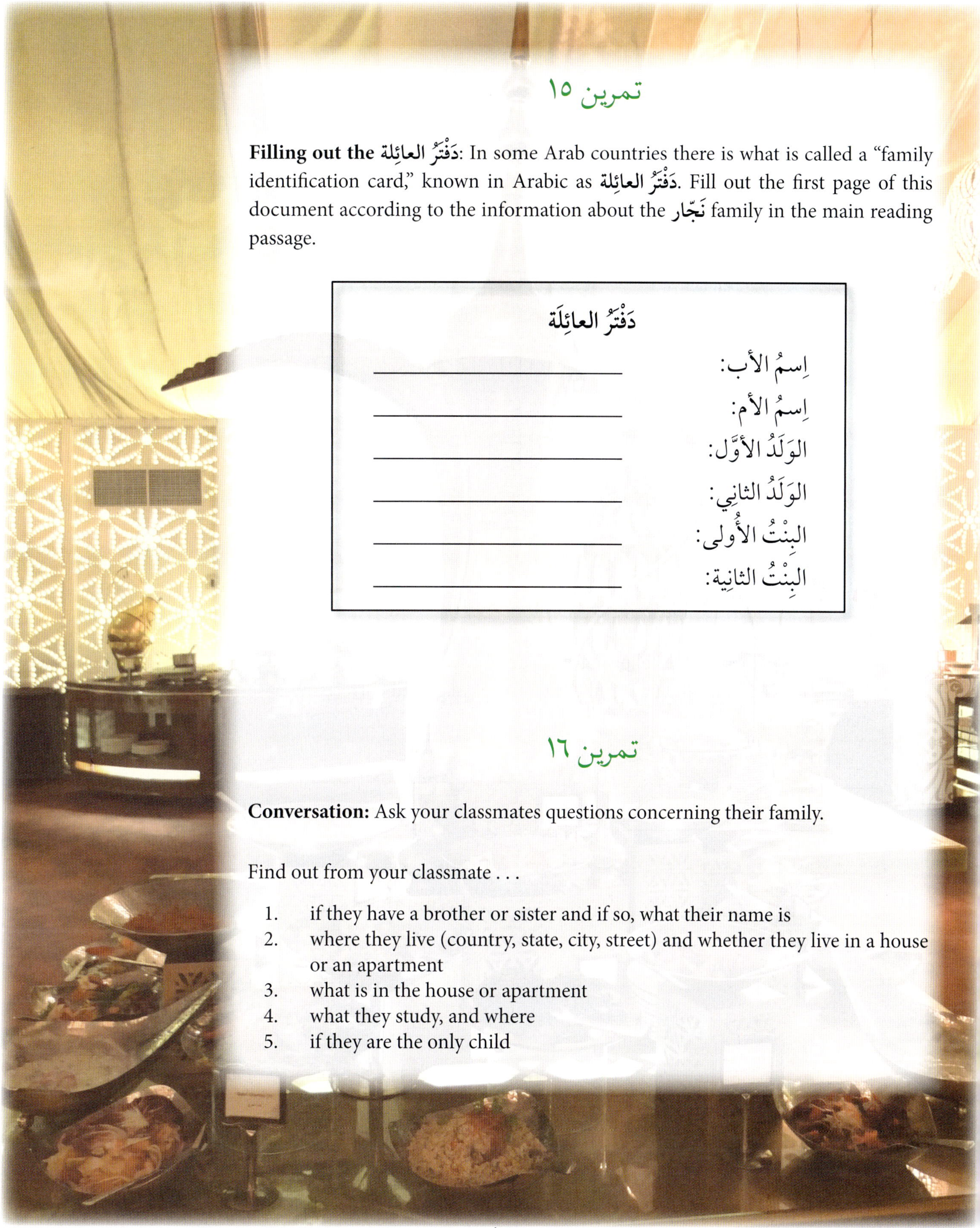

الإفطار في دُبي

تمرين ١٧

A. Listen and select: Check the box that matches the information as expressed in the listening passages for this lesson.

١- نَدى أستاذَةُ اللُغَةِ . . .

☐ الإنكليزيَّة ☐ الفَرَنسيَّة ☐ العَرَبيَّة

٢- نَدى لَها . . .

☐ ابن واحِد ☐ ابنان ☐ ثَلاثة أبناء

٣- اِسم زَوْج نَدى . . .

☐ سامِر ☐ رامِز ☐ سَميح

٤- ابنُها رامِز في الصَفّ . . .

☐ الثالِث ☐ الخامِس ☐ السابع

B. صواب أم خطأ: Mark the following sentences صواب (true) or خَطأ (false) according to the information in the listening passage and correct any false statements.

٥- تَسكُن أُمّ سَميح في دارِها. ________________.

٦- سَميح بارودي هُوَ زَوْج نَدى حَفّار. ________________.

٧- يَسكُن سَميح وعائلَتُه في مَدرَسة بَنات. ________________.

٨- لِهذِه العائلة ابنان وابنَة. ________________.

تمرين ١٨

A. Verb conjugations: Let's take a moment to review some verb conjugations. Give the independent pronoun with respect to the conjugated verb.

مِثال: أحمَد يَدْرُس في المَدرَسَةِ الابتِدائيَّة. ____هو____

١- هالة تَدْرُس في سوريَّة. ________

٢- هَلْ تَدْرُسين في كَنَدا؟ ________

٣- أدْرُس في جامِعة بَيْروت. ________

٤- رانية تَدْرُس في المَكْتَبة. ________

٥- نَدْرُس في غُرفَةِ الصَفّ. ________

B. Conjugate the verb with respect to the given pronoun. All verb conjugations are in the present tense.

مثال: هُم (دَرَسَ) ____يَدْرُسونَ____ عِلمَ الحاسوب.

أنا (دَرَسَ) ________ اللُغَة العَرَبيَّة في جامِعَة وِلاية أوهايو. وأنتَ، هَل (دَرَسَ) ________ في هذِه الجامِعَة؟ ونَحْنُ (عَرَفَ) ________ أنَّ مايكل براون (دَرَسَ) ________ في الجامِعَةِ الأمريكيَّة في القاهِرة وهالَة بُستاني وسَحَر حَلّاق (دَرَسَ) ________ في جامِعَة حَلَب. ولكِنْ أينَ (سَكَنَ) ________ هالَة وسَحر؟ هَلْ (سَكَنَ) ________ في شَقَّة أم في بَيت؟

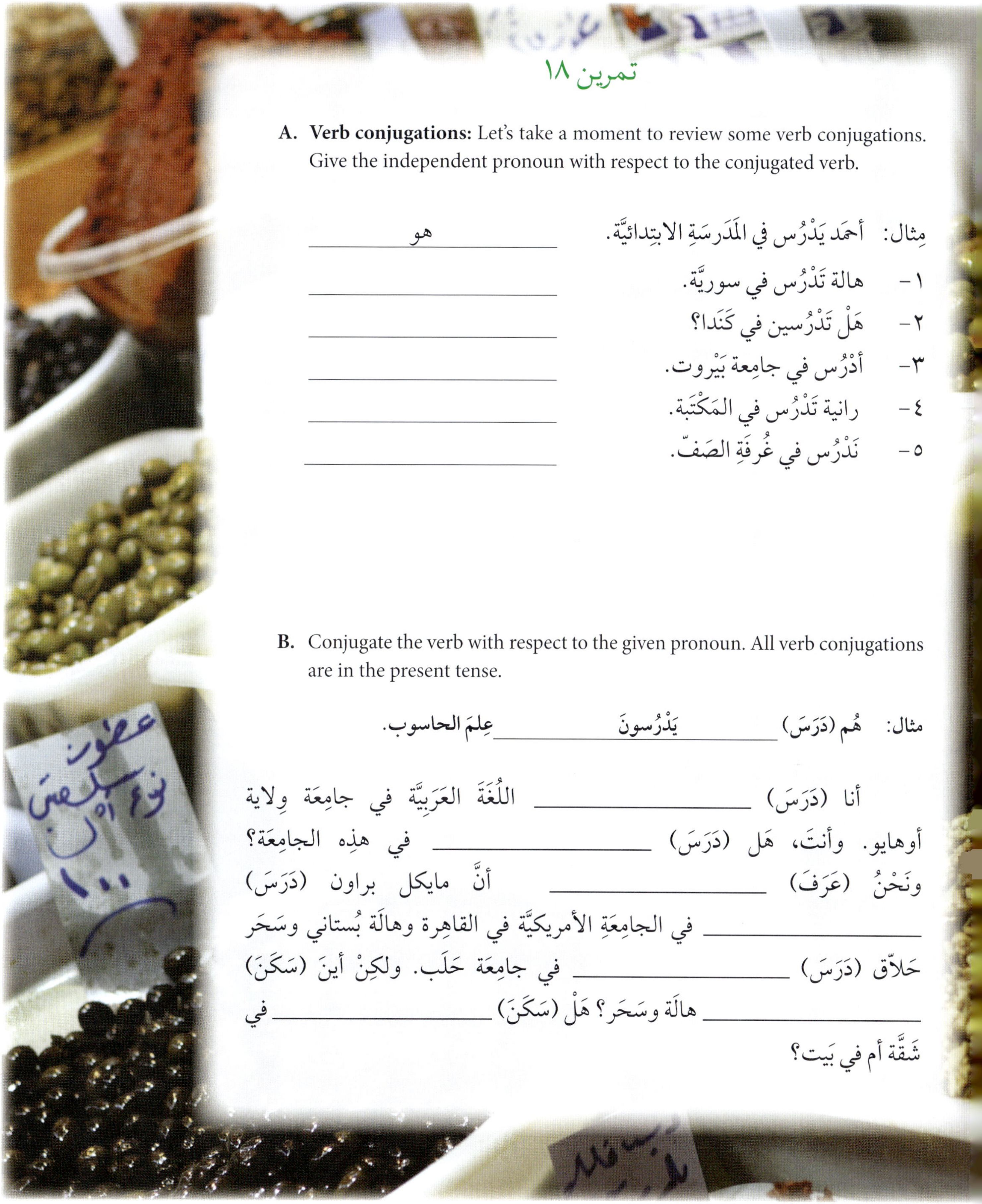

سوق العطّارين في حَلَب

المُفْرَدات

Listen to the vocabulary items on the CD and practice their pronunciation.

father . . . . (n., m.) أب ج آباء

elementary. (adj.) ابْتِدائيّ

son . . . . (n., m.) ابْنٌ ج أبْناء

daughter . . . . (n., f.) ابْنَة ج بَنات

brother. (n., m.) أَخ ج إخوة

sister . . . . (n., f.) أُخْت ج أَخَوات

mother. (n., f.) أُمّ ج أُمَّهات

English. (n., m.) إنْكليزيّ

first . . . . (n., m.) أوَّل ج أوائِل

girl . . . . (n., f.) بِنْت ج بَنات

ninth . . . . (adj.) تاسِع

differential equations. . . . . (n., m.) تَفاضُل

third . . . . (adj.) ثالِث

eighth . . . . (adj.) ثامِن

second . . . . (n., m.) ثانٍ (الثاني)

fifth. . . . . (adj.) خامِس

of school, academic. . . . . (adj.) دِراسِيّ

fourth . . . . (adj.) رابع

husband . . . . (n., m.) زَوْج ج أزْواج

wife. . . . . (n., f.) زَوْجَة ج زَوْجات

seventh. (adj.) سابِع

خان الشونة في حَلَب

sixth . . . . (adj.) سادِس

small; young. . . . . (adj.) صَغير

child . . . . (n., m.) طِفْل ج أطْفال

tenth . . . . (adj.) عاشِر

nuclear family. . . . . (n., f.) عائِلَة ج عائِلات

(academic) term, season . . . . (n., m.) فَصْل ج فُصول

only; no more than . . . . (particle) فَقَطْ

physics . . . . (n., f.) فيزياء

big . . . . (adj.) كَبير

chemistry . . . . (n., f.) كيمياء

nice. . . . . (adj.) لَطيف

who. . . . . (question particle and relative noun) مَنْ

sole, only. (n., m.) وَحيد ج وَحيدون

middle . . . . (adj., f.) وُسْطى

boy . . . . (n., m.) وَلَد ج أَوْلاد

الدرس السادس

Objectives

- Using terms of address
- Expressing regret or apology
- Expressing lack of knowledge
- Expressing degree
- Introduction to the negation and conjugation of the present tense verb
- Secrets of the language: prefixes and suffixes
- Introduction to cardinal numbers 11–999

رُكنُ مُفْرَداتِ المَشْهَدِ الأوّل

Do you know where _______ is?	هل تَعْرِف أَيْنَ _______؟
sorry	آسِف ج آسِفون
(I / you / we) can	يُمْكِنُ + (ني / ك / نا)
to ask (s.o.) a question	سأل / يَسأل / سُؤال
employee	مُوَظَّف ج مُوَظَّفون
information	اِسْتِعْلامات
(I'm / you're / we are) right	معَ + (ي / ك) حَقّ
please, if you would	مِن فَضْلك
floor	طابَق ج طَوابِق
help, assistance	مُساعَدة
don't worry about it, no problem	لا شُكْرَ على واجِب

Presentation: Address students with the proper terms. For example:
يا آنسة ريم، يا أخ مايكل، يا أستاذ، يا سيّد
Ask the learners to correctly address you with يا أستاذ/ يا أستاذة followed by your name. Note that in the Arab world the titles are followed by the first name, not the last as in the West. Remind the learners that in writing, the forms of address should take a definite article.

Practice: Conduct a chain drill in which students greet one another using their names with the appropriate terms of address.
١- مَرحباً يا آنسة ليسا.
٢- أهلاً يا أخ مايكل. مرحباً يا آنسة جينيفر
٣- أهلاً يا آنسة ليسا. مرحباً يا سيِّد آلن.

أَيْنَ مَكْتَبُ المُدير؟

تمرين ١

أملأ الفراغاتَ الآتية حَسَب معلوماتِ النَصِّ المَرئي:

المَشْهد الأوَّل

- عفواً، هَل ______ أَيْنَ مَكْتَبُ المُدير؟
- آسِف. لا أعرِفُ. ______ أنْ تَسأَلَ مُوَظَّفَ الاسْتِعلامات.
- آه. ______ ______، شكراً.
- مساءُ الخير.
- مساءُ النور.
- ______ ______، هل تَعرِفُ أَيْنَ مَكْتَبَ المُدير؟
- مَكْتَبُ المُديرِ في ______ الثاني الغُرْفَةُ رقمُ ثلاثة، بِجانِبِ غُرْفةِ المَكْتَبةِ.
- شُكراً جزيلاً على ______.
- لا شُكْرَ على ______.

من آثار بعلبك الرومانية

رُكنُ مُفْرَداتِ المَشْهَدِ الثاني

اللهُ أعلَم	*God knows*
ما رأيُك	*what's your opinion*
مُوافِق ج مُوافِقون	*I / you / we agree*
الوِلايات المُتّحِدة	*the United States*
زارَ / يَزورُ / زيارة	*to visit*
سَنة ج سَنوات	*year*
عادَ / يَعودُ / عودة	*to return*
بَرنامَج ج بَرامِج	*program*

المَشْهد الثاني

- هل ______ من أَيْنَ أُستاذتُنا الجديدة؟
- ______ ______. ما رأيُكِ أن نَذْهَب ونَسألَها.
- أنا ______.
- مَرحباً يا أستاذة سَماح.
- أهلاً وسهلاً.
- نَحنُ طالِبتان في ______.
- تَشَرّفنا.
- هل ______ أن نَعرِف من أَيْنَ أنتِ؟
- أنا من لُبنان من مَدينة بَعْلَبَك، ولكنّني أسكُن في ______ ______ ______ مُنذُ عِشرين سَنة.
- هل تَزورين لُبنان كُلّ سنة؟
- لا. أزورُها كُلّ ثلاث أو أربع ______.
- هل ______ إلى لُبنان وتَعيشين فيه؟
- ______ ______. لا أعرِف الآن.

1. Terms of Address

يا آنِسَة!

As in many languages, when people speak to each other, they use terms of address. Some Arabic terms of address also serve as titles. For example, the term آنِسة is equivalent to the English "Miss"; سَيِّدة is similar to "Mrs."; and the word سَيِّد is like "Mr." However, people may also use the words أخ "brother" and أخت "sister" to address strangers. The use of these terms is perceived to make the addressee feel safe, respected, and close—like a family member. In direct oral interaction, these terms may be preceded by the vocative يا, which is a particle used to call attention, as you may recall from Lesson 3. However, in indirect speech (e.g., when referring to someone) or in writing, the definite article الـ may be prefixed to the different terms of address (e.g., الأستاذ أحمد).

Presentation: Express apology (at tripping over a student's book bag) or regret (at not knowing the answer to a question) using آسف/ آسفة. Explain that these forms change according to gender and number.

Practice: Conduct a chain drill in which each student asks another what a word means in Arabic. If the student does not know the word, then he/she should respond using آسف/ آسفة.

١ – ما معنى program بالعربية؟
٢ – آسف/ آسفة لا أعرف.

Application: Group Work. Scavenger Hunt: Choose a number of items (five to seven) and have students ask each other if they have with them مع or own عند them, or if they know a certain person, celebrity, or location. If they do not have that item, then they should use the appropriate response.

تمرين ٢

Check out the manner in which the recipient is addressed in this old Egyptian telegram. How is he addressed? What is his name? What is his address?

EGYPTIAN STATE TELEGRAPHS AND TELEPHON

P.S. 109

R O.H.E.M.S. No. 3949

21.JL.36.4.-P.

٢٧/ ٧ ٢٤٣٠١٤م٢

حضرة المحترم الاستاذ محمد افندى كامل عبد الباقى

المحامى ٣٠ شارع العطرى بالعباسية مصر

In speech you may use the article يا with either the first or the last names (e.g., an educated person named خَليل حدّاد may be addressed as يا أُسْتاذ خَليل or يا أُسْتاذ حَدّاد).

The plural forms of سَيِّد (سادة) and سَيِّدة (سَيِّدات) may be used to address groups of people, as in public gatherings. Consider the following example, where the MC is introducing a man named حُسَيْن زاهِر:

Use of Terms of Address	
Oral (information)	**Written (formal)**
يا سَيِّد أحمَد!	السَيِّد أحمَد ناجي
يا سَيِّدة رَنا!	السَيِّدة رَنا غَلاييني
يا آنِسَة هَنادي!	الآنِسَة هَنادي زَيْتونة
يا أُستاذ خَليل!	الأُستاذ خَليل حَدّاد
يا أخ مُنذِر!	الأخ مُنذِر الدَجاني
يا أُخت مُزْنة!	الأُخْت مُزْنة القايِد

تمرين ٣

Read and select: Review the dialogues in this lesson once more and check the box that corresponds with that information.

١- مَكْتَب أستاذِ الرِياضِيّات في . . .

☐ جامعة حَلَب　　☐ مكان لا نعرفه　　☐ الغُرفة

٢- تَسكُن هالَة بُستاني في . . .

☐ شَقّة　　☐ غُرفة　　☐ شارِع

٣- اِسم أَمينَةِ المَكتَبة . . .

☐ هالَة بُستاني　　☐ سامية　　☐ نِداء خَيّاط

٤- صَلاح . . .

☐ لَيْسَ مَعَهُ كِتاب　　☐ لَيْسَ مَعَهُ مِحفَظة　　☐ لَيْسَ في الصَفّ

٥- الآنِسة . . . أَيْنَ كُلِّيَّةُ الحُقوق.

☐ تَعرِف　　☐ لا تَعرِف　　☐ لا تَتَكَلَّم

٦- صَلاح . . .

☐ طالِب　　☐ أستاذ　　☐ أمين مَكتَبة

تمرين ٤

Terms of address in use: On a separate sheet of paper, write how you would address these people appropriately according to the contexts below. Imagine that you are . . .

1. writing an official business letter to **وَليد طَرَزي**, who has a university degree
2. addressing **محمود سالِم**, a lower-level employee in your office
3. addressing a young, single female secretary named **ريم مَعلوف** in person
4. writing to a lady whose name is **رَباب كَحّال**
5. writing to an older man who is not very educated, whose name is **عبد الرحيم حُسَين**
6. addressing your professor **فَريد قَدّورة** in person
7. writing to a female student whose name is **زَينَب حَمدي**

2. Expressing Regret or Apology Using آسِف

One way of expressing regret or apology is by using the word آسِف "I'm sorry." The word آسِف is an active participle in Arabic (= the doer of the action like "runner," "walker," "swimmer," etc.) and is treated like a noun. This means that in the nominative case—when it is the subject of the sentence—it will take the dual ـانِ and the masculine plural ونَ or the feminine plural ات.

The Sound Plural الجمع *Suffix*: ونَ / ات	The Dual المُثَنّى *Suffix*: ـانِ	The Singular المُفْرَد	Gender الجِنْس
آسِفون	آسِفان	آسِف	**Masculine** المُذَكَّر
آسِفات	آسِفتان	آسِفة	**Feminine** المُؤَنَّث

Note: When the dual suffix ان is appended to the feminine form, the feminine suffix تاء مربوطة is retained, but it changes into a regular تاء. However, when the plural feminine ending ات is suffixed to the word آسِفة, the تاء مربوطة is dropped.

تمرين ٥

Conducting an official interview: Seek out one of your classmates whose name you do not know. Apologize for not knowing their name and then conduct an interview with them using the correct term of address throughout. Find out and write down as much information as you can. Possible topics are: place of origin, where they are living now, how many brothers and sisters they have, how many languages they know, what they are studying this term, if they have a car or bike. After you have exhausted your questions, switch roles. Be prepared to share your information with your classmates.

تمرين ٦

Write down the correct form of آسِف in the bubbles according to gender and number:

Presentation: Present the phrase الله أعلم as an alternative to لا أعرف to express a lack of knowledge.

Presentation: Ask students questions to which you expect they will have no answer so that they will use الله أعلم

١- ما أوّلُ كتابٍ في الإنكليزية؟
٢- مَن في هذا الصف يكتب اليابانية؟
٣- ما أوّلُ لغةٍ في التاريخ؟
٤- أين كلية الـ . . . ؟

3. Expressing Lack of Knowledge Using اللهُ أعلَم

You already know the phrase لا أعْرِف "I don't know," and you saw it in the first exchange in Section 1. There are, however, other ways of expressing lack of knowledge. One of them involves the use of the phrase اللهُ أعلَم (pronounced *allāhu a'lam*), which means "God knows / God only knows." It is one of many phrases that involve the use of the word الله that we will cover over the course of this book.

4. Expressing Degree

Expressing degree refers to how well one does something. In the exchange below the woman tries to find out whether Hiba speaks تَكَلَّمَ English well. Her response shows that she does not.

هَل تَتَكَلَّمينَ الإنكليزيَّة جَيِّداً يا هِبة؟

لا، أتَكَلَّمُها قَليلاً.

The adverb جَيِّداً "well" is derived from the adjective جَيِّد "good," just as قَليلاً "a little" is derived from قَليل "little" by suffixing تَنوين seated on a silent أَلِف.

Note: These adverbs generally occupy the final position of a sentence.

تمرين ٧

التطابق: اكتب الكلمات المتطابقة في العمود الأوسط:

١-	جَيِّداً		لُغَةً
٢-	آنِسة		أعْلَم
٣-	يَتَكَلَّمُ		خَمسة
٤-	أمينَةُ		قَليلاً
٥-	اللهُ		سَيِّدَة
٦-	سَيِّداتي		مَكتَبة
			سادَتي
			لُبنان

تمرين ٨

أملأ الفراغاتَ الآتية بالكَلِمةِ المُناسَبة من المُربَّعات:

اللهُ أعْلَم	الأخ	قَليلاً	الآنِسة	سَيِّداتي	سادَتي	آسِفة

١- ________ هالَة لا تَسكُن هُنا بَلْ في سَكَنِ الطالِبات.

٢- أنا ________ قَلَمي لَيسَ مَعي.

٣- أينَ مِفتاحُ السَيّارَة؟ ________

٤- ________ وَسادَتي، أهلاً بِكُم.

٥- أتَكَلَّمُ اللُغَةَ الإنكليزيَّة جَيِّداً والفَرَنسِيَّة ________.

تمرين ٩

Read and respond: On a separate sheet of paper, respond to the following questions in Arabic with reference to the main reading passages in this lesson. Improve your Arabic by writing your answers in complete sentences.

1. Does the woman know where the School of Law is?
2. What is Hala Boustani's address?
3. How would you introduce your favorite celebrity to an audience in Arabic?
4. How do you say that you speak a little Arabic?
5. What would you say if someone asks you about your professor's address, but you have no idea?
6. How would a woman express regret for not knowing how many students are in her son's class?
7. How would a man express regret for not knowing the name of his daughter's instructor?

مَدينة القرائش في المَغرِب

تمرين ١٠

اخترِ الكلِمةَ المُناسِبَة

١- أدْرُس في الإسكَندريَّة __________ يسكُن أخي.

☐ حَيْثُ ☐ عَلى ☐ في

٢- هذا كِتاب __________.

☐ عَليم ☐ جَيِّد ☐ أمين

٣- ريم عَلاّف __________ مَكتَبة في جامِعَة تِشرين.

☐ صيدلانية ☐ قليلاً ☐ أمينَة

٤- __________ لا أعرِف أينَ كُلِّيَّةُ الصَيْدَلَة.

☐ شُكْراً ☐ آسِف ☐ مِن

٥- __________ هالَة الإنكليزيَّة جَيِّداً.

☐ تَتَكَلَّم ☐ أعْلَم ☐ تَسكُن

صَيْدلانيّة

5. The Present Tense: Negation and Conjugation

A. Negation

You have already used the present tense of the verb سَكَنَ "to live," "to reside" in order to describe where one lives. For example, to indicate that you live in an apartment, you say: أَسْكُنُ في شَقة. However, if you do not live in an apartment, you can express that by inserting the negative particle لا in front of the verb:

١ لا أسكُنُ في شَقَّة.

Note: Negating present-tense verbs مُضارِع with the negative particle لا does not change either the structure of the verb or the word order of the sentence.

B. Conjugation

The following table lists all thirteen verb conjugations in the present tense according to person. All changes to the root verb تَكَلَّمَ are shown in red.

تَكَلَّمَ (في المُضارِع)		
Verb الفِعْل	**Pronoun** الضَمير	**Person**
أَتَكَلَّمُ	أنا	First المُتَكَلِّم
نَتَكَلَّمُ	نَحْنُ	
تَتَكَلَّمُ	أَنْتَ	Second المُخاطَب
تَتَكَلَّمِينَ	أَنْتِ	
تَتَكَلَّمانِ	أَنْتُما	
تَتَكَلَّمونَ	أَنْتُم	
تَتَكَلَّمْنَ	أَنْتُنَّ	
يَتَكَلَّمُ	هُوَ	Third الغائِب
تَتَكَلَّمُ	هِيَ	
يَتَكَلَّمانِ	هُما (m. d.)	
تَتَكَلَّمانِ	هُما (f. d.)	
يَتَكَلَّمونَ	هُم	
يَتَكَلَّمْنَ	هُنَّ	

6. Secrets of the Language: Prefixes and Suffixes

While memorizing the verb conjugations might seem to be a daunting task at first, here are some tips in terms of patterns that might simplify the matter. The generalizations that follow apply to every single Arabic verb in the indicative.

A. Overall

As you can see, all present/imperfect-tense verbs take a prefix. The suffixes to present-tense verbs indicate either *gender* or *number*.

Suffixes for Present-Tense Verbs	
ـانِ	for all duals, feminine and masculine
ـونَ	for masculine plurals
ـنْ	for feminine plurals

What is the difference between the present-tense conjugation of أنْتَ and هِيَ?

No differences exist. They are exactly the same and can only be distinguished through context.

B. First Person

The similarities between the conjugation of first-person singular and plural should be obvious. Examine the chart above to see what you can deduce.

As you can see, the conjugation for the singular uses the هَمزة from أنا as the first letter of its verbs; similarly, the conjugation for the plural uses the نون from نَحْنُ as the first letter of its verbs.

٢	أنا	←	أتكَلّمُ
٣	نَحْنُ	←	نَتكَلَّمُ

C. Second Person

Take a close look at the second-person independent pronouns. Do you see any patterns?

They all start with the same two letters أنْـ. It is the third letter of these pronouns that indicates gender and number.

Now take a look at all of the second-person verbs. Do you see a pattern there?

Each verb starts with a تـ, while their suffixes indicate *gender*, *dual*, or *plural* as can be seen in the Present-Tense Conjugation chart at the top of this page.

D. Third Person

All masculine verbs start with a يـ. You would think that all feminine verbs would start with a تـ to follow a pattern. Unfortunately we have an anomaly that has to be memorized.

The feminine plural starts with a يـ.

تمرين ١١

أملأ الفراغات الآتية بتصريف الفعل الصحيح في المضارع:

___________ (عَرَفَ) سَناء أربَعَ لُغات ولكِنْ هَل ___________ (تَكَلَّمَ) ها جَيِّداً؟ كَمْ لُغَةً ___________ (تَكَلَّمَ) مايكل براون؟ هُوَ ___________ (عَرَفَ) اللُغَةَ الإنكليزيَّة جَيِّداً لكِنَّهُ ___________ (تَكَلَّمَ) اللُغَةَ العَرَبيَّة قليلاً. هُوَ ___________ (سَكَنَ) في مَدينَةِ القاهِرة حَيْثُ ___________ (دَرَسَ) في الجامِعَةِ الأمريكيَّة. سَحَر وهالَة مِن دِمَشق لكِنَّهُما ___________ (سَكَنَ) في حَلَب حَيْثُ ___________ (دَرَسَ) في جامِعَتِهما. وأَنْتُم، أينَ ___________ (سَكَنَ) وماذا ___________ (دَرَسَ) في هذا الفَصْل؟

تمرين ١٢

Conversation: Find out how many people speak the following languages and how well they speak them. If your classmates know other languages that are not included here, write them down and indicate how well they speak them. Be prepared to report your findings to your instructor in Arabic.

١- الإنكليزيَّة ___________________.

٢- العَرَبيَّة ___________________.

٣- الإسْبانِيَّة ___________________.

٤- الفَرَنسِيَّة ___________________.

٥- اللاتينِيَّة ___________________.

7. Cardinal Numbers 11–999 الأعداد الأصْليّة

A. Cardinal Numbers 11 and 12

These compound numbers *precede* the noun they modify and agree with the specified noun in gender.

Feminine	Masculine	Case
إحْدى عَشْرَة سَيّارَة	أحَدَ عَشَرَ كِتاباً	Nominative, Accusative, and Genitive
اِثنتاعَشْرَةَ سَيّارَة	اِثنا عَشَرَ كِتاباً	Nominative
اِثنتَي عَشْرَةَ سَيّارَةً	اِثني عَشَرَ كِتاباً	Accusative and Genitive

Note that the number 11 is indeclinable; that is, it does not change with respect to case.

However, the number 12 does change its form with respect to case. The forms اِثنا (m.) and اِثنتا (f.) are used in nominative case, while the forms اِثنَي (m.) and اثنتَي (f.) are used when the noun is the object of a verb (accusative case) or a preposition (genitive case).

B. Cardinal Numbers 13–19

Like the numbers 3–10, these numbers have reverse gender agreement with the singular of their modified noun.

However, the reverse gender agreement is limited to the "ones" or single digits, not the tens, as you can see in the following example:

٤ ثَلاثَةَ عَشَرَ كِتاباً　　　ثَلاثَ عَشْرَةَ سَيّارَةً

Presentation: Present and practice the numbers 11–999 as described in Lessons 5 and 6.

Activity: Bookstore: You may wish to introduce the phrase بِكَم (= how much) to students in order to practice the numbers. Make some copies of a foreign currency, if you do not already have some authentic Arab currency. It would be best to have both coins and paper money. Make some signs in Arabic marking the name and the amount of each of your items: book bag, pens/pencils, calculator, books, notebooks, etc. You will play the part of the merchant, and a couple of students will play the part of the customer.

Pass out the money and talk about the amounts on each of the coins/paper bills that you are using, what country it comes from, and the name of the currency. For additional practice, allow the learners to haggle, reflecting a habit used when shopping, as illustrated in the dialogue below.

Practice: Repeat the names and numbers of the money that you handed out and review the names of the items you are selling. Do not review the price of the items that you are selling since it would be best if the students barter with you.

Application on page 117.

Application: Have some students attempt to purchase the items in front of you. Greet them as a vendor would greet his/her customers.

أ - أهلاً وسهلاً ومرحباً بكَ يا سيّدي! كيف حالك هذا الصباح؟
ط - الحمد لله. وأنت، كيف الحال؟
أ - الحمد لله. أي خدمة؟
ط - بكم هذا الدفتر هنا؟
أ - هذا الدفتر بخمسين ليرة.
ط - لا. هذا ليس جيداً. بخمسة وثلاثين ليرة!
أ - ماشي الحال. تفضّل يا سيّدي.
ط - شكراً
أ - عفواً.

Once you have modeled an exchange such as this with a couple of students, have a student play the part of the seller, while others play the part of the buyer.

Feminine المؤنّث	الأعداد	Masculine المُذكّر
ثَلاثَ عَشْرَةَ سَيّارَةً	١٣	ثَلاثَةَ عَشَرَ كِتاباً
أربعَ عَشْرَةَ سَيّارَةً	١٤	أربعَةَ عَشَرَ كِتاباً
خَمسَ عَشْرَةَ سَيّارَةً	١٥	خَمسَةَ عَشَرَ كِتاباً
سِتَّ عَشْرَةَ سَيّارَةً	١٦	سِتَّةَ عَشَرَ كِتاباً
سَبعَ عَشْرَةَ سَيّارَةً	١٧	سَبعَةَ عَشَرَ كِتاباً
ثَماني عَشْرَةَ سَيّارَةً	١٨	ثَمانِيَةَ عَشَرَ كِتاباً
تِسعَ عَشْرَةَ سَيّارَةً	١٩	تِسعَةَ عَشَرَ كِتاباً

Reverse gender agreement exists between the first word of the number (the ones digit) and the noun. Notice that ثلاثة and كتاباً exhibit a reverse gender agreement, while the tens digits agree in gender (e.g., عَشَرَ and كتاباً are both masculine).

Note: All numbers 11 through 19 (except for the number 12, which shows a case marker) are invariable, with a فتحة on the end in all cases.

Remember: The counted nouns are *singular indefinite accusative* (e.g., كِتاباً, سيّارَةً).

C. Cardinal Numbers 20–90

These numbers (i.e., the tens) are nouns and therefore change in form according to case. The ending ونَ is used for the nominative case (subject) (e.g., عِشرون) and ينَ for the accusative and genitive cases (e.g., عِشرينَ). Like the numbers 11–19, the noun following them is singular, indefinite, and accusative in that تَنوين (ً) appears on the last radical. They are invariable with regard to gender; that is, they do not vary in form to match the gender of the counted noun. In the examples below the number 30 changes with respect to case, but not gender.

Feminine المُؤنّث	Masculine المُذكّر	Case الحالَة
هُناكَ ثَلاثونَ جامِعَةً	عِندي ثَلاثونَ كِتاباً	**Nominative**
في ثَلاثينَ جامِعَةً	في ثَلاثينَ كِتاباً	**Genitive/Accusative**

Tens العُقود (20–90) with masculine and feminine nouns:

Feminine المؤنَّث	الأعداد	Masculine المُذَكَّر
عِشرونَ سَيّارَةً	٢٠	عِشرونَ كِتاباً
ثَلاثونَ سَيّارَةً	٣٠	ثَلاثونَ كِتاباً
أربَعونَ سَيّارَةً	٤٠	أربَعونَ كِتاباً
خَمسونَ سَيّارَةً	٥٠	خَمسونَ كِتاباً
سِتّونَ سَيّارَةً	٦٠	سِتّونَ كِتاباً
سَبعونَ سَيّارَةً	٧٠	سَبعونَ كِتاباً
ثَمانونَ سَيّارَةً	٨٠	ثَمانونَ كِتاباً
تِسعونَ سَيّارَةً	٩٠	تِسعونَ كِتاباً

SUMMARY

- **The numbers 11 and 12 أحْكامُ العَدَد**

  Both words in the number agree in gender with the noun. The number 11 is indeclinable (i.e., it does not change with case), exhibiting a **فتحة** on the final radical of both words, whereas the words **اِثنا** and **اثنتا** in the number 12 change to **اثنَي** and **اثنتَي** in the accusative and genitive cases.

- **The numbers 13–19**

  The first word of the number (the ones digit) has a reverse gender agreement with the noun, while the second word (ten) agrees with the noun in gender. Neither the ones digits nor the tens digits change with case; they always have a **فتحة** on their final radical.

- **The numbers 20–90**

  These numbers have two forms: (1) nominative (e.g., **عِشْرون**) and (2) accusative and genitive (e.g., **عِشْرين**). The noun following these numbers is singular, indefinite, accusative (e.g., **سِتّون/ ستّين سيّارةً**).

D. Inside the Numbers

As we have seen, the numbers 1 and 2 always agree in gender with the singular noun. This applies to 21, 22; 31, 32; 41, 42, etc.

٥	المُؤَنَّث	واحِدةٌ وعِشرونَ سَيّارةً	اِثنَتان وعِشرونَ سَيّارةً
٦	المُذَكَّر	واحِدٌ وعِشرونَ كِتاباً	اِثنانِ وعِشرونَ كِتاباً

As we have noted, the numbers 3–9 are always opposite the gender of the modified noun. This also applies to numbers 23–29; 33–39; 43–49, etc.

٧	المُؤَنَّث	ثلاثٌ وعِشرونَ سَيّارةً
٨	المُذَكَّر	أربعةٌ وعِشرونَ كِتاباً

E. The Number 100 (مِئة)

This is also a noun, which means that its case varies according to its position in the sentence. The counted noun following it is always singular indefinite. It forms an **إضافة** structure with the following noun, which is therefore genitive and indefinite, and takes a double **كسرة**:

٩	مِئَةُ كِتابٍ	مِئَةُ سَيّارَةٍ

Since the word **مِئة** is a noun, it is subject to being made dual and plural. The dual is formed by suffixing **انِ** for the nominative case or **ـَيْنِ** for both the genitive and accusative cases. The plural is formed by suffixing **ات** because it is a feminine noun, thus resulting in **مِئات** "hundreds." However, the plural form **مِئات** is never used with the numbers 100–999, but it is used in phrases such as:

١٠	مِئاتُ الكُتُبِ	*hundreds of books*

Note: In this usage, the counted noun (highlighted in red) is plural, definite, and genitive.

Here is a list of multiples of 100 used with nouns:

Feminine المُؤنَّث	الأعداد	Masculine المُذَكَّر
مِئتا (مِئتي) سَيّارةٍ	٢٠٠	مِئتا (مِئتي) كِتابٍ
ثَلاثُمِئةِ سَيّارةٍ	٣٠٠	ثَلاثُمِئةِ كِتابٍ
أربَعُمِئةِ سَيّارةٍ	٤٠٠	أربَعُمِئةِ كِتابٍ
خَمسُمِئةِ سَيّارةٍ	٥٠٠	خَمسُمِئةِ كِتابٍ
سِتُّمِئةِ سَيّارةٍ	٦٠٠	سِتُّمِئةِ كِتابٍ
سَبعُمِئةِ سَيّارةٍ	٧٠٠	سَبعُمِئةِ كِتابٍ
ثَمانُمِئةِ سَيّارةٍ	٨٠٠	ثَمانُمِئةِ كِتابٍ
تِسعُمِئةِ سَيّارةٍ	٩٠٠	تِسعُمِئةِ كِتابٍ

Note: The number 200 loses its final **نون** because it is the first word of an **إضافة** structure, which is known in Arabic as **المُضاف**.

تمرين ١٣

Conversation: Numbers in use: Find out how many . . .

1. people in class know whose picture is on the 20-dollar **دولار** bill; the 50; the 100
2. TVs your classmates have in their homes
3. students are taking biology this term
4. watches they have
5. phones they have
6. pens your classmates each have in their book bags

And now write your answers down on a separate sheet of paper in complete sentences. Be prepared to share your answers with your classmates. A word bank of plurals follows.

نَظّارة ج نَظّارات	طالِب ج طُلّاب	دَفتَر ج دَفاتِر	تِلْفاز ج تِلْفازات
هاتِف ج هَواتِف	قَلَم ج أقْلام	ساعَة ج ساعات	دَرّاجَة ج دَرّاجات

تمرين ١٤

A. Listen and select: Check the box that matches the information as expressed in the listening passage for this lesson.

١- يَسكُن عادِل مَحمود في . . .

☐ الإسكَندَريّة ☐ طَنطا ☐ القاهِرة

٢- عادِل مَحمود هُوَ . . . سامية.

☐ أخو ☐ أبو ☐ أخت

٣- تَدرُس سامية في جامِعَة . . .

☐ طَنطا ☐ القاهِرة ☐ الإسكَندَريَّة

٤- لِعَبدِ الحَليم . . .

☐ أخت واحِدَة ☐ أختان ☐ ثَلاث أخَوات

٥- تَسكُن سامية مَحمود الآن في . . .

☐ سَكَنِ الطالِبات ☐ بَيت أبيها ☐ كُلِّيَّةِ التِجارة

B. Answer these questions with reference to the listening passage.

٦- كَم أخاً لِسامية؟ ________________________.

٧- مَن زَينَب؟ ________________________.

٨- أهِيَ في المَدرَسة أم في الجامِعَة؟ ________________________.

٩- مَن تَهاني وماذا تَدرُس؟ ________________________.

C. Describe Samia's room in Arabic.

D. Compose a biographical sketch about yourself modeled after the listening passage.

Grammar note: As can be seen in this lesson, the preposition لِـ "to have" is very similar to عِندَ. Traditionally speaking, there has been a slight difference in usage in that لِـ was generally used for humans (= I have a son, daughter, friend, etc.), whereas عِندَ was used for everything else. In modern usage, عِندَ can be used in both cases.

المُفْرَدات

Listen to the vocabulary items on the audio and practice their pronunciation.

to be able	اِسْتَطاعَ (يَسْتَطِيعُ) اِسْتِطاعة (v.)
sorry	آسِف (m.) / آسِفة (n., f.)
most knowledgeable	أعلَم (n. superlative)
God knows	الله أعْلَم
librarian	أمينُ/ أمينةُ مَكتَبةٍ (n., m./f.)
program	بَرْنامِج ج بَرامِج (n., m.)
to speak	تَكَلَّمَ (يَتَكَلَّمُ) تَكَلُّم (v.)
abundant	جَزيلاً
good	جَيِّد (adj.)
well	جَيِّداً (adv.)
where, when	حَيْثُ (adv.)
pharmacology	صَيْدَلَة (n., f.)
group of ten	عَقْد ج عُقود (n., m.)
knowledgeable	عَليم (adj.)
little	قَليل (adj.)
a little	قَليلاً (adv.)
to, for, by	لِـ (prep.)
Don't worry about it (response to "thank you")	لاَ شُكْرَ على واجِب
boss; director	مُدير ج مُدَراء (n., m.)
help, assistance	مُساعَدة (verbal noun)
agreement	مُوافَقَة (verbal noun)
worker, employee	مُوَظَّف ج مُوَظَّفون (n., m.)
hundred	مِئة ج مِئات (n., f.)
you (m. sg.) are able	يُمْكِنُكَ (v.)

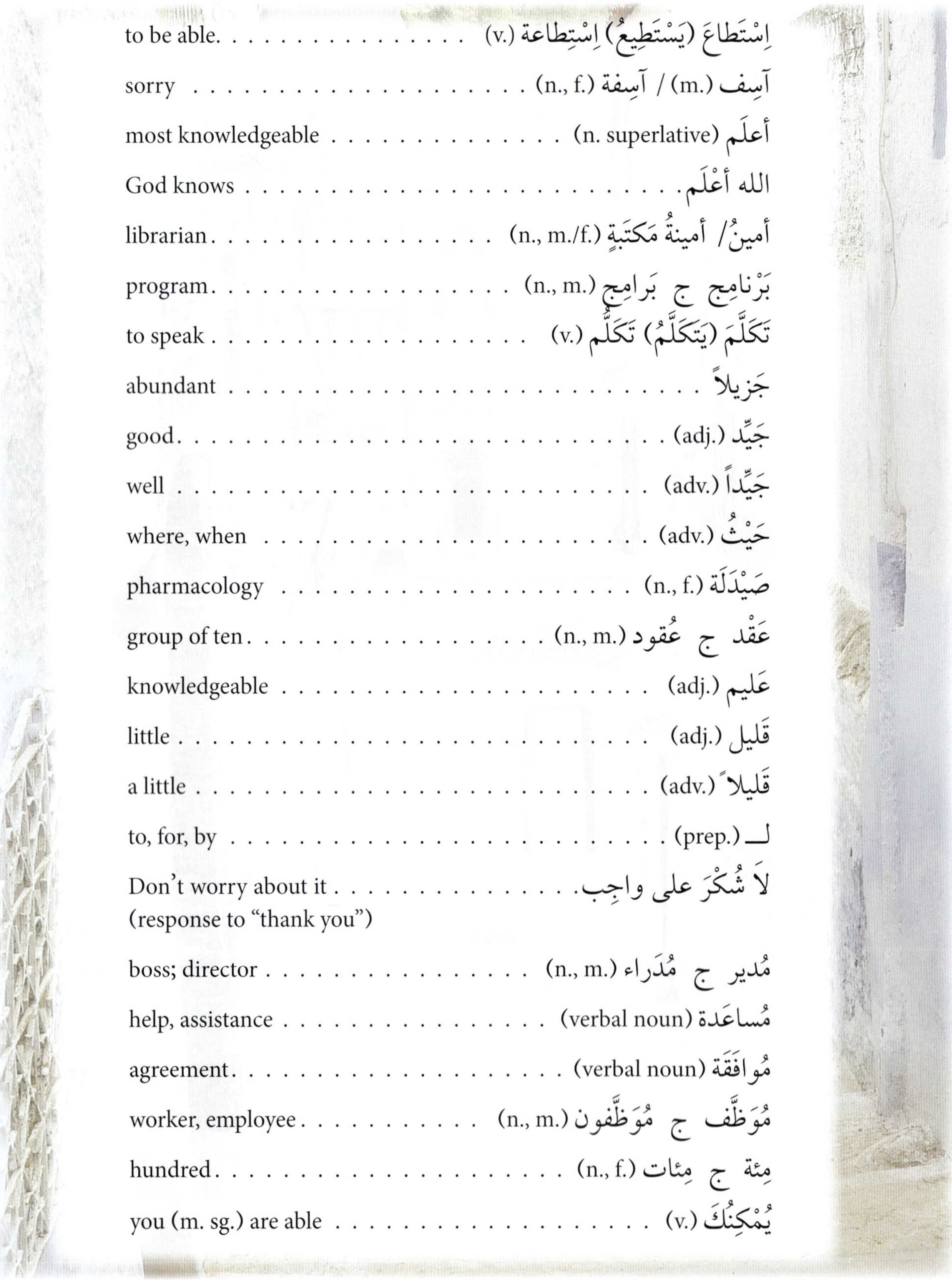

مَدينة شفشاون في شَمال المَغرِب

2

الدرس السابع

شارع المتنبي في بغداد العراق

Presentation: Bring some Arabic-language newspapers and magazines into the classroom, or connect to the Internet and display them on the classroom screen. Introduce and practice the words جريدة ومجلة along with the names of two or three publications. Make sure students pronounce the *tā' marbūṭa* at the end of each of these two words when used in conjunction with their names.

جَريدةُ الشرق الأوسط

مَجَلَّةُ العربي

Name the Arabic and English publications that you read and show them to students.

Practice: Conduct a chain drill in which students tell the student sitting next to them which newspapers and magazines they read.

Application: Pair Activity. Have the students break down into groups of two or three and ask each other: how many publications they read, what they are, how many days they read the newspaper, when they read the newspaper (morning, evening), and whether they read Arabic newspapers or magazines.

You may also wish to have the students do a survey of who among them reads certain newspapers and magazines, such as *Time*, *Newsweek*, the *New York Times*, the *Washington Post*, *USA Today*, etc.

Objectives

- Learning about Arabic print media
- Inquiring about and describing activities or objects
- Making polite requests and offers using the imperative
- Doubly transitive verbs
- The pronunciation of the pronoun ه
- Introduction to the cases of the noun
- Expressing possession with لِـ and مَعَ
- Introduction to attached pronouns suffixed to verbs
- Revisiting Arabic names

الكَلِماتُ المُفيدَة في صُوَر عَديدة

قَرَأ (يَقرَأُ) قِراءة

كَتَبَ (يَكْتُبُ) كِتابة

مَجَلّة ج مَجَلاّت

جَريدة ج جَرائد

رُكنُ مُفْرَداتِ المَشْهَدِ المرئي

to like or love s.th.	أحَبَّ / يُحِبُّ / حُبّ
in order to (+ present-tense verb)	لِـ + يَفْعَلَ
to learn	تَعَلَّم / يَتَعَلَّم / تَعَلُّم
vocabulary item	مُفْرَدة ج مُفْرَدات
to give s.th. to s.o.	أعْطى / يُعْطي / إعْطاء
another, additional s.th.	غَيْر
to sell s.th.	باعَ / يبيع / بَيْع
store	مَحَلّ ج مَحَلّات
near, neighboring	قُرْب
to buy, to purchase	اِشْتَرى / يَشْتَري / شِراء
to go (to)	ذَهَبَ / يَذْهَب / ذَهاب (إلى)

تمرين ١

أملأ الفراغات الآتية حَسَب معلومات النص المرئي:

صَباحُ الخَيْر.

صَباحُ الخَيْر.

ماذا تَفْعَل يا جون؟

________ الجَريدةَ العربية.

أنْتَ ________ قِراءةَ الجرائد؟

نَعم، ________ أنْ أقرأَ الجَريدةَ العَربيّة ________ المُفْرَدات الجَديدة.

ما الجَريدةُ الّتي ________؟

________ جَريدةَ الشَرْق الأوسَط.

هل عِندَكَ جَريدة ثانية ________ إياها؟

آسِف. ما عِندي ________ هذِه الجَريدة ولكِن هناك

________ قَريب ________ الجَرائدَ العَربيّة.

أين هو؟

خَلْفَ الجامِعة، ________ المَطْعَم الهِنْديّ.

عَرَفْته. سأذْهَب وأشْتَري واحدة. شكراً جزيلاً.

عَفواً.

تمرين ٢

تَمرينُ المُشاهَدة: شاهِدوا الدَرْسَ السابع على الشابِكة.

١- لماذا يُحِبُّ جون قِراءةَ الجَرائدِ العَرَبيَّة؟ ____________

____

٢- أيّة جَريدة يَقرَأ جون؟ ____________

____

٣- أينَ المَحَلُّ الّذي يَبيعُ الجَرائدَ العَرَبيَّة؟ ____________

____

جَرائِد ومَجلاّت عَرَبيّة

هُناكَ جَرائِد ومَجلاّت عَرَبيَّة في مَكتَبةِ الجامِعة.

جَريدةُ الأهْرام مِصْريّة.

جَريدة تِشْرين سوريَّة.

جَريدةُ الشَرْقِ الأوْسَط سُعوديّة.

جَريدةُ الرافِدَيْن عِراقيّة.

جَريدةُ الفِكْر تونِسيّة.

مَجَلَّةُ الإكليل يَمَنيّة.

مَجَلَّةُ الفُنون مَغْرِبيّة.

مَن يَقرَأ هذِه الجَرائِد والمَجلّات؟

يَقرأُ المَجلاّت والجَرائدَ العَرَبيّة طُلاّب عَرَب في الجامعة وطُلاّب أمريكيّون يَدرُسون اللُّغةَ العَربيّة.

ماذا يَقرَأون؟

يَقرأُ الطُلاّبُ العَرَب في أمريكا الجَرائِد والمَجلاّتِ العَرَبيّة في مَكتبَةِ الجامِعة عادَةً. يَقرَأ عَدنان مارتيني جَريدة «تِشْرينَ» ومَجلَّة «المَعرِفة» السوريّتَين عادَةً ويقرَأ أحياناً مَجلّة «روز اليوسِف» المِصْريّة.

يَقرَأ وَليد صايغ عادَةً جَريدة «النَهارِ» اللُبنانيّة ومَجلَّة «المَجلّةِ» السُعوديّة، ويَقرَأ أحْياناً جَريدة «الأهرامِ» المِصريّة.

يَقرَأ زياد نابلسي عادةً جَريدة «الرافدين» العِراقيّة، لكِنَّهُ يَقرَأ جَريدة «الشَرقِ الأوْسَط» السُعوديّة و«الأخبارَ» المِصْريّة أيضاً. يَقرَأ زِياد أحْياناً مَجلَّة «الرافِد» الإماراتية ومَجلَّة «المَوْقِف الأدَبيّ» السوريّة.

- أيّة جَريدَة تَقرَأ يا عَبدَ اللطيف؟
- أقرَأ جَريدَةَ النَهار عادَةً.
- هَل جَريدَةُ النَهار سوريّة؟
- لا. هِيَ لُبنانيّة. المُجاهِد جَزائريّة.
- هَل تَكتُب في جَريدة؟
- لا. أنا لا أكتُب في أيّة جَريدة. أنا أقرَأُ الجَرائِد.

Reflecting on our reading: The word أيّ is used as a question particle. Can you deduce its meaning from context?

Presentation: Pretend that you are reading and then tell students what you are doing; then start writing and ask them what you are doing. Randomly ask students what they are doing and then check for comprehension by asking what each one is doing in the third person.

أ – ماذا تفعل يا جون؟
ط – أتكلم مع أستاذي.
أ – ماذا يفعل جون يا سارة؟
ط – يتكلم جون مع أستاذه.

Practice: Choose about five pictures that show people conducting some activity and ask students what the people in the pictures are doing.

Activity: Have students ask one another what they do in the classes that they are taking.

١. Using أيّ "which"

The focus of the exchange between ʻAbd al-Latīf and his friend is on the newspaper, not the action of reading. In instances such as these, we use أيّ for both feminine and masculine objects to ask "which" (originally, no feminine form of it existed, but you may encounter أيّةُ in use, which is acceptable). As we have already seen, when we want to ask about an action we use ماذا followed by a verb.

If the nature of the activity is known—reading, for example—then we would use that verb (e.g., "what are you reading?"). But if the activity is not known, then the generic verb فَعَلَ is used meaning "to do." Consider the following question and answer exchange.

The question word أيٌّ is a noun; therefore, it forms an إضافة with a following noun and functions as the subject or object in a sentence.

In summary, the interrogative (question) word used to inquire about objects is أيّ "which," and the question word used to inquire about actions is ماذا "what."

If the request cannot be fulfilled, the words (m.) آسِف / (f.) آسِفة may be used, as in the exchange above.

2. Making Polite Requests with مِن فَضْلِك and Using تَفَضَّل

As you can see in the previous exchange, the phrase مِن فَضل is used along with the attached pronoun كَ. Any of the second-person attached pronouns (= كَ، كِ، كُما، كُم، كُنَّ) can be attached to this phrase to denote a polite request from someone or a group of people. A positive response to a request usually involves the use of a particular imperative verb تَفَضَّل/ تَفَضَّلي, which also signifies politeness. This verb carries many meanings that differ with respect to context.

Note: In this instance, تَفَضَّل can be roughly translated as "here you go." If you open the door for someone while saying تَفَضَّل, the meaning would be "come in"; if you seat someone while saying تَفَضَّل, it would mean "please (be seated)."

A. The Imperative

Requesting and offering something might involve the use of the imperative form of the verb you are using. Two imperative verbs أَعْطِ and تَفَضَّلْ are used in the dialogue found later in section C. The verb أَعْطِ "give!" represents the second-person masculine singular conjugation, because it is *addressed to a man.*

The imperative verb is not conjugated for the person speaking; it is conjugated for the person being addressed.

Likewise, the form تَفَضَّلي can be said by anyone, in fact, by any group of people, but it is addressed to an individual woman. There are basically five imperative forms of the Arabic verb corresponding to the five second-person pronouns seen in the table below.

Imperative Forms of the Verb تَفَضَّل					
أنتُنَّ	أنتُم	أنتُما	أنتِ	أنتَ	**Pronoun**
تَفَضَّلْنَ	تَفَضّلوا	تَفَضَّلا	تَفَضَّلي	تَفَضَّلْ	**Imperative**

B. Forming the Imperative

You may be wondering how you can come up with the imperative (command) form of any verb on your own. All you have to do is follow these few, easy steps:

1. If the letter following the prefix is a سكون, replace the prefix with a همزة (*hamzat wasl*):

Write!	أُكْتُبْ	←	يَكْتُبُ	١

To figure out the middle short vowel of the imperative, look at the middle short vowel of the present-tense verb. If there is a ضَمّة, then the imperative will begin with a ضَمّة, just as in examples 1, 2, and 3.

Get out!	أُخْرُجْ	←	يَخْرُجُ	٢
Enter!	أُدْخُلْ	←	يَدْخُلُ	٣

When the second short vowel of the present-tense verb is a كسرة or a فَتْحة, then the imperative will start with a كسرة:

Understand!	اِفْهَمْ	←	يَفْهَمُ	٤
Sit down!	اِجْلِسْ	←	يَجْلِسُ	٥

2. For words that have four letters or more, drop the prefix of the present-tense verb. If the letter following the prefix has a short vowel on it, do nothing (e.g., يَتَفَضَّلُ becomes تَفَضَّلْ; the تاء is followed by a فتحة).

Note that the final ضَمّة is also dropped:

Drop ضَمّة Retain فَتحة

٦ يَتَفَضَّلُ ← تَفَضَّلْ

Drop ياء

3. For past-tense verbs that have four letters, place a فتحة on the initial همزة.

أَعْطِ	←	أعطى	٧

Conjugation of أعطى (يُعْطي)

Imperative	Present	Past	Pronoun	Person
	أُعطي	أعطَيْتُ	أنا	المُتكَلِّم
	نُعطي	أَعطَيْنا	نَحنُ	
أَعْطِ	تُعطي	أَعْطَيْتَ	أنتَ	المُخاطَب
أَعْطي	تُعطِينَ	أَعطَيْتِ	أنتِ	
أَعطِيا	تُعطِيانِ	أَعْطَيْتُما	أنتُما	
أَعْطوا	تُعْطونَ	أَعطَيْتُم	أنتُم	
أَعْطينَ	تُعْطينَ	أَعْطَيْتُنَّ	أنتُنَّ	
	يُعْطي	أَعْطى	هُوَ	الغائب
	تُعْطي	أَعطَتْ	هِيَ	
	يُعْطِيانِ	أَعْطَيا	هُما	
	تُعْطِيانِ	أَعطَتا	هُما	
	يُعْطونَ	أَعْطَوْا	هُم	
	يُعْطِينَ	أَعطَيْنَ	هُنَّ	

Presentation: Go around the class requesting things from the students:

أ – أعطني . . . مِن فضلك. شكراً

ط – تفضل. عفواً.

With the objects in your possession, instruct the students to request them back from you. Practice the forms well enough to enable the students to interact with you and with each other.

ط – أعطيني قلمي من فضلك.

أ – تفضّل/ تفضّلي

ط – شكراً

أ – عفواً

Practice: Conduct Exercise 5.

C. Doubly Transitive Verbs

Verbs that take an object are called transitive verbs. For example, in the sentence "I wrote a letter," the verb "wrote" is transitive because the word "letter" is the direct object of the verb "wrote." A limited number of verbs are transitive to two objects. One of them is the verb **أعْطى** "to give." In the sentence **أعْطِني جَريدةً** "give me a newspaper" in the dialogue below, the two objects are the pronoun **ني** "me" suffixed to the verb and the noun **جَريدةً** "newspaper."

Note: The direct object of **أعْطى** will be in the accusative case; when indefinite, as in the example below, it will take a double **فتحة** on the final radical. When the direct object of a verb is definite, however, it will take a single **فتحة**.

- أَعْطِني جَريدة مِن فَضْلِكَ!
- أيّة جَريدة؟
- جَريدَة «الدُسْتور» مِن فَضْلِك.
- تَفَضَّل!
- شُكراً!
- عَفواً!

D. Pronunciation of the Attached Pronoun هُ

As you know, this pronoun (pronounced *hu*) can only function as a suffix. However, if the preceding vowel is a **كسرة** (i.e., the short vowel *i*) or the long vowel **ي**, then, due to vowel harmony, it is pronounced *hi*. Listen to the recording and repeat during the pauses:

فيهِ   إلَيْهِ   بِهِ   في بيتِهِ   أعْطِهِ

تمرين ٣

وافِقْ بَيْنَ الكَلِماتِ في العَمودَين، واكتُبهما في الوَسَط:

١-	جَريدة		تَفَضَّلْ
٢-	عادَةً		مَعَهُ
٣-	أعطِني		مَجَلَّة
٤-	يَقرأ		أحْياناً
٥-	العَرَبي		يَكْتُبُ
			الأهْرام

تمرين ٤

أكمِلِ الجُمَلَ التاليةَ بكلماتٍ من المستطيل:

تَفَضَّلي	اِجلِسي	أعطِني	جَيِّداً	أيّ	مِن فَضْلِك	تَشَرَّفْنا	تَقرَأ	تكتُب

١- ____________ مَجَلّة تَقرَأينَ يا هُدى؟

٢- أعطِني مَجَلَّةَ العَرَبيّ ____________.

٣- يا سَيِّد، ____________ جَريدَةَ الأهْرام، مِن فَضْلِك.

٤- يا كَريمة، ____________ هنا في هذا الكُرْسيّ بِجانِبِ الشُبّاك.

٥- يا طالِبَ اللُغةِ العَرَبيّة، هَل ____________ جَريدة تشرين ؟

٦- يا أُسْتاذ، أعْطِني مَجَلّةَ المَجَلّة مِن فَضْلِك. ____________ يا آنسة.

تمرين ٥

Conversation: Imperatives in use. In groups of two, one person should pretend to be a newspaper vendor while the other is the buyer. The buyer will ask about various Arabic newspapers and magazines that were introduced in this lesson. Use the imperatives "give!" and "here you go" during this business transaction. **For a challenge** the vendor may wish to ask "which newspaper/magazine?" and ask for a lot of money, for example, "give me five American dollars!" Remember to be creative with the language and to use as much of your vocabulary as you can.

تمرين ٦

اِختَرِ الكَلِمَةَ المُناسِبةَ حَسَبَ النَصّ:

١ - «الرافدين» ____________ عِراقيّة.

☐ مَكتَبَة ☐ مَجَلّة ☐ جَريدَة

٢- هُناكَ ____________ عَرَبيّة في مَكتَبةِ الجامِعة.

☐ طالِبات ☐ طُلاّب وطالِبات ☐ مَجَلاّت وجَرائِد

٣- الفُنون ____________ مَغرِبيَّة.

☐ جَريدة ☐ مَجَلَّة ☐ طالِبة

٤- يَقْرَأُ الجَرائِدَ العَرَبيَّة في المَكتَبةِ طلاّب ____________.

☐ أمريكيّون ☐ مِصْريّون ☐ يَعرِفونَ العَرَبيّة

٥- يَقرَأ عَدنان مارتيني عادةً مَجَلَّةَ ____________.

☐ النَهار ☐ المَجَلَّة ☐ المَعرِفة

٦- أَعطى الرَجُل جَريدة ____________.

☐ الأهرام ☐ الدُسْتور ☐ تِشرين

٧- يَقرَأ زِياد نابُلسي جَريدة ____________ عادةً.

☐ الأهرام ☐ الرافِدين ☐ تِشرين

٨- يَقرَا عَبدُ اللَطيف ____________.

☐ جَريدة لُبنانيَّة ☐ جَريدة سوريّة ☐ مَجَلَّة جزائريّة

تمرين ٧

Conversation: Scavenger hunt, using أعْطى، مِن فَضْلِك، تَفَضَّلْ. In Arabic, politely ask for and return the following items to your classmates. Be sure to write down the names of the people who gave you these items. Of course, the first one who completes the scavenger hunt wins.

1. one biology or computer science book
2. three pencils
3. one identity card
4. two notebooks
5. a pair of glasses

Be prepared to report your "treasure" to your class.

3. Cases of the Noun

There are three cases of the noun in Arabic:

A. The Nominative Case الرَّفْع

A noun is nominative مَرْفوع if:

1. it is the doer of the action, the agent, the *-er* form in English (like runner, writer, swimmer, etc.), or the subject of a verb in a verbal sentence. Like English, many Arabic words follow a form, that of **فاعِل**, which by no mere coincidence is the name for the active participle (or the "doer") in Arabic اِسمُ الفاعِل. Consider the word **الطالِبُ** "student" in the following example:

٨	يَقرَأُ الطالِبُ جَريدَةً.	*The student reads/is reading a newspaper.*

2. it is the subject مُبْتَدَأ of a nominal sentence **الطالِبُ**, as in example 9:

	المُبْتَدَأ	الخبَر
٩	يَقرَأُ الطالِبُ	جَريدَةً.

3. it is the predicate خَبَر of a nominal sentence **أمريكيٌّ**, as in example 10:

	المُبْتَدَأ	الخبَر
١٠	الطالِبُ	أمريكيٌّ.

Note that both nouns in example 10 are nominative, because they are the subject and predicate (topic and comment) of a nominal sentence, yet **الطالِبُ** is marked with a ضَمّة because it is definite, while **أمريكيٌّ** is marked with a double ضَمّة because it is indefinite.

Grammar note: Singular Arabic nouns take two short vowels if indefinite and one short vowel if definite—exceptions are certain nouns called diptotes (see Lesson 15, section 2).

In the nominative case, the ending انِ is suffixed to dual nouns, and ونَ to sound masculine plurals.

The two students are American.	الطالِبانِ أمريكيّانِ.	١١
The students are American.	الطُلاّبُ أمريكيّونَ	١٢

B. The Genitive Case الجَـرُّ

A noun is in the genitive case مَجْرور if:

1. it is the object of a preposition مَجْرورٌ بِحَرْفِ الجَرِّ

in the house	في البَيْتِ	١٣

2. it is the second part of an إضافة structure known as مُضاف إلَيْه

the chemistry lab	مَخْبَرُ الكيمْياءِ	١٤

The Genitive Markers		
after definite nouns	في البيتِ	كسرة
after indefinite nouns	في بيتٍ	تنوين كسرة
dual nouns	في البَيْتَيْنِ	ـَيْنِ
sound masculine plurals	مع المُوَظَّفينَ	ينَ

C. The Accusative Case النَّصْب

This case is a bit more complex to define. But it can be readily said that if the noun is neither nominative nor genitive, then it is accusative مَنْصوب. We are already familiar with how to use النَّصْب in two instances:

1. the direct object of a verb المَفْعول بِهِ:

Sana knows the French language.	تَعرِفُ سَناء اللُغةَ الفَرَنسِيّة.	١٥

2. the specification of quantity **التَمْييز**:

How many books do you have?	كَمْ كِتاباً عِندَكَ؟	١٦
50 books.	خَمْسونَ كِتاباً.	١٧

The accusative markers include the **فتحة**, double **فتحة**, ـَيْنِ (*-ayni*) for dual nouns, and ينَ (*-īna*) for sound masculine plurals.

The Accusative Markers		
after definite nouns	رأيْتُ الرَجُلَ	فتحة
after indefinite nouns	رأيْتُ رَجُلاً	تنوين فتحة
dual nouns	رأيْتُ رَجُلَيْنِ	ـَيْنِ
sound masculine plurals	رأيْتُ المُوَظَّفينَ	ينَ

تمرين ٨

Cases of the noun: On a separate sheet of paper, rewrite each sentence giving the case of the underlined word(s) in each sentence. Provide the short vowels and then offer an explanation of why you chose that particular diacritic using Arabic terminology:

١- أستاذُ الصفّ مِن مَدينَةِ سوسة في تونِس.

٢- السَيّارة في الشارِع.

٣- كَمْ طالِب في الصفّ؟

٤- يَعرِفُ أحمَد عُنوان هالَة.

٥- يَعرِفُ مايكل اللُغة العَرَبيّة قليلاً.

٦- تَكتُبُ الطالِبة على وَرَقة في دَفْترِها.

٧- يَقرَأُ عَبدُ اللطيف كِتاب.

٨- مِفتاح سَيّارة الأستاذ في سَيّارتِه!

Presentation: Demonstrate the difference in meaning between عندي and لي on the one hand, and معي on the other. The first two signify possession, or ownership, whereas the latter denotes accompaniment or having something on you, but which is not necessarily yours.

Application: Pair Activity. Break the class down into groups of two or three, and have one person ask the other questions that require the distinction between these prepositions. Have them ask if the student has a car, bike, sunglasses, computer, calculator, book bag, keys, notebook, books, pencils, brothers, sisters, etc. Have about five students report their answers by writing them on the board.

Have the class correct the answers as a group.

4. Expressing Possession with the Prepositions لِـ and مَعَ

Possession has been expressed so far with the adverb of place عِندَ followed by a noun or an attached pronoun. Consider the example:

١٨	عِندَ سامي سَيّارةٌ.	*Sami has a car.*
	عِندي سَيّارةٌ.	*I have a car.*

Possession may also be expressed with the preposition لِـ by attaching either a pronoun or a noun to لِـ:

١٩	لي أُخْتانِ.	*I have two sisters.*
	لِعادِلٍ أُخْتانِ.	*Adil has two sisters.*

Like عِندي, the prepositional phrase لي may be translated as "I have;" although neither are verbs in Arabic.

Note that لِـ and عِندَ may not be used interchangeably. With reference to people, both the preposition لِـ and the adverb عِندَ may be used to express possession of something whether acquired or inherent (e.g., I have a car; I have two hands).

When it is used with reference to inanimate objects, however, only لِـ may be used:

٢٠	لِغُرفَتي شُبّاكان.	*My room has two windows.*

Note: When the preposition لِـ (*li-*) is prefixed to a noun, it is pronounced *li*, but when prefixed to a pronoun, it is pronounced *la* (e.g., لَهُ، لَنا، لَكِ).

The phrase that occurred in our main reading passage, مَعي قَلَم means "I have a pen with me." مَعي can be thought of as "along with," or "on my person," to be differentiated from عِندَ which alludes to a worldly possession.

Error Prevention: Use ذَهَبْتُ إلى الجامِعةِ بِالسَّيّارة

Do not use

ذَهَبْتُ إلى الجامِعةِ مَعَ السَّيّارة

This would mean that you and your car came to the university together.

تمرين ٩

Translation: Express possession, using عِندَ ,لـ, and مَعَ:

1. Reema [feminine name] has two bicycles.

   ____.

2. Our house has three doors.

   ____.

3. Ahmed has got a car [with him] now.

   ____.

4. I have a brother and a sister.

   ____.

5. Do you have your eyeglasses on you?

   ____.

6. Mrs. Boustani has a son and a daughter.

   ____.

5. Attached Pronouns Suffixed to Verbs

So far, we have seen attached pronouns suffixed to nouns where they function as possessive pronouns (e.g., كِتابي "my book," قَلَمُها "her pen"). However, when these pronouns are suffixed to verbs and prepositions they serve as object pronouns, such as the English "him," "them," etc.

٢١	أعرِفُ ثَلاثَ لُغاتٍ وأتَكَلَّمُها جَيِّداً.	*I know three languages and speak them well.*

In example 21, the highlighted suffix ها (third-person feminine singular) in أتَكَلَّمُها means "them" (not "it" or "she") because this attached pronoun refers back to لُغات, which is a non-rational plural.

Remember: Non-rational (i.e., inanimate) plurals are treated as feminine singular. This means that *any reference to such plurals is made in the third-person feminine singular, regardless of the gender of the singular noun.*

You will notice that pronouns attached to verbs are the very same pronouns that we attach to nouns and prepositions. There exists one exception, however; the first-person singular pronoun ي becomes ني when suffixed to verbs:

Nadia knows me from the university.	٢٢ تَعرِفُني نادية مِنَ الجامِعة.

Attached Pronouns Suffixed to Verbs

الضمير المُنْفَصِل	أنا	نَحنُ	أنتَ	أنتِ	أنتُما	أنتُم	أنتُنَّ	هُوَ	هِيَ	هُما	هُما	هُم	هُنَّ
	↓	↓	↓	↓	↓	↓	↓	↓	↓	↓	↓	↓	↓
الضمير المتصِل	ني	نا	كَ	كِ	كُما	كُم	كُنَّ	هُ	ها	هُما	هُما	هُم	هُنَّ

تمرين ١٠

Convey the meanings of the following sentences in Arabic:

1. I know her.

 ______________________________.

2. He gave us a newspaper.

 ______________________________.

3. They (m.) know Arabic and speak it at home.

 ______________________________.

4. Give me (addressing a man) that magazine, please.

 ______________________________.

5. They (f.) know me.

 ______________________________.

6. Do you (f.) know them (m.)?

 ______________________________.

7. Give him (addressing a woman) your phone number.

 ______________________________.

تَذَوّق الثّقافة العَربيّة

Most Arabic first names have meanings. For example, the name وَليد (m.) means "boy" or "newborn," and the name تَهاني (f.) means "congratulations." There are also compound names (e.g., عَبْدُ الله). Such compound names containing عَبْدُ are only for males. The first word عَبْدُ means "servant, slave, creature." The second word is either الله "God" or any one of the 99 other names of Allah, such as عَبْدُ اللَطيف and عَبْدُ الهادي (pronounced *abdu-l-laṭīf* and *abdu-l-hādī*). Thus, the popular belief that the word *Abdul* is an Arabic name is partially mistaken, since this word represents only the first part of the name عَبْدُ plus the definite article الـ of the second part.

تمرين ١١

Foreign names in news articles: Examine these excerpts from an Arabic magazine and circle the foreign names that you can identify and then transcribe them in English. Five names appear in the first excerpt (on the right) and three in the second.

يقول جون كلارك غيبل "لقد قررت أن أجرب حظي في التمثيل عندما أحضر كلايد وير نص الفيلم (جيم السيئ) لأنني أحببته كثيراً. سأمثل هذا الفيلم مع ممثلين مجربين هما جيمس برولين وريتشارد راوندتري."

ساهم الكاتبان غراهم غرين وجون لو كاريه في ظهور نوع جديد من أدب الرواية الجاسوسية يتحدث عن جرائم فظيعة ترتكب على كلا الجانبين من جدار برلين أيام الحرب الباردة.

تمرين ١٢

Listen and select:

A. Listen to the recorded passage and check the best alternative according to the passage.

١- أحمَد زَوج ____________ .

☐ فاطِمة ☐ رانِية ☐ سَميرَة

٢- يَقرَأُ أحمَد جَريدَةَ ____________ أحياناً.

☐ الدُستورِ ☐ الشَرقِ الأوسَطِ ☐ الأهرامِ

٣- فَريد ____________ فاطِمة.

☐ اِبنُ ☐ زَوجُ ☐ أبو

B. Complete these sentences according to the information in the passage:

٤- فاطِمة لَها اِبنَتانِ هُما ____________ و____________.

٥- تَقرَأُ فاطِمةُ جَريدَةَ ____________ .

٦- يَقرَأُ أحمَد عادةً جَريدَةَ ____________ .

C. صواب أو خطأ On the basis of the information in the recorded passage, mark these statements خَطَأ or صَواب and correct the false ones.

٧- يَقرأُ أحمَدُ مَجَلّةَ الهِلال.

٨- سَميرة أُخْتُ بَشير.

٩- تَسكُنُ عائِلَةُ أحمَد في عُمان.

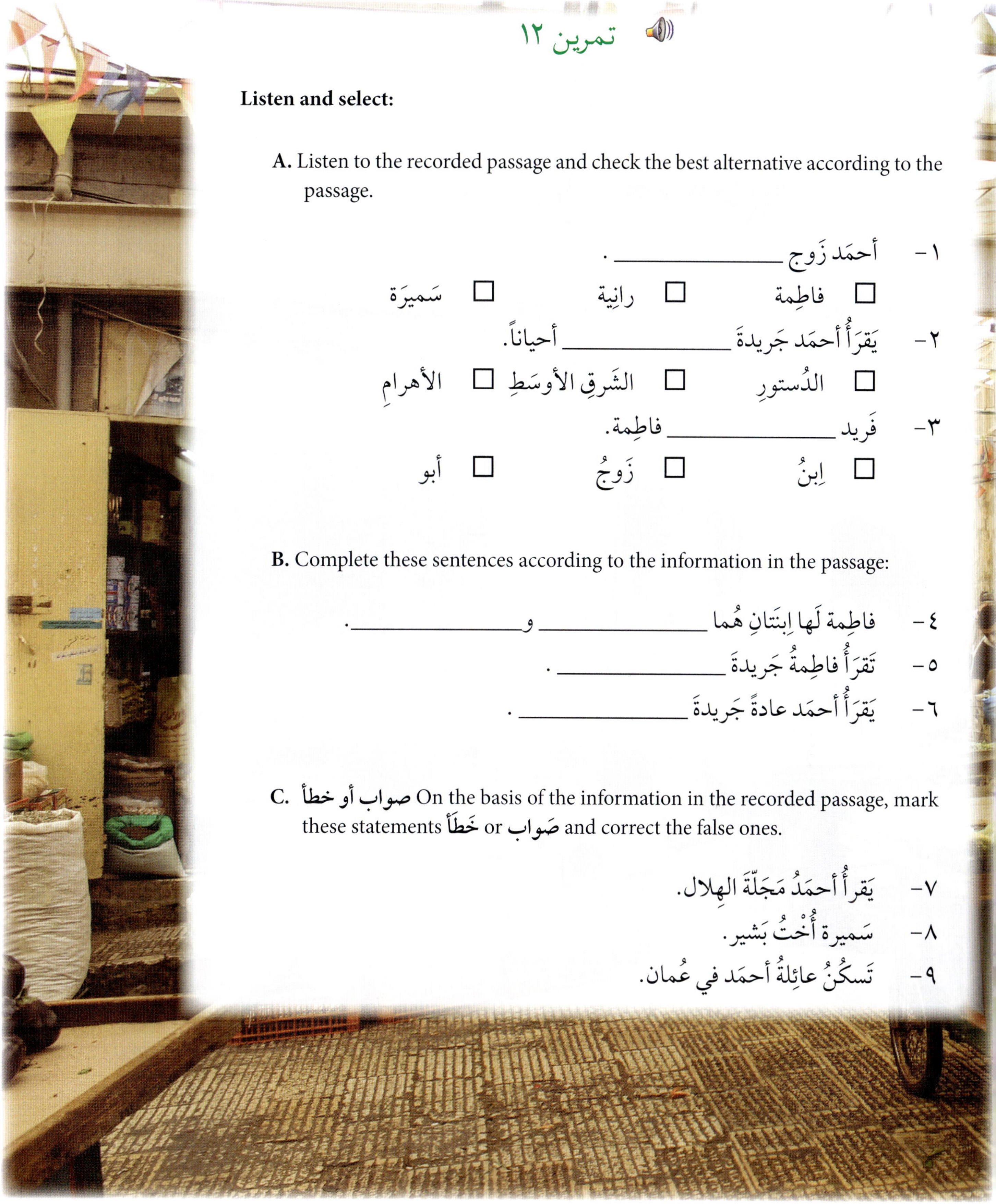

إحدى الأسواق القديمة في مدينة نابلس

تمرين ١٣

Listen and select:

Listen to the recorded passage and fill in the blanks with the words you hear:

١- ________ أمس إلى مَكتَبةِ الجامِعة، و________ كُتُباً كَثيرة. ________ عن مَجَلّةِ العَرَبيّ الكوَيتيّة، وجَريدة تِشرين السوريّة، ثمّ ________ في المَقهى، و________ عَصيرَ البرتقال، وعِندَ الساعة الخامِسة تَقريباً ________ إلى البيت.

٢- ________ صَديقي أمس إلى بيتِه لِتَناوُل طَعام العَشاء. جَلَستُ مع والِده ووالِدَته وإخوَتِه و________ عَن الدِراسة والأخبار السياسيّة. وبَعدَ العَشاء ________ عن والِدي وعمله في جَريدة النَهار اللُبنانيّة، و________ والِدَتُه عن عَمَل والِدَتي فـ________ إنَّها تَعمَل أستاذةً في الجامِعة. ثُمَّ ________ الحلوى و________ الشاي، وفي الساعة العاشِرة والنِصف ________ و________ على ________ لي.

مطابع صحيفة الجزيرة

المُفْرَدات

أحَبَّ (يُحِبُّ) حُبّ، مَحَبّة (.v) .... to like

أحياناً (.adv) .... sometimes

أرادَ (يُريدَ) إرادة (.v) .... to want

اِشْتَرى / يَشْتَري / شِراء .... to buy, to purchase

أعطى (يُعطي) أَعْطِ (imperative) (.v) .... to give

إعْطاء (verbal noun) .... giving

أيّ (.n., m) / أيّةُ (.n., f) .... which

باعَ (يَبيعُ) بَيْع (.v) .... to sell

تَعَلَّم / يَتَعَلَّم / تَعَلُّم .... to learn

تَفَضَّلْ / تَفَضَّلي (imperative) (.v) .... if you please

ذَهَبَ / يَذْهَب / ذَهاب (إلى) .... to go (to)

عادَةً (.adv) .... usually

غَيْر .... another, additional s.th.

فَعَلَ (يَفعَلُ) فِعْل (.v) .... to do

قَرَأَ (يَقرَأُ) قِراءة (.v) .... to read

قُرْب (.adv) .... near, close

كَتَبَ (يَكْتُبُ) كِتابة (.v) .... to write

لِـ + يَفْعَلَ .... in order to + (present-tense verb)

مَجَلَّة ج مَجَلّات (.n., f) .... magazine

مَحَلّ ج مَحَلّات .... store

مُفْرَد ج مُفْرَدات .... vocabulary item

مِنْ فَضْلِك (polite phrase) .... please

الدرس الثامن

Objectives

- Requesting and declining things politely
- Describing daily activities
- Expressing likes and dislikes
- Introduction to adverbials of time صَباحاً، مَساءً
- Revisiting the imperative
- Introduction to food and drink
- Revisiting prepositions and attached pronouns
- Introduction to plurals of nouns
- Revisiting the إضافة structure (multiple إضافة)

الكَلِماتُ المُفيدة في صُوَر عَديدة

أَكَلَ (يأْكُلُ) أَكْل

شَرِبَ (يَشْرَبُ) شُرْب

أَحَبَّ (يُحِبُّ) حُبّ

شاي

بَيْض

خُبْز

جُبْن

حَليب

فنجان قَهْوة

زُبْدة

تُفّاحة

بُرتُقالة

تمرين ١

وافِق بَينَ الكَلِماتِ في العَمودَين واكتبهما في الوسط:

١-	شاي		مَساءً
٢-	مُرَبّى		حاضِر
٣-	لَحْم		قَهوَة
٤-	صَباحاً		بُرتُقال
٥-	مَعَ		عَسَل
٦-	مَطْعَم		كَأس
٧-	يَشرَب		خِنزير
٨-	عَصير		دونَ
			مَقصَف
			يأكُل

تمرين ٢

اِختَر الكلمة الّتي لا تُناسِب باقي الكلمات في كُلّ مجموعة وبَيِّن السَبَب:

١-	فول	طَعْمِيّة	مُرَبّى	فَلافِل
٢-	دون	ظُهْر	صَباح	مَساء
٣-	عَصير	شاي	قَهوة	بُرتُقال
٤-	ماء	حَليب	خُبْز	شاي

شاي مِن فَضلِك!

- تُريدين قَهْوَة يا آنِسة؟
- لا. شُكراً. أُريد شاياً مِن فَضلِك.
- مَعَ السُكَّر؟
- نَعَم.
- حاضِر.

- تُريد قَهوة يا سَيِّد؟
- لا شُكراً. أُريد عَصير بُرتُقال مِن فَضلِك.

Reflecting on our reading: Notice the use of أرادَ in the preceding dialogues. In the cartoon bubbles the people are able to express the same idea without using the verb أرادَ. Based on this information, can you deduce the meaning of our mystery verb?

١. Requesting and Declining Things Politely

In the preceding dialogues, the woman and the man politely decline what the waiter is offering by using the expression **لا شُكراً**. They request their preferences politely by directly stating what they want followed by the phrase **مِن فَضلِك** "if you please."

Note how the two waiters have used the appropriate terms to address their patrons (**آنسة** and **سَيِّد**). Also, notice how the waiter responds to a request by using the word **حاضِر** "ready, all set," meaning that the order will be placed right away.

العَرْض: حدّد السياق بعرض صور زبائن مطعم ما يطلبون مأكولات ومشروبات.

قدِّم المفردات الجديدة الخاصة بالمأكولات والمشروبات باستخدام صور أو أشياء حقيقية (ملاحظة: إن المشروب السائل اسمه **القهوة** إنما الحبوب الكاملة أو المطحونة معروفة باسم **البُنّ**).

كرِّر نطق كل الكلمات على حدة واجعل الطلاب يعيدون وراءك. وبهذه الطريقة، قدِّم كل المفردات بتكرار الكلمات المعروضة سابقا.

التطبيق الجماعي:اطلب من كل طالب الذكر ما يريد الأكل والشرب وكذلك زميل الصف الذي أجاب قبله حتى تتراكم أجوبة الطلاب وأقوالهم.

مثلاً:

ط آ – أريد فلافل وحمصا وشايا.
ط ب – أريد قهوة ومارك يريد فلافل وحمصا وشايا.
ط ج – أريد عصير برتقال وجون يريد قهوة ومارك يريد فلافل وحمصا وشايا.

وفي حالة أن الطالب قد نسي ما ذكره زميله، شجعه على طرح سؤالاً على زميله قبل الانتقال إلى الطالب التالي.

التطبيق الفردي: الأنشطة: اجعل الطلاب يجدون من يأكل فطوراً في الصف ومن (لا) يأكل طعاماً معيناً على الفطور / الغداء / العشاء ومن (لا) يحب تناول الطعام في مطعم ومن يتناول الطعام في سكن الطلاب ومن يتناوله في البيت إلخ.

ماذا يَشرَبون ويأكُلون صَباحاً؟

هذا مايكل براون. يَشرَب مايكل صَباحاً فِنجان قَهوَة مَعَ الحَليب والسُكَّر. ويأكُل مايكل في الصَباح الحُبوب مَعَ الحَليب عادةً. لكِنَّ مايكل الآن في القاهِرة ويَأكُل هُناكَ صَباحاً الخُبْز والجُبْن والبَيْض ويَشرَبُ الشاي. يُحِبّ مايكل القَهوَةَ العَرَبّيّة أيْضاً.

الحُبوب مَعَ الحَليب

عَسَل

كأس ماء

هذِه هالة بُستاني. تَشرَب هالة كأس ماء صَباحاً وتأكُل الخُبْز والجُبْن والزَيتون مَعَ فِنجان شاي. تَشرَب هالة الشاي مَعَ السُكَّر عادةً في الصَباح لكِنَّها تَشرَبُ القَهوة دون سُكَّر أحياناً.

هذِه كاثي وايت. هي تَدرُسُ اللُغَةَ العَرَبيّة في جامِعَة آركانسو. تَشرَب كاثي فِنجان قهوة صَباحاً دونَ سُكَّر أو تَشرَب كَأس عَصير بُرتُقال، لكِنَّها لا تَشرَبُ الشاي. تَأكُل قِطْعَة خُبز مَعَ الزُبدَة ومُرَبّى البُرتُقال أو العَسَل.

- يَأْكُل الأمريكيّون صَباحاً الحُبوب مَعَ الحَليب عادةً أو البَيْض ولَحْم الخِنْزير ويَشرَبون عَصيرَ البُرتُقال أو القَهْوة أو الحَليب.
- يَأْكُلُ الفِرَنسِيّون عادةً الخُبْز والمُرَبّى في الصَباح ويَشرَبون القَهْوة.
- يَأكُل العَرَب عادةً الخُبْز والجُبْن والزَيْتون صَباحاً ويَشرَبونَ الشاي.

وأنتَ يا طالِب اللُغَةِ العَرَبِيَّة ماذا تَشرَب صَباحاً وماذا تأكُل؟

العرض: أشِرْ إلى حبك لبعض أنواع الطعام والشراب:

«أشرب القهوة الأمريكية لكنّني أحبُّ القهوة العربيّة.»
«أحبّ التفّاح لكنّني لا أحبُّ البرتقال.»

الممارسة: اسأل الطالب ما يحب ولا يحب الأكل والشرب. اطلب من الطالب المستمع الإفادة بما فهم من زميله حتى يخلص كل تصاريف فعل (أحبّ). استمر في هذا النشاط حتى يحقق الطالب ضربة من الدقة.

التطبيق الجماعي: اطلب من الطالب أن يجد من يحب ولا يحب القهوة الأمريكية / العربية / التركية والطعام الأمريكي / العربي / المكسيكي / الإيطالي / الصيني إلخ. أطلب من الطالب الإفادة بما وجد واكتب الأجوبة على السبورة في أصناف معينة من الطعام والشرب. اكتب عدد الطلاب الذين يحبون طعاماً أو شراباً معيناً ثم اطلب منهم ذكر عدد الطلاب الذين اندرجت أسماءهم تحت صنف معين.

«مثلا:
– ثلاثة طلاب قالوا إنها يحبون البيتزا ولكن طالبين قالا إنهما لا يحبانها.»

2. Describing Daily Activities

Describing activities involves the use of verbs. Some activities are performed habitually (e.g., eat), others are in progress (e.g., am eating). The former type of activity is described by the simple present in English and the latter by the present continuous, or progressive. In Arabic, the simple present is called the indicative, or **المُضارِع المَرفوع**, which is used for both the habitual and progressive aspects (e.g., **أقرأ** "I read/am reading").

ماذا يَفْعَلُ مايكل براون؟

أنا مايكل براون. أدْرُسُ اللُغَةَ العَرَبيَّة في الجامِعَةِ الأمريكيَّة في القاهِرة في هذا الفَصْلِ الدِراسيّ. أسْكُن في شَقَّة في شارِعِ المازِنيّ. آكُل عادةً في شَقَّتي صَباحاً الخُبز والبَيْض وأشرَبُ الشاي. عِندَ الظُهْر آكُل أحْياناً في مَطعَم إسمُه «نِعْمة». آكُل هُناكَ الفول أو الطَعمِيَّة (الفلافِل). أُحِبُّ الفول والطَعْمِيَّة كثيراً، لكِنَّني لا أُحِبُّ اللَحْم. أحْياناً آكُل سَلَطة في مَقْصَفِ الجامِعَة. مَساءً آكُل في مَقْصَفِ الجامِعَة أو في مَطعَم أو في شَقَّتي.

زِياد يَقْرَأُ الجَريدة

مَرْحَباً زِياد. ماذا تَفْعَل هُنا؟

أقْرَأ الجَريدة وأشرَب قَهوَة. تَعالَ إلى هُنا واشْرَب فِنْجان مَعي، يا هاني.

لا شُكراً. أنا مَشْغول قَليلاً. أيّ جَريدَة تَقْرَأ؟

أقْرأ جَريدةَ النَهار. هُنا عَلى الطاوِلة جَريدةُ الأخْبار، تَفَضَّلْ إقْرأها.

شُكراً. سأقرأُها بَعْدَ قَليل.

تمرين ٣

Conversation: Eating in the Middle East. In groups of two, pretend that you, like Michael, are eating breakfast, lunch, and dinner in an Arab city. Ask your partner how much, or how little, they would like the Middle Eastern plates that Michael mentioned. Record your answers on a separate sheet of paper and be prepared to report them to your class.

تمرين ٤

آ- اِختَر الكَلِمة المُناسِبة من نصوصِ هذا الدَرس وحِواراتِها.

١- الآنِسة في ________ .

☐ غُرفَةِ الصَفِّ ☐ المَطْعَم ☐ البَيْت

٢- يُريدُ الرَجُلُ ________ .

☐ كأس ماء ☐ فِنجان قَهوة ☐ عَصير بُرتُقال

٣- مايكل براون في مِصر الآن. يَأكُل صَباحاً ________ .

☐ البَيْض ☐ الفول ☐ الحُبوب

٤- يُحِبّ مايكل ________ أيْضاً.

☐ القَهوةَ الأمريكيّة ☐ القَهوةَ العَرَبيّة ☐ الشاي

٥- تَشرَب هالة بُستاني القَهوة ________ .

☐ مَعَ سُكَّر ☐ دونَ سُكَّر ☐ مَعَ العَسَل

٦- تأكُل كاثي وايت صَباحاً الخُبز و ________ .

☐ لَحم الخِنزير ☐ البَيْض ☐ العَسَل

٧- يأكُل مايكل الطَعْميّة في ________ .

☐ مَقْصَفِ الجامِعَة ☐ مَطْعَم نِعمَة ☐ شَقَّتِه

٨- لا يُحِبّ مايكل ________ .

☐ السَلَطة ☐ الفَلافِل ☐ اللَحْم

٩- يَقرَأ زِياد ________ .

☐ كِتاباً ☐ مَجَلّة ☐ جَريدة

١٠- يُريد هاني أن ________ .

☐ يَشْرَب قَهوة ☐ يَقرَأ جَريدة ☐ يَقرَأ مَجَلّة

الطعام في الدار البيضاء في المَغرِب

ب- اكتُب «صواب» أو «خطأ» إلى جانِب كُلّ جُملة حَسَب نُصوصِ القِراءة ثُمَّ صَحِّح الخَطأ مِنها.

١١- يَشرَب مايكل القَهوة مَعَ الحَليب والسُكَّر.
١٢- تأكُل هالَة قِطعة خُبز مَعَ الزُبدة والعَسَل صَباحاً.
١٣- تَشرَب كاثي كأس عَصير بُرتُقال صَباحاً.
١٤- يُريد هاني أن يَشْرَب عَصير بُرْتُقال.

ج- أسئلة لِلفَهم: اكتُب إجابات عَن الأسئلة على وَرَقة مُنفَصِلة وَفق نُصوصِ القِراءة.

١٥- مَتى يَشرَب مايكل الشاي في القاهِرة؟
١٦- مَتى تَشرَب هالَة الشاي؟
١٧- ماذا تأكُل كاثي صَباحاً؟
١٨- أينَ يأكُل مايكل ظُهْراً؟

3. Expressing Likes and Dislikes

The verb أحَبّ / يُحِبّ "to like" is used in roughly the same manner as its English counterpart. In order to express dislike, we precede the same verb with the negative particle لا.

١	أُحِبّ عَصيرَ البُرتُقال.	*I like orange juice.*
٢	لا أُحِبّ الحَليبَ.	*I don't like milk.*

Remember that the noun (e.g., عَصيرَ البُرتُقال، الحليبَ) following أُحِبّ "I like" is the object of this verb and it must, therefore, be in the accusative case marked by a red فتحة in examples 1 and 2 above for singular definite nouns, or يْنِ for dual and ينَ for sound masculine plurals.

4. Adverbials of Time

An adverbial modifies a verb and indicates the time, place, or manner in which an action occurred. Usually, the adverbial is an indefinite noun to which a double فتحة is suffixed, indicating that it is in the accusative case نَصْب. The adverbial meaning may also be expressed with a prepositional phrase. For example, صَباحاً "in the morning" may be expressed as a prepositional phrase: في الصَباحِ. Consider these two examples:

٣	صَباح	←	صَباحاً	=	في الصَباح
	مَساء	←	مَساءً	=	في المَساء
٤	ظُهر	←	ظُهْراً	=	عِنْدَ الظُهر

Note that the noun in the prepositional phrase is always definite. The same preposition may be used to refer to the evening في المَساءِ.

With reference to noontime, however, another preposition is used: عِندَ الظُهْرِ. While the use of prepositions with respect to time may not seem intuitive at first, look again—for the Arabic pattern exactly mirrors the English "in the morning/evening" = في الصَباح/ المَساءِ and "at noon" = عِندَ الظُهْرِ.

Adverbials are extremely handy words that can describe frequency such as عادَةً "usually; habitually" and أحْياناً "sometimes." Another adverbial that can readily become part of your linguistic repertoire is كَثيراً "a lot." It is based on the adjective كَثير "much." This adverbial is used in the following passage to modify the verb أُحِبُّ, expressing degree, as in أُحِبُّ العَسَلَ كَثيراً "I like honey very much."

Error Prevention: A common mistake among language learners is to confuse كثيرة (an adjective used to modify a single feminine noun or an inanimate plural) with كثيراً (an adverb that is used to modify verbs). Consider the examples:

٥	هُناكَ أوْراق كثيرة على مَكتَبي.	*adjective*
٦	أُحِبّ البيتزا كثيراً وآكُلُها كثيراً.	*adverb*

العرض: اعرض خريطة العالم التي تذكر كل أسماء الدول بالعربية. أخبر الطلاب بما يأكل بعض المجتمعات على الفطور والغداء والعشاء.

- يأكل الأمريكيون صباحاً الحبوب مع الحليب على الفطور ويشربون عادة القهوة الأمريكية.

الممارسة: أشِرْ إلى دولة ما واطلب من الطالب الذكر ما يأكل أهلها في الوجبات الرئيسية الثلاثة. ركز على الدول التي قد عاش الطالب فيها أوقد زارها.

التطبيق الجماعي: (في الصف أو خاريجه) اطلب من الطلاب إيجاد الأجوبة عمّ يأكل أهل مجتمعات معينة في اليوم سواء أكان على الشابكة أو من زملاء غرفة الصف. تتأكد من سلامة جملهم من حيث ترتيبها العربي أي (فعل / فاعل / مفعول به).

تمرين ٥

Adverbials in conversation: With a partner, make a list of foods that you like and the degree you like them (a lot, a little). Mention the times of day (morning/afternoon/evening) that you (sometimes/usually) eat these foods. Be prepared to report both your and your partner's responses to the class.

تمرين ٦

اِخْتَرِ الكَلِمةَ المُناسِبة:

١- أشرَب صَباحاً ________________ .

☐ قِطعَة خُبْز ☐ عَصير بُرتُقال ☐ لَحْم خِنزير

٢- يأكُل سامي في ________________ عِندَ الظُهْر.

☐ مَطْعَم ☐ مَكتَب ☐ كُلِّيَّة

٣- يأكُل أبي صَباحاً الزُبدة مَعَ ________________ .

☐ الزَيتون ☐ الجُبْن ☐ العَسَل

٤- تَشرَب أخْتي صَباحاً ________________ فَقَط.

☐ الماء ☐ المَقصَف ☐ المُرَبّى

٥- يأكُل الأمريكيّون في الصَباح عادةً ________________ مَعَ الحَليب.

☐ القَهوة ☐ السُكَّر ☐ الحُبوب

تمرين ٧

رَتِّب كَلِمات كُلّ سُؤال في جُملة.

١- مِن، كأس، أريد، فَضلِك، ماء

____

٢- صَباحاً، سَمير، وَالجُبْن، الشاي، ويَشرَب، الخُبْز، يأكُل

____

٣- اللَحْم، الفَلافِل، يُحِبّ، يُحِبّ، لكِنَّهُ، مايكل، لا

____

رُكنُ مُفْرَداتِ المَشْهَدِ المرئي

light (in weight)	خَفيف
to bring s.th. to s.o.	أحْضَر / يُحْضِر / إحْضار
if you please	لَو سَمَحت
dinner	عَشاء
to prepare s.th.	حَضَّر / يُحَضِّر / تَحْضير
boiled	مَسْلوق
fried (over easy for eggs)	مَقْلي
to end s.th.; to finish s.th.	أنْهى / يُنْهي / إنْهاء
to help	ساعَد / يُساعِد / مُساعَدة
appetizing	شَهيّ
what's your opinion	ما رأيُك

تمرين ٨

١ - تَمرينُ المُشاهَدة: شاهِدوا المَشْهَدَ الأوَّلَ وأجِبْ عَن الأسئِلة الآتيّة:

١- تَطْلُبُ الآنِسة . . .

☐ فِنْجان قَهوة ☐ عَصير لَيمون ☐ كأسَ شاي

٢- تُريدُ الآنِسة أيضاً . . .

☐ خُبْزاً ☐ مُربّى عَسَل ☐ كأس ماء

٣- تُحِبُّ الآنِسة . . .

☐ الدِراسة ☐ القِراءة ☐ الكِتابة

٤- تُريدُ الآنِسة مَعَ الفِنْجان . . .

☐مَجَلّة ☐ كِتاباً ☐ جَريدة

٥- يُحْضِرُ النادِل للآنِسة . . .

☐ قَهوة وجَريدة ☐ فِنجان قَهوة فَقَط ☐ فِنجان شاي وجَريدة

ب – تَمرينُ المُشاهَدة: شاهِدوا المَشْهَدَ الثاني وأَجِبْ عَن الأَسئِلة الآتيّة:

١- تُريد أن تَشْرَبَ الآنِسةُ الثانية . . .

☐ فِنْجان شاي ☐ فِنجان قَهوة ☐ كأسَ حَليب

٢- تُريدان أن تُحَضِّرا على العَشاء . . .

☐ الحُبوب مع الحَليب ☐ لَحْمة مَفْرومة ☐ بَيْضاً

٣- تُحِبُ الآنِسةُ الثانية أيْضاً . . .

☐ الجُبْنة ☐ الزُبْدة ☐ المُرَبّى

٤- تُحَضِّرُ العَشاء . . .

☐ الآنِسةُ الأولى فَقَط ☐ الآنِسةُ الثانية فَقَط ☐ الآنِستان معاً

٥- تَقرأُ الآنِسةُ الثانية قَبْلَ تَحْضير العَشاء . . .

☐ جَريدة ☐ مَجَلّة ☐ كِتاب

ج – تَمرينُ المُشاهَدة: شاهِدوا المَشْهَدَ الثالِث وأَجِبْ عَن الأَسئِلة الآتيّة:

١- حَضَرَت الآنِسة إلى الجامِعة . . .

☐ صَباحاً ☐ مَساءً ☐ ليلاً

٢- تَناولَت فَطوراً . . .

☐ لا بأس به ☐ شَهيّاً ☐ خَفيفاً

٣- تُحِبُّ الآنِسةُ الثانية . . . على الغَداء

☐ الخَضروات ☐ الفَواكه ☐ الزَعتر

٤- تُحِبُّ الآنِسةُ الأولى . . .

☐ الخُبز مع المُرَبّى ☐ اللَبَنة ☐ المَعكَرونة

٥- ستأكُلان . . . معاً.

☐ الفَطور ☐ الغَداء ☐ العَشاء

تمرين ٩

تَمرينُ المُشاهَدة: شاهِدوا الدَرْسَ الثامِنَ على الشابِكة.

المَشْهَدُ الأوَّل

١- ماذا تُريد الآنِسة؟ ________________________

٢- متى تُحِبُّ الآنِسة قِراءةَ الجَرائد؟ ________________________

____

المَشْهَدُ الثاني

١- ماذا تُريد أن تَشْرَبَ الآنِستان؟ ________________________

____

٢- ماذا ستُحَضِّرُ الآنِستان على العَشاء؟ ________________________

____

3. From context, try to guess the meaning of the word حَسَناً: ________________________

المَشْهَدُ الثالِث

1. Circle the foods the woman with the glasses ate for breakfast (فَطور):

لَحْم	زَعْتَر	بَيْض	لَبَنة	أَرُزّ	مُرَبّى	خَضْراوات	زُبْدة	زَيْتون

٢- ماذا ستأكل الآنِستان على الغَداء؟ ________________________

تمرين ١٠

ما تُحِبُّ وما لا تُحِبّ: اكتب أسماء ثلاثة أشياءَ تحِبُّها وثلاثة لا تُحِبُّها، وشَكِّلِ الكَلِمات.

١- ________________________.

٢- ________________________.

٣- ________________________.

٤- ________________________.

٥- ________________________.

٦- ________________________.

5. The Imperative

Let's take a look at the imperative form of the verb جَلَسَ "to sit" = اِجلِسْ, which was used in the main dialogue. It followed another imperative verb تفضَّلي "if you please" to create the phrase تفضَّلي اِجلِسْي.

احفَظْ تصريفات «جَلَسَ» في الأمر.

Conjugation of جَلَسَ (يَجْلِسُ)			
Person	**Pronoun الضَمير**	**Present المُضارِع**	**Imperative الأمْر**
المُتكَلِّم	أنا	أجْلِسُ	
	نَحْنُ	نَجْلِسُ	
المُخاطَب	أنْتَ	تَجْلِسُ	اِجْلِسْ
	أنْتِ	تَجْلِسينَ	اِجْلِسي
	أنْتُما	تَجْلِسانِ	اِجْلِسا
	أنْتُم	تَجْلِسونَ	اِجْلِسوا
	أنْتُنَّ	تَجْلِسْنَ	اِجْلِسْنَ
الغائب	هُوَ	يَجْلِسُ	
	هِيَ	تَجْلِسُ	
	(المُذَكَّر) هُما	يَجْلِسانِ	
	(المؤنَّث) هُما	تَجْلِسانِ	
	هُم	يَجْلِسونَ	
	هُنَّ	يَجْلِسْنَ	

6. Food and Drink

The types of foods and drinks consumed in different cultures and the manner in which people consume them vary tremendously. The paragraphs in the main reading passages illustrate the types of food and drink consumed at breakfast in the Arab and American cultures.

تمرين ١١

اكتُبِ العِبارةَ المُناسِبة لِكُلّ من الأشخاص المَذكورين كَما في المِثال:

مِثال:		اِجلِسا مِن فَضْلِكُما

1. A woman		.________________
2. A mixed group of five		.________________
3. A man		.________________
4. Four women		.________________
5. Three boys		.________________

7. Prepositions and Attached Pronouns

Attached pronouns may be suffixed to prepositions. In the exchange below, the first-person singular attached pronoun ي "me" is suffixed to the preposition مِن "from," resulting in مِنّي *minnī* "from me."

8. Plurals of Nouns

A. Sound Masculine Plurals جَمْع مُذَكَّر سالِم

Some masculine nouns do not undergo any internal changes when put into the plural form. Such a noun usually refers to humans and is made plural by suffixing ونَ to it if it is the subject of a sentence (nominative رفع) and by ينَ if it is the object of a verb (accusative نصب) or a preposition (genitive جر). Such nouns are called **sound masculine plurals:**

الجَرّ والنَّصب	الرَّفْع	المُفرَد
أمريكيّينَ	أمريكيّونَ	أمريكيّ

Such nouns are called "sound" because no internal changes in the word occur and the same sequence of letters is retained in the plural form.

B. Sound Feminine Plurals جَمْع مُؤنَّث سالِـم

Some feminine plurals display the ending ات (e.g., ساعات / ساعة). These are called **sound feminine plurals**, since no internal changes ever take place. Note that the ة must be dropped before the suffix ات is attached. Case markers are indicated on the end of the plural suffix. Only two types exist and they are illustrated below:

1. A ضَمّة or double ضَمّة for the nominative رَفع:

٧	ساعاتُ	ساعاتٌ

2. A كسرة or double كسرة for the accusative نَصب and the genitive جَرّ:

٨	ساعاتِ	ساعاتٍ

C. Broken Plurals جَمْع تَكسير

Other nouns, feminine and masculine, are made plural through internal changes whereby addition and/or deletion of long and short vowels occur. These are called **broken plurals**. A small sampling of those we have come into contact thus far follows. We have endeavored to put them in order:

المُفرَد	الجَمع
صَفّ	صُفوف
عِلم	عُلوم
بَيت	بُيوت
حَقّ	حُقوق
باب	أبواب
وَرَقة	أوراق
قَلَم	أقلام
حاسوب	حَواسيب
مِفتاح	مَفاتيح
طالِب	طُلاّب
جِدار	جُدران

المُفرَد	الجَمع
حَقيبة	حَقائب
جَريدة	جَرائد
صورة	صُوَر
غُرفة	غُرَف
كِتاب	كُتُب
مَدينة	مُدُن
أستاذ	أساتِذة
هاتِف	هَواتِف
دَفتَر	دَفاتِر
مَكتَب	مَكاتِب
كُرسي	كَراسٍ

Note that the consonants remain unchanged in the plural form. Only short and long vowels are dropped, added, or their positions changed. Case markers appear on the end of the plural form just as they would on the end of a singular form:

الجَرّ	النَصْب	الرَفْع
كُتُبٍ	كُتُباً	كُتُبٌ

You are strongly advised to memorize and practice the plural form of a noun along with the singular.

SUMMARY

- Sound masculine plural nouns are formed by suffixing ون to subjects and ين to objects.
- Sound feminine plural nouns are formed by suffixing ات to the noun.
- Broken plurals are formed through internal changes in the word.

تمرين ١٢

Grammar identification: Underline all sound masculine plural nouns and adjectives, place a dotted line under sound feminine plurals, and draw a box around broken plurals, as in the examples. There may be more than one plural form in each sentence.

مِثال: أساتِذة أمريكيّون   أمينات مَكتَبات   طُلاب عَرب

١- السَيّارات اليابانِيَّة سَيّارات جَيِّدة.

٢- هؤلاء طُلاّب ماليزيّون.

٣- هُناكَ بَنات وأبناء كثيرون في عائِلات المِصريّين.

٤- في كُلِّيَّتي حواسيب كَثيرة.

٥- يأكُل السوريّون الجُبن والزَيتون صَباحاً.

٦- مَن مَعَهُ أقلام في حَقيبتِه؟

تمرين ١٣

Convey these sentences in Arabic in which the broken plural has been used. Use the broken plural chart on the previous page.

1. There are three French (female) students in our class.

   ______________________________.

2. I have three pencils with me.

   ______________________________.

3. There are five telephones in this room.

   ______________________________.

4. Do you know any Egyptian students (m.)?

   ______________________________.

5. There are three tables and six chairs in the teachers' room.

   ______________________________.

9. المُضاف والمُضاف إليه Structures Revisited

In this lesson, extensive use of the إضافة structure is made. There are 17 instances of it altogether throughout the passages and dialogues, including repeated ones. One example is قِطعةُ خُبزٍ "a piece of bread." This phrase is indefinite because the second (or last) noun of the phrase is indefinite خُبزٍ, whereas the phrase عَصير البُرتُقال is definite because of the definite article that is prefixed to the second noun البُرتُقال.

One of the إضافة structures is كَأس عَصير بُرتُقالٍ. Literally, it means "a glass of juice of orange." This phrase is a multiple إضَافة because it contains more than two successive nouns. كَأس عَصيرِ بُرتُقال is an indefinite إضافة phrase.

تمرين ١٤

Grammar identification: On a separate sheet of paper, write down at least six إضافة structures from the reading passages that appear at the beginning of this lesson, provide their meanings, and note whether or not they are definite.

تمرين ١٥

A Taste of the Middle East: Take a close look at the menu below. See if you can identify the three foreign words. Once you are through, split up into groups of three. One person will play the waiter, and the other two people will play the part of the patrons. Emulate the dialogues that appeared at the beginning of this lesson by using the proper greetings, terms of address, and language used for taking and giving orders. Use the menu to make your orders. Be creative with the language, and use as much vocabulary from this lesson and the menu as possible.

مشويات

كباب	٦٠٠
كباب خشخاش	٧٠٠
شيش طاووق	٦٠٠
مشكل مشاوي	١٢٠٠
طبق مشاوي	٤٠٠٠
ريش	١٥٠٠

مقبلات

حمص	٣٠٠
بابا غنوج	٣٠٠
فتوش	٣٥٠
تبولة	٤٠٠
زبادي بالخيار	٣٠٠
سلطة خضراء	٣٠٠

شطائر

برجر لحم	٤٠٠
برجر دجاج	٤٠٠
شطيرة كباب	٦٠٠
شطيرة كبدة	٣٠٠
شطيرة تكة لحم	٣٠٠
شطيرة كلاوي	٣٠٠

مشروبات

مشروبات غازية

مشروبات ساخنة

تمرين ١٦

آ- إختَر الجواب المُناسب لِلنصّ المُسَجَّل.

١- تَشرَب سُعاد صَباحاً ________________ .

☐ قَهوة ☐ ماء ☐ سُكَّراً

٢- تَشرَب سُعاد الشايَ صَباحاً مَعَ ________________ .

☐ السُكَّر والحَليب ☐ الخُبْز والجُبن ☐ الدَجاج واللَحْم

٣- تَأكُل سُعاد ظُهراً ________________ .

☐ الدَجاج أو اللَحْم ☐ الجُبن أو الزَيْتون ☐ العَسَل أو المَربّى

ب- ضَع «صَح» أو «خَطَأ» إلى جانبِ كلِّ جُملة وصَحِّح الخَطَأ.

٤- لا تُحِبّ سُعاد صيداوي أكل اللَحْم.

٥- تَأكُل سُعاد السَلَطة مَساءً.

٦- تَشرَب سُعاد القَهوة العَرَبيّة.

المُفْرَدات

استمِع إلى المُفرَدات على القُرص وحاول أن تُتقن النطق

أحْضَرَ (يُحْضِرُ) إحْضار (v.) . . . . to bring

أرُزّ (n., m.) . . . . rice

أكَلَ (يأكُلُ) أكْل (v.) . . . . to eat

أنْهى / يُنْهي / إنْهاء (v.) . . . . to finish s.t

بُرتُقال (n., m.) . . . . orange

بَيْض (n., m.) . . . . egg

تَعالَ (imperative, m., sg.) تَعالي (f., sg.) . . . . Come here!

تُفّاح (n., m.) . . . . apple

تَناوَلَ (يَتَناوَلُ) تَناوُل (v.) . . . to eat; to take; to reach for something

جُبْن ج أجْبان (n., m.) . . . . cheese

جَلَسَ (يَجلِسُ) جُلوس (اِجلِسْ) (imperative) (v.) . . . . to sit

حاضِر (participle) . . . . ready, all set (polite expression)

حَبّ ج حُبوب (n., m.) . . . . grain, cereal

حَسَناً (adv.) . . . very well, okay (a response denoting agreement)

حَضَّرَ (يُحَضِّرُ) تَحضير (v.) . . . . to prepare

حَليب (n., m.) . . . . milk

خُبْز (n., m.) . . . . bread

خَضْراوات (n., f.) . . . . vegetables, greens

خَفيف (adj.) . . . . light (in weight)

خِنزير ج خَنازير (n., m.) . . . . pig, swine

دَجاج (n., m.) . . . . chicken without . . . . (prep.) دونَ

butter . . . . (n., f.) زُبْدة

wild thyme . . . . (n., m.) زَعتَر

olive . . . . (n., m.) زَيْتون

to help. . . . . (v.) ساعَد (يُساعِد) مُساعَدة

sandwich . . . . (n., f.) شَطيرة ج شَطائر

sugar . . . . (n., m.) سُكَّر

salad. . . . . (n., f.) سَلَطة ج سَلَطات

tea . . . . (n., m.) شاي

to drink . . . . (v.) شَرِبَ (يَشْرَبُ) شُرْب

appetizing. . . . . (adj.) شَهي

morning. . . . . (n., m.) صَباح

patty made from ground beans . . . . (n., f.) طَعْمِيّة
and spices fried in oil (Egypt)

noon . . . . (n., m.) ظُهْر

honey . . . . (n., m.) عَسَل

dinner. . . . . (n., m.) عَشاء

juice . . . . (n., m.) عَصير

breakfast . . . . (n., m.) فَطور

patty made from ground beans . . . . . . (n., m.) فُلفُل ج فَلافِل
and spices fried in oil (Syria)

cup . . . . (n., m.) فِنْجان ج فَناجين

fava beans. . . . . (n., m.) فول

piece. (n., f.) قِطْعة ج قِطَع

coffee	قَهْوة (n., f.)
glass	كَأس ج كُؤوس (n., f.)
a great deal	كَثيراً (adverbial)
meat	لَحْم ج لُحوم (n., m.)
if you please	لَو سَمَحْت
What's your opinion?	ما رأيُك
water	ماء ج مِياه (n., m.)
when	مَتى (question particle)
jam, preserve	مُرَبّى ج مُرَبَّيات (n., m.)
boiled	مَسْلوق (passive particle)
evening	مَساء (n., m.)
kitchen	مَطْبَخ ج مَطابِخ (n., m.)
restaurant	مَطْعَم ج مَطاعِم (n., m.)
cafeteria	مَقْصَف ج مَقاصِف (n., m.)
boiled	مَقْلي (adj.)
agree	مُوافِق (active participle)

مَحَلّ بهارات في حَلَب

سوق حَلَب

الدرس التاسع

ساعة مائية في فاس المغرب العتيقة

Objectives

- Telling time formally and informally
- Describing daily activities
- Giving background information
- Introduction to mass and count nouns
- Counting in the hundreds and thousands

١ - قِراءةُ الساعة

كَم الساعَة ؟

السّاعَةُ الحادية عَشرة والرُبْع

إنَّنا نَستَخْدِم العَدَدَ التَرْتيبي في قراءةِ الساعة كَما تَعَلَّمْناه في الدَرْس الخامِس:

	الاسْم المُؤنَّث	العَدَد التَرْتيبي	الوَزْن
١	الطالِبة	الثانية، الثالِثة، الرابِعة، الخامِسة إلخ	الفاعِلة
٢	الساعة	الثانية، الثالِثة، الرابِعة، الخامِسة إلخ	

العرض: أحضر ساعة إلى الصف سواء أكانت حقيقية أو ورقية واعرض على الطلاب أوقات مختلفة. مارس نطق قراءة الساعة ممارسة مكثفة.

الممارسة الشفهية: ابدأ بالأوقات السهلة (أي الساعة الواحدة أو الثانية أو الثالثة إلخ) وتقدم تدريجياً إلى تقسيمات الساعة (أي الثالثة والنصف أو الرابعة والربع أو التاسعة إلا ثلثا أو الحادية عشرة إلا ربعا إلخ). اعرض على الطلاب أوقات مختلفة عشوائياً واطلب منهم قراءة الساعة وتسارع في العرض وتغيير الأوقات تدريجيا.

الممارسة التحريرية: ضع عدداً من الساعات في الصف واطلب من الطلاب العمل على السبورة في الأزواج لاستنتاج كم الساعة عندهم واجعلهم يكتبون الوقت على السبورة. بعد ذلك، اطلب من الصف أن يصحح الكتابة عند الخطأ.

التطبيق: العمل في الأزواج: اطلب من كل مجموعة من طالبين أن يسأل زميله ماذا يفعل في اليوم العادي ووفي أي ساعة يقوم بهذا الشيء. على سبيل المثال: «**في أي ساعة يستيقظ ويتناول الوجبات الرئيسية ويقرأ الجريدة ويكمل الواجب وينام إلخ.**»

وعِنْدما نَقْرأ الساعة، نَسْتَخْدِم نَفْسَ الوَزَن أي الفاعِلة:

العدد	الأصل	الساعة
واحِد	وحد	الواحِدة
اِثْنانِ	ثني	الثانية
ثَلاثة	ثلث	الثالِثة
أَرْبَعة	ربع	الرابِعة
خَمْسة	خمس	الخامِسة
سِتّة	سدس	السادِسة
سَبْعة	سبع	السابِعة
ثَمانية	ثمن	الثامِنة
تِسْعة	تسع	التاسِعة
عَشَرة	عشر	العاشِرة

A. Grammatical Structure

The phrase used in telling time is a noun/adjective phrase:

٣ الساعَةُ الثانِيَةُ

As you can see in example 3, **الساعَة** is a feminine noun, while **الثانية** is its adjective. When we tell time in Arabic, the noun and adjective must agree in number, gender, case, and definiteness—in fact, *telling time is always definite in* **الفُصحى**. Consider the example:

الكلِمة الّتي تَلي حَرْف جَرّ (في) تأخُذ كَسْرة كَما تَرى في المَثالَيْن الآتِيَيْن:

٤	في الساعةِ الواحدةِ
٥	في الساعةِ الثانيةِ

The compound numbers 11 and 12 are the exception to the rule because, as we mentioned in Lesson 6, they are indeclinable. That is to say, numbers 11 and 12 adhere to one set form regardless of case. Consider examples 4 and 5, paying close attention to how **الساعةُ** (nominative) changes to **الساعةِ** (genitive) following the preposition **في**, whereas the number does not change:

٦	الساعةُ الحادِيةَ عَشْرَةَ	في الساعةِ الحادية عَشْرَةَ
٧	الساعةُ الثانِيةَ عَشْرَةَ	في الساعةِ الثانيةَ عَشْرَةَ

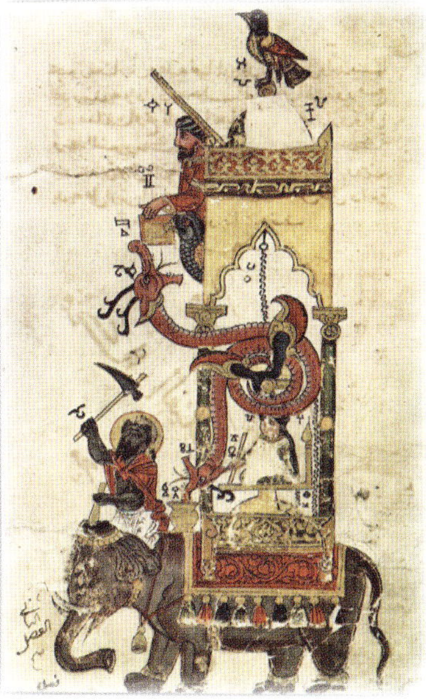

ساعة الفيل المائية في
مخطوطة من آل الجزري

ب – تَقسيم الساعة:

نُقَسِّم الساعة إلى الأقْسام الآتية:

٨	الرُبْع	الثُلْث	النِصف

	العاشِرة والرُبْع	الثانية والثُلْث	العاشِرة والنِصْف

٩

الدقيقة الساعة

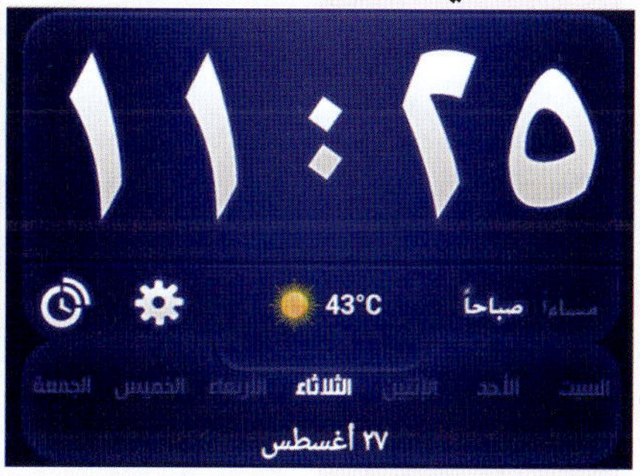

اليوم

التاريخ الشهر

تَقسيم الوَقْت			الجمع
سِتّون (٦٠) ثانية	=	دَقيقة	دَقائِق
سِتّون (٦٠) دَقيقة	=	ساعة	ساعات
أَرْبَعة وعِشرون (٢٤) ساعة	=	يَوْم	أَيّام
ثلاثون (٣٠) يَوْماً	=	شَهْر	أَشْهُر
اثْنا عَشَر (١٢) شَهْراً	=	سَنة	سَنَوات
عَشْر (١٠) سَنوات	=	عَقْد	عُقود
مئة (١٠٠) سَنة	=	قَرْن	قُرون

السّاعَةُ الآن الواحِدة وعَشْر دَقائِق مَساءً في التِلفزيون العَرَبيّ السوريّ.

هُنا القاهِرة. السّاعَةُ الآن الثانية والثُلْث بَعْدَ الظُهْر.

Note that hours and fractions are connected with the conjunction وَ, and that all divisions of the hour are definite with the *exception* of minutes.

السّاعَةُ الآن الخامِسة وخَمْس دقائق

السّاعَةُ الآن الرابِعة والرُبْع

السّاعَةُ الآن الثالِثة والثُلْث

السّاعَةُ الآن الثامِنة والنِصْف

Notice that the minute hand of the four clocks that appear on the previous page is on the right-hand side of the clock dial, therefore the particle وَ "and" is used. When the minute hand is on the left-hand side, إلاّ "till" (as in, "a quarter till five," etc.) is used with hours and fractions. إلاّ is used for all times when the minute hand is on the left-hand side of the clock face except for the first nine minutes after the half hour mark (see clock face 10:35 below). The noun following إلاّ is accusative مَنصوب and indefinite, as in the highlighted examples:

الساعَةُ العاشِرة
والنِصْف وخَمْسُ دَقائق

الساعَةُ العاشِرة
إلاّ خَمْسَ دَقائق

الساعَةُ الثانِية
إلاّ رُبْعاً

الساعَةُ العاشِرة
إلاّ ثُلْثاً

A variation to saying 10:35 is: **الساعَة العاشِرة وَخَمْسُ وَثَلاثون دَقيقة**

The clock face below summarizes the information about the uses of و and إلاّ.

quarter till	إلاّ رُبْعاً
twenty till	إلاّ ثُلْثاً
quarter after	والرُبع
twenty after	والثُلث

ساعة مِصريّة قَديمة
نُسَمّيها مِسَلّة

SUMMARY

- The number indicating the time is an ordinal number: الساعَة الثانية وَالنِصف.
- The numbers 11 and 12 are invariable: الساعة الثانيةَ عَشْرَةَ.
- The fractions of an hour used are: نِصف، ثُلْث، رُبع، دَقيقة.
- The particle وَ is inserted between the hour and fractions.
- The particle إلاّ is used to indicate times until the hour (40–59 minutes).

تمرين ١

Under each clock face, indicate the time shown. Provide the short vowels on the ends of all words, assuming that الساعة is nominative مَرفوع.

١-

٢-

٣-

٤-

٥-

٦-

٧-

٨-

٩-

تمرين ٢

العَلاقات الدُوَلِيَّة

Conversation: Making a مَوْعِد. Make a **مَوْعِد** "date" with someone in class to eat at a restaurant or to study at a friend's house or in the library. In order to mention as many times as possible, please do not settle on the first time mentioned; in fact, disagree as much as possible. Tell the person that you are in class, or that you are not at home, or that you have another appointment at that time; try to make up as many excuses as possible to elicit as many times as possible as you see in the example below.

آسِفة، عِندي مَوْعِد في الساعَة السادِسة والنِصْف.

هَل تُريدين أن تَدْرُسي مَعي في سَكَن الطالِبات في الساعة السابِعة؟

العرض: اعرض على الطلاب جدولك وصف لهم بتفاصيل ما تقوم به في اليوم العادي. وفي حالة أن يومك فيه أنشطة غير معروفة للطلاب، بسطها وغير الموقف حتى يناسب كلامك مستوى الطلاب اللغوي.

وفي متابعة النشاط، اعرض على الطالب جدولك الحقيقي أو المعدل سواء أكان مطبوعا أم مكتوبا بخط اليد. وفي حالة أنه مكتوب بخط اليد تأكد بأن الخط سهل القراءة. وفي حالة أنه جدول حقيقي، تأكد بأن الغالبية العظمى من الكلمات والحوادث معروفة للطالب.

التطبيق الجماعي: اطلب من الطالب أن يجد من عنده موعد في الصف اليوم ومع من الموعد وفي أي ساعة وأين.

سَحَر في جامِعة حَلَب

تَدرُس سَحَر حَلاّق التِجارة في جامِعة حَلَب في سوريا. هِي مِن دِمَشق وتَسكُن مَعَ طالِبَة مِن دِمَشق أيضاً اِسمُها هالَة بُستاني. عِندَ سَحَر أربَع مَوادّ في هذا الفَصل هِي الرِياضِيّات واللُغَة الإنكليزيَّة والمُحاسَبة والإحْصاء.

الإحْصاء

مَوْعِد دَرْس الرِياضِيّات في الساعَة التاسِعَة صَباحاً، ومَوْعِد دَرْس اللُغَة الإنكليزيَّة في العاشِرَة. بَعْدَ دَرْس الإنكليزيَّة تَقرَأ سَحَر مَجَلاّت وجَرائِد إنكليزيَّة في المَكتَبَة. عِندَ الظُهْر تَأكُل سَلَطَة أو فَلافِل أو حِمَّصاً في مَقْصَف الجامِعَة. أحْياناً تَأكُل الكَباب الحَلَبِيّ. في الساعَة الواحِدَة مَوْعِد دَرْس المُحاسَبة، وفي الساعَة الثالِثَة تَدرُس الإحْصاء. بَعْدَ ذلِكَ تَدرُس سَحَر في المَكتَبَة مِنَ الساعة الرابِعَة إلى السادِسَة مَساءً مَعَ طُلاّب وطالِبات مِن صَفِّها.

المُحاسَبةُ

مايكِل براون في القاهِرة

اِسمي مايكل براون. أنا من وِلاية أوهايو في الوِلاياتِ المُتَّحدِةِ الأمريكيّة. يَسكُن أبي وأُمّي جاك ومارثا براون في مَدينة سينسيناتي وتَسكُن أُختي لين في توليدو وهي لا تدرُس الآن. يَدرُس أخي ريتشارد في جامِعة وِلاية أوهايو في كَلَمبَس. هٰذِه جامِعتي أيضاً أدرُس فيها العَلاقات الدُوَليّة.

أنا الآن في الجامِعَةِ الأمريكيَّة بِالقاهِرَة أدرُسُ اللُغَةَ العَرَبيَّة وأدَبَها. مَوْعِد دَرْسِ اللُغَةِ العَرَبيَّة في الساعَةِ الثامِنَة صَباحاً وأستاذَة هٰذِهِ المادّة هِي الدُكتورة زَيْنَب طَه. ومَوْعِد دَرْسِ الأدَب العَرَبيّ في الساعَة الحادِيَة عَشْرَة واسمُ الأسْتاذ عَبّاس التونسي. أُحِبّ دُروسَ العَرَبيَّة كَثيراً.

في مَقْصَف جامِعَةِ القاهِرة أتكَلَّم عادةً بِالعَرَبيَّة مَعَ سَمير عَبد الفَتّاح وهُو طالِب مِصريّ مِن مَدينَة طَنْطا في مِصْر. هذا هُو أوَّل حَديث بِاللُغَة العَرَبيَّة مَعَ سَمير.

الجامِعَةِ الأمريكيَّة بِالقاهِرَة

سَمير	مايكِل
مَرحباً!	أهلاً!
اِسمي سَمير عَبدُ الفَتّاح.	تَشَرَّفْنا. أنا مايكِل براون.
تَشَرَّفْنا. مِن أينَ أنتَ؟	أنا مِن وِلايَة أوهايو في أمريكا.
ماذا تَفعَل هُنا في القاهِرة؟	أدرُسُ اللُغَةَ العَرَبيَّة. وأنتَ؟
أنا أدرُسُ الهَنْدَسَة. تَتكَلَّمُ العَرَبيَّة جَيِّداً!	شُكراً. لَيسَ جَيِّداً جِدّاً. وأنتَ، هَل تَتكَلَّمُ الإنكليزيَّة؟
أينَ تَسكُنُ الآن؟	هُنا في القاهِرة.
أعرِف . . . يَعني هَل تَسكُن في سَكَن الطُلّاب؟	لا، في شَقَّة.
مَن يَسكُن مَعَك؟	لا يسكُن مَعي أحَد. أسكُن وَحْدي.
فُرصَة سَعيدة! مَعَ السَلامة.	مَعَ أَلْف سَلامة.

تمرين ٣

آ- أكمِل الجُمَلَ الآتية بالاختيار المُناسِب وَفق نَصّ القراءة:

١- سَحَر حلاّق مِن مَدينة ____________ .

☐ دِمَشق ☐ حَلَب ☐ القاهِرة

٢- تَسكُن سَحَر ____________ .

☐ وَحْدَها ☐ مَعَ طالِبة ☐ مَعَ ثَلاث طالِبات

٣- تَدرُس سَحَر في هذا الفَصْل ____________ .

☐ مَجلاّت وجَرائِد ☐ اللُغَة الإنكليزيَّة ☐ اللُغَة العَرَبيَّة

٤- تَأكُل سَحَر عِندَ الظُهْر في ____________ الجامِعَة.

☐ مَكتَبَة ☐ مَقْصَف ☐ مَطْعَم

٥- مَوْعِد دَرْسِ المُحاسَبَة في الساعَة ____________ .

☐ العاشِرَة صَباحاً ☐ الواحِدَة بَعْدَ الظُهْر ☐ الثالِثَة بَعْدَ الظُهْر

٦- اِسم أُخت مايكِل براون ____________ .

☐ مارثا ☐ لين ☐ كاثي

٧- يَدرُس مايكِل الآن في مَدينَة ____________.

☐ سِنسِناتي ☐ كَلَمبَس ☐ القاهِرة

٨- يَتكَلّم مايكِل العَرَبيّة في مَقْصَفِ الجامِعَة مَعَ ____________.

☐ سَمير عَبد الفَتّاح ☐ زَينب طَه ☐ عَبّاس التونسيّ

٩- يَدرُس سَمير عَبدُ الفَتّاح ____________ .

☐ العَلاقات الدَوْليّة ☐ الأدَب العَرَبيّ ☐ الهَنْدَسَة

ب- اكتُب «صَح» أو «خطأ» إلى جانِب كُلّ جُملة حَسَب نُصوصِ القِراءة ثُمَّ صَحِّح الجُمَلَ الخطأ.

١٠- عِندَ سَحَر حَلاّق ثَلاث مَوادّ في هذا الفَصْل.

____

١١- تَقرَأ سَحَر الجَرائِد في المَكتَبَة بَعْدَ دَرْسِ المُحاسَبة.

____

١٢- تَدرُس سَحَر مَعَ طُلّاب وطالِبات مِن صَفِّها بَعْدَ دَرْسِ الإحْصاء.

____

١٣- يَدرُس مايكِل الأدَبَ العَرَبِيّ مَعَ الأستاذ عَبّاس التونِسيّ.

____

١٤- يَدرُس أخو مايكِل في جامِعَة وِلايَة أوهايو.

____

تمرين ٤

آ- املأ الفَراغات الآتية بِما تَفعَلُه سَحَر في اليومِ العادي.

الساعة	ماذا تَفعَل سَحَر؟
٨	في الساعَةِ الثامِنَة تأكُل سَحَر الفَطور.
٩	
١٠	
١١	
١٢	
١	
٢	
٣	
٤	
٥	
٦	

ب- املأ الفَراغات الآتية بِما يَفعلُه زَميل غُرْفةِ الصَفّ في اليومِ العادي.

الساعة	ماذا يَفعَل طالِب اللُغَة العَرَبِيَّة في صَفِّك؟

ج- املأ الفَراغات الآتية بِما تَفْعَلُه أنْت يا طالِب اللُغةِ العربيّة في اليومِ العادي.

الساعة	ماذا أفعَل كلَ يوم

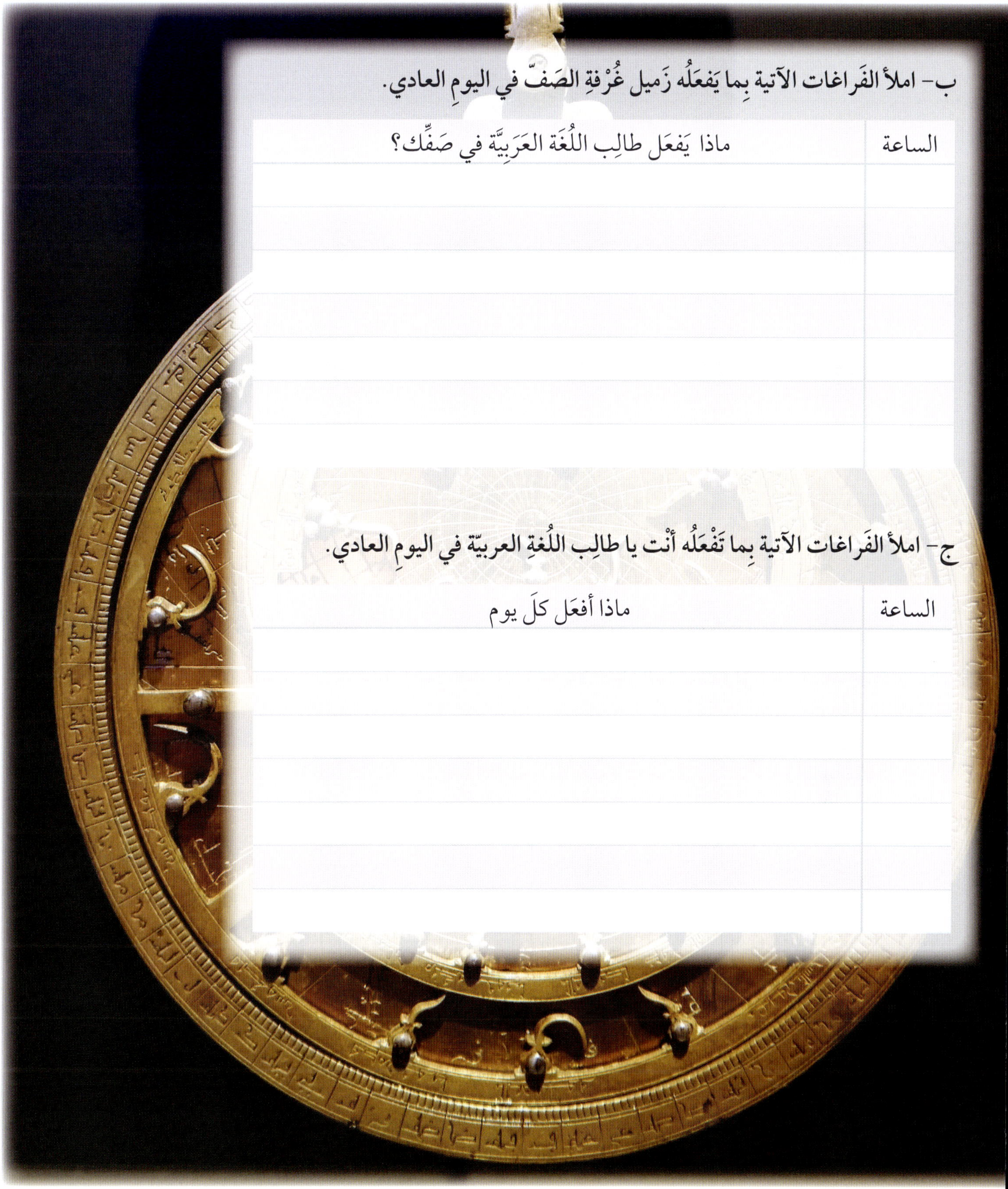

الإسطرلاب: مِقياس فلكية

رُكنُ مُفْرَداتِ المَشْهَدِ المرئي

health	صِحّة
to go to	ذَهَب / يَذْهَب / ذَهاب (إلى)
good	جَيِّد
every	كُلّ
to start	بَدَأ / يَبْدَأ / بِداية
to end	اِنْتَهى / يَنْتَهي / اِنْتِهاء
noon	ظُهْر
to sleep	نام / يَنام / نَوْم
to wake up	اِسْتَيْقَظ / يَسْتَيْقِظ / اِسْتيقاظ

تمرين ٥

تَمرين المُشاهَدة: أكْمِل الجُمَلَ الآتية بالاخْتيار المُناسِب وَفْق نَصِّ المُشاهَدة:

١- يَذْهَب إلى الجامِعة في الساعة . . .

☐ الثامِنة ☐ الثامِنة والنِصْف صَباحاً ☐ الثامِنة والنِصْف ليلاً

٢- يَبْدأ الدَرْس في الساعة . . .

☐ التاسِعة تَماماً ☐ الحادية عَشْرة ☐ الثامِنة والنِصْف صَباحاً

٣- يَنْتَهي الدَرْس في الساعة . . .

☐ العاشِرة تَماماً ☐ الواحِدة ظُهْراً ☐ الحادية عَشْرة صَباحاً

٤- يَسْتَيْقِظ في الساعة . . .

☐ السابِعة والرُبْع ☐ السابِعة والثُلْث ☐ السابِعة والنِصْف

٥- ينام في الساعة . . .

☐ الحادية عَشْرة ☐ الحادية عَشْرة والنِصْف ☐ العاشِرة ليلاً

تمرين ٦

آ- املأ المُرَبَّعات بِأسماء عائلة مايكل براون.

عائِلَة براون

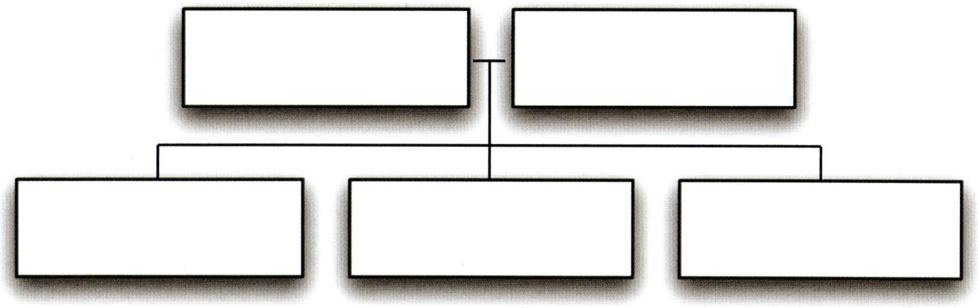

ب- املأ المُرَبَّعات بِأسماء عائلتك يا طالِب اللُغةِ العَرَبيّة.

عائِلَة ....

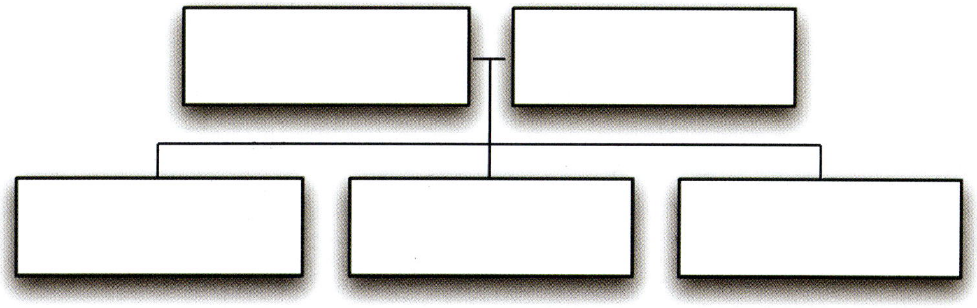

ج- اكْتُب فِقْرة عن عائلة براون أو عائلتك.

تمرين ٧

وافِقْ بَيْنَ الكَلِمات في العَمودَين واكتُبْهُما في الوسط.

١-	أوَّل		دَقيقَة
٢-	الوِلايات المُتَّحِدَة		العَلاقات الدُوَلِيَّة
٣-	ساعَة		واحِد
٤-	مادَّة		صَفّ
٥-	نِصْف		أمريكا
			ثُلْث

تمرين ٨

اِختَر الكَلِمةَ الّتي لا تُناسِب باقي الكَلِمات في كُلّ مَجموعة وبَيِّن السَبَب.

١-	رُبْع	نِصْف	ثُلْث	كَثير
٢-	مَوْعِد	حِمَّص	كَباب	فلافِل
٣-	إحْصاء	مُحاسَبَة	دَقيقَة	عِلْم الحاسوب
٤-	ثالِث	تاسِع	واحِد	أوَّل

2. Telling Time Informally

In many Arabic colloquial varieties, cardinal numbers are used instead of ordinal numbers to tell time informally. Also, the forms are not definite. Thus, to indicate 7:30 or 10:15, for example, in an informal way, you say:

١٠	الساعة سَبعة ونِصف
١١	الساعة عَشَرة ورُبْع

This practice may still be acceptable in a formal setting when used orally, so long as the phonology and morphology (pronunciation and structure) of the words comply with the standard norms. Remember, however, that in writing it is recommended that you use the standard forms discussed above.

Also in informal speech, when indicating the minutes after or before the hour, you may drop the word for "minutes." Consider these examples:

السّاعة سَبعة وعَشَرة	١٢
السّاعة أربعة إلاّ خمسة	١٣

Bear in mind that the conjunction وَ (*wa*) is pronounced *w* without the *fatḥa* (e.g., *sab'a w 'ashara*).

تمرين ٩

المُحادَثة: اسأل زملاء غُرْفة الصَفّ ماذا يُحِبّون في التِلفاز؟ واكْتُب ما يقولون لَك في المُرَبّعات الآتية:

كَم ساعة؟	مَتى (مِن أيّ ساعة إلى أيّ ساعة)	ماذا يُحِبّ في التَلفزيون	اِسمُ الطالِب

3. Suppressing the Initial Sound of the Article

With any prefix, take for instance the prefix بِـ, the *a-* part of the definite article is dropped (e.g., *bil-* + *word*). The same elision occurs when the conjunction وَ is prefixed (e.g, *wal-* + *word*). So, don't say *bi* + *al* + word; rather, merge them together.

bil	بالـ	=	الـ	+	بِـ	١٤
wal	والـ	=	الـ	+	وَ	١٥

4. Mass and Count Nouns

A noun may refer to the general class of something, for example, cheese, water, air, etc. This type of noun is known as a mass noun. In Arabic, one way of creating a count noun from a mass noun is by simply adding a *tā' marbūṭa* to the noun:

an apple	تُفّاحة	*apples*	تُفّاح	١٦
a grape	عِنَبة	*grapes*	عِنَب	
a banana	مَوْزة	*bananas*	مَوْز	

العرض: اعرض مفهوم العدد باستخدام فواكه سواء أكانت حقيقية أو صناعية أو صورا) وعُد كم عندك. أبدأ بالترتيب العادي:

«هذه تفاحة والآن تفاحتان والآن ثلاث تفاحات».

استمر في عرض كذا نوعا من الفواكه حتى يحقق الطالب ضربة من الطلاقة.

الممارسة: اسأل الطالب كم (تفاحة / موزة / قطعة بيتزا / قطعة دجاج) يأكله في الأسبوع وكم يوماً يأكله.

التطبيق الجماعي: اطلب من الطالب أن يجد كم طالباً في الصف يأكل (طعاماً ما) وكم يوماً يأكله في الأسبوع.

تمرين ١٠

Forming count nouns: Form count nouns from the following mass nouns that occurred in Lesson 8. Provide the meaning of each count noun you form.

١- بُرتُقال ________________ ٢- خُبز ________________

٣- زَيتون ________________ ٤- بَيْض ________________

٥- فول ________________ ٦- سُكَّر ________________

5. Numbers: Reading Hundreds and Thousands

The Arabic word for thousand is **ألف** (plural **آلاف**). **ألف** is a noun and, therefore, forms an **إضافة** structure with a counted noun. The following noun must be singular, genitive, and indefinite—hence it takes **تَنوين كَسرة**:

١٧	ألف رَجُلٍ	*one thousand men*
	ألْف كِتابٍ	*a thousand books*
	ألْف لَيْلة ولَيْلةٍ	*a thousand and one nights*

Traditionally, Arabic numbers were read from right to left; that is, moving from the ones, tens, hundreds, and then thousands. When the number 1246 is read from right to left it appears in this manner:

١٨ سِتّ وأربَعون ومِئتان وألف

Although this style is still practiced by a few radio and television announcers, another style of reading numbers is more prevalent today. When reading a number, you start with the highest category. Thus, in order to read 5246, read from left to right, as in English. Start with the thousands, then read the hundreds, *skip the tens*, read the ones, and then read the tens. Consider the example:

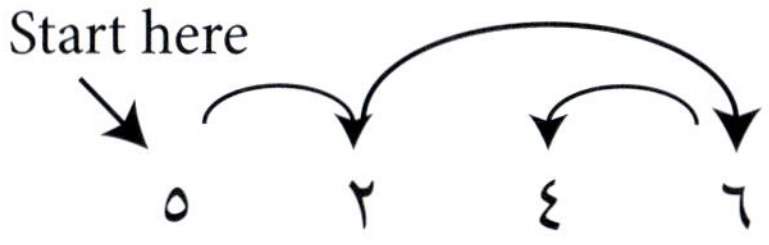

١٩ خَمسة آلاف ومِئتان وسِتّ وأربَعون

Note that unlike English, the conjunction وَ is inserted before every category, highlighted in red in the examples above.

تمرين ١١

Writing out numbers: Spell out these numbers in words:

١- ٩٠٧ ______________________

٢- ٤٧٨٣ ______________________

٣- ١٣٦٨٥ ______________________

٤- ١٩٨٤ ______________________

٥- ٢٠١٠ ______________________

تمرين ١٢

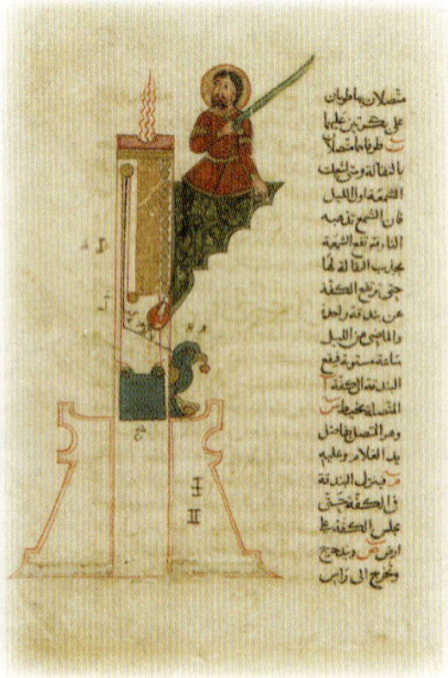

شرح الجزري للساعة الشمعية

اكْتُب الجُمَل الآتية بالعربيّة:

مِثال: ما اسْم أخْت مايكِل؟ اِسم أخْت مايكِل لين.

1. When does Saḥar eat in the cafeteria? (**مَتى**)

____

2. At what time does Saḥar have statistics? (**في أيّ ساعَة**)

____

3. What's the name of Michael Brown's Arabic language professor? (**ما**)

____

4. Where do Michael's parents live? (**أين**)

____

تمرين ١٣

آ- اِختَرِ الجوابَ المُناسِب حَسَبَ النَصِّ المُسَجَّل.

١- اِسم هذا الطالِب ________ .

☐ عَبدُ الله ☐ عادِل ☐ أشْرَف

٢- يَدرُس هذا الطالِب الأدَب ________ .

☐ العَرَبيّ ☐ الإنكليزيّ ☐ الفَرَنسِيّ

٣- أستاذ مادّةِ اللُغَةِ الإنكليزيَّة هُو الدُكتور ________

☐ جَزائِريّ ☐ ديـڤيس ☐ عَبدُ السلام

٤- أستاذ مادَّةِ الأدَبِ الإنكليزيّ مِن ________ .

☐ الأردُن ☐ مِصْر ☐ بريطانيا

ب- ضَع «صَح» أو «خَطَأ» إلى جانِب كُلِّ جُملة وصَحِّح الخَطَأ.

٥- يَدرُس عادِل في جامِعَة بريطانيَّة.

____

٦- أشرَف طالِب في الجامِعَةِ الأردُنِيَّة.

____

٧- أستاذ مادةِ اللُغَةِ الإنكليزيَّة بَريطانيّ.

____

٨- مَوْعِد مادَّةِ الأدَب في الساعةِ الواحِدَة.

____

ج- على وَرَقة مُنْفَصِلة، اكْتُب الآتي:

9. Write out the daily schedule of the person described in the listening passage.

10. Give the title used to refer to a university professor in the listening passage.

المُفْرَدات

استمِع إلى المُفردات على القُرص وحاول أن تُتقن النطق.

أحَد ج آحاد (n., m.) . . . . one

اِسْتَيْقَظَ (يَسْتَيْقِظُ) اِسْتيقاظ (v.) . . . . to wake up

إحْصاء (n., m.) . . . . statistics

انْتَهى (يَنْتَهي) اِنْتِهاء (مِن) (v.) . . . . to come to an end

إلاّ (particle) . . . . till, except, minus

ألْف ج آلاف (n., m.) . . . . thousand

بَدَأ (يَبْدأُ) بِداية (v.) . . . . to begin

بَعْدَ (prep.) . . . . after

ثُلْث ج أثْلاث (n., m.) . . . . a third

جَيِّد (adj.) . . . . good

حَديث ج أحاديث (n., m.) . . . . conversation

حِمَّص (n., m.) . . . . dip prepared from chick peas, sesame seed paste, lemon juice

دَقيقَة ج دَقائِق (n., f.) . . . . minute

دُوَلِيّ (n., m.) . . . . international

ذَهَبَ (يَذْهَب) ذَهاب (v.) . . . . to go

رُبْع ج أرْباع (n., m.) . . . . quarter

ساعَة ج ساعات (n., f.) . . . . o'clock, hour

صِحّة (n., f.) . . . . health

عَلاقة ج عَلاقات (n., f.) . . . . relation

عَنى (يَعْني) (v.) . . . . to mean

فُرْصَة سَعيدة . . . . literally "a happy opportunity" meaning “good to meet you”

kebāb, minced meat on a skewer. . . . . (n., m.) كَباب
with parsley and onion

every . . . . (n., m.) كُلّ

united . . . . (adj., m.) مُتَّحِد

accounting . . . . (n., f.) مُحاسَبة

time, appointment . . . . (n., m.) مَوْعِد ج مَواعيد

to fall asleep, to sleep . . . .(v.) نامَ (يَنامُ) نَوْم

half . . . .(n., m.) نِصْف ج أَنْصاف

here . . . . (demonstrative) هُنا

alone, by himself . . . . (adv.) وَحْدَهُ

the United States of America. . (n., f.) الوِلاياتُ المُتَّحِدةُ الأمريكيّة

ساعة الجزري
الفلكية العملاقة

الدرس العاشر

بُرج خَليفة في إمارة دُبي

أهداف الدرس

- تعلُّم وصف الأشخاص والممتلكات والأنشطة
- تذوّق عادات العائلة العربية وجغرافية الخليج
- تعلُّم معلومات عن المرأة الخليجية وزي الرجل العربي
- تعلُّم تصريف الفعل الماضي والنفي
- تعلُّم المصدر
- مراجعة مطابقة الصفة للموصوف
- تعلُّم تركيب الأسماء العربية

المُفْرَدات الجَديدة في صُوَر عديدة

ذَهَبَ (يَذْهَبُ) ذَهاب إلى

عَمِلَ (يعمَلُ) عَمَل

سائِق ج سائِقون

فَتاة جَميلة

صَديقتان

طَويل قَصير

قَويّ

العرض: استخدم المواد التي في متناول اليد كي تعطي الطلاب فكرة عن الصفات الموجودة في هذا الدرس والذي سبقه: «**جميل،وسيم، طويل، قصير، كبير، صغير، جديد،حديث قديم، لطيف، إلخ . . .**»

قد تود أن تستخدم (ليس / ليست) لتوضح الصفات المتعلقة بالمواد وكذلك التي لا تتعلق بها. «**هذه صورة لفتاة جميلة وطويلة. لكنها ليست كبيرة.**»

«**هذا رجل قصير، لكنّه وسيم.**» «**أنا طويل/ لست طويلاً.**»

الممارسة: اطلب من الطلاب أن يصفوا صوراً جاءوا بها من البيت أو من الهواتف الذكية باستخدام الصفات التي تعلموها حتى الآن.

التطبيق الأول: في مجموعات من طالبين أو ثلاثة، اطلب من طالب أن يسأل الآخر عن إخوته، أين يسكن وماذا يدرس وماذا يحب أن يفعل ويقرأ ويأكل ويشرب بالإضافة إلى أسئلة عن سماته. وفي نهاية النشاط، اطلب من المجموعات الإفادة بما عندهم من المعلومات.

التطبيق الثاني: اطلب من الطالب جمع معلومات عن مَن مِن الزملاء عنده سيارة (أو أي شيء غيره مثل شقة أو بيت، أو دراجة إلخ): ١_ جديدة أو٢_ قديمة أو٣_ كبيرة أو٤_ صغيرة أو٥_ اقتصادية أو٦_ رياضية أو ٧_ مكشوفة.

واطلُب من الطلاّب الإبلاغ عمّا جمعوا من المعلومات وكتابتَها على السبورة ثم اطلُب منهم ذِكر أسماء الطلاب الذين عندهم تلك الأشياء بالتحديد.

تأكّد من أن الطلاب قد بدأوا حفظ الأفعال الجديدة بقراءتها جهراً في صيغة الماضي والمضارع والمصدر لكل من المفردات الجديدة. مارس هذا التمرين معهم في الصف حتى تعودهم على إيقاع العربية وأوزان الفعل المزيد.

لُؤلُؤة القَطامي فَتاة عَرَبِيّة مِن قَطَر

مَدينة الدوحة عاصِمة قطر

لُؤلُؤة القَطامي فَتاة مِن الدَوْحَة في قَطَر. هِيَ طالِبَة في جامِعَة قَطَر في كُلِّيَّةِ الآداب وتَدرُسُ اللُغَة الإنكليزيّة. تَسكُن لُؤلُؤة مَعَ أسرتِها في الدَوْحَة في دار كَبيرة جَديدَة فيها سَبعُ غُرَفِ نَوم.

دار كَبيرة في الدوحة

غُرفة نَوْم في الدوحة

جامعة قطر

تَذْهَب لُؤلُؤة إلى الجامِعَة بِالسَيّارَة مَعَ سائِق هِنْديّ. هُناكَ سائِق ثانٍ مِنَ الباكِسْتان تَذهَبُ مَعَهُ أمُّها إلى السوقِ وإلى بُيوت صَديقاتِها. لِعائِلَةِ القَطامي ثَلاث سَيّارات. الأولى سَيّارة أمريكيّة كَبيرة (كاديلاك) وهِيَ لِلأُمّ. والسَّيّارَةُ الثانِيّة (مَرسيدس) ألمانِيَّة وهِيَ لِلأب. والسَّيّارةُ الثالِثة (تويوتا) يابانِيَّة تَذهَب بِها لُؤلُؤة وإخوَتُها إلى الجامِعَة والمَدارِس.

لُؤلُؤة فَتاة جَميلَة. هِيَ لَيسَتْ طَويلة ولَيْسَتْ قَصيرة لكِنَّ أُختَها الصَغيرة عائِشة طَويلَة. تُحِبّ لُؤلُؤة دِراسَةَ اللُغَةَ الإنكليزيَّة، وهِيَ تَذهَب إلى مَكتَبَةِ الجامِعَة بَعْدَ الظُهْر وتَقرَأ هُناكَ الجَرائِد والمَجَلاّتِ الإنكليزيّة.

لِلُؤلُؤة أُختان وأخَوان. أُخْتاها دانَة وعائِشة في المَدرسة الثانَوِيَّة. أخوها الصَغير حَسَن في الصَفِّ العاشِرِ الثانَويّ. أخوها الكَبير حُسَيْن في الكُوَيْت الآن. وهُوَ يَسكُن ويَعمَل هُناكَ. يَسكُن حُسَيْن في شَقَّة في شارِع حَمَد المُبارَك. عِندَ حُسَين سَيّارة (پورش) ألمانِيَّة وهِيَ سَيّارَة حَديثَة وجَميلَة لَها مُحَرِّك قَويّ.

سَيّارة قَديمة

سَيّارة جَديدة وحَديثة

مُحَرِّك

حُسَين

دَرَس حُسَيْن التِجارة في لَنْدَن وسَكَن فيها أربَع سَنوات. يُحِبّ حُسَيْن العَمَل بِالحاسوب لكِنَّهُ ما دَرَس عِلمَ الحاسوب. حُسَيْن رَجُل طَويل ووَسيم، لكِنْ لَيْسَ لَهُ زَوْجة الآن ولا يَسكُن أحَد مَعَهُ في شَقّتِه. يَلبَس حُسَيْن الكوفيّة والعِقال.

تمرين ١

تأمّل القِراءة: اشرَح مَعاني التَعبيراتِ الآتية بالعَرَبيّة وَفق سياقِها في نَصِّ القِراءة.

١- الدَوْحَة ________________________

٢- سَيّارة حُسَيْن ________________________

٣- شارِع حَمَدِ المُبارَك________________________

تمرين ٢

آ- **أكمِل الجُمَل الآتية بِكَلِمات مُناسِبة وَفْق نَصِّ القِراءة.**

١- لُؤلُؤة فَتاة مِن ____________ .

☐ الكُوَيْت ☐ قَطَر ☐ الباكِسْتان

٢- تَدرُس لُؤلُؤة ____________ .

☐ اللُغَة الإنكليزيّة ☐ التِجارة ☐ العَلاقاتِ الدُوَليّة

٣- تَقرأُ لُؤلُؤة المَجلاّتِ الإنكليزيّة في ____________ .

☐ البَيْت ☐ الصَفّ ☐ المَكتَبَة

٤- تَسكُن لُؤلُؤة في ____________ .

☐ سَكَنِ الطالِبات ☐ شَقّة ☐ دار أُسْرَتِها

٥- عِند عائِلةِ القَطامي ________ .
☐ سَيّارتان ☐ ثَلاث سَيّارات ☐ أربَع سَيّارات

٦- دَرَس حُسَيْن التِجارة في ________ .
☐ الدَوْحَة ☐ الكُوَيْت ☐ لَندَن

٧- يَعمَل حُسَيْن في ________ .
☐ الكُوَيْت ☐ الدَوْحَة ☐ لَندَن

٨- لِحُسَيْن سَيّارةٌ________ .
☐ أمريكيَّة ☐ يابانِيّة ☐ ألمانِيَّة

ب- بيِّن إنْ كانَت الجُمَل الآتية صَواباً أو خَطأ وَفْق النَصّ وصَحِّح الخَطأ مِنها:

٩- في دار عائِلة القَطامي تِسع غُرَف.

____

١٠- تَذهَب أمّ لُؤلُؤة مَع السائِق إلى السوق.

____

١١- تَقرَأ لُؤلُؤة المَجلاّت الإنكليزيّة في كُلِّيَّةِ الآداب.

____

١٢- سَيّارة حُسَيْن لَها مُحَرِّك قَويّ وجَميل.

____

١٣- يَسكُن حُسَيْن مَعَ زَوْجَتِه في بَيْت كَبير.

____

ج- **المُحادَثة وكِتابةُ السيرة:** اِجْلِس مَعَ زَميل مِن زُملاء الصَفّ وأُجرِ مُقابَلة مَعه بِالعَرَبيّة حَتّى تَكْسِب أكْبَر قَدْر مِن المَعلوماتِ الشَخصيّة عَنْهُ وعَن أُسْرَتِه. حاوِل تَقْليدَ وَصْفٍ مِن أوْصاف نَصِّ القِراءةِ الرَئيس بِاسْتِخْدام الأسْئِلة عَن البَيْت / الشَّقّة (كَبير أم صَغير) والسَّيّارة (جَديدة أم قَديمة والنَوْع) وأين يَعْمَل وإذا كان يُعْجِبُه عَمَلُه وماذا يَدْرُس وإذا كانَت دُروسه تُعْجِبُه وكَم مادّةً يَدْرُس. اكْتُب على وَرَقة مُنْفَصِلة وَصْف الشَّخْص الّذي تَعَرَّفْت عليه.

تمرين ٣

أكمِل الجُمل الآتية بأنسب كلمة من الاختيارات.

١- سَيّارَتي لَها ________ قَويّ.

☐ باب ☐ شُبّاك ☐ مُحَرِّك

٢- في شَقّتي ________ نَوْم واحِدَة.

☐ غُرفة ☐ باب ☐ شُبّاك

٣- يَسكُن أبي في ________ كَبيرة.

☐ بَيْت ☐ دار ☐ بِناء

٤- لي ________ مِنَ اليابان.

☐ قَديم ☐ قَصير ☐ صَديق

٥- يَعمَل حامِد ________ في القاهِرة.

☐ سائِقاً ☐ طَويلاً ☐ جَميلاً

تمرين ٤

اِختَر الكَلِمَةَ الّتي لا تُناسِب باقي الكَلِمات في كُلّ مَجموعة وبَيِّن السَبَب:

١-	قَصير	مَكتَبَة	مَجَلاّت	كُتُب	جَرائِد
٢-	سَيّارة	مُحَرِّك	صَديق	سائِق	كاديلاك
٣-	اليابان	ألمانيا	الهِند	دِراسة	سوريّا
٤-	أخ	أخت	أب	لَبِسَ	أم
٥-	قَصير	كَبير	صَغير	طَويل	فَتاة

تمرين ٥

وافِقْ بَيْنَ الكَلِماتِ في العَمودَين:

١-	سَيّارة		جَميلة
٢-	كَبير		مَجَلات
٣-	دار		بِنْت
٤-	طَويل		حَديث
٥-	وَسيم		صَغير
٦-	قَديم		قَصير
٧-	فَتاة		سائِق
٨-	مَكْتَبَة		قَويّ
			بَيت

يمكن أن تطلب من الطالب كتابة بحث علمي مبسط بشأن موضوع من المواضيع الثقافية الواردة في هذا الباب.

تَذَوَّق الثَقافة العَربيّة

العائلة:

مِن خَصائِص العائلةِ العَرَبيّة أنّها تُحافِظ على أبْنائِها حَقّ المُحافَظة حَتّى بَعْدَ بُلوغ الثامِنة عَشْرة مِن أعْمارِهِم. عُموماً، يَبْقى الأبْناء مُعْتَمِدين على آبائهم مالياً ويَسْكُنون في البَيْت حَتّى يَتِمّ زواجُهم.

المَرأة العَرَبيّة:

لا يُسْمَح للبِنْت العَرَبيّة بِالذّات بالخُروج مِن البَيْت بِنَفْسِها، خُصوصاً في مِنْطَقة الخَليج. ومَعَ أنَّ الشّابّةَ العَرَبيّة تَتَمَكَّن مِن قيادة السيّارة شَرْعيّاً، فَإنّها عادةً لا تقوم بها (إنَّ المَمْلكةَ العَرَبيّةَ السُعوديّة هي الدَوْلةُ الوَحيدةُ الّتي تَمْنَعُ المَرأة مِن السّياقة لِذلِك تُوجَد فيها حاجة إلى السائق). ومُعْظَم هَؤلاء السائقين مِن الهِنْد وباكِسْتان وبَنْغلادِيش. وَبِفَضْل العَوائد المُكْتَسَبة مِن النِفْط، فَإنّ تَوْظيفَ السائقين على نِطاق واسع صار عادةً مَيْسورة التَكْلِفة.

إنّ فُرَصَ العَمَل لِلمَرأة في مِنطَقةِ الخَليج مَحدودة بِمِهَن مُعَيَّنة كَالتَّعْليم لأنَّها لا تَعْمَل مَعَ الرِّجال في هذا المجال. مِن المُلاحَظ أنّ هذه القُيود قَد أثّرَت تأثيراً إيجابياً في المَرأة وَرَغْبَتِها في أنْ تَنْجَحَ نَجاحاً باهِراً وَتَتفوّق على الرَّجُل. وَقَد أنْجزَت المَرأةُ العَرَبيّة إنْجازات مُتَميِّزة في مَجالات عِدّة، خاصّةً في التَّعْليم والأدَب والفَنّ.

وفي الدُوَلِ الأكثر عِلْمانيّة (secular) مِثْل الجزائر ومِصْر وسوريا ولبُنان وفِلَسْطين والعِراق، تَتَمَتَّع المَرأة العَرَبيّة بِنَفْس القَدْر مِن فُرَص العَمَل كالرَجُل وتَتَوَظَّف في مُعْظَم المَجالات حَتّى في مَناصِب عالية في الحُكومة.

هذا مِن ناحية، ومِن ناحية أُخْرى (on the other hand) فَالرَجُل العَرَبيّ يَتَمَتَّع بِحُريّة شِبْهِ مُطْلَقة مِن حَيْثُ (in terms of) خُروجُه مِن البَيْت وبِعَدَد أكْبَر مِن فُرَص العَمَل لِلمُحْتَرِفين. لا يُتَوقّعُ مِن الشّاب أنْ يَتْرُكَ بَيْت العائلة حَتّى يَتِمَّ الزَّواج.

الخَليج:

تُسَمّي الدُوَلُ العَرَبيّة الخَليجَ (الخَليج العَرَبيّ) بَيْنَما تُسَمِّيه إيران (الخَليج الفارِسيّ). تُطِلّ إيران على الخَليج مِن الشَّرْق، والإمارات العَرَبيّةُ المُتَّحِدة وقَطَر والمَمْلكةُ العَرَبيّةُ السُعوديّة والكوَيْت تُطِلّ عليه مِن الغَرْب والعِراق يُطِلّ عليه مِن الشَّمال. إنَّ دَوْلَةَ البَحْرَيْن جَزيرة صَغيرة وتَقَع في الجُزءِ الغَرْبيّ مِن الخَليج.

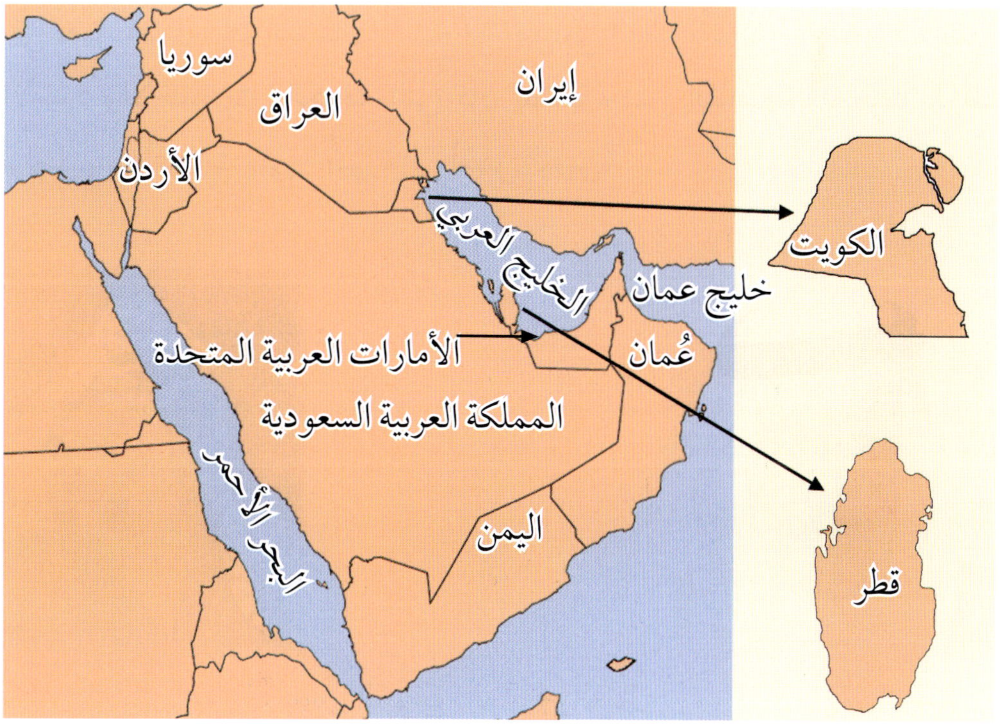

أينَ قَطَر والكُوَيْت؟

- الكُوَيْت وقَطَر على الخَليج العربي.

أسماء الشَخْصيّاتِ الوارِدة في الدَّرْس وعلاقَتُها بِالتاريخ الحَديث:

إنّ الاسْمَ (لُؤلُؤة) اِسْم نِسائيّ مُنْتَشِر في مِنْطَقةِ الخَليج. ويَرْجِع إلى الفَتْرةِ الّتي سَبقَت اِكْتِشاف النَفْط حَيْثُ كانَ الإيراد (income) مِن الغَوْص لِصَيْد اللُّؤلُؤ جُزءاً كَبيراً مِن الدَخْل.

اللُغة في الخَليج:

كَما يَحْدُث في مُعْظَم اللَهجاتِ العَرَبيّة إنَّ حَرْفَ الهَمْزة (ء) يَتَحَوَّل إلى واو أو ياء، لِذلِكَ يُنْطَق اِسْم لُؤلُؤة (لولْوَة = *lulwa*) في هذِه المِنْطَقة. وَجَدير بالذِكْر أنَّ اِسْماً آخَر مَذْكوراً في الدَّرْس (دانة = *big pearl*) يَرْجِع إلى مِهْنةِ الغَوْصِ القَديمة قِدَمِ التَّاريخ.

الغُتْرة أو الكوفيّة:

زَيُّ الرَّجُل في الخَليج وفي بَعض البِلاد الأُخرى: في مِنْطَقة الخَليج، تُسَمَّى قِطْعَةَ النَّسيج الّتي تُوضَع على الرَّأس وتَتَدَلّى إلى الكَتِفَيْن (غُتْرة) بَيْنَما تُعْرَف بِـ(كوفيّة) في بِلاد الشّام حَيْثُ تُلبَس في المَناطِق الرِّيفيّة. وفي الصُّورة إلى أسْفَل اليَسار، تَرى الزَّيَّ الرَّسْميّ المَصْنوع مِن حَرير ناعِم أبْيَض اللَوْن ويُوضَعُ فَوْقَه (عِقال) وهو جَديلة (cord) لَوْنُها أسْوَد ومَصْنوعة مِن الصُوف أو الحَريرِ المُقَصَّب تُوضَع على الغُترة أو الكوفيّة ويُلبَس على مَدار السَنة ومِن مزاياها أنّها تَحْمي اللابِس مِن شِدّةِ الحَرارة والبُرودة. وفي فَصْلِ الشِّتاء، يَتِمّ اِسْتِبْدالُ النَّسيج الأبْيَض مِن القُطْن بِقُماش مِن الصُّوفِ المُقَلَّم بالأسْوَد والأحْمَر مِثْل الكوفيّة الّتي كان يَلْبَسُها رَئيس السُلْطةِ الفِلَسْطينيّةِ الوَطَنيّةِ الراحِل ياسِر عَرَفات (في الصُّورة إلى أسْفَل اليَمين).

الكوفيّة (الغُتْرة) والعِقال

١ – الفِعْل الماضي The Past-Tense Verb

الفِعْلُ الماضي هو فِعْل يَلْحَقُ بِه (attach to it) في آخِرِه ضَمير مُتَّصِل. فَتَكون كَلِمة الفِعْل بالعَرَبيّة كأَنَّها جُمْلة بالإنكليزيّة.

ونَسْتَخْدِمه (we use it) حين نَتَكَلَّم في صيغةِ الماضي يَعْني شَيْء قَد مَضى، فَتَتأَمَّل (contemplate) معنا تَصْريف الفِعْل الماضي بِالعَرَبيّة:

آ– فِعْل دَرَسَ في صيغة الماضي

الفاعِل	الضَمير المنفصِل	الفِعْل الماضي	الضَّمير اللاحِق
المُتَكَلِّم	أنا	دَرَسْتُ	ـتُ
	نَحْنُ	دَرَسْنا	ـنا
المُخاطَب	أَنْتَ	دَرَسْتَ	ـتَ
	أَنْتِ	دَرَسْتِ	ـتِ
	أَنْتُما	دَرَسْتُما	ـتُما
	أَنْتُم	دَرَسْتُم	ـتُم
	أَنْتُنَّ	دَرَسْتُنَّ	ـتُنَّ
الغائب	هُوَ	دَرَسَ	ـَ
	هِيَ	دَرَسَتْ	ـَتْ
	(مُذَكَّر) هُما	دَرَسا	ـا
	(مُؤَنَّث) هُما	دَرَسَتا	ـتا
	هُم	دَرَسوا	ـوا
	هُنَّ	دَرَسْنَ	ـنَ

أساسُ اللُغةِ العَرَبيّة هو الجَذْر (root) ونَرْبُط حَرْفاً (a letter) أو أكْثَر بِنِهايةِ الفِعْلِ العَرَبيّ حين نَتَكَلَّم في الماضي. وكَما تَرى في الجَدْوَل أعلاه، الأحْرُفُ المُظَلَّلة بِاللَوْن الأَزْرَق هي الّتي قَد أَضَفْناها إلى جَذْر دَرَسَ كَيْ نُبَيِّنَ الفاعِل.

العرض: قدّم للطلاب كلمة (الماضي). أنا عادةً أحرّك يدي من الأمام إلى الخلف جانب أذني كما لو كنت أنش الذباب كي أشير إلى صيغة الماضي وأنا أقول الكلمة جهرياً. تساعد هذه الحركة الطالب في القيام بالتصحيح الذاتي حين يُخطئ في زمن الفعل بدلاً من أن أقاطعه وأقطع سلسلة التفكير.

الممارسة: اسأل الطلاب ماذا فعلوا هذا الصباح، وماذا أكلوا، وماذا قرأوا، ومع من تكلّموا، ومتى استيقظوا إلخ. حين يُفْهَم التمرين جيّداً، انتقل إلى صيغة الغائب واسأل الطلاب عن زملاءهم في الصف. مثلاً:

«أ – ماذا فعل مارك اليوم في الصباح يا سارة؟»

«ط آ – الله أعلم. يا مارك، ماذا فعلتَ اليوم صباحاً؟ »

«ط ب – استيقظت في الساعة كذا وأكلت كذا وشربت كذا وذهبت إلى الجامعة بسيّارتي. »

«ط آ – مارك استيقظ في الساعةِ كذا وأكلَ كذا وشرب كذا وذهب إلى الجامعةِ بسيّارتِه.»

التطبيق: النشاط الجماعي: في مجموعات من طالبين أو ثلاثة، اطلب منهم أن يسألوا بعضهم بعضاً أسئلة مثل: أين سكنتَ، وأين درستَ، وماذا أكلتَ وشربتَ صباح اليوم، ومع من تكلّمتَ، وإذا قرأتَ الجريدة اليوم وما اسمُها إلخ.

متابعة النشاط: اطلب من مجموعات معينة أن تخبر الأخرى ما وجدت من المعلومات، ثم اكتُب بعض الجمل على السبورة واطلُب من الطلّاب تصحيحها إن كانت خطأ. حاول ألا تقاطع الطالب حتى تصححه لأنّ هذا يعكر جو التعلم ويبطئ الدرس. انتظر حتى ينهي كلامه، ثم دع الطلاب يصحّحون. وفي حالة أنهم جميعاً لا يعرفون الجواب، قدم التصحيحات بنفسك.

هَل لاحَظْت (notice) الحَرْفَ المُشْتَرَك بَيْن الضَّميرِ المُنْفَصِل (independent pronoun) والفِعْل في صيغةِ المُخاطَب؟ نَعَم! إنَّ حَرْفَ التاء (ت) هو الحَرْفُ المُشْتَرَك في هذِه الصيغة. طالما أنَّك تَعْرِف الضَّميرَ المُنْفَصِل، فسَوْفَ تَعْرِف التَّصْريف الصَّحيح!

	أنْتَ	دَرَسْتَ
	أنْتِ	دَرَسْتِ
١	أنْتُما	دَرَسْتُما
	أنْتُم	دَرَسْتُم
	أنْتُنَّ	دَرَسْتُنَّ

مُلاحَظة: إنَّ الألِف في آخِر فِعْل دَرَسوا صامِتة، يَعْني لا تُنْطَق:

دَرَسوا: *darasū*

ب– نَفي الفِعْل الماضي Negating the Past-Tense Verb

نَسْتَطيع نَفي الفِعْلِ الماضي بِاسْتِخدام أداة مِن أدَواتِ النَفي ألا وهي حَرْف ما قَبْل الفِعْل، وهذِه العَمَلية سَهْلة لِلغاية لأنَّنا لا نُغَيِّر أي شَيْء آخَر في الفِعْل أو في تَرْتيبِ الجُمْلة:

٢ دَرَسْتُ التِجارةَ. *I studied business.* ← ما دَرَسْتُ التِجارةَ. *I didn't study business.*

تمرين ٦

لِلمُحادَثة: اكتُب أسماء الزُملاء في غرفةِ الصَفّ الّذين ما . . .

1. drank coffee this morning
2. read the paper this morning
3. ate breakfast this morning
4. studied this lesson
5. worked this morning

والآن أخبِر الأستاذ بِما عَلِمْت من الأصدقاء في الصف.

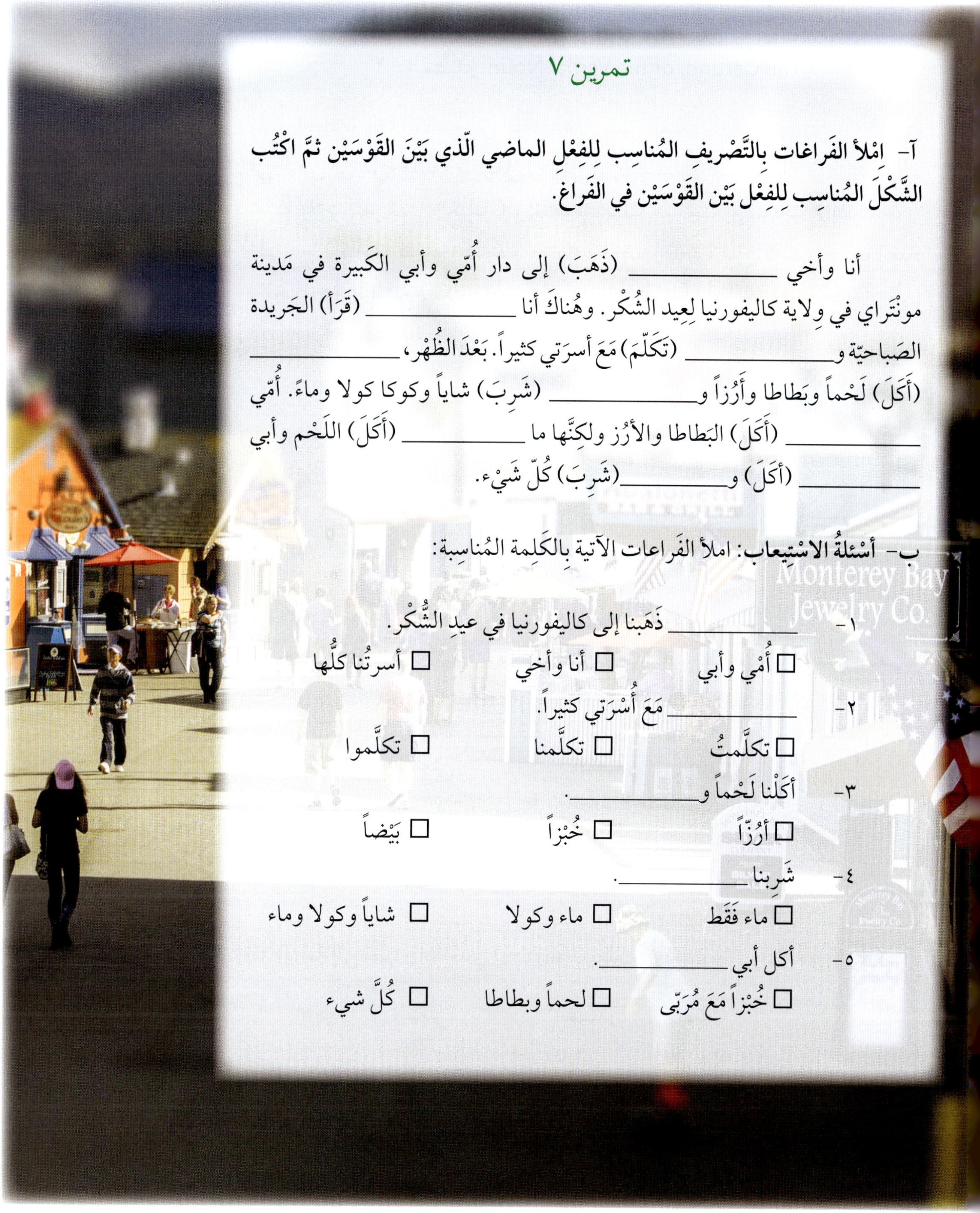

تمرين ٧

آ- اِملأ الفَراغات بِالتَّصْريفِ المُناسِب لِلفِعْلِ الماضي الّذي بَيْنَ القَوْسَيْن ثمَّ اكْتُب الشَّكْلَ المُناسِب لِلفِعْل بَيْنَ القَوْسَيْن في الفَراغ.

أنا وأخي ـــــــــــــ (ذَهَبَ) إلى دار أُمّي وأبي الكَبيرة في مَدينة مونْتَراي في وِلاية كاليفورنيا لِعيد الشُكْر. وهُناكَ أنا ـــــــــــــ (قَرَأ) الجَريدة الصَباحيّة وـــــــــــــ (تكَلّم) مَعَ أسرَتي كثيراً. بَعْدَ الظُهْر، ـــــــــــــ (أكَلَ) لَحماً وبَطاطا وأَرُزاً وـــــــــــــ (شَرِبَ) شاياً وكوكا كولا وماءً. أُمّي ـــــــــــــ (أكَلَ) البَطاطا والأرُز ولكِنّها ما ـــــــــــــ (أكَلَ) اللَحْم وأبي ـــــــــــــ (أكَلَ) وـــــــــــــ(شَرِبَ) كُلّ شَيْء.

ب- أسْئلةُ الاسْتيعاب: املأ الفَراغات الآتية بِالكَلِمة المُناسِبة:

١- ـــــــــــــ ذَهَبنا إلى كاليفورنيا في عيدِ الشُّكْر.

☐ أُمّي وأبي ☐ أنا وأخي ☐ أسرتُنا كلُّها

٢- ـــــــــــــ مَعَ أُسْرَتي كثيراً.

☐ تكلّمتُ ☐ تكلَّمنا ☐ تكلّموا

٣- أكَلْنا لَحْماً وـــــــــــــ.

☐ أرُزّاً ☐ خُبْزاً ☐ بَيْضاً

٤- شَرِبنا ـــــــــــــ.

☐ ماء فَقَط ☐ ماء وكولا ☐ شاياً وكولا وماء

٥- أكل أبي ـــــــــــــ.

☐ خُبْزاً مَعَ مُرَبّى ☐ لحماً وبطاطا ☐ كُلَّ شيء

٢– المَصْدَر The Gerund, or the Verbal Noun

نَشْتَقُّ (we derive) المَصْدَر مِن الفِعْل، على سَبيل المِثال: دِراسَة (studying)، الوارِدة في النَصّ الرَئيس، مُشْتَقّة مِن فِعْل (دَرَسَ). إنَّ المَصْدَر اِسْم (a noun) فَنَسْتَطيع أنْ نُعَرِّفَهُ بِلام التَّعْريف (الكِتابة) ونَسْتَطيع كَذلِكَ أنْ نُثْبِت بِه المُلْكيّة (possession) لِشَيْء ما (كِتابَتُه، كِتابَتُها، كِتابَتُهُم . . .)، والمَصْدَر يَتَغَيَّر، مِثْل الاِسْم، حَسَب العَدَد والحالة—أي: الرَفْع (الكِتابةُ) أو النَصْب (رأَيْتُ الكِتابةَ) أو الجَرّ (في الكِتابةِ). يَدُلّ (denotes) المَصْدَر والفِعْل على حَدَث ما:

	الفِعْل	المَعْنى		المَصْدَر	المَعْنى
٣	سافَر	*he traveled*	←	سَفَر	*a trip, traveling*
	سَبَحَ	*he swam*	←	سِباحة	*a swim; swimming*

ملاحظة: المَصْدَر يَخْتَلِف عَن الفِعْل مِن حَيْثُ الزَمَن، فَالمَصْدَر لا يَدُلّ على زَمَن الحَدَث.

إنّ مَصادِر الأفْعال الثلاثيّة كَثيرة مُتَعَدِّدة لكِنّ هُناكَ ضَوابِط غالِبة تَدُلّ على المَعْنى. مَثَلاً: إنْ دَلّ على حِرْفة (profession) فَغالِباً ما يَكون مَصْدَرُه (فِعالة):

	الفِعْل	المَعْنى		المَصْدَر	المَعْنى
	كَتَبَ	*he wrote*	←	كِتابة	*writing*
٤	تَجَرَ	*he did business*	←	تِجارة	*business*
	زَرَعَ	*he planted*	←	زِراعة	*planting*

أمّا بِالنِسْبة إلى مَصْدَر المُتَعَدّي (transitive) يَغْلُب أنْ يَكون على وَزْن (فَعْل) مِثْل:

	الفِعْل	المَعْنى		المَصْدَر	المَعْنى
	أَكَلَ	*he ate*	←	أَكْل	*eating*
٥	فَهِمَ	*he understood*	←	فَهْم	*understanding*
	ضَرَبَ	*he hit*	←	ضَرْب	*hitting*

لِبَعْض الأفْعال مِن ثَلاثة حُروف مَصْدَران، مِثْل: دِراسة ودَرْس مِن فِعل (دَرَسَ). إليكَ بَعْضُ الجُمَل فيها المَصْدَران:

٦	دِراسةُ العَرَبيَّةِ جَيِّدةٌ.	*Studying Arabic is good.*
٧	أُحِبُّ دَرْسَ العَرَبيَّةِ.	*I like Arabic class.*
٨	في دَرْسِ العَرَبيَّةِ. . .	*In the Arabic lesson. . .*

إليكَ بعضُ الأفعال بالعربيةِ التي تُشْبِه (resemble) مَصادِرَها كتابةً:

	الفِعل	المَعنى		المَصْدَر	المَعنى
٩	شَرِبَ	*to drink*	←	شُرْب	*drinking*
	لَبِسَ	*to wear*	←	لُبْس	*wearing, attire*
	عَمِلَ	*to work*	←	عَمَل	*work*
	سَكَنَ	*to reside*	←	سَكَن	*residing, residence*
	فَعَلَ	*to do*	←	فِعْل	*doing, deed*
	دَرَسَ	*to study*	←	دَرْس	*studying, lesson*

تمرين ٨

لِلمُحادَثة: إسْأل زَميلك في غُرْفةِ الصَّفّ الأسْئلةَ الآتية ثُمَّ اكْتُب الأجْوِبة على ورقة مُنْفَصْلة. اِسْتَخْدِم المَصْدَر في السُّؤال والجَواب كَما في المِثال:

مِثال: تُحِبُّ لُؤلُؤة دِراسَةَ اللُّغَةِ الإنكليزيَّة.

مَن في الصَّفّ:

1. likes reading in the morning
2. wants to study (studying) mathematics
3. lives in the dorm (residence of students)
4. likes drinking coffee with his/her friends
5. has a family member who likes Arab food
6. knows anyone who wants to work (working) in Kuwait
7. wants to wear (wearing) the *kūfiyya*

والآن أخبِر الأستاذ ما عَلِمت من الأصدِقاء.

٣– مُراجَعة مُطابَقة الصِفة لِلمَوْصوف Noun-Adjective Agreement Revisited

تَذَكَّر أنَّ الصِّفة تُطابِقُ المَوْصوف في الحالاتِ الأرْبَع الآتية: ١_ الإفراد والتَّثْنية والجَمْع (number)، ٢_ والتَّذْكير والتَّأنيث (gender)، ٣_ والحالةُ الإعرابية (case)، ٤_ والتَّنْكير والتَّعْريف (definiteness). هَيّا بِنا نُراجِع كُلّ هذِه الحالات الآن:

آ– المُفرَد والمُثنّى والجمع Number (Singular, Dual, Plural)

تأتي الصِّفة بَعْدَ المَوْصوف في اللُّغةِ العَرَبيّة كَما تَرى في المِثال ١٠، أي يأتي مُتَعَلِّمٌ بَعْدَ وَلَدٌ. ونَسْتَطيع أنْ نُحَوِّل المَوْصوف: وَلَدٌ، مِن الإفْراد إلى التَّثْنية بِزيادة ألِف ونون (ان) في آخِره كَما تَرى في المِثال ١١. وعِنْدَ تَحْويلِ المَوْصوف مِن التَّثْنية إلى الجَمْع، نَسْتَخْدِم جَمْع الصِّفة: مُتَعَلِّمون، كَما تَرى في المِثال ١٢.

١٠	وَلَدٌ	مُتَعَلِّمٌ	*an educated lad*
١١	وَلَدانِ	مُتَعَلِّمانِ	*two educated lads*
١٢	أولادٌ	مُتَعَلِّمون	*educated lads*

تَذَكَّر: وَصْف جَمْع غَيْر العاقِل (plural non-rational nouns) بِالمُفْرَدة المُؤَنَّثة (feminine singular) كَما تَرى في المِثالين ١٣–١٤:

١٣	كُتُبٌ	قَديمَةٌ	*old books*
١٤	سَيّاراتٌ	قَديمَةٌ	*old cars*

في المِثال ١٣، نَرى أنَّ كُتُبٌ جَمْع التَّكْسير المُذَكَّر (broken masculine plural) لِكَلمة (كِتاب). وفي المِثال ١٤، نَرى أنَّ سَيّاراتٌ جَمْع مُؤَنَّث سالِم لِغَيْر العاقِل (non-rational feminine sound plural) لِكَلِمة سَيّارة ولكِن نَسْتَخْدِم نَفْس الصِّفة أي قَديمة التي هي مُفْرَدة مُؤَنَّثة.

تمرين ٩

Adjective identification (number):

1. Underline the adjectives in the following sentences.
2. Write **صواب** next to those that show correct noun–adjective agreement in number and **خطأ** next to those that do not.
3. Correct any and all mistakes.

١- عِندي هاتِف يابانِيّة. ____________________

٢- تَأكُل سَلمى في مَطعَم صَغير. ____________________

٣- عِندَ أخي كُتُبٌ قَديمات. ____________________

٤- إخْوَةُ مَحمود طِوال. ____________________

٥- هَل أولادُها الصَغيرُ مَعَها؟ ____________________

٦- في صَفِّنا كَراسٍ قَديم. ____________________

ب- التَذْكير والتَأنيث Gender

يَجِب أنْ يُطابِقَ الاسْم والصِّفةَ في التَّذْكير والتَّأنيث. فإذا كان المَوْصوف مُذَكَّراً مِثْل مَطعَمٌ في المِثال ١٥، كَذلِكَ الصِّفة: حَديثٌ، وإذا كانَ الاسْم مُؤَنَّثاً مِثْل مَدرَسَةٌ في المِثال ١٦، كَذلِكَ الصِّفة: حَديثَةٌ.

١٥	مَطعَمٌ	حَديثٌ	*modern restaurant (m.)*
١٦	مَدرَسَةٌ	حَديثَةٌ	*modern school (f.)*

هذا كِتابٌ قديمٌ وفيه أوراقٌ قديمةٌ مَكتوبٌ عليها اللغةُ العربيةُ القديمةُ.

تمرين ١٠

Adjective identification (gender):

1. Underline the adjectives in the following sentences.
2. Write **صواب** next to the sentences that show correct noun-adjective agreement in gender and **خطأ** next to those that do not.
3. Correct any and all mistakes.

١- باريس مَدينةٌ فَرَنسيٌ. ____________________

٢- عَدنان طالِبٌ سوريٌ. ____________________

٣- مينيسوتا وِلايةٌ أمريكيّةٌ. ____________________

٤- جامِعَتُنا كَبيرٌ. ____________________

٥- صَفُّنا صَغيرٌ. ____________________

٦- حُسَيْن رَجُلٌ قَطَرِيَّةٌ. ____________________

ج- حالة الإعراب Case

يَجِب أنْ تَتَطابَق الصِّفة والمَوْصوف في الحالةِ الإعْرابيّة أي حَرَكات الضَّمّة والفَتْحة والكَسْرة كَما تَرى في الأمْثِلة:

١٧	لُغَتي الأولى اللُغَةُ العَرَبيّةُ.	مَرفوع بالضَمّة	*My first language is Arabic.*
١٨	يَعرِفُ مايكِل اللُغَةَ العَرَبيَّةَ.	مَنصوب بالفَتحة	*Michael knows Arabic.*
١٩	أتَكَلَّمُ مَعَ أستاذي بِاللُغَةِ العَرَبيَّةِ.	مَجرور بالكَسرة	*I speak with my teacher in Arabic.*

وفي المِثال ١٧، نَرى أنَّ الصِّفة العَرَبيَّةُ في حالة الرَّفْع (nominative case) لأنَّ المَوْصوف اللُغَةُ خَبَر الجُمْلة (predicate of the sentence). وكَما تَرى أنَّ الكَلِمَتَيْن تأخُذان ضَمّة في آخِرِهما. وفي المِثال ١٨، نَرى أنَّ الصِّفة العَرَبيَّةَ في حالةِ النَصْب (accusative case) لأنَّ المَوْصوف اللُغَةَ مَفعول بِه (direct object). وفي المِثال ١٩، نَرى أنَّ الصِّفة العَرَبيَّةِ في حالةِ الجَرّ (genitive case) لأنَّ المَوْصوف اللُغَةِ مَجْرور بِحَرْف الجَرّ (بـ).

هُناكَ بَعْضُ الحالات لَمْ نَذْكُرْها بَعْدُ وهي كَالآتي:

لِلتَّثْنية: نَزيد (ان) في آخِرِ الصِّفة كَما تَرى في المِثال ٢٠، وفي حالة الرَّفْع و (يْنِ) في حالتَيْ النَّصب والجَرّ، كَما تَرى في المِثالَيْن ٢١-٢٢.

٢٠	الكِتابان قَديمان . . .	حالةُ الرَّفع	*the two old books . . .*
٢١	رأيتُ سَيّارتَيْن قَديمَتَيْن	حالةُ النَّصب	*I saw two old cars.*
٢٢	مَشَيْنا أمامَ سَيّارتَيْن قَديمَتَيْن	حالةُ الجَرّ	*We walked in front of two old cars.*

لِلجَمْع: نَزيد (ون) في آخِرِ الصِّفة في حالةِ الرَّفْع، كَما تَرى في المِثال ٢٣، و (ين) في حالتَيْ النَّصْب والجَرّ، كَما تَرى في المِثالَيْن ٢٤-٢٥.

٢٣	المُدَرِّسونَ مُتَعَلِّمونَ	حالةُ الرَّفْع	*The teachers are educated.*
٢٤	رأيتُ المُدَرِّسينَ المُتَعَلِّمينَ	حالةُ النَّصب	*I saw the educated teachers.*
٢٥	تَكَلَّمتُ مَعَ المُدَرِّسينَ المُتَعَلِّمينَ	حالةُ الجَرّ	*I spoke with the educated teachers.*

تمرين ١١

Adjective identification (case):

1. Underline the adjectives in the following sentences.
2. Write صواب next to the sentences that show correct noun-adjective agreement in case and خطأ next to those that do not.
3. Correct any and all mistakes.

١- عِندي كِتابانِ جَديدَيْن. ______________________

٢- يَدرُسُ سامي لُغَةً جَديدةٌ. ______________________

٣- يَدرُسُ عَدنان في الجامِعَةِ الأمريكيَّةِ. ______________________

٤- أعرِفُ رِجالاً وَسيمونَ. ______________________

٥- هذِه شَقّةُ الطالِبَةِ السوريَّةُ. ______________________

د- النَكِرة والمَعرِفة Definiteness

يَجِب أنْ تَتَطابَقَ الاسْم والصِّفة في التَّنْكير والتَّعْريف. إلَيْك بَعْض حالاتِ التَّعْريف مع أمْثِلة بَيْن القَوْسَيْن:

	الاسْم المُعَرَّف
٢٦	التَعريف بأل (مِثْل: الكتاب، السَيّارة، الرَجُل، المرأة، إلخ)
٢٧	التَعريف بالضمير (مِثْل: كتابي، سَيّارتكَ، ولدها، بنته، إلخ)
٢٨	التَعريف بالـإضافة (مِثْل: كِتابُ الطالِبِ، مِفْتاحُ بابِ السَيارةِ، إلخ)
٢٩	التَعريف بالعَلَمية، أي اِسْم شَخْص ما (مِثْل: طارِق، لينا، جابِر، إلخ)

تَذَكَّر أنَّ الجُمْلَةَ الاسْميّة (a nominal sentence) تَتَكَوَّن مِن المُبْتَدَأ (subject) والخَبَر (predicate). وكَما نَرى في المِثال ٣٠، أنَّ المُبْتَدَأ الباب مُعَرَّف والخَبَر كَبيرٌ صِفة مُنَكَّرة. أمّا في المِثال ٣١، فيأتي الاسْم والصِّفة مُعَرَّفَيْن، فَنَعْتَبِره مُبْتَدَأ جُمْلة اِسْميّة ولَيْسَ جُمْلة مُفيدة.

٣٠	البابُ كَبيرٌ.	*subject and predicate*	*The door is big.*
٣١	البابُ الكَبيرُ . . .	*subject of a nominal sentence*	*The big house . . .*

وعِنْدَما يأتي الاسْم والصِّفة مُعَرَّفَيْن (البابُ الكَبيرُ) أو نَكِرَتَيْن (بابٌ كَبيرٌ) فَنُسَمِّيه شِبْه جُمْلة (a noun phrase).

أمّا إذا أتى الاسْم مُعَرَّفاً (الباب) والصِّفة نَكِرة (كَبيرٌ) فَنَعْتَبِره جُمْلة مُفيدة.

٣٢	البَيْتُ كَبيرٌ.	*complete sentence*	*The house is big.*
٣٣	البَيْتُ الكَبيرُ . . .	*incomplete sentence*	*The big house . . .*
٣٤	بَيْتٌ كَبيرٌ	*incomplete sentence*	*A big house . . .*

تمرين ١٢

Definiteness: *phrase* or *sentence*?

1. Label the following items "phrase," "sentence," or "both."
2. Write **صواب** if the phrase is grammatically correct and **خطأ** if it is incorrect.
3. Correct any and all mistakes. An example is provided.

مِثال:	الدَرّاجةُ الإيطاليّةٌ	phrase	خطأ	الدرّاجةُ الإيطاليةُ
١-	أستاذُ العَرَبِيَّةِ.	________	________	________
٢-	المَدينةُ القَديمَةُ.	________	________	________
٣-	الكُرسيُّ صَغيرٌ.	________	________	________
٤-	سَيّارةٌ حَديثَةٍ.	________	________	________
٥-	صورةٌ الجَميلةٌ.	________	________	________
٦-	الفَتاةُ قَطَرِيَّةٌ.	________	________	________
٧-	هاتِفٌ جَديدٌ	________	________	________
٨-	رَجُلُ الوَسيمُ.	________	________	________
٩-	مُدُنُ الخَليجِ.	________	________	________
١٠-	سَيّارَتُكَ جَديدةَ.	________	________	________
١١-	مَكتَبُها كَبيرٌ.	________	________	________
١٢-	حاسوبٌ قَديمٌ.	________	________	________

تَذَوّق الثَقافة العَربيّة

العائلةُ العَربيّة والأُسْرةُ العَربيّة: كَما لاحَظْت، هُناكَ كَلِمَتان في اللُغة العَربيّة تَدُلان على معنى family. تُشير كَلِمة العائلة إلى مَن يَعيش في بَيْت واحِد مِثْل الأمّ والأب والأوْلاد. أمّا كَلِمة الأسْرة فَتَدُلّ على جَماعة أفْراد الأُسْرة الكَبيرة مِن أب وجَدّ وعَمّ وخال وخالة وعَمّة وجدّة أو أفراد تربِطُهم صِلاتُ القُربى.

تمرين ١٣

أكْمِل الجُمَلَ الآتية بالاختيارِ المُناسِب وَفْق قواعِد اللُغة العَرَبيّة:

١- تِلكَ هِيَ كُلِّيَّةُ الآدابِ ________ .

☐ جَديدَةٌ ☐ جَديدٍ ☐ الجَديدةُ ☐ الجديدِ

٢- أينَ الكُتُبُ ________ ؟

☐ القَديمُ ☐ القَديمَةُ ☐ القُدَماءُ ☐ القَديماتُ

٣- تُحِبُّ هالَة مَدينَةَ دِمَشقَ ________ .

☐ قَديمٌ ☐ القَديمَ ☐ قَديمَةٌ ☐ القَديمَةَ

٤- عِندي دَرّاجَتانِ ________ .

☐ فَرَنسِيٌّ ☐ فَرَنسِيّانِ ☐ فَرَنسِيَّتانِ ☐ فَرَنسِيّاتٍ

٥- اِسمُ الطالِبِ ________ سامي.

☐ الجَديدَ ☐ الجَديدُ ☐ الجَديدِ ☐ جَديدٌ

٦- تَسكُنُ الطالِباتُ ________ في سَكَنِ الطالِباتِ.

☐ الجَديدُ ☐ الجُدُدُ ☐ الجَديدةُ ☐ الجَديداتُ

تمرين ١٤

أكْمِل الجُمَلَ الآتية بالصِّفةِ المُناسِبة كَما تَرى في المِثال. لاحِظ بأنَّ جَمْع صَغير هو صِغار:

مِثال: عِندي بَيت صَغير

أُختي صَغيرَة

١- عِندَ سالِمٌ سَيّارة ________ .

٢- أذهَبُ إلى الجامِعَة بِالسَّيّارةِ ________ .

٣- يُحِبّ أبي الأولادَ ________ .

٤- ريما وغادَة بِنتان ________ .

٥- ثَلاثَةُ مَفاتيح ________ .

٦- هَل دِمَشق وبَغداد مَدينَتان ________ .

٧- هَل أخوكِ ________ يا سَميرة؟

٨- يَجلِس عِماد في المَكتَبِ ________ .

تمرين ١٥

آ- **أكْمِل الجُمَلَ الآتية بِالاخْتِيارِ المُناسِب وَفْق نَصِّ الاسْتِماع:**

١- سَعيد طالِب ________.

☐ سوريّ ☐ تونسيّ ☐ أمريكيّ

٢- يَدرُس سَعيد ________.

☐ عِلمَ الحاسوب ☐ الكيمياء ☐ الطِبّ

٣- يَسكُن سَعيد في ________.

☐ شَقَّة ☐ بَيت ☐ سَكَنِ الطُلاّب

٤- لِسَعيد ________.

☐ أختان ☐ ثَلاثُ أخَوات ☐ أربَعُ أخَوات

ب- **اكتُب «خطأ» أو «صواب» إلى جانِب كُلّ جُمْلة ثُمَّ صَحِّح الجُمَلَ الخَطأ:**

٥- يَدرُس سَعيد في جامِعَة ماساتشوسِتس. ________

٦- يَدرُس برايَن الطِبَ الآن. ________

٧- فَرَح صَديقة سَعيد. ________

٨- تَدرُس عَلياء في الجامِعَة. ________

٩- عِندَ برايَن سَيّارة. ________

١٠- سَعيد لَيسَ عِندَهُ دَرّاجة. ________

ج- **لَخِّص نَصَّ الاستِماع بِالإنكليزيّة:**

المُفْرَدات

استمِع إلى الكَلِمة بالعَرَبيّة ثُمَّ أعِد نُطقَها مرّتَين.

أسْرة ج أسَر (f., s.) .... extended family

ألمانيا (n., f.) .... Germany

ألمانيّ (adj.) .... German

الباكِسْتان (n., f.) .... Pakistan

بَنْغلاديش (n., f.) .... Bangladesh

ثانَوِيّ (adj.) .... secondary

جَديد ج جُدُد (adj., m.) .... new

جَميل ج (ون) (adj.) .... beautiful, good-looking

حَديث (adj.) .... modern

دار ج دور (n., f.) .... house

دَجاج (n., m) .... chicken

دِراسة ج دِراسات (n., f.) .... study

ذَهَبَ (يَذْهَبُ) ذَهاب (إلى) (v.) .... to go

سائِق ج سائقون (n., m.) .... driver, chauffeur

سوق ج أسْواق (n., f.) .... market

صَديق ج أصْدِقاء (n., m.) .... friend.

صَغير ج صِغار (n., m.) .... small child, young child

طَويل ج طِوال (n., m.) .... tall

عائلة ج عوائِل \ عائلات (f., s.) .... nuclear family

عِقال ج عُقُل (n., m.) .... cord used to hold a headdress in place

عَمِلَ (يَعْمَلُ) عَمَل (v.) .... to work.

غُتْرة ج غُتَر/ غُترات (n., f.) a man's headdress . . . .

فَتاة ج فَتَيات (n., f.) girl, young woman . . . .

قَديم ج قُدَماء (adj.) old, ancient . . . .

قَصير ج قِصار (n., m.) short . . . .

قَويّ ج أقوِياء (adj.) powerful, strong . . . .

كَبير ج كِبار (n., m.) big, large; old (in age) . . . .

كوفِيّة ج كوفيّات (n., f.) headdress . . . .

لَبِسَ (يَلبَسُ) لُبْس (v.) to wear . . . .

ما (particle) particle used to negate past-tense verbs . . . .

مُحَرِّك ج مَحَرِّكات (n., f.) engine, motor . . . .

الهِنْد (n., f.) India . . . .

وَسيم ج (ون) (adj., m.) handsome . . . .

اليابان (n., f.) Japan . . . .

الفَنّ المِعماريّ في المَغرِب

الدرس الحادي عشر

أهداف الدرس

- وَصْف أنْشِطة في الماضي والمُضارِع والمُسْتَقْبَل
- تَعَلُّم كَيْفيَّة اِسْتِخْدام قَبْلَ وبَعْدَ
- تَعَلُّم كَيْفيَّة اِسْتِخْدام أظُنّ أنَّ
- تَعَلُّم كَيْفيَّة اِسْتِخْدام قال إنَّ
- تَعَلُّم اِسْم التَفْضيل
- تَعَلُّم كان وأخواتها
- وَصْف التَقْويم الهِجْريّ
- تَعَلُّم حَرْف الجَرّ بـ
- تَعَلُّم الأسْماء الخَمْسة: أبو، أخو، حَمو، ذو، فو

المُفْرَدات الجَديدة في صُوَر عديدة

مَشى (يَمشي) مَشْي

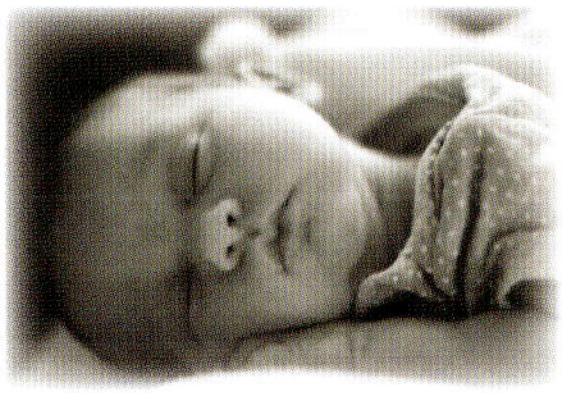

نامَ (يَنامُ) نَوم

فُندُق

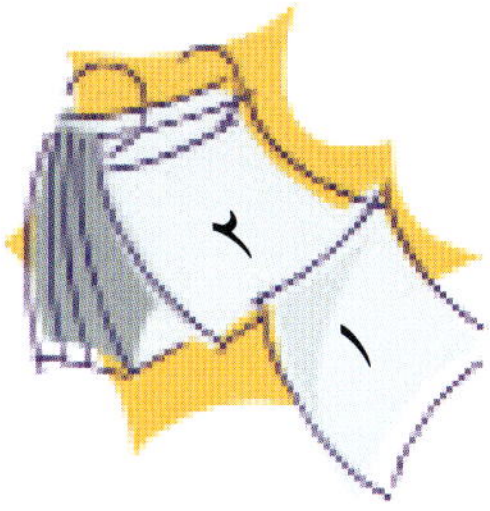

أمْس اليَوْم غَداً

قَميص ج قُمصان

رُكْنُ المُفرداتِ الجَديدة	
نَزَلَ (يَنْزِلُ) نُزول (في)	to stay at
وَصَلَ (يَصِلُ) وُصول (إلى)	to arrive
ظَنَّ (يَظُنُّ) ظَنّ (أنَّ)	to think (that)
قالَ (يَقولُ) قَوْل (إنَّ)	to say (that)
بَعيد (عَن)	far (from)
قَريب (مِن)	close (to)
قَبْلَ	before
بَعْدَ	after

الوقت	
دَقيقة ج دَقائق	minute(s)
ساعة ج ساعات	hour(s)
يَوْم ج أيّام	day(s)
أُسْبوع ج أسابيع	week(s)
شَهْر ج شُهور/ أشْهُر	month(s)
فَصْل ج فُصول	season(s)
سَنة ج سِنون / سَنَوات	year(s)

انْظُر إلى الجَدْوَل إلى الأسْفَل بِعُنْوان «أيّام الأُسْبوع» وتأمَّل مَعي (consider with me) جَذْر كَلِمة أُسْبوع. أي نَعَم! إنَّ جَذْرَها: س / ب / ع وهذِه الأحْرُفُ الثَلاثة أيضاً جَذْركَلِمة أُخْرى نَعْرِفُها: سَبْعة! لأن هُناكَ سَبعة أيّام في الأُسْبوع.

أيّام الأسْبوع

			يَوْم			
السَبت	الجُمْعة	الخَميس	الأرْبِعاء	الثُلاثاء	الإثْنَين	الأحَد
Saturday	Friday	Thursday	Wednesday	Tuesday	Monday	Sunday

حين نَسْتَخْدِم يَوْم الـ في جُمْلة لا نَقول: ~~على يوم~~ وإنَّما نَقول: في يَوْم الـ أو نَسْتَخْدِم: يَوْم الـ كَما نَفْعَل بالإنْكليزيّة:

١	يَوْمَ الجُمْعةِ، حَضَرْتُ الصَفَّ الصَباحيّ.	Friday, I attended my morning class.
٢	في يَوْمِ الجُمْعةِ، حَضَرْتُ الصَفَّ الصَباحيّ.	On Friday, I attended my morning class.
٣	لا نَقول: ~~على~~ يَوم الـ	We never use على to mean "on" in this context.

تمرين ١

اِختر الكَلِمةَ الّتي لا تُناسِب باقي الكَلِمات في كُلّ مَجموعة وبيِّن السَبَب:

١-	وَصَلَ	شَهْر	ذَهَبَ	نامَ
٢-	نَزَل في	فُندُق	مَطعَم	مَقصَف
٣-	الجُمْعَة	يَوْم	الإثْنَيْن	أيْلول
٤-	كَبير	بَعيد	حينَ	قَريب
٥-	وِسادَة	ساعَة	بَطّانِيَّة	شَرشَف

تمرين ٢

وافِقْ بَيْنَ الكَلِمات في العَمودَين.

١-	آب		أُسْبوع
٢-	مَساءً		سَوفَ
٣-	نَزَلَ في		المِكسيك
٤-	شُباط		السَبْت
٥-	وِسادَة		فُنُدق
٦-	فاهيتا		سَرير
٧-	شَهْر		ظُهْراً
٨-	الأَحَد		فِبرايِر
٩-	كانون الثاني		طائِرة
١٠-	مَطار		يَنايِر أغُسطُس

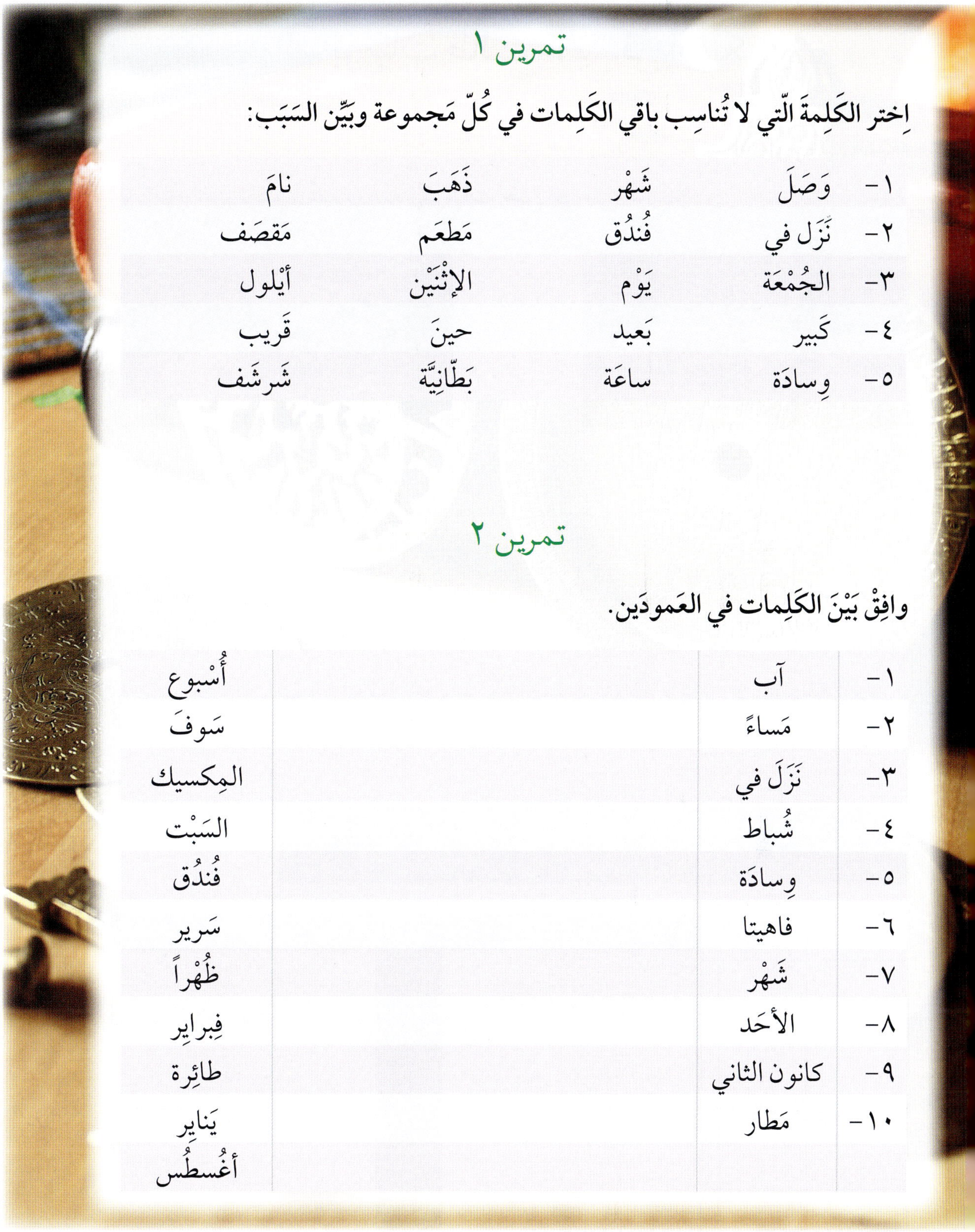

الأَسْطُرلاب

يَوْمِيّات طالِب عَرَبيّ في أمريكا

هذا عَدنان مارتيني هو طالِب عَرَبيّ مِن سوريا يَدرُس عِلمَ الحاسوب في جامِعة وِلاية أوهايو. كَتَب عَدنان هذِه اليَوْمِيّات حين أتى إلى أمريكا.

مَطار

طائِرَة

الخَميس ١٣ أيْلول ٢٠١٨

وَصَلْتُ اليَوْم إلى مَطار كَنيدي في نيويورك في الساعَةِ السادِسة مَساءً. ذَهَبتُ إلى فُندُق شيراتُن في المطار وأكَلتُ في مَطعَمِ الفُندُق. بَعْدَ ذلِكَ ذَهبتُ إلى غُرفَتي ونِمْتُ حَتّى الساعة السابِعة مِن صَباح يَوْمِ الجُمْعة. مَوعِد طائِرَتي في الساعةِ العاشِرة والنِصْف صَباحاً.

أيلول ٢٠١٧

يوم السبت	يوم الأحد	يوم الإثنين	يوم الثلاثاء	يوم الأربعاء	يوم الخميس	يوم الجمعة
						١
					٧	٨
					١٤	١٥
					٢١	٢٢
					٢٨	٢٩

الخميس ١٤ أيلول	الساعة	الجُمعة ١٥ أيلول
اللغة الإنكليزية	٩	
	١٠	مَوْعِد الطائرة العاشِرة والنصف
	١١	
الرياضيات	١٢	مَوْعِد الوُصول إلى مطار كلمبس
	١	
	٢	
الكيمياء	٣	
	٤	
	٥	
مَوْعِد الوُصول إلى مطار كَنيدي	٦	

مَواعِيد عَدنان اليومية

الجُمْعَة ١٤ أيْلول ٢٠١٨

مطار كَلَمبَس الدُوَليّ

وَصَلتُ إلى مَطار كَلَمبَس في الساعةِ الثانِية عَشْرة ظُهْراً. حين وَصلتُ إلى المَطار كانَ هِشام هُناك (هِشام هو صَديق أخي رامي). نَزَلتُ في شَقَّة هِشام. يُوجَد في شَقَّتِه غُرفَتا نَوْم وغُرفة جُلوس واحِدة. غُرفة نَوْم هِشام أكْبَر مِن الغُرفة الثانية. أظُنّ أنّي سأسكُن مَعَهُ في هذا الشَهْر.

ذَهبْنا أنا وهِشام أمْس إلى السوق بِالسَيّارة وهي بَعيدة عَن الشَقّة. اِشْتَرَيْتُ وِسادة وشَرشَفين وبَطّانِيّتَين لِسَريري، واشْتَرى هِشام قَميصاً جَديداً بِخَمسة وعِشرين دولاراً. بَعْدَ ذلِك أكَلنا في مَطعَم مِكسيكيّ قَريب مِن شَقَّتِه. أكَلَ هِشام فاهيتا بِاللَحْم وأنا أكَلتُ فاهيتا بِالدّجاج. يُحِبّ هِشام الأكْل المِكسيكيّ. سآكُل غداً في مَطعَم عَرَبيّ إنْ شاءَ الله.

الأرْبِعاء ١٩ أيلول ٢٠١٨

بُحَيرة المرآة في جامعة ولاية أوهايو

كُنْتُ اليَوْم في الجامِعَة. ذَهَبْتُ إلى دُروسي ومَشَيْتُ في الجامِعة. أظُنّ أنّ جامِعَة ولاية أوهايو كَبيرة جِدّاً. يَقولُ هِشام إنَّها مِن أكْبَر جامِعاتِ الوِلاياتِ المُتَّحِدَةِ الأمريكيّة. في الساعةِ الخامِسة مَساءً مَشَيْتُ إلى الشَقَّة. قَبْلَ ذلِك مَشَيْتُ إلى مَكتَبَة «إس بي إكس» القَريبة مِن الجامِعة واشْتَرَيْتُ كُتُبي مِنها. اِشْتَرَيْتُ سَبعَة كُتُب وثَلاثة دَفاتِر بِمِئتَين وسِتَّة وسَبعين دولاراً. سأقرَأُ قَليلاً قَبْلَ النَوْم وسَوْفَ أكتُب إلى أبي وأمّي.

تمرين ٣

لِلمُحادَثة: افرض (suppose) أنّك وَصَلْتَ اليَوْم إلى مَطار القاهِرة وَقَد اِتَّصَلْتَ بِصَديقك المِصْريّ بالهاتِف حَتّى تَقول لَهُ:

to arrive	وَصَلَ (يَصِل) وُصول (إلى)	*to come*	أتى / يأتي / إتيان (إلى)
to do	فَعَلَ (يَفْعَلُ) فِعل	*to buy*	اِشْتَرى / يَشْتَري / شِراء

1. your plane's time of arrival
2. what street your new apartment is on
3. when your friend wants to eat lunch and who is buying (paying)
4. what you want to do in Cairo and on what day
5. when you want to go to the markets so you can buy some new

____

عُطلة نِهاية الأسبوع في البِلاد العَرَبيّة

يَذهَب الطُلّاب إلى المَدارس سِتَّة أيّام في الأُسْبوع في بَعْضِ البِلادِ العَرَبيَّة ويَعمَلُ الناس سِتّة أيّام في الأُسْبوع أيْضاً. ويَوْم الجُمْعَة هو عُطلَة نِهايةِ الأُسْبوع. في سوريا عُطْلَة نهايةِ الأُسبوع هي يَوْما الجُمْعة والسَبْت، لكِنّ عُطْلَة نِهايةِ الأُسْبوع في لُبنان هي يَوْما الجُمْعَة والأحَد.

تمرين ٤

آ - **أكْمِل الجُمَلَ الآتية بِكَلِمات مُناسِبة وَفْق نَصِّ القِراءة.**

١- وَصَل عَدنان إلى مَطار كَنيدي ____________ .

☐ في الساعةِ العاشِرة ☐ في الساعةِ السادِسة ☐ بِالسَيّارة

٢- كان مَوْعِد طائِرة كَلَمبَس في الساعة ____________ .

☐ السادِسة ☐ العاشِرةِ والنِصْف ☐ الثانِيَة عَشْرة

٣- هِشام ____________ .

☐ صَديق عَدنان ☐ أخو رامي ☐ صَديق رامي

٤- حين وَصَل عَدنان إلى مَطار كَلَمبَس كان هِشام في ____________ .

☐ المَطار ☐ الجامِعة ☐ الشَقَّة

٥- يوجَد في شَقَّة هِشام ____________ .

☐ غُرفَة نَوْم واحِدة ☐ غُرفَتا نَوْم ☐ ثَلاث غُرَف نَوْم

٦- في هذا الشَهر سَوفَ يَسْكُن عَدنان في ____________ .

☐ شَقَّة هِشام ☐ فُنْدُق ☐ سَكَن الطُلاّب

٧- اِشْتَرى هِشام ____________ .

☐ كُتُباً ☐ قَميصاً ☐ وِسادَةً

٨- اِشْتَرى عَدنان كُتُباً بِـ ____________ دولاراً.

☐ ٧٢٦ ☐ ٦٢٧ ☐ ٢٧٦

ب - بيِّن إن كانَت الجُمَل الآتية صواباً أو خَطأ وَفْق النَصّ وصَحِّح الخَطأ مِنها:

٩- سَيَسكُن عَدنان في غُرفَة كَبيرة.

١٠- وَصَل عَدنان إلى كَلمبَس يَوْم الجُمْعَة.

١١- ذَهَب عَدنان إلى دُروسِه في الجامِعَة يَوْم الثُلاثاء.

١٢- يَظُنّ عَدنان أنَّ جامِعَة وِلايَّة أوهايو أكبَر مِن جامِعَة دِمَشق.

العرض: أخبر الطلاّب ما عملته اليوم قبل المجيء إلى الصف، مثلاً:
«أ - أتيت إلى الجامعة هذا الصباح في الساعة الثامنة والنصف صباحاً وبعد ذلك ذهبت إلى مكتبي وتكلمت مع صديقي فلان هناك ولكن قبل ذلك شربت قليلاً من القهوة وبعد شرب القهوة قابلت صديقي فلان. وبعد ذلك جئت إلى غرفة الصف هذه.»

ثمّ، اسأل الطلاّب عمّ فهموا من القصة.
للممارسة: اسأل الطلاّب ماذا فعلوا البارحة. وعند إتمام الفكرة، اسألهم ماذا فعلوا قبل أو بعد ذلك حتّى تجعلهم يستخدمون هذين الحرفين في أجوبتهم وحديثهم اليومي.
التطبيق في مجموعات من اثنين: اطلب من الطلاّب الإفادة بما فعلوا هذا الصباح، أو الأمس، أو الأسبوع الماضي، واطلب من المستمع أن يسأل المتكلّم ماذا فعل قبل أو بعد ذلك.

١ - وَصْفُ الأنْشِطة في الماضي والمُضارِع والمُسْتَقْبَل

Describing Activities in the Past, Present, and Future

لَقَد تَعَلَّمْنا تَصريف الفِعْل العَرَبيّ في صيغتَي الماضي والمُضارِع. تَدُلّ صيغة الماضي على فِعْل (action) قد تمّ (completed)، ونسمّي الضَمائر المُستَخْدَمة فيه، الضَمائر المُسْتَتِرة (hidden pronouns) وهي تأتي في آخِر الجَذْر. أما صيغة المُضارِع فَتَدُلّ على فِعْل لم يَتِمّ بَعْدُ (not yet completed)، والضَمائر المُسْتَتِرة المُستَخْدَمة فيها تأتي في بِدايةِ الجَذْر مع بَعْضِ الأحْرُف في النِهاية الّتي تَدُلّ على التأنيث والتَثْنية والجَمْع. وأخيراً، تَدُلّ صيغة المُسْتَقْبَل على فِعْل لم يَحْصُل بَعْدُ لكِنَّه سيَحْصُل في وَقْت لاحِق (at a later time). وكَيْف نَدُلّ على المُسْتَقْبَل؟ نَزيد الحَرْف سَـ في بِدايةِ الفِعْلِ المُصَرَّف (conjugated verb) وحَرْفُ السين هذا (سَـ) مأخوذ مِن الحَرْف سَوْفَ الّذي يَدْخُل على الفِعْل المُضارِع ويُشير إلى المُسْتَقْبَل. لَيسَ هُناكَ أي فَرْق بَيْن (سَـ) و(سَوْفَ) من حَيْثُ المَعنى.

	المُضارِع		المُسْتَقْبَل
١	يَدْرُس	←	سَيَدْرُس / سَوْفَ يَدْرُس

ملاحَظة: لَيسَ هُناكَ أي فَرْق بَيْنَ استِخدام حَرْفَي (سَـ) و(سَوْفَ) من حَيْثُ التَصريف.

تمرين ٥

لِلمُحادثة: حاوِل اِسْتِخْدام حَرْفَي (سـَ) و (سَوْفَ) في الأجْوِبة لِلأسْئلة مِثل: ماذا تَفعَل يوم الـ ______؟ كَذلِك، حاوِلْ أنْ تَسْتَخْدِم (أظُنّ أنّ) كَما في المِثال:

مِثال: ماذا تَفعَلُ يَوْمَ الجُمْعة؟	*What are you doing this Friday?*
أظُنّ أنّني سأقْرَأ في المَكتَبَة يَوم الجُمْعة مَساءً.	*I think that I am going to read at the library Friday evening.*

في ما يَلي، بَعْضُ المَواضيعِ الّتي قَدْ تُساعِدُك في القِيام بالمُحادَثة:

الأكْل	النَوْم	الكِتابة	القِراءة	الشِراء	المُحادَثة	الذَهاب إلى مَكان	المَشي

والآن، اكْتُب أجْوِبَتك على وَرَقة مُنْفَصِلة (separate sheet of paper) وأخْبِر الزُملاء بِما وَجَدْتَ مِن المَعلومات.

٢- اِسْتِخْدام قَبْلَ وبَعْدَ

تَجِد كَلِمة (adverb) مُقابِلها بالعَرَبيّة في كَلِمة ظَرْف الّتي تَدُلّ على وِعاء أو إناء (vessel or container) أي كُلّ ما يَسْتَقِرّ غَيْرُه فيه ولَها نَوْعان نحوياً: ١_ظَرْف الزَمان و٢_ظَرْف المَكان (adverb of place and time).

٢	أشْرَبُ القَهوةَ صباحاً.	ظَرْف الزَمان	*I drink coffee in the morning.*
٣	قَرَأَ الجَريدةَ أمامَ التِلْفازِ.	ظَرْف المَكان	*He read the newspaper in front of the TV.*

في المِثال ٢، نَجِد أنّ الفِعْل (أشْرَبُ) يَحْدُث في الصَباح، وهو ظَرْف الزمان لأنّه يَدُلّ على وَقْت الحَدَث. وفي المِثال ٣، نَجِد أنّ الفِعل (قَرَأ) يَحْدُث في مَكان مُعَيَّن (certain) أي أمامَ التِلْفاز. لِنَتَكَلّم (let's talk) عن ظَرْفَي (قَبْلَ) و (بَعْدَ) اللّذان يُفيدان ظَرْفَي المَكان والزَمان. تأمَّل معي الأمْثِلة الآتية:

٤	سأراكَ قَبْلَ (أو بَعْدَ) الدَرسِ.	ظَرْف الزَمان	*I'll see you before (or after) class.*
٥	داري قَبْلَ (أو بَعْدَ) الفُنْدُقِ.	ظَرْف المَكان	*My house is before the hotel.*

العرض: اعرض على الطلاّب تقويماً عربياً حتّى تسألهم أسئلة مستخدماً فيها الماضي والحاضر والمستقبل. قد تجري الأسئلة على الوتيرة الآتية:
- «أين أكلتَ يوم الثلاثاء يا سامر؟»
- «أكلتُ في المطعم يوم الثلاثاء.»
- «وأين ستأكل يوم السبت؟»
- «سآكل في بيت أبي وأمّي يوم السبت.»

وهنا، اطرح بعض الأسئلة على الزملاء بالنسبة إلى قصة سامر. وبعد ذلك، اطرح بعض الأسئلة على طالب من طلاّب الصفّ فيها أسماء الشهور:
- «يا بدر، أين سافرتَ في تشرين الثاني؟»
«والله يا أستاذ، سافرتُ إلى كاليفورنيا في تشرين الثاني. سأزور دمشق في حزيران.»

ثمّ، اطرح أسئلة على الطلاّب عمّ سيفعل بدر في تشرين الثاني وحزيران.
الممارسة: أشِر إلى يوم من أيام الشهر في التقويم واسأل طالباً ما سيفعل فيه. في حالة أنه يرتكب خطأً من حيث زمن الفعل، حاول أن تصحّحه عن طريق الإشارات اليدوية كي تجعله يصحّح نفسه أو يصحّحه طالب من الطلاّب.
التطبيق في مجموعات من اثنين أو ثلاثة: اطلب منهم أن يتكلّموا عن الأمس واليوم والغد. وبعد هذا، اطلب من الطالب أن يتكلّم عمّ فعل / يفعل / سيفعل زميله.

إن الكَلام الّذي يَلي هذَين الظَرْفَيْن في حالةِ الجَرّ مِثْلُه مِثْل حالة أحْرُف الجَرّ الّتي تَجُرّ الكَلِمة الّتي تَليها، على سَبيلِ المِثال (by way of example) الاسمُ المُعَرَّف (definite nouns) مَجْرور بالكسرة (مَثْل: بَعْدَ الفُنْدُقِ) والمُثَنّى مَجْرور بالـ ـَيْنِ (مِثْل: قَبْلَ ساعتَيْن) والجَمْع المُذَكَّر السالِم مَجْرور بالـ ينَ (مِثْل: أمامَ المُعَلِّمين).

تمرين ٦

الكتابة: صِف (describe) ما يَحْدُث في جَدْوَل عَدْنان باسْتِخْدام الظَرْفَين (قَبْلَ وبَعْدَ). تَذَكَّر (remember) إذا أرَدْت أنْ تُحَدِّد (pinpoint) كَم ساعة مَضت مُنْذُ الحَدَث أو كَم ساعة تَتَبَقّى حَتّى الحَدَث، اسْتَخْدِم حَرْف الجَرّ (بِـ):

مِثال: دَرْس اللُغة الإنكليزيّة بَعْدَ الفطور بساعة وقَبْلَ دَرْس الرياضيّات بثَلاث ساعات.

الخَميس ٧ أيلول ٢٠١٧	الساعة
الفَطور	٨
اللُغة الإنكليزية	٩
	١٠
	١١
الرياضيّات	١٢
	١
	٢
الكيمياء	٣
	٤
الذَهاب إلى السوق	٥

١- دَرْسُ الرياضيّات ______________________________

____

٢- دَرْسُ الكيمياء ______________________________

____

٣- اِستِخدام ظَنَّ أنَّ

مِن المُمْكِن أنْ نَسْتَخْدِمَ الفِعْل ظَنَّ أنَّ حين نَشُكّ (we have doubt) في أمْر ما والمُرادِف (synonym) لَهُ بالعَرَبيّة هو: اِعْتَقَد أنَّ (to think that). وعادةً يَلي هذا الفِعْل الحَرْف أنَّ (that) الّذي يَدْخُل على بِداية جُمْلة اِسْميّة (nominal sentence) كَما تَرى في المِثالَيْن ٦-٧ لَكِن أحْياناً لا نَسْتَخْدِم أنّ كَما نَفْعَل بالإنْكِليزية اُنْظُر إلى المِثال ٨.

٦	أظُنُّ أنَّها في المَدرَسَةِ الآن.	I think that she is at school now.
٧	أظُنُّ أنَّ الأسْتاذَ يَقرَأه.	I think that the professor is reading it.
٨	أظُنُّ البِنْتَ ناجِحة.	I think the girl is successful.

العرض: يمكن أن تُبدي رأيك ببعض الأشياء المعروفة، على سبيل المثال:
«أظن أنّ مدينة نيويورك مدينة كبيرة وحديثة.»
«أظن أنّ محرك سيارة مرسيديس قوي جداً.»
«أظن أنّ أودري هيبورن جميلة.»

والآن، اعرض على الطلاّب بعض الصور المعروفة من الشابكة أو من عندك، واسألهم رأيهم بها:
«هل تظن أنّ مدينة نيويورك جميلة؟»
«هل تظنين أن مطار هيثرو مطار كبير؟»

التطبيق: دع الطلاّب القيام باستطلاع الرأي في الصف واطلب منهم طرح أسئلة مثل:
«هل تظن أنّ جامعة ولاية أوهايو أكبر جامعة في أمريكا؟»
«هل تظنين أن محرك السيارات الألمانية هو الأقوى؟»
«هل تظن أن موسيقا فلان جميلة؟»

وعند نهاية التمرين، اطلب من بعض الطلاّب الإفادة بما جمع من المعلومات مثلاً:
«خمسة طلاّب يظنون أنّ موسيقا فلان جميلة.»

آ- اِسْتِخدام الحَرف أنّ

كَما تَرى في الأمْثِلة أعلاه (above)، يَدْخُل الحَرْف أنَّ على الجُمْلة الإسْميّة، أي بَعْدَ الحَرْف أنَّ نَسْتَخْدِم إما ضَمير مُتَّصِل (ها في المثال ٦) وإما جُمْلة اِسْميّة (الأسْتاذَ في المِثال ٧). ولاحِظ أنَّ الاسْم الأسْتاذَ مَنصوب بالفَتْحة لأنَّ الحَرْف أنَّ يَنْصُب الاسْم ويَرْفَع الخَبَر.

٩	القَهْوةُ في الصَباحِ جَيِّدةٌ.	جُملة عادية	Coffee in the morning is good.
١٠	أظُنُّ أنَّ القَهْوةَ في الصَباحِ جَيِّدةٌ.	جُملة فيها أنَّ	I think that coffee in the morning is good.
١١	هذِهِ الجَريدةُ سياسيّةٌ.	جُملة عادية	This newspaper is political.
١٢	أظُنُّ أنَّ هذِهِ الجَريدةَ سياسيّةٌ.	جُملة فيها أنَّ	I think that this paper is political.

في المِثال ١٠، اسْم أنَّ القَهْوةَ لِذلِك هو مَنْصوب بالفَتْحة، كَذلِك في المِثال ١٢ اسْم أنّ الجَريدةَ لِذلِكَ هو مَنْصوب بالفَتْحة. أما بالنِسبة إلى خَبَر أنَّ فَهو مَرفوع بالضَمَّة، كَما نرى في المِثال ١٠ جَيِّدةٌ (علامة الرَفْع تَنْوين الضَّمّ) كَذلِك سِياسيّةٌ في المثال ١٢.

ب- الفِعْل المشدَّد Verbs with Doubled Consonants

إنَّ أصْل الفِعْل ظَنَّ هو: (ظ نَ نَ) لكِنْ سُكِّنَت النُون الأُولى وأدْغِمَت (= أدْخِلَت) في النُون الثانية. ونَقول لَكَ هذا، لأنَّ تَصْريف الفِعْل المُشَدَّد يَخْتَلِف اِخْتِلافاً بسيطاً عن تَصريف الفِعْل الثُلاثيّ المجرّد (triliteral root or three-letter root). تأمّل (consider) الجَدْوَل الآتي:

تَصريف الفِعْل ظَنَّ			
	الضمير المنفصل	الماضي	المُضارِع
المُتَكَلِّم	أنا	ظَنَنْتُ	أظُنُّ
	نَحْنُ	ظَنَنّا	نَظُنُّ
المُخاطَب	أنْتَ	ظَنَنْتَ	تَظُنُّ
	أنْتِ	ظَنَنْتِ	تَظُنّينَ
	أنْتُما	ظَنَنْتُما	تَظُنّانِ
	أنْتُم	ظَنَنْتُم	تَظُنّونَ
	أنْتُنَّ	ظَنَنْتُنَّ	تَظْنُنَّ
الغائب	هُوَ	ظَنَّ	يَظُنُّ
	هِيَ	ظَنَّتْ	تَظُنُّ
	هُما (مُذَكَّر)	ظَنّا	يَظُنّانِ
	هُما (مُؤَنَّث)	ظَنَّتا	تَظُنّانِ
	هُم	ظَنّوا	يَظُنّونَ
	هُنَّ	ظَنَنَّ	يَظْنُنَّ

كَما نُلاحِظ في الجَدْول أعلاه، في صيغةِ المُتَكَلِّم والمخاطَب، تَظْهَر النُون المُشَدَّدة كَحَرْفَيْن مُنْفَصِلَيْن أي: (ظَنَنْ + ضمير = ظَنَنْتُ أو ظَنَنت أو ظَنَنْتِ). لكِنَّ في صيغةِ الغائب، حَرْفُ النُون مُشّدَّد (ظَنَّ أو ظَنَّتْ أو ظَنّوا).

تمرين ٧

المُحادثة فيها اِسْتِخْدام ظَنَّ أنّ: اسأل (ask) زَميل الغُرْفة ما هي سَيّارتُه المُفَضَّلة أو فيلمُه المُفَضَّل أو فَريقُه الرياضيّ المُفَضَّل أو أُغْنيتُه المُفَضَّلة أو مَن هو مُمَثِّله المُفَضَّل إلخ. وإذا لم يُحِبّ زَميلك فيلمَك المُفَضَّل، قُلْ لَه لِماذا تَظُنّ أنّه جيّد.

وبَعْد أنْ تُكْمِل باب (اسم التَفْضيل) في هذا الدرس، تَسْتَطيع أن تُعيد (re-do) هذا التَمْرين مرّة أُخرى تَسْتَخْدِم فيه اسم التَفْضيل وتَقول لَهُ لِماذا تَظُنّ أنّ فيلمَك / سَيّارتك / أُغْنيتكَ المُفَضَّل(ة) جيّد(ة) إلى هذِه الدَرَجة (to this extent).

رُكنُ مُفْرداتِ المَشْهدِ المرئي

جاء / يَجيء / مَجيء (إلى)	*to come (to)*
زار / يزور / زيارة	*to visit*
البارِحة	أمس أو الأمسِ
ما رأْيك؟	*what's your opinion?*
تَعَرّف / يَتَعَرَّف / تَعَرُّف (على)	*to become acquainted (with)*
مانِع (لَيْسَ عِنْدي مانِع)	*objection (I have no objection)*
رائع	*wonderful*
مُتَحَمِّس (لِـ)	*I am excited (to)*
ضَيْف ج ضُيوف	*guest*
قابَل / يُقابِل / مُقابَلة	*to meet with*
مُوافِق	*agree*

تمرين ٨

اِملأ الفَراغاتَ الآتية بالكَلِمةِ المُناسِبة وَفْق النَصّ المرئيّ.

- عِنْدي صَديق اسمُه عَدْنان مارتيني وهو مِن مَدينة حَلَب يَدْرُس ______________
______________ في جامِعة وِلاية أوهايو وهو الآن في سوريا ______________
لِزيارة عائلتِه لَقَد ______________ إلى مَطار دِمَشْق الدُوَليّ ______________

مساءً. ما ______________ أنْ تأتي مَعي وتَتَعَرَّف عليه؟

- لَيْسَ عِنْدي مانِع، وصَديقي مايكل الّذي يَدْرُس في القاهِرة سَيَصِل غداً أيضاً.

- رائع! أنا ______________ جداً للقاءِه. فَلَقَد تَكَلَّمْت مَعهُ على الحاسوب ______________ مرّات.

- أكيد. وهو أيضاً يُريد أن يُقابِلك.

- هل قُلْتَ لَهُ إنَّه سَيَكون ______________ أيضاً؟

- أكيد!

- حسناً! سَنَذْهَب إلى النَوْم، وغداً نَذْهَب ______________ عَدْنان.

- ______________.

تمرين ٩

تَمرين المُشاهَدة: أَجِب عن الأسْئلة الآتية وَفْق نَصِّ المُشاهَدة.

١- لِماذا يَذْهَب سامِر وستيف إلى مَطار دِمَشْق الدُوَليّ؟ ______________

____

٢- مَتى وَصَل عَدنان إلى سوريا؟ ______________

____

٣- مَتى سَيَصِل مايكل إلى دِمَشْق؟ ______________

____

٤- كَيْف تَعَرَّف سامِر على مايكل؟ ______________

____

٥- مَن سَيُقابِل عَدنان وستيف غداً؟ ______________

____

6. Try to guess what the word **أكيد** means from context and write your answer here:

____

٤ – اِسْتِخدام قالَ إنَّ Using "to say that" in Reported Speech

حين نُريد أنْ نُخْبِر شَخْصاً ما (someone) بِحَدَث ما (an event) نَسْتَخْدِم الفِعْل قال الّذي يليه الحَرْف إنَّ (that)، وهذا الحَرْف يَنْصُب الاسْم ويَرْفَع الخَبَر مِثْل الحَرْف أنّ الّذي تَعَلّمْناه في باب «اِسْتِخْدام الحَرْف أنَّ» في هذا الدَّرْس.

حِوار فيه: قالَ وإنَّ ولِـ ولَـ

– ماذا قُلْتَ؟

– قُلْتُ إنّني أُريد أنْ أذْهَب إلى المَطار.

– لِماذا؟

– لأني تَكَلَّمتُ مَع أُمّي اليوم بالهاتِف وقالَت لي إنّها تُريد أن تَزورَنا في العُطْلة.

– وماذا قُلْتَ لِأُمِّكَ؟

– قُلْتُ لَها إنَّ الطَقْسَ في دِمَشْق بارد الآنَ!.

وكَما تَرى في الحِوار أعلاه، نَسْتَخْدِم الحَرْف إنَّ بَعْدَ قال حَتّى نُفيد شَخْصاً بالخَبَر ونُوَجِّه الكَلام إلى هذا الشَّخْص باسْتِخْدام (لَـ + ضَمير مُتَصِل) أو (لِـ + اسم).

١٣	أُريدُ أنْ أقولَ لَكَ شَيئاً.	*I want to tell you something.*
١٤	أُريدُ أنْ أقولَ لِزَيْدٍ شَيئاً.	*I want to tell Zayd something.*

تَذَكَّر: نَسْتَخْدِم إنَّ بَعْدَ الفِعْل قالَ وأنَّ بَعْدَ ظَنَّ كما تَرى في الجَدول أدناه:

١٥	قالَ إنَّ	*qāla 'inna*
١٦	ظَنَّ أنَّ	*ẓanna 'anna*

العرض: تظاهر كأنك تتكلّم بالهاتف مع قريبك أو صديقك أمام الصفّ وبَعده اسألهم عمّ قلت، أو حضّر مكالمة خيالية مثل:

«تكلّمتُ مع أمّي هذا الصباح وقالت لي إنها تريد أن تذهب إلى السوق. فقلتُ لها أنا أيضاً أريد الذهاب إلى السوق. قالت لي إنها ستذهب في الساعة كذا وقلت لها أنا مشغول في الساعة كذا وأريد الذهاب في الساعة كذا إلخ . . .»

والآن، اسألهم ماذا قيلَ ومَن قاله.

للممارسة: اسأل الطلاّب إذا تحدثوا مع شخص بالهاتف صباح اليوم وماذا قالوا، وأين كانوا، وماذا قال لهم المتكلّم الآخر ، إلخ. وبعد أن تعوّدوا على استخدام (قال لي إنّ)، اطرح عليهم اسئلة الاستيعاب مثل:

أ – «ماذا قال ماهر؟»

ط – «قال ماهر إنه تكلّم مع صديقه عبدالله هذا الصباح.»

التطبيق: في مجموعات من اثنين أو ثلاثة: اعمل تمرين ٩، وبعده، اطلب منهم الإفادة بما فهموا من شريكهم.

تمرين ١٠

اِسْتِخْدام أَنَّ أو إِنَّ: اِملأ الفَراغات بالحَرْف المُناسِب وشَكِّل (provide the correct endings) الكَلِمات الّتي بَيْن القَوسَيْن (between parentheses):

١- يَظُنّ سَميح ________ (الجامِعَة) بَعيدة.
٢- تَقول ريم ________ (سَيّارتها) قَديمة.
٣- هَل تَظُنّين ________ (الكِتاب x ٢) بِعِشرين دولاراً؟
٤- أظُنّ ________ (مَدينَة) سان فرانسيسكو جَميلة.
٥- يَقول صَديقي بَشّار ________ (الطُلّاب) لَيْسوا في الصَفّ.
٦- تَقول سُعاد ________ (السَيّارة x ٢) (جَديدَة x ٢).

تمرين ١١

لِلمُحادَثة: اِسْتَخْدِم قالَ إِنَّ مع زَميل من زُملاء الغُرْفة واسأله إذا تَكَلَّم مع أحَد اليَوْم، ثُمَّ اسأله ماذا قال لِهذا الشَخْص.

مِثال: **هَل تَكَلَّمْتَ مَع صَديق مِن أَصْدِقائك اليَوْم؟ ماذا قُلْتَ لَهُ وماذا قالَ لَكَ؟**

٥- اِسْم التَفْضيل Comparative and Superlative

حين نُقارِن بَيْن شَيْئَين، نَنْظُر إلى صِفة مُعَيَّنة مُشْتَرَكة بَيْنَهُما وزادَ أَحَدُهُما على الآخر وتَجِد مُقابِلَها بالإنْكليزيّة في (taller, shorter, older, younger). أما بِالعَرَبيّة، فَنَسْتَخْدِم وَزن أَفْعَل مِن كَما تَرى في الأَمْثِلة الآتية:

١٧	هالة أَطْوَل مِن لينا.	*Hālā is taller than Līnā.*
١٨	لينا أَقْصَر مِن هالة.	*Līnā is shorter than Hālā.*
١٩	تامِر أَكْبَر مِن خالِد.	*Tāmer is older than Ḳālid.*
٢٠	خالِد أَصْغَر مِن تامِر.	*Ḳālid is older than Tāmer.*

العرض: راجع مع الطلّاب بعض الصفات الّتي قد تعلّموها حتّى الآن واكتبها على السبّورة، مثلاً:
طويل، قصير، جميل، وسيم، كبير، صغير، قريب، بعيد
قارن بعض الأشياء الموجودة في غرفة الصف وحاول أن تجعل الطلّاب استخدام اسم التفضيل (أفْعل) و(أفعل من)، على سبيل المثال اعرض عليهم قلمين وضعهما جنباً إلى جنب وقل:

«هذا القلم طويل . . . طويل جداً ولكن هذا القلم الثاني قصير . . . هذا القلم أطول من ذاك وذلك القلم أقصر من هذا إلخ.»

قارن بين الأشياء في الصور مثلاً:
«سيارتي كبيرة. هي أكبر من سيارة فلان.»
«شقة ليسا قريبة من الجامعة. هي أقرب من شقة مايكل.»
«باريس أجمل من القاهرة. القاهرة أكبر من باريس.»

للممارسة: اسأل الطلّاب أسئلة فيها اسم التفضيل:

«مَن أطول طالب في هذا الصف؟
ما أصغر/ أكبر ولاية في أمريكا.
ما أجمل/ أكبر مدينة في بلد كذا.»

التطبيق: اعمل تمرين ١٣.

وإذا أَرَدْنا أن نَقول (tallest, shortest, oldest, youngest) بالعَرَبيّة، فَنَسْتَخْدِم نَفْس الوَزَن أَفْعَل، ولكِنّنا لا نَسْتَخْدِم مِن بَعْده ويأتي مُعَرَّفاً باللام التَعريف أو الإضافة:

٢١	هالة هي الأَطْوَل.	مُعَرَّف باللام التَعريف	Hālā is *the tallest.*
٢٢	هالة أَطْوَل البَنات.	مُعَرَّف بالإضافة	Hālā is *the tallest of the girls.*
٢٣	تامِر هو الأَصْغَر.	مُعَرَّف باللام التَعريف	Tāmer is *the youngest.*
٢٤	تامِر أَصْغَر البَنين.	مُعَرَّف بالإضافة	Tāmer is *the youngest of the boys.*

ونَسْتَطيع أن نَشْتَقّ (derive) اِسْم التَفْضيل من وَزَن (فَعيل) المَعروف لَك لأنّهُ وَزَن الصِفة العَرَبيّة مِثْل:

الوَزَن: فَعيل						
١	٢		٣			
فـ	ـعـ	ـيـ	ـل	←	فعيل	
كـ	ـبـ	ـيـ	ـر	←	كَبير	
صـ	ـغـ	ـيـ	ـر	←	صَغير	
ط	ـو	يـ	ـل	←	طَويل	

وحين نَتَكَلّم عن أَوْزانِ الفِعْل العَرَبيّ (forms of the Arabic verb)، نَسْتَخْدِم الأَحْرُف الثلاثة الآتية: (فـ / عـ / ـل) نَموذجاً له (as a model of verbs) بِحَيْثُ إنَّ حَرْفَ الفاء يَدُلّ على أوّل حَرْفِ الفِعْل وحَرْفُ العَيْن على ثاني حَرْفِ الفِعْل وحَرْفُ اللام على ثالِث حَرْفِ الفِعل. وإذا أَرَدْنا أن نَشْتَقّ اِسْم التَفْضيل من وَزَن (فَعيل) فَقَط علَيْنا أن نَحْذَف (omit) الياء ونُضيف هَمْزة إلى الفاء كَما تَرى في الأَمْثِلة الآتية:

٢٥	كَبير	ـيـ	←	كبر	←	أ + كبر	=	أكْبَر
	بَعيد	ـيـ	←	بعد	←	أ + بعد	=	أبْعَد
	قَريب	ـيـ	←	قرب	←	أ + قرب	=	أقْرَب
	جَميل	ـيـ	←	جمل	←	أ + جمل	=	أجْمَل

كَذلِك، نَسْتَطيع أنْ نَسْتَخْدِم اِسْم التَفْضيل في صيغةِ الإفْراد (المِثال ٢٦) والتَّثْنية (المِثال ٢٧) والجَمْع المُعَرَّف والمُنكَّر (المِثال ٢٨).

٢٦	هِشام أطْوَلُ طالِبٍ في الصَفِّ.	*Hishām is the tallest student in the class.*
٢٧	هِشام وسامي أطْوَلُ طالِبَيْن في الصَفِّ.	*Hishām and Sāmī are the two tallest students in the class.*
٢٨	هِشام وسامي وعَبدُ الرَحيم أطْوَلُ طُلاّبٍ (أو :الطُلاّبِ) في الصَفِّ.	*Hishām, Sāmī, and ʿabdul-Raḥīm are the tallest students in the class*

مُلاحَظة: إذا أَرَدْنا أنْ نَسْتَخْدِم ضَميراً بَدَلاً مِن (instead of) اِسم، فَيدْخُل على نُون حَرْف الجَرّ (مِن) مَثَلاً:

٢٩	هالَة أطْوَلُ مِنها.	*minhā*	*Hālā is taller than she is.*
٣٠	هِشام أطْوَلُ مِنه.	*minhu*	*Hishām is taller than he is.*
٣١	هِشام أطْوَلُ مِني.	*minī*	*Hishām is taller than I am.*

في المِثال ٢٩، نَرى أنّ (مِن + هِيَ = مِنْها) كَما نَرى في المِثال ٣٠ (مِن + هُوَ = مِنْهُ)، وفي المِثال ٣١، نَرى أنّ (مِن + أنا = مِني).

تمرين ١٢

على وَرَقة مُنْفَصِلة: قارِن (compare) بَيْن الصورتَيْن إلى اليَسار بِاسْتِخْدام اِسْمِ التَفْضيل، وقَد تُساعِدك الكَلِمات الآتية: طَويل، قَصير، كَبير، صَغير

تمرين ١٣

قارِنوا بَينَ الصُوَر الآتية باستِخدام اسمِ التَفضيل (أفعل من) كَما في المِثال.

مِثال: (كَبير / صَغير)

الرَجُل أكبر من الشاب.   الشاب أصغَر من الرَجُل

(سَريع / بَطيء)

(قَصير / طَويل)

(غالٍ / رَخيص)

(قَديم / حَديث)

تمرين ١٤

استمعوا إلى المقارنة بين دمشق والقاهرة وسجّلوا المعلومات التي سمعتموها.

دِمشَق	القاهِرة

تمرين ١٥

إسْم التَفْضيل: على وَرَقة مُنْفَصِلة، حوِّل (change) الصِفة الّتي بَيْن القَوْسَيْن إلى اِسْم التَفْضيل باِسْتِخْدِم وَزن (أَفْعَل) أو (أَفْعَل مِن) حَسَب السياق (according to context).

١- سان فرانْسيسكو (جَميل) ديترويت.

٢- جامِعة ويسكونسن واحِدة مِن (كَبير) الجامِعات في أمريكا.

٣- سَناء (طَويل) طالِبة في الصَفّ.

٤- أريحا (قَدَم) مَدينة في العالَم.

٥- حاسوب هُدى (كَبير) حاسوبي.

٦- اِشْتَرى هاني (حَديث) سَيّارة في السوق.

٧- باريس وروما (جَميل) مَدينَتَيْن في أوروبا.

٨- سَناء (طَويل) أنا.

٩- الطائِرة (سريع) من القِطار.

١٠- مَدينة لاباز (عالٍ) عاصِمة في العالَم.

تمرين ١٦

لِلمُحادَثة: اِسْأل زُملائك في الصَّفّ حَتّى تَجِد مَن هُو في الصَفّ:

1. is the oldest
2. is the youngest
3. is the tallest
4. is the shortest
5. has a car newer than your instructor's car
6. lives closest to the university/college you attend
7. lives farther away from the university/college than your instructor

وحين تَمّ التَمرين، أخْبِر الزُملاء بِما وَجَدت مِن المَعلومات.

٦- مُراجَعة الإضافة

تَتَألَّف (is comprised of) الإضافة مِن جُزئين: المُضاف والمُضاف إلَيْهِ. فَنقول:

	الأَصْل	الإضافة	التَغيُّر عِنْد الإضافة	الحال
٣٢	مُعَلِّمٌ	مُعَلِّمُ المَدْرَسةِ	حَذف التَنوين	
٣٣	مُعَلِّمان	مُعَلِّما المَدْرَسةِ	حَذْف النُون ـن	المُثَنّى
٣٤	مُعَلِّمون	مُعَلِّمو المَدْرَسةِ	حَذْف النُون ـن	الجَمْع

في المِثال ٣٢، عِندَنا إضافة مُؤَلَّفة مِن (made up of) المُضاف ((مُعَلِّم)) والمُضاف إليه ((المَدْرَسة)). إذاً، القاعِدة كالآتي: نَحْذَف تَنْوينَ المُضاف عِنْدَ الإضافة مِثْل ٣٣، ونَحْذَف نونَ المُضاف إذا كان مُنَوَّناً كَما رأَيْنا في المِثالين ٣٣-٣٤.

	المُضاف		المُضاف إليه		الإضافة	
٣٥	غُرْفَتانِ	+	نَوْمٍ	=	غُرفَتا نَوم	المُثَنّى
٣٦	سائِقونَ	+	السَيّارات	=	سائقو السَيّاراتِ	الجَمْع

تمرين ١٧

إسْتِخْراج الإضافة: ارْسُم دائرةً حَوْلَ الأسْماء المُضافة الثلاثة عشرة في الإعلانات الآتية.

سيارة بسعرمغر. يرجى الاتصال على الهاتف ٦٦٧٤٦٣٢-إياد.	للمراجعة الرجاء الاتصال بالهاتف ٤٥٧٩٨٤٤.
مطلوب سائقي شاحنات للعمل في شركة المطاحن. يتراوح الراتب الشهري من مئتي دينار إلى ثلاثمئة دينار.	دار في شارع الجلاء مع هاتف وبرّاد وغسالة وتلفاز. ثلاث غرف نوم وغرفتا جلوس وغرفة طعام مع المفروشات. الإيجار السنوي ٦٠٠ ألف ليرة.
قطعة أرض في صحنايا صالحة	محل تجاري في وسط المدينة

٧- كانَ وأخَواتُها

((كانَ / يَكونُ / كَوْن)) تَدْخُل على المُبْتَدَأ والخَبَر في الجُمْلة الاسْمية وتَرْفَع الاسْم وتَنْصُب الخَبَر. أوّلاً، دَعْنا نَنْظُر إلى بَعْض الأمْثِلة:

		المُبْتَدَأ	الخَبَر	المَعنى
٣٧		الطالِبُ	مُجْتَهِدٌ.	*The student is diligent.*
٣٨	كانَ	الطالِبُ	مُجْتَهِداً.	*The student was diligent.*

وكَما نَرى في المِثال ٣٨، حين تَدْخُل (كانَ) على الجُمْلة الاسْمية، تُغَيِّر الزَمَن مِن المُضارِع إلى الماضي. كذلِكَ، نَسْتَطيع أن نَسْتَخْدِم (كانَ) في كُلّ الأزْمِنة:

٣٩	كُنْتُ	أمْسِ في مَكتَبي في الساعةِ الثامِنةِ.
٤٠	سَأكونُ	في مَكتَبي في الساعةِ الثامِنةِ غَداً.
٤١	أكونُ	في مَكتَبي في الساعةِ الثامِنةِ صباحاً.

هَل تَعْرِف قَواعِد الكَلِمات المُظَلَّلة في اللَوْن الأزْرَق؟ أي نَعم! إنَّها ظَرْف الزَمان وكُلُّها تَدُلّ على زَمَن مُعَيَّن، مَثَلاً: في المِثال ٣٩، أمْسِ يَدُلّ على الماضي لِذلِكَ نَسْتَخْدِم كُنْتُ، وغَداً، في المِثال ٤٠، يَدُلّ على المُسْتَقْبَل لذلِكَ نَسْتَخْدِم سَوْفَ أو سَـ ويَكون بَعدَها. أمّا المِثال ٤١، فَـ أكونُ يَدُلّ على اِستِمراريّة الفِعل (continuous action).
وهذا الفِعْل مِن مَجْموعة أفْعال نُسَمّيها ((الأفْعال الناقِصة)) نِسْبةً لِلمَعنى الناقِص في الجُمْلة أي المَعنى لا يَتِم بِدون الخَبَر، مَثَلاً:

	الفِعْل الناقِص	المُبْتَدَأ	الخَبَر
٤٢	كانَ	الوَلَد . . .	
٤٣	كانَ	الوَلَد	شاطِراً

فَفي المِثال ٤٢، لا نَعْرِف ماذا حَدَث لِلوَلَدحَتّى يَدْخُل على الجُمْلة خَبَراً يُفيدُها بِما حَدَث لَه. ونَعْرِف فِعْلاً آخر مِن هذِه المَجْموعة: لَيْسَ الّتي بِدَوْرِها تُؤَثِّر في الجُمْلة

بِنَفْس الطَريقة، كَما نَرى في المِثالَين ٤٤-٤٥.

	الفِعْل الناقِص	المُبْتَدَأ	الخَبَر
٤٤	لَيْسَ	الوَلَد . . .	
٤٥	لَيْسَ	الوَلَد	شاطِراً

والآن، دَعْنا نَنْظُر ونَتَأمّل الجَدْوَل الآتي الّذي يُبَيِّن (shows) لَنا كَيْف نُصَرِّف الفِعْل كانَ:

تَصريف الفِعْل كان			
	الضمير المنفصل	الماضي	المُضارِع
المُتكَلِّم	أنا	كُنْتُ	أكونُ
	نَحْنُ	كُنّا	نكونُ
المُخاطَب	أَنْتَ	كُنْتَ	تكونُ
	أنْتِ	كُنْتِ	تكونينَ
	أَنْتُما	كُنْتُما	تكونانِ
	أَنْتُم	كُنْتُم	تَكونونَ
	أَنْتُنَّ	كُنْتُنَّ	تَكُنَّ
الغائب	هُوَ	كانَ	يَكونُ
	هِيَ	كانَتْ	تكونُ
	هُما (مُذَكَّر)	كانا	يَكونانِ
	هُما (مُؤَنَّث)	كانَتا	تكونانِ
	هُم	كانوا (silent *alif*)	يَكونونَ
	هنَّ	كُنَّ	يَكُنَّ

تمرين ١٨

اِملأ الفَراغ: بِتَصْريف الفِعْل كانَ المُناسِب وَفْق السياق:

١- ________ تامِر في الدارِ البَيضاء غَداً. * Casablanca

٢- صَديقي أحمَد وزَوجَتُه ________ في المَطعَم أمس.

٣- مَن ________ في المَطارِ حينَ وَصَلَتْ طائِرَةُ دانة؟

٤- أنا وعائِلَتي ________ عِندَكُم في الأسْبوعِ المُقْبِل.

٥- الأستاذُ والطُلاّبُ ________ أمامَ بابِ الجامِعَة بَعْدَ ظُهْرِ أمس.

٦- هِيَ وأخوها ________ في المَطعَمِ يَوْمَ الأحَدِ الماضي.

٧- أينَ ________ أمْس يا هالَة؟

٨- مَتى ________ في مَكتَبِكَ يا أستاذ عادَةً؟

تمرين ١٩

اِسْتِخْدام كانَ في المُحادَثة: اِفْرِض (suppose) أنّك رأَيْت مُطْرِبك (celebrity) المُفَضَّل في المَطار. أخْبِر صَديقك بما رأيْت، ومَن كان مَعك، ومَن كان مع المُطرِب، وماذا قُلْتَ وماذا قال وأي شَيْء آخَر تَجِدُه مُثيراً (interesting) سواء أكانت مُصادفةً (chance encounter) أو بالخيال (fictional).

٨- التَقويم في العالَم العَرَبيّ Calendars in the Arab World

عُموماً (generally)، نَسْتَخْدِم نَوْعي التَقويم في العالَم العَرَبيّ: التَقويم الهِجْريّ القَمَريّ (the Islamic lunar calendar) والتَقويم الغَرْبيّ أو التَقويم الميلاديّ (the Gregorian calendar) الّذي تَخْتَلِف أسْماء شُهوره مِن بَلَد لآخَر. في سوريا الكُبرى والعِراق (Mesopotamia) تُستَعمَلُ أسْماء الشُهور من السُريانيّة (Syriac) الّتي أصولُها اللُغة الأرامية (Aramaic)، بَيْنما تُسْتَخْدَم أسْماء الشُهور اللاتينيّة (Latin) في مِصْر وشَمال إفريقيا الّتي كانت مُستَخدمة في الإمبراطورية الرومانية (جوليان) نِسْبةً إلى يوليوس قَيصَر.

العرض: أحضر تقويماً عربياً من عندك واعرضه إلى الطلاّب. قدّم أسماء الشهور أسوةً بالطريقة الّتي استخدمتها لتقديم الأعداد ١٠- ٠. قدّم شهرين شهرين وأعِد كل اسمَين معاً.
للممارسة: قد ترغب في كتابة أسماء الشهور على السبورة وبجانبها رقمها في الترتيب. وكلما يتذكّر الطالب اسم شهر ما، امسح الاسم تاركاً الرقم. أعيد هذا حتّى تتبقّى الأرقام فقط.
أعِد أسماء شهور التقويم الآخر مستخدماً نفس الطريقة.
التطبيق: اطلب من الطلاّب كتابة تاريخ اليوم كلّما يسلّمون الواجب.
النشاط: تاريخ الولادة: قدّم المبني للمجهول (وُلِدَ) واطلب من الطلاّب أن يسألوا بعضهم بعضاً تاريخ الولادة وسجّلوه على ورقة. ثمّ اطلب منهم أن يجمعوا التواريخ حتّى يروا مَن ولد في كل شهر، ثمّ دعهم يخبرون بما جمعوا.

في مُعْظَمِ البِلاد العَرَبيّة، عُطْلة نِهايةِ الأسْبوع هي يَوْم الجُمْعة، ويَبْدأ أسْبوع العَمَل يَوْم السَبْت في بَعْضِ البِلاد، بَيْنَما (whereas) في بِلاد أخْرى يَبْدأ أسْبوع العَمَل يَوْم الأحَد. على سَبيل المِثال، عُطْلة نِهاية الأسْبوع في سوريا يَوْمَي الجُمْعة والسَبْت، لكِن في لُبْنان حَيْثُ يَكْثُر عَدَدُ المَسيحيين، يُعْتَبَر يَوْم الأحَد يَوْم تَعْطيل (a day off).

آ- التَقْويم الهِجْريّ

إن التَقْويم الهِجْريّ مَبْني على (based on) دَوْرة القَمَر (lunar cycle) وقد بدأ التَقْويم عِنْد هِجْرة رَسول الله مُحَمَّد مِن مَكّة المُكَرَّمة إلى يَثْرِب (وهُو الاسْم السابِق لِلمَدينة المُنَوَّرة) في عام ٦٢٢ ميلاديّ ولِهذا السَبَب (for this reason) اِخْتِصار التَقْويم الهِجْريّ حَرْف هـ وهذا الحَرْف يأتي بَعْد التاريخ مَثَلاً: عام ١٤٠١ هـ. إنَّ عَدَد أيّام السَنة القَمَريّة أقَلّ من السَنة الغَرْبيّة بأحَد عَشَر يَوماً.

شُهورُ السَنةِ الهِجريّة			
١	مُحَرَّم	٧	رَجَب
٢	صَفَر	٨	شَعبان
٣	رَبيعُ الأوَّل	٩	رَمَضان
٤	رَبيعُ الآخِر	١٠	شَوّال
٥	جُمادى الأولى	١١	ذو القِعْدة
٦	جُمادى الآخِرة	١٢	ذو الحِجّة

رَجَب ١٤٢٨ هـ						
السبت	الأحد	الإثنين	الثلاثاء	الأربعاء	الخميس	الجمعة
	١	٢	٣	٤	٥	٦
٧	٨	٩	١٠	١١	١٢	١٣
١٤	١٥	١٦	١٧	١٨	١٩	٢٠
٢١	٢٢	٢٣	٢٤	٢٥	٢٦	٢٧
٢٨	٢٩	٣٠				

التقويم الهِجْريّ (الإسلاميّ)

ب- التَّقْويم الغَرْبيّ

تَرْجع جُذور التَّقْويم الغَرْبيّ إلى التَّقْويم الغَريغوري نِسْبَةً لِلبابا غَريغوريوس الثالِث عشر (Pope Gregory XIII) الّذي قامَ بِتَعديل نِظام السَّنة الكَبيسة (leap year system). وتَرْجِع جُذور التَّقْويم الميلاديّ إلى وِلادة السَيِّد المَسيح (the Messiah) ونَسْتَخْدِم الحَرْف « م » لِيَدُلّ على كَلِمة « الميلاديّ » مَثْلما نَسْتَخْدِم الحَرْف « هـ » لِيَدُلّ على كَلِمة « الهِجْرة » وهُما يأتيان بَعْد السَنة مُباشَرةً: ٢٠١٧ م / ١٤٣٨ هـ. إنَّ أسماء الشُهور المُسْتَخْدَمة في مِصْر تأتي في العَمود الأَزْرَق بَيْنَما أَسْماء الشُهور المُسْتَخْدَمة في الشام الكُبرى (Greater Syria) والعِراق تأتي في العَمود الأَبْيَض في الجَدْوَل إلى الأَسْفَل:

شُهورُ السنةِ الميلاديّة					
١	كانون الثاني	يَنايِر	٧	تَمّوز	يوليو/ يولية
٢	شُباط	فِبرايِر	٨	آب	أغسطَس
٣	آذار	مارِس	٩	أيلول	سَبْتَمْبَر
٤	نيسان	أبريل	١٠	تِشرين الأَوَّل	أكْتوبَر
٥	أيّار / مايِس	مايو	١١	تِشرين الثاني	نوفَمْبَر
٦	حَزيران	يونيو / يونية	١٢	كانون الأَوَّل	ديسَمْبَر

تشرين الأول ٢٠١٧ م						
السبت	الأحد	الإثنين	الثلاثاء	الأربعاء	الخميس	الجمعة
						١
٢	٣	٤	٥	٦	٧	٨
٩	١٠	١١	١٢	١٣	١٤	١٥
١٦	١٧	١٨	١٩	٢٠	٢١	٢٢
٢٣	٢٤	٢٥	٢٦	٢٧	٢٨	٢٩
٣٠	٣١					

التقويم الميلاديّ

تمرين ٢٠

اِملأ الفَراغات باسْمِ الشَهرِ المُناسِب

١- يَأتي شَهْر تمّوز بَعْد شَهْر ________________ .
٢- يَأتي شَهْر آذار قَبْل شَهْر ________________ .
٣- شَهْر ________________ هُوَ الشَهْر السادِس في التَقويم الميلاديّ.
٤- الشَهْر الثاني عَشَر هُو ________________ .
٥- شَهْر ________________ هُوَ الشَهْر الثامِن في التَقويم الإسلاميّ.
٦- في الأُسْبوع ________________ الأيّام.
٧- يَأتي يَوْم الخَميس قَبْل يَوْم ________________ .
٨- يَوْم الإثْنَيْن بَعْد يَوْم ________________ .
٩- يَوْم عُطْلَة نِهايَة الأُسبوع في البِلاد العَرَبِيّة هُوَ ________________.
١٠- عُطْلَة نِهايَة الأُسْبوع في أمريكا هِيَ يَوْما ________________ .

٩- حَرف الجَرّ الباء

كَما هُوَ الحال في مُعْظم حُروف الجَرّ، إنّها تَتّخِذ المَعنى مِن السياق، وحَتّى الآن اِسْتَخْدَمْنا مَعنيين مِن المَعاني الثَلاثة عَشَرة لِحَرْف الباء في هذا الكِتاب وهِيَ كالآتي:

	الجُمْلة	مَعنى الباء
٤٦	اِشْتَرَيْتُ كِتاباً بِعِشْرينَ دولاراً.	المُقابَلة أو العِوَض
٤٧	أنا أكبَرُ مِن أُخْتي بِسَنَتَيْن.	الظَرْفيّة
٤٨	ما مَعْنى "police" بِالعَرَبِيَّة؟	الظَرْفيّة

وكَما تَرى في الأمْثِلة أعْلاه، الكَلِمات الّتي تَلي أي حَرْف جَرّ سَيَكون في حالةِ الجَرّ. في المِثال ٤٦، عِنْدَنا باء المُقابلة وهِي تَدْخُل على التَعْويض (compensation). أمّا المِثال ٤٧، فهُوَ ظَرْف الزَمان والمِثال ٤٨ حَرْف الباء بِمَعنى «في» وهو كَذلِكَ ظَرْف الزَمان.

١٠- مِن الأسماء الخَمسة الخاصّة Of the Five Special Nouns

تُوجَد في اللُغة العَرَبيّة خَمْسة أسْماء تَخْتَلِف عَن غَيْرِها بإعرابِها (declension) بالحُروف لا بالحَرَكات « أي الضَمّة والفَتْحة والكَسْرة ». لَقَد تَعَلّمْنا اثْنين منها: أخ وأب. انْظُر إلى الجَدْوَل الآتي ولاحِظ (notice) أنّنا نُضيف إلى الاسْم الخاصّ الحَرْف المُقابِل للحَرَكة: الواو لِلضَمّة في حالةِ الرَفع (المِثال ٤٩) والألِف لِلفَتْحة في حالةِ النَصب (المِثال ٥٠) والياء لِلكَسْرة في حالةِ الجَرّ (المِثال ٥١).

	الحَرَكة		الحَرْف المُقابِل	الحالة
٤٩	ـُ	←	و	المَرْفوع
٥٠	ـَ	←	ا	المَنْصوب
٥١	ـِ	←	ي	المَجْرور

	الحَرَكة العادية		الاسْم الخاصّ	
٥٢	هذا كِتابُ حازِم.	مَرْفوع بالضَمّة	هذا أبو حازِم.	مَرْفوع بالواو
٥٣	اِشتَرَيْتُ كِتابَ حازِم.	مَنْصوب بالفَتْحة	إنَّ أبا حازِم في الدارِ.	مَنْصوب بالألِف
٥٤	لِكِتابِ حازِم.	مَجْرور بالكَسْرة	لأبي حازِم	مَجْرور بالياء

في المِثال ٥٢، أبو خَبَر الجُمْلة الاسمية لِذلِكَ كَلِمة أبو مَرْفوع بالواو، وفي المِثال ٥٣، أبا خَبَر إنَّ وكَما تَعْلَم الحَرْف إنَّ يَنْصِب الخَبَر وهُنا نَجده مَنْصوباً بالألِف، أمّا المِثال ٥٤، فأبي مَجْرور لأنّه يَلي حَرْف الجَرّ اللام.

تمرين ٢١

اِسْمان من الأَسْماء الخَمْسة الخاصّة: بَيِّن (indicate) الأَسْماء الخَمْسة في الجُمَل الآتية وإعرابَها:

مِثال　تَكَلَّمْنا مَع أبيكَ.　أبيك مَجْرور بِالياء لأنّه يأتي بَعْد حَرْف الجَرّ (مَع).

١ – رأَيْتُ أخا زَيْد في الدُكّان. ______________

٢ – زار أبو أحْمَد صَديقَه تامِر. ______________

٣ – سَكَن سَليم في بَيت أبيه وأمّه. ______________

٤ – إنَّ أبا وَليد شاطِر. ______________

٥ – ساعَد أبو خالِد أخاه الصَغير في الواجِب. ______________

تمرين ٢٢

اِسْمان من الأَسْماء الخَمْسة الخاصّة: أَعْرِب (provide the case markers) الأَسْماء الخَمْسة في الجُمَل الآتية.

١– هَل هذا الكِتاب لـ (أخ + هِيَ). ______________

٢– أدرُسُ (اللُغَة) العربِيَّة. ______________

٣– يَعمَلُ (أب) سامية في الدار البَيضاء. ______________

٤– هذا (الكِتاب) لَيْسَ لي. ______________

٥– يَدرُس صَديقي في (جامِعَة) دِمَشق. ______________

٦– إنَّ (أب) سَليم صَديق أبي. ______________

تمرين ٢٣

آ- أكْمِل الجُمَل الآتية بالاخْتِيار المُناسِب وَفْق نَصّ الاسْتِماع:

١- ذَهَب حَسّان إلى ________________ .

☐ دِمَشق ☐ الرِياض ☐ القاهِرة

٢- حَسّان لَهُ ________________ .

☐ ابن واحِد ☐ اِبن وبنت ☐ ثَلاثة أبناء

٣- نَزَلَ حَسّان في ________________ .

☐ فُنْدُق ☐ شَقَّةِ أخيهِ ☐ دار أبيه

٤- في بَيْت أبي حَسّان ________________ .

☐ غُرفَتا نَوْم ☐ ثَلاث غُرَف نَوْم ☐ أربَع غُرَف نَوْم

من السوق
في حَلَب

ب- اكْتُب ((خطأ)) أو ((صواب)) على الخَطّ ثُمَّ صحِّح الجُمَل الخَطأ:

٥- ذَهَب حَسّان إلى الرِياض بِالسَّيّارة مَع زَوْجَته.

____

٦- كانَ أبو حَسّان في المَطار حين وَصَل حَسّان وعائِلَته.

____

٧- حَسّان طالِب في مَدرَسَة ثانَوية في دِمَشق.

____

٨- رانِية أصغَر مِن رائِد بِسَنَتَيْن.

____

المُفْرَدات

استمِع إلى المُفْرَدة بالعَرَبيّة ثم أعِد نُطْقَها مرّتين.

August . . . . (n., m.) آب

to come . . . . (v.) أتى (يَأتي) إتيان (إلى)

Monday . . . . (n., m.) الإثْنَين

Sunday . . . . (n., m.) الأَحَد

March . . . . (n., m.) آذار

Wednesday . . . . (n., m.) الأرْبِعاء

week . . . . (n., m.) أُسْبوع ج أَسابيع

to buy . . . . (v.) اِشتَرى (يَشتري) شِراء

certainly, surely . . . . (exclamation) أكيد

yesterday. . . . . (adv.) أَمْسِ

that (after verbs similar to "think") . . . . (particle) أَنَّ

that (after the verb for "say") . . . . (particle) إنَّ

hopefully (lit. "God willing") . . . . (set phrase) إنْ شاءَ الله

May. . . . . (n., m.) أيّار

September . . . . (n., m.) أَيْلول

some . . . . بَعْض

October . . . . (n., m.) تِشرين الأوَّل

November . . . . (n., m.) تِشرين الثاني

to be acquainted with. . . . . (v.) تَعَرَّفَ (يَتعَرَّفُ) تَعَرُّف (على)

calendar . . . . (n., m.) تَقويم ج تَقاويم

July . . . . (n., m.) تَمّوز

Tuesday . . . . (n., m.) الثُلاثاء

to come . . . . (v.) جاء (يَجيءُ) مَجيء

sitting . . . . (verbal noun) جُلوس

Islamic month (Jumādī al-āḳira) . . . . (n., f.) جُمادى الآخِرة

Islamic month (Jumādī al-ʻūlā) . . . . (n., f.) جُمادى الأولى

Friday . . . . (n., m.) الجُمعة

till, until . . . . (particle) حَتّى

June . . . . (n., m.) حَزيران

when . . . . (adv.) حينَ

Thursday. . . . . (n., m.) الخَميس

lesson. . . . . (n., m.) دَرْس ج دُروس

Islamic month (d̲ū al-ḥijja) . . . . (n., m.) ذو الحِجّة

Islamic month (d̲ū al-Qiʻda). . . . . (n., m.) ذو القِعدة

wonderful, awesome . . . . (active participle) رائع

Islamic month (Rabīʻal-āḳira) . . . . (n., m.) رَبيع الآخِر

Islamic month (Rabīʻal-ʻawwal) . . . . (n., m.) رَبيع الأوَّل

Islamic month (Rajab) . . . . (n., m.) رَجَب

Islamic month (Ramaḍān). . . . . (n., m.) رَمَضان

to visit . . . . (v.) زارَ (يَزورُ) زِيارة

shall, will. . . . . (future particle) سَـ

Saturday. . . . . (n.,m.) السَبْت

year. . . . . (n., f.) سَنة ج سَنَوات / سُنون

shall, will. . . . . (future particle) سَوْفَ

February . . . . (n., m.) شُباط

bed sheet. . . . .(n., m.) شَرْشَف ج شَراشِف

Islamic month (šaʿbān). . . . . (n., m.) شَعبان

month . . . . (n., m.) شَهْر ج أشْهُر / شُهور

Islamic month (šawwāl) . . . . (n., m.) شَوّال

Islamic month (ṣafar) . . . . (n., m.) صَفَر

guest . . . .(n., m.) ضَيْف ج ضُيوف

airplane . . . . (n., f.) طائِرة ج طائِرات

to think, to believe . . . . (v.) ظَنَّ (يَظُنُّ)

tomorrow . . . . (adv.) غَداً

hotel . . . . (n., m.) فُنْدُق ج فَنادِق

to meet. . . . . (v.) قابَلَ (يُقابِلُ) مُقابَلة

to say. . . . . (v.) قالَ (يَقولُ) قَوْل

before . . . . (adv.) قَبْلَ

close, near . . . . (adv.) قَريب

shirt . . . . (n., m.) قَميص ج قُمْصان

to be (was, were) . . . . (v.) كانَ (يَكونُ) كَوْن

December . . . . (n., m.) كانون الأوَّل

January. . . . . (n., m.) كانون الثاني

objection. . . . . (active participle) مانِع

enthusiastic . . . .(active participle) مُتَحَمِّس

Islamic month (muḥarram) . . . . (n., m.) مُحَرَّم

to walk. . . . . (v.) مَشى (يَمْشي) مَشي

airport . . . . (n., m.) مَطار ج مَطارات

to sleep. . . . . (v.) نامَ (يَنامُ) نَوم

to stay (in a place) . . . . (v.) نَزَلَ (يَنْزِلُ) نُزول

sleeping . . . . (verbal noun) نَوْم

April . . . . (n., m.) نيسان

pillow . . . . (n., f.) وِسادة ج وَسائِد

to arrive, to reach a destination . . . . . . (v.) وَصَلَ (يَصِلُ) وُصول

day . . . . (n., m.) يَوْم ج أيّام

today . . . . (adv.) اليَوْم

diary, daily journal . . . . (n.) يَوْمِيّة ج يومِيّات

الساعةُ الشَمسيّة المِزوَلة

الدرس الثاني عشر

أهداف الدرس

- تعلُّم وَصْف الفَصول الأرْبَعة
- تَعَلُّم وَصْف الطَقْس
- تَعَلُّم (بَعْض / كُلّ / مُعْظَم)
- التَحْويل من المئوية إلى الفَهْرِنْهايت والعَكْس

المُفْرَدات الجَديدة في صُوَر عديدة

صَحْو / سَماء صافية

الشَمْس

غَيْمة ج غُيوم

غائِم

مُشْمِس

ماطِر

شَجَرة ج أشْجار

زَهْرة ج أزْهار

نَهار

٢٤ ساعة =

لَيْل

حارّ

دافِئ

مُعْتَدِل

بارِد

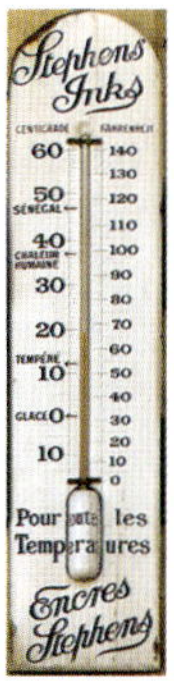

تمرين ١

وافِقْ بَيْنَ الكَلِمات في العَمودَين

١-	رَبيع		مَطَر
٢-	حارّ		مِئَوِيَّة
٣-	غائِم		خَريف
٤-	شاطِئ		صَحوٌ
٥-	لَيْل		سَماء
٦-	ثَلْج		بَحْر
٧-	دَرَجة		نَهار
			بارِد

تمرين ٢

اِختر الكَلِمة الّتي لا تُناسِب باقي الكَلِمات في كُلّ مجموعة وبيِّن السَبَب:

١-	شَجَرة	زَهْرة	خَضراء	ثَلْج
٢-	طَقْس	بُحَيْرة	مُعْتَدِل	دَرَجة حَرارة
٣-	مَطَر	شاطئ	بَحْر	بُحَيْرة
٤-	دافِئ	بارِد	فَصْل	حارّ
٥-	ريح	مَطَر	ثَلْج	أسْبوع

الفُصول الأربَعة والطَقْس

في السَنة أربَعَة فُصول هي الرَبيع والصَّيْف والخَريف والشِتاء.

فَصْلُ الرَّبيع

فَصْلُ الرَبيع جَميل. الأشْجار خَضْراء والأزْهار من كُلّ لَوْن. يَسْقُطُ المَطَر أحْياناً، لِكنَّ الطَقْس مُعْتَدِل دائِماً. الشَمس ساطِعَة في مُعْظَمِ الأيّام. أشْهُر هذا الفَصْل هي آذار ونيسان وأيّار.

يَسْقُط المَطَر

فَصْلُ الصَّيْف

يَأتي فَصْلُ الصَيْف بَعْدَ فَصْلِ الرَبيع. الطَقْس حارّ في الصَيْف والسَماء صافِية. يَذهَبُ النَاس في الصَيْف عادةً إلى شاطِئ البَحْر أو البُحَيْرة ويَسْبَحونَ هُناك. شُهور الصَيْف هي حَزيران وتَمّوز وآب.

شاطِئ البَحْر

فَصْلُ الخَريف

أشْهُر فَصْلِ الخَريف هي أيْلول وتِشرين الأوَّل وتِشرين الثاني ويَأتي هذا الفَصْل بَعْدَ فَصْلِ الصَيْف. هُناكَ غُيوم في السَماء في الخَريف وتَهُبُّ الرِياح وتَسقُط أوراقُ الأشْجار. يَذهَب كُلُّ الطُلّاب إلى المَدارِس والجامِعات في هذا الفَصْل.

تَسْقُط الأوراق

فَصْلُ الشِّتاء

هُناكَ ثَلاثة أشْهُر في الشِتاء أيْضاً وهي كانون الأوَّل وكانون الثاني وشُباط. في هذا الفَصْل يَسْقُط المَطَر أو الثَلْج ويَكون الطَقْس بارِداً عادَةً. يَذهَب بَعْضُ النَاس في أمريكا في الشِتاء عادةً إلى وِلايَتيْ أريزونا وفلوريدا لأنَّهُما دافِئَتان في هذا الفَصْل.

يَسْقُط الثَلْج

هَيّا نَتَأمَّل ما قَرَأنا: اِستُخْدِمَ (was used) الفِعْل سَقَطَ في عَدّة سِياقات في هذا الدَرْس. هل تَسْتَطيع أن تَسْتَخْدِم هذِه السياقات المُخْتَلِفة كَيْ تَسْتَنْتِج (deduce) مَعناها؟

العرض: استخدم تقويماً مصوّراً تتمثّل فيه فصول السنة المختلفة وأسماء الشهور. اذكر للطلاّب اسم الشهر الجاري والفصل الحالي. وبعد ذلك اذكر الشهور التي قبله وبعده وفصلها. وصِفْ لهم بعض سمات كل فصل من فصول السنة، مثلاً:

«في فصل الربيع يسقط المطر والأشجار خضراء ويأتي فصل الصيف بعد فصل الربيع وفيه الطقس حارّ جداً والسماء صافية إلخ.»

الممارسة: اسأل الطلاّب أي فصل من فصول السنة يحبونه ولماذا:

أ- «أي فصل من فصول السنة تحبه ولماذا؟»

ط- «أحب فصل الربيع لأنّ الطقس جميل والأزهار كذلك.»

أ- «وماذا تفعلين في فصل الربيع؟»

ط- «أحب الذهاب إلى شاطئ البحر حيث أسبح وأمشي.»

أ- «عظيم! يا تامر، أي فصل من فصول السنة تحب لينا؟»

ط- «لينا تحب فصل الربيع لأن الطقس جميل إلخ.»

التطبيق: في مجموعات من اثنين أو ثلاثة: اطلُب من الطلاّب أن يسألوا بعضهم بعضاً أسئلة عن فصول السنة، مثلاً: أي فصل يحبونه وماذا يفعلون فيه. وعند نهاية التمرين، اسأل الطلاّب ما علموا من أصدقائهم.

الجُمْعة ١٣ آذار ٢٠٢٠
الطَقْس اليَوم
ماطِر
مَطَر كُلّ اليَوم. تَصِل دَرَجة الحَراراة إلى ١٢ مِئَوِيَّة نَهاراً و٦ دَرَجات لَيْلاً. رياح خَفيفة.

الثُلاثاء ١٧ تمّوز ٢٠٢٠
الطَقْس اليَوم
حارّ وصَحو
تَصِل دَرَجة الحَرارة إلى ٣٦ مِئَوِيَّة. رِياح خَفيفة. السَماء صافية.

الإثنين ١ تِشرين الأوَّل ٢٠٢٠
الطَقْس اليَوم
مُعْتَدِل وغائِم
تَصِل دَرَجة الحَرارة إلى ١٨ مِئَوِيَّة نَهاراً و١٢ دَرَجة لَيلاً. رِياح قَوِيّة. غُيوم في النَهار.

الجُمْعة ٢٦ كانون الثاني ٢٠٢٠
الطَقْس اليَوم
بارِد
يَسْقُط الثَلْج مِن الصَباح حتّى المَساء. تَصِل دَرَجة الحَرارة إلى -٢ مِئَوِيَّة. لَيسَ هُناكَ رِياح.

مُلاحَظة: تَذَكَّر أنَّ كَلِمة يَوْم بِمَعنى (day) بَيْنَما كَلِمة اليَوْم المُعَرَّفة بِمَعنى (today).

تمرين ٣

آ- **أكمِل الجُمَلَ الآتية بِكَلِمات مُناسِبة وَفْق نَصِّ القِراءة.**

١- في السَنة أربعَة ________ .

☐ شُهور ☐ فُصول ☐ أسابيع ☐ أيّام

٢- شَهْر تِشرين الأوَّل مِن أشْهُر ________ .

☐ الخَريف ☐ الشِتاء ☐ الرَبيع ☐ الصَيْف

٣- الطَقْس في الرَبيع ________ .

☐ حارّ ☐ بارِد ☐ مُعْتَدِل ☐ كَبير

٤- يَذهَب بَعْضُ الناس في أيّامِ الصَيْفِ الحارّة إلى ________ .

☐ البَحْر ☐ الغُيوم ☐ الرِياح ☐ الشِمْس

٥- يَذهَب بَعْضُ الأمريكيّين في الشِتاء إلى ________ .

☐ المَدينة ☐ ألاسكا ☐ الغُيوم ☐ أريزونا

٦- تَهُبُّ الرِياح في فَصْل ________ .

☐ الرّبيع ☐ الصَيْف ☐ الخَريف ☐ الشِتاء

ب - **أجِب عن الأسْئلة الآتية وَفْق نَصّ القِراءة الرئيس:**

٧- في أيِّ فَصْل تَكونُ الأشْجار خَضْراء؟ ________

٨- مَتى تَكونُ الشَمْس ساطِعة في مُعْظَم الأيّام؟ ________

٩- هَل توجَد بُحَيرة قَريبة مِن مَدينَتِك؟ ما اسْمُها؟ ________

١٠- في أيِّ فَصْل يَكونُ الطَقْس حارّاً؟ ________

ج – بيِّن إن كانَت الجُمَلُ الآتية «صواباً» أو «خطأ» وَفْق النصّ وصَحِّح الخطأ مِنْها:

١١- يَسقُطُ الثَلْج في الخَريف.

____

١٢- تَصِل دَرَجةُ الحَرارة في الشِتاء إلى -٢ (ناقِص اِثنَين) مِئَويَّة.

____

١٣- الطَقْس غائِم في الصَيْف في مُعْظَمِ الأيّام.

____

١٤- طَقْسُ اليَوم ماطِر.

____

تمرين ٤

تَقريرُ الطَّقْس: اُكْتُب، أنْت وشَريكُك، أحْوال الجَوْ اليَوْم بِكُلّ تَفاصيلِها (details) مِثْلَما يُقَدِّمُها مُذيعُ الأحْوالِ الجَويّة المَحَلّيّة (the local weather reporter). ولا تَنسَ أنْ تَتَكَلّم عن الطَقْس الوَطَنيّ والمَحَلّيّ مِن حَيْثُ:

١- الطَقْس غَداً في الصَباح والمَساء واللَيل.
٢- أحْوال الطَقْس لِأرْبَعة أيّام (واذْكُر أسْماء أيّام الأُسْبوع).
٣- أحْوال الطَقْس في عُطْلة نِهاية الأُسْبوع.
٤- المُدّة الّتي سَيَكون الطَقْس مُشْمِساً أو غائماً أو ماطِراً.

وعِنْدَما تَنْتَهي من الكِتابة، إقرأ الأحْوال الجَوّيّة على زُمَلائك.

تمرين ٥

اِسْتِخْدام وَصَلَ في جُمَل: على وَرَقة مُنْفَصِلة، تَرْجَم (translate) الجُمَلَ الآتية إلى العَرَبيّة مُسْتَخْدِماً وَصَلَ ووَصَلَ إلى.

1. Hani's هاني flight arrived at 9:30.
2. I arrived in this city in 2006.
3. The temperature in the summer reaches 40 degrees Celsius in my city.
4. We have reached lesson 12.
5. The temperature will reach negative five at night.

العرض: اعرض على الطلاّب صوراً على اختلاف الأحوال الجوّيّة واسألهم أن يصفوها مستخدمين المفردات الجديدة في هذا الدرس. وبعد ذلك، اسألهم كيف كان الطقس بالأمس وقبله، وفي الأسبوع الماضي، وكيف سيكون الطقس غداً.

الممارسة على المدى البعيد: في بداية كلّ صفّ، عوّد الطلاّب على ذكر التاريخ والأحوال الجوّيّة في مرحلة الإحماء من كلّ درس.

التطبيق: في مجموعات من اثنين أو ثلاثة: اطلُب من الطلاّب أن يسألوا بعضهم بعضاً أسئلة عن نوع الطقس الذي يحبونه وماذا يفعلون فيه. عليك أن تقدّم كلمة (نَوْع) للقيام بهذا النشاط. قد تكون الأسئلة كالآتي:

«أي نوع من الطقس تحبين؟» «ولماذا تحبين هذا النوع من الطقس؟»

وماذا تفعلين في الطقس كهذا؟

اطلُب من الطلاّب أن يقدّموا ما عِلموا من أصدقائهم.

تمرين ٦

أعِدّ تَرْتيب الكَلِمات في كُلّ مَجْموعة لِتُشَكِّل جُمَلاً مُفيدة.

١- تِلْكَ – ما – في – البُحَيْرة – سَبَحْتُ
٢- أختي – مِفتاحُ – هذا – شَقّةِ – بابِ
٣- أيّار – حَزيران – شَهْرُ – شَهرِ – بَعْدَ – يَأتي
٤- غَدٍ – الطَقْسُ – بَعْدَ – سَيَكونُ – صَحْواً
٥- الصَيْفِ – شاطِئِ – في – إلى – الناسُ – البَحْرِ – يَذهَبُ
٦- لِصَديقاتِها – غَداً – قالَت – إلى – إنَّها- زَينَب – المَغرِبِ- سَتَذْهَبُ
٧- جَيِّدَةٌ – العَرَبِيَّةَ – إنَّ – لي – لُغَتي- أُستاذي – قالَ
٨- مِن – السَبتِ – إلى – في – بِالقِطارِ – حَلَبَ – دِمَشقَ – ذَهَبْتُ – يَوْمِ

تمرين ٧

المُحادَثة عن الطَقْس والسَفَر: اِفْرِض (suppose) أنَّك الآن رَجَعْت من السَفَر إلى الإسْكَنْدَريّة في مِصر، ويُريد صَديقُك أنْ يَعْرِف:

1. when you arrived (on what day and at what time)
2. what the weather was like in Alexandria
3. when you went to the beach and what you did at the beach
4. what hotel you stayed at
5. how many days you were there
6. with whom you went
7. with whom you spoke and whether you spoke to them in Arabic
8. what you talked about
9. how long you were on the plane

بَعْض الكَلِمات المُفيدة:

قالَ (إنَّ)	وَصَلَ (إلى)	تَكَلَّمَ (مَعَ)	نَزَلَ (في)
الطَقْس	فُنْدُق	طائِرة	شاطِئ

تمرين ٨

تَمرين المُشاهَدة: شاهِدوا الدَّرْس الثاني عَشَر على الشابِكة.

١- لماذا يُحِبّ فَصْلَ الصَّيْف؟ ____________________

____

٢- لماذا يُحِبّ فَصْل الرَّبيع؟ ____________________

____

٣- لماذا يُحِبّ فَصل الشِتاء؟ ____________________

____

٤- كَم شَهْراً في السَنة؟ ____________________

____

أذْكُر (recite) أَسْماءَ الشُهور مع ((جون)). وإذا واجَهَتْك مُشْكِلة في تَذَكُّر (remembering) الأَسْماء، راجِع باب ٨ الدَّرْس الحادي عَشر.

تمرين ٩

تَمرينُ المُشاهَدة: إملأ الفَراغات في نَصِّ المُشاهَدة:

- الجَوّ جَميل اليَوْم.
- مَعَك حَقّ. نحن في فَصْل ________.
- هل تَعْرِف أَسْماء الفُصول بِالعَرَبيّة؟
- طَبْعاً. تَعَلَّمْتُها في الصَفّ.
- ما هي؟
- بَعْدَ فَصْلِ الرَبيع، يأتي ________ وثُمّ ________ وبَعْدَ ذلِكَ ________.
- أي فُصول تُحِّب؟
- أُحِبّ فَصْلَ الصَيْف لأَنَّني أذْهَب إلى ________ فأنا أُحِبُّ السِباحة.
- أنا أُحِبّ فَصْلَ الرَبيع. ________ تِكون مُزْهِرة والطَقْس جَميل و________.

العرض: اكتب (مُعْظَم وبَعْض وكُلّ) في عمود على السبورة ومارس مع الطلاّب النطق السليم مركّزاً على اللام المشدّدة في كلمة كُلّ.

وبعد ذلك، وفي عمود بجانب الأول، اكتب كلمات معروفة للطلاّب مثل:

طلاّب، اليوم، الأيام، الأسبوع، القهوة، العصير، شيء، الأشياء، شهر، الشهر، إلخ

يجب أن تناسب الكلمات في العمود الثاني المضاف.

الممارسة: اطلُب من الطلاّب أن يرّكبوا المضاف والمضاف إليه من العمودين مركزاً معهم على النطق السليم.

التطبيق: في مجموعات من اثنين: اطلُب من الطالب أن يسأل صديقه ماذا يفعل: **((معظم أيام الأسبوع، كلّ يوم / كلّ اليوم / كل يوم أحد/ كلّ يوم الأحد / بعض أيام الصيف / بعض شهور الشتاء إلخ.))**

واطلُب من الطالب أن يسأل صديقه مع مَن يفعل هذه الأشياء يعني **مع معظم الأصدقاء، بعضهم، كلّهم إلخ**

وعند نهاية النشاط، اطلُب منهم أن يفيدوا بما علِموا من أصدقائهم.

- أنا أيْضاً أُحِبّ فَصْل ________. فأنا أُحِبّ ________ و________.
- هل تَعْرِف أسْماء ________ بِالعَرَبيّة؟
- نَعَم. في السَنة إثنا عَشَرَ شَهْراً هي كانون الثاني، شُباط، ________، نيسان، أيّار، حَزَيْران، ________، آب، ________، تِشْرين الأوّل، تِشْرين الثاني، وكانون الأوّل.
- جَيِّد، أنت تَعْرِف أشْياء كَثيرة بِالعَرَبيّة.

١- بَعْض / كُلّ / مُعْظَم Partitive Nouns

تَدُلُّ الكَلِمات في هذِه المَجْموعة على جُزء من الكُلّ أشْهرُها: بَعْض / مُعْظَم كُلّ / نِصْف / ثُلْث، ونُسَمِّي هذِه الكَلِمات المُضاف لأنّها أوّل كَلِمة في الإضافة. ويأتي بَعْدَه المُضاف إليه.

وجَدير بالذِّكْر أنَّ مَعنى هذِه الكَلِمات يَتَغيَّر حَسَب حالةِ المُضاف إليه سَواء أكان مَعْرِفة أو نَكِرة أو إفراداً أو جَمْعاً. والآن، تَمَهَّل (take some time) في قِراءةِ الجَدْوَل إلى الأسْفَل وتَتَأمَّله.

مُعْظَم	مُعْظَمُ اليَوْمِ	*most of the*
	مُعْظَمُ الأيّامِ	*most of the*
	مُعْظَمُ أيّامِ الأسبوعِ	*most of the*
بَعْض	بَعْضُ اليَوْمِ	*part/some of the*
	بَعْضُ يَوْمٍ	*part of a*
	بَعْضُ أيّامٍ	*a number of*
	بَعْضُ الأيّامِ	*some of the*
	بَعْضُ أيّامِ الأسبوعِ	*some of the*

the whole	كُلّ اليَوْمِ	كُلّ
every	كُلّ يَوْمٍ	
all of the	كُلّ الأيّامِ	
all of	كُلّ أيّامِ الأسبوعِ	

إنَّ المُضاف إليه دائماً مَجْرور وعَلامَتاه كَسْرة (حين يَكون الإسْم مَعْرِفة) أو تَنْوين كَسْرة (حين يكون الإسم نكرة). مَثلاً، أنْظُر إلى الأمْثِلة أعلاه، كُلّ الأيّامِ وأيّامِ الأسْبوعِ مَعْرِفة، لِذا تَدْخُل عليها كَسْرة. أمّا بِالنِسْبة إلى يَوْمٍ فيَدْخُل عليها تَنْوين كَسْرة لأنَّها نَكِرة.

تَفادي الأخْطاء: الفَرْق بَيْن كُلّ + إسْم نَكِرة وكُلّ + إسْم مَعْرِفة يُشْبه (resembles) مُقابِلَه بالإنْكليزيّة بِحَيْثُ كُلَّما نُريد أنْ نَقول (every day/week/month)، فأنّنا نَسْتَخْدِم كُلّ + إسْم نَكِرة أمّا إذا أَرَدْنا أن نَقول (*the* whole day/week/month)، فَأنّنا نَسْتَخْدِم كُلّ + إسم مَعْرِفة مَثلاً (كُلّ اليَوْمِ أو الـأسْبوعِ أو الشَّهْر)، فَنَسْتَخْدِم التَّعريف في كِلتَيْ اللُغتَيْن.

تمرين ١٠

إسْتِخْدام كُلّ وبَعْض ومُعْظَم: تَرْجَم الفِقْرة الآتية إلى اللُغةِ العَرَبيّة ورَكِّز (concentrate) على الإسْتِخْدام الصَحيح لِهذِه المَجْموعة.

Every weekend during the summer, some of my friends and I go to the beach. Friday night I usually walk on the beach with my friend Leila and we talk about all of our classes. On Saturday, I usually read or swim most of the day. Some of my friends do not like reading and studying on the beach, but I like it. We are in our car most of the day Sunday on our way home. Summer is a beautiful season of the year.

ساحة النجمة بيروت

٢- تَحويل دَرَجة الحَرارة Converting Temperature Scales

نَسْتَطيع أن نُحَوِّل من دَرَجةِ الفَهْرِنْهايت إلى الدَرَجة المِئَوِيَّة حَسَب المُعادَلة (equation) الآتية: الدَرَجة المِئَوِيَّة = (°F - ٣٢) x ٥ /٩. مَثَلاً إذا أرَدْنا أن نُحَوِّل ٧٨° F إلى الدَرَجة المِئَوِيَّة، فَنَقوم بالآتي:

١	٧٨ - ٣٢	=	٤٦
٢	٤٦ × ٥	=	٢٣٠
٣	٢٣٠ ÷ ٩	=	٢٥,٥٥

لِذا، ٧٨°F = ٢٥،٥٥°C.

وإذا أرَدْنا أن نُحَوِّل الفَهْرِنْهايت إلى الدَّرَجة المِئَوِيَّة، فأنّنا نَقوم بِعكْس العَمَليّة: الفَرِنْهايت = ٣٢ + (٩/٥ ×°C).

تمرين ١١

تَحْويل دَرَجة الحَرارة: حَوِّل الدَرَجات الآتية مِمّا هي إلى مُقابِلها.

١- ٣٨ مِئَوِيَّة ______________

٢- ٨٤ فَرنهايت ______________

٣- ٣٢ فَرنهايت ______________

٤- ٢٠ مِئَوِيَّة ______________

٥- ٩٢ فَرنهايت ______________

تمرين ١٢

آ- **أكْمِل الجُمَلَ الآتية بالاخْتِيارِ المُناسِب وَفْق نَصِّ الاسْتِماع:**

١- في أوّل يَوم كانَ الطَقْس في النَهار ____________ .

☐ بارِداً ☐ مُعْتَدِلاً ☐ حارّاً

٢- ذَهَبَ الزَوْج والزَوْجة إلى صافيتا في فَصْلِ ____________ .

☐ الشِتاء ☐ الرَبيع ☐ الصَيْف

٣- وَصَلَ الزَوْج وزَوْجَتُهُ إلى صافيتا يَوم ____________ .

☐ الخَميس ☐ الجُمْعة ☐ السَبْت

٤- يَعمَلُ الزَوْج في مَدينَة ____________ .

☐ صافيتا ☐ دِمَشق ☐ حَلَب

ب- **اكْتُب «خطأ» أو «صواب» على الخَطّ ثُمَّ صحِّح الجُمَل الخَطأ:**

٥- ذَهَبَ الزَوْج والزَوْجة إلى صافيتا بِالقِطار.

____

٦- كانَت الأشْجار خَضْراء في صافيتا.

____

٧- تُريد الزَوْجَة السَكَن في حَلَب.

____

٨- الطَقْس بارِد في صافيتا.

____

ج- **لَخِّص** (summarize) **نَصَّ الاِسْتِماع بِحَوالي** (roughly) **خَمْسين كَلِمة.**

المُفْرَدات

استمِع إلى المُفْرَدة بالعَرَبيّة ثم أعِد نُطْقَها مرّتين.

أخْضَر ج خُضْر (adj., m.) .... green

بارِد (adj., m.) .... cold

بَحْر ج بِحار (n, m.) .... sea

بُحَيْرة ج بُحَيْرات (n., f.) .... lake

بَعْض (n.) .... some

ثَلْج ج ثُلوج (n., m.) .... snow

حارّ (adj., m.) .... hot

حَرارة (n., f.) .... heat

خَريف (n., m.) .... autumn

خَضْراء ج خُضْر (adj., f.) .... green

دافِئ (adj., m.) .... warm

دَرَجة ج دَرَجات (n., f.) (درجة حرارة) degree (temperature), step

رَبيع (n., m.) .... spring

ريح ج رِياح (n., f.) .... wind

زَهْرة ج زَهَرات / أزْهار (n., f.) .... flower

ساطِع (adj., m.) .... brilliant, shining

سَبَح (يَسْبَحُ) سِباحة (v.) .... to swim

سَقَطَ (يَسْقُطُ) سُقوط (v.) .... to fall

سَماء ج سَماوات (n., f.) .... sky

شاطِئ ج شَواطِئ (n., m.) .... beach

شِتاء (n., m.) .... winter

tree . . . . (n., f.) شَجَرة ج شَجَرات

sun . . . . (n., f.) شَمْس ج شُموس

pure; clear, not cloudy . . . . (f.) صافِيَة (adj., m.) صافٍ

clear, fine (of weather) . . . . (adj., m.) صَحْوٌ

way, road. . . . . (n., f.) طَريق ج طُرُق، طُرُقات

weather . . . . (n., m.) طَقْس ج طُقوس

worker, laborer (Labor Day) . (عيد العُمّال) (n., m.) عامِل ج عُمّال

cloudy, overcast . . . . (adj., m.) غائِم

rain cloud . . . . (n., f.) غَيْمة ج غُيوم

every, all, the whole. . . . . (n.) كُلّ

color . . . . (n., m.) لَوْن ج أَلْوان

night . . . . (n., m.) لَيْل

rainy . . . . (adj., m.) ماطِر

abloom. . . . . (adj., m.) مُزْهِر

rain. . . . . (n., m.) مَطَر ج أَمْطار

moderate. . . . . (adj.) مُعْتَدِل

most . . . . (n.) مُعْظَم

minus . . . . (n., m.) ناقِص

daytime . . . . (n., m.) نَهار

الفصول الأربعة من العصر الروماني في تونس

الدرس الثالث عشر

الحياة اليَوْميّة في بَيْروت

أهداف الدرس

- وَصْف ما نَقوم بِه يَوْمِيّاً
- مُراجَعة المُضاف: كأْسُ حَليبٍ - فِنْجانُ شاي - قِطْعَةُ خُبْزٍ
- تَعَلُّم نَفي فِعْل الأمْر
- تَعَلُّم الفِعْل المُعْتَلّ الآخِر
- اِسْتِخْدام لأنَّ
- تَرْكيب الجُمْلة العَرَبيّة: الفِعْل / الفاعِل / المَفْعول بِه
- اِسْتِخْدام واو القَسَم

المُفردات الجَديدة في صُوَر عَديدة

فُرشاةُ الأسنانِ ومَعجون

نَظَّفَ (يُنَظِّفُ) تَنْظيف

اِسْتَحَمَّ (يَسْتَحِمُّ) اِسْتِحْمام

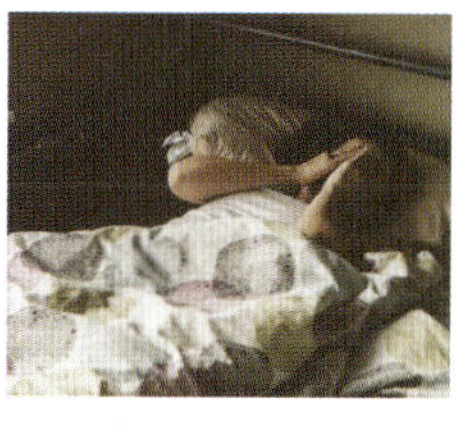

نَهَضَ (يَنْهَضُ) نُهوض

شاهَد (يُشاهِدُ) مُشاهَدة

تمرين ١

واِفِقْ بَيْنَ الكَلِمات في العَمودَين:

١-	اِسْتَحَمَّ		مَعْجون أسْنان
٢-	فُرشاة		ذَقْن
٣-	نَسِيَ		حافِلَة
٤-	سَرير		غَسَلَ
٥-	كَباب		مَطعَم
٦-	حَلَقَ		فَلافِل
٧-	مَقْصَف		مَوْعِد
			نَوْم

تمرين ٢

اِختَر الكَلِمة الّتي لا تُناسِب باقي الكَلِمات في كُلّ مجموعة وبيِّن السَبَب:

١-	فُرشاة	ماء	قَهوة	شاي
٢-	فَطور	غَداء	طِبّ	عَشاء
٣-	حافِلَة	سَيّارَة	دَرّاجة	حاسِبَة
٤-	كَباب	صابون	فَلافِل	فول
٥-	سِنّ	وَجْه	لَبَن	يَد
٦-	مادَّة	مُسَلسَل	بَرنامَج	تِلفاز
٧-	نَهَضَ	اِسْتَحَمَّ	غَسَلَ	مَرَّة
٨-	وَرَقَة	مُشاهَدَة	كِتاب	رِسالة

ماذا تَفعَل هالَة بُستاني كُلَّ يَوْم؟

هالَة بُستاني طالِبة تَدرُسُ الطِبّ في جامِعَة حَلَب. تَسكُن في شَقَّة مَعَ صَديقَتِها سَحَر حَلّاق.

تَغسِلُ يدَيْها

تَنهَض هالَة مِن النَوم في الساعةِ السابِعة والرُبْع صَباحاً وتَذهَب إلى الحَمّام وتَسْتَحِمّ أو تَغْسِل يَدَيْها وَوَجهَها بِالماء والصابون وَتُنَظِّف أَسْنانَها بِفُرشاةِ الأَسْنان والمَعْجون.

تُحَضِّر الفَطور

بَعدَ ذلِك تَذهَب إلى المَطْبَخ وتُحَضِّر طَعامَ الفَطور. تَأكُل هالَة على الفَطور عادَةً بَيضَتَين أو قِطْعَة خُبْز وقِطْعَة مِن الجُبْن مَعَ كأس حَليب.

الفول المُدَمَّس

في يَومِ الجُمْعة تُحَضِّر هالَة وسَحَر البَيْض أو الفول المُدَمَّس على الفَطور وتَشربان الشاي بَعدَ الطَعام.

حافِلة

في الساعةِ الثامِنَة تَذهَب هالَة إلى الجامِعَة بِالحافِلة. لا تَذهَب إلى الجامِعَة بِالسَيّارة لأنَّها لَيْس عِندَها سَيّارة.

في السَاعةِ الثّامِنة والنِصْف تَصِل إلى الجامِعَة وتَذهَب إلى المَكتَبَة وتَدرُس هُناكَ حَتّى السَاعة الحادِيَة عَشْرة.

الكَباب الحَلَبيّ

في الساعةِ الحادِيَة عَشْرة تَذهَب إلى دَرْسِ الكيمياء مَعَ صَديقَتِها غادة. وفي السَّاعةِ الثّانِية عَشْرة تَذهَبان مَعاً إلى مَقْصَفِ الجامِعَة وتَأكُلان الغَداء هُناك. تَأكُل هالَة أَحْياناً الكَباب الحَلَبيّ وأَحْياناً الفَلافِل، لكِنَّ غادة تَأكُل لَبَناً أو سَلَطَة فَقَط، وأَحْياناً تَأكُل التَبّولَة.

العرض: صِف ما تفعله كلّ يوم مستخدماً الحركات اليدوية الدالّة والأغراض والصور الملائمة.

الممارسة: اسأل الطلاّب أن يصفوا ما يفعلونه كل يوم وأي يوم من أيام الأسبوع وفي أي ساعة، وكم مرة في الأسبوع. حاول أن تساعد الطلاّب في تركيب جمل معقدة بإضافة الظرف لجمل بسيطة، مثلاً: «أنهض في الساعة السابعة والنصف صباحاً وأتناول الغداء في الساعة الواحدة والربع ظهراً ولكنّي عادةً لا آكل الفطور.»

التطبيق: في مجموعات من اثنين: اطلُب من الطالب أن يخبر زميله ما يفعله كل يوم، ثمّ اطلُب من زميله أن يخبر الطلاّب ما علمه.
إليك بعض الأسئلة التي قد تفيدك في القيام بالنشاط:

«في أيّةِ ساعة: تنام، تنهض، تحضر الفطور، تشاهد التلفاز، ترجع إلى البيت إلخ.»

بَعدَ ذلِك تَذهَب هالَة إلى المَخْبَر من السَاعةِ الواحِدة إلى السَاعةِ الثالِثة. بَعدَ المَخبَر تَذهَب إلى دَرْسِ الأحْياء.

طعام العَشاء

في السَاعةِ الخامِسَة تَرْجِع إلى البَيْت وتكون في شَقَّتِها في السَاعةِ الخامِسَة والرُبع. في المَساء تُحَضِّر هالَة طَعامَ العَشاء، وتَأكُل عادةً الزَيْتون والجُبْن أو الخُضَر أو البَيْض المَقْليّ وتَشرَب فِنجان شاي بَعدَ العَشاء.

الأخبار

تُشاهِد هالَة التِّلفاز قَليلاً كُلّ لَيْلة. تُحِبّ مُشاهَدةَ المُسَلْسَلات العَرَبيّة والأمريكيّة وبَرامِجَ الأخْبار مِنَ العالَم. تَذهَب هالَة عادةً إلى سَريرِها في السَاعةِ العاشِرة والنِصْف عادةً أو في السَاعةِ الحادِيَة عَشْرة على الأكْثَر.

رُكْنُ المُفْرَداتِ الجَديدةِ			
نَسِيَ (يَنْسى) نِسيان	*to forget*	مَشْغول ج مَشْغولون	*busy*
مُتأخِّر	*late*	مُبَكِّر	*early*

يَوميّات عَدنان مارتيني

الثُلاثاء ٩ تِشرين الأوَّل ٢٠١٨

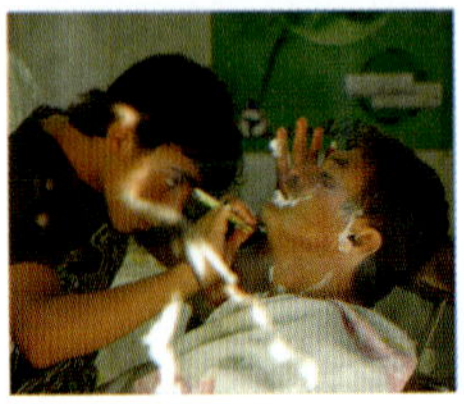
حَلَقْتُ ذَقْني

نَهَضْتُ اليَوْمَ مِنَ النوم في السَاعةِ السَابعة إلاّ ثُلْثاً. اِسْتَحَمْتُ وحَلَقْتُ ذَقْني بِرُبع ساعة ثُمَّ أكَلْتُ فَطوري (كأس حَليب وقِطعَة خُبْز مَعَ الجُبْن) ومَشَيْتُ إلى الجامِعة.

وَصَلتُ إلى صَفّي في السَاعةِ الثامِنة والنِصْف تَماماً. لا أحِبُّ هذِهِ المادَّة (لُغاتَ الحاسوب) لأنَّها في وَقْت مُبَكِّر جِدّاً. وَصَل بَعْضُ الطُلّاب مُتأخِّرين إلى الصَفِّ اليَوْم. حين رَجَعْتُ إلى البَيْت مَساءً كانَ هُناكَ وَرَقة مِن زِياد على باب غُرفَتي. كَتَبَ فيها: «لا تَنسَ العَشاءَ اليَوْم في مَطعَم علي بابا في السَاعةِ السَابِعة مَع تِم وليسا.» نَسِيتُ مَوْعِد هذا العَشاء واللهِ.

الأربِعاء ١٠ تِشرينَ الأوَّل ٢٠١٨

بَعدَ دَرس لُغاتِ الحاسوب ذَهَبْتُ إلى المَكتَبَة وقَرأتُ ساعَتَين ثُمَّ أكَلْتُ الغَداء في مَقصَفِ الجامِعة وذَهَبْتُ إلى عَمَلي في مَخْبَرِ الحاسوب. أعْمَل هُناكَ خَمس عَشْرة ساعة في الأسبوع. بَعدَ الظُهْر ذَهَبْتُ إلى دَرسَيْ الرِياضِيّات واللُغة الإنكليزيّة. رَجَعْتُ إلى المَكتَبَة مَرّةً ثانِيَةً وقَرَأتُ دُروسي حَتّى السَاعة الثامِنة مَساءً. بَعدَ ذلِكَ مَشَيْتُ إلى شَقَّتي وأكَلتُ العَشاء مَعَ زِياد في الشَّقَّة.

ما أكَلْنا أمْس في مَطْعَم علي بابا. تَكَلَّمَتْ ليسا أمس بِالهاتِف وقالَتْ إنَّها مَشْغولة جِدّاً. سَنأكُل مَعاً (أنا وزِياد وليسا وتِم) مَساء يَوْم الجُمْعَة إن شاءَ الله. ذَهَبْتُ إلى النَوْم في السَاعة الحادِيَة عَشْرَة بَعدَ مُشاهَدة بَرنامَج «سِتّونَ دَقيقة» على التِلفاز. أُحِبّ مُشاهَدَة هذا البَرنامَج. لا أُحِبّ كِتابَةَ الرَسائِل عادةً لكِنَّني سَأكتُب رِسالَة إلى أبي وأمّي غَداً إنْ شاءَ الله.

تمرين ٣

لِلمُحادَثة: اِسْأل صَديقَك في غُرْفة الصَفّ الأسْئلة الآتية ثُمَّ اكْتُب الأجْوِبة على ورقة مُنْفَصِلة:

1. what time they wake up in the morning
2. when they shower/brush their teeth
3. when/where they eat breakfast/lunch/supper
4. what they usually eat for breakfast/lunch/supper
5. what time they go to school, and how they get to school
6. what subjects they study and on what days
7. what time they return home
8. what time they go to bed

والآن أخبِر الأستاذ ما عَلِمت من الأصدِقاء.

مَطعم في دِمشق

تمرين ٤

آ- **أكْمِل الجُمَل الآتية بِكَلِمات مُناسِبة وَفْق نَصّ القِراءة.**

١- تسكُن هالَة بُستاني الآنَ في ________ .

☐ حَلَب ☐ القاهِرة ☐ دِمَشق

٢- تَنْهَض هالَة مِنَ النَوْم في الساعةِ ________ .

☐ السادِسَة ☐ السابِعَة ☐ الثامِنَة

٣- تذهَب هالَة إلى الجامِعَة ________ .

☐ بِالحافِلَة ☐ بِالسَيّارة ☐ مَشْياً

٤- تَأكُل هالَة الغَداءَ مَعَ صَديقَتِها ________ .

☐ سُعاد ☐ غادَة ☐ سَحَر

٥- مَوْعِد دَرسِ الأحْياء في السَاعةِ ________ .

☐ الواحِدَة ☐ الثانِيَة ☐ الثالِثَة

٦- يَأكُل عَدنان على الفَطورِ ________ .

☐ الزَيْتون ☐ البَيْض ☐ الجُبْن

٧- وَصَلَ عَدنان إلى دَرس لُغاتِ الحاسوب ________ .

☐ في مَوْعِدِهِ ☐ مُبكِّراً ☐ مُتأخِّراً

٨- ما أكَلَ عَدنان العَشاء مَعَ أصْدِقائِهِ يومَ الثُلاثاء لأنَّ ليسا كانَت ________ .

☐ مُبكِّرَةً ☐ مَشْغولَةً ☐ مُتأخِّرَةً

٩- يَعمَل عَدنان في مَخبَرِ الحاسوب ________ في الأسبوع.

☐ عَشْرَ ساعات ☐ خَمسَ عَشْرَةَ ساعة ☐ عِشْرونَ ساعة

١٠- يُحِبّ عَدنان ________ .

☐ مُشاهَدَة التِّلفاز ☐ كِتابَةَ الرَسائِل ☐ بَرنامَج سِتّون دقيقة

إحدى الأسواق في عمان الأردن

ب- اِملأ الفَراغات الآتية بالكَلِمة المُناسِبة وَفْق نَصّ القِراءة.

١١- تَسْكُن هالَة بُستاني مَعَ ____________.

١٢- تَرْجِع هالَة إلى شَقّتِها في الساعةِ ____________ .

١٣- تذهَب هالَة إلى السَرير في الساعةِ ____________.

١٤- لا يُحِبّ عَدنان مادّةَ لُغاتِ الحاسوب لأنّها ____________.

١٥- نَسِيَ عَدنان مَوْعِدَ ____________.

١٦- يَقرأ عَدنان دُروسَهُ عادةً في ____________.

ج - بيِّن إن كانَت الجُمَلُ الآتية صواباً أو خَطأ وَفْق النَصّ وصَحِّح الخَطأ مِنْها:

١٧- تأكُل هالَة بُستاني الفول على الفَطور كُلّ يوم.

١٨- تذهَب هالَة إلى النَوم في الساعةِ العاشِرة مَساءً.

١٩- تُنَظِّف هالة وَجهَها بِالفُرشاة والمَعْجون.

٢٠- لَيْسَ عِندَ هالَة سَيّارة.

٢١- تُحِبّ هالَة مُشاهَدَة بَرنامَج سِتّون دَقيقة.

٢٢- يَحلِق عَدنان ذَقنَهُ قَبْلَ النَوم.

٢٣- نَسِيَ عَدنان دَرس لُغاتِ الحاسوب.

٢٤- تَكَلَّمَ عَدنان بِالهاتِف وقالَ إنَّهُ مَشْغول.

٢٥- سَيَأكُلُ الأصْدِقاءُ الأرْبَعَة العَشاءَ مَعاً يومَ الجُمْعَة.

٢٦- سَيَكتُب عَدنان رِسالة يَومَ الأربِعاء.

تمرين ٥

أعِدّ تَرْتيب الكَلِمات في كُلّ مَجْموعة لِتُشَكِّل جُمَلاً مُفيدة:

١- على - الفولَ - هالَة - الغَداءِ - تَأكُلُ - المُدَمَّس
٢- صَباحاً - مُشاهَدَةَ - الأخْبارِ - أُحِبُّ - بَرامِجِ
٣- السَبْتِ - السَيّارَةَ - زَوْجي - يَوْمَ - يَغسِلُ

تمرين ٦

أعِدّ تَرْتيب الجُمَل لِتُشَكِّل فِقْرة كامِلة. الجُمْلة الأولى في مَكانِها المُناسِب:

١- اِسْمي رَوضَة قَطّان.
أُحَضِّر عادَةً فَطوراً كَبيراً لي ولِزَوجي وأولادي.
نَرجِع إلى البَيْت في الساعةِ الثامِنَة مَساءً
في الساعةِ الرابِعَة بَعدَ الظُهْر أذهَب وأولادي إلى دار أبي وأمّي.
أعْمَل أمينَة مَكتَبَة في الجامِعَةِ الأُردُنِيَّة في عَمّان.
لكِنَّني أنهَض مُتَأخِّرَةً في يَوْمِ الجُمْعة (في التاسِعَة أو العاشِرة).
وأحْياناً نَأكُلُ الحِمَّص إلى جانِبِ الزَيتون والجُبْن.
حَيْثُ أتَكَلَّم مَعَهُما ومَعَ أُختي وأَخي.
بَعدَ الفَطور أُنَظِّفُ الدار وأغسِلُ القُمْصان.
أُحَضِّر أحْياناً الفولَ المُدَمَّس والبَيْض المَقْليّ.
أذهَب إلى عَمَلي في الساعةِ السابعَة كُلَّ يَوْم.

مَطعم في جُبَيل لُبنان

تمرين ٧

الكِتابة: اُكْتُب، على ورقة مُنْفَصِلة، فِقْرة (paragraph) واذْكُر (mention) فيها

١- ماذا تَفْعَل كُلّ يَوْم

٢- وماذا تَفْعَل عادةً

٣- وماذا تَفْعَل أحياناً، كَما تَرى في المِثال:

مِثال: آكُلُ الكَبابَ الحَلَبيّ على الغَداء عادةً.

تمرين ٨

املأ الفَراغات: أكمَل الجُمَل بالكَلِمات المَوجودة في المُرَبَّعات أدناه:

الحَلوى تَنهَضينَ عيد المَعجونِ الشايَ تَبّولَةً فَجْر الصابونِ

١- تَشرَب هالَة ____________ بَعدَ الفَطور.

٢- أغسِل يَدَيَّ بِالماء و____________ .

٣- هَلْ تَأكُل ____________ بَعدَ الطَعام؟

٤- مَتى ____________ مِن النَوم يا لَيْلى؟

٥- أُنَظِّف أسْناني بِالفُرشاة و____________ .

٦- آكُل ____________ فَقَط على الغَداء.

تمرين ٩

لِلكِتابة: اُكْتُب، على ورقة مُنْفَصِلة، ماذا تَفْعَل في حياتِك اليَوْميّة من الصَّباح حَتّى المَساء في أُسْبوع العَمَل وكَذلِك في عُطْلة نِهايةِ الأُسْبوع. حاوِل أن تُقَلِّد (copy) نَصّ القِراءة الرئيس في هذا الدَّرس.

تمرين ١٠

لِلمُحادَثة: إسْأل صَديقَك الأسْئِلة الآتية:

1. what time they go to sleep
2. where they go at night, and with whom
3. what time they get back home
4. what they like to do (watch movies or television, go out to eat, go to a friend's house)
5. when/what they eat/drink
6. what they like to watch on the weekends

والآن، أخْبِرِ الأسْتاذة والطلاّب الآخَرين ما عَلِمت من صَديقِك.

١ – كَلِمات مِثل بَعْض Partitive Nouns

كَما تَعَلّمْنا سابِقاً، تَدُلُّ كَلِمة بَعْض على جُزء من الكُلّ، وتُوجَد كَلِمات أُخرى بِاللُغة العَرَبيّة لَها نَفْس الدَلالة (connotation). وفي هذا الدَرْس، رأيْنا ثلاث كَلِمات مِن هذِه المَجْموعة ألا وهي: كَأْسُ ماء وفِنْجانُ شاي وقِطْعَةُ خُبْز. لاحِظ بأنَّ الكَلمة الأولى (مُظَلَّلة بالأزْرَق) تَدُلُّ على جُزء مُعَيَّن من الكُلّ.

مُلاحَظة: نَسْتَطيع إسْتِخْدام حَرْف الجَرّ مِن لِيَدُلَّ على جُزء من شَيء، على سَبيل المِثال: قِطْعَةٌ مِنَ الخُبْز أو كَأْس مِن الماء أو فِنْجان من الشّي ولَها نَفْس دَلالة الإضافة تَماماً.

تمرين ١١

إسْتِخْدام بَعْض وقِطْعة وكَأْس وفِنْجان في جُمَل: تَرْجَم (translate) الفِقْرة الآتية إلى العَرَبيّة وحاوِل أن تَسْتَخْدِم الإضافة ومِن لِلتَّعْبير عن مَعانيها.

I woke up this morning and then fixed breakfast. For breakfast I ate *some eggs*, a *slice of bread*, and *some pieces of cheese*, and I drank *two glasses of orange juice* and a *cup of coffee*.

تمرين ١٢

تَمرينُ المُشاهَدة: شاهِدوا الدَّرْسَ الثالث عَشَر على الشابِكة.

Place a number next to the following sequence of events in the order that is described in the scene. Her first daily activity is already given:

١	**تَسْتَيْقِظ في الساعةِ السابعة والنِصْف.**
	تَستَمِع إلى الموسيقا وهي تَشرَبُ القهوة مع زَوْجِها.
	في الساعةِ الثالثة تَعود إلى البيت وتُحَضِّرُ الغداء.
	في المساء تَذهَب وزَوجُها لزيارةِ العائلة أو الأصدقاء.
	تُشاهِدُ التِلفاز وتَنام في الساعةِ الثانية عشرة ليلاً.
	تَغسِل وَجهَها وتُنَظِّفُ أسنانَها.
	تَغسِلُ الصُحون ثُمَّ تُغيِّر ملابِسَها.
	تَعود إلى البيت لِتُحَضِّرَ العَشاء وتُرَتِّبَ البيت.
	تُحَضِّرُ الفَطور.

٢- نَفي فِعْل الأمْر Negating Imperative Verbs

نَسْتَخْدِم فِعْل الأمْر حين نَطْلُب فِعْلاً ما (مِثْل هاتْ أو أعطِ) أو نُصْدِر أمْراً (مِثْل اِجْلِسْ أو تَفَضَّلْ) كَما تَعَلّمْنا في الدَّرْس السابِع. وإذا أرَدْنا أنْ نَنْفي الأمْر (مِثْل لا تَجلِسْ هُنا)، فأنّنا نَسْتَخْدِم لا، وهو يَسْبُق الفِعْل ويَجْزِمه أي في المُضارِع المَجْزوم. اُنْظُر إلى المِثال:

	المُضارِع المَرفوع		المُضارِع المَجْزوم		نَفي فِعْل الأمْر
١	أَكْتُبُ	←	أُكْتُبْ	←	لا تَكْتُبْ

كَما تَرى في المِثال ١، أنَّ فِعْل الأمْر (أُكْتُبْ) يُشْبِه المُضارِع المَرْفوع (أَكْتُبُ) إلاّ في الحَرَكة أي الضَّمَّة في المُضارِع المَرْفوع والسَّكون في الأمْر ونَفي الأمْر.

العرض: اسأل الطلاّب أسئلة باستخدام الحركة اليدوية المناسبة لتشير إلى صيغة نفي فعل الأمر، مثلاً:
«لا تكتب/ تكتبي/ تكتبوا على الجدار.»
«لا تنسَ/ تنسي، تنسوا موعد درس العربية.»
«لا تأتِ/ تأتي/ تأتوا متأخِّراً/ متأخِّرةً/ متأخِّرين.»
«لا تأكل/ تأكلي/ تأكلوا في ذلك المطعم.»

الممارسة: تظاهر كأنك تحدّد موعداً مع شخص ما كي تدرس معه أو تشاهد التلفاز أو تود شرب فنجان شاي أو قهوة معه وما إلى ذلك.
التطبيق: أطلُب من الطلاّب تحديد موعد مع زميله كي يدرس العربية معه في مقهى أو كي يشاهد فيلماً في دار السينما أو ما إلى ذلك.
أخبر الطالب أن يذكّر زميله بألا ينسى الموعد أو ينصحه بشيء يجعله يستخدم صيغة نفي فعل الأمر،أسوة بما ورد في الأمثلة المظللة بالأخضر أعلاه.

عِنْدَما نَنْفي فِعْلَ الأمْر في المُخاطَب (second person)، نَرى أنَّ النّون تُحْذَف (is omitted) في كُلِّ الحالات إلاّ في تَصْريف أَنْتُنَّ كَما تَرى في المِثال ٣:

	الضَّمير	المُضارِع المُخاطَب		المُضارِع المَجزوم
٢	أَنْتُم	تكتُبونَ	←	تكتُبوا
٣	أَنْتُنَّ	تكتُبنَ	←	تكتُبنَ

مُلاحَظة: إنَّ الألِف في فِعْل (تكتُبوا) في المُضارِع المَجْزوم صامِتة (silent) كَما نَرى في المِثال ٢. وعِنْدَما نُضيف ضَميراً مُتَّصِلاً لِفِعْلِ المُضارِعِ المَجْزوم، تَسْقُط الألِف كَما تَرى في المِثال ٤:

	المُضارِع المَجْزوم		الضَّمير		
٤	لا تكتُبوا	+	ها	←	لا تكتُبوها

٣- الفِعْلُ المُعْتَلّ Weak Verbs

نُسَمّي نَوْع الفِعْل هذا فعلاً مُعْتَلا لأنَّ حَرْفاً مِن حُروفِه الثَّلاث حَرْف عِلّة (long vowel) في مَكان الفاء (المِثال ٥) أو في مَكان العَيْن (المِثال ٦) أو في مَكان اللام (المِثال ٧). وكُلّ مِن المَجْموعات الثلاث لَها اِسْم خاصّ بِها:

٥	وَصَلَ أو وَقَفَ أو وَزَنَ	الفِعْلُ المِثال	*assimilated verb*
٦	قال أو زار أو قام	الفِعْلُ الأجْوَف	*hollow verb*
٧	نَسِيَ أو مَشى أو قَضى	الفِعْلُ الناقِص	*defective verb*

بِالنِسْبة إلى فِعْلِ الأمْر في صيغةِ المُخاطَب، فأنَّ الضَّمير أَنْتَ هو الضَّمير الوَحيد الّذي يُحْذَف حَرْفُ العِلّة مِنه في المُضارِع المَجْزوم ويُسْتَبْدَل (it can be substituted) بِمُقابِله الحَرَكة: وفي الصفحة التالية، نرى أنّ الواو تَصير ضَمّة (المِثال ٨) والألِف تَصير فَتْحة (المِثال ٩) والياء تَصير كَسْرة (المِثال ١٠)

	المُضارِع المُخاطَب		المُضارِع المَجزوم			
٨	تَقولُ	←	تَقُلْ	الواو	←	ضَمّة
٩	تنسى	←	تَنسَ	الألِف	←	فَتحة
١٠	تَقْضي	←	تَقْضِ	الياء	←	كِسْرة

ونَقوم بِنَفْسِ العَمَلية في نَفي الفِعْلِ المُضارِع كَما فَعَلناه في المُضارِعِ المَجْزوم، فَقَط علَيْنا أن نُضيف حَرْف النَّفي لا قَبْلَ الفِعْل.

	المُضارِع المُخاطَب		المُضارِع المَجزوم			
٨	تَقولُ	←	لا تَقُلْ	الواو	←	ضَمّة
٩	تَنسى	←	لا تَنسَ	الألِف	←	فَتحة
١٠	يَقْضي	←	لا تَقْضِ	الياء	←	كِسْرة

تمرين ١٣

إسْتِخْدام نَفي فِعْل الأمْر: على ورقة مُنْفَصِلة، إسْتَخْدِم نَفي فِعْلِ الأمْر لِكُلّ من هذِه المَواقِف (situations):

1. In order to decrease the amount of graffiti, you write a sign asking people not to write on the walls.
2. You remind a male friend not to forget the time of his flight.
3. Ask a woman not to give her phone number to someone (him).
4. Ask a man not to sit on a particular chair.
5. Inform your friends that there is no class today (ask them not to go to class).

العرض: استخدم لأنَّ في موقف حقيقي أو خيالي، مثلاً:
«أنا متأخِّر. لماذا؟ لأنّي ليس عندي سيّارة.»
«مايكل ليسَ هنا. لماذا؟ لأنّه يدرس في المكتبة.»
«لماذا لا تسكن في فلوريدا في الصيف؟ لأنَّ الطقسَ حارَ.»
«لماذا تأتي بالسيّارة؟ لأنّ الجامعة بعيدة.»

الممارسة: أعطِ الطلاّب بعض الأجوبة لسؤال (لماذا) واطلُب منهم أن يأتوا بالسؤال المناسب، مثلاً:
«لأنّه كان يدرس في المكتبة.
لأنّها أرادت أن تأكل معك.
لأننا أردنا أن نسبح في البحر.
لأننا كنّا بردانين.»

التطبيق: تظاهر كما لو انسرق شيء ما من الصف. قسم الصف إلى مجموعات من اثنين أو ثلاثة، واطلُب منهم أن يأتوا بدليل البراءة. على طالب من طلاّب الصفّ لأن يلعب دور محقق الشرطة. اختر مجموعة من المجموعات أن تخرج من الصف وتنتظر قليلاً عند الباب، واستدعِ فرداً من هذه المجموعة لأن يدخل الصف. اطلُب من المحقق أن يسأله أسئلة لإثبات براءته، ثمّ استدعِ فرداً آخر من المجموعة وأعِد نفس الأسئلة والعملية مع كل فرد وكل مجموعة. وتفوز المجموعة التي تأتي بحجة البراءة الأكثر إقناعاً.

٤- اِسْتِخدام لأنَّ

تَتَألَّف (is comprised) لأنَّ من حَرْفَيْن: لِـ (for) وأنَّ (that) = (for that; because). وكَما تعَلَّمْنا، إنَّ وأنَّ، تأتي بَعْدَهُما جُمْلة اِسْمية، وكَذلِكَ بَعْدَ لأنَّ. مَثَلاً: إذا أَرَدْنا أنْ نَقول (because I)، نَسْتَخْدِم لأنَّني. أُنْظُر إلى الجَدْوَل إلى الأَسْفَل الّذي فيهِ بَعْض الأَمْثِلة:

١١	لأنَّ	+	أنا	←	لأنَّني
		+	نَحْنُ	←	لأنَّنا
		+	أَنْتَ	←	لأنَّكَ
		+	أَنْتِ	←	لأنَّكِ
		+	هو	←	لأنّه
		+	هي	←	لأنّها

كَما رأَيْنا في الدَرْسِ الحادي عَشْر، حَرْف أنَّ يَنْصِبُ الاسْم ويَرْفَعُ الخَبَر،كذلِكَ لأنَّ:

١٢	- لِماذا تَسْكُن هُنا؟	*Why do you live here?*
	- أَسْكُن هُنا لِـأَنَّ المَدينةَ جَميلةٌ،	*I live here because the city is beautiful,*
١٣	ولِـأنَّ سُكّانَها مُحْتَرَمون.	*and its residents are respectable.*

نَرى في المِثال ١٢، المَدينةَ اِسْم مَنْصوب بالفَتْحة وجَميلةٌ اِسْم مَرْفوع، عَلامتُه تَنوين الضَّمّ. وفي المِثال ١٣، سُكّانَها مَنْصوب بالفَتْحة ومُحْتَرَمون مَرْفوع، عَلامتُه الواو.

تَذَكَّر: نُجيب عن (we answer) أداة الاِسْتِفْهام لِماذا بِـ: لأنَّ

تمرين ١٤

صِلوا بَين العَمود (أ) والعَمود (ب) لِتَكوين جُملة صَحيحة.

(أ)	(ب)
١- هو لا يأكُل كَثيراً	لأنّها تُحِبّ الرياضة.
٢- تَمشي إلى الجامِعة كُلّ يَوم	لأنّها مُزدَحِمة.
٣- سأنام باكِراً	لأنّه مَريض.
٤- هو سَعيد	لأنّهم يُحِبّون مُشاهَدة الأفلام الجَديدة.
٥- لِماذا لا تُحِبّ الدِراسة في القاهِرة؟	لأنّه اِشترى سيّارة جَديدة.
٦- يَذهَبون إلى السينما	لأنّ دَرسَ العَرَبيّة في الساعة السابِعة صَباحاً.
	لأنّهنّ متأخِّرات.

تمرين ١٥

Conversation: In pairs, one person should play the role of the "interrogator" who is going to be asking a lot of probing questions. The other person should come up with reasonable excuses. Choose your reason or reasons for (1) coming to class late; (2) returning home late last night; or (3) not showing up to your dinner date with your friends. Both partners should take a couple of minutes to prepare the questions they want to pose or the excuses they want to make. Switch roles after the role-play has reached its conclusion.

Follow-up exercise: Report everything that happened in your role-play to your classmates, using the verb "to say."

٥- تَرْكيب الجُملة العَرَبيّة: الفِعْل Verb Position in Arabic Sentences

نَعرِف أنَّ الجُمْلة في اللُغةِ العَرَبيّة نَوْعان: الجُمْلةُ الاِسْميّة والفِعْليّة. وفي هذا الباب، نَتكَلَّم عن الجُمْلةِ الفِعْليّةِ الّتي عُموماً تَتكَوَّن من: الفِعْل والفاعِل (المِثال١٣) أو الفِعْل والفاعِل والمَفْعول بِهِ (المِثال ١٤):

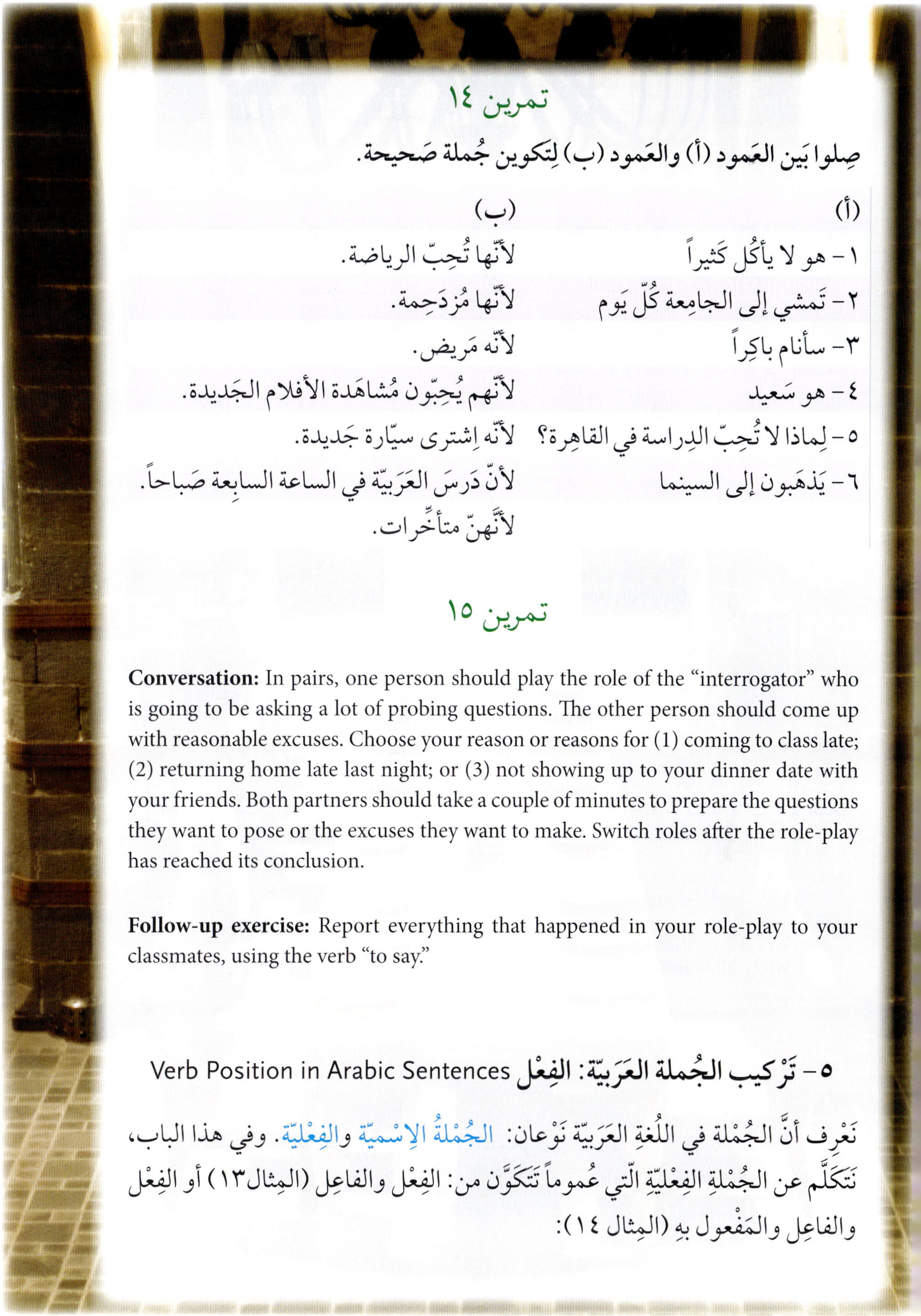

داخِل مَطعم في سوريا

	الفاعِل	الفِعْل	
The professors stood up.	الأَسَاتِذةُ.	قامَ	١٤

	المَفعول بِهِ	الفاعِل	الفِعْل	
The students (f.) study Arabic.	العَرَبيّةَ.	الطالِباتُ	تَدْرُسُ	١٥

على الفِعْل العَرَبيّ أن يُطابِقَ الفاعِل في التَذْكير والتأْنيث، ولكِنّه لا يُطابِقه في الجَمْع، إنْ كانَ الفِعْل مُتَقَدِّماً (preceding) عن الفاعِل كَما نَرى في المِثالين ١٤ و١٥.

والآن دَعْنا نَنْظُر إلى نَفْس الجُمْلتَيْن ولكِن هذِه المَرّة الفاعِل يَسْبُق الفِعْل:

	الفاعِل	الفِعْل	
The professors stood up.	قاموا	الأَسَاتِذةُ	١٦

	المَفعول بِهِ	الفاعِل	الفِعْل	
The students (f.) study Arabic.	العَرَبيّةَ.	يَدرُسْنَ	الطالِباتُ	١٧

في حالة أنَّ هُناكَ فاعِلان (two subjects) واحِد مُذَكّر وواحِد مُؤنَّث، فَنُصَرِّف الفِعل وَفْق تَذْكيرِ الإِسْم الأول أو تأْنيثه، كَما نَرى في المِثال ١٨:

	المَفعول بِهِ	الفاعِلان	الفِعْل	
My brother and sister live in my house.	في بَيْتي.	أخي وأختي	يَسْكُنُ	١٨

هيّا نَتَأمّل جُمْلة من نَصّ القِراءة الرَّئيس:

	المَفعول بِهِ	الفاعِل المُثنّى	الفِعْل	
Hala and Sahar are preparing eggs for breakfast	البَيْضَ على الفَطور	هالَة وسَحَر	تُحَضِّرُ	١٩
and drink tea.	الشاي.		وتَشْرَبان	

في المِثال ١٨، (تُحَضِّرُ) في صيغةِ الإفراد (singular) لأنه يَسْبُقُ الفاعِلَيْن هالَة وسَحَر بَيْنَما (تَشْرَبان) في صيغةِ التَّثْنية (dual) لأنَّه يأتي بَعْدَ الفاعِلَيْن.

تمرين ١٦

تَصْريفُ الفِعْلِ العَرَبيّ: صَرِّف (conjugate) الفِعْلَ الّذي بَيْنَ القَوْسَيْن حَسَب الزَمَن والإفْراد والتَّثْنية والجَمْع والتَذْكير والتَأْنيث. فَكِّر في (consider) السياق حَتّى تَعْرِف زَمَن الفِعْل.

مِثال: أَخَوات صَديقي (عَمِلَ) الآن في سوق كَبيرة.
أَخَوات صَديقي يَعْمَلنَ الآن في سوق كَبيرة.

١- كُلُّ الطُلّاب (دَرَسَ) ________ اللُغَةَ الإنكليزِيَّة في المَدارِس الآن.
٢- (وَصَلَ) ________ صَديقاتي مِنَ الرِباط أَمْسِ.
٣- (عَمِلَ) ________ أبي وأُمّي في مَدينَةِ الرِياض حين كُنْتُ صَغيراً.
٤- أخي وزَوجَتُه (سَكَنَ) ________ في مَدينَة حَلَب في سورية حَتّى الآن.
٥- صَديقي وعائِلَتُه (اِنْتَقَلَ) ________ إلى دار جَديدة في الشَهْرِ الماضي.
٦- (لَبِسَ) ________ سامي وأخوه الكوفِيَّة والعِقال عادَةً.
٧- (دَرَسَ) ________ مُعْظَم صَديقات هالَة اللُغَة الإنكليزِيَّة الآن.

٦- إسْتِخدام واو القَسَم Giving an Oath

تَعَلَّمْنا سابِقاً أنَّ حَرْف الواو حَرْف جَرّ وهو أيضاً حَرْف قَسَم ونَجِد مُقابِلَها بِالإنْكليزيّة في التَعْبير (by God). والإسْمُ الّذي يليه في حالةِ الجَرّ، علامتُه كَسْرة الّتي تأتي في آخِر حَرْفِ الإسْم مَثَلاً:

	واللهِ	*by God*
٢٠	والشَّمْسِ	*by the sun*
	والتينِ والزَيْتون	*by the figs*

تمرين ١٧

آ- **أكْمِل الجُمَلَ الآتية بِالاخْتِيارِ المُناسِب وَفْق نَصِّ الاسْتِماع:**

١- سَيَغسِل هاني قُمصانَهُ يَوْم ________ .

☐ الجُمْعة ☐ السَبْت ☐ الأحَد

٢- سَيَذهَب هاني عِندَ الظُهر إلى ________ .

☐ مَكتَبَةِ الفارابي ☐ مَطعَمِ الصَحّة ☐ دارِ صَديقِه

٣- يَدرُس غَسّان في جامِعَة ________ .

☐ دِمَشق ☐ بِرمِنغهام ☐ حَلَب

٤- في السَنَةِ المُقْبِلَة سَيَكون غَسّان في ________ .

☐ سورِيَة ☐ بريطانيا ☐ أمريكا

٥- سَيَأكُل الأصْدِقاءُ الثَلاثَة العَشاء في مَطعَمِ ________ .

☐ الفارابي ☐ الصَحّة ☐ الجامِعَة

ب- **اكْتُب «خطأ» أو «صواب» على الخَطّ ثُمَّ صحِّح الجُمَل الخَطأ:**

٦- عِندَ هاني سَيّارة.

____

٧- يَدرُس غَسّان الأدَبَ الأمريكيّ.

____

٨- سَيَأكُل الأصْدِقاءُ الثَلاثَة العَشاء في الساعةِ السابِعة.

____

٩- عامِر صَديق هاني وغَسّان.

____

ج- بِالعَرَبيّة، صِف (describe) ماذا سَيَفْعَل المُتَحَدِّث (narrator) في صَباح عُطْلة نِهاية الأسْبوع.

د- اُكْتُب كُلّ ما تَعرِفه عن صَديق المُتَحَدِّث

المُفْرَدات

استمِع إلى المُفْرَدة بالعَرَبيّة ثُمَّ أعِد نُطْقَها مرّتين.

اسْتَحَمَّ (يستَحِمُّ) استِحْمام (v.) . . to bathe, to take a bath or shower

اِنتَقَلَ (يَنتَقِلُ) اِنْتِقال (v.) . . . . to move, to relocate

بِحاجةٍ (إلى) . . . . in need of

بَرنامَج ج بَرامِج (n., m.) . . . . program

تَبّولة (n., f.) . . . . salad made with finely chopped parsley, cracked wheat, tomatoes, lemon juice, and olive oil

ثُمَّ (conjunction) . . . . then, and again

جَهَّزَ (يُجَهِّزُ) تَجْهيز (v.) . . . . to prepare

حافِلة ج حافِلات (n., f.) . . . . bus, tram

حَضَّرَ (يُحَضِّرُ) تَحْضير (v.) . . . . to prepare, to make

حَلَقَ (يَحْلِقُ) حَلْق / حِلاقة (v.) . . . . to shave

حَمّام ج حمّامات (n., f.) . . . . bathroom

خَبَر ج أخْبار (n., m.) . . . . news story

خُضرة ج خُضَر (n., f.) . . . . vegetables

ذَقْن ج ذُقون (n., f.) . . . . chin (when used with "to shave," it signifies shaving one's beard)

رَتّبَ (يُرَتِّبُ) تَرْتيب (v.) . . . . to organize

رَجَعَ (يَرْجِعُ) رُجوع (v.) . . . . to return, to go back

رِسالة ج رَسائِل (n., f.) . . . . letter, message

سِنٌّ ج أسْنان (n., f.) . . . . tooth

شاهَدَ (يُشاهِدُ) مُشاهَدة (v.) . . . . to watch

صابون (n., m.) . . . . soap plate . . . . (n., m.) صَحْن ج صُحون

to return . . . . (v.) عادَ (يَعودُ) عَوْدة

world . . . . (n., m.) عالَم ج عَوالِم

dinner . . . . (n., m.) عَشاء ج أعْشِية

break; vacation . . . . (n., f.) عُطْلة ج عُطْلات/ عُطَل

lunch . . . . (n., m.) غَداء ج أغْدِية

to wash . . . . (v.) غَسَلَ (يَغْسِلُ) غَسْل

to change something . . . . (v.) غَيَّرَ (يُغَيِّرُ) تَغيير

brush . . . . (n., f.) فُرْشاة ج فَراشٍ

breakfast . . . . (n., m.) فَطور

to spend time . . . . (v.) قَضى (يَقضي) قَضاء

writing . . . . (verbal noun) كِتابة

much, a great deal . . . . (n., m.) كَثير ج كَثيرون / كِثار

because. . . . . (particle) لأَنَّ

yogurt . . . . (n., m.) لَبَن

why. . . . . (particle) لِماذا

one coming early . . . . (n., m.) مُبَكِّر ج مُبَكِّرون

one coming late . . . . (n., m.) مُتَأَخِّر ج مُتَأَخِّرون

stewed . . . . (adj.) مُدَمَّس

once, one occurrence. . . . . (n., f.) مَرّة ج مَرّات

show, (television) series . . . . (n., m.) مُسَلسَل ج مُسَلسَلات

watching . . . . (verbal noun) مُشاهَدة

busy . . . . (n., m.) مَشْغول ج مَشْغولون

together . . . . (adv.) مَعاً

paste . . . . (n., m.) مَعْجون ج مَعاجين

fried . . . . (adj.) مَقليّ

to forget . . . . (v.) نَسِيَ (يَنسى) نِسْيان

to clean. . . . . (v.) نَظَّفَ (يُنَظِّفُ) تَنْظيف

to get up . . . . (v.) نَهَضَ (يَنهَضُ) نُهوض

by God, I swear, really (used to add emphasis) . . . . وَاللّهِ

face. . . . . (n., m.) وَجْه ج وُجوه

hand . . . . (n., f.) يَد ج أَيْدٍ

وادي رُم في الأُرْدُنّ

الدرس الرابع عشر

أهداف الدرس

- وَصف الفِعْل في الماضي والمُضارِع والمُسْتَقْبَل
- اِسْتِخْدام حَرْف الشَّرْط أمّا . . . فـَ
- اِسْتِخْدام الكَلِمة المُرَكَّبة لِذلِكَ
- تَعَلُّم اِسْتِخْدام حَرْف الجَرّ لِـ بعد الفِعْل قال
- تَعلُّم اِسم الإشارة
- تَعَلُّم اِسم النِّسْبة

المُفرَدات الجَديدة في صُوَر عديدة

الصِحافة

قِطار

مَحَطّة ج مَحَطّات

مَشْهور ج مَشْهورون

مُهَنْدِس ج مُهَنْدِسون

زار (يَزورُ) زيارة

تمرين ١

أ- أكْمِل الجُمَل الآتية بِكَلِمات مُناسِبة.

١- جِمي كارتَر رَجُل __________ .

☐ مَشْهور ☐ مُتَوَسِّط ☐ مُهَندِس

٢- ذَهَب سالِم إلى تونِس في __________ الصَيف.

☐ بَلْدة ☐ بِطاقة ☐ عُطْلة

٣- تَسكُن سَناء في __________ «القَنَوات» في مَدينة دِمَشق.

☐ حَديث ☐ حَيّ ☐ حَبّ

٤- سَتَدرُس أختي في جامِعَةِ الجَزائِر في فَصلِ الخَريفِ __________ .

☐ الحارّ ☐ الأوَّل ☐ المُقْبِل

ب- اِختَر الكَلِمة الّتي لا تُناسِب باقي الكَلِمات في كُلّ مَجموعة وبَيِّن السَبَب:

٥-	شَمْس	حارّ	بَصَل	صَيْف
٦-	مَوْعِد	سَرير	قِطار	مَحَطّة
٧-	أرُزّ	عَدَس	بَصَل	طَقْس
٨-	عيد	شاطِئ	بَحْر	بُحَيْرة

تمرين ٢

أَعِدّ تَرْتيبَ الكَلِمات في كُلّ مَجْموعة لِتُشَكِّل جُمَلاً مُفيدة:

١- فِلَسطينِيَّةٌ - «المُسَخَن» - مَشْهورَةٌ - أَكْلَةٌ

٢- الإسْكَندَرِيَّة - بْراون - زارَ - مايكل - مَدينَة

٣- شاطِئِ - هُناكَ - على - البَحْرِ - ناسٌ - كانَ - كَثيرونَ

٤- مَساءً - القِطارِ - سامية - مَحَطَّةِ - وَصَلَتْ - إلى

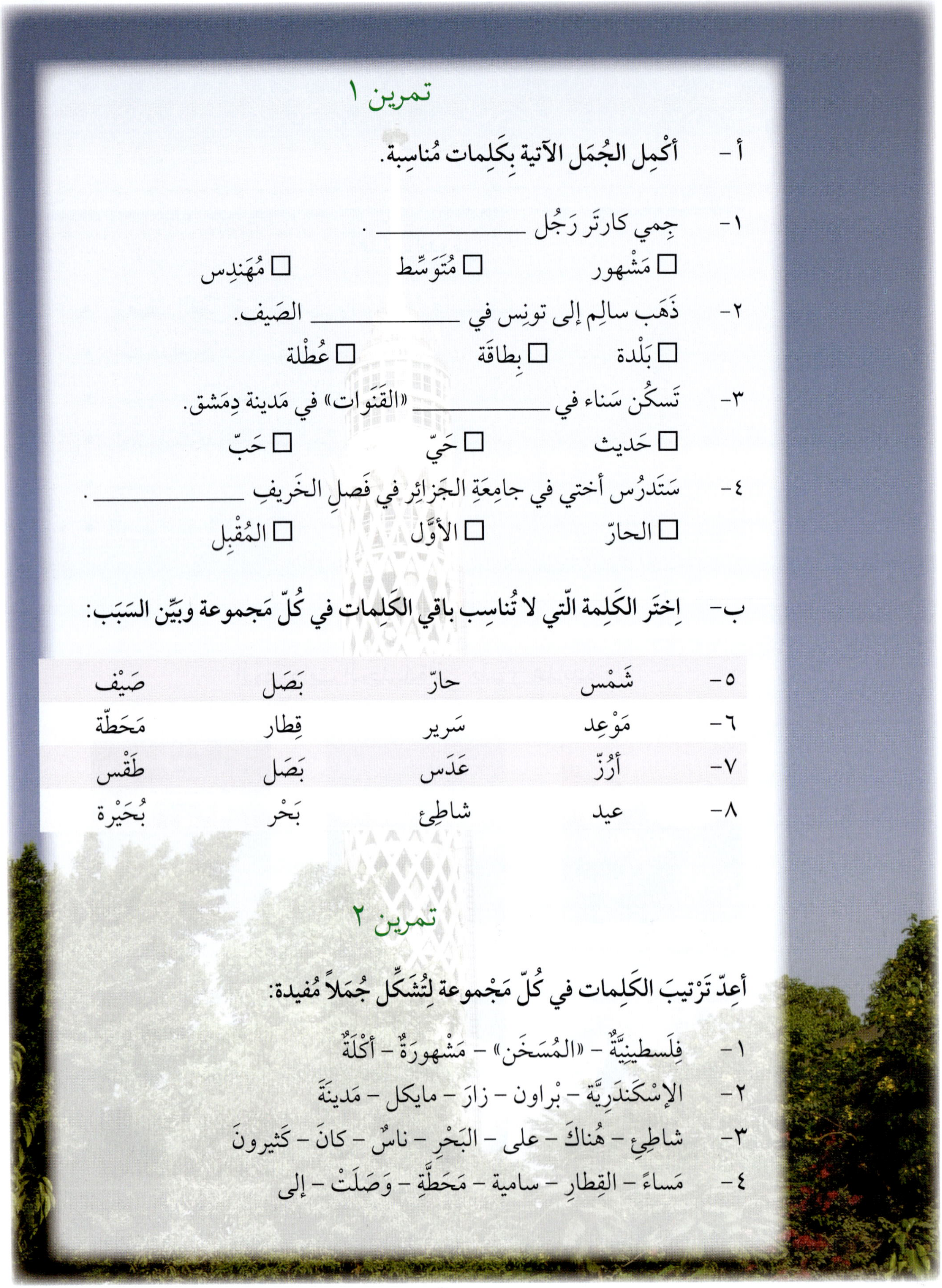

برج القاهرة

تمرين ٣

أعِدّ تَرْتيبَ الجُمَل لِتُشَكِّل فِقْرة كامِلة. الجُمْلة الأولى في مَكانِها المُناسِب:

١- أَحْمَد حِجازي رَجُل مِن مَدينَة حَلَب.
بَعدَ أربَع ساعات ونِصْف وَصَلوا إلى طَرْطوس.
لكِنَّ طَرطوس لَيْسَتْ قَريبَة ولَيْسَ عِندَ أَحْمَد سَيّارة.
بَعدَ خَمسة أيّام رَجَعوا إلى حَلَب بِالقِطار أَيْضاً.
أراد أَحْمَد زِيارة مَدينَة طَرطوسَ مع عائِلَتِه.
نَزَلوا في طَرطوس في فُنْدُق قَريب مِن شاطِئِ البَحْر.
وطَرطوس مَدينَة صَغيرَة على الشاطِئِ السورِيّ.
كانوا في مَحَطَّةِ القِطار في حَلَب في الساعةِ السابِعَة صَباحاً.
لِذلِكَ ذَهَبوا إلى هُناكَ بِالقِطار

يَوميّات مايكِل براون

الثُلاثاء ٢١ أغُسْطُس (آب) ٢٠١٨

بَعدَ دَرسِ العَرَبيَّة بَعدَ ظُهرِ اليَوم ذَهَبتُ إلى مَطعَم مَشْهور في حَيِّ المُهَندِسين اِسْمُهُ «العُمْدَة» مَعَ أصدِقائي حُسَيْن أحْمَد وهِبَة عَبد الله وجِنِفَر كولي. يَدرُس حُسَيْن التِجارة وتَدرُس هِبَة الصِحافَة. أمّا جِنِفِر فَهي طالِبَة أمريكيَّة مِن جامِعَة واشِنطَن في سانت لويس تَدرُسُ اللُغَةَ العَرَبيَّة في الجامِعَةِ الأمريكيَّة في القاهِرة. أَكَلْنا هُناكَ «الكُشَري» وهي أَكْلَة مِصريَّة مِنَ الأَرُزّ والعَدَس والمَعكَرونَة والبَصَل. أُحِبُّ الكُشَريّ كَثيراً، لكِنَّني حين آكُلُ الكُشَريّ أشرَب كَثيراً مِن الماء بَعدَ الطَعام. لِذلِكَ ما أَكَلْتُ كَثيراً مِنَ الكُشَريّ. كانَ المَطعَم نَظيفاً وكانَ هُناكَ بَعضُ الناسِ البريطانيّين والإيطالِيّين.

العمدة

الكُشَري

إن هذا الدرس مراجعة الأفعال اليومية الواردة في الدروس السابقة بشأن ما نفعل في اليوم، وفي أي ترتيب، وكم مرة في اليوم نفعله وفي أي وقت.

العرض: صف الأشياء التي فعلتها اليوم، وتفعلها الآن وستفعلها في المستقبل نموذجاً للطلاب، مثلاً:

«ذهبت إلى فلوريدا في الصيف (أو أي فصل).»
«أشاهد الأخبار في الساعة العاشرة.»
«سأزور أمّي وأبي في حزيران (أو أي شهر).»

الممارسة: اسأل الطلاب ماذا يفعلون في ساعات معيّنة من اليوم، وفي أيام معيّنة من الأسبوع وأشهر معيّنة من السنة وفصل معيّن من فصول السنة.

شجع الطلاّب على تقديم المعلومات على مستوى الفقرة مستخدمين أدوات الربط. وكذلك، اطلب منهم أن يحكوا حكايات مفصّلة بقدر ما استطاعوا ويُظهروا معرفتهم باللغة العربية على أحسن حال.

في حالة أن الطالب يجيب عن السؤال بكلمتين أو ثلاثة، شجعه على تقديم أكبر مقدار من المعلومات مستخدما اللغة العربية والإشارات اليدوية.

التطبيق: في مجموعات من اثنين أو ثلاثة: اطلب من الطلاب أن يسألوا بعضهم بعضاً أسئلة متعلقة بما يفعلون كل ساعة / يوم / أسبوع / شهر / فصل دارسي وسنوي.

الأربعاء ٢٢ أغسطس (آب) ٢٠١٨

يَقول حُسَيْن إنَّ الطَقس غَداً سَيكون حارّاً. قُلْتُ لَهُ إنّي سَأذهَب في عُطلَة نِهايَةِ الأسبوع هذِهِ إلى مَدينَةِ المِنيا. قالَ لي إنَّ المِنيا حارّة أيْضاً، وهي أحَرّ من القاهِرَة. سَأزور أُسرَة صَديقي سَمير أحْمَد هُناكَ وسَأنزِل عِندَهُم. سَأذهَب بِالقِطار من مَحطَّةِ الجيزة. ثَلاث ساعات ونِصْف من هذِهِ المَحطَّة إلى المِنيا. مَوعِدُ القِطار في الساعةِ السابِعة صَباحاً مِن كُلّ يَوْم. سَيَكون أخو سَمير في مَحطَّةِ القِطار حين أصِل إلى هُناك.

مَحطة المنيا

يَوميّات عَدنان مارتيني

الخَميس ٢٣ آب ٢٠١٨

بَعدَ دُروسي اليَوم ذَهَبْتُ إلى المَكتَبَة وقَرَأتُ أكْثَر من ساعَتَيْن. كانَ هُناكَ صَديقي تِم نِكَلز وقالَ لي إنَّ الطَقس سَيكون حارّاً غَداً وبَعدَ غَد وإنَّ عُطلة نِهايَةِ الأسبوع هذِهِ طَويلة لأنَّ يَومَ الإثنَيْن ٣ أيلول هو عيدُ العُمّال، لِذلِكَ سَيَذهَب يَومَ السَبت مع صَديقَيْنِ إلى «سيدَر پوينت» وهي مَدينَة مَلاه على شاطِئ بُحَيْرة إيري، والطَقس هَناكَ أبْرَد من طَقس كَلَمبَس. قالَ لي تِم «تَفَضَّلْ مَعَنا». سَأذْهَب مَعَهُم إنْ شاء الله لأنَّني ما زُرتُ «سيدَر پوينت» حَتّى الآن.

مَدينَة مَلاهٍ

الأحَد ٢ أيلول ٢٠١٨

كانَ الطَقس جَميلاً جِدّاً في «سيدَر پوينت» وكانَت الشَمْس ساطِعة ودَرَجَةُ الحَرارة مُعْتَدِلَة. بُحَيْرة إيري كَبيرَة، وهي أكبَر مِن كُلِّ البُحَيراتِ القَريبَة من كَلَمبَس. كانَ هُناكَ ناس كَثيرون على شاطِئِ البُحَيْرة وكانَ بَعْضُ الناس يَسبَحون في الماء. كانَ يَومُ السَبْت هذا من أجْمَل أيّامِ الصَيف. سَأزور «سيدَر پوينت» مرةً ثانية مع أصدِقائي في الصَيْفِ المُقبِل إن شاءَ الله.

العرض: حضّر فقرة صغيرة عمّا فعلت وتفعل وتنوي الفعل واذكر فيها الوقت واليوم والشهر والفصل بتحديد. اطلُب من الطلاّب أن يستمعوا إليك ويكتبوا ملاحظات.

الممارسة: استيعاب الاستماع: اسأل الطلاّب أسئلة عامة بصدد ما علموا من الفقرة، مثلاً:

«ماذا فهمتم من هذه القصة؟»)

((هل سمعتم أيّة كلمة عرفتموها؟»

اكتب كل الأجوبة على السبورة بما فيها الخطأ. اكتب علامات استفهام فوق الأجوبة التي اختلف فيها الطلاّب، ثمّ أعِد قراءة القصة كي توضح هذه النقاط. لا تشدّد على أي جزء من النص في القراءة واطلب من الطلاّب أن يصحّحوا أجوبتهم.

التطبيق: اطلُب من الطلاّب أن يسألوا زملاءهم أسئلة كالآتي:

«مَن يشاهد الأخبار في الساعة السادسة والنصف؟»

«مَن زار سيدَر پوينت؟»

«مَن سافر إلى مصر ومِن أكل الكشري هناك؟»

«مَن سبح في بحيرة إيري؟»

قسم الطلاّب إلى مجموعات من اثنين أو ثلاثة واكتب أجوبتهم على السبورة لتقارنها وترى إذا كان هناك التطابق بين المجموعات أم لا.

تمرين ٤

آ- **أكْمِل الجُمَل الآتية بِكَلِمات مُناسِبة وَفْق نَصّ القِراءة.**

١- «العُمْدة» اِسْم ________ .

☐ صَديق مايكِل ☐ حَيّ في القاهِرة ☐ مَطعَم

٢- الكُشَريّ أكْلَة ________ .

☐ مِصْريَّة ☐ بريطانيّة ☐ إيطاليّة

٣- كانَ «العُمْدة» ________ .

☐ قَريباً ☐ نَظيفاً ☐ جَميلاً

٤- سَيَذهَب مايكِل إلى المِنيا من ________ .

☐ مَطارِ القاهِرة ☐ مَحطَّةِ الجيزَة ☐ حَيِّ المُهَندِسين

٥- ذَهَبَ عَدنان بَعدَ دُروسِهِ إلى ________ .

☐ المَكتَبَة ☐ الصَفّ ☐ الشارِع

٦- ذَهَبَ عَدنان في عُطلَة نِهايَةِ الأسبوع إلى مَدينَة ________ .

☐ كَلَمبَس ☐ دِمَشق ☐ مَلاهٍ

٧- عيدُ العُمّال في يَومِ ________ .

☐ السَبْت ☐ الأحَد ☐ الإثْنَيْن

٨- اِسْم صَديق عَدنان ________ .

☐ تِم ☐ مايكِل ☐ جِنِفَر

ب- **اكْتُب «خطأ» أو «صواب» على الخَطّ ثُمَّ صحِّح الجُمَل الخَطأ:**

٩- مِنَ القاهِرَة إلى المِنيا خَمس ساعات بِالقِطار.

١٠- مَوعِد قِطار المِنيا في الساعةِ التاسِعَة.

١١- كانَ الطَقس في «سيدَر پوينت» غائِماً.

١٢- سَيَذهَب عَدنان إلى «سيدَر پوينت» في الصَيفِ المُقبِل.

ج- **اكْتُب ثلاثة أسْئلة عن نَصِّ القِراءة.**

نَهْر النيل في مَدينة المِنيا

تمرين ٥

المُحادَثة: صِف سَفْرةً (a trip) قُمْت بها في حياتِك. اِشْرَح (explain) لِماذا أَعْجَبَتْك أم لَم تُعْجِبْك وأين سافَرْت، وماذا حَدَث فيها، وكيف وَصَلْت إلى المَكان وفي أي فَصْل من فُصول السَنة سافَرْت، ومع مَن سافَرت، وكَم يَوْماً قَضَيْت هُناكَ ومَتى رَجَعْت منها.

وعِنْدما اِنْتَهَيْت من قِصّتِك عن السَفْرة، اُطْلُب من صَديقِك أن يَقول لَك ما عَلِم من سفرتِك وقارِن بَيْن ما يَقول وما حَدَث فِعْلاً. والآن، بَدِّل الدَوْرَين وصَديقُك يَشرَح.

١ - اِسْتِخدام حَرف الشَرط أمّا . . . فـ

غالباً ما لا يدرك الطالب أن الحرف (الفاء) يدخل على كل كلمة سواء أكان فعلاً أو حرف جر أو اسم أو صفة. تأكّد من أن هذه النقطة القواعدية واضحة بالنسبة لهم.

نَسْتَطيع أنْ نُقارِن اِسْماً واِسْماً آخَر بِاسْتِخْدام حَرْفِ الشَّرْط أمّا الّذي يُلْزِمُه (needs) حَرْفَ الفاء بَعدَه. اُنْظُر إلى المِثال ١:

١ سَيّارَةُ يوسُف قَديمةٌ	أمّا	سَيّارةُ أحْمَد،	فَجَديدَةٌ.	*Yousef's car is old, as for Ahmed's car, it is new.*

في المِثال ١، ذَكَرْنا المُبتَدأ (سَيّارةُ يوسُف) وأضَفْنا إليه الخَبَر قَديمةٌ، وفي هذِه الحالة نَسْتَطيع أنْ نَسْتَخْدِم حَرْفَ الشَّرْط (أمّا) كَيْ نقارِن هذِه الجُمْلة الاسْمية وجُمْلة اِسْمية أخرى مِثل سَيّارةُ أحْمَد الّتي خَبَرُها جَديدةٌ.

نَرى هُنا بأنَّنا نَسْتَطيع أنْ نَذْكُر أي جُمْلة اِسْمية مُؤلَّفة من مُبْتَدأ وخَبَر ونُقارِن خَبَرَها وخَبَر جُمْلة اِسْمية أخْرى، كَما يُوجَد في المِثال ٢:

٢ المُبْتَدَأ	الخَبَر	أمّا	مُبْتَدَأ آخَر	فَخَبَر آخَر.

أمّا بالنِسبة إلى الجُمْلة الفِعْلية، فحَرْف الفاء غالباً ما يأتي قَبْل الفِعْل الثّاني مباشرةً (directly). تأمَّل معي المِثال ٣:

	الفِعْل الأول		الفِعْل الثاني	
٣	أَتَكَلَّمُ	اليابانيّة جيّداً أمّا كَريم	فيتكلَّمُها	قليلاً.

نَرى في المِثال ٣، أنَّ هذه الجُمْلة فيها فِعْلان: أَتَكَلَّمُ ويَتَكَلَّمُ لِذا يَلْصَق حرفُ الفاء بالفِعْلِ الثّاني. ونُقارِن هُنا بَيْنَ كَيفَ أتكلَّم اليابانية (جَيّداً) وكَريم الّذي يَتكَلَّمُها (قَليلاً).

أحياناً، تُواجِه طالِبَ اللُغةِ العَرَبيّة صُعوبة في المَكانِ المُناسِب لِلفاء، أين يَضعه؟ نَسْتَطيع أن نَعْتَمِد على مَعْرفتِنا باللُغةِ الإنْكليزيّة بِالمَكانِ المُناسِب لِلفاصِلة (comma) لأَنَّهُما يأتيان في نَفْسِ المَكان في الجُمْلة. اُنْظُر إلى المِثالين:

٤	أُحِبُّ الحِمَّص أمّا أمّي فَتُحِبُّ التبولة.	*I like* ḥimmus. *As for my mother, she likes* tabūleh.
٥	مايكِل براون في القاهِرةِ أمّا عَدنان فَهُوَ في كَلَمبَس.	*Michael Brown is in Cairo. As for Adnan, he is in Columbus.*

تمرين ٦

لِلمُحادَثة: اِسْأل أصدقائك في الصَفّ الأَسْئِلَةَ الآتية واِسْتَخْدِم فيها حَرْف الشَّرْط أمّا . . . فَـ. مَن في الصَّفّ:

1. likes German cars/Italian cars
2. has visited the city of Aleppo, Syria/the city of Paris, France
3. watches the news/reads the paper
4. bought a new telephone/bought a new computer
5. wants to visit *ḳān el-ḳalīlī* bazaar in Egypt/*el-ḥamidiyya* bazaar in Syria

على ورقة مُنْفَصِلة اكْتُب ما عَلِمتَ مِن أصدِقائك مُسْتَخْدِماً جُمَل فيها أمّا . . . فَـ ورَكِّز على المَكان المُناسِب لِحَرْف الفَاء. أخْبِر الأَسْتاذ بما عَلِمتَ من أصْدِقائك.

تمرين ٧

اِسْتِخْدام أمّا . . . فـَ في جُمَل: على ورقة مُنْفَصِلة، كَوِّن جُمْلة واحِدة من الجُمْلتَيْن كَما تَرى في المِثال:

مِثال: **مَدينة نيويورك كَبيرَة / مَدينَة توليدو صَغيرَة**

مَدينة نيويورك كَبيرَة أمّا مَدينَة توليدو فَصَغيرَة.

١- نَهْرُ النيلِ طَويل / نَهْر بَرَدى قَصير

٢- يَسكُن نادِر في شَقّة / ناديا تَسكُن في سَكَنِ الطالِبات

٣- أخي مُهَندِس / أختي أستاذة

٤- اِشتَرَيْتُ مِحْفَظة / زَوْجَتي اِشْتَرتْ نَظّارة

٥- مَدينَة طَرابُلُس الشام في لُبنان / مَدينة طَرابُلُس الغَرْب في ليبيا

٦- أُحِبّ عَصيرَ البُرتُقال / أنْتِ تُحِبّينَ الحَليب

٢- اِسْتِخدام لِذلِكَ

نَسْتَخْدِم هذِه الكَلِمة الّتي تَتَألَّف من لام الجَرّ لِـ (for) واسْم الإشارة ذلِكَ (that) لِتَدُلَّ على سَبَب (reason). ونَجِد مُقابِلَها بِالإنْكليزيّة (for that reason). وحين تأتي هذِه الكَلِمة في جُلْمتِك، سواء أكانَ كِتابةً أو قَوْلاً، العِبارة تُحَسِّنها (improves it) وتَجعَلُها أفْصَح (more eloquent). اُنْظُر إلى المِثالين ٦ و٧:

٦	أُحِبُّ الدِراسات الدُوَليّة لِذلِكَ أدْرُس اللُغة العَرَبيّة.	*I like International Studies, therefore, I study Arabic.*
٧	تُريد لَيْلى أنْ تُسافِر إلى الوَطَن العَرَبيّ، لِذلِكَ اِشْتَرَت تَذْكَرة طائرة.	*Layla wants to travel to the Arab world, therefore she bought a plane ticket.*

العرض: قدّم بعض الجمل للطالب التي فيها **لذلك**، مثلاً:

«الطقس حارّ لذلك سأسبح في البحيرة أو المسبح.»
«ليس عندي دروس الآن لذلك سأقرأ في المكتبة.»
«مايكل ليس عنده مطبخ لذلك يأكل في المطعم.»

الممارسة: اطلُب من حوالي خمسة طلاّب أن يكتبوا جملة بسيطة على السبورة (قد تكون الجملة مثبتة أو منفية)، مثلاً:

«(ليس) عندي تلفاز.»
«(ليس) هناك طعام في ثلاجتي.»
«(لا) أحبّ التاريخ.»

ثم اطلُب منهم أن يقدموا أسباباً لما كتبوا، مثلاً:

«ليس عندي تلفاز (لذلك أقرأ كثيراً).»
«ليس هناك طعام في ثلاجتي (لذلك آكل في مقصف الجامعة).»
«أحبّ التاريخ (لذلك أدرسه).»

التطبيق: في مجموعات من اثنين أو ثلاثة: اطلُب من طالب أن يسأل الآخر أسئلة فيها **لماذا** ويكتب الأجوبة على ورقة. بدِّل الأدوار بعد أن انتهى الطالب من الأسئلة. وفي الختام، اطلُب من الطلاّب أن يكتبوا ما علموا من زملاءهم على السبورة، ثم اسأل الطلاّب أسئلة مثل:

«هل هناك أية مشكلة في هذه الجملة؟»
«هل هذه الجملة صحيحة أم خطأ؟»

دع الطلاّب أن يقدّموا اقتراحاتهم في تصحيح الأجوبة وتحسينها وناقش سبب صحة التصحيح.

تمرين ٨

آ- **أكمِل الجُمَل الآتية كَما في المِثال:**

مِثال: عِندي عُطلة طَويلة؛ لِذلِكَ سأُسافِر إلى البَحر.

١- أنا مُتأخِّر عَن الجامِعة، لِذلِكَ ________________ .

٢- أنا عَطشان، لِذلِكَ ________________ .

٣- المُفرَدات صَعبة، لِذلِكَ ________________ .

٤- أسكُن في غُرفة صَغيرة مع صَديقي، لِذلِكَ ________________ .

٥- سأطبُخ اليَوم، لِذلِكَ ________________ .

٦- أنا مَريض، لِذلِكَ ________________ .

٧- أحِبّ الأماكِن القَديمة ؛لِذلِكَ ________________ .

٨- أحِبّ القِراءة، لِذلِكَ ________________ .

ب- **أكمِلوا الجُمَل الآتية باستخدام (لأنّ/ لِذلِكَ) كما في المِثال:**

مثال: سأُنظِّفُ البَيت لأنّه وَسِخ (dirty).

١- الجوّ حارّ ________________ .

٢- لا أسمَع ما تَقول ________________ .

٣- الأستاذ غاضِب ________________ .

٤- الجامِعة بَعيدة ________________ .

٥- الرياضة جَيِّدة ________________ .

٦- أحِبُّ الصَيف ________________ .

٣- اِسْتِخدام حَرف الجَرّ لِـ بَعْد الفِعْل قالَ

يَلي الفِعْل قال حَرْف الجَرّ لِـ حين نَذْكُر الشَخص الّذي أخْبَرناه بِالقَوْل، مَثَلاً:

٨	قُلْتُ لِعَدنان إنَّني جاهِز.	*I told Adnān that I was ready.*

لكِن، يَخْتَلِف نُطْق (pronunciation) اللام حين تَدْخُل على الأسماء (لِـ) وحين تَدْخُل على الضمائر (pronouns) (لَـ):

٩	قالَ لِـ + اسْم	li
	قُلْتُ لِنور، قال لِصَديقِه	
١٠	قالَ لَـ + ضَمير	la
	قُلْتُ لَها، قالَ لَه	

تمرين ٩

اِسْتِخْدام قالَ: على ورقة مُنْفَصِلة، تَرْجِم الجُمَل الآتية إلى العَرَبيّة مُسْتَخْدِماً قالَ.

1. My professor told me that he would be in his office at nine.
2. Maḥmūd told his wife that he stayed at the Sheraton Hotel in Damascus.
3. He told her also that he ate at al-Sharq Restaurant every day.
4. Marwān says that his brother will arrive at the train station at 4 p.m.

٤ – مَحَلّ اِسم الإشارة في الجُملة العَرَبيّة

في اللُغة العَرَبيّة، أسْماءُ الإشارة مِثل هذا أو هذِه تَلْعَب أدْوار (roles) عَديدة في الجُمْلة العَرَبيّة:

١١	أَعْطِني هذا	المَفْعول بِه
١٢	أَعْطِني مِن هذا	في حالة الجَرّ
١٣	هذا هُوَ أُسْتاذُ العَرَبِيَّة.	المُبْتَدأ
١٤	هذا الكِتاب . . .	مُبْتَدَأ شِبه جُمْلة

أمّا بالنِسبة إلى اسْم الإشارة + الإضافة فهُناكَ بَعْض الأشْياء علَيْنا أنْ نَتَذَكَّرَها، على سَبيلِ المِثال، يأتي اسْمُ الإشارة بعد الإضافة في حالةِ المُبْتَدَأ:

١٥	كِتابي هذا . . .	*this book of mine . . .*
١٦	عُطلَةُ الأسْبوعِ هٰذِهِ . . .	*this weekend . . .*

في المِثال ١٥، الكَلِمة الأخيرة في المُبْتَدأ هو هذا، كذٰلِكَ هٰذِهِ في المِثال ١٦، ونُكْمِل الفِكْرة بإضافة الخَبَر:

	المُبْتَدأ	الخَبَر	
١٧	كِتابي هذا	جَديدٌ	*This book of mine is new.*
١٨	عُطلَةُ الأسْبوعِ هٰذِهِ	مُمْتِعةٌ	*This weekend is fun.*

وَلكِنْ إذا سَبَق اسم الإشارةُ الفاعِلَ، فَتُصْبِح جُمْلة:

	المُبْتَدأ	الخَبَر	
١٩	هذا هو	كِتابي.	*This is my book.*
٢٠	هٰذِهِ هي	عُطلَةُ الأسْبوعِ.	*This is the weekend.*

تمرين ١٠

اِسْتِخدام أسماءِ الإشارة: تَرْجَم هذه الجُمَل والتعابير إلى العَرَبيّة مُسْتَخْدِماً اسم الإشارة المُناسِب في المَكان المُناسِب:

1. This is our professor. ______________________
2. this holiday of yours (f., sg.) ______________________
3. these friends of mine ______________________
4. This is my car. ______________________
5. these eyeglasses (sg.) of my mother's ______________________

٥- مُراجَعة اِسم النِسبة مِئَويّ

نَشْتَقّ اِسْمَ النِسْبة مِئَوِيّ من كَلِمة مِئة بِحَذْفِ التاء المَربوطة وإضافة حَرْف الواو ثُمَّ نُلْحِقُها بالياء المُشَدَّدة دَلالةً على نِسبة شَيء إليه.

٢١	مِئة	+	و	+	يّ	=	مِئَويّ

وهُناكَ بَعْضُ الأسْماء مَثَل مِئَويّ:

	أُسْرة	←	أُسْرَويّ
٢٢	سَنة	←	سَنَويّ
	شِتاء	←	شَتَويّ

تمرين ١١

اِشْتَقّ اِسْمَ النِسْبة من الكَلِمات الآتية:

١- أوروبا ________________

٢- سَنَة ________________

٣- سَماء ________________

٤- شِتاء ________________

٥- ميلاد ________________

٦- مِئَة ________________

٧- خَريف ________________

٨- أُسْرَة ________________

تمرين ١٢

لِلكتابة ثمّ المُحادَثة: على ورقة مُنْفَصِلة، صِف زيارةً قُمْت بِها إلى مَكان حَقيقيّ أو خياليّ. أُذْكُر أَيْنَ ذَهَبْت ولِماذا سافَرت إلى ذلِكَ المَكان، وماذا فَعَلْت هُناكَ، وأين نَزَلْت وكَم مِن الوَقْت بَقِيت هُناكَ ومَتى رَجَعْت. صِف المَكان مِن حَيْثُ المِساحة وعدد السُكّان والطَّقْس. والآن، احْكِ لِزَميلك القِصة الّتي كَتَبتها وتَكَلّم عَمّا رأيت ومع مَن تَكَلّمت وماذا قُلت وماذا قالوا لَكَ في قِصّتك.

تمرين ١٣

آ- **أكْمِل الجُمَل الآتية بالاخْتِيارِ المُناسِب وَفْق نَصّ الاسْتِماع:**

١- رامِز الخولي من مَدينَة ________ .

☐ طَرابُلْس ☐ حِمْص ☐ دِمَشق

٢- أكَل رامِز وزوجَتُهُ فَطوراً صَغيراً لأَنَّهُما ________ .

☐ لا يَأْكُلانِ الفَطور ☐ في طَرابُلْس ☐ سَيَأْكُلان غَداءً كَبيراً

٣- وَصَلَ رامِز وَزَوجَتُهُ إلى طَرابُلْس في الساعَةِ ________ .

☐ التاسِعة ☐ الحادِيَةَ عَشْرَة ☐ الواحِدة

٤- أكَلَ رامِز وَزَوجَتُهُ على الغَداء ________ .

☐ فولاً ☐ كَباباً ☐ أطعِمة لُبنانِيَّة

الميناء في مَدينة طَرابلُس الشام

ب- **اِمْلأ الفَراغات** بِالكَلِمة المُناسِبة وَفْق نَصّ الاسْتِماع:

٥- يَعمَل رامِز ________ .

٦- يَسكُن رامِز وَزَوجَتُهُ في مَدينَة ________ .

٧- ذَهَبَ رامِز وَزَوجَتُهُ إلى طَرابُلْس في فَصْلِ ________ .

٨- أكَلَ رامِز وَزَوجَتُهُ طَعامَ الغَداء في مَطعَم اسْمُهُ ________ .

ج- **اكْتُب «خطأ» أو «صواب» على الخَطّ ثُمّ صحِّح الجُمَلَ الخَطأ:**

٩- اِسْم زَوجَة رامِز سِهام.

____

١٠- مَشى رامِز وَزَوجَتُهُ في السوق بَعدَ الغَداء.

____

١١- كانَ الطَقس بارِداً وجلَسا في غُرفَة دافِئة.

____

١٢- ذَهَبَ رامِز وَزَوجَتُهُ إلى طَرابُلْس بِالحافِلة.

____

تمرين ١٤

تَمرينُ المُشاهَدة: شاهِدوا الدَرْسَ الرابع عَشَر على الشابِكة.

المَشْهَدُ الأوَّل

١- لماذا جاءَ مايكل إلى دِمَشق؟ ______________________

____

٢- كَم يَوماً سَيَبقى مايكل في دِمَشق ولماذا عليهِ أنْ يَرجِع إلى القاهِرة؟ ______________________

____

٣- كَيْفَ الحياة بِالقاهِرة في رأي مايكل؟ ______________________

____

٤- مَن يَنْتَظِرُ مايكل عِند قَوس باب شَرقيّ؟ ______________________

____

المَشْهَدُ الثاني

١- ماذا يَدرُس سامِر وفي أيّةِ كُلّيّة؟ ______________________

____

٢- ماذا يُفَضِّل مايكل العامية أم الفُصحى؟ ______________________

____

٣- إلى أين سَيذهَب كُلٌّ مِن ستيف وسامِر ومايكل؟ ______________________

____

____

____

حارة في دِمَشْق القديمة

المُفْرَدات

استمِع إلى المُفْرَدة بالعَرَبيّة ثم أعِد نُطْقَها مرّتين.

أرُزّ (n., m.) . . . . rice

أُسْرة ج أُسَر (n. f.) . . . . extended family

اِنتظَرَ (يَنْتَظِرُ) اِنتِظار (v.) . . . . to wait

بَصَل (n., m.) . . . . onion

حَيّ ج أحْياء (n., m.) . . . . neighborhood, borough

زارَ (يَزورُ) زِيارة (v.) . . . . to visit

ساوى (يساوي) (v.) . . . . to do (Syrian colloquial)

شو (interrogative particle) . . . . what (Syrian colloquial)

صِحافة (n., f.) . . . . journalism

عامِل ج عُمّال (n., m.) . . . . worker, laborer

عاميّة (active participle) . . . . colloquial

عَدَس (n., m.) . . . . lentils

عُطلة ج عُطَل/ عُطلات (n., f.) . . . . break, vacation

عُطْلَةُ نِهايَةِ الأُسْبوعِ (n., f.) . . . . weekend

عُمْدَة ج عُمَد (n., m.) . . . . mayor

عيد ج أعْياد (n., m.) . . . . celebration, festivity, feast day, day, holiday, *Eid*

عيدُ العُمّال . . . . Labor Day

فُصْحى (superlative) . . . . . Classical Arabic (lit., "most eloquent")

فَضَّلَ (يُفَضِّل) تَفْضيل (v.) . . . . to prefer

قِطار ج قِطارات (n., m.) . . . . train

قَوْس ج أقْواس (n., m.) . . . . arch.

lightly salted, partially dehydrated yogurt with olive oil . . . . (n., f.) لَبَنة

for this reason, therefore . . . . (demonstrative) لِذلِكَ

station . . . . (n., f.) مَحَطّة ج مَحَطّات

crowded . . . . (adj.) مُزْدَحِم

famous, well known . . . . . (participle) مَشْهور ج (ون)، مَشاهير

pasta, macaroni . . . . (n., f.) مَعْكَرونة

place of entertainment . . . . (n., m.) مَلْهىً ج مَلاهٍ

engineer . . . . (n., m.) مُهَنْدِس ج مُهَندِسون

clean . . . . (adj., m.) نَظيف

end . . . . (n., f.) نِهاية ج نِهايات

حي القَنوات في دِمَشْق

سوق تجاريّ أثريّ في دمشق

الدرس الخامس عشر

أهدافُ الدرس

- وَصْف المُناسَبات مِثل الأعياد الوَطَنيّة والدينيّة
- تَعَلُّم تَقْديم مَعلومات شَخْصيّة
- مُراجَعةُ الأسماء الخمسة
- مُراجَعةُ المَمنوع من الصَرْف
- تَعَلُّم المَبْني لِلمَجْهول

رُكنُ المُفْرَداتِ الجَديدة

اِحْتَفَلَ (يَحْتَفِلُ) اِحْتِفال (بِـ)	*to celebrate*
صامَ (يَصومُ) صَوْم / صِيام	*to fast*
عيد ج أعياد	*feast / holiday*
ثَوْرة ج ثَوْرات	*revolution*
مَسيح	*Messiah*
نَوْع ج أنْواع	*type / kind*
اِسْتِقلال	*independence*
تَعليم	*education*

تمرين ١

اِختر الكَلِمة الّتي لا تُناسِب باقي الكَلِمات في كُلّ مجموعة وبيِّن السَبَب:

١-	تَربية	تَعليم	فَجْر	مَدرَسة
٢-	الأضْحى	الفِطر	الفِصْح	الجَزيرة
٣-	إسلاميّ	اِبْتِدائيّ	مُتَوَسِّط	ثانَويّ
٤-	فَجْر	حَلوى	ظُهر	مَغرِب

تمرين ٢

وافِقْ بَيْنَ الكَلِمات في العَمودَين.

١-	إسلاميّ		المَسيح
٢-	عيدُ الشُكْر		رَمَضان
٣-	عيدُ الأضْحى		ثانَويّة
٤-	عيدُ الميلاد		٤ تَمّوز
٥-	عيدُ الفِطْر		مَسيحيّ
٦-	عيدُ اسْتِقلال أمريكا		الحَجّ
			ديك حَبَش

أعياد عَرَبيّة وإسلاميّة ومَسيحيّة وأمريكيّة

في البِلادِ العَرَبيَّة هُناكَ أعياد عَرَبيَّة وإسلامِيَّة ومَسيحِيَّة. يَحْتَفِل كُلّ بَلَد عَرَبيّ عادةً بِعيد اسْتِقلالِه أو بِعيد ثَوْرته. هٰذِه أعيادُ الاسْتِقلال والثَورة في بَعضِ البِلادِ العَرَبيَّة.

البَلَد	عيدُ الاسْتِقلال	عيدُ الثَوْرة	العَلَم
تونس	٢٠ آذار	----	
الجَزائِر	----	١ تِشرين الثاني	
سورية	١٧ نيسان	----	
العِراق	----	١٧ تَمّوز	
عُمان	١٨ تِشرين الثاني	----	
لُبنان	٢٢ تِشرين الثاني	----	
مِصْر	----	٢٤ تَمّوز	
المَغْرِب	٣ آذار	----	
اليَمَن	٢٢ أيّار	----	

تَحتَفِل كُلُّ البِلادِ العَرَبيَّة بالأعيادِ الإسْلاميَّة، لكِنَّ بَعضَ البِلادِ العَرَبيَّة تَحْتَفِل بِالأعيادِ المَسيحيَّة أيْضاً، ويَكون هذا في سوريا ولُبنانَ وفِلَسطينَ والأردُنِّ والعِراقِ ومِصْر.

العرض: أحضِر بعض المواد التعبيرية من البيت أو حضّرها من الشابكة بشأن مختلف الأعياد والمناسبات سواء أكانت إسلامية أو غربية.

أشِر إلى غرض أو صورة واشرحه من حيث أهميته في العيد أو المناسبة وتحدّث عن الطريقة التي تحتفل به في بلدك.

الممارسة: أشِر إلى الغرض أو الصورة واسأل أسئلة موجّهة واكتبِ الأجوبة على السبورة، مثلاً:

«ما هذا؟ (شجرة)»
«أيّ شجرة هذه؟ (شجرة عيد الميلاد)»
«متى يأتي عيد الميلاد؟ (في شهر كانون الأوّل)»
«في أيِّ يوم من الشهر؟ (في الخامس والعشرين)»
«ماذا يأكل الناس في عيد الميلاد؟ (ديك حبش، حلوى)»
«ماذا تفعل بعد الأكل؟ »
«أينَ ستكون في عيد الميلاد؟ (في بيتي مع أسرتي)»

التطبيق: في مجموعات من اثنين أو ثلاثة: اطلُب من الطلّاب أن يسألوا زملائهم في الصفّ أسئلة عن عيدهم المفضل وكيف يحتفلون به، مثلاً:

«ما هي عطلتك المفضّلة وكيف تحتفل(ين) بها؟»

وبعد أن ينهوا النشاط، اطلُب من الطالب أن يقدّم ما علِم من زملائه.

تمرين ٣

املأ الفَراغات: أكمِل الجُمَل بالكَلماتِ المَوجودة في المُربَّعات أدناه:

الاسْتِقلال	وُلِدَ	ذو الحِجّة	تَعليم	إسلاميّ	رَمَضان	طَعام	لأنَّ	نَوْع

١- إيران بَلَد ________ لكِنَّهُ لَيس بَلَداً عَرَبيّاً.

٢- اِنتَقَلَتْ أُختي إلى قَطَر ________ عَمَلَ زَوجِها صارَ هُناكَ.

٣- ________ جورج واشنطُن في وِلاية فرجينيا في سَنة ١٧٣٢.

٤- تَحتَفِل سورية بِعيدِ ________ في ١٧ نيسان.

٥- ما ________ سَيّارتِك يا أستاذ؟

٦- يَصومُ المُسلِمون في شَهرِ ________.

عيدان إسلاميّان

مِن الأعيادِ الإسلاميَّة عيدُ الفِطْر ويَأتي بَعدَ شَهر رَمَضان. في شَهر رَمَضان يَصومُ المُسْلِمون عَنِ الأكْل والشُرْب مِن الفَجْر حَتّى المَغرِب. بَعدَ رَمَضان كُلُّ المُسلِمين يَحتَفِلون بِعيدِ الفِطْر ثَلاثة أيّام، يَأكُلون كُلّ أنواعِ الطَعام والحَلْوى ويَشرَبونَ القَهْوة.

العيدُ الثاني هُوَ عيدُ الأضْحى ويَأتي في شَهر ذي الحِجّة بَعدَ الحَجّ. ويَكونُ الحَجّ في مَكّةَ في السُعوديّة. يَحتَفِلُ المُسلِمون بِهذا العيد أربَعَة أيّام (بَعضُهُم يَحتَفِل بِهِ يوماً أو يَومَين فَقَط).

بَعضُ البِلادِ الإسلامِيَّة تَحتَفِل بِعيد ميلاد رَسولِ الله مُحَمَّد صلّى اللهُ عَلَيهِ وسَلَّمَ وبَعضُ البِلاد لا تَحتَفِل بِهِ، ويُسَمّى هذا العيد «عيدُ المَوْلِد.»

عيدان مَسيحيّان

شَجَرَةُ عيدِ الميلاد

عيدُ الميلاد يَعني مِيلادُ السَيِّدِ المَسيح عيسى عَلَيْهِ السلام ويَحتَفِل بِهِ المَسيحيّون في ٢٥ كانون الأوّل.

عيدُ الفِصْح

العيدُ المسيحيُّ الثاني هو عيدُ الفِصْح ويُحْتَفَل بِهذا العيد في يَوم أحَد في فصلِ الربيع (في آذار أو نيسان أو أيّار).

أعياد أمريكيّة

عيدُ الشُكْر

ديك حَبَش

يَحتَفِلُ الأمريكيّون بِعيدِ الشُكْر في رابع يَومِ خَميس من شَهرِ تِشرينَ الثاني. يَأكُلُ الأمريكيّون في هذا اليَوم ديكَ حَبَش (ديك رومي) وحَلوى تُسَمّى فَطيرةَ القَرْع.

عيدُ الاسْتِقلال

تَحتَفِل أمريكا بِعيدِ الاسْتِقلال في اليَومِ الرابعِ من شَهر تَمّوز.

عيدُ العُمّال

تَحتَفِل أمريكا بِعيدِ العُمّال في أوَّل يَوم إثنين من شَهر أيلول.

عيدُ مارتِن لوثَر كِنغ

تَحتَفِل مُعظَمُ الوِلاياتِ الأمريكيّة بِهذا العيد في ثالِث يَومِ إثنين من شَهر كانونَ الثاني.

سُعاد ريماوي

سُعاد ريماوي فَتاة عِراقيّة مِن مَدينة بَغداد. تَدرُسُ التِجارة في جامِعة بَغداد تَسكُن مَعَ أبيها وأُمِّها وثَلاثَة إخْوة في بَيت كبير في شارِع دِجلة.

وُلِدَتْ سُعاد في مَدينة بَغداد وعيد ميلادِها في ٢٠ آذار. هي أكبَر إخوَتِها. دَرَسَتْ في مَدارِسِ بَغداد مِن الصَفِّ الأوَّلِ الابْتِدائيّ إلى الصَفِّ الثامِنِ المُتَوَسِّط. حين كانَتْ في سِنِّ الرابِعة عَشْرة اِنتَقَلَتْ مَعَ أبيها وأمِّها مِن بَغداد إلى مَدينةِ المَوصِل لأنَّ أباها صارَ مُديرَ التَربية والتَعليم فيها. دَرَسَت هُناكَ في مَدارِسِ المَوصِل ثَلاث سَنوات. بَعدَ ذلِكَ رَجَعوا إلى بَغداد. حين تَخَرَّجَتْ مِن المَدرَسةِ الثانَويّة ذَهَبَتْ إلى جامِعَة بَغداد.

سُعاد في سِنِّ العِشرين الآن. تَقول سُعاد إنَّها حين تَتَخَرَّج مِنَ الجامِعة بَعدَ سَنَتَين سَوفَ تَرجِع إلى المَوصِل وتَعمَل هُناكَ لأنَّها تُحِبّ تِلكَ المَدينة.

تمرين ٤

آ- **أكمِل الجُمَلَ الآتية بِكَلِمات مُناسِبة وَفْق نَصِّ القِراءة.**

١- عيدُ الثَورة في مِصْر في ________ .

☐ ٤ تَمّوز ☐ ١٧ تَمّوز ☐ ٢٤ تَمّوز

٢- عيدُ ________ عيد إسلاميّ.

☐ الفِصْح ☐ الفِطر ☐ الثَورة

٣- عيد اِستِقلال سورية في ________ .

☐ ١٧ نيسان ☐ ٨ آذار ☐ ٢٢ أيّار

٤- يُحتَفَل بعيدِ ________ في شَهر كانون الأوَّل.

☐ الفِصْح ☐ الأَضْحى ☐ الميلاد

٥- سَكَنَتْ سُعاد ريماوي في المَوصِل ________ .

☐ سَنة واحِدة ☐ ثَلاث سَنوات ☐ خَمس سَنوات

٦- رَجَعَتْ سُعاد إلى بَغدادَ حينَ كانتْ في سِنِّ ____________ .

☐ الثالِثة عَشْرة ☐ السابِعة عَشْرة ☐ الثامِنة عَشْرة

٧- تَدرُس سُعاد ____________ في جامِعة بَغداد.

☐ التِجارة ☐ الطِبّ ☐ اللُغَة الإنكليزيّة

٨- تَسكُن سُعاد ____________ .

☐ في شَقّة ☐ مَعَ أسرتِها ☐ في سَكَنِ الطالِبات

ب- اكْتُب «خطأ» أو «صواب» على الخَطّ ثُمَّ صحّح الجُمَل الخَطأ:

٩- تَحتَفِلُ الجزائرُ بِالأعْيادِ الإسلاميّةِ والمَسيحيّة.

١٠- يُحْتَفَل بِعيدِ الفِصْحِ في ٢٢ آذار.

١١- يَأكُلُ الأمريكيونَ ديك حَبَش في عيدِ الفِصْح.

١٢- تَحتَفِل كُلُّ الوِلاياتِ الأمريكيّة بِعيد مارتِن لوثَر كِنغ.

١٣- سُعاد أكبَر مِن إخوتِها الثَلاثة.

١٤- سَوفَ تَتَخرَّج سُعاد مِنَ الجامِعَة بَعد سَنة واحِدة.

تمرين ٥

المُحادَثة: في مَجموعات من اثنَيْن، صِف عيداً تَتَذَكَّره جَيِّداً. إليكَ بَعض الأفْكار الّتي قد تُفيدُكَ:

١- ماذا فَعَلْت في ذلِك اليَوْم؟

٢- ماذا حَدَثَ لَك في ذلِك اليَوْم؟

٣- مع مَن كُنْت؟

٤- عَمّا (عن + ماذا) تَكَلَّمْت مع عائلتك أو أصدِقائك؟

وفي حال أنّك لا تتذكّرُ العيدَ جيّداً، تَسْتَطيع أن تَحْكي قِصة خيالية تُقَلِّد فيها النَصَّ الرئيس في هذا الدَرْس وحاوِل أن تَسْتَخْدِمَ المُفرَداتَ الجَديدة فيها. وبَعد أن تَنْتَهي من التَمْرين، بَدِّل الأدوار ثُمّ احْكِ لأصدقائك ما فَهِمت من زَميلك.

تمرين ٦

أعِد تَرْتيبَ الكَلِمات في كُلّ مَجْموعة لِتُشَكِّل جُمَلاً مُفيدة:

١- يَحتَفِلُ - ميلادِهِ - بِعيدِ - أخوكَ - مَتى؟
٢- شَهر - أختي - آب - وُلِدَتْ - في
٣- جِدّاً - أستراليا - كَبيرةٌ - جَزيرةٌ
٤- في - إلى - الخَريف - هذِهِ - اِنتَقَلتُ - فَصْلِ - الشَقّة

تمرين ٧

أعِد تَرْتيبَ الجُمَل لِتُشَكِّل فِقْرة كامِلة. الجُمْلةُ الأولى في مَكانِها المُناسِب:

١- وُلِدَ مازِن المُدَرِّس في مَدينةِ حَلَب،
ثُمَّ رَجَعَ إلى حَلَب ودَرَسَ في جامِعَةِ حَلَبَ في السَنةِ الأولى.
بَعدَ ذلِكَ دَرَسَ في مَدرَسَةٍ ثانَويّةٍ في مَدينةِ دِمَشق.
يَقول مازِن إنّه سَوفَ يَرجِعُ إلى حَلَب حينَ يَتَخَرَّج.
دَرَسَ في مَدارِسِ حَلَبَ الابْتِدائيّةِ والمُتَوَسِّطة.
ثُمَّ اِنتَقَلَ إلى جامِعَة دِمَشق في السَنةِ الثانية.

تمرين ٨

المُحادَثة: اسْأل زُملاءك في الصفّ الأسئلة الآتية وبَعد أن تَنْتَهي من التَمرين، أخْبِر الأستاذ والأصدقاء ما عَلِمتَ مِنهُم.

اسأل زُملائك:

١- كَيْفَ تَحْتَفِل(ين) بِعيدِ ميلادِك؟
٢- كَيْفَ يَحْتَفِلُ المَسيحيونَ بِعيدِ الميلاد؟
٣- كَيْفَ يَحْتَفِلُ المُسْلِمونَ بِعيدِ الفِطْر؟
٤- كَيْفَ اِحْتَفَلْت بِعيدِ رأسِ السَّنة؟

تمرين ٩

الكِتابة: اُكْتُب فِقرة عن عيد أو مُناسَبة (festive event) مَذْكورة أو غَيْر مَذْكورة في هذا الدَرس وتَصِفها مُسْتَخْدِماً نَفْس الأُسْلوب الوارِد في النَص الرئيس. لا تَنْسَ أن تَذْكُر: في أي شَهْر من شُهور السَنة يَحْتَفِل بِها الناس، وكَيف ومَن يَحْتَفِل بِها. وإذا أردتَ، تَسْتَطيع أن تَقرأ قِصتَك على زُملائك في الصَفّ. وكَما فَعلْنا في تَمرين ٥، تَسْتَطيع أن تَكْتُب قِصة خياليّة غَيْر واقِعيّة إذا أرَدْت.

١ – الأسماء الخَمسة

العرض: عادةً، حين أقدّم الأسماء الخمسة، أذكر القصة الإنكليزية الشهيرة «جاك وشجرة الفاصولياء» التي يرجع أصلها إلى أكثر من ٥،٠٠٠ سنة، لأن فيها عملاق يلقي بضعة أبيات شعرية ذات الصلة بالأسماء الخمسة من حيث النطق على الأقل فيقول:

Fee-fi-fo-fum!

I smell the blood of an English-man.

فالبيت الأوّل عبارة عن تصريف الاسم ((فم)) في كل حالاته: في فا فو فم. وبما أنّ معظم الطلاّب في الغرب قد سمعوا وحفظوا هذا البيت، فنستطيع كأساتذة اللغة العربية أن نستغل هذه المعرفة كي نعلّق هذه المعلومات الجديدة بمعلوماتهم الذهنية القديمة وبالتالي نسهّل عملية الاستيعاب والفهم والحفظ عندهم.

لقد تَعَلَّمنا اسمَيْن من الأسماءِ الخَمْسة في الدُروس السابِقة ألا وهُما: أب وأخ. وفي هذا الباب، سَنُقَدِّم ذو (of, with, owner of) وهو نَفْس اسم الشَهرِ الّذي تَعَلَّمْناه في الدَرْسِ الحادي عشر ذو الحِجّة. ونَرى تَصْريفَه في السياق (شَهر ذي الحجة) حَيْثُ يَتَحوّل حَرف الواو إلى ياء، هَل تَعْلَم لِماذا؟

أي نَعم، لأنَّه المُضاف إليه الّذي نَعرِف جَيِّداً بأنّه يأتي في صيغةِ المَجْرور، وكَما هو الحال في الأسماءِ الخَمْسةِ الأخرى، نَسْتَخْدِمُ الواو والألِف والياء بَدلاً من الحَرَكات، الضَمّة والفَتْحة والكَسْرة.

وفي الجَدول أدناه، نَرى كُلَّ الأسماءِ الخَمْسة بِما فيها: حَمو (father-in-law) وفَم (mouth).

مَرفوع	أبو	أخو	ذو	فو	حَمو
مَنصوب	أبا	أخا	ذا	فا	حما
مَجرور	أبي	أخي	ذي	في	حمي

دَعْنا الآن نُراجِع الحالاتَ الثلاث: نَسْتَخْدِمَ المَرْفوع لِلفاعِل ولِلمُبْتَدأ والخَبَر. أمّا المَجْرور، فَنَسْتَخْدِمُه لِلاسم المَجرور والمُضاف إليه. وأخيراً، نَسْتَخْدِمُ المَنْصوب لِلمَفعول بِه وعِدّة سياقات أخرى سَنَتَعَلّمُها في مِشوارِنا (our journey) في تَعَلُّمِ اللُغة العَرَبيّة.

مُلاحَظة: في صيغةِ التأنيث، تأتي كَلِمة ذو بشَكْل ذات. وكَما تَرى في الجَدْوَل أدناه، لَها عِدّة أشْكال حَسَب وَظيفَتِها (*its function*) في السياق، ونُقَدِّم هُنا أشْكالَها المُخْتَلِفة في حالاتِ الرَفْع والنَصْب والجَرّ.

أشْكال ذو			
	المَرفوع	المَنصوب	المَجرور
المُثنّى المُذَكَّر	ذَوا	ذَوَيْ	ذَوَيْ
المُثنّى المؤنَّث	ذَواتا	ذَواتَيْ	ذَواتَيْ
جَمع المُذَكَّر	ذَوو	ذَوي	ذَوي
جَمع المؤنَّث	ذَواتُ	ذواتِ	ذَواتِ

مُلاحَظة: هُناك تَطابُق تامّ بَيْن الاسم وذو فهو يُرفَع بالواو ويُنصَب بالألف ويُجَرّ والياء كَما نَرى في الأمْثِلة الآتية:

١	رَجُلٌ ذو عِلْم	**حالة الرَفع**	*a man of knowledge*
٢	شاهَدتُ رَجُلاً ذا عِلْمٍ.	**حالة النَصْب**	*I saw a man of knowledge.*
٣	تَكَلَّمْتُ مَعَ رَجُلٍ ذي عِلْمٍ	**حالة الجَرّ**	*I spoke with a man of knowledge.*

تأتي كَلِمة ذو بِمَعنى صاحِب (possessor, owner) في صيغةِ الإضافة فَهو المُضاف والاسمُ الّذي يَليه، أي عِلْم في الأمْثِلة أعلاه، المُضاف إليه في حالةِ الجَرّ. قَد يُفيدُك أنْ تُفَكِّر به كَبَديل (as an alternative to) كَلِمة صاحِب وإذا اِسْتَبْدَلناه في الأمْثِلة أعلاه فَستَكون: ١_ رَجُلٌ صاحِبُ عِلْمٍ، و٢_ شاهَدتُ رَجُلاً صاحِبَ عِلْمٍ، و٣_ تَكَلَّمْتُ مَعَ رَجُلٍ صَاحِبِ عِلْمٍ وهي تَدُلّ على نَفْس المَعنى تماماً.

أمّا بِالنِسْبة إلى لام التَعريف (الـ + اسم)، فَهو يَدْخُل على الاسم ولا يُغيِّر المَعنى.
أُنْظُر إلى المِثال الآتي:

٤	رَجُلٌ ذو عِلْم	*a man of knowledge*	الرَجُلُ ذو عِلْمٍ	*the man of knowledge*
٥	امرأةٌ ذاتُ عِلْم	*a woman of knowledge*	المَرأةُ ذاتُ عِلْمٍ	*the woman of knowledge*

في الواقِع، إنَّ التَغَيُّر في شَكْل ذو في المِثال ٤ إلى ذات في المِثال ٥، سَبَبُه التَغيير من التَذكير إلى التأنيث.

تمرين ١٠

إِسْتِخْدامُ الأَسْماءِ الخَمسة: إِسْتِناداً إلى الجَداول المَعروضة في هذا الباب، أُكْتُب الشَكْل الصحيح لِلاسمِ المَوجود بَين القَوْسَيْن (paranthesis).

١- ما اسمُ (أب + كَ)؟ ____________
٢- إِشتَرَيتُ بَيْتاً (ذو) أربَعِ غُرَف. ____________
٣- (أخ + ها) طالِب في هذِهِ الجامِعَة. ____________
٤- (أب) أحْمَد رَجُلٌ مِن مَدينةِ دُبَيّ. ____________
٥- هَل هذِهِ السَيّارة لـ (أخ + ك)؟ ____________
٦- (ذو) الحِجّة اسْمُ شَهر مِن الأَشْهُرِ العَرَبيّة. ____________
٧- أَتَتْ سامية إلى هذِهِ الجامِعة لأنَّ (أخ + ها) يَدرُس فيها. ____________
٨- أينَ (أب + كِ) يا مَها؟ ____________

تمرين ١١

تَمرينُ المُشاهَدة: شاهِدوا الدَرْسَ الخامس عَشَر على الشابِكة.

المَشْهَدُ الأوَّل:

١- ارسُم دائرة حَولَ الأعيادِ الإسلاميّة واكْتُب خَطّاً تَحْتَ الأعيادِ المَسيحيّة

عيد الميلاد	عيد المَوْلِد النبَويّ
عيد رأْس السَنة الهِجْرِيَّة	عيد الفِصْح
عيد الفِطْر	عيد الأضْحى المُبارَك

٢- ما الأعيادُ الخاصّة بِسوريا؟ ________________

____

____

٣- ما العِباراتُ الخاصة بالمُناسِبات؟ ________________

____

____

المَشْهَدُ الثاني

٤- كَم يَوْماً يَحتَفِلُ المُسلِمون بِعيدِ الفِطْر وبِعيدِ الأضْحى المُبارَك؟ ________

____

٥- كَيفَ يَصومُ المُسلِمون في شَهر رَمَضان؟ ________________

____

٦- كَيفَ يُزَيِّنُ المَسيحيّون بُيوتَهُم لِعيدِ الميلاد؟ ________________

____

٧- ما الأعيادُ المُهِمّة في أمريكا؟ ________________

____

٢ – المَمْنوع مِن الصَرف Diptotes

لا يَجوز (it isn't permissible) أن تدْخُل على بعض الكَلِمات في اللُغة العربيّة الكَسرة إنما تَدْخُل عليها الضَمّة والفَتحة بَدلاً منها ونُسَمِّي هذه الكَلِمات المَمْنوع من الصَرْف. وقد وَرَدت (appeared) في النَصّ الرئيس كَلِمة من هذا النَوع أي مَكّةَ التي دَخَلَت عليها فَتْحة بَدلاً من الكَسرة المَفروضة لأنّها مَجْرورة بِحَرْفِ الجَرّ في. انْظُر إلى الجُملة من النَصّ في المثال ٦:

٦	ويَكونُ الحَجّ في مَكّةَ في السُعوديّة	حالة الجَرّ

كَذلِكَ، لا يَدْخُل على المَمنوع من الصَرف التَنوين في حالة النكرة (الأمْثِلة ٧ و٨ و٩) وتَدْخُل عليها الفَتْحة في حالتي النَصب والجَر (الأمثِلة ٨ و٩ و١١ و١٢). دَعْنا نَتَأمّل الكَلِمتَين دِمَشق وشَوارِع في الأمثِلة الآتية:

٧	مَرفوع	هذِهِ دِمَشقُ الفَيحاءُ	١٠	هذِهِ شَوارِعُ نَظيفةٌ.
٨	مَنصوب	وَصَلتُ دِمَشقَ الفَيحاءَ.	١١	أعرِفُ شَوارِعَ نَظيفةً.
٩	مَجرور	في دِمَشقَ الفَيحاءِ.	١٢	في شَوارِعَ نَظيفةٍ.

إنّ الاسم دِمَشق والجَمع شَوارِع مَمنوعَان من الصَرْف، لِذلِكَ تَدْخُل عليهما الفَتحة في حالتَي الرَفع والنَصب بَيْنما تَدْخُل على الصِفتَين نَظيفة والفَيحاء الحَرَكة المُناسِبة وَفْقاً لِلسياق.

مُلاحَظة: حين يَكون المَمنوع من الصَرْف مُعَرَّفاً بالإضافة أو لام التَعريف، فيُعْرَب مِثل الأسماء المَعَرَّبة. أنظُر إلى الأمثِلة ١٣ و١٤ و١٥:

١٣	مَرفوع	هذِهِ الشَوارِعُ النَظيفةُ.
١٤	مَنصوب	أعرِفُ الشَوارِعَ النَظيفةَ.
١٥	مَجرور	في الشَوارِعِ النَظيفةِ.

الخُلاصة

* الممنوعُ مِن الصرف لا يُنوَّن ويُنصَبُ ويُجَرُّ بِالفَتحة *

تمرين ١٢

المَمنوع من الصَرْف: وَرَدت سَبعة أسماء مَمنوعة من الصَرْف في النَصّ الرئيس، اكْتُبها على السَطرَين إلى الأسْفَل:

تمرين ١٣

في الجُمَل إلى الأسْفَل، أعرِب (provide short vowels) الكَلِمات الّتي لَيست مُعْرَبة.

١- دَرَسَتْ سامية في مَدارِس مِصْريَّة.

٢- في مَدينةِ الرِياضِ شَوارِع حَديثة.

٣- يَحُجُّ المُسلِمون إلى مَكَّة والمَدينة.

٤- ذَهَبنا في شَهر نيسان الماضي إلى لُبنان والأردُن بِالحافِلة.

فوانيس على سجاد

٣- الفِعْل المَبْني لِلمَجهول The Passive Voice

هُناكَ نَوعان من الفِعلِ العربيّ: الفِعْلُ المَبني لِلمعلوم الّذي نَعرِف من خِلالَه الفاعِل يَعني مَن فَعَل الفِعْل، مَثلاً:

١٦	كَتَبَ عُمَرُ القِصّةَ.	عُمَر = الفاعِل

مَن كَتَب القِصّة؟ عُمَرُ هو الّذي كَتَبَ القِصّة فَهو الفاعِل.
أمّا النَوع الآخَر فهو الفِعْلُ المَبني لِلمَجهول بِحَيثُ لا نَعرِف الفاعِل، على سَبيل المَثال:

١٧	كُتِبَت القِصّةُ.	كُتِبَت = فِعل مَبني لِلمَجهول

نَستَخدِمُ الفِعلَ المَبني لِلمَجهول حين لا نُريد أن نَذكُر الفاعِل. ونَستَطيع أن نُحَوِّل فِعلاً مُتَعَدّياً (transitive verb) إلى فِعل مَبني لِلمَجهول بِالطَريقةِ المَشروحة في البابِ الآتي:

آ- الفِعْل المَبْني لِلمَجهول: الفِعْل الماضي

إذا أرَدت أن تُحَوِّل فِعلاً ماضياً ثُلاثياً صَحيحاً (sound triliteral past-tense) إلى فِعل مَبني لِلمَجهول، فَعليكَ أن تَضُمّ أوّلَهُ وتَكسِر ما قَبل آخِره، مَثلاً:

فَعَلَ ← فُعِلَ

	المَبني لِلمَعلوم			المَبني لِلمَجهول	
١٨	وَلَدَ	*to give birth*	←	وُلِدَ	*was born*

لا نَقوم بِأي تَغييرات أخرى في الفِعلِ الماضي غير أن نَضُمّ أوّل حَرف ونَكسِرُ الحَرف قَبلَ الأخير.

العرض: حضّر فقرة قصيرة تتكاثر فيها الفعل المبني للمجهول، مثلاً:

«وُلِدتُ في مدينة تُسمى التفاحة الكبيرة في شهر كذا في سنة كذا. ويقال الذي وُلِدَ في هذا الشهر سيُعرَف بقوته العظيمة وذكائه العالي ويقال أيضاً إنه كُتِبَ عليه أن ينجح في الحياة.»

الممارسة: اسأل الطلاّب أسئلة عن الفقرة التي قرأتها لهم مركّزاً على استخدام الفعل المبني للمجهول. وعند نهاية هذا التمرين، اسألهم أسئلة بشأن حياتهم وتجاربهم، مثلاً:

«أين وُلِدت؟ (أو أين وُلِدَ أي فرد من عائلة الطالب)»
«ماذا يُقال عن مدينتك؟»
«ماذا تُسمّى مدينة باريس (أو أي مدينة لها لقب معروف)»
«متى كُتِبَ كتابُ «ألف ليلة وليلة»؟ (أو أي كتاب مشهور)»

التطبيق: في مجموعات من اثنين أو ثلاثة: اطلُب من الطلاّب أن يسألوا بعضهم بعضاً في أي شهر من السنة وُلِد وماذا يقال عن الشخص الذي وُلِد في ذاك الشهر، مثلاً:

«في أي شهر وُلِدت؟»
«ماذا يقال عن الشخص الذي وُلِدَ في ذاك الشهر؟»

اطلُب من الطلاّب أن يخبروا بما علموا من زملائهم. ساعد الطلاّب في التعبير عن بعض الصفات والسمات.

الفِعلُ الماضي الأجوَف

إنَّ الأفعالَ الّتي يَتَوَسّطُها حَرفُ العِلة (أي الواو أو الألف أو الياء)، نُسَمّيها الفِعل الأجوَف. إذا أرَدتَ أن تُحَوِّلَ الفِعل الّذي بوسطِهِ ألِف مِثل قال أو باع إلى فِعل مَبني لِلمَجهول، ، فتَتَحَوَّل الألف إلي ياء، مَثلاً:

	المَبني لِلمَعلوم			المَبني لِلمَجهول	
١٩	قالَ	to say	←	قِيلَ	was said
	باعَ	to sell	←	بِيعَ	was sold

الفِعلُ الماضي الناقِص

إنَّ الأفعالَ الّتي في آخِرِها حَرفُ العِلة (مِثل: سَمّى أو رَمى)، فَنَضُمّ أوّل حَرف ونَكسِر ما قبلَ الآخِر، لكِنَّ الكَسرة تُغيِّر الألِفَ المَقصورة إلي ياء، مَثلاً:

	المَبني لِلمَعلوم			المَبني لِلمَجهول	
٢٠	سَمّى	to name	←	سُمِّيَ	was named
	رَمى	to throw	←	رُمِيَ	was thrown

ب- الفِعْل المَبْني لِلمَجهول: الفِعْل المُضارِع

إذا أرَدتَ أن تُحَوِّل فِعلاً مُضارِعاً ثُلاثياً صَحيحاً (sound triliteral present-tense) إلى فِعل مَبني لِلمَجهول، فَعليكَ أن تَضُمّ أوّلَهُ وتَفتَح ما قَبل آخِره، مَثلاً:

يُفْعَلُ

	المَبني لِلمَعلوم			المَبني لِلمَجهول	
٢١	يَكتُبُ	to write	←	يُكتَبُ	is written

الفِعلُ المُضارِع المِثال

نَستَطيع أن نُحَوِّلَ الفِعلَ المُضارِع المَبني لِلمَعلوم الّذي يَبدأ بَحَرفِ العِلة الواو، مِثل وَلَد إلى فِعل مُضارِع مَبني لِلمَجهول بِضَمّ أوّله وفتَح ما قَبل آخِره وإضافة الواو الأصليّة:

	المَبني لِلمَعلوم			المَبني لِلمَجهول	
٢٢	يَلِدُ	is giving birth	←	يُولَدُ	is born

الفِعلُ المُضارِع الأجوَف

نَستطيع أن نُحَوِّل الفِعلَ المُضارِع المَبني لِلمَعلوم الّذي بِوَسطِه حَرف الواو، مِثل يَقولُ، إلى فِعل مُضارِع مَبني لِلمَجهول بِضَمّ أوّلِه وألْف (نُعطيه ألِفاً) ما قَبل آخِره، مَثَلاً:

	المَبني لِلمَعلوم			المَبني لِلمَجهول	
٢٣	يَقولُ	is saying	←	يُقالُ	it is said

الفِعلُ المُضارِع الناقِص

نَستَطيع أن نُحَوِّلَ الفِعلَ المُضارِع المَبني لِلمَعلوم الّذي يَنتَهي بحَرف الألِف أو الياء، مِثل يُسَمّي، إلى فِعل مُضارِع مَبني لِلمَجهول بِضَمّ أوّله وإضافة ألِف مَقصورة قَبل آخِره، مَثَلاً:

	المَبني لِلمَعلوم			المَبني لِلمَجهول	
٢٤	يُسَمّي	to name	←	يُسَمّى	to be named

ج- الفاعِل ونائِب الفاعِل

يُسَمّى نائبُ الفاعل لأنّه يَحلّ مَحَلَّ الفاعِل بَعد حَذفِه من الجُملة، وفي جُملة كَهذِه، لا نَعرِف مَن قام بِالعَمل فيها فيَصير الفاعِل مَجهولاً. إنّ نائبَ الفاعِل اسم مَرفوع ويأتي بَعد فِعل مَبني لِلمَجهول، انظُر إلى المِثال الآتي:

	المَبني لِلمَجهول	نائِب الفاعِل		
٢٥	تُسَمّى	مَدينةُ نيويورك	«التُفّاحَة الكَبيرة.»	The city of New York *is known as* the Big Apple

الخُلاصة

الفِعلُ الماضي المَبني لِلمَجهول

* نُحَوِّل الفِعلَ الماضي الثُلاثي الصَحيح المَبني لِلمَعلوم إلى المَبني لِلمَجهول بِضَمّ أوَّلِه وكَسر ما قَبل آخِره، ونَرى هذا في الوَزن | **فُعِلَ**

* **الفِعل الأجوَف** | قال ← قيلَ

* **الفِعل الناقِص** | أتى ← أُتِي

الفِعل المُضارِع المَبني لِلمَجهول

* نُحَوِّل الفِعلَ المُضارِع الثُلاثي الصَحيح المَبني لِلمَعلوم إلى المَبني لِلمَجهول بِضَمّ أوَّلِه وفَتح ما قَبل آخِره، ونَرى هذا في الوَزن | **يُفْعَلُ**

* **الفِعل المِثال** | يَلِدُ ← يُولَدُ

* **الفِعل الأجوَف** | يَبيعُ ← يُباعُ

* **الفِعل الناقِص** | يَرْمي ← يُرْمَى

الفاعِل ونائِبُ الفاعِل

* نُسَمّي الاسمَ الّذي يلي الفِعل المَبني لِلمَجهول نائِب الفاعِل وهو في حالةِ الرَفع لأنّه يحَلّ مَحَلَّ الفاعِل.

تمرين ١٤

اِستِخدامُ الفِعلِ المَبني لِلمَجهول: في الجُمَلِ الآتية، حَوِّل الفِعل المَبني لِلمَعلوم إلى فِعل مَبني لِلمَجهول وأعرِب (provide full voweling) الفِعل ونائب الفاعِل كَما تَرى في المِثال:

	المَبني لِلمَعلوم		الفِعل المَبني لِلمَجهول	نائِب الفاعِل	
مِثال	(كَتَبَ سامي) رِسالةً مِن باريس.	←	كُتِبَتْ	رِسالةٌ	مِن باريس.

١- (يَقولُ أصْدِقائي) إنَّ باريس مَدينةٌ جَميلة.

٢- (وَلَدَتْ أمّي) هالَةَ في بَيروت سَنَةَ ١٩٨٥.

٣- (يُسَمّي الأمريكيّونَ) وِلايَةَ نيويورك «إمباير ستيت.»

٤- (يَشرَبُ النّاسُ) القهوةَ بَعدَ الطعامِ عادةً.

٥- (سَمّى العَرَبُ) بَغدادَ «مَدينةَ السلام.»

تمرين ١٥

حَوِّلوا الفِعل المَبني لِلمَعلوم إلى فعل مبني للمجهول كما في المثال:

مثال: كَتَبَ سامي رِسالةً مِن باريس. ← كُتِبَتْ رِسالةٌ مِن باريس.

١- كَتَبَ الطالِبُ المُفرَداتِ الجَديدة. ← ________________ .

٢- شَرَحَ الأستاذُ دَرسَ القَواعِد. ← ________________ .

٣- سَمّى العَرَبُ بَغدادَ مَدينةَ السَلام. ← ________________ .

٤- يَشرَبُ الناسُ القَهوةَ بَعدَ الطعامِ عادةً. ← ________________ .

٥- وَلَدَتْ أمّي هالَةَ في بَيروت سَنَةَ ١٩٨٢. ← ________________ .

٦- يَقولُ أصْدِقائي: إنَّ باريس مَدينة جَميلة. ← ________________ .

حين أقدّم الأفعال الناقصة مثل (صار) و(كان)، أقول للطالب، «ليس عليك أن تبني مخططاً ذهنياً جديداً لهذه المجموعة من الأفعال على الرغم من أن الأسماء مختلفة (أي المبتدأ والخبر يختلف اسمياً عن الفاعل والمفعول به)، فأنها تتشابه من حيث حالة الرفع والنصب. على سبيل المثال: إذا قارننا الفعلين (كتب) و(صار) في جملتين فنرى التشابهات:»

«كتب الرجلُ كتاباً.»
«صار الرجلُ مشهوراً.»

أقول لهم الفرق بينهما يكمن في مفهوم (الحركة)، فالأفعال العادية تدل على حركة ما بينما الأفعال الناقصة تدل على التغيير في حالة ما. وقد تسهّل على الطالب هذه المعرفة في اكتساب هذه المجموعة الفعلية.

الحِناء أو الحنة على يد امرأة

٤ - الفِعْل الناقِص: صارَ

مع أنّ مَعنى الفِعل الناقِص صار (to become) يَختَلِف عن الفِعل الناقِص كانَ (was, were)، فأنّهُما يشاركان بِنَفْس الوَظيفة القَواعديّة ألا وهي أنّهُما يَنتَميان إلى نَفس المَجموعة: كانَ وأخواتُها الّتي تَدخُل على جُملة اسميّة فتَرفَع المُبتَدأ وتَنصُب الخَبَر، انظُر إلى المِثال ٢٤:

جُملة اسميّة		الفِعل الناقِص	المُبتَدأ	الخَبَر
٢٤ الطَقسُ جَيِّدٌ.	←	صارَ	الطَقسُ	جَيِّداً.

في المِثال ٢٤، نَرى أنّ المُبتَدأ مَرفوع بِالضمّة والخَبَر مَنصوب بِتَنوين الفَتح.

تمرين ١٦

استِخدام صارَ في الجُملِ الآتية: تَرجَم (translate) الجُمَلَ الآتية إلى اللُغةِ العَربيّة مُستَخدِماً الإعراب المُناسِب:

1. The sky was cloudy, but it cleared up (became clear).

____

2. The weather was cold in February, but it has become much warmer.

____

3. She was a girl, but she has become a woman.

____

4. The city turned (became) beautiful.

____

5. I am starting to understand what I watch in Arabic.

____

تمرين ١٧

آ- **أكْمِل الجُمَلَ الآتية بِالكَلِمةِ المُناسِبة وَفْق نَصِّ الاسْتِماع:**

١- اِسم زَوْجَةِ مَحْمود ____________ .

٢- مَحمود لَهُ صَديق أمريكيّ اِسمُهُ ____________ .

٣- يَعمَل صَديق مَحمود في مَدينةِ ____________ .

٤- تَخَرَّجَ مَحمود وصَديقُه مِنَ الجامِعَة في ____________ .

ب- **أجِب عن الأسئِلةِ الآتية وَفْق نَصِّ الاسْتِماع.**

٥- كَم مَدينة أمريكيّة زارَها مَحمود وزَوْجَتُه؟ ما هِيَ؟

____

٦- ماذا يَعمَل صَديق مَحمود؟

____

٧- في أيّ يَوم وشَهر احْتَفَلَ الأصْدِقاءُ الأربَعَة بِعيدِ الشُكْر؟

____

٨- ماذا أكلوا في عيدِ الشُكْر؟

____

ج- **اكْتُب «خطأ» أو «صواب» على الخَطّ ثُمَّ صحِّح الجُمَل الخَطأ:**

٩- يَسكُن مَحمود وزَوجَتُه في الوِلاياتِ المُتَّحِدَةِ الأمريكيّة.

____

١٠- كانَ مَحمود وصَديقُه طالِبَين في جامِعَة واحِدة.

____

١١- يَسكُن صَديق مَحمود في بَيت مَعَ زَوجَتِه كارلا.

____

١٢- أحَبَّتْ زَوجة مَحمود الطَعام كَثيراً في بَيت صَديق مَحمود.

____

المُفْرَدات

استمِع إلى المُفْرَدة بالعَرَبيّة ثم أعِد نُطْقَها مرّتين.

to celebrate .... اِحْتَفَلَ (يَحْتَفِلُ) اِحْتِفال بِـ (v.)
independence .... اِسْتِقلال (n., m.)
Islam .... إسلام (n., m.)
to move, to relocate.............. اِنتَقَلَ (ينتقِلُ) اِنْتِقال (v.)
country .... بَلَد ج بِلاد (n., m.)
to graduate .... تَخَرَّجَ (يتخرَّجُ) تَخَرُّج (v.)
education, upbringing .... تَرْبية (n., f.)
instruction, education .... تَعليم (n., m.)
revolution .... ثَوْرة ج ثَورات (n., f.)
pilgrimage .... حَجّ (n., m.)
dessert, sweets. .... حَلْوى ج حَلَوِيات (n., f.)
special, particular (to) .... خاصّ (adj.)
cock, rooster. .... ديك ج دِيَكة (n., m.)
turkey .... ديك حَبَش (n., m.)
with, of, owner of. .... ذو ج ذَوو (n., m.)
head .... رأس ج رُؤوس (n., m.)
Ramadan, the month of fasting .... رَمَضان (n., m.)
to adorn, to decorate .... زَيَّنَ (يُزَيِّنُ) تزيين (v.)
square, courtyard .... ساحة ج ساحات (n., f.)
to save, to protect .... سَلَّمَ (يُسَلِّمُ) تَسْليم (v.)
age of a person .... سِنّ (n., m.)
to become .... صارَ (يَصيرُ) صَيْر، صَيْرورة، مَصير (v.)
to fast. .... صامَ (يَصومُ) صَوْم (v.)
to pray, to bless .... صَلّى (يُصَلّي) (v.)
to manufacture, to make............ صَنَعَ (يَصنَعُ) صِناعة (v.)
food .... طَعام ج أطْعِمة (n., m.)

phrase . . . . (n., f.) عِبارة ج عِبارات

to be off from work . . . . (v.) عَطَّلَ (يَعَطِّلُ) تَعْطيل

Feast of Immolation/sacrifice (after Haj), Greater Bairam . . (n., m.) عيدُ الأَضْحى

Thanksgiving . . . . (n., m.) عيدُ الشُكْرِ

Easter . . . . (n., m.) عيدُ الفِصْحِ

feast of breaking the Ramadan fast . . . . (n., m.) عيدُ الفِطْرِ

Christmas . . . . (n., m.) عيدُ الميلاد

dawn, daybreak . . . . (n., m.) فَجْر

pie . . . . (n., f.) فَطيرة ج فَطائِر

pumpkin . . . . (n., m.) قَرْع

blessed . . . . (n., m.) مُبارَك

intermediate . . . . (adj., m.) مُتَوَسِّط

director, manager . . . . (n., m.) مُدير ج مُدَراء

Muslim, one of the Islamic faith . . . . . (n., m.) مُسْلِم ج مُسْلِمون

Christ . . . . (n., m.) المَسيح

teacher . . . . (active participle) مُعَلِّم ج مُعَلِّمون

information . . . . (n., f.) مَعلومة ج مَعلومات

sunset . . . . (n., m.) مَغْرِب

occasion . . . . (n., f.) مُناسَبة ج مُناسَبات

region . . . . (n., f.) مِنْطَقة ج مَناطِق

birthday, birthplace . . . . (n., m.) مَوْلِد

birth, birthday . . . . (n., m.) ميلاد ج مَواليد

prophet . . . . (n., m.) نَبيّ ج أَنْبياء

to congratulate, to felicitate (on the occasion of) (v.) هَنَّأَ (يُهَنِّئُ) تَهنئة

to be born (passive) . . . . (v.) وُلِدَ (يولَدُ) وِلادة / مَوْلِد

الدرس السادس عشر

أهداف الدرس

- وَصْف شَخصِيّات وأنشِطة وأحداث صارَت في الماضي
- أسرارُ اللُغة العَرَبيّة: أوزانُ الفِعلِ المَزيد
- مُراجَعةُ الأعدادِ التَرتيبيّة

رُكنُ المُفْرَداتِ الجَديدة

قامَ (يَقومُ) قِيام	to occur; to start (war)
اِنْتَخَبَ (يَنْتَخِبُ) اِنْتِخاب	to elect
اِغْتال (يَغتالُ) اِغتيال	to assassinate
تُوُفِّيَ	to pass away
التَمييز العُنْصُريّ	discrimination
دَخَلَ (يَدْخُلُ) دُخول	to enter
نُفِيَ (يُنْفى) نَفْي	to be sent into exile

تمرين ١

اِختَر الكَلِمة الّتي لا تُناسِب باقي الكَلِمات في كُلّ مَجموعة وبيِّن السَبَب:

١-	وُلِدَ	نُفِيَ	تُوفِّيَ	اُغْتيلَ
٢-	شاعِر	جَيْش	ضابِط	قائِد
٣-	أمير	زَعيم	رَئيس	مُحامٍ
٤-	كاتِب	حَصَلَ	قِسّيس	خَطيب
٥-	مَدينة	قَرْية	بَلْدة	فَلْسَفة

تمرين ٢

وافِقْ بَيْنَ الكَلِمات في العَمودَين.

١-	حَرْب		خَرَجَ
٢-	كِتاب		الأندَلُس
٣-	تُوُفِّيَ		مَلِك
٤-	قانون		اجْتِماع
٥-	غَرْناطة		سَلام
٦-	دَخَلَ		مُقَدِّمة
٧-	رَئيس		وُلِدَ
			مُحامٍ

تمرين ٣

أكْمِل الجُمَلَ الآتية بِكَلِمات مُناسِبة.

١- والت ويتمان ____________ أمريكيّ مَشْهور.

☐ شاعِر ☐ زَعيم ☐ رَئيس

٢- ____________ باراك أوباما رئيساً مَرَّتَين.

☐ تُوُفِّيَ ☐ وُلِدَ ☐ أُنْتُخِبَ

٣- أفلاطون أشْهَر ____________ في العالَم. * Plato

☐ مَلِك ☐ فَيْلَسوف ☐ مُحامٍ

٤- مَتى صارَتْ إليزابث الثانية ____________ بريطانيا؟

☐ قَرية ☐ جائِزة ☐ مَلِكَة

٥- فِرساي بَلْدَة صَغيرة ____________ باريس.

☐ قُرْب ☐ حَرْب ☐ جَيْش

٦- كانَ هوميروس أوَّل ____________ كَتَبَ التاريخ. * Homer

☐ مُؤَرِّخ ☐ قِسّيس ☐ قائِد

تمرين ٤

أعِد تَرْتيب الكَلِمات في كُلّ مَجْموعة لِتُشَكِّل جُمَلاً مُفيدة:

١- شاعِرةً - كانَتْ - إميلي دِكِنسَن - مَشْهورةً - أمريكيّةً

______

٢- مَكْتَبِ - أختي - مُحامٍ - تَخَرَّجَتْ - عَمِلَتْ - مِنَ - في - ثُمَّ - الجامِعةِ

______

٣- الأمريكيّةِ - مَرَّتَيْنِ - بِل كلنتَن - المُتَّحِدةِ - رَئيساً - أُنْتُخِبَ - لِلوِلاياتِ

______

٤- سَنَةَ - كِنيدي - في - دالاس - أُغْتيلَ - بِمَدينةِ - ١٩٦٣ - الرَّئيسُ

______

تمرين ٥

أعِد تَرْتيب الجُمَل لِتُشَكِّل فِقْرة كامِلة. الجُمْلة الأولى في مَكانِها المُناسِب:

١- مُحَمَّد بن موسى الخوارِزمي عالِم رِياضِيّات مُسْلِم مَشْهور.

وكَتَبَ كِتاباً في حِسابِ الجَبْر وتُرْجِمَ إلى اللاتينيّة.

عَرَفَتْ أوروبا عِلْمَ الجَبْرِ مِن هذا الكِتاب.

تُوُفِّيَ الخُوارِزمي سَنَةَ ٨٤٠ ميلاديّة.

كَلِمةُ *algorithm* مأخوذة مِن اسْمِه.

وكَتَبَ أَيْضاً عَنِ الصِفْر في الرِياضيّات.

وُلِدَ الخُوارِزمي في مَدينة خُوارِزم.

أَسَّسَ الخُوارِزمي عِلْمَ الجَبْر.

شَخصيّات أمريكيّة وعَرَبيّة

جورج واشنِطَن
١٧٣٢-١٧٩٩

هُوَ أوّل رَئيس لِلوِلاياتِ المُتَّحِدةِ الأمريكيّة. وُلِدَ في وِلاية فِرجينيا وتُوُفِّيَ فيها. كان قائِدَ الجَيش في الثَّوْرةِ الأمريكيّة وحارَبَ البِريطانيّين بَينَ سَنتَيْ ١٧٧٦ و١٧٨١. صار رَئيسَ الجُمهوريّة في سَنَةِ ١٧٨٩ وأُنْتُخِبَ رَئيساً مَرّةً ثانِيّةً في ١٧٩٣، لكِنَّهُ رَفَضَ في المَرّةِ الثالِثة ورَجَعَ إلى دارِه في «ماونت ڤِرنَن» في فِرجينيا في سَنةِ ١٧٩٧ حَيْثُ تُوُفِّيَ بَعدَ سَنَتَيْن.

إبراهام لِنكَن
١٨٠٩-١٨٦٥

هُوَ رَئيسُ الجُمْهوريَّةِ الأمريكيُّ السادِس عَشَر. وُلِدَ في وِلايَة كِنتكي سَنةَ ١٨٠٩. اِنتَقَلَ إلى وِلاية إلينوي في سَنة ١٨٣١. دَرَسَ لِنكَن القانون، وفي سَنةِ ١٨٣٦ صار مُحامِياً ثُمَّ صار رَئيسَ الجُمْهوريَّة في سَنةِ ١٨٦٠. بعدَ ذلِك قامَت الحَربُ الأهْليّةُ الأمريكيّة. أُنْتُخِبَ مَرّةً ثانيةً في سَنةِ ١٨٦٤. أُغْتيلَ إبراهام لِنكَن في واشِنطَن العاصِمة في شَهر نيسانَ سَنةَ ١٨٦٥.

العرض: قدّم المفردات الرئيسة كلمة كلمة واكتبها على السبورة وأنت تقولها بصوت عالٍ وتستخدمها في سياق. قدّم شخصية تاريخية بارزة غير موجودة في هذا الدرس يمكن أن تكون شخصية عربية أو أمريكية. تأكّد من استخدام صور عديدة كي تدب فيها الحياة.

الممارسة: اطلب من الطلاب أن يختاروا شخصية أو شخصيتين بارزتين غير موجودتين في هذا الدرس، ثمّ اطلب منهم أن يفكروا في الشخصية المختارة واكتب سيرتها مستقاة من أقوال الطلاب من حيث خلفيتها وأنشطتها ومساهماتها المهمة إلخ. من الممكن أن تقدّم بعض المفردات الإضافية حسب حاجات الطلاب. اكتب على السبورة بعض الأسئلة التي قد تساعد فتح الموضوع لهم، مثل:

«متى وُلِدَ جون كِنيدي؟ أين وُلِد؟»
«أين درس وماذا درس؟»
«هل هو من أسرة غنية أم فقيرة؟»
«ماذا عمل قبل أن يكون رئيساً؟»
«هل له إخوة وأخوات؟ هل تعرف بعضهم؟»
«ما اسم زوجته؟»
«من حارب الرئيس كنيدي؟»
«هل توفي أم اغتيل؟»
«أين اغتيل؟»
«ما اسم الرجل الذي اغتاله؟»
«كم كان عمر الرئيس كنيدي حين اغتيل؟»

التطبيق: الممارسة الجماعية: قسم الصف إلى مجموعات من اثنين أو ثلاثة واطلب منهم أن يكتبوا سيرة شخصية أو عدة شخصيات مثلما وردت في هذا الدرس. اطلب من كل مجموعة أن تخبر المجموعات الأخرى بما حصلت عليه من المعلومات.

مارتِن لوثَر كِنغ
١٩٢٩-١٩٦٨

زَعيم أمريكيّ أسْوَد. وُلِدَ في مَدينة أتلانتا في وِلاية جورجة. كان قِسّيساً وخَطيباً وحارَبَ التَميزَ العُنْصُريّ. حَصَلَ على جائِزَة نوبِل لِلسَلام سَنَةَ ١٩٦٤. أُغْتيلَ في مَدينة مِمْفِس في وِلاية تِنيسي سَنَةَ ١٩٦٨. تَحتَفِلُ مُعظَمُ الوِلاياتِ الأمريكيّة بِعيد مارتِن لوثَر كِنغ في ثالِث يَوْم إثنين مِن شَهر كانونَ الثاني.

عَبدُ القادِر الجَزائِري
١٨٠٧-١٨٨٣

أمير وزَعيم جَزائِريّ. وُلِدَ في قَرية قُرْب «وَهْران» في الجَزائِر. حينَ دَخَلَتْ فَرَنسا الجَزائِر في سَنَةِ ١٨٤٣ حارَبَ الأمير عَبدُ القادِرِ الفَرَنسيّين خَمسَ عَشْرَة سَنة ثُمَّ نُفِيَ إلى طولون. وفي سَنَة ١٨٦٨ انتقَلَ إلى دِمَشق حَيْثُ سَكَنَ وتُوُفِّيَ فيها في سَنَة ١٨٨٣. كانَ الأمير عَبدُ القادِر كاتِباً وشاعِراً أيْضاً.

يوسُف العَظْمة
١٨٨٤-١٩٢٠

قائِد سوريّ وُلِدَ في مَدينة دِمَشق في سَنَةِ ١٨٨٤. كان ضابِطاً في الجَيْشِ العُثْمانيّ ثُمَّ صار ضابِطاً في الجَيْشِ السوريّ. حين دَخَلَ الفَرَنسيّون سوريا في سَنَةِ ١٩٢٠ كان وَزيرَ الدِفاع وخَرَجَ على رَأْس جَيْش صَغير وحارَبَهُم في «مَيْسَلون» قُرْب دِمَشق واسْتُشْهِدَ هُناكَ.

جَمال عَبْدُ الناصِر

١٩١٨-١٩٧٠

زَعيم عَرَبيّ مِن مِصر وُلِدَ في قَرية «بَني مُرّ» قُرْب مَدينة «أسْيوط» في مِصر. انتَقَلَ إلى القاهِرة وهُوَ في سِنِّ الثامِنة وسَكَن مَعَ عَمِّهِ خَليل ودَرَس بِها ثُمَّ بِالإسْكَندَريَّة. دَرَس بِالكُلِّيَّةِ الحَربيّة وتَخرَّج مِنها وصار ضابِطاً بِالجَيْشِ المِصْريّ. حارَبَ في فِلَسطين سَنَةَ ١٩٤٨ حَيْثُ جُرِحَ في الحَرْب. في سَنَة ١٩٥٢ قام بِثَوْرة على المَلِك وصارَتْ مِصْر جُمْهوريّة. صار رَئيسَ الجُمْهوريّةِ المِصْريّة في سَنةِ ١٩٥٦ ثُمَّ رَئيسَ الجُمْهوريّةِ العَرَبِيَّةِ المُتَّحِدة (مِصرَ وسوريا) في سَنَةِ ١٩٥٨. تُوُفِّيَ بِالقاهِرة في سَنَةِ ١٩٧٠.

عَبدُ الرَحْمن بن خَلْدون

١٣٣٢-١٤٠٦

مُؤَرِّخ وفَيْلَسوف وعالِم اجتِماع عَرَبِيّ. وُلِدَ في تونِس وتُوُفِّيَ بِالقاهِرة. كَتَبَ كُتُباً في التاريخ والاجْتِماع والفَلْسَفَة والأدَب. أَسَّسَ عِلْمَ الاجْتِماع في مُقَدِمَتِه المَشْهورة لِكِتابِهِ «العِبَر.» عَمِل وسَكَن في مَدينة غَرناطَة في الأندَلُس وفي فاس في المَغرِب وفي تِلمسان في الجَزائِر وفي القاهِرة في مِصْر حَيْثُ دَرَّس في الجامِعِ الأَزْهَر.

تمرين ٦

آ - **أكْمِل الجُمَلَ الآتية بِكَلِمات مُناسِبة وَفْق نُصوصِ القِراءة.**

١- تُوُفِّيَ الأمير عَبْد القادِر الجَزائِريّ في سَنَة ____________ .

☐ ١٨٤٣ ☐ ١٨٦٨ ☐ ١٨٨٣

٢- كان يوسُف العَظْمة ضابِطاً في الجَيْشِ ____________.

☐ العُثمانيّ ☐ الفَرَنسيّ ☐ الجَزائِريّ

٣- دَرَس جَمال عَبد الناصِر ____________ .

☐ بِجامِعَةِ القاهِرة ☐ بِالجَيْشِ المِصْريّ ☐ بِالكُلِّيَّةِ الحَرْبيّة

٤- أسَّس ابنُ خَلدون عِلْمَ ____________ .

☐ الاجْتِماع ☐ الفَلْسَفَة ☐ التاريخ

٥- صار جورج واشِنطَن رَئيساً ____________ .

☐ مَرَّةً واحِدة ☐ مَرَّتَيْن ☐ ثَلاث مَرّات

٦- أُنْتُخِبَ إبراهام لِنكَن رَئيساً لِلوِلاياتِ المُتَّحِدة أوَّل مَرّة في سَنَة ____________ .

☐ ١٨٣٦ ☐ ١٨٦٠ ☐ ١٨٦٤

٧- حَصَل مارتِن لوثَر كِنغ على جائِزَة نوبِل لِلسلامِ في سَنَة ____________ .

☐ ١٩٦٠ ☐ ١٩٦٤ ☐ ١٩٦٨

ب- **أكْمِل الجُمَلَ الآتية بِكَلِمات مُناسِبة وَفْق نُصوصِ القِراءة.**

٨- نُفِيَ الأمير عَبد القادِرِ الجَزائِريّ إلى ____________.

٩- حارَب يوسُف العَظْمة الفَرَنسِيّينَ في ____________ .

١٠- كان ____________ رَئيسَ الجُمْهوريّةِ العَرَبيّةِ المُتَّحِدة.

١١- دَرَّس ____________ في الجامِعِ الأزْهَر.

١٢- وُلِدَ ____________ في سَنَة ١٧٣٢.

١٣- صار ____________ مُحامِياً في سَنَة ١٨٣٦.

١٤- حارَب مارتِن لوثَر كِنغ ____________ .

ج- **اكْتُب ((خطأ)) أو ((صواب)) على السَطْر ثُمَّ صحِّح الجُمَل الخَطأ:**

١٥- سَكَنَ الأمير عَبد القادِر الجزائِريّ مَدينة دِمَشق بَعد سَنَة ١٨٦٨ .

١٦- كان يوسُف العَظْمة رَئيس سورية حين دَخَلَها الفَرَنسيّون.

١٧- وُلِدَ يوسُف العَظْمة في دِمَشق سَنَة ١٨٨٤ .

١٨- حارَب جَمال عَبد الناصِر البريطانيّين في مِصْر.

١٩- كان ابن خَلدون شاعِراً.

٢٠- تُوُفِّيَ جورج واشِنطَن في مَدينة واشِنطَن.

٢١- قامَت الحَرْبُ الأهْليّةُ الأمريكيّة قَبْلَ سَنَةِ ١٨٦٠ .

٢٢- وُلِدَ مارتِن لوثَر كِنغ في مَدينة مِمفِس.

تمرين ٧

نُبذة (a summary) **عن حياة شَخصيّة تاريخية الأكثر شيوعاً وعشرون سؤالاً:** اختَر شَخصيّة تاريخيَة تَجِدُها مُثيرة واكتُب فِقرة عن حياتها. حاوِل أن تُقَلِّد أُسلوب النُصوص الرئيسة في هذا الدَرس. ابحَث في الشابِكة عن مَعلوماتِ الشَخصيّة الّتي اختَرتها.

وبَعد أن تَنتَهي من الكِتابة، اِلعَب لُعبَةَ الشَخصيّة (عِشرون سؤالاً) مع صَديقك أو مَجموعة من الأصدِقاء في غُرفةِ الصَفّ كي تَرى إذا استَطاع أن يَحزَر (guess) شَخصيّتَك المُختارة. بالمُناسَبة، كُلّ الأسئِلة والإجوِبة يَجِب أن تَكون بِالعَرَبيَة. طَبعاً، بَعضُ الأسِئلة غَير مَسموحة في اللُعبة مِثل: (ما اسم الشَخصية، أو مَن هو؟).

تمرين ٨

المُحادَثة: اِسأل صَديقك ثَلاثة أو أربَعة من الأسئلة الآتية:

١- أعطِني اِسم طالِب تَعرِفُه صار رئيس صَفِّه بالمَدرَسة الثانوية.

٢- مَن تَعرِف مِن الفلاسِفة؟

٣- هل في أسرتِك مُحام؟

٤- مَن مِنَ الشَخصيّات السياسية كانوا ضُبّاطاً في الجَيش؟

٥- مِن مِن أصدقائك دَرَس أو يَدرُسُ القانون؟

٦- اعطِني اسم كاتِبَين أمريكيَّين.

٧- أعطِني اسم شاعِرة واسم شاعِر.

٨- مِن مِن الناس الّذين تَعرِفُهُم لَهُ شَخصيّة قَويّة؟

والآن، أخبِر الأستاذ ما عَلِمت من أصدقائك في الصَفّ.

تمرين ٩

تَمرينُ المُشاهَدة: شاهِدوا الدَرْسَ السادس عَشَر على الشابِكة.

المَشْهَدُ الأوَّل

١- مَن هو عَبد القادِر الجَزائري وماذا فَعَل؟ ______

______

______

٢- ماذا قال ستيف عن جَمال عَبد الناصِر؟ ______

______

٣- أيّ عِلم أسَّسَهُ ابن خَلدون؟ ______

______

٤- لماذا يَستطيع ستيف أن يَتكَلَّمَ اللغةَ العربيَّة جَيِّداً؟ ______

______

المَشْهَدُ الثاني

١- ما أنواعُ العَصير لَدى أبي سمير؟ ______

______

______

٢- ماذا طَلَب مايكل؟ ______

٣- كَم دَفَع كُل من مايكل وسامِر وستيف؟ ______

______

مدرسة عربية في القرن التاسع عشر

١ – أسرار اللُغة العَرَبيّة: أوزان الفِعْل المَزيد
Secrets of the Language: Forms of the Arabic Verb

في الحِقيقة، قَد يَكون هذا الباب أكثَر الأبواب فائدةً في هذا الكِتاب من حَيثُ فَهم اللغُة العربيّة والطَريقة المِثاليّة لِاستِخدامِها كِتابيّاً وشَفَهياً (orally). لِماذا؟ فإذا فَهِمتَ أوزانَ الفِعل المَزيد فَهماً سَليماً واستَوعِبتَها حَقّ الاستِيعاب (comprehension)، فَسَوف يَتَبَيَّن لَك نِظامُ اللُغةِ العَربيّة وتَرتيبُها وتَركيبُها. فَستَتَعَلَّمُ الاِستِخدامَ الصَحيح لِهذِه المَعرِفة كي تَستَنتِج (deduce) مَعنى الكَلام وتُوَلِّدَه (generate)، وبِذلِكَ لا يَنقَطِع سَيلُ الكَلِمات والمَعاني الّتي نَستَطيع اِشتِقاقها (derive it) من الجَذر (انظُر الصَفحة ٣٤٤).

هُناكَ نَوعان من الفِعل: المُجَرَّد والمَزيد.

الفِعلُ المُجَرَّد

يَتأَلّفُ الفِعلُ المُجَرَّد من الحَدِّ الأدنى من الأحرُف، مِثل: سَكَنَ. فإذا سَقَط أي حَرف من حروفِه الثلاثة الأصليّة، فَلَم يعُدْ يَدُلّ على مَعنى الفِعل.

الفِعلُ المَزيد

إذا زِدنا حَرفاً على الجَذر، فَيدُلّ على مَعنى مُرتَبِط بالمَعنى الأصليّ، مَثَلاً، إذا زِدنا ميماً في أوّل الفِعل سَكَن، فَيُصبِح مَسْكَن أي مَكان السَكن.

	الفِعل المُجَرّد					ميم المَكان	
١	سَكَنَ	to reside	+	مـَ	←	مَسْكَن	*place of residence*

وإذا زِدنا ألَفاً بعد حَرفِه الأوّل فَيُصبِح ساكِن أي المُقيم وهو اسم فاعِل لسَكَن. ونُسَمّي الأفعالَ الّتي فيها أحرُف زيادة: الفِعل المَزيد.

	الفِعل المُجَرّد					اسم الفاعِل	
٢	سَكَنَ	to reside	+	ا	←	ساكِن	*resident*

اطلب من الطلاب قراءة هذا الباب بإمعان واهتمام قبل المجيء إلى الصف. قدم لهم أمثلة عديدة من أوزان الفعل المزيد كي تدعم المفاهيم المقدمة هنا. إذا سأل طالب عن أهمية أوزان الفعل المزيد، فقد تقول له إن معرفتها تسمح لك بأن تقوم بـ ١_ خلق كلمات جديدة من وضع جذر جديد في الأوزان المختلفة الأمر الذي يوفر لهم ما يعادل ٩٠ شكل من أشكال الجذر، ٢_ استخدام الكلمة المناسبة في السياق المناسب لأنه يفهم دلالاتها الدقيقة لفعل ما و٣_ استنتاج معاني كلمات مجهولة من معرفة معاني الأوزان ودلالاتها، و٤_ التمكن من استنتاج معنى جذر مجهول من معرفة معاني الأوزان ودلالاتها، و٥_ تسهيل حفظ المفردات الجديدة على أساس معرفة الأوزان.

إليكم بعض المراجع التعليمية التي قد تجدها مفيدة في الصف: Wright's *A Grammar of the Arabic Language*, Wehr's *Dictionary of Modern Written Arabic*, and *Using Arabic* by Alosh.

لهذا الدرس بالذات، يستحسن أن يُحضِر الطلاب قاموسهم إلى الصف. وقد تودّ أن تعرض لهم صورة لصفحة مأخوذة من القاموس كي تشرح لهم استخدامه.

حين تقدّم لهم الأوزان، تأكّد أن تشرح لهم العدد الروماني جَنب مع أوزان الفعل المزيد.

أوزان الفِعل العشرة

I	II	III	IV	V	VI	VII	VIII	X
سَكَنَ	دَرَّسَ	حارَبَ	أرادَ	تَكَلَّمَ	تَفاضَلَ	اِنْكَسَرَ	اِحْتَفَلَ	اِسْتَخْدَمَ

على الرَغم من أنّ هذه الأفعال كُلَّها في صيغةِ المُذَكَّرِ الغائب، فأنّها تَتَنوّع (vary) في الوَزن، وهذا من خَصائص (characteristics) الصَرف العَرَبيّ (Arabic morphology). لاحِظ في الجَدوَل أعلاه أنّ الفِعل يَصير أكبَر وأطوَل مع التَقَدُّم في الرَقم. ولِكُلّ وَزن من هذه الأوزان، مَعنى خاصّ بِهِ وتَختَلِف وَظيفتُه اختِلافاً بسيطاً تارةً وكبيراً تارةً حَسَب السِياق والجَذر.

في هذا الباب وَصف دِقيق لِلميزان الصَرفيّ (morphological patterns) مِمّا سَيُعطيك خَريطة طَريق (a road map) لإدراكِ القُدرة (ability) على استِخدام مَعنى الكَلِماتِ الدَقيق.

هذا، وإنّ مَعرِفة أوزانِ الفِعلِ المَزيد لا تُمَكِّنُك من تَحديد نَوعِ الكلمة ووَظيفتِها فَحسبُ، بَل تُسَهِّل عَمليّةَ البَحث عن الكَلِمات في القاموس، لأنَّ الكلمات مُرتّبة (are ordered) في مُعظَمِ القَواميس المُعاصِرة حَسَب جَذرِها، غَير القَواميس التي تَترَتَّب الكَلِمات فيها حَسَب تَرتيب حُروف الهِجاء (alphabetical order) وخَير مِثال على ذلِكَ قاموس المَورِد من تأليف مُنير البَعلبَكيّ.

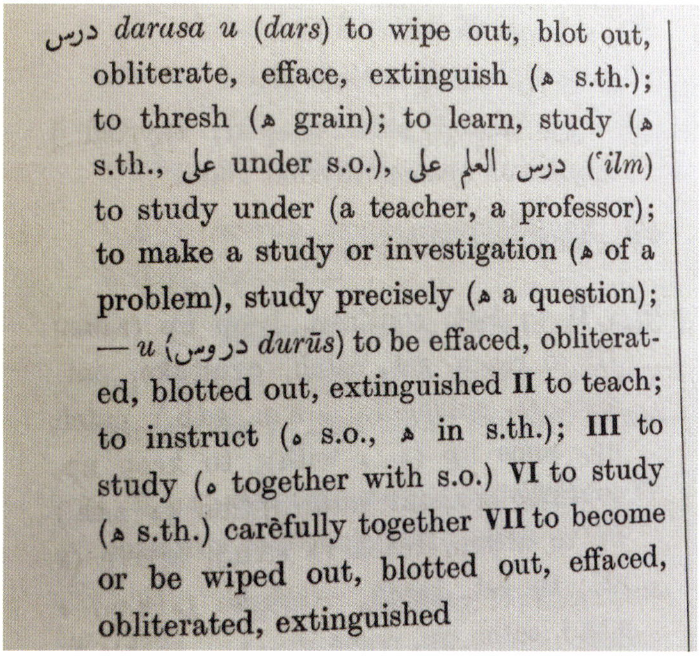
درس *darasa* u (*dars*) to wipe out, blot out, obliterate, efface, extinguish (ه s.th.); to thresh (ه grain); to learn, study (ه s.th., على under s.o.), درس العلم على (*ʿilm*) to study under (a teacher, a professor); to make a study or investigation (ه of a problem), study precisely (ه a question); — *u* (دروس *durūs*) to be effaced, obliterated, blotted out, extinguished **II** to teach; to instruct (ه s.o., ه in s.th.); **III** to study (ه together with s.o.) **VI** to study (ه s.th.) carefully together **VII** to become or be wiped out, blotted out, effaced, obliterated, extinguished

تأمّل معنا فِعل دَرَس كَما وَرَد في قاموس Hans Wehr ولاحِظ كَيف يَتَغيّر مَعناه في الأوزان المُختَلِفة

ممارسة استخدام القاموس:

الاسم: اختر حوالي عشر كلمات يجب على الطلاب البحث عنها في القاموس (أو المُعجَم). اطلب منهم أن يبحثوا عن الجذر والمصدر واسم الفاعل واسم المفعول.

الفعل: اطلب من الطلاب البحث عن حوالي خمسة أفعال وتحديد الجذر وتقديم بعض أوزانها. حاول قدر الإمكان أن تختار الأفعال التي تظهر بوضوح مفاهيم الأوزان كما وردت في هذا الدرس.

٢- أوزان الفِعْل المَزيد: مَعانيُها ودلالاتُها

Patterns and the Root System

يَتألّف الجَذر الأساسيّ من ثَلاثة حُروف وهي بِدَورِها تُمَثِّل الحُروفَ الثلاثة في الفِعل العَرَبيّ المُجَرَّد (أي الفِعل الثُلاثيّ). وكَما ذَكَرنا في الدَرس الحادي عشر (الباب الخامِس) تُستَخدَم الحُروف الفاء والعين واللام نَموذجاً (as a model) لِتَحديد وَزن الفِعل أو اِشتِقاق كَلِمات منه.

وفي هذا النَموذِج، يُمَثِّل حَرف الفاء أوّل حُروف الكَلِمة والعَين ثاني حُروف الكَلِمة واللام ثالِث حُروف الكَلِمة وآخِرَها. إذا أخَذنا الفِعل سَكَن مِثالاً فَسَنَجِد أنَّ وَزنَها فَعَل بِحَيثُ كُلّ حَرَكات النَموذِج تَبقى كَما هي في الفِعل أي حَرفُ السين مَفتوح وكَذلِك حرفُ الكاف مفتوح كَما نَرى في المِثال ٣.

٣	سَكَن	←	فَعَل

وإذا دَخلَت ضَمّة على الحَرف الثاني في الفِعل مِثل كَبُر، فَستَصير العَين في النَموذِج مَضمومة (المثِال ٤)

٤	كَبُر	←	فَعُل

وإذا دَخلَت كَسرة على الحَرف الثاني في فِعل مِثل فَهِم، فَستَصير العَين في النَموذِج مَكسورة (المِثال ٥).

٥	فَهِم	←	فَعِل

وإذا دَخَل على الفِعل المُجَرَّد أي حَرف إضافيّ، فَسيَظهَر في النَموذَج أيضاً. دَعنا نَتَأمّل الجَدوَل أدناه كي نَفهَم كَيفية قُبول النَموذَج الأحرُف الإضافيّة المُظَلّلة بالأحمر:

I	II	III	IV	V	VI	VII	VIII	X
فَعَلَ	فَعَّلَ	فاعَلَ	أفْعَلَ	تَفَعَّلَ	تَفاعَلَ	اِنْفَعَلَ	اِفْتَعَلَ	اِسْتَفْعَلَ

كَما تَرى في الجَدوَل في الصفحة السابقة، أنَّ كُلَّ الأحرُف ذات اللَون الأحمَر، هي أحرُف إضافيّة، ونُسمّي هذِه الأشكال: أوزان الفِعل المَزيد ولِها مزايا (features) خاصّة نَستَطيع استِخدامَها من أجلِ:

١ـ **تَحديد نَوع الكَلِمة**: نَستَطيع أن نُميِّز بَين الاسم والفِعل على أساس وَزن الكَلِمة، على سَبيل المِثال: إذا قَرأنا كَلمة تَكَلُّم ولَم نَعرِف إذا كانَت اسماً أو فِعلاً فَنَرجِع إلى وَزنِها تَفَعُّل ونَستَنتِج (deduce) مِنه أنَّه اسم.

٢ـ **تَحديد جَذر الكَلِمة**: بَعد تَجريد (stripping) الكَلِمة من الأحرُف الإضافية، نَرى الفِعل المُجَرَّد أي الجَذر.

٣ـ **البَحث عن الكَلِمة في القاموس**: أنَّ مُعظم القَواميس مُرَتَّبة (are arranged) حَسَب الجَذر، وبِما أنَّنا نَستَطيع استِخراج الجَذر، فَعَمَليّة إيجاد الكَلِمة في القاموس تَصير أمراً سَهلاً.

٤ـ **تَحديد وَزن الكَلِمة**: لِكُلّ وَزن مَعنى خاصّ بِه، لِذا، حين نَعرِف الوَزن والجَذر، نَستطيع استخدام هذه المَعرِفة كي نَستَنتِج مَعنى الكَلِمة الجديد، أو إذا أَرَدنا أن نَشتَقّ (to derive) كَلِمة جَديدة، فَبِإمكانِنا أن نَستَخدِم مَعرِفة الجَذر والوَزن كَي تُفيدَنا في اِشتِقاقِها.

كَي نُحَدِّد جَذر الاسم، لَيس علَينا إلاّ أن نُوافِق بَين الاسم والوَزن المُناسِب الّذي نَراه في الصَفحة التالية، وبَعد ذلِكَ، نحذِف (omit) كُلَّ الأحرُف غَير الفاء والعين واللام (ف – ع – ل)، فالأحرُف المُتبَقِّية هي جَذر الاسم المُراد (desired).

في هذا الدَرس، نُقَدِّم لَك جَدوَل الاسم في الصَفحة التالية ثُمَّ نُقَدِّم لكَ جَدوَل الفِعل. نُشَجِّعُك على حِفظ (memorize) الجَدوَلَين بِما في ذلِك مَعاني كُلّ وَزن من الأوزان العَشرة والعَدَد الرومانيّ الّذي يُرافِقه. اقرأ هذَين الجَدوَلَين كُلّ يَوم بِصَوتٍ عالٍ بالطَريقة التالية: الفِعل الماضي والمضارع والمَصدَر وافعَل هذا التَمرين مع كُلّ فِعل جَديد تَتَعلَّمُه من الآن فَصاعِداً (from now on).

الاسم					
NOUN OF PLACE & TIME اِسْمُ المَكان والزَمان	RECIPIENT (Passive Participle) اِسْمُ المَفْعول	AGENT (Active Participle) (Doer) اِسْمُ الفاعِل	VERBAL NOUN (Masdar) المَصْدَر	FORM الوَزن	MEANING, USE, AND RELATIONSHIP المعنى والاستعمال والعلاقة
مَفْعَلٌ (ة)	مَفْعُولٌ	فَاعِلٌ	فَعْلٌ فُعُولٌ فِعَالَةٌ إلخ	I	REGULAR
مُفَعَّلٌ	مُفَعَّلٌ	مُفَعِّلٌ	تَفْعِيلٌ	II	CAUSATIVE OR INTENSIVE
مُفَاعَلٌ	مُفَاعَلٌ	مُفَاعِلٌ	مُفَاعَلَةٌ فِعَالٌ	III	RECIPROCAL (Mutual Action)
مُفْعَلٌ	مُفْعَلٌ	مُفْعِلٌ	إِفْعَالٌ	IV	CAUSATIVE
مُتَفَعَّلٌ	مُتَفَعَّلٌ	مُتَفَعِّلٌ	تَفَعُّلٌ	V	REFLEXIVE OF II
مُتَفَاعَلٌ	مُتَفَاعَلٌ	مُتَفَاعِلٌ	تَفَاعُلٌ	VI	REFLEXIVE OF III
مُنْفَعَلٌ	———	مُنْفَعِلٌ	اِنْفِعَالٌ	VII	PASSIVE OF I (No Agent)
مُفْتَعَلٌ	مُفْتَعَلٌ	مُفْتَعِلٌ	اِفْتِعَالٌ	VIII	REFLEXIVE OF I
———	———	مُفْعَلٌّ	اِفْعِلَالٌ	IX	COLORS OR PHYSICAL DEFECTS
مُسْتَفْعَلٌ	مُسْتَفْعَلٌ	مُسْتَفْعِلٌ	اِسْتِفْعَالٌ	X	TO SEEK I

شارع المعز في القاهرة

لِكُلّ كَلِمة أصلُها عَرَبيّ، وَزن من هذِه الأوزان، وهذا بِمَعنى أن الكَلِمات الأجنَبيّة عموماً لَيس لَها وَزن من أوزان الفِعل المَزيد. تُشَكِّل هذه الأوزان قالَباً (representation) أو نَموذَجاً (model) لِكَلِمة قَد تَكون فِعلاً أو صِفة أو اسماً في المُفرَد أو الجَمع أو المُذَكَّر أو المُؤَنَّث وتُبيِّن (shows) الأحرُف الإضافيّة لأي كَلِمة. دَعنا نَنظُر إلى كَلِمة (طالِب) ونُحاوِل أن نَجِدَها في الجَدوَل في الصَفحة السابِقة.

الاسم					
المعنى والاستعمال والعلاقة	الوَزن	المَصْدَر	اِسْمُ الفاعِل	اِسْمُ المَفعول	اِسْمُ المَكان والزَمان
REGULAR	I	فَعْلٌ فُعُولٌ فِعَالَةٌ إلخ	فَاعِلٌ	مَفْعُولٌ	مَفْعَلٌ(ة)

نَجِد أنَّ كَلِمة طالِب هو اسمُ الفاعِل في الوَزن الأوَّل الّذي يقابِلُه بالإنكِليزيّة (-*er* form) أي (resid*er*, writ*er*, play*er*).

٦	لَعِب	←	لَـ	+	ا	+	عِب	=	لاعِب	*player*
٧	كَتَب	←	كَـ	+	ا	+	تِب	=	كاتِب	*writer*
٨	سَكَن	←	سَـ	+	ا	+	كِن	=	ساكِن	*resider*

وعِند تَرجمة كَلِمة طالِب إلى الإنكليزيّة، نَتوَقّع أن نَجِد فيها الـ(-*er*). وفي الواقِع، إنّ التَرجَمة لَها فيها الـ(-*er*)! عِندما نَنظُر إلى جَذر كَلِمة طالب نَجِد أنّ أصل الكَلِمة طَلَب الّتي تَعني "to request, to seek". فإذا تَرجَمنا كَلِمة طالِب حَرفيّاً (literally) فَسَنَجِد أنّها تَعني (request*er* or seek*er*). فكَلِمة طالِب تَعني (requester or seeker of knowledge) أو «طالِب العِلم».

ومن هذا المُنطَلَق (from this point of departure)، نَستَطيع أن نَستَخدِم مَعرِفَتنا بأوزان الفِعل المَزيد كَي نشتَقّ كَلِمات جَديدة تُساعِدُنا في استِخدام الكَلِمة المُناسبة في الوَقت

المُناسِب وكَما يُقول المَثَل العَرَبيّ: لِكُلِّ مَقام مَقالٌ = *A saying for every setting*. والآن، نُريد أن نُطَبِّق (to apply) ما تَعَلّمنا: حاوِل أَنْ تُحَوِّل الفِعل (دَرَس = to study) لِاسمِ الفاعِل (studier).

٩	دَرَس	←	فاعِل	=	؟

وإذا قُلتَ (دارِس)، فهذا صَحيح! هَيّا نَتَدَرّب على بَعضِ التمارين مُستَخدِمين اسم الفاعِل في الوزن الأوّل.

تمرين ١٠

اسمُ الفاعِل: اكتُب الفاعِل المُناسِب.

1. drinker ______________
2. studier ______________
3. worker ______________
4. walker ______________
5. inside ______________
6. outside ______________

حَوِّلْ الأفعال الآتية إلى اسمِ الفاعِل ثُمَّ استخدِمها في جُمَل صَحيحة كَما هو في المِثال:

	الفِعل	اسم الفاعِل	الجُملة
	مِثال: خَرَج	خارِج	يَلعَب الأولاد في الخارِج.
١-	سَمِع		
٢-	رَجَع		
٣-	دَخَل		
٤-	وَقَف		
٥-	عَمِل		
٦-	فَهِم		
٧-	جَلَس		

٣- مُراجَعة العَدَد التَرتيبيّ Review of Ordinal Numbers

هل لاحَظت أنّنا نَستَخدِم العَدَد التَرتيبيّ في دُروس هذا الكِتاب أي: الدَرس الأوّل والثاني والثالِث إلخ. وكَما ذَكرنا أنّ العَدَد التَرتيبيّ (أوّل) يَختلِف عن العَدَد الأصلي cardinal (واحد). ولكن وَزن كُلّ الأعداد التَرتيبيّة غير المُفرَد فاعِل، على سَبيل المِثال: ثلاثة تَصير ثالِث وأربَعة تَصير رابع وهكذا من رَقم اثنَين إلى عَشَرة.

إلَيك العَدَد التَرتيبيّ في حالات الرَفع والنَصب والجَرّ:

١١	هذا هُوَ الدَرسُ الثالِثُ.	الرَفع	Nominative
١٢	قَرَأتُ الدَرسَ الثالِثَ.	النَصب	Accusative
١٣	في الدَرْسِ الثالِثِ.	الجَرّ	Genitive

والأعداد التَرتيبيّة من رَقم العَشَرة فَما فَوق لَها خاصّيتان (two characteristics) مُهِمتان ألا وهما:

آ- العَدَد التَرتيبيّ من ١١-١٩ مَبني (invariable) أي لا مَحلَ لَهُ من الإعراب (they do not inflect in case).

١٤	هذا هُوَ الدَرْسُ الثالِثَ عَشَرَ.	الرَفع
١٥	قَرَأتُ الدَرْسَ الثالِثَ عَشَرَ.	النَصب
١٦	في الدَرْسِ الثالِثَ عَشَرَ.	الجَرّ

لاحِظ معنا أنّ في الأمثِلة ١٤-١٦، يَظهَر الاسم الدَرس في الحالات الثَلاثة أي الرَفع والنَصب والجَرّ ومع ذلِك تَنتَهي كُلّها بِنَفسِ الإعراب أي الفَتحة (المُظلَّلة بِالأحمَر أعلاه).

ب- يَختَلِف العَدَد التَرتيبيّ عن العَدَد الأصليّ من حَيثُ تَطابُق التأنيث والتَذكير بَينَهُ والفاعِل، انظُر إلى الأمثِلة أدناه:

١٧	الدَرْسُ الثالِثَ عَشَرَ	المُذَكَّر
١٨	الصورةُ الثالِثةَ عَشْرَةَ	المُؤنَّث

العرض: أحضر بعض الصور لرؤساء الولايات المتحدة الأمريكية، وخرائط بعض الولايات وقائمة أسماء فائزين رياضيين في رياضات مثل بطولة كرة المضرب أو بطولة العالم في بيسبال أو كأس العالم إلخ) وراجعها مع الطلاب:

«كانت أوهايو الولاية السابعة عشرة.»
«كانت رود آيلند الولاية الثالثة عشرة.»
«أي شخص أو أي فريق يحتل المرتبة الـ (أولى، ثانية، ثالثة) في رياضة كذا.»

الممارسة: اسأل الطلاب الأسئلة الآتية:

«مَن كان الرئيس السادس عشر للولايات المتحدة؟»
«أي درس ندرسه الآن وما هو آخر درس في هذا الكتاب؟»
«في أية ساعة نأكل الغداء؟»

أمّا بِالنِسبة إلى العُقود أي ٢٠ / ٣٠ / ٤٠ إلخ، فَالأمر لَيس مُعَقَّداً (complex)، فَقَط علَيك أن تَزيد الـ التَعريف (the definite article) في بِداية العَدَد لِلحُصول على العَدَد التَرتيبيّ:

	العَدَد الأصليّ			العَدَد العَدَد التَرتيبي	
١٩	عِشْرونَ دَرْساً	20 lessons	←	الدَرْسُ العِشْرونَ	the 20th lesson
٢٠	ثَلاثونَ دَرْساً	30 lessons	←	الدَرْسُ الثَلاثونَ	the 30th lesson

أمّا بِالنِسبة إلى الأعداد المَعطوفة فَتُطابِق الفاعِل من حَيثُ الإعراب كَما نُلاحِظ في الحَرَكات المُظَلَّلة بالأحمَر في الجَدول أدناه:

٢١	هذا هُوَ الدَرْسُ الثالِثُ والعِشْرونَ.	الرَفع
٢٢	قَرَأتُ الدَرْسَ الثالِثَ والعِشْرينَ.	النَصب
٢٣	في الدَرْسِ الثالِثِ والعِشْرينَ.	الجَرّ

إنّ إعراب الجزء الأوّل يُطابِق الاسم الدَرس وكَذلِك الجزء الثاني أي العِشرون الّذي لَهُ شَكلان ألا وهُما العِشرون لِحالة الرَفع والعِشرين لِحالَتي النَصب والجَرّ كَما نَرى في الأمثِلة أعلاه المُظَلَّلة بالأحمَر.

أمّا بِالنِسبة إلى الأعداد فَوق المِئة، فَيَدخُل حَرف الجَرّ بَعْدَ على العَدَد بعد عَشَر كَما نَلاحِظ في المِثال أدناه:

٢٤	الدَرْسُ الخامِسَ عَشَرَ بَعْدَ المِئة	*the fifteenth lesson after the hundredth (115th)*

تمرين ١١

أ- **أكْمِل الجُمَلَ الآتية بالاخْتِيار المُناسِب وَفْق السياق:**

١- الصورةُ ____________ في هذا الدَرس هي صورة جورج واشنِطَن.

☐ الأوَّلُ ☐ الأولى ☐ الواحِدةُ

٢- قَرَأنا عَن هالَة بُستاني في الدَرس ____________.

☐ عَشْرة ☐ عاشِر ☐ العاشِر

٣- دَرسُ الكيمياء في الساعةِ ____________ والنِصْف.

☐ الثانيةُ عَشْرَةُ ☐ الثانيةَ عَشْرَةَ ☐ الثانيةِ عَشْرَةِ

٤- سَيكون الدَرسُ ____________ عَن الدِراسة والمَواعيد.

☐ الثالِثِ والعِشْرينَ ☐ الثالِثَ والعِشْرينَ ☐ الثالِثُ والعِشْرونَ

٥- كان لِنكَن في السَنَةِ ____________ حين أُغْتيلَ في واشنطَن العاصِمة.

☐ الرابِعةِ والخَمْسينَ ☐ الرابِعةَ والخَمْسينَ ☐ الرابَعةُ والخَمْسونَ

ب- **العَدَد الترتيبيّ**: اكتُب الأعداد التَرتيبيّة الآتية وشكِّلها (provide the short vowels):

مِثال: الرَجُل ١٥ **الرَجُلُ الخامِسَ عَشَر**

٦- البِنتُ ٩ ____________

٧- الكِتابُ ١٨ ____________

٨- في السَنةِ ٢٥ ____________

٩- في عيدِ الثَورةِ ١٠٥ ____________

١٠- على الصَفحةِ ١٢٢ ____________

١١- الطالِبُ ١ ____________

تمرين ١٢

أ- **اِملأ الفَراغات** بالكَلِمة المُناسِبة وَفْق نَص الاسْتِماع:

١- كانَتْ هذِهِ الشَخْصيّة زَوْجة رَئيس ________ .

٢- أُغْتيلَ زَوْجُها في ________ .

٣- اِسمُ الزَوْجِ الثاني هُوَ ________ .

ب- **أَكْمِل الجُمَل الآتية بالاخْتِيار المُناسِب وَفْق نَصِّ الاسْتِماع:**

٤- صارَتْ هذِهِ الشَخْصيّة زَوْجة ________ .

☐ مَرَّةً واحِدة ☐ مَرَّتَيْن ☐ ثَلاثَ مَرّات

٥- اِسْم هذِهِ الشَخْصيّة ________ .

☐ أمريكيّ ☐ فَرَنسيّ ☐ عَرَبيّ

٦- بَعد وَفاة زَوْجِها الثاني سَكَنَتْ في ________ .

☐ مَدينةِ نيويورك ☐ مَدينةِ واشِنطَن ☐ وِلايةِ تكساس

ج- **اكْتُب «خطأ» أو «صواب» على الخَطّ ثُمَّ صَحِّح الجُمَل الخَطأ:**

٧- هذِهِ الشَخْصيّة فِرَنسيّة.

____

٨- صارَتْ زَوْجة مَرّة ثانية في سَنَةِ ١٩٦٨.

____

٩- الزَوْجُ الثاني أمريكيّ.

____

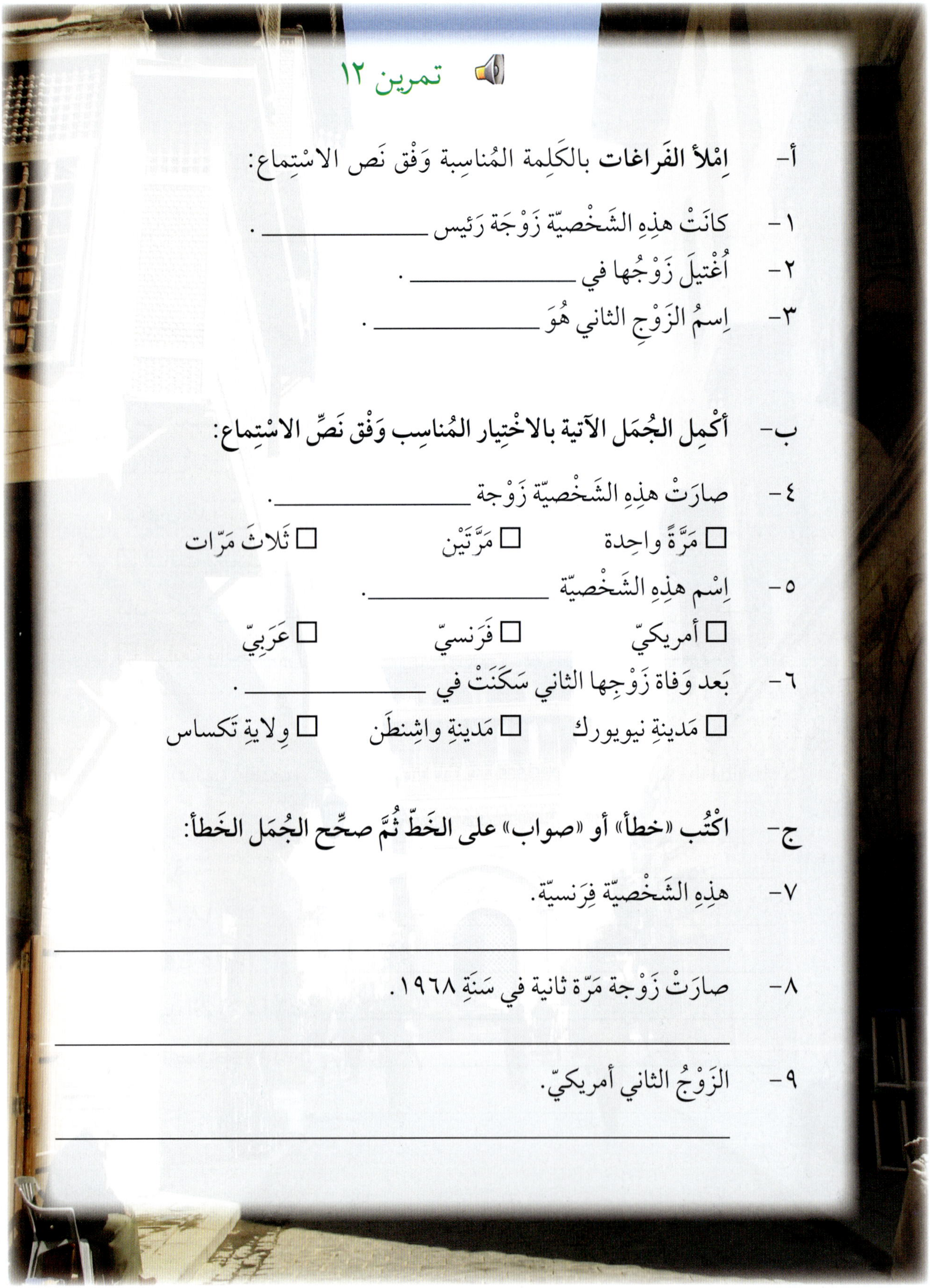

القاهِرة القَديمة

المُفْرَدات

استمِع إلى المُفْرَدة بالعَرَبيّة ثم أعِد نُطْقَها مرّتين.

اِجْتِماع ج اِجْتِماعات (n., m.) . . . . . . meeting, social gathering

اِستَخدَمَ (يَستَخدِمُ) اِستِخدام (v.) . . . . to use, to utilize, to employ

اُسْتُشْهِدَ (يُستَشْهَدُ) اِسْتِشهاد (passive v.) . . . . . to become a martyr

أسَّسَ (يُؤَسِّسُ) تأسيس (v.) . . . . to establish, to found

أسْوَد ج سُود (n., m.) . . . . black

اُغتيل (يُغتال) اِغتِيال (passive v.) . . . . to be assassinated

أمير ج أُمَراء (n., m.) . . . . prince

اِنْتَخَبَ (يَنْتَخِبُ) اِنْتِخاب (v.) . . . . to elect

الأنْدَلُس (n., f.) . . . . Andalusia, Muslim Spain

تاريخ ج تَواريخ (n., m.) . . . . history

تَمييز (verbal n., m.) . . . . discrimination

تُوُفِيَ (يُتَوَفّى) وَفاة (passive v.) . . . . to pass away

جامِع ج جَوامِع (n., m.) . . . . mosque

جائِزة ج جَوائِز (n., f.) . . . . prize, award

الجَبْر (n., m.) . . . . algebra

جُرِحَ (يُجرَحُ) جَرح (passive v.) . . . . . . to be wounded, to be hurt

جُمهوريّة ج جُمهوريّات (n., f.) . . . . republic

جَيْش ج جُيوش (n., m.) . . . . army

حارَبَ (يُحارِبُ) حَرْب / مُحارَبة (v.) . . . . to fight

حَرْب ج حُروب (n., f.) . . . . war

حِساب ج حِسابات (n., m.) . . . . account to acquire, to obtain, to get . . (v.) حَصَلَ (يَحصُلُ) حُصول + على

to tell a story; to talk . . . . (v.) حَكَى (يَحْكي) حِكاية

to go out, to exit. . . . . (v.) خَرَجَ (يَخرُجُ) خُروج

orator, preacher, speaker . . . . (n., m.) خَطيب ج خُطَباء

to enter. . . . . (v.) دَخَلَ (يَدخُلُ) دُخول

to pay. . . . . (v.) دَفَعَ (يَدْفَعُ) دَفْع

defense. . . . . (n., m.) دِفاع ج دِفاعات

head . . . . (n., m.) رأس ج رُؤوس

to reject . . . . (v.) رَفَضَ (يَرفُضُ / يَرفِضُ) رَفْض

leader, president. . . . . (n., m.) رَئيس ج رُؤَساء

leader (popular). . . . . (n., m.) زَعيم ج زُعَماء

young man. (n., m.) شابّ ج شَباب

poet. . . . . (n., m.) شاعِر ج شُعَراء

personality, character. . . . . (n., f.) شَخصِيّة ج شَخصِيّات

ranking officer. . . . . (n., m.) ضابِط ج ضُبّاط

to request, to order (i.e., in a restaurant) . . (v.) طَلَبَ (يَطْلُبُ) طَلَب

Toulon (a town in southern France) . . . . (n., f.) طولون

scholar, scientist. . . . . (n., m.) عالِم ج عُلَماء

sociologist . . . . (n., m.) عالِم اجْتِماع

sociology. . . . . (n., m.) عِلْم اجْتِماع

to introduce s.o. to s.o. else . . . . (v.) عَرَّفَ (يُعَرِّفُ) تَعريف (على)

race, element . . . . (n., m.) عُنصُر ج عَناصِر

racial . . . . (adj.) عُنصُريّ

philosophy. . . . . (n., f.) فَلْسَفة ج فَلسَفات

philosopher . . . . (n., m.) فَيْلَسوف ج فَلاسِفة

to do, to perform . . . . (v.) قامَ (يَقومُ) قِيام

law . . . . (n., m.) قانون ج قَوانين

leader (military) . . . . (n., m.) قائد ج قُوّاد / قادة

nearby, close. . . . . (adv.) قُرْب

village . . . . (n., f.) قَرية ج قُرى

priest . . . . (n., m.) قِسّيس ج قِسّاوِسة

writer, scribe. . . . . (n., m.) كاتِب ج كُتّاب / كَتَبة

for the sake of (Syrian colloquial) . . . . كرمال

generous . . . .(adj.) كَريم ج كُرَماء

necessary . . . . (active participle) لازِم

lawyer, attorney-at-law, counsel. . . . . (n., m.) مُحامٍ ج مُحامون

mixed . . . . (passive participle) مُشَكَّل

introduction. . . . . (n., f.) مُقَدِّمة ج مُقَدِّمات

place, location. . . . . (n., m.) مَكان ج أَمْكِنة

king. . . . . (n., m.) مَلِك ج مُلوك

جَيِّد (Syrian colloquial) . . . . (adj.) مْنيح ج امْناح

historian . . . . (n., m.) مُؤَرِّخ ج مُؤَرِّخون

to be sent into exile, to be expelled . . . (passive v.) نُفِيَ (يُنْفى) نَفْيٌ

now (Syrian colloquial) . . . . هَللأ / هَلَّق

minister . . . . (n., m.) وَزير ج وُزَراء

قُرطُبة في الأندَلُس

الدرس السابع عشر

أهداف الدرس

- تَعَلُّم تَحديد مواعيد وكِتابة جَداول ووَصفُ فَعاليات العيد
- تَعَلُّم المُثَنّى والجَمع في الإضافة
- إستِخدام كُلّ - مَرّة - مَرَّتين
- إستِخدام ما عدا
- إستِخدام لِأنَّ + الجُملة الاسميّة
- إستِخدام اسمُ الفاعِل واسمُ المَفعول
- إستِخدام لَم + المُضارع المَجزوم
- مُراجعةُ الفِعل المُعتلّ

رُكنُ المُفْرَداتِ الجَديدة

أَخذ (يَأْخُذُ) أخْذ	to take
أرْسَلَ (يُرْسِلُ) إرْسال	to send
اِنْتَهى (يَنْتَهي) اِنْتِهاء	to end
بَدَأَ (يَبْدَأُ) بِداية	to begin
رأى (يَرى) رأي / رؤية	to see
سَاعَدَ (يُساعِدُ) مُساعَدة	to help
عَلِمَ (يَعْلَمُ) عِلْم	عَرَفَ (يَعْرِف) مَعْرِفة
وَجَدَ (يَجِدُ) وُجود	to find
ما عَدا	إلاّ
بَعْضُهُم بَعْضاً / بَعْضُهُم البَعْض	each other
عام	سَنَة

تمرين ١

اخترَ الكَلِمةَ الّتي لا تُناسِب باقي الكَلِماتِ في كُلِّ مَجْموعةٍ وبَيِّن السَبَب.

١-	لأنَّ	بِسَبَب	ما عَدا	لِماذا
٢-	عَرَب	رَمَضان	صامَ	غُروب
٣-	عيد	الشام	مُعايَدة	حَلوى
٤-	اِلتِهاب	طائِرة	مَطار	بَوّابة
٥-	عِيادة	حَبّة	صَديق	طَبيب
٦-	رَأى	جالِس	زارَ	اِستَقبَلَ
٧-	طَبيب	مُدَرِّس	مُدير	طالِب

تمرين ٢

وافِقْ بَيْنَ الكَلِماتِ في العَمودَيْنِ.

١-	أَخَذَ		نَسِيَ
٢-	أَلِمَ		فَقير
٣-	بَدَأَ		طَبيب
٤-	عَلِمَ		اِنتَهى
٥-	غَنِيّ		أعطى
			أسبِرين

تمرين ٣

المُحادَثة: اسأل زَميلك وأخبِر الجَميع بِما عَلِمت من مَعلومات:

١- في أي سِن بدأت تَتكَلّم(ين)؟

٢- أيّ لُغة بدأت تَتكَلّم(ين) بِها أولاً . . . ثانياً؟

٣- في أي ساعة يَبْدأ ويَنْتَهي دَرْسُ اللُغةِ العَرَبيّة ؟

٤- مَن يُساعِدُك وكَيْف؟

٥- لِماذا تُحِبّ(ين) أو لا تُحِبّ(ين) زيارة طَبيب الأسنان؟

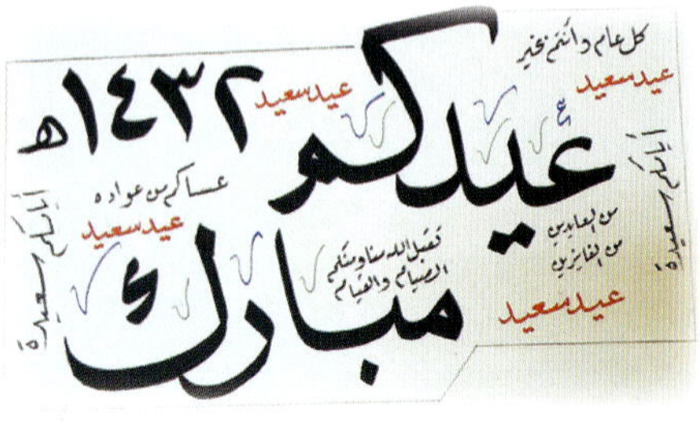

تمرين ٤

أعِدْ ترتيبَ الكَلِماتِ في كُلِّ مَجموعةٍ لِتُشَكِّلَ جُمَلاً مُفيدة.

١- المُسلِمون – رَمَضان – في – شَهْر – يَصوم.

٢- عاصِمةِ – ما – تَعلَم – هَلْ – اِسمُ – الأرْدُن؟

٣- الخَميس – المَكتَبَةِ – في – كُلَّ – ما عَدا – أدرُس – يَومٍ – يَومَ.

٤- شَهرِ – الدِراسةُ – حَزيران – تَنتَهي – الجامِعةِ – في – في.

٥- بَعد – السينَما – وَصَلتُ – الفيلم – دارِ – إلى – بِدايَةِ.

تمرين ٥

المُحادَثة قبل القِراءة: اسأل زَميلك:

١- ماذا تَعرِف عن عيد الفِطر؟

٢- كَم يَوماً يَحتَفِل المُسلِمون بِعيد الفِطر؟

٣- ما هي العِبارة الّتي يَقولُها المُسلِمون في عيد الفِطر؟

٤- مَتى تَبدأ عُطلة نِهاية الأسبوع في بَلَدِك؟

٥- كَم مَرّة تَزور طَبيب الأسنان في السَنة؟

عيدُ الفِطْر

مايكِل براون، كَما تَعلَمون، مَوْجود الآن في القاهِرة لِدِراسةِ العَرَبيّة. يَذهَب كُلَّ يَوم إلى دُروسِهِ في الجامِعة ما عَدا يَومَ الجُمعة لأنَّ هذا اليَوم عُطلَة نِهايَةِ الأسبوع في مِصر وفي مُعظَمِ البِلادِ العَرَبيّة. كَتَب مايكِل في يَوميّاتِهِ هذِهِ الكَلِمات:

الثُلاثاء ٢٠ فِبْراير (شُباط) ٢٠١٨

اليَوم عُطلة بِسبَب عيدِ الفِطر، وهو عيد يَأتي بَعدَ شَهر رَمَضان. صام مُعظَم زُمَلائي المِصريّين في رَمَضان. فَفي هذا الشَهر يَصومُ الناس عَنِ الطَعام والشَراب مِنَ الصَباح حَتّى غُروبِ الشَمس. أمّا في العيد فَيَزورُ الناس بَعْضُهُم بَعْضاً عادةً ويَأكُلون كَثيراً مِنَ الطَعام والحَلوى ويَشربونَ الشاي والقَهوة.

العَرض: اشرح ما يفعل المسلمون في شهر رمضان مستخدماً صوراً من عندك أو من الشابكة لتَدُب فيها الحياة. إليك مِثال:
يصوم المسلمون ويزورون بعضهم بعضاً ويستقبلون بعضهم بعضاً ويكتب المسلمون بطاقات معايدة أو يرسلونها عبر وسائل التواصل الاجتماعي إلى بعضهم بعضاً ويقول الناس «كلّ عام وأنتم بخير» أو تعبير خاص ببلدك.
الممارسة: اعرض للطلّاب صوراً تُبيّن لهم فعاليات شهر رمضان واطلب منهم أن يشرحوها.
التطبيق: في مجموعات من اثنين: وزّع على كلّ مجموعة صورة لفعاليات قد يقوم بها مسلم عادي في شهر رمضان. اتركهم يفعلون النشاط خمس دقائق تقريباً واطلب منهم تحضير قصة قصيرة حقيقية أو خيالية بما يحدث في الصورة، ثمّ اطلب منهم أن يحكوها للصفّ.

العرض: تظاهر كأنّ ضرسك يؤلمك كثيراً واشرح للطلاّب وضعك. اسألهم أين يجب عليك الذهاب وأخبرْهم بدرجة الألم ومتى صار يؤلمك ضرسك وكم مرة تفرّش أسنانك في اليوم وكم مرة تزور طبيب الأسنان في السنة. إليك مثال:

«آه يا جماعة . . . لا أعرف ما العمل، يؤلمني ضرسي كثيراً والألم لم يعد يطاق. ما رأيكم؟ ما العمل؟ إلى أين سأذهب. فالألم يزداد وكلما آكل وأشرب شيئاً ساخناً أو بارداً أحسّ بألم شديد في ضرسي. آه . . . هل أحد يعلم ما العمل؟ لقد آلمني ضرسي منذ شهر وأنا أفرش أسناني يومياً. لماذا يؤلمني ضرسي يا ترى؟»

التَطبيق: دع الطلاب يبدون رأيهم في ما عليك الفعل وأين يجب عليك الذهاب، ومن سيرافقك وكم من الوقت يستغرق المشوار إلخ.

التَطبيق: في مجموعات من اثنين أو ثلاثة: اطلب من طالب من كل مجموعة أن يتظاهر كأن ضرسه يؤلِمه وعلى الآخرين مساعدته. قد تحتاج إلى بعض الكلمات ومصطلحات جديدة للقيام بهذا النشاط.

متابعة النشاط: اطلب من طالب متطوّع القيام بهذا النشاط أمام الصفّ.

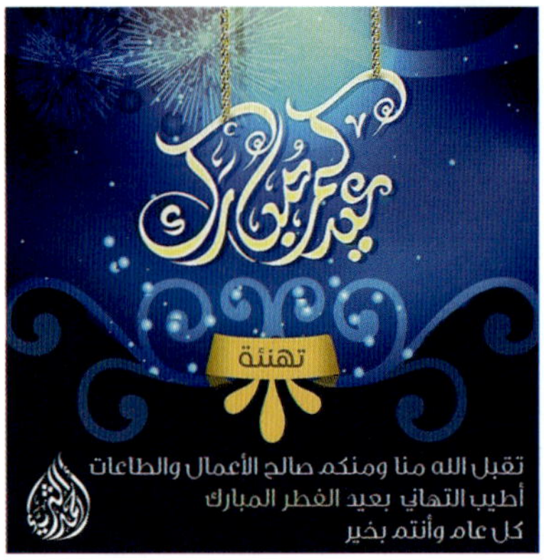

بِطاقَتا مُعايَدة

أرسَلتُ أمس بِطاقات مُعايَدة لِبَعض أصدِقائي المِصريّين. وَجَدتُ في المَكتَبَة بِطاقات مَكتوب علَيْها «كُلَّ عام وأنتُم بِخَير» وبِطاقات مَكتوب علَيْها «عيد مُبارَك.» اِشْتَرَيْتُ مِنَ النَوعِ الأوَّل، أمّا الناس فَيَقول بَعْضُهُم لِبَعض «كُلَّ سَنَة وأنتَ طَيِّب.» وقال لي سَمير إنّ الناس في بِلادِ الشام يَقولون «كُلَّ سَنَة وأنتَ سالِم.»

الخميس ١ مارِس (آذار) ٢٠١٨

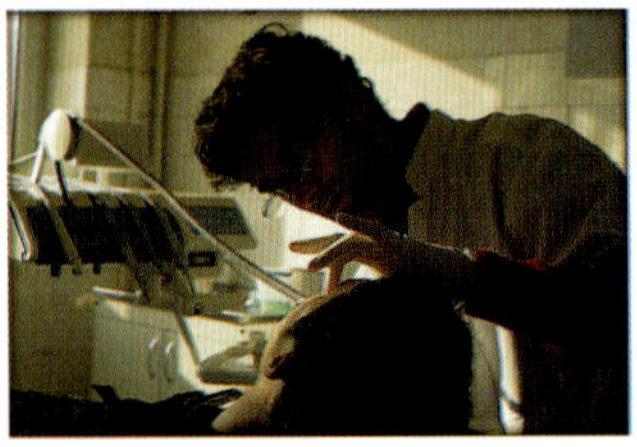

آلَمَني ضِرسي

أمس كان عِندي مَوعِد عِندَ طَبيبِ الأسْنان في الساعةِ الثانية والنِصْف. آلَمَني ضِرسي كَثيراً في اللَيلةِ الماضِية وأخَذتُ حَبَّتَي أسبِرين دون فائدة كَبيرة. لَمْ أنَمْ تِلكَ اللَيْلة مِن ألَمي.

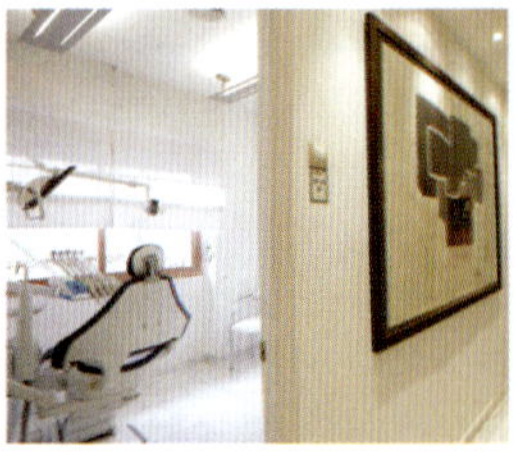

عيادة الطَبيب

وَصَلتُ إلى عِيادةِ الطَبيب قَبل مَوعِدي بِخَمس دَقائق فَقَط، لكِنَّ الطَبيب لَمْ يَرَني حَتّى الساعةِ الثالِثة وعَشْر دَقائق. قال لي إنَّ هُناكَ الْتِهاباً في الضِرْس. أعطاني حُبوباً ضِدَّ الالْتِهاب. سَأرجِع إلى الطَبيبِ بَعدَ ثَلاثة أيّام.

عام دِراسيّ جَديد

كَتَب عَدنان مارتيني هذِهِ اليَوْمِيّات حين كان طالِباً في جامِعة وِلاية أوهايو يَدرُس عِلمَ الحاسوب، وكانَت هذِهِ هِيَ بِدايَةُ السَنةِ الثانِية لَهُ في كَلمبَس.

السَبت ٢٢ أيلول ٢٠١٨

بَعد ثَلاثة أيّام يَبدَأُ العامُ الدِراسيُّ الجَديد. في فَصلِ الصَيفِ الماضي لَمْ أرجِع إلى سوريا بَل دَرَستُ ثَلاث مَوادّ وهِيَ عِلمُ الحاسوب والرياضيّات والكيمياء. اِنتَهَت الدِراسة في الشَهرِ الماضي وذَهَبتُ إلى نيويورك وأورلاندو وزُرتُ تورنتو في كَندا أيضاً. رَجَعتُ إلى كَلَمبَس في الأسبوعِ الماضي.

اليَوم وغَداً سَأذهَب بِسيّارتي إلى مَطار كَلَمبَس الدُوَليّ ثَلاث مَرّات لأستَقبِل بَعضَ الطُلاّبِ العَرَب الجُدُد. أنا لا أعرِفُهُم لكِنّي عَلِمتُ أسماءَهُم مِن مَكتَبِ الطُلاّبِ الأجانِب في الجامِعة. اليَوم سَأستَقبِل هِشام تَميمي وخَديجة عَبد السلام. ولا أعرِف عَنْهُما شَيْئاً الآن. سَتَصِل طائِرة هِشام في الساعةِ الحادية عَشْرة والرُبع صَباحاً، أمّا مَوعِد طائِرة خَديجة فَهُوَ في الساعةِ الرابِعة والنِصْف بَعدَ الظُهر.

الإثنين ٢٤ أيلول ٢٠١٨

ذَهَبتُ أمس وأمسِ الأوَّل إلى المَطار. اِسْتَقْبَلْتُ هِشام تَميمي وخَديجة عَبد السَلام أمسِ الأوَّل. وَصَلَت طائرة هِشام مُتأخِّرةً عِشرين دَقيقة. كان مَعَهُ حَقيبَتان. حَمَلنا الحَقيبَتَين إلى السَيّارة ثُمَّ أخَذْتُهُ إلى سَكَنِ الطُلاّب حَيثُ سَيسكُنُ هذِهِ السَنَة.

تحمِلُ حَقيبة

رَجَعتُ مَرَّةً ثانِيةً إلى المَطار بَعدَ الظُهر لأسْتَقبِل خَديجة. وَصَلَت طائِرَتُها في مَوعِدِها. وَجَدْتُ خَديجة جالِسة بِجانِبِ البَوّابَة رَقْم تِسعة. كان مَعَها حَقيبَتان أيضاً. أخذتُها بِالسَيّارة بَعد ذلِكَ إلى سَكَنِ الطالِبات حَيثُ سَتسكُنُ هذِهِ السَنَة.

عَرَفتُ مِن هِشام أنَّهُ مِن مَدينةِ الخَليل في فِلَسطين. أتى إلى الوِلاياتِ المُتَّحِدة لِيَدرُسَ الهَندَسةَ الكَهرَبائيّة. هُوَ مِن أُسرة مُتَوَسِّطة. أبوهُ مُدير مَدرسة ثانَوية وأمُّهُ مُدَرِّسَة عُلوم في مَدرَسة مُتَوَسِّطة لِلبَنات. عِندَهُ أربَعة إخْوة: اِثنان في المَدرَسةِ الابتِدائيّة، واحِد في الصَفِ الرابع والثاني في السادِس، والأخُ الثالِث في الصَفِّ الثامِن في المَدرَسةِ المُتَوَسِّطة، والأخُ الرابع في الصَفِّ الحادي عَشَر في المَدرَسَةِ الثانَويّة. لَهُ أختان، واحِدة تَسكُن في مَدينةِ القُدْس والثانية طالِبة في جامِعَة «بيرزَيْت».

هشام تَميمي

عَرَفْتُ مِن خَديجة أنَّها تونِسيّة مِن مَدينة تونِس أتَتْ إلى جامِعة وِلاية أوهايو لِتَدرُسَ الأدَبَ الأمريكيّ. عِند خَديجة أخَوان وأخت واحِدة. أخوها الكَبير مُنير يَسكُن ويَعمَل في باريس. وأخوها الصَغير في المَدرَسةِ الثانَوية في تونِس. أمّا أختُها فَهِيَ مُتَزَوِّجة وتَسكُن مَعَ زَوْجِها في تونِس. قالَت خَديجة إنَّها فَقيرة، لكِنَّ أخاها الكَبير يُساعِدُها.

فُؤاد عَبد الرَحيم

سامِر العاني

خديجة عبد السلام

اِستَقبَلتُ طالِبَين أمس وهُما فُؤاد عَبد الرَحيم وسامِر العاني. فُؤاد مِن مِصر وأتى مِنَ القاهِرة لِيَدرُس عِلمَ الحاسوب. يَقول إنَّه مِن أسرة لَيسَت غَنيّة، فأبوهُ ساعي بَريد وأمُّه رَبّة بَيت، لكنَّه حَصَل على مِنحة دِراسيّة مِن حُكومَتِه.

ساعي بَريد

أمّا سامِر فَهُوَ عِراقيّ، لكِنَّهُ لَمْ يَأت مِن العِراق بَل مِن دُبَيْ حَيثُ يَعمَل أبوه وتَسكُن أسرتُه. يُريدُ سامِر دِراسةَ الطِبّ لأنّ أباهُ طَبيب، لكِنَّهُ لَيس في كُلِّيَّةِ الطِبّ الآن. سَيسكُن سامِر وفُؤاد في سَكَنِ الطُلاّب في فَصلِ الخَريف، لكِنَّهُما يُريدانِ السَكَن في شَقّة بَعدَ ذلِك.

تمرين ٦

اختَر التكْمِلةَ المُناسِبةَ حَسَب النَص.

١- يَأتي عيد الفِطر ________ شَهر رَمَضان.

☐ قَبْلَ ☐ بَعْدَ ☐ مَعَ

٢- عُطلَة نِهايَةِ الأسبوع في مُعظَمِ البِلادِ العَرَبيّة هِيَ يوم ________ .

☐ الجُمْعة ☐ السَبت ☐ الأحَد

٣- ________ المُسلِمون في شَهر رَمَضان من الصباح إلى المساء.

☐ يَأكُلُ ☐ يَصومُ ☐ يَشرَبُ

٤- ________ الناس بَعْضُهُم بَعْضاً في العيد.

☐ يَأخُذُ ☐ يَنتَهي ☐ يَزورُ

٥- وَجَد مايكِل براون بِطاقات ________ في المَكتَبَة.

☐ حَلْوى ☐ مُعايَدة ☐ قَهْوة

٦- وَصَل مايكِل إلى عِيادَةِ طَبيبِ الأسنان ________ .

☐ مُتَأخِّراً ☐ في مَوعِدِه ☐ قَبْلَ مَوْعِدِه

٧- عَدنان مارتيني طالِب في السَنَةِ ________ .

☐ الأولى ☐ الثانية ☐ الثالِثة

٨- دَرَس عَدنان ________ في فَصْلِ الصَيف.

☐ مادّة ☐ مادّتَيْن ☐ ثَلاثَ مَوادّ

٩- اِنتَهَت الدِراسة في جامِعة عَدنان في شَهر ________ .

☐ تَمّوز ☐ آب ☐ أيلول

١٠- اِستَقبَل عَدنان ________ طُلاّب عَرَب في المَطار.

☐ ثَلاثَةَ ☐ أربَعَةَ ☐ خَمسَةَ

١١- وَصَلَت طائرة خَديجة إلى المَطار ___________ .

☐ في مَوعِدِها ☐ مُتَأَخِّرة ☐ قَبْلَ مَوْعِدِها

١٢- أبو هِشام تَميمي ___________ .

☐ مُدَرِّس عُلوم ☐ ساعي بَريد ☐ مُدير مَدرَسة

١٣- كانَت خَديجة جالِسة بِجانِب ___________ في المَطار.

☐ البَوّابة ☐ الكُرسيّ ☐ الطائرة

١٤- تُريدُ خَديجة دِراسة ___________ .

☐ الأدَبِ الأمريكيّ ☐ عِلمِ الحاسوب ☐ الطِبّ

١٥- فُؤاد عَبد الرَحيم طالِب ___________ .

☐ عِراقيّ ☐ سوريّ ☐ مِصريّ

تمرين ٧

اكتُب بِطاقة مُعايدة لِصَديق مُستَخدِماً عِبارات مُناسِبة ووقِّع اسمَك عليها.

تمرين ٨

عَرِّف هؤلاءِ الأشْخاص كَما في المِثال حَسَبَ نَصّ القِراءة.

مِثال: رَبّةُ بَيت — **هِيَ أمُّ الطالِب المِصريّ فُؤاد عَبد الرَحيم.**

١- طَبيب الأسنان ________________

٢- مُدَرِّسةُ عُلوم ________________

٣- ساعي بَريد ________________

٤- أختُها مُتَزَوِّجة ________________

٥- طَبيب ________________

تمرين ٩

أجِبْ عَن هذِهِ الأسئلةِ على صَفحة مُنفَصِلة حَسَبَ نَصّ القِراءة.

١- لِماذا لا يَذهَبُ مايكِل إلى الجامِعةِ في القاهِرةِ يَومَ الجُمْعة؟

٢- لِماذا ذَهَبَ مايكِل إلى طَبيبِ الأسنانِ؟

٣- أيّةَ مُدُن زارَ عَدنان مارتيني في الصَيف؟

٤- مِن أينَ حَصَلَ عَدنان على أسماءِ الطُلاّبِ العَرَب الجُدُد؟

٥- لِماذا يُريدُ سامِر دِراسَةَ الطِبِّ؟

تمرين ١٠

أكتُبْ «خطَأ» أو «صَواب» جانِبَ كُلِّ جُمْلَة وصَحِّح الجُمَلَ الخَطَأ.

١- سَيَرى مايكِل طَبيبَ الأسنانِ مَرَّتَين.

٢- رَجَعَ عَدنان إلى سوريَّة في عُطلةِ الصَيف.

٣- مَدينةُ الخَليل في تونِس.

٤- تَدرُسُ أختُ خَديجة في جامِعةِ «بير زَيت».

٥- وَصَلَ سامِر إلى كَلَمبَس مِن بَغداد.

تمرين ١١

مَن هؤلاءِ الأشخاصِ حَسَب نَصّ القِراءة ومن أي بَلَد عَرَبيّ جاءوا؟ اكتُب اسْمَ بَلَدِ كُلٍّ مِنهُم على الخَريطة.

١ - سامِر

٢ - خَديجة

٣ - هِشام

٤ - فُؤاد

٥ - عَدنان

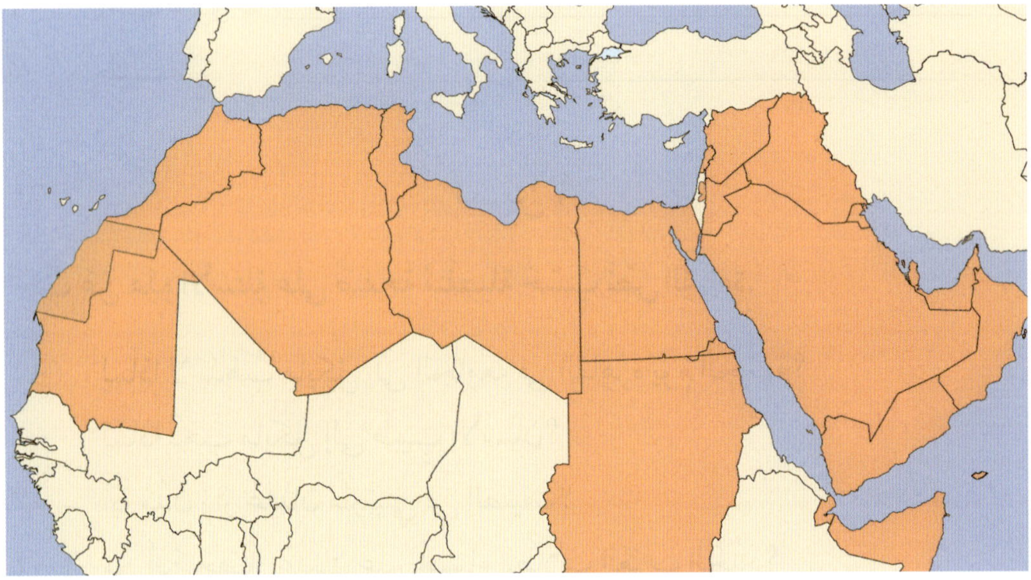

تمرين ١٢

تَمرينُ المُشاهَدة: شاهِدوا الدَرْسَ السابع عَشَر على الشابِكة.

١ - لِماذا قالَتْ أمّ سامِر العِبارة «البيت بيتك»؟ ________________________

____

٢ - لماذا لا يُريد مايكل أنْ يشرب؟ ________________________

____

٣ - أينَ يَدرُس هاني وهنادي؟ ________________________

٤ - ماذا تَدرُس هنادي؟ ________________________

٥ - لِماذا يَذهَب مايكل وستيف إلى باب توما؟ ________________________

____

تَذوّق الثَقافة العَربيّة

في المَشهَد المَرئي، قالَت أم سامِر لِمايكل «نَوَّرت الشام»، وهذا التَعبير شائع (common) في البِلاد العَربية والمَقصود مِنه (you light Damascus up). نَستطيع اِستِخدام هذا التَعبير في سياقات مُختلِفة مَثَلاً: نَوّرت البَيت / المَحَلّ / الغُرفة إلخ. وقد تَقول رَداً على هذا التَعبير الجميل: النور بِوجودك (the light is from your presence) أو النور نورك (the light is your light) أو قَول آخَر من هذا القبيل.

١ - الإضافة: نون المُثَنّى ونون جَمْع المُذَكَّر السالِم

كما تَعلَم، أنّ المُثَنّى يَنتهي بالـ(انِ) مِثل: كِتابانِ في حالة الرَفع أو (ـَينِ) مِثل (كِتابَينِ) في حالتَي النَصب والجَرّ. ولكِن، تَسقُط النون في كُلّ هذه الحالات في الإضافة. انظُر إلى المِثالَين أدناه:

١	حَبَّتان	two pills	+ أسبِرين	←	حَبَّتا أسبِرين	two pills of aspirin
٢	بِطاقتانِ	two cards	+ مُعايَدة	←	بِطاقتا مُعايَدةٍ	two greeting cards

كَذلِك تَسقُط النون في الإضافة في جَمع المُذَكَّر السالِم الّذي يَنتهي بِالـ(ونَ) مِثل: (مُعَلِّمونَ) في حالة الرَفع أو (ينَ) مِثل (مُعَلّمينَ) في حالتي النَصب والجَرّ.

٣	مُدَرِّسونَ	teachers	+ العُلوم	←	مُدَرِّسو العُلوم	science teachers
٤	مُهَندِسونَ	engineers	+ الشَرِكة	←	مُهَندِسو الشَرِكة	the company's engineers

٢- اِستِخدام كُلّ ومَرّة

كَلِمة كُلّ (every, each, all) مُضاف ويأتي بَعده مُضاف إليه مِثل:

every book	كُلّ كِتابٍ	every day	كُلّ يومٍ
the whole book	كُلّ الكِتابِ	all day	كُلّ اليومِ
all of the books	كُلّ الكُتُبِ	all of the days	كُلّ الأيّامِ

ومن المُمكِن أن تأتي في إضافة مُرَكَّبة مِثل:

every Thursday	كُلّ يومِ خميسٍ
all day Thursday	كُلّ يومِ الخَميسِ

تَذكّر أنّ الاسم كُلّ مُضاف لِذلِك يَظهَر في كُلّ الحالات الثلاثة (أي الرَفع والنَصب والجَرّ)، لكِن الكَلِمات الّتي تَليه مُضاف إليه وتأتي في حالة الجَرّ فقط لاغير.

نَستَعمِل كَلِمة مَرّة (one time, one instance) كَي نَعبِّر عن فِعلة واحدة ودائماً تأتي في حالة النَصب، كَما نَرى في الأمثِلة الآتية:

٥	زُرتُ دِمَشق مَرّةً.
٦	زُرتُ دِمَشق مَرّتَين.
٧	زُرتُ دِمَشق ثَلاثَ مَرّاتٍ.

السَبَب أنَّ مَرّة في حالة النَصب هو أنّها مَفعول مُطلق (absolute object) وهو دائماً مَنصوب.

العرض: استخداماً حركات يدوية وبدنية مناسبة، تُبيّن للطلاب كم مرة قمتُ أو لا تزال تقوم بشيء، على سبيل المثال:

«أحب عائلتي كثيراً لذلك أزورها مرّةً كلّ شهر. كذلك أحبّ الشاطئ وخاصة الساحل الغربي حيث سكنت لمدة سنتين. أسافر إلى كاليفورنيا مرّة كل سنة وأمشي على الشاطئ وأسبح في البحر.»

الممارسة: اسأل الطلاّب كم مرّة يقومون بنشاط ما:

«وأنت يا سامر، كم مرّةً في الشهر تذهب إلى الشاطئ؟ مرّة واحدة فقط؟!؟ ألا تحبّ الشاطئ؟»

«يا ماري كم مرّة يذهب سامر إلى الشاطئ في الشهر؟»
«ماري: يذهب سامر إلى الشاطئ مرّة واحدة في الشهر فقط لا غير.»
«ولماذا يذهب إليه مرّة واحدة في الشهر فقط؟»
«ماري: لا أعرف. سأسأله. يا سامر لماذا تذهب إلى الشاطئ مرّة واحدة فقط في الشهر.»

التَطبيق: في مجموعات من اثنين: وزّع على الطلاّب ورقة مكتوب عليها حوالي خمسة أسئلة عن كم مرّة يقومون بأنشطتهم اليومية--كما فعلوا في تمرين ١١. اطلب منهم استخدام مرّة وكلّ وما عدا في أجوبتهم. إليك مثال:
«كم مرّة تذهب إلى الجامعة في الأسبوع؟»
«كل يوم ما عدا يومي السبت والأحد.»
«كم مرّة تزور أهلك في الشهر؟»
«كل عطلة نهاية أسبوع.»
«كم مرّة تركب درّاجتك في الأسبوع؟»
«أركبها مرّة واحدة في الأسبوع فقط.»
«كم مرّة زرت ديزني ورلد؟ لقد زرتها مرّة واحدة فقط ولكنها أعجبتني كثيراً.»
«مَن جاء إلى الصف اليوم؟»
«جاء كل الطلاّب إلى الصف اليوم ما عدا فلان.»

٣- اِستِخدام ما عَدا

تأتي كَلِمة ما مع عَدا في التَعبير ما عَدا الّذي يَعني "except"، لكِن نَستطيع اِستِخدام عَدا بِنفسِها وتَدُلّ على نَفس المَعنى. إنَّ الاسم الّذي يلي ما عَدا في حالة النَصب دائماً.

٨	اِسْتقبَلَ عَدنان في المَطارِ كُلَّ الطُلاّبِ الجُدُدِ ما عَدا طالِبَينِ.	مَنصوب بِالـ(ينِ)
٩	كَتبتُ إلى كُلِّ أصدِقائي ما عَدا ثَلاثةً مِنهُم.	مَنصوب بِالـ(ً)

٤- اِستِخدام لِـ + الجُملة الاسميّة

آ- **التَذَكُّر**

سَبَق وتَعَلَّمنا اِستِخدام لأنَّ (because) لِلتَعبير عن التأويل(explanation). تَتألَّف لأنَّ من حَرفَين ألا وهما: لِـ (لام التَعليل = the *lām* of reason) وأنَّ (لِلتَوكيد = emphasis).

١٠	لِـ	+	أنَّ	←	لأنَّ	*because*

حَرف أنَّ من (إنَّ وأخواتُها) فَينصُب الاسم ويَرفَع الخَبَر كَما نَرى تَحتَ:

١١	لا نَسبَحُ في البُحَيرةِ لأنَّ الماءَ بارِدٌ.	*We don't swim in the lake because the water is cold.*
١٢	أسْكُنُ في هذِهِ المَدينةِ لأنَّ الطَقسَ جَميلٌ.	*I live in this city because the weather is pretty.*

في المِثالَين أعلاه ماءَ والطَقسَ اِسمان مَنصوبان بالفَتحة وبارِدٌ وجَميلٌ خَبَران مَفروعان بِتَنوين الضَمّ.

مُلاحَظة: نَستَطيع أن نَزيد ضَميراً مُتصلاً على لأنَّ وباقي الجُملة يَبقى كَما هو:

١٣	لا نَسبَحُ في البُحَيرةِ لأنَّها باردةٌ.	*We don't swim in the lake because it is cold.*
١٤	أسْكُنُ في هذِهِ المَدينةِ لأنَّها جَميلةٌ.	*I live in this city because it is pretty.*

في هذا الدرس، نقدّم ثلاثة طرق للتعبير عن التعليل ألا وهي: لِـ + جملة اسمية وبسبب + جملة اسمية ولِـ + فعل مضارع منصوب. قدّم للطلاّب هذه العبارات كلّ واحدة على حدة واشرح لهم كيفية استخدامها بطريقة سليمة في المحادثة التواصلية. مارس معهم كلّ واحدة حتى يُظهر لك أنّ الطلاّبَ فهموا استخدامها فهماً صحيحاً ثمّ تقدّم للأخرى.

العرض ١: لأنَّ
قُل لهم جملاً واضحةً في السياق واشرحها مستخدماً لأنَّ. أوضح لهم أيضاً أنّ الاسم الذي يلي لأنَّ منصوب. إليك بعض الأمثلة:

يسكن سالم في حلب لأنّه يعمل فيها. (ضمير متصل)
ما أكلتُ فطوري لأنّي متأخِّر. (ضمير متصل)
أمشي من بيتي لأنَّ الجامعةَ قريبةٌ. (اسم إنَّ)
آكل في ذلك المطعم لأنَّ الفولَ ممتاز هناك!
(اسم إنَّ)

العرض ٢: بِسبب
تابع ترتيب النشاط أعلاه وأوضح لهم أنَّ بِسَبَب مضاف والاسم الذي يليه مضاف إليه:

«اليوم عطلةٌ بِسَبَبِ الثلج.»
«ما مشيتُ اليوم بِسَبَبِ المطر.»

تأكّد بأنّك تترجم بِسَبَب of because لأنّ المقابل بالإنكليزية يتطلب جملة اسمية بعده أسوة بالعربية ولا يسمح لنا بأن نستخدم جملة شاملة بعده.

العرض ٣: لِـ + مضارع منصوب
تابع ترتيب الشرح أعلاه.
قد ترغب في ترجمة لِـ كَـ *in order to* بالإنكليزية.

التطبيق: افعل تمرين ١١.

ب- بِسَبَب **because of**

في هذا الدَرس، نُلاحِظ أنّ هُناكَ كَلِمة أخرى مُستخدِمة لِلتَعبير عن التأويل، أي بِسَبَب *because of*، المُتألّف من حَرف الجَرّ بِـ والاسم سَبَب *reason, cause*.

١٥	بِـ	+	سَبَب	←	بِسَبَب	*because of*

وَكَما هو الحال بِالإنكليزيّة، لا نَستَطيع اِستِخدام جُملة فِعليّة بَعد بِسَبَب، بَل لابُدّ من أن تليه جُملة إسميّة:

١٦	اليومُ عُطلةٌ بِسَبَبِ العيدِ.	*Today is a day off because of the holiday.*
١٧	لَم أحضُر الدَرْس بِسَبَبِ الطَقْسِ.	*I didn't attend class today because of the weather.*

لاحِظ في المِثالَين أعلاه ١٦-١٧، لا نَستَطيع اِستِخدام فِعل بَعد بِسَبَب، لأنّ بِسَبَبِ مُضاف والاسم الّذي يَليه مُضاف إليه.

ج- لِـ + المُضارِع المَنصوب

هُناك طَريقة أخرى كي نُعَبِّر عن التَعليل وهو اِستِخدام الحَرف لِـ قَبل الفِعل المُضارِع المَنصوب. تُبَيِّن الجَداول في الباب السابع في هذا الدَرس المُضارِع المَرفوع والمَنصوب والمَجزوم وكَذلِك المُلحَق «ج» في نِهاية هذا الكِتاب.

الحَرف لِـ هذا في مَجموعة حُروف التَعليل وكُلُّها تَدُلّ على نَفس المَعنى:

لِـ / كَي / حَتّى	+	فِعل مُضارِع مَنصوب	*in order to*

١٨	ذَهَبَتْ أختي إلى المَطارِ لِتَأخُذَ أوّلَ طائرةٍ إلى تونِس.	مَنصوب بالفَتحة
١٩	جِئتِ إلى هذه المدينةِ لِتَزوري صَديقَتَكِ.	تَسقُط نون النسوة
٢٠	أتى سامِر وفؤاد إلى الولاياتِ المُتَّحِدَةِ لِيَدرُسا في الجامِعة.	تَسقُط نون المُثَنّى
٢١	ذَهبوا إلى المَطعَمِ لِيَحتَفِلوا بِعيدِ ميلادِ صَديقِهِم.	تَسقُط نون الجَماعة

تمرين ١٣

المُحادَثة: اسأل زَميلك مُستَخدِماً الكَلِمات بَينَ القَوسَين في الإجابة.

١- لِماذا تُرْسِل(ينَ) بِطاقاتِ مُعايَدة؟ (لِـ . . .)
٢- إلى مَن أرْسَلْت بِطاقاتِ مُعايَدة؟ (كُلّ . . . ما عَدا)
٣- مَن اِسْتَقْبَلْت في المَطارِ ومِن أينَ أتى المُسافِر؟
٤- إلى أينَ سافَرْت ولماذا سافَرت إلى ذلك البَلَد؟ (بِسَبَب)
٥- كَمْ مَرّةً زُرت بَلَداً أجْنَبيّاً؟

أخبِر الجَميع بِما عَلِمت من المَعلومات.

٥- اِستِخدام اسم الفاعِل واسم المَفعول

كما تَعلَم الحُروف الفاء والعين واللام تَرمُز إلى الحَرف الأوّل والثاني والثالِث للفِعل العَرَبيّ وفي الوَزَن الأوّل اسمُ الفاعِل يأخُذ شَكْل فاعِل مِثل طالِب أو ساكِن أو عالِم كَذلِك اسم المَفعول في الوَزَن الأوّل الّذي يأخُذ شَكْل: مَدروس أو مَقبول أو مَسموع.

٢٢	هُوَ طالِبٌ في هذِهِ الجامِعة.	اسمُ الفاعِل
٢٣	هُوَ عالِمٌ في مَجال الطِبّ.	
٢٤	ما المَطلوب مِني؟	اسمُ المَفعول
٢٥	هذا الأمر مَعلوم.	

من المَعلوم أنّ لِلاسم العَرَبيّ مُثَنّى وجَمْع كَذلِكَ اسمُ الفاعِل والمَفعول، تأمّل الجَدوَل الآتي:

	المُفرَد	المُثَنّى	الجَمْع	المَعنى
٢٦	ذاهِبٌ	ذاهِبانِ	ذاهِبونَ	*goer*
٢٧	طالِب	طالِبانِ	طُلّاب	*requester/seeker*
٢٨	مَشْهور	مَشْهورانِ	مَشهورونَ / مَشاهير	*famous*
٢٩	مَحْصول	مَحْصولانِ	مَحاصيل	*(crop) yield*

العَرض: تقديم اسم الفاعِل:
اكتب _ ا _ _ على السبورة وأخبرهم بأنّ هذا النموذج يوازي الوَزن **فاعِل** حيث نستبدل الفراغات بحروف الجذر. ومقابله بالإنكليزية "er" مثل -runner, walk er, sleeper. ثم اطلب من الطلاّب إعطاءك جذر فعل في الوزن الأول. اسألهم سؤالاً مثل:
«أعطني فعلاً في الوزن الأوّل.»

عادةً يُقدِّم الطلاب فعلاً صحيحاً مثل **كتب** أو **شرب**. اكتب الفعل على السبورة بجانب النموذج واملأ الفراغات بحروف الفِعل، وبعد ذلك أسألهم ما معنى **كاتِب**؟
تابع هذه العملية مستخدماً ثلاث كلمات أو أربعة حتى يفهم الطلاّب الدرس جيداً.
ذكّرهم بأنّ هذه العملية تنفع الوزن الأول فقط لاغير، أما الأوزان المتبقية أي الثاني إلى العاشر، فلها شكل خاص مع أنّها كلها تبدأ بميم مضمومة وعين الفِعل مكسورة أي مُفعِل.
تأكّد بأنّ الطلاّب يدركون أنّ الكسرة في الوزن الأول هي نفس الكسرة الموجودة في الأوزان الأخرى وتدل على نفس المعنى أي أن هذه الكلمة اسم فاعِل.

العرض: تقديم اسم المفعول:
اكتب مَـ _ _ و _ على السبورة وبجانبه **مَفعول** وقل للطلاّب أنّ هذا الوزن يدل على اسم عليه يقع حكم فعل ومقابله بالإنكليزية:
"that which is done to the root."

تابع ما فعلنا سابقاً باسم الفاعِل.

وكما فعلنا أعلاه، تأكّد بأنّ الطلاب يدركون أنّ العين المفتوحة أي مُفَعَّل تدل على أنّ هذه الكلمة **اسم مفعول**.

اسمُ الفاعِل واسمُ المَفعول في الوَزَن الثاني إلى العاشِر

١- يَدخُل حَرف الميم على بِداية كُلّ اسم فاعل واسم مَفعول في الوَزَن الثاني إلى العاشِر: مـُ + فعل.

٢- اسمُ الفاعِل: العين مَكسورة أي تَدخُل على الحَرف الثاني كَسرة:

٣- اسمُ المَفعول: العين مَفتوحة أي تَدخُل على الحَرف الثاني فَتحة:

X	VIII	VII	VI	V	IV	III	II
مُسْتَخْدِم	مُنْتَخِب	مُنْكَسِر	مُتَساقِط	مُتَكَلِّم	مُخْرِج	مُخاطِب	مُدَرِّس
user	*elector*	*broken*	*falling*	*speaker*	*director*	*addresser*	*teacher*

X	VIII	VII	VI	V	IV	III	II
مُسْتَخْدَم	مُنْتَخَب	--	مُتَساقَط	مُتَكَلَّم	مُخْرَج	مُخاطَب	مُدَرَّس
used	*elected*	--	*fallen*	*spoken*	*outcome*	*addressed*	*taught*

إفطار رمضان

اسمُ الفاعِل واسمُ المَفعول

	الوَزَن	مِثال	اِسمُ الفاعِل	مِثال	اِسمُ المَفعول	مِثال
II	فَعَّل	دَرَّس	مُفَعِّل	مُدَرِّس *teacher*	مُفَعَّل	مُدَرَّس *taught*
III	فاعَل	حارَب	مُفاعِل	مُحارِب *warrior*	مُفاعَل	مُحارَب *fought, resisted*
IV	أفْعل	أعْطى	مُفْعِل	مُعْطي *giver*	مُفْعَل	مُعْطى *given*
V	تَفَعَّل	تَعَلَّم	مُتَفَعِّل	مُتَعلِّم *educated*	مُتَفَعَّل	مُتَعَلَّم *learnable*
VI	تَفاعَل	تَقاسَم	مُتَفاعِل	مُتَقاسِم *sharer*	مُتَفاعَل	مُتَقاسَم *shared*
VII	اِنْفَعَل	اِنْكَسَر	مُنْفَعِل	مُنْكَسِر *broken; defeated*	------	------
VIII	اِفتَعَل	اِحتَفَل	مُفْتَعِل	مُحْتَفِل *celebrator*	مُفْتَعَل	مُحتَفَل *celebrated*
IX	اِفْعَلّ	اِخْضَرّ	-----	-----	مُفْعَلّ	مُخْضَرّ *colored green*
X	اِسْتَفْعَل	اِسْتَقْبَل	مُسْتَفعِل	مُسْتَقْبِل *receiver*	مُسْتَفْعَل	مُسْتَقْبَل *received*

تمرين ١٤

آ- اِستَخرِجوا **اسم الفاعل** أو **اسم المفعول** من الجُمَل الآتية:

	اسم الفاعِل	اسم المَفعول
مِثال: أخي مُتَزَوِّج مُنذُ سَنة.	مُتَزَوِّج	غَير مَوجود
١- هالة بُستاني ساكِنة في حَلَب الآن.	______	______
٢- تَحتاج الرياضة إلى مُشَجِّعين.	______	______
٣- قال الأستاذ إنَّ الامتِحان قَبلَ العُطلة مُفيد.	______	______
٤- هُناك عِدة مُفرَدات مُشتَرَكة بين الفُصحى والعاميّة.	______	______
٥- تَمَّت الوِلادة بِسلامة والمَولود ووالِدتُه بِخَير.	______	______
٦- في رَمَضان الشَوارِع مُزَيَّنة بِالأضواء المُلوَّنة.	______	______
٧- يَريد المُعَلِّم مُساعَدةَ الطُلّاب المُبتَدِئين.	______	______
٨- قرأتُ مَجموعةً مِن الكُتُبِ المُتَرجَمة إلى العَرَبيّة.	______	______
٩- اللاذقية مِن المُدُن الواقِعة على الساحِل السوريّ.	______	______
١٠- وَضع الشاري المُشتَرَيات في العَرَبة.	______	______

ب- اكتبوا **اسم الفاعل** أو **اسم المفعول** مِن الأفعال المَوضوعة بَين قَوسَين.

١- في السنوات الأخيرة، قَلّ عدد ______ (يُدَخِّن).

٢- يَجِب على كُلّ ______ (يَدرُس) الوُصول إلى الصَفّ في الوَقت المُحَدَّد.

٣- اِستَقبَلَتُ الطُلاب ______ين (وَصَل) إلى الجامِعة.

٤- اِنكَسَرَت الكأس ______ (يَضَع) على الطاوِلة.

٥- هذا الحاسوب ______ (يُصنَع) في اليابان.

٦- أخي يَعمَل ______ (يُصوِّر) في التِلفاز.

داخل المسجد الاقصى

٧- يُعَدّ حَليم بَركات مِن أهَمّ ______ (يُفكِّر) العَرَب في القَرنِ العِشرين.

٨- ما أكلتُ اليوم، لِذلِكَ فإنَّني______ (جاع).

٩- عَمِل أبي ______ (يُترجِم) جَريدة النَهار اللُبنانيّة.

١٠- البَرنامَج ______ (يُسَجِّل) على شَريط فيديو.

٦- اِستِخدام لَمْ + المُضارِع المَجزوم

حَتّى الآن، اِستَخدَمنا الحَرف ما لِنَنفي الفِعل الماضي، وكَما تَعلَم لا تؤثِّر ما لا على الفِعل ولا على تَركيب الجُملة *word order*:

٣٠ زُرنا بَيروت. *We visited Beirut.* ← ما زُرنا بَيروت. *We didn't visit Beirut.*

كَذلِك، نَستَطيع اِستِحدام الحَرف لَم لِنَنفي الزَمَن الماضي الّذي يُوفِّر لَنا نَفياً رَسمياً *formal* حاسِماً *emphatic*. وَلكِن، خِلافاً لِلحَرف ما، تُؤثِّر لَم على الفِعل فَيَجعلُه في المُضارِع المَجزوم. فَلنِنظُرْ إلى ما يَحدُث لِلفِعل حين يَدخُل عليهِ حَرف النَفي لَم مُقارَنةً بالمُضارِع المَرفوع:

شارع من شوارع القدس في رمضان

العَرض: إقرأ فقرة قصيرة كتبتها للطلاّب تكاثر فيها حرف النفي لَمْ، مثلاً: «لَم أذهب إلى السينما مع صديقي جون لأنّي لم أرد أن أشاهد ذلك الفيلم الذي كان جون يريد مشاهدته. كنت أريد أن أستقبل صديقي عدنان في المطار ولكن لم يرد جون أن يذهب معي. لا أعرف لماذا لم تعجب جون فكرة الذهاب إلى المطار لأنّنا لم نرَ عدنان منذ عدّة أشهر.»

الممارسة: اسأل الطلاّب بعض أسئلة الاستفهام التي تتطلب منهم استخدام حرف النفي لَمْ، مثلاً:
«لماذا لم أذهب إلى السينما؟»
«لماذا لم يذهب جون إلى المطار؟»
«هل رأينا عدنان في الشهر الماضي؟»

التطبيق: في مجموعات من اثنين: وزّع على الطلاّب صوراً قصصية أو لوحات قصصية وأخبرهم بأن عليهم رواية قصة تناسب الصور مركزين على استخدام لَمْ فيها. وبعد انتهاء الرواية، اطلب منهم أن يحكوها لزملائهم.

مُقارَنة بَين المُضارِع المَرفوع والمَجزوم			
الضَمير	المَرفوع	المَجزوم	
أنا	أكْتُبُ	لَمْ أكْتُبْ	
نَحْنُ	نَكْتُبُ	لَمْ نَكْتُبْ	
أنتَ	تَكْتُبُ	لَمْ تَكْتُبْ	
أنتِ	تَكْتُبينَ	لَمْ تَكْتُبي	تَسْقُط النون
أنتُما	تَكْتُبانِ	لَمْ تَكْتُبا	تَسْقُط النون
أنتُم	تَكْتُبونَ	لَمْ تَكْتُبوا	تَسْقُط النون
أنتُنَّ	تَكْتُبْنَ	لَمْ تَكْتُبْنَ	نَفس التَصريف
هُوَ	يَكْتُبُ	لَمْ يَكْتُبْ	
هِيَ	تَكْتُبُ	لَمْ تَكْتُبْ	
هُما	يَكْتُبانِ	لَمْ يَكْتُبا	تَسْقُط النون
هُما	تَكْتُبانِ	لَمْ تَكْتُبا	تَسْقُط النون
هُمْ	يَكْتُبونَ	لَمْ يَكْتُبوا	تَسْقُط النون
هُنَّ	يَكْتُبْنَ	لَمْ يَكْتُبْنَ	نَفس التَصريف

كَما لاحَظنا في الجَدوَل أعلاه، تَسقُط النون في كُلّ التَصريفات ما عَدا جَمع المؤنَّث أي أنْتُنَّ وهُنَّ.

٧- مُراجَعة الفِعْل المُعتَلّ

في اللُغة العَرَبيّة يُوجَد هُناك بعَض الأفعال لَها حَرف عِلّة في الجَذر مِثل الواو أو الياء، وهذه الأفعال المُعتَلّة تُصرَّف تَصريفاً خاصّاً في المُضارِع المَجزوم. دَعنا نَنظُر إلى الفِعلين زار (الّذي لَهُ واو العين = زور) ومَشى (الّذي لَهُ ياء اللام = مَشي).

لاحِظ في المُضارِع المَجزوم أنَّ حَرف العِلّة يتَحوَّل إلى حَركة مِثل الواو تَصير ضَمة (المِثال ٣١) أو الياء تَصير كَسرة (المِثال ٣٢).

٣١	سنَزور بَيروت.	We will visit Beirut.	←	لَمْ تَزُرْ بَيروت.	We didn't visit Beirut.
٣٢	سَنَمشي.	We will walk.	←	لَمْ نَمْشِ.	We haven't walked.

في الجَدوَل أدناه، تَرى تَصريف الفِعل زارَ بواو العَين الّذي يَتَحوَّل إلى ضَمّة في المُضارِع المَجزوم، وهكَذا نُصَرِّف كُلّ فِعل أجوَف في المُضارِع المَجزوم:

تَصريفُ الفِعلِ زارَ بِالمُضارِعِ المَرفوعِ والمَجزومِ

الضَمير	المَرفوع	المَجزوم	
أنا	أزورُ	أزُرْ	
نَحنُ	نَزورُ	نَزُرْ	
أنتَ	تَزورُ	تَزُرْ	
أنتِ	تَزورينَ	تَزوري	تَسْقُط النون
أنتُما	تَزورانِ	تَزورا	تَسْقُط النون
أنتُم	تَزورونَ	تَزوروا	تَسْقُط النون
أنتُنَّ	تَزُرْنَ	تَزُرْنَ	نَفس التَصريف
هُوَ	يَزورُ	يَزُرْ	
هِيَ	تَزورُ	تَزُرْ	
هُما	يزورانِ	يَزورا	تَسْقُط النون
هُما	تَزورانِ	تَزورا	تَسْقُط النون
هُمْ	يَزورونَ	يَزوروا	تَسْقُط النون
هُنَّ	يَزُرْنَ	يَزُرْنَ	نَفس التَصريف

في الجَدوَل أدناه، تَرى تَصريف الفِعل مَشى بياء اللام، وهكَذا نُصَرِّف كُلّ فِعل ناقِص في المُضارِع المَجزوم:

تَصريفُ الفِعْلِ مَشى بِالمُضارِعِ المَرفوعِ والمَجزومِ			
الضَمير	المَرفوع	المَجزوم	
أنا	أمشي	أمشِ	
نَحْنُ	نَمشي	نَمشِ	
أنتَ	تَمشي	تَمشِ	
أنتِ	تَمشينَ	تَمشي	تَسْقُط النون
أنتُما	تَمشِيانِ	تَمشِيا	تَسْقُط النون
أنتُم	تَمشونَ	تَمشوا	تَسْقُط النون
أنتُنَّ	تَمشينَ	تَمشينَ	نَفس التَصريف
هُوَ	يَمشي	يَمشِ	
هِيَ	تَمشي	تَمشِ	
هُما	يَمشِيانِ	يَمشِيا	تَسْقُط النون
هُما	تَمشِيانِ	تَمشِيا	تَسْقُط النون
هُمْ	يَمشونَ	يَمشوا	تَسْقُط النون
هُنَّ	يَمشينَ	يَمشينَ	نَفس التَصريف

لاحِظ أنّ النون لا تَسقُط في الفِعل المُؤنَّث المُضارِع المَجزوم المُظَلَّل بالأحمَر في الجَدوَلين السابِقَين.

زي البَنات التَقليديّ لعيد الفِطر

تمرين ١٥

أعِدْ تَرتيبَ الجُمَلِ لِتُشكِّلَ فِقرةً مُفيدة.

١- لَمْ أذْهَبْ (= ما ذَهَبتُ) اليومَ إلى المَدرَسةِ بِسَبَبِ عيدِ الاستِقلال.
سَبَحنا في البَحْرِ ساعَتين.
ثُمَّ أخذنا القِطارَ في الساعةِ الرابِعةِ والنِصْفِ ورَجَعنا إلى بُيوتِنا.
لِهذا السَبَبِ ذَهَبتُ أنا وأصدِقائي إلى شاطِئِ البَحْر.
بَعدَ الظُهرِ سَبَحنا قَليلاً مَرّةً ثانية.
ذَهَبنا إلى الشاطِئِ بِالقِطار.
بَعدَ ذلِكَ أكَلنا الغَداءَ في مَطعَمٍ صَغيرٍ على الشاطِئِ.
وَصَلنا إلى الشاطِئِ في الساعةِ العاشِرةِ والنِصْفِ صَباحاً.

تمرين ١٦

أكْمِلِ الجُمَلَ الآتيةَ بِكَلِماتٍ مُناسِبةٍ وَفْقَ قَواعِدِ اللُغةِ العَرَبيّة.

١- عِندي ________ كَبيرتانِ.
☐ دَرّاجتانِ ☐ دَرّاجتا ☐ دَرّاجتَيْنِ

٢- يَعمَلُ في الشَرِكةِ ________ سَيّاراتٍ مِن بِلادٍ عَديدة.
☐ سائِقونَ ☐ سائِقو ☐ سائِقَيْنِ

٣- يَأكُلُ مازِن العَشاءَ مَعَ زَوجَتِهِ في المَطعَمِ ________ يَومِ جُمْعة.
☐ كُلَّ ☐ مَرَّةً ☐ ما عَدا

٤- زُرْتُ مَدينةَ باريس ________ .
☐ مَرّتانِ ☐ مَرَّتَيْنِ ☐ مَرَّتا

٥- تَدرُسُ هالَة في المَكتَبَةِ كُلَّ يَومٍ ________ يَومَ الجُمْعة.
☐ ما عَدا ☐ كُلَّ ☐ مَرَّة

٦- يَسكُنُ مايكِل براون القاهِرَةَ الآنَ بِسَبَبِ ________ .
☐ يُريدُ أن يَدرسَ العَرَبيّة ☐ دِراسةِ العَرَبيّة

٧- عِندَ سالي سَيّارةُ تويوتا لأنَّ ________ .
☐ السَيّاراتِ اليابانيّةَ جَيِّدةٌ ☐ تُحِبُّ اليابان

تمرين ١٧

١- اِبحَث عن اسم فاعِل في الفِقرة فَوق صورة خَديجة واسم فاعِل آخر في يَوميّة عَدنان (يوم الإثنين) واكتُبْهُما في أسفَلِ الصَفحة (كُلّ أشكال وُرودِها).

____

٢- اِبحَث عن اسم مَفعول في صَفحة ٣٥٨ واكتُبْه تَحت.

____

٣- اِبحَث عن فِعلَي مُضارِع مَجزوم في يَوميّة مايكل براون (يوم الجُمعة) وفِعل مُضارِع مَجزوم وفِعل مُضارع مَنصوب في يَوميّة عَدنان (يَوم السَبت) اكتُبْها تَحت.

____

٤- اِبحَث عن عَدَدَينِ تَرتيبيَّينِ في الفِقرة بِجانِب صورة هِشام واكتُبْهُما تَحت.

____

٥- اِبحَث عن الأفعال في الأوزان الآتية: فَعَلَ / أفْعَلَ / اِفْتَعَلَ في صَفحة ٣٥٨ واكتُبْها تَحت.

____

٦- اِبحَث عن فِعلَينِ مُعتَلَّينِ في نَصّ القِراءة صَفحة ٣٣٥ وفِعل مُعتَلّ في صَفحة ٣٥٨ واكتُبْها في صيغة الغائب (= هُوَ) في الماضي والمُضارِع.

____

٧- اِبحَث عن إضافة في يَوميّة مايكل براون (يوم الخَميس) حَيثُ المُضاف في صيغة المُثَنّى واكتُبْها تَحت.

____

تمرين ١٨

اخترِ التَصْريفَ المُناسِبَ لِلفِعلِ لِتُكمِلَ الجُملَ التالية:

١- أتى سامِر إلى أمريكا لـ ________ الطِبّ.

☐ يَدرُسُ ☐ يَدرُسَ ☐ يَدرُسْ

٢- لَمْ ________ الطَبيبُ هذا الشَيء.

☐ يَقولُ ☐ يَقولَ ☐ يَقُلْ

٣- ما ________ هاوائي حَتّى الآن.

☐ زُرنا ☐ نَزورَ ☐ نَزُرْ

٤- لَمْ ________ بِعيدِ ميلادِ ابنَتِهِم هذا العام.

☐ يَحتَفِلونَ ☐ اِحتَفَلوا ☐ يَحتَفِلوا

٥- ذَهَبَ عَدنان إلى كاليفورنيا لِـ ________ ديزني لاند.

☐ يَرى ☐ يَرَ ☐ رأى

٦- لَمْ ________ الفَتاةُ في اللَيلِ بِسَبَبِ الألَم.

☐ تَنامُ ☐ تَنامَ ☐ تَنَمِ

بعد الإفطار

تمرين ١٩

آ- **أكْمِل الجُمَل الآتية بالكَلِمة المُناسِبة وَفْق نَصّ الاسْتِماع:**

١- الشَخْص في هذا التَمرينِ هُوَ ________ .

☐ أُم ☐ أب ☐ طَبيب

٢- «اللاذِقيةُ» هُوَ اسمُ ________ .

☐ بَحْر ☐ عِيادَة ☐ مَدينة

٣- لَمْ تَنَمِ البِنت بِاللَيل بِسَبَب ________ .

☐ البَطْن ☐ الألَم ☐ الأسْبرين

٤- سَوفَ تَنامُ البِنت في النَهار بِسَبَب ________ .

☐ الإبْرَة ☐ الألَم ☐ حَبّاتِ الأسبِرين

ب- أكمِلِ الجُمَلَ التاليةَ بِعِباراتٍ مِنَ النص:

٥- اسم أبي البِنت ____________ .

٦- يَعمَل أبو البِنتِ ____________ .

٧- أعطى الطَبيب لِلبِنتِ ____________ في العِيادة.

٨- اسْمُ البِنتِ ____________ .

ج- اكتُبْ «خَطأ» أو «صَواب» جانِبَ كُلِّ جُمْلَةٍ وصَحِّحِ الجُمَلَ الخَطأ.

٩- الأمُّ لا تَعمَل.

١٠- لَم تَنَمِ الأمّ كَثيراً بِسَبَب أَلَم في بَطنِها.

١١- أخَذَتِ البِنتُ الإبرةَ في عِيادَةِ الطَبيب.

١٢- سَتَأخُذ البِنت حَبّة أسبِرين بَعد كُلّ طَعام.

د- أجِبْ عَن هذِه الأسئِلةِ حَسَبَ النَصّ:

١٣- كَم وَلَداً في هذِهِ العائِلة؟

١٤- ماذا فَعَلَت الأمّ في اللَيل لِتُساعِد ابنَتَها؟

١٥- إلى أين أخَذَت الأمُّ ابنَتَها في الصَباح؟

١٦- ما سَبَب أَلَم البِنت؟

١٧- في نَصّ الاستِماع، هُناكَ ثلاثة مُفرَدات لا نَعرفُها. اكتُبْها على وَرَقة مُنفَصِلة وفَكِّر فيها من حَيثُ الجذر والوَزن وحاوِل أن تَستَنتِج معناها مُستَخدِماً السياق كَدَليل.

١٨- اكتُب اسم البَحر المَذكور في نَصّ الاستِماع بالعَرَبيّة والإنكِليزيّة.

من الأكلات الرَمَضانيّة

المُفْرَدات

استمِع إلى المُفْرَدة بالعَرَبيّة ثم أعِد نُطْقَها مرّتين.

أَجْنَبيّ ج أَجانِب (n., m.) . . . . foreigner

أَجْنَبيّ / أَجْنَبيَّة (adj.) . . . . foreign

أَخَذَ (يَأْخُذُ) أَخْذ (v.) . . . . to take

أَرْسَلَ (يُرسِلُ) إرْسال (v.) . . . . to send

اِسْتَقبَلَ (يَسْتَقبِلُ) اِستِقبال (v.) . . . . to receive (someone)

اِعتَقَدَ (يَعتَقِدُ) اِعتِقاد (v.) . . . . to believe.

اِلْتِهاب ج اِلتِهابات (n., m.) . . . . inflammation, infection

أَلَم ج آلاَم (n., m.) . . . . pain.

آلَمَ (يُؤلِمُ) (v.) . . . . to hurt

أمّا (particle) . . . . as for, but, yet, however

اِنْتهى (يَنْتَهي) اِنتِهاء (v.) . . . . to finish, to come to an end

بَدَأَ (يَبدَأُ) بَدْء (v.) . . . . to begin

بِداية ج بِدايات (n., f.) . . . . beginning

بَسّ . . . . only (standard usage in most Arab varieties)

بَوّابة ج بَوّابات (n., f.) . . . . gate

جالِس ج جالِسون (n., m.) . . . . sitting

حَبّة ج حَبّات (n., f.) . . . . pill

حُكومة ج حُكومات (n., f.) . . . . government

حَمَلَ (يَحْمِلُ) حَمْل (v.) . . . . to carry.

رَأى (يَرى) رُؤية (v.) . . . . to see

رَبّةُ بَيْت ج رَبّات بُيوت (n., f.) . . . . housewife future marker (= *will* in Syrian colloquial) . . . . رَح

colleague, coworker. . . . . (n., m.) زَميل ج زُمَلاء

mail carrier . . . . (n., m.) ساعٍ ج سُعاة (ساعي بَريد)

to help, to assist . . . . (v.) ساعَدَ (يُساعِدُ) مُساعَدة

safe, secure; healthy. . . . . (n., m.) سالِم ج سالِمون

reason, cause . . . . (n., m.) سَبَب ج أسْباب

Syria, Damascus, Greater Syria . . . . (n., f.) الشام

drink, syrup, sherbet . . . . (n., m.) شَراب ج أشْرِبة، شَرابات

opposite, anti-, adversary, opponent . . . . (n., m.) ضِدٌّ ج أضْداد

molar tooth . . . . (n., m.) ضِرْس ج أضْراس، ضُروس

physician, doctor . . . . (n., m.) طَبيب ج أَطِبّاء

good . . . . (n., m.) طَيِّب ج طَيِّبون

year. . . . . (n., m.) عام ج أعْوام

crowded (Syrian colloquial) . . . . (n., f) عَجْقة

to know . . . . (v.) عَلِمَ (يَعْلَمُ) عِلْم

sunset . . . . (n., m.) غُروب

rich, wealthy. . . . . (n., m.) غَنيّ ج أغنِياء

and, then, so. . . . . (coordinating particle) فَـ

benefit, use, advantage . . . . (n., f.) فائِدة ج فَوائِد

poor . . . . (n., m.) فَقير ج فُقَراء

to worry . . . . (v.) قَلِقَ (يَقْلَق) قَلَق

as . . . . (particle) كَما

electricity . . . . (n., f.) كَهْرَباء

not (particle used to negate past-tense verbs) . . . . . . (particle) لَمْ

لَيْلة ج لَيالٍ (n., f.)	(a) night
ما عَدا (particle)	except
ماضٍ (الماضي) (adj.)	previous, last, past
مُبارَك (n., m.)	blessed
مَدْرَسة ج مَدارِس (n., f.)	school
مُعايَدة ج مُعايَدات (n., f.)	greeting
مَكْتوب (n., m.)	written
مِنْحة ج مِنَح (n., f.)	scholarship, grant, gift
مَوْجود ج مَوْجودون (n., m.)	existing, present
نَوْع ج أنْواع (n., m.)	kind, sort
وَجَدَ (يَجِدُ) وُجود (v.)	to find

عيد الأضحى في مِصر

الدرس الثامن عشر

أهداف الدرس

- وَصْف أنشِطة وأحداث في المُضارِع والماضي
- قراءة إعلانات صُحُفيّة
- وَصْف مُخَطَّط شَقّة أو بَيت والأثاث فيها
- وَصْف مَحَلّات تِجاريّة ومَكانها في الحَي.
- اِستِخدام: أريدُ أنْ + المُضارِع

المُفرداتُ الجَديدة في صُوَرٍ عَديدة

مَوْقِد

بَرّاد / ثَلّاجة

خِزانة كُتُب

مِصْباح

مِرآة

حَوْض

مِرحاض

مَغسَلة

رُكنُ المُفْرَداتِ الجَديدة

to rent	اِسْتَأجَرَ (يَسْتَأجِرُ) اِسْتِئجار
it pleases	أعْجَبَ (يُعْجِبُ) إعْجاب
announcement; advertisement	إعلان ج إعلانات
rent	إيجار ج إيجارات
part(s)	جُزء ج أجْزاء
company	شَرِكة ج شَرِكات
to place	وَضَعَ (يَضَعُ) وَضْع
to fall; to be located	وَقَعَ (يَقَعُ) وُقوع
there is; there are	يوجَدُ

تمرين ١

وافِقْ بَيْنَ الكَلِماتِ في العَمودَين.

١-	بَرّاد		مِترو
٢-	خُبْز		تَليفون
٣-	مَحَطّة		ثَلاّجة
٤-	عِيادة		خَلْفَ
٥-	بِناية		عَيْش
٦-	بَنْك		دُكّان
٧-	هاتِف		طَبيب
٨-	بَقّال		شَقّة
			مَصْرِف

تمرين ٢

اخترَ الكَلِمةَ الّتي لا تُناسِب باقي الكَلِمات في كُلِّ مَجْموعة وبيِّن السَبَب.

١-	خبّاز	بقّال	نَوْع	خُضَريّ
٢-	مِرحاض	غسّالة	برّاد	جلاّية
٣-	مَغسَلة	حَوْض	هاتِف	مَجلى
٤-	فَوْقَ	شارِع	تَحْتَ	أمامَ
٥-	غُرفة	شَقَّة	مَوْقِف	بِناية

تمرين ٣

أكمِلِ الجُمَلَ التالِيَة بِأفضَل كَلِمَة مُناسِبَة:

١- ________ مايكِل إلى شَقَّة جَديدة.

☐ اِسْتأجَر ☐ اِنتَقَلَ ☐ أعْجَبَ ☐ أحَبَّ

٢- أتَكَلَّم مَعَ أصدِقائي بِـ________ .

☐ البَرّاد ☐ المِصْباح ☐ المِرآة ☐ الهاتِف

٣- أجلِس ________ التِلفاز.

☐ أمامَ ☐ خَلْفَ ☐ تَحْتَ ☐ فَوْقَ

٤- تَضَع هالَة مَلابِسَها في ________ .

☐ الثَلاّجة ☐ الخِزانة ☐ المِرحاض ☐ السَرير

٥- يَعمَل أبو هِشام في ________.

☐ مَصرِف ☐ مَوقِف ☐ مَجلى ☐ خِزانَة

٦- يَجلِس صَديقي أحمَد إلى ________ .

☐ نَوْمي ☐ يَميني ☐ مَلابِسي ☐ خِزانَتي

٧- ________ مايكِل سَيّارَةً لِيَومَين حينَ كانَ في الإسكَندَرِيَّة.

☐ اِشتَرى ☐ باعَ ☐ اِسْتأجَر ☐ اِنْتَقَلَ

مَسجَد السُلطان حَسَن في القاهِرة

شَقَّة مايكِل الجَديدة

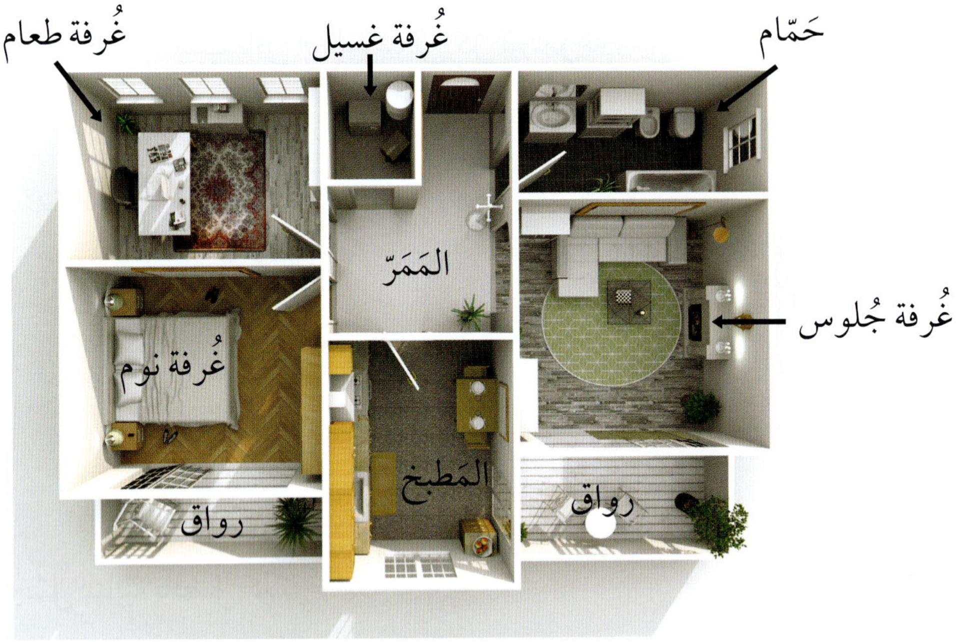

مُخَطَّط شَقَّة مايكِل

يَسكُن مايكِل براون، كَما تَعلَم، في القاهِرة الآن لأَنَّه يَدرُس اللُغَةَ العَرَبيَّة في الجامِعةِ الأمريكيَّة بِالقاهِرة. أرادَ مايكِل أنْ يَنتَقِل مِن شَقّتِهِ القَديمَة إلى شَقّة أخرى أقْرَب إلى الجامِعة فيها هاتِف وبَرّاد. قرأ في الجَريدة هذا الإعلان عَن شَقّة لِلإيجار:

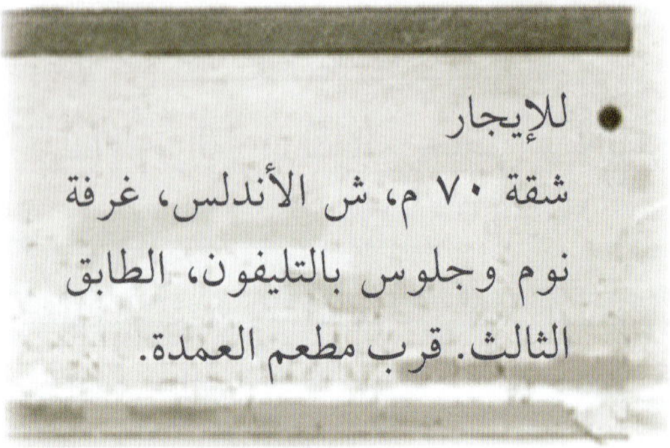
للإيجار
شقة ٧٠ م، ش الأندلس، غرفة نوم وجلوس بالتليفون، الطابق الثالث. قرب مطعم العمدة.

رَأى مايكِل تِلكَ الشَقّة، وهِيَ تَقَع في «بابِ اللَوق» وأعْجَبَتْه، فاسْتأجَرَها مِن سَيِّدة عَلِم أنَّها عَمِلَتْ في الكُويت عِدّة سَنَوات. أُجْرةُ الشَقّةِ الشَهريَّة ٧٠٠ جُنَيه مِصريّ بِالإضافةِ إلى الماء والكَهرباء. تُوجَد غُرفَة جُلوس واحِدة في الشَقَّة لكِنَّ هذِهِ الغُرفة واسِعة. هُناكَ طاوِلَة وأربَعَة كَراسٍ في جُزْء مِنَ الغُرفَة يَسْتَعمِلُها مايكِل لِلطَعام

العرض: أحضر معك صورة لمخطط بيت أو شقّة من عندك أو من الشابكة وتأكّد من أنّ كلّ غرفة واضحة في الصورة. صِف للطلاّب كلّ غرف البيت من حيث الاسم والاستخدام وكم مرة في اليوم تستعملها ومتى تستعملها. إليك مثال:

«هذه صورة غرفة جلوسي وعادة نجلس فيها أنا وزوجتي حين نشاهد التلفاز أو نستقبل الضيوف. ويوجد فيها أريكة طويلة ومقعد وطاولة قهوة ومكتبة التلفاز.»

الممارسة: اطلب من بعض الطلاّب أن يصفوا شقتهم / بيتهم ثم اسأل الآخرين أسئلة الاستيعاب مثل:

أ- «يا سارة، ماذا يوجد في شقّتك؟»
سارة- «في شقّتي يوجد غرفتا نوم ومطبخ وغرفة جلوس وغرفة طعام وحمام.»
أ- «وماذا يوجد في غرفة جلوسك؟»
سارة- «يوجد في غرفة جلوسي كذا وكذا وكذا.»
أ- «عظيم! يا ليسا، ماذا يوجد في غرفة جلوس سارة؟»
ط-«يوجد في غرفة جلوس سارة كذا وكذا وكذا.»

التطبيق: في مجموعات من اثنين أو ثلاثة: اطلب من الطلاّب أن يسألوا بعضهم بعضاً أسئلة مثل:
«أين تسكن وكم غرفة في سقتك/ بيتك وأي نوع من غرف هي وماذا يوجد فيها من الآثاث.»

وللدِراسة أيضاً، وفي الجُزْءِ الآخَر أريكة كَبيرة لِلجُلوس يُوجَد مُقابِلُها تِلفاز وخِزانَةُ كُتُب صَغيرة وَضَعَ مايكِل فيها كُتُبَهُ وعَلَّق على الجِدار صورة أُسرتِه. إلى جانِبِ الأريكَة هُناكَ مِصْباح وهاتِف.

غُرفَة جُلوس

غُرفَة طَعام ومَطبَخ

أمّا في غُرفَةِ النَوم فَهُناكَ سَرير وطاوِلَة صَغيرَة علَيْها مِصْباح كَهْرَبائِيّ وخِزانَة مَلابِس. إلى جانِبِ غُرفَةِ النَوم يُوجَد الحَمّام وفيهِ حَوْضُ الاسْتِحْمام ومِرْحاض أوروبيّ ومَغْسَلة. فَوْقَ المَغْسَلة هُناكَ مِرْآة.

غُرفَة نَوم

حَمّام

المَطبَخ لَيْسَ واسِعاً. فيهِ ثَلاّجة ومَوْقِد يَعمَل بِالغاز ومَجْلى، لكِنْ لَيْسَ فيهِ غَسّالة ولا جَلاّية كَهْرَبائيَّة. مَطبَخُهُ هذا أكبَر مِن مَطبَخِهِ القَديم. يَستَعمِل مايكِل المَطبَخ كُلَّ يوم لأنَّهُ يَأكُل فطورَه في البَيت وأحْياناً يَأكُل الغَداء والعَشاء أيضاً.

حينَ انتَقَل مايكِل مِن شَقَّتِهِ القَديمَة إلى شَقَّتِهِ الجَديدة أتى صَديقاهُ المِصريّان سَمير عَبدُ الفَتّاح وحُسَيْن أحْمَد لِيُساعِداهُ في الانتِقال. حَملوا كُتُبَ مايكِل وحَقائِبَهُ ثُمَّ اسْتأجَروا شاحِنة صَغيرة وذَهَبوا إلى الشَقَّةِ الجَديدة. لَمْ يَذهَبوا في ذلِكَ اليَوم إلى الجامِعة.

شاحِنة

في مَساء يَومِ الخَميس مِنَ الأسبوعِ التالي زارَهُ في شَقَّتِهِ الجَديدة أصدِقاؤُهُ سَمير وحُسَين وجِنِفَر وهِبة. قالَت هِبة إنَّ الشَقّة أعْجَبَتْها لأنَّها مُطِلّة على شارِع كَبير، وقال حُسَين إنَّها تُعجِبُهُ لأنَّها في بِنايَة نَظيفَة، وقال سَمير إنَّ الشَقَّة تُعجِبُهُ لأنَّها قَريبة مِنَ السوق. أمّا جِنِفَر فَقالَت إنَّها لا تُريد أنْ تَسكُن في شَقَّة لأنَّها لا تُحِبّ أنْ تُنَظِّفَها كُلَّ يَوم. لكِنَّ مايكِل قالَ لَها إنَّ خادِمة تَأتي مَرَّتَين في الأسبوع لِتُنَظِّفَ الشَقَّة، وإنَّها تُساعِدُه أحْياناً في تَحضيرِ الطَعام.

شَقَّة مايكِل

مُحام

طَبيب أسنان

شَرِكة تَأجير سَيّارات

شَرِكة تَأمين

بَنك مِصر

مَطعَمُ الصِحة

تَقَع شَقَّة مايكِل في بِنايَة في بابِ اللَوق قَريبة مِن وَسَطِ المَدينة. هُناكَ مَصْرِف في الطابَقِ الأرضِيِّ هُوَ «بَنْك مِصر» ومَطعَم صَغير يُسَمّى «مَطعَمُ الصِحّة». وفي الطابَق الأوَّل تُوجَد شَرِكَة تَأجير سَيّارات وشَرِكة تَأمين. أمّا في الطابَقِ الثاني فَهُناكَ عِيادَة طَبيب أسْنان ومَكتَب مُحام.

مَوقف حافلات

أمامَ البِنايَة هُناكَ مَوقِف حافِلات، ويُوجَد مُقابِلَها مَكتَبة. إلى يَمينِ المَكتَبة هُناكَ دُكّان بَقّال وإلى يَسارِها دُكّانُ الخُضَريّ. مَحَطّةُ المِترو «سَعْد زَغلول» لَيْسَتْ بَعيدة جِدّاً عَنِ البِنايَة. في الشارِع التالي بَعدَ شارِع شَريف، ويُسَمّى شارِعَ مُحَمّد فَريد، يُوجَد مَخبَز يَبيع أنواعاً مِن الخُبزِ العَرَبيّ. اِشترى مايكِل مِنَ الخَبّاز الخُبزَ الشاميَّ والعَيْش البَلَديّ وأعجَبَهُ النَوعانِ جِدّاً. هُناكَ أيضاً حَديقَة عامَّة في ذلِكَ الشارِع تَقَع خَلفَها مَدرَسة بَنات ابتِدائيّة.

تمرين ٤

آ- أجِبْ عَن هذِهِ الأسئِلة حَسَب نَصّ القِراءة:

١- لِماذا اِنتَقَل مايكِل مِن شَقَّتِه القَديمة؟
٢- في أيّ طابَق تُوجَد شَقَّة مايكِل الجَديدة؟
٣- ما مَعنى الحَرفَين (م) و (ش) في الإعْلان؟
٤- مَن ساعَدَهُ في الانْتِقال مِن الشَقَّةِ القَديمة إلى الجَديدة؟
٥- في أيّ مَكان مِن القاهِرة تُوجَدُ الشَقّةُ الجَديدة؟
٦- هَل تُعجِبُ الشَقَّةُ الجَديدة حُسَين؟ لِماذا؟

ب- أكتُبْ «خَطَأ» أو «صَواب» بِجانب كُلّ جُملَة وصَحّح الجُمَلَ الخَطَأ:

٧- هُناكَ هاتِف وبَرّاد في الشَقَّةِ الجَديدة.
٨- عَمِلَتْ هِبة عِدّة سَنَوات في الكُوَيت.
٩- عَلَّق مايكِل على الجِدار صورَة صَديقَتِه.
١٠- لا يَسْتَعمِل مايكِل المَطبَخ كَثيراً.
١١- اِنتَقَل مايكِل إلى الشَقَّةِ الجَديدة بِالحافِلة.
١٢- يَعمَلُ المَوقِد في الشَقَّةِ الجَديدة بِالكَهرَباء.
١٣- المَخبَز في شارِعِ الأندلُس.
١٤- اِنتَقَل مايكِل إلى الشَقَّةِ الجَديدة يَوم الجُمْعة.

ت- اكتُبْ أسئِلَة لِهذِهِ الإجابات كَما في المِثال:

مِثال: لأَنَّهُ يَدرُسُ اللُغةَ العَرَبيّة بِالقاهِرة. ← لِماذا يَسكُنُ مايكِل بِالقاهِرة؟

١٥- بِشاحِنة صَغيرة. ________________

١٦- لأَنَّها قَريبة مِنَ السوق. ________________

١٧- في الطابَقِ الثاني. ________________

١٨- تَقع خَلْفَ الحَديقَةِ العامَّة. ________________

تمرين ٥

المُحادَثة: اسأل زَميلك:

١- مَتى اِسْتَأجَرْتَ شقة أو سَيّارة؟ (ماضٍ)
٢- لِماذا يُعْجِبُك بَيْتُك / شَقّتُك أو لِماذا لا تعجِبُك؟
٣- أينَ يَقع بَيْتُك / شَقَّتُك؟ (مُقابِل، أمام، خَلْف، يَسار، يَمين)
٤- ما مُخَطَّط بَيْتِك / شَقَّتِك؟
٥- مَن مِن أصْدقائك يَعْمَل في شَرِكة وما اسمُها؟

تمرين ٦

أكمِل الجُمَلَ التالية بِالكَلِمَةِ المُناسِبَة حَسَب النَصّ.

١- شَقَّة مايكِل الجَديدة في الطابَقِ ________ .

☐ الأوَّل ☐ الثاني ☐ الثالِث

٢- عَلِمَ مايكِل عَنِ الشَقّة مِن ________ .

☐ حُسَين ☐ الجَريدة ☐ المَجَلّة

٣- أجرَةُ الشَقَّةِ السَنَوِيّة ________ جُنَيه مِصريّ.

☐ ٧٠٠ ☐ ٤٨٠٠ ☐ ٨٤٠٠

٤- الهاتِف في غُرفَةِ ________ .

☐ الجُلوس ☐ النَوم ☐ الطَعام

٥- يأكُل مايكِل طَعام ______________ دائِماً في البَيت.

☐ الفَطور ☐ الغَداء ☐ العَشاء

٦- المِرآة فَوقَ ______________ .

☐ المَجلى ☐ المَغسَلة ☐ الأريكة

٧- أصدِقاء مايكِل زاروه ______________ .

☐ صَباحاً ☐ ظُهراً ☐ مَساءً

٨- شَرِكةُ التَأمين في الطابَقِ ______________ .

☐ الأوَّل ☐ الثاني ☐ الثالِث

٩- يُوجَد ______________ مُقابِل بِنايَة مايكِل.

☐ مَكتَبَة ☐ مَدرسَة ☐ مَحَطّة مِترو

١٠- اِشتَرى مايكِل العَيشَ البَلَديّ مِن ______________ .

☐ الخُضَريّ ☐ البَقّال ☐ الخَبّاز

تمرين ٧

أعطِ مُقابِلَ هذِهِ الكَلِمات:

١- يَمين ______________ ٢- فَوْق ______________

٣- أمامَ ______________ ٤- واسِع ______________

تمرين ٨

أعِدْ تَرتيبَ الكَلِمات في كُلّ مَجموعة لِتُشَكِّل جُملاً مُفيدة.

١- بَيتي - اِبتِدائية - هُناكَ - خَلفَ - مَدرَسة

٢- التِلفاز - الكَبيرة - وَضَعْتُ - مُقابِلَ - الأريكة

٣- أصدِقائي - سَيّارَتي - مِن - في - ساعَدَني - غَسْلِ - اِثنانِ

٤- لِلإيجار - اليوم - قَرَأتُ - شَقَّةٍ - إعلاناً - في - عَن - جَريدةٍ

تَحضير القَهوة

تمرين ٩

أعِدْ تَرتيبَ الجُمَل لِتُشكِّل فِقرة مُفيدة.

١- مَرحباً. أنا مُنى الأسوَد وأعمَل مُدَرِّسَةً في وَسَطِ المَدينة.
لأنَّ فيها غُرفة مَكتَب لَهُ وغُرفة طَعام ومَطبَخاً واسِعاً.
قالوا إنَّ الشَقّة أعجبَتْهُم لأنَّها مُطِلّة على حَديقَة جَميلة.
اِنتَقَلْتُ وعائِلَتي في الشَهرِ الماضي إلى شَقَّة كَبيرة.
لِذلِكَ أركَبُ الحافِلة كُلَّ يوم إلى المَدرَسة.
تَقع شَقَّتي الجَديدة في شارِع بَعيد عَن وَسَطِ المَدينة.
زارَنا أمسِ بَعض أصدِقائِنا لِيُشاهِدوا الشَقَّةَ الجَديدة.
تُعجِبُني شَقّتي كَثيراً وتُعجِبُ زَوْجي كَذلِكَ.

تمرين ١٠

لَوحات قِصَصيّة (Storyboard): اكتب جُملة لِكلِّ صورة حتى تُشَكِّل قِصة في النِهاية.

١- 

____
____
____
____

٢- 

____
____
____
____

٣-

٤-

٥-

٦-

٧-

تمرين ١١

إقرأ هذَين الإعلانَين ثُمَّ أجِبْ عَنِ الأسئِلةِ التالية:

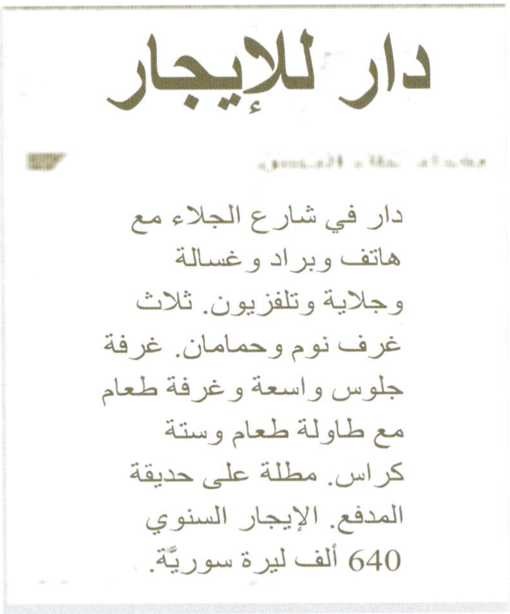

١- في أيّ بَلَد تُوجَد كُلّ مِنَ الدار والشَقَّة؟

٢- كَمْ غُرفَة في الشَقَّة؟

٣- ما عُمْلات (currencies) كُلٍّ مِن مِصر وسوريَّة والكُويْت؟

٤- اِقرأ الإعلانَين في هذا التَمرين والإعلان في أوَّلِ الدَرس والإعلان في الدَرس ١١ تَمرين ١٢ مَرَّةً ثانيةً ثُمَّ اكتُب إعلاناً مِثلَ هذِه الإعلانات في جَريدة عَرَبيّة عَن غُرفتِك أو شَقّتِك أو بيتِك.

١ – اِستِخدام: أرادَ أنْ + المُضارِع المَنصوب

نُعَبِّر عن الرَغبة أو النِيّة أو الحاجة بِاستِخدام الفِعل أراد + أنْ + المُضارِع المَنصوب مَثلاً:

١ أرادَ مايكِل + أنْ + ينتَقِل — *Michael wanted to move.*

العرض: احكِ للطلاّب قصة قصيرة تستخدم فيها الفعلين أراد أن وأحب أن كثيراً كما ترى في المِثال:

«تريد زوجتي أن تشتري قميصاً في السوق ولكني لا أريد الذهاب إلى السوق لأنّني لا أريد أن أشتريَ شيئاً. أريد أن أقرأ جريدة فيها إعلانات عن شقق للإيجار لأنّنا نريد أنا وزوجتي الانتقال من شقّتنا القديمة إلى شقّة جديدة.»

الممارسة: اسأل الطلاّب أسئلة تتطلب استخدام الفعلين أراد أن وأحب أن مثلاً:

أ- «هل تريد أن تستأجر شقّة جديدة يا مارك؟»
مارك- «لا. لا أريد أن أستأجر شقّة جديدة.»
أ- «يعني تعجبك الشقّة التي تسكن فيها كثيراً؟»
ط- «لا. لا تعجبني شقتي كثيراً ولكن لا أحب الانتقال.»
«معك حق. يا ليسا، هل يريد مارك أن يستأجر شقّة جديدة ولماذا أو لماذا لا؟»

التطبيق: نشاط جماعي: حضّر قائمة أشياء يجب على الطلاّب أن يعرفوها من زملائهم. مثلا:

من في صفك:
- يريد أن ينتقلَ
- تعجبه شقته
- ينوي شراء أثاث
- يعيش قرب حديقة عامة
- يستأجر بيتاً

الحِفاظ على سَلامة اللُغة:

- بِما أنّ الحَرف أنْ يُترجَم (is translated) باللُغة الإنكليزيّة كَـ(the infinitive) كَما نَرى في المِثال ١ "to move"، فَأنَّ كَثيراً من الطُلّاب يَستَخدِمون الفِعل الماضي مع الضَمير الغائب (third-person past tense) ، مع أنّ قَصدُهم المُتَكلِّم أي أنا، إنّما علينا أنْ نُصَرِّف الفِعل الّذي يليه حَسَب الضَمير المَقصود.
- لا تَخلِط (confuse) بَين أنْ (الّذي يليه فِعل) وأنَّ وإنَّ (اللّذين تَليهُما جُملة اسميّة).

أنْ	+	جُملة فِعليّة
أنَّ	+	جُملة اسميّة
إنَّ	+	جُملة اسميّة

حين يَلي الفِعلان أعجَبَ وأحَبّ الحَرف أنْ، فَنستخدِم المُضارِع المَنصوب كَما نَفعَل في الفِعل أرادَ + أنْ + المُضارِع المَنصوب. لاحِظ هذا في المِثالَين ١و٢:

٢ أُحِبُّ أنْ آكُلَ عَشائي في المَطعَم. *I like to eat my dinner in the restaurant.*

في هذِه الحالة، نُسَمّي الحَرف أنْ أنْ المَصدَريّة لأنّه يُوازي (is equivalent) المَصدَر من حَيثُ المَعنى. لِذا نَستطيع أن نَستبدِل (to replace) أنْ يَنتَقِلَ في المِثال ١ وأنْ آكُلَّ في المِثال ٢ بالمَصدر كَما تَرى في المِثالَين أدناه:

٣ أرادَ مايكِل + الانْتِقالَ. *Michael wanted relocation.*

٤ أُحِبُّ + أكْلَ عَشائي في المَطعَم. *I like eating my dinner in the restaurant.*

كَما نُلاحِظ في المِثالَين ٣ و٤ في الصَفحة السابِقة أنّ المَصدَر مُعرَّف (definite) ومع أنّ المِثال ٤ يَبدو المَصدَر نَكرة، فأنَّه مَعرفة لأنّه مُضاف في الإضافة أَكْلَ عَشائي.

دَعنا أن نَنظُر إلى الفِعل إعجاب في جُملتَين واحدة فيها أن المَصدَريّة (المِثال ٥) والأخرى فيها المَصدَر (المِثال ٦):

٥	يُعْجِبُه	+	أنْ يَدرُسَ	اللُّغَةَ العَرَبيَّة.	*[It] pleases him to study Arabic*

قَد يُفيدُنا أن نُتَرجِم أعجَبَ بالإنكليزيّة كـ *to please* لأنّه يُشبِه (resembles) تَركيب الجُملة الإنكليزيّة. نَشرَح اِستِخدام هذا الفِعل في باب الإعجاب أدناه في هذِه الصَفحة. أمّا الآن، فَنودّ أن نَنظُر إلى الفِعل أعجَبَ + أنْ + جُملة فِعليّة (المِثال ٥ أعلاه) وأعجَبَ + المَصدَر (المِثال ٦ أدناه).

٦	تُعْجِبُه	+	دِراسةُ	اللُّغَةِ العَرَبيَّة.	*Studying Arabic pleases him.*

لاحِظ أنّ المَصدَر دِراسةُ مُؤنَّث لِذلِكَ الفِعل أعجَبَ في صيغة الفِعل المُضارِع المُؤنَّث تُعْجِبُ. لاحِظ أيضاً أنَّ المَصدَر دِراسةُ مُضاف في المِثال ٦ أعلاه دِراسةُ اللغُةِ.

الفِعل أعْجَبَ

قد يُحيِّرُك (confuse you) الفِعل أعجَبَ لأن أحياناً يُترجَم كـ "to like" وفي هذِه الحالة الفاعِل هو ضَمير مُستَتِر (implied pronoun) ولكِن حَرفيّاً نُتَرجِمُه "to please" لأنْ يَبدو كأنّ الفاعِل يَحلّ مَحلّ المَفعول بِه. قارِن (compare) بَين الجُملتَين أدناه:

٧	أُحِبُّ	الطَعامَ	العَرَبيّ.	*I like Arabic food.*
٨	يُعْجِبُني	الطَعامُ	العَرَبيّ.	*Arabic food pleases me.*

في المِثال ٧، الطَعامَ هو المَفعول بِه في حالة النَصب بَينما (whereas) الطَعامُ في المِثال ٨ هو الفاعِل في حالة الرفع.

نَستَطيع أن نُغيِّر تَركيب الجُملة حَتّى يَتَبيَّن لَنا الفاعِل والمَفعول بِه:

٩ يُعْجِبُ	الطَّعامُ العَرَبيُّ (أنا).	*Arabic food pleases (me).*

يُوضِح لَنا المِثال ٩ أنَّ الطَّعامُ فاعِل الجُملة والضَمير أنا هو المَفعول بِه. إذا اِستبدَلنا الضَمير المُنفَصِل أنا بِمَفعول بِه ظاهِر (انظُر المِثال ١٠)، فَنستطيع أن نَرى أنّه في حالة النَصب:

١٠ يُعْجِبُ	الطَّعامُ العَرَبيُّ الطالِبَ.	*Arabic food pleases the student.*

الخُلاصة

بَعضُ الأفعال، مِثل أرادَ وأحَبَّ يَليها الحَرف أنْ الّذي تَليه جُملة فِعلية في المُضارِع المَنصوب.

تمرين ١٢

التَرجَمة: اكتُب جُملتَين لِكُلّ من الجُمَل الآتية استِخداماً أَحَبَّ أن في واحدة منهما ويُعْجِبُ + المَصدَر للأخرى كَما تَرى في المِثال:

المِثال:	I like to swim.	Swimming pleases me.
	أُحِبُّ أنْ أسْبَحَ أو	تُعْجِبُني السِباحةُ.

1.	Rāmī likes to write to all his friends.	Writing to all of his friends pleases Rāmī.
2.	My friends like to go to the beach.	Going to the beach pleases my friends.
3.	Hāla likes to help her younger brother with his studies.	Helping her younger brother with his studies pleases Hāla.
4.	My sister likes to sleep late.	Sleeping late pleases my sister.
5.	I like to live in this city.	Living in this city pleases me.
6.	Rānya likes to read before going to sleep.	Rānya enjoys reading before going to sleep.
7.	Hanān likes to travel to Cairo.	Traveling to Cairo pleases Hanān.

تمرين ١٣

أُكتُب الحالات القَواعديّة الآتية مِن نُصوص القِراءة:

١- أربع حالات اسم النِسبة ______________________

٢- حالتان من المَصدَر ______________________

٣- حالتان من المُضارِع المَنصوب ______________________

٤- حالة من المُضارِع المَجزوم ______________________

٥- حالتان من اسم التفضيل ______________________

٢- **إستِخدام: اسم الآلة** The Noun of Instrument

في اللُغة العَرَبيّة، تُوجَد أوزان نَستخدِمُها كَي نَشتقّ منها اسم الآلة. ونَذكُر هُنا الأكثر استِخداماً مع أمثِلة، ثلاثة منها تَعرِفها أي ١١ و١٢ و١٤

	الوَزن	المِثال	
١١	مِفْعال	مِفْتاح	
١٢	مِفْعَلة	مِسْطَرة	
١٣	مِفْعَل	مِقَصّ	*scissors*
١٤	فاعول	حاسوب	

مع الحاجة لاشتِقاق كَلمات جَديدة لأجهِزة حَديثة في العالَم اليَوم، فإنّ هُناكَ أوزان أخرى تَدُلّ على اسم الآلة ونَذكُر سِتّة منها مع أمثِلة وَرَدَت في هذا الكِتاب حَتّى الآن:

الوَزن	المِثال
فاعِل	هاتِف
فاعِلة	حاسِبة
مُفَعِّل	مُحَرِّك
مُفَعِّلة	مُسَجِّلة
فَعّال	بَرّاد
فَعّالة	غَسّالة

العرض: أحضِر معك بعض الصور لشقة أو بيت (من عندك أو من الشابكة) وحدّد اسماء الآلة الموجودة في ذلك المكان. أخبِر الطلاب بمكانها في البيت / الشقة وكم مرة تستعملها في (الساعة / اليوم / الشهر) وماذا تفعل هذه الآلة، مثلاً: **«هذه صورة حاسوبي وهو موجود في شقّتي على طاولة في مكتبي. أستخدمه كل يوم \ يومياً ما عدا يوم الأحد. أنا عادةً أستخدمه حين...»**

الممارسة: أرِ للطلاّب صوراً لأسماء الآلة الموجودة في محيطها الطبيعي واطلب منهم أن يصفوها من حيث وجود الآلة في الصورة وكيف تُستعمَل وإذا أعجبتهم أم لا. إليك مثال نصِف فيه الهاتف النقال / الجوّال أو المحمول أو الخلوي:

أ- **«ما هذا»**
ط- **«هذا هاتف.»**
أ- **«هل معك هاتف؟»**
ط- **«نعم. معي هاتف.»**
أ- **«كم مرّة في اليوم تستخدمه؟»**
ط- **«أستخدم هاتفي ثلاث أو أربع مرّات كل يوم.»**
أ- **«هل يعجبك هاتفك؟»**
ط- **«نعم، كثيراً لأنّني أحبّ أن أتكلّم مع أصدقائي.»**

التطبيق: في مجموعات من اثنين: وزّع على الطلاّب صوراً فيها أسماء الآلة واطلب منهم أن يسألوا بعضهم بعضاً إذا امتلكوا الآلة الموجودة في الصورة أم لا، وكم مرة يستعملونها في الساعة / اليوم / الشهر / ومتى يستعملونها وإذا أعجبتهم إلخ. وعند انتهاء النشاط اطلب منهم أن يخبروا زملاءهم بما علموا.

تمرين ١٤

تَحديد الوَزَن: أُكتُب الأسماء المَوجودة في المُرَبَّعات تَحت الوَزَن الصَحيح:

مِرحاض	حاسِب	مِبراة	حافِلة	دَرّاجة	بَرّاد	ثَلاّجة
جَلاّية	هاتِف	شاحِنة	خَلاّط	مِسْطَرة	مِصْباح	حاسِبة

فاعِل	فاعِلة	فَعّالة	فَعّال	مِفْعَلة	مِفعال

٣- اِستِخدام: حُروف الجَرّ

يُحَدِّد السياق مَعنى حُروف الجَرّ إلى حَدٍّ بَعيد. نأخُذ في عَين الاعتبار (take into consideration) حَرف الجَرّ في الّذي لَهُ عِدّة معانٍ حَسَب السياق وغَرَض الجُملة، كَما نَرى في الأمثِلة أدناه:

١٥	يَدرُسُ الطِبَّ في جامِعَةِ بِرِنْسْتَن.	*at (signifying a place)*
١٦	سَأستَقبِلُهُ في الساعةِ الثانِيَةِ.	*at (signifying a time)*
١٧	نَحنُ في الصَفِّ.	*in (place)*
١٨	زُرتُهُ في يَومِ الخَميسِ.	*on (time)*

العرض: أحضَر بعض الصور للصف (من عندك أو من الشابكة) تتمثّل فيها أحياء / حارات الحضارتين الشرقية والغربية. تصِفها استخداماً حروف الجر الموجودة في الباب إلى اليمين.

الممارسة: اطلب من الطلاّب أن يصِفوا الصور التي عرضتها لهم وبعض صور الأحياء التي لم تقدمها لهم حتّى الآن.

التطبيق: في مجموعات من اثنين: اطلب من الطالب أن يعرف من زميله أين توجد بعض المحلات حيث يسكن كما ترى في المثال أدناه:

«أين توجد/ يوجد عيادة طبيب/ شركة تأمين/ مصرف/ موقف حافلات/ مكتب محام حيث تسكنين؟» «ماذا يوجد مقابل/ بجانب/ فوق/ تحت/ قرب/ خلف/ إلى يسار بيتك/ شقّتك؟»

آ- حُروف الجَرّ في فِئَتَين (two categories)

تَندَرج حُروف الجَر الّتي وَرَدَت في هذا الكِتاب حَتّى الآن في فِئَتَين: المُتّصِلة أي الّتي تَدخُل على بِداية الاسم المَوصوف والمُنفَصِلة أي الّتي تَستقِل عن الاسم المَوصوف في الجُملة. تَذَكّر أنّ الاسم الّذي يَلي حَرف جَرّ هو مَجرور بالكَسرة.

١٩	بِـ	أكتُبُ بِالقَلَمِ.	*(write) with*
٢٠		أسكُنُ بِبيروت.	*in (place)*
٢١		اِشتَرَيتُ الكِتابَ بِخَمسينَ دولاراً.	*for ($50)*
٢٢		وَصَلنا بِالطائِرة.	*by (plane)*
٢٣		تَكَلَّمتُ بِاللُغةِ العَرَبيَّة.	*in (Arabic)*
٢٤	كَـ	الأستاذ، كَما تَعلَم، لُبنانيّ.	*as (you know)*
٢٥	لِـ	لِسامِيَة أربَعَةُ أولاد.	*has*
٢٦		كَتَبتُ لِجَميعِ أصدِقائي.	*to (all of my friends)*
٢٧	مِن	هِيَ مِن مَدينةِ بَغداد.	*from (the city of Baghdad)*
٢٨	إلى	ذَهَبتُ إلى المَكتَبَةِ.	*to (the library)*
٢٩	عَن	تَكَلَّمَ عَن أُسرَتِه.	*about (his family)*
٣٠	على	الكِتابُ على الطاوِلَةِ.	*on (the table)*
٣١	في	هُوَ في غُرفَتِه.	*in (his room)* [see examples 12–15]
٣٢	حَتّى	دَرَستُ حَتّى الساعةِ الثانِيَة.	*till (two)*
٣٣	وَ	وَالله	*by God (I swear)*
٣٤	عَدا	نَعمَلُ كُلَّ يَومٍ عَدا يَومِ الجُمعة.	*except (Friday)*

مع أنّ في المِثال الأخير ٣٤ عَدا يُعتبَر حَرف جَرّ، فأنّنا نَستطيع كَذلِكَ اِعتِباره فِعلاً حين يُستَخدَم مع ما، والاسم الّذي يَليه في حالة النَصب، كَما نَرى في المِثال ٣٥:

٣٥ زارَني أصدِقائي ما عَدا واحِداً.	*My friends visited me except for one.*

ب- ظَرف المَكان

يَعتبِر بَعض النَحويين (grammarians) عَدَداً من الظُروف (adverbs) والأسماء حُروف الجَرّ. لأن هذِه الظُروف والأسماء تَصِف العَلاقة بَين أشياء من حَيثُ المكان. إن الصُوَر أدناه تُصَوِّر مَعاني بَعض هذِه الكَلِمات:

على

أمامَ

خَلْفَ

في

بِجانِب

تَحْتَ

فَوْقَ

بَيْنَ

نَذكُر بَعض الكَلمات الشَبيهة لِحُروف الجَر (الّتي أيضاً تُعتبَر ظَرفا زَمان ومَكان) في قائمة في الصَفحة الآتية. لاحِظ أنّ هذه الكَلِمات هي أسماء في حالة النَصب وأنّها مُضاف ومضاف إليه في حالة الجَرّ.

٣٦	عِندَ	سَأراكَ عِندَ بابِ المَكتَبة.	at the door
٣٧	أمامَ	هُناكَ شَجَرةٌ أمامَ بابِ داري.	in front of
٣٨	قَبْلَ	المَخبزُ قَبْلَ الحَديقةِ.	before the park (place)
٣٩		سَأراكَ قَبلَ المَغرِبِ.	before (time)
٤٠	بَعْدَ	دُكّانُ البَقّالِ بَعدَ المَحطّةِ.	after (the station)
٤١		سَتزورُنا بَعدَ العُطلةِ.	after (the break)
٤٢	بَيْنَ	الحَديقةُ بَينَ دارِ جاري ودارِك.	between
٤٢	خَلْفَ	هُناكَ مَصرِفٌ خَلْفَ بَيتي.	behind
٤٤	جانِبَ	أُحِبُّ أنْ أجلِسَ جانِبَ الشُبّاكِ.	by, next to
٤٥	بِجانِبِ	أُحِبُّ أنْ أجلِسَ بِجانِبِ الشُبّاكِ.	by, next to
٤٦	تَحْتَ	هُناكَ مَطعَمٌ تَحْتَ شَقَّتي.	under
٤٧	فَوْقَ	المِصباحُ فَوْقَ الطاوِلةِ.	over
٤٨	دونَ	أشرَبُ الشاي دونَ سُكّرٍ.	without
٤٩	مُقابِلَ	مَحطّةُ القِطارِ مُقابِلَ المَخبَزِ.	across from
٥٠	مَعَ	وَصَلَتِ الطائِرةُ مَعَ اللَيلِ.	at (night)
٥١		سَكَنتُ مَعَ طالِبَةٍ لُبنانِيّة.	with

تمرين ١٥

المُحادَثة: اِسأل زُملائك: مَن في الصَفّ:

1. rents an apartment or house
2. lives close to/far from campus
3. lives on the ground floor of their apartment building
4. likes their coffee with/without sugar
5. has a garden in front/back/on the side of their house
6. lives across from a bank

أُكتُب أجوِبة زُملائك على وَرَقة مُنفَصِلة حَتّى تُخبِر الجَميع بِما علِمتَ من الآخَرين.

تمرين ١٦

أكمِلِ الجُمَلَ التاليَةَ بِحَرفِ الجَرِّ المُنفَصِلِ أو الظَرْف المُناسِب.

في	إلى	حَتّى	مِن	على	مَعَ	عَن

١- وَصَلَتِ الطائِرَةُ ____________ مَوعِدِها.

٢- ذَهَبنا ____________ الجَزائِرِ بِالطائِرة.

٣- وَجَدتُ كِتابي ____________ طاوِلَةِ الأستاذ.

٤- سَأدرُسُ في المَكتَبةِ ____________ الساعةِ الرابِعة.

٥- تَسكُنُ أمّي ____________ القُدسِ.

٦- قَرَأنا ____________ الأميرِ عَبدِ القادِرِ الجَزائِرِيِّ في هذا الكِتابِ.

٧- هذِهِ الأزهارُ ____________ صَديقي.

٨- ذَهَبتُ إلى السينَما ____________ ثَلاثَةٍ مِن أصدِقائي.

أكمِلِ الجُمَلَ التاليَةَ بأحَدِ حُروفِ الجَرِّ المُتَّصِلةِ (لَ - بِ - كَ).

٩- اِشتَرَتْ هالَةَ هذا الكِتابَ ____________ خمسينَ دولاراً.

١٠- هِيَ، ____________ ما تَعلَم، مَغرِبِيَّة.

١١- هَل تَسكُنينَ ____________ هذِهِ الشَقَّة؟

١٢- هَل ____________ك إخوة؟

تمرين ١٧

اخترِ الكَلِمةَ المُناسِبةَ لِتُكمِلَ الجُمَلَ التالية.

١- هَل شَقّتُك ________ عِيادةِ الطَبيب؟

☐ إلى ☐ بَيْنَ ☐ فَوْقَ ☐ عِنْدَ

٢- جَلَسْتُ في سَيّارةِ الأجرة ________ السائِق.

☐ خَلْفَ ☐ بَيْنَ ☐ مُقابِل ☐ أمامَ

٣- هَل تَشرَبينَ القَهوة ________ سُكَّر؟

☐ بَعْدَ ☐ قَبْلَ ☐ دونَ ☐ جانِبَ

٤- لَم يَرجِعْ أحمَد إلى المَدرَسة ________ الغَداء.

☐ أمامَ ☐ خَلْفَ ☐ تَحتَ ☐ بَعْدَ

٥- تَقَعُ بَلَدَتي ________ مَدينَتَين كَبيرتَين.

☐ مُقابِل ☐ دونَ ☐ بَيْنَ ☐ خَلْفَ

٦- عَلَّقتُ صورة أمّي ________ صورةِ أبي.

☐ جانِبَ ☐ عِنْدَ ☐ دونَ ☐ بَعْدَ

٧- هَل هُناكَ مَوقِف حافِلة ________ بابِ الشَرِكة؟

☐ خَلْفَ ☐ أمامَ ☐ فَوْقَ ☐ تَحْتَ

٨- هُناكَ مَخبَز ________ دُكّانِ البَقّال.

☐ بَيْنَ ☐ مُقابِلَ ☐ فَوْقَ ☐ مَعَ

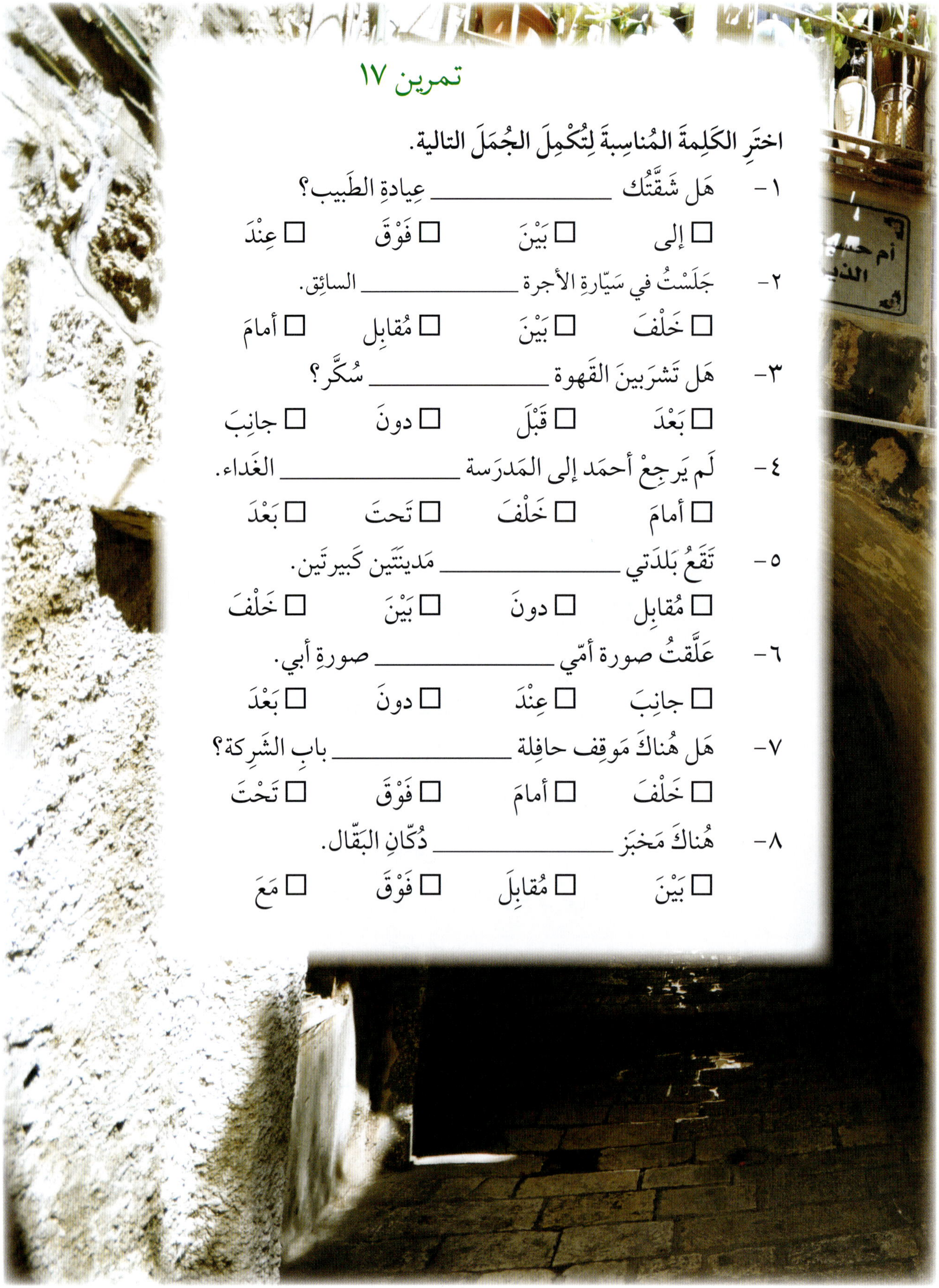

حارة المُسلِمين في القُدس

تمرين ١٨

المُحادَثة: الطَريق إلى البَيت: لقد وَصَل صَديقُك العَرَبيّ إلى مَدينتِك اليَوم ويُريد أن يَقوم بزِيارة لَك. قُل لَه مَتى تَرجِع إلى البَيت من العَمَل ومَتى يَستطيع القيام بالزيارة. دُلّهُ على الطريق إلى بَيتِك من المَطار مُستَخدِماً العديد من حُروف الجَرّ الوارِدة في هذا الدَرس. وبَعد أن يَصِل صَديقُك إلى بَيتِك / شَقّتِك، أخبِرْهُ بالأشياء الآتية مُستخدِماً صُورة مَخطَّط الشَقّة أدناه.

١- دَع صَديقَك يَرى شَقّتَك وأخبِره أين وَضعتَ كُلّ الآثاث والأشياء الأخرى في بَيتِك.

٢- تَخيَّل أنّك في المَطبَخ ويُريد صَديقُك أن يَضع حَقائبَه في مَكان ما. قُل لَهُ أين غُرفة الضُيوف وكَذلِكَ أين يَضع حَقائبَه.

٣- تَخيَّل أنّك وصَديقك في غُرفةِ الجُلوس ويُريد إستِخدامَ الحَمّام كَي يَستحِمّ بعد السَفرة الطَويلة. دُلّهُ على الطريق إلى الحَمّام بِكُلّ التَفاصيل مُستَخدِماً: بِجانب . . . وأمامَ الـ . . .

تمرين ١٩

استَمِع إلى النَصّ الأوّلِ ثُمَّ أجِبْ عَنِ الأسئِلة التالية:

١- لِماذا انْتَقَلَتِ العائِلةُ إلى شَقّةٍ جَديدة؟

٢- لِماذا تُعْجِبُ الشَقّةُ الجَديدةُ الزَوجة؟

٣- أينَ تَقعُ الشَقّةُ الجَديدة؟

اكتُبْ «خَطأ» أو «صَواب» جانِبَ كُلِّ جُمْلَةٍ وصَحِّحِ الجُمَلَ الخَطأ.

٤- الشَقّةُ القَديمةُ أكبَرُ مِنَ الجَديدة.

٥- تَعمَلُ الزَوجةُ في شَرِكة.

٦- اِشتَرَت الزَوجةُ تِلفازاً.

تمرين ٢٠

أكمِلِ الجُمَلَ بِالكَلِماتِ المُناسِبةِ حَسَبَ نَصِّ الاستِماع.

١- الزَوجة والزَوج لَهُما ________ .

☐ وَلَد واحِد ☐ وَلَدان ☐ ثَلاثَة أولاد ☐ أربَعَة أولاد

٢- في الشَقّة الجديدة ________ نوم.

☐ غُرفة ☐ غُرفتا ☐ ثَلاث غُرَف ☐ أربَع غُرَف

٣- الشَقّة الجَديدة قَريبَة مِن ________ .

☐ عَمَلِ الزَوج ☐ بَيت أسرةِ الزَوجة

☐ بَيت أسرةِ الزَوج ☐ الجامِعة

٤- سَوفَ تَشتَري هذِهِ العائِلة ________ .

☐ غَسّالة ☐ بَرّاداً ☐ جَلاّية ☐ أريكة

٥- الشَقّة الجَديدة مَوجودة في الطابَقِ ________ .

☐ الأوَّل ☐ الثاني ☐ الثالِث ☐ الرابِع

تمرين ٢١

المُحادَثة: في مَجموعات من اِثنَين، طالِب من الطالبَين يَدُل الآخر على الطَريق إلى بَيته / شَقّته من الصَفّ. يجب على الطالِب المُستمِع أن يَرسُم خَريطة بِما عَلِم من صَديقِه دون أن يُري المُتكَلِّم الخَريطة. وعِند الاِنتِهاء، يُري الطالِب المُستمِع الخَريطة إلى المُتكَلّم الّذي يُقارِنها بالحَقيقة. بَدِّل الأدوار عِند اِنتِهاء التَمرين.

تمرين ٢٢

استَمِعْ إلى النَصِّ الثاني ثُمَّ اكتُبْ أسماءَ الشوارِع والأماكِن على المُخَطَّط حَسَبَ النَصّ.

تمرين ٢٣

تَمرينُ المُشاهَدة: شاهِدوا الدَرْسَ الثامن عَشَر على الشابِكة واكتبوا ما يقولون.

سامر: تَفَضَّل. هُنا أرْضُ الديار ________ فيها بَحْرة وشَجَرةُ النارنج وفي ________ العُلْوي ________ غُرفةُ ________ أبي وأمّي وتِلكَ غُرفةُ ________ هَنادي، وهذِه غُرفة ________ فَقَط، هذا هوَ ________ ________ فيه ________ ________ ومايكرويف و________ و________ وطاولة طَعام نَجتَمِع حَوْلَها وهو **مُشتَرَك** ________ ستيف أيضاً وهذِه الغُرفة هيَ غُرفةُ ________ ________ فيها ________ كَبيرة وتِلفاز وطاوِلة في وَسَطِ الغُرفة.

هذِه غُرفتي وهذِه غُرفة ستيف تعالَ لأُريكَ إياها هذِه غُرفة ستيف فيها سَرير و________ أدراج وفَوْقَها ________ وبِجانِبِها كُرسي مِن الخَشَب وطاوِلة ________ و________ كَبيرة وقُرْبَ الغُرفة ________ ________ خاصّ بِستيف ________ فيه سَخّان للماءِ ودُوش و________ مع ________.

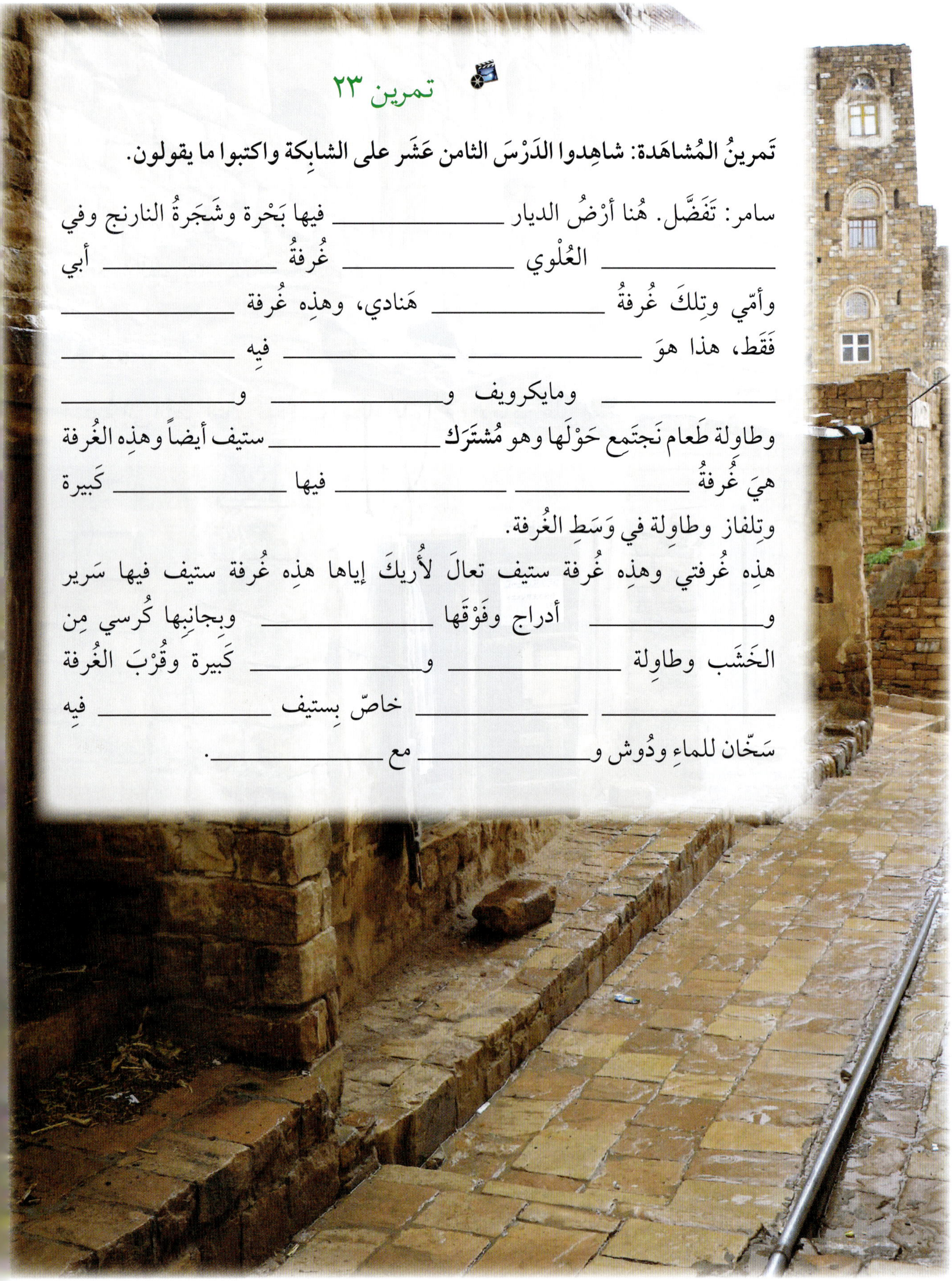

شارِع في مَدينة ثلاء في اليمن

المُفْرَدات

استمِع إلى المُفْرَدة بالعَرَبيّة ثم أعِد نُطْقَها مرّتين.

furniture . . . . (n., m.) أثاث

to meet; to gather . . . . (v.) اِجْتَمَعَ (يَجْتَمِع) اِجْتِماع

to lease, to let . . . . (v.) أجَّر (يؤجِّر) تأجير

rent, wage, fare . . . . (n., f.) أُجْرة ج أُجور

other . . . . (n., m.) آخَر ج آخَرون

ground, land. . . . . (n., f.) أرض ج أراضٍ

couch. . . . . (n., f.) أريكة ج أرائِك

to rent, to hire. . . . . (v.) استأجَرَ (يَستأجِرُ) استِئجار

to use, to utilize, to employ . . . . (v.) اِستَخدَمَ (يَستَخدِمُ) اِستِخدام

to please . . . . (v.) أَعْجَبَ (يُعْجِبُ) إعْجاب

advertisement. . . . . (n., m.) إعْلان ج إعْلانات

in front of . . . . (prep.) أمامَ

to (infinitive) . . . . (particle) أنْ

Europe . . . . (n., f.) أوروبا

rent. . . . . (n. m.) إيجار ج إيجارات

to sell. . . . . (v.) باعَ (يَبيعُ) بَيْع

refrigerator (Syria) . . . . (n., m.) بَرّاد ج بَرّادات

far. . . . . (adv.) بَعيد

grocer . . . . (n., m.) بَقّال ج بَقّالون

local, popular . . . . (adj.) بَلَديّ

bank (colloquial) . . . . (n., m.) بَنْك ج بُنوك

to be late . . . . (v.) تَأخَّرَ (يَتَأخَّرُ) تَأخُّر

insurance . . . . (n., m.) تأمين ج تأمينات

telephone (colloquial) . . . . (n., m.) تَليفون ج تَليفونات

refrigerator (Egypt). . . . . (n., f.) ثَلاّجة ج ثَلاّجات

part. . . . . (n., m.) جُزْء ج أجْزاء

dishwasher. (n., f.) جَلاّية ج جَلاّيات

[Egyptian] pound. . . . . (n., m.) جُنَيه ج جُنَيْهات

park, garden . . . . (n., f.) حَديقة ج حَدائِق

[bath] tub . . . . (n., m.) حَوْض ج أحْواض

servant . . . . (n., m.) خادِم ج خَدَم

baker . . . . (n., m.) خَبّاز ج خَبّازون

closet, cupboard. . . . . (n., f.) خِزانة ج خَزائِن / خِزانات

wood, lumber, timber . . . . (n., m.) خَشَب ج أخْشاب

greengrocer . . . . (n. m.) خُضَريّ ج خُضَريّون

behind . . . . (prep.) خَلْفَ

shop, store . . . . (n., f.) دُكّان ج دَكاكين

dinar (currency in Algeria, Bahrain, Iraq, Kuwait) . . . . (n., m.) دينار ج دَنانير

water heater. . . . . سَخّان لِلماء

truck . . . . (n. f.) شاحِنة ج شاحِنات

company. (n., f.) شَرِكة ج شَرِكات

health . . . . (n.) صِحّة

floor, storey, flat . . . . (n., m.) طابَق ج طَوابِق

in general, generally . . . . على العُموم

عَلَّقَ (يُعَلِّقُ) تَعْليق (v.)	to hang
عِيادة ج عِيادات (n., f.)	doctor's practice, clinic
عَيش (n., m.)	bread (Egypt)
غاز ج غازات (n., m.)	[butane] gas
غَسّالة ج غَسّالات (n., f.)	washing machine
فاخِر (adj.)	deluxe, fancy, excellent, luxurious
لَيْرة ج لَيْرات (n., f.)	[Syrian] pound; lira
م (مِتْر) ج أَمْتار (n., m.)	meter
مِترو (n., m.)	metro
مَجْلى ج مَجالٍ (n., m.)	kitchen sink
مَخْبَز ج مَخابِز (n., m.)	bakery
مُخَطَّط ج مُخَطّطات (n., m.)	[floor] plan, map
مِرْآة ج مَرايا (n., f.)	mirror
مِرْحاض ج مَراحيض (n., m.)	toilet
مُرْتَفِع (active participle)	elevated
مُريح (adj.)	comfortable
مِصْباح ج مَصابيح (n., m.)	lamp
مَصْرِف ج مَصارِف (n., m.)	bank
مُطِلٌّ (verbal noun)	overlooking
مَغْسَلة ج مَغاسِل (n., f.)	washbasin, bathroom sink
مُقابِل (adv.)	opposite, across from
مَلبَس ج مَلابِس (n., m.)	clothes
مَوْقِد ج مَواقِد (n., m.)	[cooking] range
مَوْقِف ج مَواقِف (n., m.)	[bus] stop, parking lot

spacious, large. . . . . (adj.) واسِع

there is/are, to exist. . . . . (passive of وَجَد) وُجِدَ (يوجَدُ)

to put. . . . .(v.) وَضَعَ (يَضَعُ) وَضْع

to be located; fall down. . . . . (v.) وَقَعَ (يَقَعُ) وُقوع / وَقْع

left . . . . (n., m.) يَسار

right . . . . (n., m.) يَمين

صناعة القهوة عام ١٨٦٠

عمارة تاريخية في القاهرة القديمة

الدرس التاسع عشر

أهداف الدرس

- وَصْف الأنشِطة في المُضارِع والماضي
- كِتابة الرِسالة والبِطاقة البَريديّة
- كِتابة بداية الرِسالة
- اِستِخدام ظَرف الزَمان والمَكان
- حَرف لَن لنَفي الزَمَن المُستَقبَل
- اِستِخدام الأسماء المَوصولة مِثل الّذي والّتي
- مُراجَعة حَرف الجَرّ
- ضمير المُلكية في الإضافة

المُفرداتُ الجَديدة في صُوَر عَديدة

رَكِبَ (يَرْكَبُ) رُكوب

سأَلَ (يَسأَلُ) سُؤال

اِلتَقَطَ (يَلْتَقِطُ) اِلْتِقاط

اِمْتَحَنَ (يَمْتَحِنُ) اِمْتِحان

حَيوان ج حَيوانات

خِزانة مَلابِس

تَذْكَرة

بَنى (يبني) بِناء

رُكنُ المُفْرَداتِ الجَديدة

أجابَ (يُجيبُ) إجابة (عَن)	to answer
اِسْتَطاعَ (يَسْتَطِيعُ) اِسْتِطاعة	to be able
اِسْتَمْتَعَ (يَسْتَمْتِعُ) اِسْتِمْتاع (بِـ)	to enjoy
اِلْتَقَى (يَلْتَقي) اِلْتِقاء (بِـ)	to meet
تَناوَلَ (يَتَناوَل) تَناوُل	to eat, take
مِثْل ج أمْثال	like, similar to
مَرَّ (يَمُرُّ) مُرور	to pass by
مَكان ج أماكِن	place
مُنْذُ	since
هامّ	مُهِمّ
والِد	أب

تمرين ١

اختَرِ الكَلِمةَ الّتي لا تُناسِب باقي الكَلِمات في كُلِّ مَجْموعة وبَيِّن السَبَب.

١-	قِطار	سَيّارة	حَديقَة	قارِب	طائِرة
٢-	شَلاّل	نَهر	بُحَيرة	مَبنى	ماء
٣-	طَيِّب	دافِئ	حارّ	بارِد	مُعتَدِل
٤-	اِستَحَمَّ	أعجَبَ	أحَبَّ	اِستَمتَعَ	هوِيَ
٥-	دِراسة	اِمتِحان	مَحَطّة	سُؤال	مَدرَسة

تمرين ٢

وافِقْ بَيْنَ الكَلِماتِ في العَمودَيْنِ.

١-	شاهَدَ		أَحَبَّ
٢-	مَشى		شَلاّل
٣-	بِنايَة		رَأى
٤-	طَريق		مَيْدان
٥-	ساحَة		دُكّان
٦-	دافِئ		سارَ
٧-	طَيِّب		حَتّى
٨-	أَعْجَبَ		شارِع
٩-	مَحَلّ تِجاريّ		مَبنى
١٠-	إلى أنْ		جَيِّد
			حارّ

تمرين ٣

أكمِلِ الجُمَلَ التالِيَة بِأفضَل كَلِمَة مُناسِبَة:

١- ________ أخي سَيّارةً حين زارَ سان فرانسيسكو.

☐ اِسْتَأجَرَ ☐ اِسْتَقبَلَ ☐ اِسْتَمتَعَ

٢- أريد أنْ أزور مَدينةَ المَلاهي ________ تَبدأَ الدِراسة.

☐ مَعَ أنَّ ☐ إلى أنْ ☐ قَبلَ أنْ

٣- تَقَع شَقَّتي ________ مَحَطّةِ القِطار.

☐ قُرْبَ ☐ شَمالاً ☐ أطوَلَ

٤- ________ عَشَراتِ الصُوَر في حَديقةِ الحَيَوانات.

☐ اِنتَقَلتُ ☐ اِلتَقَطتُ ☐ اِحتَفَلتُ

٥- هَل __________ الغَداء.

☐ شاهَدتُم ☐ زُرتُم ☐ تَناوَلتُم

٦- __________ نَهرَ النيل أطوَلُ نَهر في العالَم.

☐ لَنْ ☐ إنَّ ☐ أنْ

٧- __________ تُشاهِدْ أختي فيلم «عيد الاستِقلال» حَتّى الآن.

☐ لَم ☐ لَن ☐ أنْ

٨- تَناوَلْتُ __________ عَرَبِيّاً في مَطعَم مَرّاكِشيّ.

☐ طَعاماً ☐ موسيقا ☐ فِرقَةً

٩- __________ الفيلمُ التِلفزيونيّ في الساعةِ الحادِيَة عَشْرَة.

☐ أعجَبَ ☐ اِلتَقَطَ ☐ اِنتَهى

١٠- __________ أدرُسَ الرِياضيّات في الفَصلِ المُقبِل.

☐ لَم ☐ لَنْ ☐ لا

مايكِل براون في القاهِرَة والإسكَندَريّة

القاهِرة، الجُمْعَة ١٤ سِبتَمبر (أيلول) ٢٠١٨

الأهرامات في الجيزة

أكتُب هذِهِ اليَوميّات كَجُزء مِن دَرسِ اللُغَةِ العَرَبيَّة، وأنا أسْتَمْتِع بِكِتابَتِها كَثيراً. وَصَلتُ إلى القاهِرة مُنذُ أسابيع وأعجَبَتْني هذِهِ المَدينة مَعَ أنَّها مَدينة كَبيرة جِدّاً فيها حوالي عشرين مِليون نَسَمة. بَعدَ وُصولي إلى القاهِرة بِمُدّة قَصيرة ذَهَبتُ مَعَ أصدِقائي إلى «الجيزة» قُربَ القاهِرة لِمُشاهَدةِ الأهْرامات، والأهرامات مَبانٍ عَظيمة بَناها الفَراعِنة مُنذُ آلافِ السِنين. اِلتَقَطتُ صُوَراً كَثيرة بِآلة تَصويري الجَديدة. ورَكِبتُ هُناكَ على الجَمَل. لَم أرَ جِمالاً إلاّ عِندَ الأهرامات وفي حَديقةِ الحَيَواناتِ الّتي زُرتُها في عُطلة عيدِ الأضحى. شاهَدتُ هُناكَ عَدَداً كَبيراً مِن الحَيَوانات مِن كُلّ بِلادِ العالَم.

جَمَلان عِند الأهرامات

العَرض: أحضر صوراً من عندك أو من الشابكة لِزيارة قمت بها. صِف للطلّاب أين التقطت الصور ومن قام بالزيارة معك ولماذا اخترت مكان الزيارة وماذا أكلت وشربت وحالة الطقس أيام الزيارة وأي شيء آخر يمكن أن يعجب الطّلاّب. إليك مِثال:

«هذه صورة الجامع الأموي في دمشق في سورية. لقد سكنت في الشام لمدة ستة أشهر في منطقة اسمها باب توما. استأجرنا أنا وزوجتي شقّة مفروشة هناك وكان الإيجار كذا ليرة في الشهر. كان الطقس بارداً جداً في الشام وخصوصاً في فصل الشتاء الذي سقط فيه الثلج أكثر من مرّة. وهنا في هذه الصورة كما ترى أنا واقف إلى اليَمين وفلان بجانبي وفلان آخر اسمه كذا إلى يَسارِ الصورة.»

الممارسة: اسأل الطُلاّب إذا كان عندهم أي سؤال بالنسبة إلى صور زيارتك. وإذا لم يكن عندهم سؤال، اطرح عليهم بعض أسئلة الاستيعاب، على سبيل المِثال:

«هل هناك أي سؤال ولو بسيط بالنسبة لصوري؟»

التطبيق: في مجموعات من اثنين: اطلب من الطُلاّب إحضار بعض الصور من عندهم كي يصِفوها لزملائهم. اجعل الطُلاّب تبديل الأدوار عند انتهاء قصة الطالب الأوّل.

تابِع نشاط التمرين، اسأل الطُلاّب إذا أرادوا أن يحكوا قصتهم الخاصة إلى زملائهم.

القاهِرة، السَبت ٢٢/ ٩/ ٢٠١٨

ميناءُ الإسكَندريّة

سافَرْتُ أوَّلَ أمس الخَميس إلى الإسكَندَريَّة بِالقِطار مَعَ بَعضِ الأَصْدِقاء. الإسكَندَريّة ميناء هامّ على البَحرِ الأَبْيَضِ المُتَوسِّط وهِيَ أقدَم مِن القاهِرة بِمِئاتِ السِنين. أَخَذنا القِطار مِن مَحَطّة رَمْسيس في مَيْدان رَمْسيس في الساعةِ الثامِنة والنِصْف صَباحاً. اِشْتَريتُ تَذكَرة ذَهاباً وإياباً بِعِشرين جُنَيهاً. مَرَرْنا في الطَريقِ إلى الإسكندَريّة بِمَدينة طَنطا ثالِث أكبَر مُدُن مِصر. وَصَلنا إلى الإسكَندَريّة بَعدَ الظُهر. ذَهَبنا أوّلاً إلى مَطعم قَريب مِنَ الشاطِئ حَيثُ تَناوَلْنا طَعاماً مِصريّاً وشَرِبنا القَهوة.

كورنَيْش الإسكَندَرية

مَشَينا قَليلاً في شارِع طَويل وجَميل بِجانِبِ الشاطِئ يُسَمّى «الكورنيش» ثُمَّ نَزَلنا إلى الشاطِئ وسَبَحنا ساعَتَين أو ثَلاث. كانَ الطَقس دافِئاً وجَميلاً والشَمس ساطِعة. نَزَلنا تِلكَ اللَيلة في فُندُق صَغير لَكِنَّهُ نَظيف. وفي اليَومِ التالي ذَهَبنا إلى الشاطِئ مَرَّة ثانية، ثُمَّ رَكِبنا القِطار ورَجَعنا إلى القاهِرة مَساءً. لَمْ أنسَ أنْ أكتُب بِطاقة بَريديَّة لأستاذتي. أَعْجَبَتْني الإسكَندَريّة كَثيراً واسْتَمتَعتُ بِهذِهِ الزِيارة بِسَبَبِ المَناظِرِ الجَميلة ولأنَّ الإسكَندَرانيّين طَيِّبون ويُحِبّون أنْ يُساعِدوا الناسَ الآخَرين.

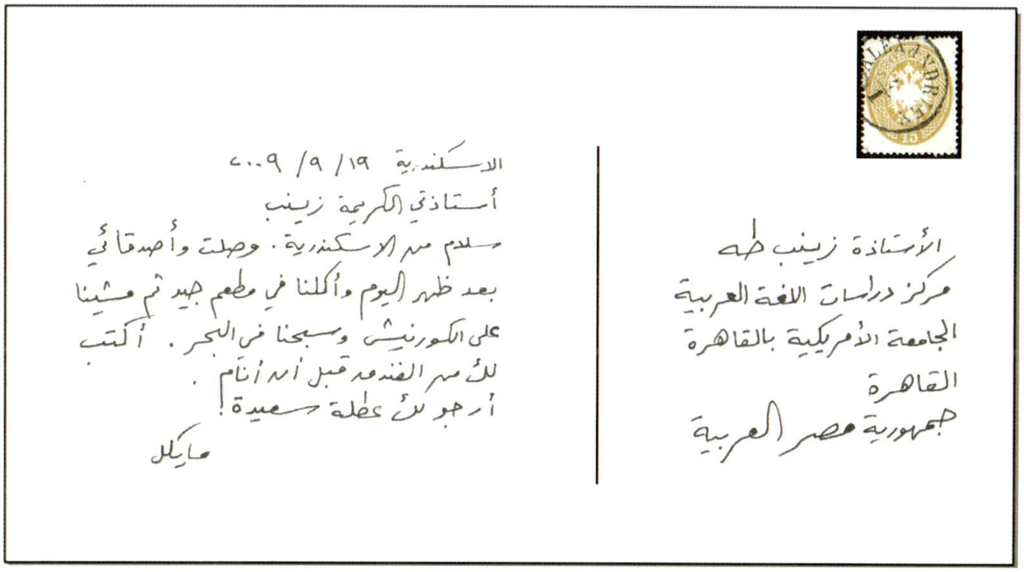

الإسكندرية ١٩/ ٩/ ٢٠٠٩
أستاذتي الكريمة زينب
سلام من الإسكندرية. وصلت وأصدقائي
بعد ظهر اليوم وأكلنا في مطعم جيد ثم مشينا
على الكورنيش وسبحنا في البحر. أكتب
لك من الفندق قبل أن أنام.
أرجو لك عطلة سعيدة!
مايكل

الأستاذة زينب طه
مركز دراسات اللغة العربية
الجامعة الأمريكية بالقاهرة
القاهرة
جمهورية مصر العربية

القاهِرة، الجُمعة ٢٣ نوفَمبر (تِشرين الثاني) ٢٠١٨

نَهرُ النيل

إنَّ الشَيءَ الَّذي أعْجَبَني في القاهِرة كَثيراً هو السَماءُ الزَرقاء ونَهرُ النيلِ العَظيمِ الَّذي يَبدَأ مِن وَسَط أفريقيا في « بُروندي ». يَسيرُ النيل شَمالاً إلى الخُرطوم عاصِمةِ السودان حَيثُ يَلتَقي نَهرا النيلِ الأبيَض والنيلِ الأزرَق، ومِن هُناكَ يَسيرُ النيل شَمالاً إلى القاهِرة ثُمَّ إلى البَحرِ الأبيَضِ المُتَوَسِّط. نَهرُ النيل أطوَل نَهر في العالَم، وطولُهُ ٦٦٩٥ كيلومِتراً، لِذلِكَ فَهُوَ أطوَل مِن نَهرِ أوهايو ونَهرِ الميسيسيبي.

القاهِرة، السَبت ٢٢ ديسمبر (كانون الأوّل) ٢٠١٨

المُتحَفِ المِصريّ

في كُلّ عُطلة نِهاية أسبوع أزور مَكاناً جَديداً. ذَهَبتُ صَباح أمس إلى المُتْحَفِ المِصريّ ووَجَدتُ فيهِ عَدَداً كَبيراً مِنَ الآثارِ الفِرعَونِيَّةِ القَديمَة وكَذلِكَ آثاراً إسلامِيَّة وعَرَبِيَّة. إنّه مُتْحَف جَيِّد جِدّاً وسَأزورُهُ مَرّة ثانِية إنْ شاءَ الله. اِشتَريتُ مِنَ المُتْحَف بَعضَ الصُوَر وكِتاباً عَن آثار مِصر. ومِن هُناكَ ذَهَبتُ إلى مَسجِد مُحَمَّد عَليّ والتَقطتُ بَعضَ الصُوَر. في الأسبوعِ المُقبِل سَوفَ أزور بَعضَ المَساجِدِ القَديمة في القاهِرة، لكِنّي لَنْ أسافِر إلى مُدُن أخرى في ذلِكَ الأسبوع.

عَدنان مارتيني في نيويورك وكَنَدا وفلوريدا

كَلَمبَس، الأربِعاء ٢٩ أغسطس (آب) ٢٠١٨

أخَذتُ أمس آخِر امتِحان في هذا الفَصلِ الدِراسيّ وكانَ في مادّةِ الرِياضِيّات. أظُنّ أنّي أجَبتُ عَنِ الأسئِلَة جَيِّداً، وأنا سَعيد أنَّ الدِراسةَ انتَهَت. أسْتَطيعُ الآن أنْ أسافِر لِزيارةِ الأماكِنِ الجَميلة في الوِلاياتِ المُتَّحِدة وكَنَدا الَّتي أريد زِيارتَها.

اِشْتَرَيتُ في الشَهرِ الماضي تَذْكَرة طائِرة إلى نيويورك ذَهاباً وإياباً بِمِئَتَين وثلاثينَ دولاراً. أرَدْتُ زيارة نيويورك مُنذُ أشهُر فَأنا لا أعرِفُها، مَعَ أنَّ لي صَديقاً

يَسكُن هُناكَ ويَدرُسُ الهَندَسَةَ الصِناعِيَّة في جامِعة نيويورك. سَوفَ يَستَقبِلُني غَسّان في المَطار. لَن أنزِل في فُندُق، بَل في شَقَّة غَسّان.

ساحة تايمز

نيويورك، الجُمعة ٣١ أغسطس (آب) ٢٠١٨

وَصَلَتْ طائِرتي إلى مَطار «لاغوارديا» في مَوعِدِها وكانَ غَسّان أمامَ البَوّابة أخذَني إلى شَقَّتِه حَيثُ وَضَعتُ حَقيبَتي وأشيائي. مَشَينا في الشَوارِعِ حَتّى وَصَلنا إلى ساحَة مَشهورة تُسَمّى «تايمز سكوير». ثُمَّ زُرْنا بَعدَ ذلِكَ مَحَلاّت تِجاريّة مِثل «ساكْس فيفث أفِنيو » و«ماسيز»، لكِنَّنا لَم نَشترِ أيّ شَيء.

مَشَينا في الشارِعِ الخامِس لِزيارة مَبْنى «إمبايَر ستيت» الَّذي يَقَع بَينَ الشارِعِ الثالِث والثَلاثين والشارِعِ الرابع والثَلاثين والَّذي بُنِيَ مُنذُ أكثَر من سبعة وثمانين عاماً. أخَذنا المِصْعَد إلى الطابَق ١٠٢ وشاهَدْنا مَدينة نيويورك مِن فَوق. كانَ هذا المَبْنى أطول مَبنىً في العالَم إلى أنْ بُنِيَ مَبنى «سِيرز» في شيكاغو وغَيرُه في كولا لامبور ودُبَي.

بَعدَ ذلِكَ تَناوَلنا طَعامَ العَشاء في مَطعَم فَرَنسيّ جَيِّد قَريب مِن مَسْرَح «راديو سيتي». كانَ الطَعام جَيِّداً لكِنَّهُ كانَ غالِياً جِدّاً. شاهَدنا فيلماً في راديو سيتي. لَن أستَطيع أن أزور جامِعة نيويورك غَداً لأنّنا سَنُسافِر بِالقِطار صَباحاً إلى شَلاّلات نياغرا.

شلاّلات نَياغَرا

شَلاّلاتُ نياغَرا، الإثنين ٣ سبتمبر (أيلول) ٢٠١٨

وَصَلنا أمس ظُهراً إلى الشَلاّلاتِ الّتي يَقَع جُزء مِنها في الوِلاياتِ المُتَّحِدَة والجُزءُ الآخَر في كَندا. ذَهبنا أوّلاً إلى الجانِبِ الكَنَديّ، وقالَ غَسّان إنَّ الشَلاّلات على الجانِبِ الكَنَديّ أجمَل. لَم أرَ أعْظَم مِن هذِهِ الشَلاّلات مِن قَبل. أعْجَبَتْني الحَدائِق والأزهارُ الجَميلة في الجانِبِ الكَنَديّ.

في اليَومِ التالي ذَهَبنا إلى الجانِبِ الأمريكيّ ورَكِبنا قارِباً مَعَ ناس آخَرين سارَ بِنا

تَحتُ الشَلاّلات. كانَ مَنظَرُ الشَلاّلات مِن تَحت عَظيماً جِدّاً، والتَقَطتُ صُوَراً كَثيرة مِنَ القارِب.

قارِبان تَحتَ الشَلالات

سَنَرجِع غداً إلى نيويورك حَيثُ سأزور تِمثالَ الحُرِيّة و«ستاتن آيلاند». شاهَدتُ صُوَرَ التِمثال في المَجلاّت والأفلام وقَرَأتُ عَنهُ كَثيراً مُنذُ كُنتُ صَغيراً، لكِنّي لَمْ أرَهُ إلى الآن.

تِمثال الحُرّية

سَنُسافِرُ أنا وغَسّان إلى «أتلانتِك سيتي» لِيَوم واحِد فَقَط بِالقِطار، وهذِهِ المَدينة مِثلُ مَدينة «لاس فيغاس» فيها أماكِن كَثيرة لِلقِمار بأنواعِه. بَعدَ ذلِكَ سَأسافِرِ وَحدي إلى فَلوريدا بِالطائِرة لِزيارة «ديزني وُرلد» في «أورلاندو».

أتلانتِك سيتي

أورلاندو، السَبت ٨ أيلول ٢٠١٨

وَصَلتُ إلى هُنا أوّل أمس بَعدَ الظُهر. نَزَلتُ في فُندُق «رامادا» وهُوَ قَريب مِن «ديزني وُرلد». في ذلِكَ المَساء ذَهَبتُ إلى العَشاء في مَطعَم يُقدِّم أطعِمَة مِن الغَربِ الأمريكيّ. لَم يُعجِبْني الطَعامُ أبَداً.

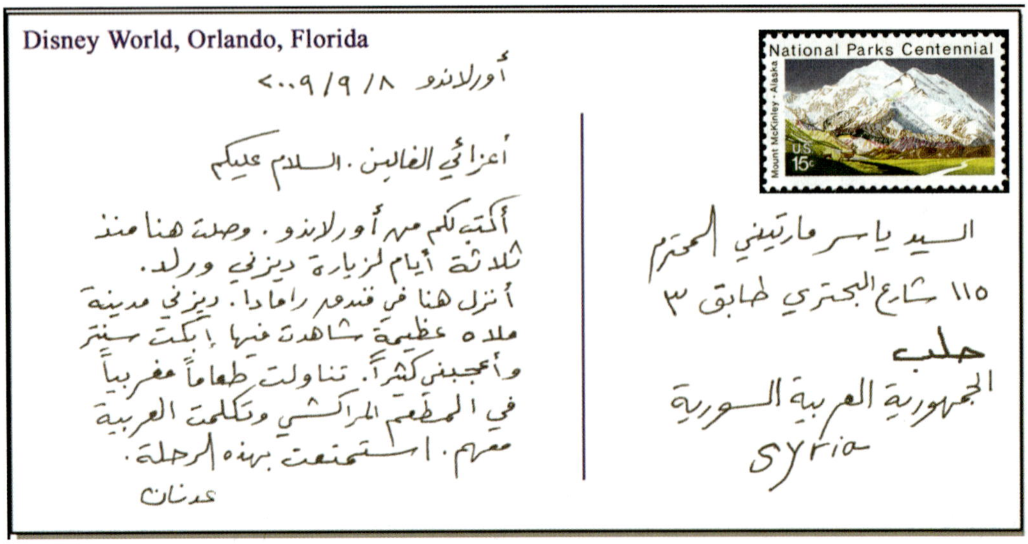
Disney World, Orlando, Florida

أورلاندو ٢٠٠٩/٩/٨

أعزائي الغالين. السلام عليكم

أكتب لكم من أورلاندو. وصلت هنا منذ ثلاثة أيام لزيارة ديزني ورلد. أنزل هنا في فندق رامادا. ديزني مدينة ملاه عظيمة شاهدت فيها إبكت سنتر وأعجبني كثيراً. تناولت طعاماً مغربياً في المطعم المراكشي وتكلمت العربية معهم. استمتعت بهذه الرحلة.

عدنان

السيد ياسر مارتيني المحترم
١١٥ شارع البحتري طابق ٣
حلب
الجمهورية العربية السورية
Syria

في صَباحِ اليَومِ التالي ذَهَبتُ مِنَ الفُندُق مَعَ بَعضِ الناسِ الآخَرين في حافِلة صَغيرة إلى «ديزني وُرلد»، وهِيَ مَدينة مَلاهٍ واسِعة جِدّاً فيها عَدَد كَبير مِن العُروض والألعاب والمَطاعِم والمَحلاّتِ التِجاريّة مِن كُلّ بَلَد في العالَم. أعْجَبَني «إبكَت سِنتَر» كَثيراً وكَذلِكَ «ماجك كِنغدَم». لَم أرَ كُلّ شَيء في اليَوم الأوّل، لِذلِكَ رَجَعتُ في اليَومِ التالي وشاهَدتُ الأشياءَ الّتي لَم أشاهِدْها وزُرتُ «إبكَتْ» مَرّة ثانِيَة. تَناوَلتُ العَشاء مَساءً في «ديزني وُرلد» في المَطعَم المَراكِشيّ الّذي يُقَدِّم أطعِمة مَغربيّة. أعجَبَني المَطعَم والموسيقا العَرَبيّة الّتي قَدَّمَتْها فِرقة مَغرِبيّة. لَم يَكُنِ الطَعام غالياً.

ماجك كِنغدَم

رِسالة عَدنان إلى صَديقِهِ مازِن:

كلمبس في ١٠ أيلول ٢٠٠٩

أخي العزيز مازن، سلام حار لك من كلمبس.

كيف حالك يا أخي؟ لم تصلني منك أية رسالة منذ مدة طويلة. كتبت لك رسالة في شهر آذار الماضي ولم يصلني منك أي شيء لذلك ظننت أنك انتقلت من عنوانك القديم في حلب. علمت من مروان بعد ذلك أنك انتقلت إلى جامعة عمان وهو الذي أعطاني عنوانك الجديد. هل يعجبك السكن والدراسة في عمان؟

أنا كما تعلم أدرس علم الحاسوب في جامعة ولاية أوهايو. بعد أيام سيبدأ العام الدراسي الجديد، وهذه هي سنتي الثانية هنا. أنا سعيد في كلمبس وأستمتع بالسكن فيها وبالدراسة كذلك.

في الأسابيع الثلاثة الماضية زرت مدينة نيويورك وأتلانتك سيتي وشلالات نياغرا في كندا وكذلك «ديزني ورلد» وهي مدينة ملاه كبيرة جداً في مدينة أورلاندو في فلوريدا. استمتعت بهذه الزيارات كثيراً. أرجو أن أزور ولاية كاليفورنيا في السنة المقبلة إن شاء الله ولاس فيغاس أيضاً.

أرجو أن تكتب لي عنك وعن دراستك. لك مني أطيب السلام وإلى لقاء قريب في حلب.

أخوك المخلص
عدنان

تمرين ٤

المُحادَثة: اسأل زَميلك:

١- لِماذا أو لِماذا لا تُحِبّ(ينَ) زيارةَ شَلاّلات نياغرا؟

٢- أيّ مكان في العالَم تُريد(ين) الذَهاب إليه؟

٣- بأيّ نوع من الموسيقا تَستَمْتِع(ينَ) ومتى تَستَمِع(ينَ) إليه؟

٤- متى تَلتَقِط(ينَ) صوراً وماذا تُحِب(ينَ) أنْ تُصَوِّر(ي)؟

٥- ماذا يُعْجِبُك أن تَفعَل(ي) في عُطْلَة نِهاية الأسْبوع ؟

تمرين ٥

أجِب عَن هذِهِ الأسئِلَة حَسَبَ نَصّ القِراءة:

١- مَتى زارَ مايكِل الأهرامات وفي أيّ مَكان تَقَع؟

٢- ماذا يُعجِب مايكِل في القاهِرة؟

٣- مِن أينَ اِشترى مايكِل كِتاباً عَن آثار مِصر؟

٤- ما اسمُ المَحطَّةِ الَّتي سافَر مِنها مايكِل إلى الإسكَندَريّة؟

٥- لِماذا أعجَبَتِ الإسكَندَريَّة مايكِل؟

٦- مَتى كَتَبَ مايكِل البِطاقَةَ البَريديّة لأستاذَتِه؟

٧- في أيّ يوم أخذَ عَدنان امتِحانَ الرِياضِيّات؟

٨- أينَ تَناوَلَ عَدنان طَعامَ العَشاء في نيويورك ومَعَ مَن؟

٩- في أيّ يوم زارَ عَدنان تِمثالَ الحُرِيَّة؟

١٠- مَعَ مَن سافَرَ عَدنان إلى أورلاندو؟

١١- أينَ تَكَلَّم عَدنان العَرَبيّة في أورلاندو؟

١٢- أينَ يَدرُس مازِن الآن؟

تمرين ٦

اخترَ التكمِلةَ المُناسِبة حَسَب نَصّ القِراءة.

١- يَومِيّات مايكِل جُزء مِن ___________.

☐ رَسائلِه ☐ دِراستِه ☐ زيارتِه

٢- رَأى مايكِل الجَمل في ___________ .

☐ حَديقةِ الحَيَوانات ☐ كُلّ مَكان ☐ شَوارِعِ القاهِرة

٣- الإسكَنْدَريّة ___________.

☐ مَدينة حَديثة ☐ أقدَم مَدينة ☐ ميناء هامّ

٤- الناس في الإسكَندَريّة ___________ .

☐ جَميلون ☐ يُحِبّون ☐ طَيِّبون

٥- يَلتَقي النيلان الأبيَض والأزرَق في ___________ .

☐ الخُرطوم ☐ القاهِرَة ☐ الإسكَندَريَّة

٦- عَدنان سَعيد لأنّ ___________ .

☐ الفَصلَ الدِراسيّ الجَديد بَدَأَ ☐ الدِراسة انتَهَتْ

☐ تذكِرةَ الطائرة بِمئتَين وثلاثين دولاراً

٧- نَزَلَ عَدنان في نيويورك في ___________ .

☐ فُندُق رَمادا ☐ إمبايَر ستيت ☐ شَقّة صَديقِه

٨- بُنِيت «إمباير ستيت» مُنذُ أكثَر مِن ___________ عاماً.

☐ ٥٥ ☐ ٨٧ ☐ ٩٥

٩- كانَ الطَعام في المَطعَمِ الفِرَنسيّ ___________ .

☐ غالياً ☐ طَويلاً ☐ جَميلاً

١٠- لَم يَزُرْ عَدنان جامِعة نيويورك بِسَبَب ___________ .

☐ العُطلَة السَنَوية ☐ زِيارَته لِلشَلاّلات ☐ الطَقس

١١- التَقطَ عَدنان صُوَراً لِلشَلاّلات مِن ___________ .

☐ الجانِبِ الكَنَديّ ☐ القارِب ☐ الحَدائِق

١٢- سافَرَ عَدنان إلى أتلانتيك سيتي ________ .

☐ بِالقِطار ☐ بِالسَيّارة ☐ بِالطائِرَة

١٣- لَم يُعجِبْ مايكِل الطَعامُ ________

☐ الفَرَنسيّ ☐ المُرّاكِشيّ ☐ الأمريكيّ الغَربيّ

١٤- تَسكُن أسرةُ عَدنان في ________ .

☐ دِمَشق ☐ حَلَب ☐ عَمّان

١٥- يُريد عَدنان زِيارة ________ في السَنةِ المُقبلة.

☐ فَلوريدا ☐ كَنَدا ☐ كاليفورنيا

تمرين ٧

أكتُبْ «خَطَأ» أو «صَواب» بِجانب كُلّ جُملَة وصَحِّح الجُمَلَ الخَطَأ.

١- اِشتَرى مايكِل صُوَراً عِندَ الأهرامات.

٢- يَسيرُ النيل شَمالاً مِنَ القاهِرة إلى الخُرطوم.

٣- الإسكَندَريّة أقدَم مِنَ القاهِرة بِمِئاتِ السِنين.

٤- نامَ مايكِل وأصدِقاؤهُ على الشاطِئ في الإسكَندَريّة.

٥- لَم يَرَ عَدنان تِمثالَ الحُريّة مِن قَبل.

٦- ذَهَبَ عَدنان إلى مَبنى إمباير ستيت بِالسَيّارة.

٧- يَظُنّ غَسّان أنَّ الشَلاّلات على الجانِبِ الأمريكيّ أجمَل.

٨- زارَ عَدنان «ديزني وُرلد» لِيَوم واحِد فَقَط.

٩- اِنتَقَلَ مازِن صَديقُ عَدنان مِن جامِعة دمشق إلى حَلَب.

كُبري قَصر النيل

تمرين ٨

وافِقْ بَيْنَ الكَلِمات في العَمودَين.

١-	شَلاّلات		حَيَوانات
٢-	بِطاقة		المَلاهي
٣-	آلَةُ		طائِرة
٤-	حَديقة		نَياغَرا
٥-	عيد		تِجاريّ
٦-	تَذْكَرة		تَصوير
٧-	مَحَلّ		تَأمين
٨-	مَدينة		بَريديّة
			الأضحى

تمرين ٩

أعِدْ تَرتيبَ الكَلِمات في كُلّ مَجموعة لِتُشَكّل جُمَلاً مُفيدة.

١- لُغاتٍ - جَيِّداً - أختي - أنْ - ثَلاثَ - تَتَكَلَّمَ - تَستَطيعُ

٢- العِشرينَ - المِصعَدَ - الطابَقِ - يَأخُذُ - إلى - الناسُ

٣- فيلماً - بِهِ - واستَمتَعتُ - في - السينَما - شاهَدْتُ - دارِ

٤- آلافِ - بُنِيَتْ - السِنين - الأهرامات - مُنْذُ

٥- الإسكَندَريّةِ - رَمسيس - إلى - رَكِبْنا - مِن - القِطارَ - مَحَطّةِ

٦- تَسْتَمتِعوا - لِمَدينَتِنا - بِزِيارَتِكُم - أنْ - أرجو

٧- تَصويري - صورةً - بِآلَةِ - لأصدِقائي - الجَديدة - التَقَطتُ

تمرين ١٠

أعِدْ تَرتيبَ الجُمَل لِتُشكِّل فِقرة مُفيدة.

١- أَردتُ أنا وعائلَتي زِيارة مَدينةِ اللاذِقيّة في عُطلةِ الرَبيع.
في الطَريق إلى اللاذِقيَّة مَرَرْنا بِمَدينتَيْ حِمص وطَرطوس.
في اليَومِ التالي ذهَبنا إلى الشاطِئ وسَبَحْنا
سارَتِ الحافِلة في الثامِنة صَباحاً.
ذَهَبنا أوَّلاً إلى الفُندُق حَيثُ وَضَعنا حَقائِبَنا.
واللاذِقيّة ميناء سورية الأوَّل على البَحرِ الأبيَضِ المُتَوَسِّط.
بَعدَ الغَداء رَكِبنا قارِباً صَغيراً لِساعة أو أكثَر.
عِندي عائِلة كَبيرة مِن أربعَة أبناء وثَلاث بنات.
ثُمَّ ذَهَبنا إلى شاطِئ البَحر حَيثُ تَناوَلنا الغَداء.
اسْتَمتَعنا كَثيراً بِهذِهِ الزِيارة.
وجَلَسْتُ أنا وزَوجَتي خَلفَ السائِق.
وَصلنا إلى اللاذِقيَّة في الثانِية بَعدَ الظُهر.
جَلَس ابني الكَبير إلى جانِبِ السائِق.
لِذلِكَ اسْتَأجَرنا حافِلة صَغيرة مَعَ سائِقِها.

حَديقةُ الأزهَر

تمرين ١١

تَمرينُ المُشاهَدة: شاهِدوا الدَرْسَ التاسع عَشَر على القُرْص الرَقْميّ.

١- لِماذا تُنادي الأم ابنَها (ماما)؟ ________________________

____

٢- لِماذا ستيف لَيسَ مَوجوداً في البَيْتِ عِندَ الفَطور مع باقي الأسرة؟ ____________

____

٣- كَيفَ حياة مايكل في القاهِرةِ في رأيه؟ ________________________

____

٤- ماذا شاهَدَ مايكل في الجيزة وماذا فَعَلَ هُناك؟ ________________________

____

٥- إلى أين سَيَذهَب سامِر ومايكل بَعدَ شُربِ القهوة؟ ________________________

____

٦- مَن عَدنان؟ ________________________

____

تمرين ١٢

تَمرينُ المُشاهَدة: بَحث مَعلوماتي من الشابِكة. اكتُب فِقرة عن المواضيع الآتية:

١- الحَكواتي
٢- الجامِعُ الأمويّ
٣- مَقهى النَوفرة

وبَعد أن انتَهَيت من كِتابةِ الفقرات، أخبِر زُملائك بِما عَلِمت من المَعلومات.

١- كِتابة الرسالة والبِطاقة البَريديّة

حِين نَكتُب بِطاقات بَريديّة ورَسائل، يجِب علَينا أن نُوجّه التَحية لِلشَخص المُرسَل إليه بِالطَريقة الصَحيحة، لِذا، نَستَخدِم كَلِمات مُعيَّنة مِثل عَزيز وحَبيب وخِلافها. بِالإضافة إلى ذلِكَ، إذا أرَدنا أن نَكتُب رِسالة أكثَر رَسميّة (more formal)، فَمِن المُمكِن أن نَستَخدِم والِد بَدَلاً مِن أب أو والِدة بَدَلاً مِن أمّ. إليكم مِثال على ذلِك:

١	والِدي الحَبيب / والِدي العَزيز	بَدَلاً من أبي الحَبيب / أبي العَزيز

وفي حالة أرَدنا أن نَكتُب إلى صَديق، فَيُمكِنُنا اِستِخدامَ التَحيات الآتية:

٢	أخي العَزيز فُلان	* فُلان(ة) = "so-and-so"
٣	أختي العَزيزة فُلانة	

مُلاحَظة: أنَّ الرَجُل لا يَستطيع اِستِخدام حَبيبتي أو الحَبيبة إلا إذا كانَت زَوجتُه أو خَطيبتُه أو أُختُه أو بِنتُه.

وفي نِهاية الرِسالة، الكاتِب عادةً يَستَخدِم واحداً من الكَلِمات الآتية:

٤	المُخلِص / المُخلِصة	*sincerely*
٥	المُشتاق / المُشتاقة	*missing you*
٦	المُحِبّ / المُحِبّة	*lovingly*

تمرين ١٣

اكتُبْ بِطاقة بَريديّة إلى صَديق عَرَبيّ سواء أكان حَقيقيّاً أم خيالياً مِن مَدينة زُرتَها في الوِلاياتِ المُتَّحِدة أو في العالَم العَرَبيّ. اكتُب بِدايتَها بِالطريقة الّتي تَعَلَّمتها في هذا الدَرس باسم الصَديق والتاريخ والعُنوان. صِف المَدينة الّتي تَنزل فيها وماذا رأيت وماذا تَنوي أن تَفعل هُناك ومَتى تَرجِع إلى بَيتك وإذا أعجَبَتك الزيارة أم لا ولِماذا. اِستعمِل البِطاقة البَريديّة في الصَفحة التالية كَي لا تتجاوَز طول البِطاقة البَريديّة العادية.

تابع نشاط تمرين ١٣: أحضر بعض البطاقات البريدية من العالم العربي ووزّعها على الطُلاّب. اطلب منهم أن يكتبوا رسالة قصيرة بالطريقة الصحيحة كي ترسلها إلى بعض الأشخاص الّذين تعرفهم في العالم العربي. وفي أحسن الأحوال، سيستلم بعض الطُلاّب أول بطاقة بريدية مكتوبة لهم بالعربية. شجّع الطُلاّب الّذين استلموا بطاقات بريدية من العالم العربي أن يعرضوها لزملائهم في الصف. ساعدهم إذا واجهتهم مشاكل بقراءة الخط.

إليك بعض المُفرَدات الّتي قد تُفيدك في إكمال هذا التَمرين:

إجازة	عيد	أَحْبَبْتُ	زيارة	احتفلتُ بـ	حَفْلة
تَناوَلَ	اِلْتَقَطَ	مُنْذُ	مَرَّة	اِلْتَقى	اِسْتَطاعَ
أَصْدِقائي	اِسْتَمْتَعْتُ بِـ	سَهِرْتُ	تَكَلَّمْتُ	مع	سَيِّد

العرض: استخدِم لوحة قصصية لخلق السياق المناسب.

الممارسة: اطلُب من الطُلاّب أن يعطوك بعض الأفكار لكتابة قصة قصيرة باستخدام ظرفي الزمان والمكان. اكتب الجمل على السبورة أو اطلُب منهم كتابتها على السبورة. إليك مِثال على ذلك:

ركب الرجل سيّارته صباحا لمدة ساعة.
ذهب الرجل شمالاً ليزور أسرته.
وصل الرجل إلى بيت أسرته الموجود فوق عيادة طبيب.
تناول الغداء عند الظهر مع أسرته وأصدقائه.
رجع إلى بيته مساءً.
جلس مع عائلته وتناول طعام العشاء معهم ليلاً.

التطبيق: وزّع على الطُلاّب لوحات قصصية واطلُب منهم أن ينشِئوا قصصاً في مجموعات من اثنين أو ثلاثة يستغرقون فيها حوالي سبع أو عشر دقائق لإكمال هذا التمرين. اسألهم إذا أرادت مجموعة من المجموعات أن تقرأ قصتها إلى الصفّ. شجّع الطُلاّب المستمعين أن يطرحوا أسئلة عن القصة الّتي سمعوها.

٢- ظَرفا الزَمان والمَكان

يُعتبَر ظَرفُ الزَمان والمَكان بِاللغُة العَرَبيّة اسماً مَنصوباً يَدُلّ على زَمان الفِعل أو مَكانه.

يَدُلّ ظَرفُ الزَمان على وَقْت وُقوع الفِعل ويُجيب عن السؤال مَتى؟

٧	وَصَلَتِ الطائِرةُ	مَساءً.

مَتى وَصَلَتِ الطائِرة؟ الجُواب: مَساءً.

إليك بَعض ظُروف الزَمان

دَقيقة	ساعة	يَوم	لَيلة	أُسبوع	شَهر	سَنَة	عام	زَمان	حين

٨	وُلِدْتُ عامَ ١٩٥٢.	أو	دَرَستُ ساعةً.	أو	قَرأتُ لَيلةً.

ويَدُلّ ظَرفُ المَكان على مَكان وُقوعِ الفِعل ويُجيب عن السؤال: أين؟

٩	مَشَيْتُ شَمالاً.
١٠	شَقَّتي تَحتَ عِيادةِ الطَبيب.

أين مَشَيْتُ في المِثال ٩؟ شَمالاً وأين تَقع شَقّتي في المِثال ١٠؟ تَحتَ عِيادةِ الطَبيب.
إلَيك بعض الأمثِلة:

أمامَ	خلفَ	تَحتَ	فَوقَ	شَمالَ	غَربَ	يَمينَ	يَسارَ	جَنوبَ	شَرقَ

١١	تَقعُ الإسكَندَريَّةُ شَمالَ القاهِرةِ.
١٢	الأهراماتُ في الجيزةِ قُرْبَ القاهِرَةِ.

مُلاحَظة: لِكُلّ ظَرف زَمان ومَكان مُقابلَه جار ومَجرور كَما تَرى في المِثالَين أدناه:

١٣	وُلِدْتُ في عامِ ١٩٥٢.
١٤	مَشَيْتُ إلى الشَمالِ.

في المِثالَين أعلاه، يأتي عامِ والشَمالِ بَعد حَرفَي الجَرّ في وإلى لِذا هُما في حالة الجَرّ، مَجروران بالكَسرة. وكَما لاحَظت، حين يأتي الظَرف في مَحلِّ الاسم، فأنّه يأتي مَجروراً بَعدَ الجار. إليك مِثالَين:

١٥	وَصَلتُ إلى المَدرسةِ صَباحاً	=	وَصَلتُ إلى المَدرسةِ في الصَباحِ.
١٦	مَشَيْتُ شَمالاً.	=	مَشَيْتُ إلى الشَمالِ.

العرض: حضِّر قصةً لتحكيها للطُلّاب وأكثِرْ فيها استخدام حَرف النفي لن، على سبيل المِثال:
«تكلمت مع أمّي بالهاتف وطلبت مني أن أزورها في عطلة نهاية الأسبوع هذا. ولكنّي لن أزورها لأني مشغول جداً بدراستي. وإن زرتها فلن أكتب واجباتي البيتية. ولكن إن بقيتُ هنا فلن أراها لمدة طويلة من الزمن. آه . . . ما العمل؟»

اسأل الطُلّاب إذا كان هناك شيء لن يقوموا به في المستقبل، مثلاً:

«هل هناك شيء لن تفعليه في عطلة نهاية الأسبوع أو الأسبوع/ الشهر المقبل؟ ولماذا لن تفعلي هذا الشيء؟»

٣- حَرف نَفي المُستَقبَل: لَنْ

كَما تَعلَم، أنّنا نَدُلّ على المُستقبَل بِاستِخدام الحَرف سَوفَ الّذي نَشتَقّ مِنه الحَرف سَـ الّذي يَتصل بِالفِعل الّذي يَليه. إليك مِثالَين على ذلِك:

١٧	سَوفَ أسافِرُ إلى مُدُنٍ أخرى.	=	سَأسافِرُ إلى مُدُنٍ أخرى.
١٨	سَوفَ أزورُ جامِعَةَ نيويورك.	=	سَأزورُ جامِعَةَ نيويورك.

كَما لاحَظت في يَوميّات مايكل براون وعَدنان مارتيني، أنّنا نَنفي زَمَن المُستقبَل بِالحَرف لَن. إلَيك مِثالَين على ذلِك:

١٩	سَوفَ أسافِرُ إلى مُدُنٍ أخرى.	≠	لَنْ أسافِرَ إلى مُدُنٍ أُخرى.
٢٠	سَوفَ أزورُ جامِعَةَ نيويورك.	≠	لَنْ أزورَ جامِعَةَ نيويورك.

تأمّل لَحظةً الأمثِلة أعلاه ١٩ و٢٠. ماذا لاحَظت من تأثير لَنْ على الفِعل الّذي يَليه؟ نَجِد أنّ الفِعلَين المَرفوعَين أسافِرُ وأزورُ حين يَليان لَنْ، يَصيران في حالة النَصب، أي مَنصوبان بالفَتحة.

الخُلاصة

١- لا نَستَخدِم سَـ أو سَوفَ مع حَرف نَفي المُستَقبَل لَن.

٢- الفِعل الّذي يَلي لَنْ في حالة النَصب، أي في المُضارع المَنصوب

تمرين ١٤

اِنْفِ (negate) الجُمَلَ الآتية:

١- سَوفَ أدرُسُ اللُغةَ العَرَبيَّة في جامُعة دِمَشق.

٢- سَتَزورُني أمّي في الشَهرِ المُقبِل.

٣- سَوفَ أشاهِد فيلمَين في عُطلةِ الأسبوع هذِه.

٤- سَأستَمتِعُ بِالسِباحة في هذا الطَقس.

تمرين ١٥

اِستَمِعوا إلى التَسجيل الآتي وسَجِّلوا الأشياءَ الّتي سَيَفعَلُها سَعيد والأشياء الّتي لَنْ يَفعَلَها.

سَيفعَلُها سَعيد . . .	لَنْ يَفعلَها سَعيد

تمرين ١٦

اكتُبوا خَمسة أشياء لَنْ تَفعَلوها في العُطلة، ثُمَّ أخبِروا زُملائكُم بِها.

١- ________________________.

٢- ________________________.

٣- ________________________.

٤- ________________________.

٥- ________________________.

٤ - الأسْماء المَوصولة: الَّذي والّتي "which" or "who"

حين يأتي اسم مُبهَم (= لا نَعلَم عَنهُ شيئاً يُذكَر)، نَستَطيع إزالة الإبهام وتَوضيح الاسم بِاستِخدام الاسم المَوصول، على سَبيل المِثال، إذا قُلتُ لَك (الطالِب)، فَماذا تَعرِف عَنهُ؟ لا شَيء. إذاً، نَستَطيع إزالةَ الإبهام وتَوضيح الكَلام بِاستِخدام الّذي، إلَيك مِثال:

٢١ الطالِبُ الَّذي يَتكَلَّمُ العَرَبِيَّةَ سَكَنَ في دِمَشق سَنَتَين.

تَصِف الكَلِمات الّتي تَلي الاسمَ المَوصول فاعِلَ الجُملة والفاعِل في المِثال ٢١ الطالِب ونُسَمي الكَلِمات بَعدَ الاسم المَوصول جُملة الصِلة وهذِه الجُملة تَتَضَمّن (includes) الضَمير العائد (referential pronoun) وهو الضَمير الّذي يَرجِع إلى الفاعِل. دَعنا نَنظُر إلى المِثال ٢٢ بالتَفاصيل:

	الفاعِل	الاسم المَوصول	جُملة الصِلة
٢٢	الطالِبُ	الَّذي	يَتكَلَّمُ العَرَبِيَّةَ سَكَنَ في دِمَشق سَنَتَين.

يُوجَد هُناكَ نَوعان من الأسماء المَوصولة ألا وهُما الاسمُ المَوصول المُختَص (الخاصّ) والاسم المَوصول المُشتَرك (العامّ). نُقَدِّمُهُما لَك في البابَين في الصَفحة التالية.

قلعة قايتباي في الأسكندرية

آ-	**الأسماء المَوصولة الخاصّة**

تَختَص الأسماءُ المَوصولة إلى باسم مُعَيَّن وتُوافِقه من حَيثُ التأنيث والتَذكير والمُفرَد والمُثنّى والجَمع. إلَيك جَدوَل فيهِ الأسماءُ المَوصولةُ الخاصّة

الأسماءُ المَوصولةُ الخاصّة				
	المُفْرَد	**المُثَنى المَرفوع**	**المُثنى المَنصوب والمَجرور**	**الجَمْع**
المُذَكَّر	الّذي	اللَذانِ	اللَذَيْنِ	الّذينَ
المؤنَّث	الَّتي	اللَتانِ	اللَتَيْنِ	اللاتي / اللَواتي

إلَيك جَدوَل يُبيِّن لَك موافَقة الفاعِل والمَوصول في حالة الرَفع، وكَما تَرى يَتَصَرَّف الاسم المَوصول حَسَب السياق.

المَرفوع		
٢٣	الطالِبُ الَّذي يَتكَلَّمُ العَرَبِيَّةَ في الصَفِّ.	**المُفردُ المُذَكَّر**
٢٤	الطالِبةُ الَّتي تَتكَلَّمُ العَرَبِيَّةَ في الصَفِّ.	**المُفرَدةُ المُؤنَّثة**
٢٥	الطالِبانِ اللَذانِ يَتكَلَّمانِ العَرَبِيَّةَ في الصَفِّ.	**المُثَنّى المُذَكَّر**
٢٦	الطالِبَتانِ اللَتانِ تَتكَلَّمانِ العَرَبِيَّةَ في الصَفِّ.	**المُثَنّى المُؤَنَّث**
٢٧	الطُلّابُ الَّذينَ يَتكَلَّمونَ العَرَبِيَّةَ في الصَفِّ.	**الجَمعُ المُذَكَّر**
٢٨	الطالِباتُ اللاتي يَتكَلَّمْنَ العَرَبِيَّةَ في الصَفِّ.	**الجَمعُ المُؤَنَّث**

في حالتَي النَصب والجرّ، تَتَحوَّل الألِف الوَسَط في المَوصول المُثَنّى إلى الياء (المُظَلَّلة بالأحمَر في المِثالَين ٢٩ و٣٠ أدناه). قارِن بَين المِثالَين ٢٥-٢٦ في الصَفحة السابِقة و٢٩-٣٠ أدناه.

	المَنصوب	
٢٩	أعرِفُ الطالِبين اللَذينِ يَتَكَلَّمانِ العَرَبيَّةَ . . .	**المُثَنّى المُذَكَّر**
٣٠	أعرِفُ الطالِبَتَينِ اللتَينِ تَتَكَلَّمانِ العَرَبيَّةَ . . .	**المُثَنّى المُؤنَّث**

بِالنِسبة إلى المَوصولِ الّذي يَصِفُ الجَمع غير العاقِل، فَيُوافِق تأنيثَه أي نَستَخدِم الّتي بَعدَه لأنّنا نَعتَبِرُ الجَمع غير العاقِل المُفرَدة المُؤنَّثة = «هِي» بِصَرفِ النَظر (regardless) عَن تأنيثِ الاسم أو تَذكيرِه. إلَيك مِثالَين:

	الجَمع غير العاقِل	
٣١	هذِهِ هِيَ الكُتُبُ الّتي اشتَرَيتُها.	كِتاب مُفرَد مُذَكَّر
٣٢	أعطِني المَجلاّتِ الّتي قَرأتَها.	مَجلّة مُفرَدة مُؤنَّثة

تمرين ١٧

اسْتَخدِم الاسمَ المَوصولَ المُناسِب في الجُمَلِ التاليةِ.

١- هَل قَرَأتِ المَجَلّةَ ________ اشتَرَيتُها أمس؟
٢- هَؤلاءِ هُنَّ الطالِباتُ ________ يَسكُنَّ في سَكَنِ الطالِبات.
٣- أحمَد وأيْمَن هُما الطالِبانِ ________ يَدرُسانِ الرِياضِيّاتِ.
٤- مَن هُوَ الأُستاذُ ________ كَتَبَ هذا الكِتاب؟
٥- أعرِفُ الرَجُلَين ________ يَعمَلانِ في هذِهِ الشَرِكة.
٦- مَن هُم أصدِقاؤكَ ________ زاروا مِصرَ؟
٧- كَتَبتُ إلى السَيِّدَتَيْنِ ________ تَسكُنانِ في تِلكَ البِناية.
٨- سَلمى وهَنا هُما ________ تَعمَلانِ في هذِهِ الدُكّان.

ب- الأسماء المَوصولة العامّة: ما ومَن

الاسمُ المَوصولُ العامّ لَهُ لَفظ واحِد لِلجَميع، أي لا تَتَغَيَّر صورتُه بِتَغيُّر نَوع الاسم. وهذا بِمَعنى أنّنا نَستَطيع أن نَستَخدِم نَفسَ الاسمِ المَوصولِ العام لِلتَذكير والتأنيث والمُفرَد والمُثَنّى والجَمع. نَعرِفُ المَوصولَ العامّ مَن جَيِّداً لأنّنا نَستعمِلُه عِندما نسأل عن هُويّة شَخص، كَما تَرى في المِثال أدناه.

٣٣	مَنْ زارَ الإسكَندَريَّة؟

حين نَستَعمِل مَن في السؤال كَما فِعلنا في المِثال ٣٣ أعلاه، فَيَدُلّ على الصورة العامّة يَعني لا يُحدِّد شَيئاً مَثَلاً يُمكِن أن نَسأل عن رَجل أو امرأة أو شَخصَين أو جَماعة. تأمّل المِثالَين أدناه:

٣٤	أعْجَبَتِ الإسكَندَريَّةَ مَنْ زارَها.
٣٥	تَكَلَّمتُ مع مَن أردتُ مِن الناس.

لاحِظ أنَّنا نَستَخدِم المَوصولَ العامّ مَن مع الناس يَعني جَمع العاقِل (rational nouns).

لاحِظ أنّنا نَستَخدِم المَوصولَ العامّ ما مع الجَمع غير العاقِل. إلَيك مِثال على ذلِك:

٣٦	إقرأي مِن تِلكَ المَجَلاّتِ ما تُريدينَ.	*Read what you would like of those magazines.*
٣٧	إقرأي مِن تِلكَ الكُتُب ما تُريدينَ.	*Read what you would like of those books.*

لاحِظ كَذلِكَ أنّ المَوصولَ العامّ ما لا يَتَغيَّر بِتَغيُّر تأنيثِ الاسم أو تَذكيره. إذ كِتاب مُفرَد مُذَكَّر ومَجَلّة مُفرَدة مُؤنَّثة.

ج- إدغام (assimilation) حَرف الجَرّ والاسم المَوصول

عِندَما يَسبُق بَعض حُروفِ الجَر الاسمَ المَوصول، فَتَصير كَلِمة مُرَكَّبة (compound word)، على سَبيل المِثال:

٣٨	عَن + ما	كَتَبَ عَدنان عَمّا فَعَلَ في العُطلةِ الصَيفِيَّة.	Adnān wrote about what he did during summer break.
٣٩	عَن + مَن	تَكَلَّمَ عَدنان عَمَّن استَقبَلَ مِن الطُلّابِ الجُدُد.	Adnān talked about whom he met of the new students.
٤٠	مِن + ما	هَل تُريدُ أنْ تَشرَبَ مِمّا أشرَب؟	Would you like to drink of what I'm drinking?
٤١	مِن + مَن	وَصَلَتْني رَسائلُ مِمَّن كَتَبتُ لَهُم.	I received letters from those I wrote.
٤٢	في + ما	قَرَأتُ فيما قَرَأتُ يومِيّاتِ طالِبٍ في القاهِرة.	Some of what I read were the journals of a student in Cairo.
٤٣	في + مَن	عَرَفتُ فيمَن عَرَفتُ في الجامِعةِ طالِبَةً تونِسيَّة.	Among those whom I knew at the university was a Tunisian female student.

د- الاسم المَوصوف في حالة النكِرة

نُلاحِظ في الأمثِلة المَذكورة في هذا الدَرس حَتّى الآن أنَّ كُلَّ الأسماءِ المَوصوفة كانَت مُعَرَّفة بِلام التعريف أو الضَمير المُتَّصِل أو اسم العَلِم. إلَيك الأسماء المَوصوفة الّتي رأيناها

الطالِب	الكُتُب	المَجلّات	أصدِقاؤك	سَلمى وهَنا	الإسكَندَريّة

ولكِنّ الأسماءَ المَوصوفة قَد تَكون نَكِرة أيضاً، وفي هذِه الحالة لا نَستَخدِم الاسمَ المَوصول إطلاقاً، كَما رأينا في يَوميّة مايكل براون:

٤٤	الأهراماتُ مَبانٍ عَظيمةٌ بَناها الفَراعِنةُ.	The pyramids are great buildings [that] the pharaohs built.

مع أنّ الاسمَ المَوصول لَيسَ مَوجوداً في المِثال ٤٤ أعلاه، فأنّ التَرجَمة بالإنكلِيزيّة تَحتاج إلَيها = *that* لأنَّ الجُملة بناها الفَراعِنة جُملة صِلة ولا نَستَطيع اِستِخدام اسم مَوصول هُنا لأنَّ الاسمَ المَوصوف نكِرة.

ي- الضَمير العائِد في صِلة المَوصول

عامِل من عَوامِلِ (feature) المِثال ٤٤ أعلاه هو الضَميرُ العائد ها ونُسَمّيه العائد لأنَّه يَعود (refers) إلى الكَلِمة مَبانٍ أي المَفعول به. حَسَب قَواعِد تَركيبِ الجُملةِ العَرَبيّة، يَجِب أن نَذكُر الضَميرَ العائد في صِلةِ المَوصول إلاّ إذا لَم يَحدُث اِلتباس (confusion) ولكِنَّه غَير مُستَخدَم في اللُغةِ الإنكلِيزيّة. قارِن نَفس الجُملة بِالعَرَبيّة والإنكلِيزيّة:

٤٥	خَديجةُ هِيَ الطالِبةُ الّتي استَقبَلَها عَدنان في المَطار.	Khadīja is the student whom Adnān met (her) at the airport.

في المِثال ٤٥، يَجِب أن نَستَخدِمَ الضَميرَ العائد ها في جُملة صِلةِ المَوصول بِالعَرَبيّة لكِن حين نُتَرجَم استَقبَلَها إلى الإنكلِيزيّة "he met her"، لا نَحتاج إليه.

تأمّل الأمثِلة أدناه:

٤٦	هذِهِ هِيَ السَيّارةُ الّتي اشتَرَيتُها.	This is the car that I bought (it).
٤٧	هذِهِ هِيَ السَيّارةُ الّتي رَكِبتُ فيها.	This is the car that I rode in (it).
٤٨	هذِهِ هِيَ السَيّارةُ الّتي أعرِفُ سائِقَها.	This is the car whose driver I know (its).

في الجَدولِ السابق، المِثال ٤٦، العائد هو المَفعول بِه وفي المِثال ٤٧ العائد هو المَجرور وفي المِثال ٤٨ العائد هو المُضاف إليه.

أمّا بِالنِسبة إلى الاسمَينِ المَوصولَين العامَّين ما ومَن، فَلا تَحتاج إلى الضَمير العائد، كَما تَرى في المِثالَين أدناه:

٤٩	اشترَيتُ مِن الكُتُبِ ما أريدُ.	*I bought books I want.*
٥٠	زُرتُ مِن الأصدِقاءِ مَن أحِبُّ.	*I visited friends I like.*

الخُلاصة

نَستَخدِمُ الضَميرَ العائد:

إذا كانَ الفاعِلَ في الجُملة غَير مَن قام بالفِعل، فَعلَينا اِستِخدام الضَميرِ العائد:

خَديجةُ هِيَ الطالِبةُ الّتي استَقبَلَها عَدنان في المَطار.	
خَديجة = الفاعِل	عَدنان = الّذي قام بِالفِعل اِستَقبَلَها

عَدَم اِستِخدام الضَميرِ العائد:

إذا كانَ الفاعِلَ في الجُملة مَن قام بالفِعل، فَلَيسَ علَينا اِستِخدام الضَميرِ العائد:

خَديجةُ هِيَ الطالِبةُ الّتي كانَت في المَطار.	
خَديجة = الفاعِل	خَديجة = الّتي قامَت بِالفِعل كانَت

يمكن أن يحيّر الطالِب متى يُستخدَم الضمير العائد. راجع معهم باب الضمير العائد في صلة الموصول في هذا الدرس واطلُب منهم حفظ القواعِد وتطبيقِها.

كذلك، ركّز معهم الاسم الموصول لا يُستخدَم إلّا بعد اسم معرّف (سنغطي الاستثناءات في الدروس القادمة).

راجع معهم معنى **الاسم المعرّف**، لأن الكثير ليس عندهم فكرة عما نقصد حين نقول المعرفة. عادةً، أقول لهُم إن الاسم المعرّف هو اسم يعرفونه وليس شيئاً عاماً.

الممارسة: اكتب على السبورة جملاً مثل الجمل الآتية واطلُب منهم أن يستخدموا الاسم الموصول وجملة الصلة:

١- هذا الدرس ____________
٢- هذه السيّارة ____________
٣- هذا هو الولد ____________
٤- أليس هذا البيت ____________
٥- ما السؤال ____________

التطبيق: اطلُب منهم أن يصفوا أشياء مثل الأسماء الآتية:

الجريدة، السيّارة، الكتاب، الجامعة، الكلية، الصديق(ة)، البيت/الشقة

أو أي اسم تعتقد أنه يُثير انتباههم ويسمح لهم بأن يستخدوا الاسم الموصول في السياق المناسب.

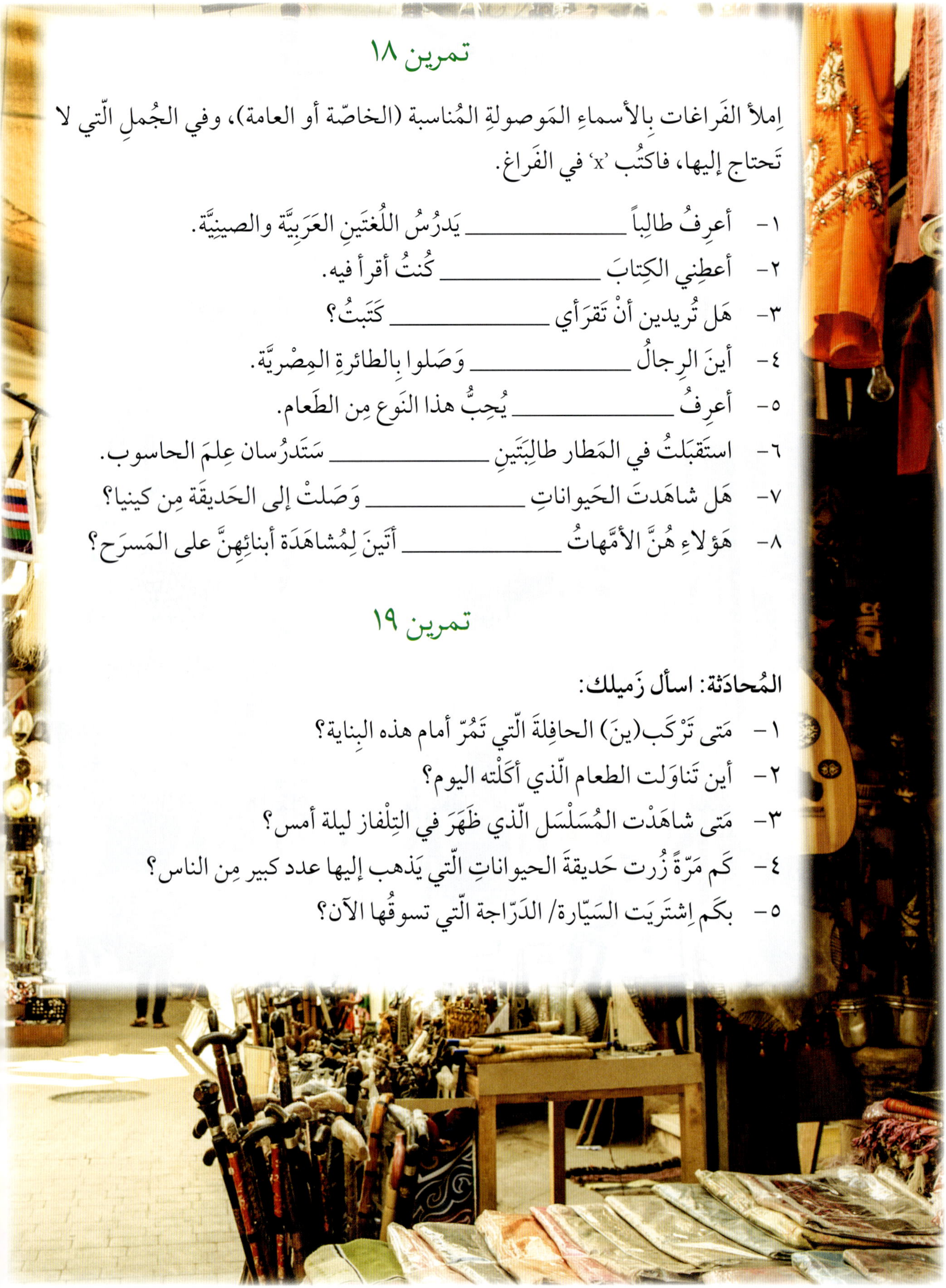

تمرين ١٨

اِملأ الفَراغات بِالأسماءِ المَوصولةِ المُناسبة (الخاصّة أو العامة)، وفي الجُملِ الّتي لا تَحتاج إليها، فاكتُب 'x' في الفَراغ.

١- أعرِفُ طالِباً ________ يَدرُسُ اللُغتَينِ العَرَبِيَّة والصينِيَّة.

٢- أعطِني الكِتابَ ________ كُنتُ أقرأ فيه.

٣- هَل تُريدين أنْ تقرَأي ________ كَتَبتُ؟

٤- أينَ الرِجالُ ________ وَصَلوا بِالطائرةِ المِصْريَّة.

٥- أعرِفُ ________ يُحِبُّ هذا النوع مِن الطَعام.

٦- استَقبَلتُ في المَطار طالِبَتَينِ ________ سَتَدرُسان عِلمَ الحاسوب.

٧- هَل شاهَدتَ الحَيواناتِ ________ وَصَلتْ إلى الحَديقَة مِن كينيا؟

٨- هَؤلاءِ هُنَّ الأمَّهاتُ ________ أتَينَ لِمُشاهَدَة أبنائِهِنَّ على المَسرَح؟

تمرين ١٩

المُحادَثة: اسأل زَميلك:

١- مَتى تَرْكَب(ينَ) الحافِلةَ الّتي تَمُرّ أمام هذه البِناية؟

٢- أين تَناوَلت الطعام الّذي أكَلْته اليوم؟

٣- مَتى شاهَدْت المُسَلْسَل الّذي ظَهَرَ في التِلْفاز ليلة أمس؟

٤- كَم مَرّةً زُرت حَديقةَ الحيواناتِ الّتي يَذهب إليها عدد كبير مِن الناس؟

٥- بكَم اِشتَرَيت السَيّارة/ الدَرّاجة الّتي تسوقُها الآن؟

سوق الأقصر في مِصر

٥- مُراجَعة حُروف الجَرّ

في نُصوصِ القِراءة في هذا الدَرس، رأَينا حُروف الجَرّ تأتي مع حُروف جَرّ أخرى وحُروف أخرى وظُروف وأسماء الإشارة. دَعنا نَنظُر إلى بَعضِ الأمثِلة لأن لِهذِه التَراكيب مَعنى خاصّاً أحياناً. تأمّل الجَدوَل أدناه:

٥١	مِن فَوق	*from above*	حَرفُ الجَرّ + ظَرفُ المَكان	
٥٢	مِن تَحتَ	*from below*	حَرفُ الجَرّ + ظَرفُ المَكان	
٥٣	إلى الآنَ	*until now*	حَرفُ الجَرّ + ظَرفُ الزَمان	
٥٤	إلى أنْ	*till; until*	حَرفُ الجَرّ + الحَرف	إلى أنْ + جُملة فِعليّة
٥٥	مَعَ أنَّ	*although*	حَرفُ الجَرّ + الحَرف	مَعَ أنَّ + جُملة اِسميّة
٥٦	كَذلِكَ	*likewise*	حَرفُ الجَرّ + اسمُ الإشارة	
٥٧	لِذلِكَ	*therefore*	حَرفُ الجَرّ + اسمُ الإشارة	

تمرين ٢٠

آ- أكمِل الجُمَلَ التالية بِكَلِمات مُناسِبة مِن الجَدوَل أعلاه.

١- اشترَى سالِم بَيتاً جَديداً و __________ سَيّارةً جَديدةً.

٢- عِصام رَجُلٌ فَقيرٌ، __________ لا يَستَطيعُ أنْ يَشتَريَ بَيتاً.

٣- لَم تَزُرْ سامية بَيروت __________ صَديقَتَها تَسكُنُ هُناكَ.

٤- جَلَسنا على شاطِئِ البَحرِ __________ غابَتِ الشَمسُ.

٥- لَم تَسمَع سَلمى خَبَراً مِن أُمِّها __________.

٦- شاهِد كَيف تَبْدو سماء القاهِرة __________ ناطِحات السَحاب.

٧- ما صَوتُ حَيواناتِ البَحْر __________ الماء؟

العرض: احكِ قصة عن زيارة قمت بها (أو أي موضوع مثل بيتك أو عملك) تُكثِر فيها استخدام الضمائر الملكية في الإضافة، مثلاً:

«أخذت آلة تصويري إلى سورية حين قمت بزيارة لها في فصل الصيف الماضي. وحين كنت هناك وضعت مفتاح باب غرفتي في حقيبة يدي وبعد ذلك نزلت وجلست إلى طاولة مطعم الفندق حيث تناولت طعام عشائي.»

الممارسة: اسأل الطلّاب أسئلة تتطلب منهم استخدام ضمائر الملكية في الإضافة، كما ترى في الأمثلة أدناه:

«هل معك مفتاح بابِ سيّارتِك؟»
«أين وضعت حقيبة يدِك؟
ما عنوان شقتِك؟»
«متى كانت آخر مرّة زرت فيها بيتَ أسرتِك؟»

التطبيق: اطلُب من الطلاّب أن يسألوا بعضهم بعضاً أسئلة مُشابهة لما قدمت لهم في الصف.

ب- اكتُب الجُمل التالية بِاللُغة العَرَبيّة:

1. So far, I haven't been able to visit the Grand Canyon.
2. The view of the city is beautiful from above.
3. He is not happy although he is rich.
4. We studied at the library until my friends wanted to go to the movies.
5. I like to travel, as does my wife.

٦- الإضافة

سَبَق وتَعَلَّمنا طَريقاً كَي نُعَرِّف (make definite) الاسم، أي نَزيد عليه ضَميراً مُلكيّاً كَما تَرى في المِثالَين أدناه:

٥٨	كِتاب + أنا	←	كِتابي	=	إضافة
٥٩	سَيّارة + هُم	←	سَيّارتُهُم	=	إضافة

إذا أَرَدنا أن نَزيد على الإضافة ضَميرَ المُلكيّة، فلَيسَ علَينا إلا أن نَفعل كَما فَعلنا في المِثالَين ٥٨ و٥٩ أعلاه، أي نَزيد ضَميراً مُلكيّاً على آخِر اسم في الإضافة أو بكَلام آخَر آخِر مُضاف إليه. تأمّل الأمثِلة الآتية:

٦٠	آلَةُ تَصوير + أنا	←	آلَةُ تَصويري	=	*my camera*
٦١	عُنوانُ شَقَّةِ + هُو	←	عُنوانُ شَقّتِهِ	=	*his apartment address*
٦٢	مِفتاحُ بابِ سَيّارةِ + هِي	←	مِفتاحُ بابِ سَيّارتِها	=	*the key to the door of her car*

تمرين ٢١

تَرجَمة: اِستَخدِم الإضافة كَي تُترجَم التَعبيرات التالية إلى العَرَبيّة.

1. my bedroom
2. her (male) friend's car
3. his wife's mother
4. their house floor plan
5. our grocer's store
6. my weekend

تمرين ٢٢

استَمِعْ إلى النَصّ المُسَجَّل ثُمَّ أجِبْ عَن الأسئِلة:

١- كَم وَلَداً في هذِه العائِلة؟

٢- أينَ هذِهِ العائِلةُ الآنَ؟

٣- أيّ فَصل مِن السَنة في هذا النَصّ؟

أكمِل الجُمَلَ التالية حَسَبَ النَصّ:

٤- لِلأردُن ________ .

☐ ميناء واحِد ☐ ميناءان ☐ ثَلاثة مَوانِئ

٥- سافَرَتِ العائِلة إلى العَقَبة ________ .

☐ بِالسَيّارة ☐ بِالطائِرة ☐ بِالقِطار

٦- زارَتْ عائِلة مَيساء العَقَبة لِمُدّة ________ أيّام.

☐ ثَلاثة ☐ أربَعة ☐ خَمسة

٧- كانَ الطَقس في العَقَبة ________ .

☐ حارّاً ☐ مُعتَدِلاً ☐ بارِداً

٨- سَبَحوا في البَحر ________ في اليَوم.

☐ مَرَّتَين ☐ ساعَتَين ☐ يَومَين

٩- اسْتَأجَرَتِ العائِلة ________ في الفُندُق.

☐ غُرفة ☐ غُرفَتَين ☐ ثَلاث غُرَف

اكتُبْ «خَطَأ» أو «صَواب» بِجانب كُلِّ جُملَةٍ وصَحِّح الجُمَلَ الخَطَأ.

١٠- المرأة في النَص مُتَزَوِّجة واسم زَوجِها هِشام.

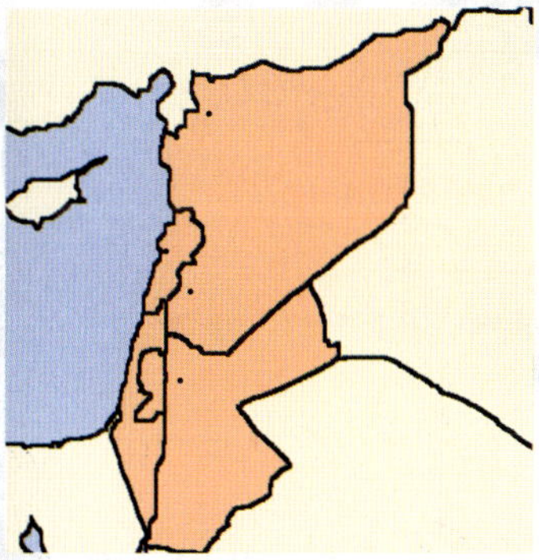

١١- تَناوَلَت مَيساء وعائِلَتُها العَشاء في مَطعَم «نَخيل».

١٢- العَقَبة ميناء على البَحرِ الأبيَضِ المُتَوَسِّط.

١٣- الفُندُق في شارِع قَريب مِن الشاطِئ.

١٤- سَتَركَبُ العائِلة قارِباً بَعدَ الظُهر.

١٥- اكتبْ على الخَريطة إلى اليسار اسمَ البَلَدِ المَوجود في النَصّ واسمَ المَدينَتَين واسمَ البَحرِ.

المُفْرَدات

استمِع إلى المُفْرَدة بالعَرَبيّة ثم أعِد نُطْقَها مرّتين.

آبَ (يَؤوبُ) إياب (v.) . . . . . to return

أبيَض ج بيض (n., m.) . . . . . white

أَثَر ج آثار (n., m.) . . . . . ruin, antiquity, artifact, relic

أجابَ (يُجيبُ) إجابة (v.) . . . . . to respond, to answer

إذاً . . . . . then, therefore

استَطاعَ (يَستَطيعُ) استِطاعة (v.) . . . . . to be able, can

استَمتَعَ (يَستَمتِعُ) استِمتاع (v.) . . . . . to enjoy

إلى أنْ . . . . . until

آلة ج آلات (n., f.) . . . . . apparatus, device, gadget, machine

التَقى (يَلتَقي) التِقاء (v.) . . . . . to meet, converge, encounter

التَقَطَ (يَلتَقِطُ) التِقاط (v.) . . . . . to take, make (a picture)

الَّتي (n., f.) . . . . . who, that

الَّذي (n., m.) . . . . . who, that

امتَحَنَ (يَمتَحِنُ) امتِحان (v.) . . . . . to examine, to test

باكِراً (adverbial) . . . . . early

بَريد (n., m.) . . . . . mail, post

بَقِيَ (يَبْقى) بَقاء (v.) . . . . . to remain, to stay

بَنى (يَبني) بِناء (v.) . . . . . to build, to construct

تَجَوَّلَ (يَتَجَوَّلُ) تَجَوُّل (v.) . . . . . to wander about, to tour

تَذكِرة ج تَذاكِر (n., f.) . . . . . ticket

تِمثال ج تَماثيل (n., m.) . . . . . statue

تَناوَلَ (يَتَناوَلُ) تَناوُل (v.) . . . to eat; to take; to reach for something

جَمَل ج جِمال (n., m.) . . . . camel

حُرِّيّة ج حُرِّيّات (n., f.) . . . . liberty, freedom

حَيَوان ج حَيَوانات (n., m.) . . . . animal

دائماً (adverbial) . . . . always

دَخَّنَ (يُدَخِّنُ) تَدْخين (v.) . . . . to smoke (e.g., a cigarette)

راح (يروح) على (v.) . . . . ذهب (Syrian colloquial)

رَجا (يَرجو) رَجاء (v.) . . . . to hope

رَكِبَ (يركَبُ) رُكوب (v.) . . . . to ride, to mount

ساحة ج ساحات (n., f.) . . . . square, courtyard

سادة . . . . straight black coffee

سارَ (يَسيرُ) سَيْر (v.) . to move, to walk, to travel, to march, to flow

سَعيد ج سُعَداء (adj., m.) . . . . happy, pleased, joyful

سُؤال ج أسئِلة (n., m.) . . . . question, query

شاهَدَ (يُشاهِدُ) مُشاهَدة (v.) . . . . to witness, to see, to watch

شَلاّل ج شَلاّلات (n., m.) . . . . waterfall

شَمال (n., m.) . . . . north

شَيْء ج أشياء (n., m.) . . . . thing, object

صَحّة وهَنا . . . . bon appétit (Syrian colloquial)

صِناعة ج صِناعات (n., f.) . . . . industry

صَوَّرَ (يُصَوِّرُ) تَصوير (v) . to make a picture, to portray, to illustrate

طَريق ج طُرُق، طُرُقات (n., f.) . . . . way, road

عَدَد ج أعْداد (n., m.) . . . . number (quantity)

عَرْض ج عُروض (n., m.) . . . show, demonstration, performance dear, esteemed, beloved . . . . (n., m.) عَزيز ج أعِزّاء

great, important, imposing . . . . . . (adj./n., m.) عَظيم ج عُظَماء

expensive, dear . . . . (n., m.) غالٍ

often, mostly, generally. . . . . (adv.) غالِباً

west. . . . . (n., m.) غَرْب

pharaoh . . . . (n., m.) فِرعَون ج فَراعِنة

band, company, troupe. . . . . (n., f.) فِرقة ج فِرَق، أفْرِقة

boat. . . . . (n., m.) قارِب ج قَوارِب

to gamble . . . . (v.) قامَرَ (يُقامِرُ) مُقامَرة، قِمار

to serve, to provide . . . . (v.) قَدَّمَ (يُقَدِّمُ) تَقديم

also, as well . . . . كَذلِكَ

kilometer . . . . (n., m.) كيلومِتر ج كيلومِترات

عِنْدَ. . . . . (prep.) لَدى

game, play, ride . . . . (n., f.) لُعبة ج لُعبات، ألعاب

building, construction . . . . (n. m.) مَبنى ج مَبانٍ

museum . . . . (n., m.) مُتحَف ج مَتاحِف

loving . . . . (n.) مُحِبّ ج مُحِبّون

sincere, faithful (sincerely yours) . . (n., m.) مُخلِص ج مُخلِصون

period, duration . . . . (n., f.) مُدّة ج مُدَد

to pass, to go by. . . . . (v.) مَرَّ (يَمُرُّ) مُرور

mosque . . . . (n., m.) مَسجِد ج مَساجِد

theater, stage. . . . . (n., m.) مَسرَح ج مَسارِح

one who is longing, yearning . . . . (n.) مُشْتاق ج مُشْتاقون

elevator, lift . . . . (n., m.) مِصعَد ج مَصاعِد

though, although . . . . مَعَ أنَّ

coming, next, following . . . . (n., m.) مُقبِل ج مُقبِلون

place, location . . . . (n., m.) مَكان ج أمْكِنة

million . . . . (n., m.) مِليون

since, for . . . . (prep.) مُنْذُ

square, field, arena . . . . (n., m.) مَيدان ج مَيادين

port. . . . . (n., m.) ميناء ج مَوانِئ

person (used in population counts). . . . . . (n., f.) نَسَمة ج نَسَمات

important, significant . . . . (n./adj.) هامٌّ ج هامّون

pyramid . . . . (n., m.) هَرَم ج أهرام / أهرامات

father, parent . . . . (n., m.) والِد ج والِدون

الدرس العشرون

أهدافُ الدَرس

- وَصْفُ الرياضات والطَعام
- التَعبير عن الِاحتِمال باستِخدام رُبَّما
- اِستِخدام فَضَّل (يُفَضِّلُ) تَفضيل
- اِستِخدام دائماً - غالِباً - أحياناً - نادِراً - أبداً
- اِستِخدام قليلاً - كَثيراً - جَيِّداً - جِدّاً
- التَقديم لِـ كانَ + المُضارِع المَرفوع
- تَعَلُّمُ الألوان
- مُراجَعةُ الفِعلِ المُعتَلّ
- اِستِخدامُ اسمِ التَفضيل الّذي لَهُ حَرف مُضَعَّف

رُكنُ المُفْرَداتِ الجَديدة

اِسْتَخْدَمَ (يَسْتَخْدِمُ) اِسْتِخْدام	to use
بَقِيَ (يَبْقى) بَقاء	to stay
تَقْريباً	almost
خُصوصاً (= خِصّيصاً أو خاصّةً)	especially
رُبَما	مُمْكِن
فَهِمَ (يَفْهَمُ) فَهْم	to understand
لَعِبَ (يَلْعَبُ) لَعْب	to play
مُباراة ج مُبارَيات	match, game
فَضَّلَ (يُفَضِّلُ) تَفضيل	to prefer
وَقْت ج أوْقات	time
شَرَحَ (يَشْرَحُ) شَرْح	to explain

المُفرداتُ الجَديدةُ في صُوَر عَديدة

جَرى (يَجْري) جَري

مُتَفَرِّج ج مُتَفَرِّجون

فازَ (يَفوزُ) فَوْز

فَريق ج فِرَق

تمرين ١

وافِق بين كلمات مِنَ العَمودِ الأيْمَن وكلِمات مِنَ العَمودِ الأيْسَر واكتُب الكَلِمَتين في الوسط.

١-	إجّاص		عَرَبية
٢-	حِصان		سودانيّ
٣-	مَوعِد		وَقت
٤-	طابَق		مُفَضَّل
٥-	فُلَيفُلة		بَقَر
٦-	لَحْم		تِجاري
٧-	فول		فاكِهة
٨-	مَحَلّ		أرضيّ
٩-	بِلاد		خَضْراء
			خَيل

العرض: اعرض على الطلاّب بعض الصور لرياضتك المفضَّلة وصِف لهم كم من الوقت مارستَها ومتى لعبتها وإذا مازلتَ تلعبها ومع من تلعبها ولماذا تعجبك. إليك مثال:

«رياضتي المفضّلة كرة المضرب لأن يمكنني أن ألعبها في الخارج مع زوجتي وأصدقائي. لقد بدأت ألعب كرة المضرب منذ سبع سنوات ولكن لم ألعبها منذ حزيران الماضي بسبب الألم الحادّ في قدمي اليمنى. والآن بدأت ألعبها كل يوم من أيام الأسبوع عدا يومي الإثنين والأربعاء. أفضّل أن ألعب لعبة كاملة غير أن أصدقائي يفضّلون أن يلعبوا ساعة واحدة فقط. أحبها كثيراً وخاصة لأنها جيدة للصحة.»

الممارسة: اسأل بعض الطلاّب ما هي رياضتهم المفضَّلة وكم مرة يلعبونها ومع مَن يلعبونها وهل يشاهدونها على التلفاز إلخ. اسأل الطلاّب الآخرين أن يفيدوك بما قال الطالب للتأكد من حسن الاستيعاب.

التطبيق الأول: في مجموعات: اطلُب من الطلاّب أن يسألوا بعضهم بعضاً عن رياضتهم المفضلة والفترة التي مارسوها ومع من يلعبونها ومتى يلعبونها ولماذا يحبونها.

التطبيق الثاني: في مجموعات: وزّع هذه الأسئلة على المجموعات بالإنكليزية حتى يحولوها إلى العربية بصورة صحيحة:

Find out who in the class:

1. likes baseball
2. has gone to one of your college's football games
3. has gone to a soccer game
4. likes to play volleyball
5. likes to cook out in public parks

التطبيق الثالث: في مجموعات: عيّن ثلاثة طلّاب أو أربعة لإيجاد المعلومات الآتية من الصف:

مَن في هذا الصف:
١- يحب كرة القدم
٢- يشاهد مباريات كرة القدم الأوروبية أو الأمريكية
٣- يتابع فريقاً معيّناً في رياضة مُعيّنة
٤- يحب لعب كرة المضرب
٥- يحب لعب الرياضة في الحدائق العامة

تمرين ٢

اختَر الكَلِمةَ الّتي لا تُناسِب باقي الكَلِمات في كُلّ مَجْموعة وبَيِّن السَبَب.

١-	مَصنوع	بَقِيَ	سَكَنَ	جَلَسَ	نَزَلَ
٢-	مَلعَب	مُتفَرِّج	شاطئ	مُباراة	فَريق
٣-	سَميط	لُبّ	مِياه غازية	عَصا	شاي
٤-	دائِماً	أحياناً	عادةً	غالِباً	تَقريباً
٥-	قَرنبيط	توت	باذِنجان	بامية	خَسّ
٦-	لَذيذ	جَيِّد	شَرَح	مُفَضَّل	مَشْويّ

رِياضات وأطعِمة مُفَضَّلة

مِن يَوميّات عَدنان مارتيني

كُرةُ السَلّةِ

حين كُنتُ في المَدرسةِ الثانوية في حَلَب لَعِبتُ كُرةَ السَلّة مع فَريقِ المَدرسة مِن الصَفِّ العاشِر حَتّى الثاني عَشَر. كانت كُرةُ السَلّة في ذلِكَ الوَقْت رِياضَتي المُفَضَّلة. كُنتُ ألعَبُها كُلَّ يوم تَقريباً. كُنتُ أذهب مع أصدِقائي إلى مُبارَيات كُرةِ السَلّة دائِماً وأشاهِدُها على التِلفاز.

كُرةُ الطاوِلةِ

أمّا هُنا في أمريكا فَلا ألعَبُ كُرةَ السَلّة كَثيراً، مَرّتَين أو ثلاث مَرّات فَقَط في الشَهر بِسَبَبِ الدِراسة. صِرتُ ألعَبُ الآن كُرةَ الطاوِلة. هُناكَ مَكان واسِع لِلألعاب في الطابَقِ الأرضيّ حَيثُ تُوجَد شَقّتي. أنزِلُ إلى هذا المَكان مَساءً وفي صَباح يَومِ السَبت وألعَبُ مع أصدِقائي أو مع بَعضِ السُكّانِ الآخَرين. تُعجِبُني كُرةُ الطاوِلة كَثيراً.

بيسبول

مُنذُ ثلاثة شُهور أخَذَني صَديقي تِم نِكلز إلى مُباراة في لُعبَة تُسَمّى هُنا «بيسبول». لا أعرِفُ لَها اسماً بالعربيّة رُبَّما لأنّنا لا نَلعَبُها في البِلادِ العَربيّة. يُحِبُّ الأمريكيّون هذه اللُعبَةَ جِدّاً، وهي تُلعَب بِعَصا طَويلة وكُرة صَغيرة بَيضاء اللَون. شَرَح لي تِم كيفَ تُلعَب

البيسبول، لكنّي لَم أفهَمْ قَواعِدَ اللُعبة مِن أوّل مَرّة. لكِنَّني الآن أفهَمُها أكثَر وبدَأتْ تُعجِبُني.

نَقانِق

بَقِينا في المَلعَب أربع ساعات تَقريباً. شَربنا كولا وأكلنا شَطائِر «هَط ضَغ»، وهذا النَوع مِن الطعام مَشهور جِدّاً في أمريكا ويأكلُه الناس في كُلّ وَقْت تَقريباً. الـ«هَط ضَغ» مِثْلُ النَقانِق في بِلاد الشام، لكِنَّها أكبَر ومَصنوعة من لَحْم البَقَر. صِرتُ أُحِبّ أنْ آكل شطائِرَ الهط ضَغ الآن وكذلك شَطائِرَ الـ«هامبَرغر»، لكنّ النَقانِق ألَذّ من الهَط ضغ لأنَّ فيها تَوابل كَثيرة.

السِباحة من الرياضاتِ الَّتي أُفَضِّلُها كَثيراً بالإضافة إلى كُرةِ السَلّة وكُرةِ الطاوِلة. هُناكَ مَسْبَح في الجامِعة أذهَب إليه دائِماً قَبلَ دُروسي في الصَباح ثَلاث مَرّات أو أكثَر في الأسبوع.

أفَضِّلُ السِباحة في البَحْرِ في فَصلِ الصَيف وكَلَمبَس لَيسَتْ على شاطِئ البَحر، لكِنَّها قَريبة مِن عَدَدٍ مِن البُحَيراتِ الكَبيرةِ الّتي يُوجَد على شواطِئها حَدائق عامّة واسِعة. سَبَحتُ في بَعضِها في الصَيفِ حينَ ذَهَبتُ إلى هُناكَ مع بَعضِ الأصدِقاء. كان في تِلكَ الحَدائق عائلات كَثيرة، وكان الكِبار والصِغار يَلعَبونَ الكُرَةَ الطائِرة وكُرَةَ القَدَم الأوروبيّة وغَيرَهُما مِن الألعاب. لَم أرَ أحَداً يَلعَب كُرةَ القَدَم الأمريكيّة.

كُرةُ القَدَمِ الأمريكيّة

كُرةُ القَدَمِ الأوروبيّة

الكُرةُ الطائِرة

يوجَد أيْضاً في هذه الحَدائِق مَشاوٍ عامّة يَستَخدِمُها الناس لِشَيِّ اللَحْم و«الهَط ضَغ»، واللَحمُ المَشويّ هو الطعامُ المُفَضَّل لِلناس في الحَدائق. هذه الحَدائق نَظيفة غالِباً وفيها الكَثير من الأشجار وأماكِن واسِعة لِلَّعب. وَصَلنا إلى الحَديقة عِندَ الظُهر تَقريباً وبَقِيْنا فيها حَتّى الساعةِ التاسِعة مَساءً. استَمتَعتُ كَثيراً في ذلك اليوم.

مِشْواة في حَديقة

من يوميّات مايكل براون

سميط بالشكولاتة

الرياضةُ المُفضَّلة عِندَ المِصريّين هي كُرَةُ القَدَم، لكِنَّها لَيسَت كُرَةَ القَدمِ الّتي نَعرِفُها في أمريكا، بَل كُرَةَ القَدَمِ الأوروبيّة. هُناك فِرَق كَثيرة لِكُرَةِ القَدَم في مِصر، لكنَّ الفَريقَينِ المَشهورَين في القاهِرة هُنا «الأهلي» و«الزَمالِك». ذَهَبتُ إلى إحدى المُبارَيات بَينَهُما مع سَمير في مَلعَبِ القاهِرة الدُوَليّ الّذي يَتَّسِع لِمِئة وعِشرين ألف مُتفَرِّج. وكانَ هُناكَ عَشرات الآلاف من المُتفرِّجين، رِجالاً ونساءً وأولاداً وبَناتاً. يأكُلُ الناس في المَلعِب عادةً «السَميط» ويَشرَبونَ الشاي والقهوة والمِياهَ الغازيّة. يأكل كَثير من الناسِ اللُبّ (أو اللِبّ كما يَقولون) وهو بُذورُ البِطّيخِ المُحَمَّصة، وكذلك الفولَ السودانيّ.

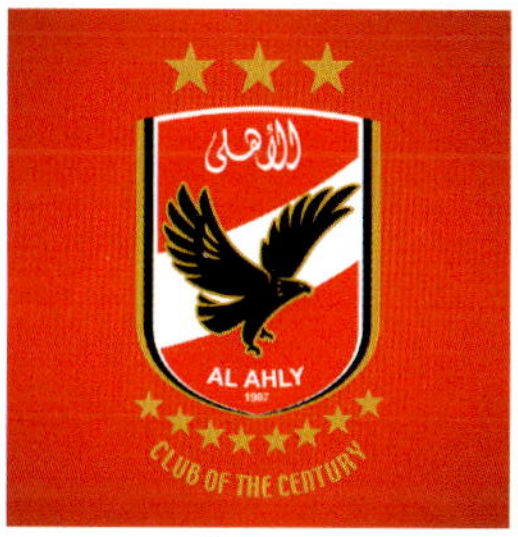

شِعار الأهلي

قال لي سَمير إنّه يَلبَس قَميصاً أحمَر لأنّ اللونَ الأحمَر هو لونُ «الأهلي»، أمّا لون «الزَمالِك» فَهو الأبيَض. وقال إنّ لِكُلّ فَريق بالقاهِرة مَلعَبَه، لكنّ الفِرَق الكَبيرة تَلعَب في مَلعَبِ القاهِرةِ الدُوَليّ عادةً. شَرَحَ لي سَمير قَواعِدَ اللُعبة وفَهِمتُها واستمتَعتُ بالمُباراةِ جِدّاً. وكان سَمير سَعيداً جِداً لأنّ فَريقَهُ «الأهلي» فاز بالمُباراة. صِرتُ أشاهِدُ مُبارَيات كُرةِ القَدَم على التِلفاز وأذهَب أحياناً إلى المَلعَب حين يكون عِندي وقت.

المَشي في شَوارِعِ القاهِرة

صار عِندي في القاهِرة رِياضة مُفَضَّلة أخرى وهي المَشي. هُنا في القاهِرة أمشي إلى كُلّ مَكان. أكثَر الناس يَمشون ولا يَركَبونَ السيّارات أو الحافِلات دائماً. أفَضِّل أنْ أمشيَ مَساءً خُصوصاً في الصَيف. أمّا في الفُصولِ الأخرى فَأيّ وَقت مِن اليَوم مُناسِب لِلمَشي. وبِسَبَبِ المَشي يَومياً صِرتُ أعرِف شَوارِعَ القاهِرة جَيِّداً ومَكانَ مُعْظَم المَحلاّت التِجاريّة القَريبة والشَركات وغَيرِها. لا تَجِدُ ناساً يَجرون في شَوارِعِ القاهِرة كَما في أمريكا. الجَري هُنا رِياضة يَلعَبُها بَعضُ الناس في المَلعَب فَقَط وليس في الشارِع. جَميعُ الألعابِ الّتي نَعرِفُها مَوجودة في مِصر وكذلكَ في البِلادِ العربيّة الأخرى كَكُرَةِ المَضرِب وكُرةِ الماء ورُكوبِ الخَيل ورُكوبِ الدَرّاجات وغَيرِ ذلك.

كُرةُ المَضرِب

كُرةُ الماء

رُكوبُ الخَيل

رُكوبُ الدرّاجات

الخُضَر والفَواكِه في مِصر لَذيذة جداً. صِرتُ آكلُ الآنَ الكَثير من الخُضَر كَالفاصولية والبازِلاء والخَسّ والبامية والباذِنجان والكوسا والفُلَيفُلةِ الخَضراء وغَيرِها. أفَضِّلُ الباذِنجان من الخُضَر.

الخُضَر

الفاصولية

البازِلاء

الخَسّ

البامية

الباذِنجان

الكوسا

الفُلَيفُلة الخَضراء

الفُلَيفُلة الحارة

لا يوجد تُفّاح كَثير في مِصر، لكِن هُناكَ فَواكِه كَثيرة أخرى كَالبُرتُقال والعِنَب والمَوْز والتوت والبِطّيخ والمَنجة والإجّاص. فاكِهَتي المُفَضّلة في مِصر هي المَنجة المِصريّة لأنَّها لَذيذة وأكبر من أيّ نَوع آخر أعرِفُه.

الفَواكِه

التُفّاح

البُرتُقال

العِنَب

المَوْز

التوت

البِطّيخ

المَنجة

الإجّاص

ومِن الأطعمةِ المِصريّة أفضَّلُ الطَعميّة والكُشري. أجِد هذه الأطعِمة لَذيذة بِسَبَبِ التَوابِلِ المَوجودة فيها. لَم أكُنْ آكل طَعاماً فيه تَوابِل كَثيرة، لكِن بَعدَ أنْ تَناوَلتهُ في مِصر صار يُعْجِبُني.

تمرين ٣

أجِبْ عن الأسئلةِ التالية حَسَب نَصّ القِراءة.

١- ما الرِياضةُ المُفَضَّلةُ الّتي كان يَلعَبُها عَدنان حين كان في المدرسةِ الثانوية؟
٢- ماذا يُوجَد تَحت شَقّةِ عَدنان؟
٣- ماذا يَأكُلُ الأمريكيّون في مُباراةِ البيسبول؟
٤- أينَ يَسبَح عَدنان في الصَيف أحياناً؟
٥- ماذا يأكُلُ الناس ويَشرَبون في مَلاعِبِ كُرَةِ القَدَم في القاهِرة؟
٦- ما الرياضاتُ الأخرى في البِلادِ العَربيّة؟
٧- لِماذا صار مايكل يَعرِف شَوارِعَ القاهِرة جيِّداً؟
٨- ما فاكِهة مايكل المُفَضَّلة في مِصر؟ لِماذا يُفَضِّلُها؟

العَرض: أحضر بعض الصور كي تبيّن للطلاّب فواكهك وخضرواتك المفضّلة. احكِ عن أنواع الطعام التي تعجبك ولاتعجبك ولماذا تحبها أو لا تحبها وكم مرة في الأسبوع تأكلها وإذا تحضّرها بطريقة خاصة.

الممارسة: اسأل الطلاّب ما هي أطعمتهم المفضلة ولماذا تعجبهم ومتى يأكلونها وكم مرة في الأسبوع يأكلونها.

التطبيق: في مجموعات من اثنين أو ثلاثة: اطلب من الطلاّب أن يجدوا من في الصف:
١- يحب الفاصولية
٢- يأكل الباذنجان
٣- يحب أكل البيتزا التي عليها الفليفلة الخضراء
٤- يأكل ((الهط ضغ)) في مباريات بيسبول.
٥- يأكل تفاحة كل يوم!

تمرين ٤

المُحادَثة: صِف لِصَديقك مباراةً حَضرتها أو فريق رياضيّ اِشترَكت فيه أو تكَلّم عن رياضتك المُفَضَّلة والسَبَب الّذي تُحِبها. حاوِل استِخدام مُعظَمِ الكَلِمات في المُرَبّعات أدناه:

فازَ	خَسِرَ	اِسْتَخْدَمَ	خُصوصاً	تَقريباً	مُفَضَّل	مُباراة	فَريق
الّذي	الّتي	الّذين	أعْجَبَ	اِسْتَطاع	فَهِمَ	أَسْتَمْتِعُ بِـ	

تمرين ٥

أكتُبْ «خَطَأ» أو «صَواب» بِجانب كُلّ جُملَة وصَحّحِ الجُمَلَ الخَطَأ.

١- يَلعَب عَدنان كُرَةَ الطاوِلة في الجامِعة.
٢- لَيسَ لِرياضةِ البيسبول كَلِمة عَرَبيّة لأنّ العَرَب لا يَلعَبونَها.
٣- النَقانِق مَصنوعة مِن اللَحم.
٤- يُوجَد في كَلَمبَس بُحَيرات كَبيرة.
٥- شاهَد مايكل مُباراة كُرة قَدَم في مَلعَب فَريق «الأهلي».
٦- كان مايكل يَلعَب رِياضَةَ الجَري في شَوارِعِ القاهِرة.
٧- لا يُوجَد تُفّاح وبِطّيخ كَثير في مِصر.
٨- الكُشَري من أطعِمَة مايكل المُفَضَّلة لأنَّ مايكل صار يأكل كثيراً من الخُضَر.

تمرين ٦

اختَرِ التَكْمِلةَ المُناسِبة حَسَب نَصِّ القِراءة.

١- لَعِب عَدنان كُرَةَ السَلّة في أمريكا ________ .
☐ يَوميّاً ☐ مَرّةً في الأسبوع ☐ مَرّتين أو ثلاث مرّات في الشَهر

٢- لُعبة عَدنان المُفَضَّلة في أمريكا هي ________ .
☐ كُرةُ السَلّة ☐ كُرةُ الطاوِلة ☐ البيسبول

٣- لَم ________ عَدنان رياضةَ البيسبول مِن أوّل مَرّة.

☐ يَفهَمْ ☐ يُشاهِدْ ☐ يُعْجِبْ

٤- أكل عَدنان في المَلعَب ________ .

☐ هامبرغر ☐ هَط ضَغ ☐ نَقانِق

٥- يَظُنّ عَدنان أنَّ النَقانِق ________ مِن الهَط ضَغ.

☐ ألَذّ ☐ أصغَر ☐ أكبَر

٦- يَسبَح عَدنان في أيّام الدِراسة في ________ .

☐ البُحيرة ☐ المَسبَح ☐ البَحر

٧- طَعامُ الناسِ المُفَضَّل في الحَدائقِ العامة هو اللَحم ________ .

☐ المَشويّ ☐ المُحَمَّص ☐ الحارّ

٨- بَقِي عَدنان في الحَديقةِ العامّة حَتّى ________ .

☐ الظُهر ☐ المَساء ☐ اللَيل

٩- يتَّسِع مَلعَب القاهِرةِ الدُوَليّ لِـ ________ ألف مُتَفرِّج.

☐ ٢٠ ☐ ٦٠ ☐ ١٢٠

١٠- يأكلُ المِصريّون في المَلعَب ________ .

☐ اللَحمَ المَشويّ ☐ النَقانِق ☐ السَميط

١١- الوَقتُ المُناسِب لِلمَشي بالقاهِرة في الصَيف هو ________ .

☐ الظُهر ☐ المَساء ☐ أيّ وَقت

١٢- يُفَضِّل مايكل مِن الخُضَر ________ .

☐ الباذِنجان ☐ المَنجة ☐ الفاصولية

١٣- تُعْجِبُ المَنجة مايكل لأنّها ________ .

☐ صَغيرة ☐ مِصريّة ☐ لَذيذة

١٤- صار مايكل يُحِبّ أنْ يَتَناول طَعاماً فيه ________ .

☐ كُشري ☐ تَوابِل ☐ طَعميّة

النَخل في المَغرِب

تمرين ٧

اخترَ التكْمِلةَ المُناسِبة لِتُكمِلَ الجُمَلَ التالية.

١- ________ كُرةَ الطاوِلة في المدرسة.

☐ أُعجب ☐ ألعَب ☐ أشتَري ☐ أُنزِل

٢- في المَبنى حيثُ أسكُن، هُناكَ ________ مِن عَدَد مِن بِلادِ العالَم.

☐ سُكّان ☐ شَطائِر ☐ مَلاعِب ☐ نَقانِق

٣- شَرَح لي صَديقي كَيفَ ________ كُرةُ القَدَمِ الأمريكيّة.

☐ تُشاهَدُ ☐ تُؤكَلُ ☐ تُفهَمُ ☐ تُلعَبُ

٤- أحِبُّ الفلافِل لأنّ فيها ________.

☐ خُضَراً ☐ تَوابِل ☐ شَطائِر ☐ فَواكِه

٥- ألعب ________ السَلّة في المدرسة.

☐ عَصا ☐ كُرَةَ ☐ ملعَبَ ☐ طابَقَ

٦- ________ ناديا اللغةَ الفَرَنسيّة وتَتكلّمُها جيّداً.

☐ تَلعَبُ ☐ تَضَعُ ☐ تَنزِلُ ☐ تَفهَمُ

٧- تُعجب أخي السيّاراتُ اليابانيّة ________ تويوتا.

☐ أحياناً ☐ دائِماً ☐ خُصوصاً ☐ جِدّاً

٨- أكلتُ ________ جُبن مع فِنجان شاي صَباحاً.

☐ شَطيرة ☐ لَذيذة ☐ فُليفُلة ☐ أطعِمة

٩- ما طَعامُك ________.

☐ اللَذيذ ☐ المَشوي ☐ النَظيف ☐ المُفَضَّل

١٠- ما اسم ________ كُرةِ السَلّةِ المَشهور في لوس أنجِلس؟

☐ جَري ☐ رِياضةِ ☐ فَريق ☐ لُعبةِ

١١- هَل تَفهمين ________ لُعبة كُرةِ القَدَمِ الأمريكيّة؟

☐ فِرَق ☐ قَواعَد ☐ رِياضات ☐ مُبارَيات

١٢- حَضَّرنا طَعامَ الغَداء على ________ في حَديقة داري.

☐ مِشواة ☐ عَصا ☐ كُرة ☐ بَقَرة

تمرين ٨

أعد تَرتيب الكَلِمات لِتُشَكِّل جملاً مفيدة.

١- بِسَبَبِ - تَوابِلِها - العَرَبيّةِ - أحِبُّ - الأطعِمةِ - بَعْض
٢- الوَطَنِ - هي - العربيِّ - القَدَمِ - اللُعبةُ - في - كُرةُ - المُفَضَّلةُ
٣- لَذيذةٌ - أنَّ - عَدنان - النَقانِق - يَظُنُّ
٤- في - المَشاوي - العامّةِ - تُستَخدَم - الحَدائقِ - اللَحمِ - لِشَيِّ
٥- على - أنْ - حُسين - الجَديد - المُبارَيات - تِلفازه - يَستَطيع - يُشاهِدَ

تمرين ٩

أعد تَرتيب الجُمَل لِتُشَكِّل فِقرة.

١- أرَدتُ أنْ أشاهِدَ مُباراةَ كُرةِ القَدَمِ مع أصدِقائي في المَلعَب.
بَدأتِ المُباراةُ في الثالِثة والنِصف.
لأنَّ فَريقَنا فازَ بِالمُباراة.
لِذلك اشترَيتُ تَذاكِرَ المُباراةِ قَبلَ يومَين.
وكانَ في المَلعَبِ آلافُ المُتَفَرِّجين.
وَصَلنا أنا وأصدِقائي إلى المَلعَبِ في الساعةِ الثالِثةِ إلاّ رُبعاً.
بَقينا في المَلعَبِ ساعتَينِ حَتّى انتهتِ المُباراة.
رَجَعنا إلى بُيوتِنا سُعَداء في الساعةِ السادِسةِ مَساءً.
الّذينَ كانوا يأكلونَ الفولَ السودانيَّ ويَشرَبونَ المياهَ الغازية.

من الطَعام المَغرِبيّ

تمرين ١٠

الكتابة: اكتُب فِقرة تَصِف فيها مُباراة رياضِيّة شاهَدتها في المَلعَب أو على التِلفاز. أيَّة لُعبة كانت؟ بينَ أيّ فَريقَين. ماذا أكلت وشرِبت أثناء المُباراة؟ هل اِستَمتَعت بِها؟ مَن فاز بِالمُباراة؟

تمرين ١١

المُحادَثة: اسأل زُملاءك في الصفّ . . .

مرّة أحياناً دائماً غالباً يَوميّاً أبداً كلّ قليلاً كثيراً جيّداً جداً

1. plays soccer a lot
2. has never played tennis
3. always goes to football games
4. studies most of the time
5. sometimes eats hot peppers
6. eats an apple a day (daily)
7. plays table tennis every weekend
8. calls his/her mother on the telephone three times a month
9. has eaten at a very expensive restaurant
10. did not sleep much last night (slept a little)

تمرين ١٢

تَمرينُ المُشاهَدة: شاهِدوا الدَرْسَ العشرين على الشابِكة.

١ – ما الأمكِنَةُ الّتي زارَها عَدنان في مَدينةِ نيويورك؟ ______________

____

٢ – لِماذا لا يَلْعَب عَدنان كُرةَ السَلّة كَما كانَ يَفْعَل في حَلَب؟ ______________

____

____

٣ – ما الرياضَتانِ اللّتان يَقومُ بِهِما عَدنان في مدينَتِهِ؟ ______________

____

____

٤ – في رأيِ عَدنان، ما أجمَلُ شيءٍ في مدينَتِهِ؟ ______________

____

____

٥ – أيْنَ سَيَذهَب سامِر ومايكل بَعْدَ هذا الاجْتِماع في الفُنُدُق؟ ______________

____

العَرض: قدّم للطلاّب بعض الجمل التي فيها الظروف الموجودة في المربعات في تمرين ١١ إلى اليسار واكتبها على السبورة ثم اطلب من الطلاّب أن يقدّموا جملاً مشابهة، على سبيل المِثال:

«أتكلّم العربية جيّداً.»
«يعجبني الطعام الإيطاليّ كثيراً.»
«أقرأ في سريري قليلا قبل النوم.»
«البحر جميل جدّاً في الإسكندريّة.»

الممارسة: اسأل الطلاب ماذا يحبون كثيراً وماذا لا يحبون كثيراً وماذا يفعلون يومياً وماذا يفعلون دائماً وكم مرة في الأسبوع يلعبون رياضة معينة أو ماذا يفعلون جيداً. إليكم مِثال على ذلك:

«ماذا تحب أن تفعل كثيراً؟»
«ماذا لا تحب أن تفعل أبداً؟»
«ماذا تحب أن تعمل كل يوم؟»
«كم مرّة تلعب رياضتك المفضلة في الأسبوع؟»
«ماذا تفعل جيّداً؟»

التطبيق: قُم بالتمرين ١١.

١- اِستِخدام كان + المُضارِع المَرفوع

حين نُريد أن نُعَبِّر عن الماضي المُستَمِرّ، أي "I used to" بالإنكلِيزيّة، فأنّنا نَستَخدِم كان + المُضارِعُ المَرفوع. أُنظُر إلى المِثال من النَصّ الرئيس:

١	كُنتُ ألعَبُ كُرةَ السَلّةِ كُلَّ يوم.	*I used to play basketball every day.*

يَختَلِف كان والمُضارع المَرفوع في المِثال ١ أعلاه، عن الفِعل الماضي لَعِبتُ الّذي لا يُعَبِّر إلاّ عمّا حَدَث في الماضي مَرّةً واحِدةً.

٢	لَعِبْتُ كُرةَ السَلّةِ.	*I played basketball.*

وإذا أرَدنا أن نُعَبِّر عن اِستِمراريةِ الفِعلِ الماضي حين يَدخُل على جُملةٍ فِعلٌ آخر نُريد أن نَصِف حالَه، فَنستَخدِم كان + المُضارع المَرفوع + حين + فِعل ماضٍ كَما نَرى في المِثال الآتي:

٣	كُنتُ أمشي في الطَريق حينَ رأيتُ صَديقتي.	*I was walking down the street when I saw my friend.*

يَختَلِفُ الفِعل الناقِص صارَ عن دَلالة كانَ لأنّه يَدُلّ على الحاضِر حين يأتي قَبل فِعل آخر، كَما رأينا في يَوميّة مايكل براون:

٤	صِرتُ أعرِفُ شَوارِعَ القاهِرةِ جَيّدًا.	*I now know (have come to know) the streets of Cairo well.*

يُمكِن أن تُعبِّر الأفعال المُتَعَلِّقة بِالحواس الخَمسة عن اِستِمرارية الفِعل، مَثَلاً:

٥	رَأى سامي هالَة تَمشي على شاطِئِ البَحر.	*Sāmī saw Hāla walking/walk on the beach.*
٦	سَمِعَتِ الأُمُّ الطِفْلَ يَضْحَك.	*The mother heard the child laughing.*

العَرض: احكِ حكاية تتكلم فيها عن شيء كنت تفعله في طفولتك، مثلاً: «في طفولتي كنت أتكلّم مع جدّي كل يوم وهو كان يحب التكلّم معي عن كرة القاعدة أي بيسبول. كان يحبّ أن يشاهد مباريات بيسبول حين عُرضت على التلفاز وكان يعجبه فريق من أفرقة بيسبول إعجاباً كبيرا. والذي أعجبني جداً كانت عادته الجميلة حين كان يتكلّم عما فعل فريقه المفضّل بعد المباراة مباشرة. ياالله كم كنت أحب جدّي ومشاهدة مباريات كرة البيسبول معه.»

الممارسة: اطرح على الطلاّب أسئلة عن قصتك للتأكد من حسن استيعابهم ثم اسأل طالباً ماذا كان يفعل في طفولته وأعِد السؤال على طالب آخر أو اثنين.

التطبيق: في مجموعات من اثنين أو ثلاثة: اطلب من الطلاّب أن يسألوا بعضهم بعضاً أسئلة عمّا كانوا يفعلون في طفولتهم، أو السنة الماضية أو في أي وقت مضى، مثلاً:

«ماذا كنت تفعل في طفولتك ولا تفعله الآن؟»
«ماذا كنت تشاهد على التلفاز في السنة الماضية.»
«أي نوع من الأكل كان يعجبك في الماضي ولكن لا تحبه الآن؟ (أو العكس)»

تمرين ١٣

حاوِل أن تُعَبِّر عن الجُمَلِ الآتية بالعَرَبيّة مُستخدِماً كانَ أو صارَ + المُضارِع المَرفوع:

1. **هالة** used to play tennis twice a week.
2. I saw **عَدنان** riding a bicycle.
3. I now know the names of all my classmates.
4. We watched the two teams play a basketball match.
5. I started to understand what people are saying in Arabic.

تمرين ١٤

المُحادَثة: اسأل زَميلك:

١- أيّ طعام كُنْت لا تُحِبُّه/ تُحِبينه ولكِنَّك صِرْت تُحِبُّه/ تُحِبّينَه الآن؟

٢- أيَ لُعبة كُنْت تَلْعَبُها/ تَلْعَبينَها كَثيراً في الماضي ولا تَستَطيع/ ينَ لُعبَها الآن؟

٣- أيّ مُسَلْسَل تَلَفِزيونيّ كُنْت تُشاهِدُه/ تُشاهِدينَه في طُفولَتِك؟

٤- هل صِرْت تَعْرِف/ تَعْرِفينَ كَيْفَ تَتَكَلَّم/ تَتَكَلَّمين اللُغة العَرَبيّة؟ (حقيقةً)

٥- ما هو العَمَلُ الّذي كُنت تُريد/ تُريدين أنْ تَعمَل/ تَعمَلي فيه في الماضي؟

تمرين ١٥

املأ الفَراغات بالتَصريفِ المُناسِب حَسَبَ السياق.

١- كانوا ___________ مُشاهَدةَ الأفلام الأمريكيّة. (أحَبَّ)

٢- كُنْتُ ___________ جَريدةَ الصَباح يَومياً. (قَرَأ)

٣- مَتى كانَ ___________ إلى عَمَلِه؟ (أتى)

٤- كانَت هالة ___________ أنّها تَفْهَمُ الدَرس. (ظَنَّ)

٥- ماذا كُنْتِ ___________ على الفَطور يا شَهيرة ؟ (أَكَلَ)

٢- اللَون

إنّ الألوان السِتة الرئيسة تَدخُل على الجُملة العَرَبيّة بِصِفةِ الاسم والصِفة لِذا تَتَصَرَّف حَسَب التأنيث والتذكير والعَدَد. في حالة التثنية (dual)، نَزيد على اللَون ان وتَتَحَوَّل الهَمزة إلى واو. تأمّل المِثال ٧ أدناه:

	المُفرَد		المُثنّى		الجمع
٧	بَيْضاء	←	بَيْضاوان	←	بيض

تَندَرِج في الجَدوَل أدناه الألوان السِتّة الرئيسة تَحتَ فِئات المُفرَد والمُثنى والجَمع في حالتَي المُذَكَّر والمُؤَنَّث.

	المُذَكَّر			المُؤَنَّث		
اللَون	المُفرَد	المُثنى	الجَمْع	المُفرَد	المُثنى	الجَمْع
	أبْيَض	أبْيَضانِ	بِيض	بَيْضاء	بَيْضاوانِ	بِيض
	أسْوَد	أسْوَدانِ	سود	سَوداء	سَوداوانِ	سود
	أخْضَر	أخْضَرانِ	خُضْر	خَضْراء	خَضْراوانِ	خُضْر
	أزْرَق	أزْرَقانِ	زُرْق	زَرْقاء	زَرْقاوانِ	زُرْق
	أحْمَر	أحْمَرانِ	حُمْر	حَمْراء	حَمْراوانِ	حُمْر
	أصْفَر	أصْفَرانِ	صُفْر	صَفْراء	صَفْراوانِ	صُفْر

مُلاحَظة: إنّ جَمعَ التأنيث والتّذكير في اللَون نَفس الشَيء

٨	بَنات	بيض	/	أولاد	بيض

العرض: أحضر بعض الصور لأي شيء له ألوان كثيرة مثل الزهور أو قوس القزح أو الأسماك الملونة. قدم الألوان واحداً واحداً في التذكير ثم تعيدها باستمرار. نستطيع أن نجعل شيئاً مثل الزهور في صيغة التذكير باستخدام النموذج الآتي: «**هذه الزهرة لونها أحمر.**»

قدّم مفهوم التذكير والتأنيث في الألوان بعد أن أثبتت أرضية التذكير في الألوان. فرّق بين ألوان الأشياء في غرفة الصف:

«**هذا الكتاب أحمر والسبورة سوداء.**»
«**قميصي أخضر وأبيض وسروالي أسود.**»

الممارسة: أسأل الطلاّب ما لون الأشياء الموجودة في جوارهم. تستطيع استخدام بعض صور الأشخاص الذين تعرفهم أو من الشابكة أو و من الطلاّب كي يصفوا لون عيون الأشخاص في صيغة المثنى.

التطبيق: في مجموعات: وزّع صوراً على الطلاّب فيها أشياء على اختلاف الألوان واطلب منهم أن يجعلوها قصة حيث الألوان هي البطل. وعند نهاية النشاط، اسألهم إذا أراد أحد إفادة الآخرين بما كتب.

تمرين ١٦

قِصّة الألوان: اكتُب القِصة الآتية في اللُّغة العَرَبيّة:

Two white clouds moved slowly (بِبُطءٍ) in the blue sky. I sat on the white beach and watched them above the blue water and the white boats. A girl wearing a red shirt and white shorts was watching the volleyball game next to a small park on the beach. She had green eyes and black hair. Her mother, wearing green shorts and a white shirt, came to take her daughter to their hotel room located across from the public park. One of the teams was wearing yellow shirts and the other was wearing green shirts. It appeared that (على ما يَبدو) the green team was winning, but everyone was happy.

٣- اِستِخدام اسم التَفضيل الّذي لَهُ حَرف مُضَعَّف

كَما تَعلَم، حين نُقارِن بَين شَيئين أو أكثَر، نَستَخدِم الوَزن أَفْعَل مِثل أَكْبَر أو أَصْغَر أو أَطْوَل أو أَقْصَر. نَستَطيع أن نَشتقّ الوَزن أَفْعَل من الوَزن فَعيل الّذي هو الصِفة أو النَعت:

٩	فَعيل	←	أَفْعَل
	كَبير	←	أَكْبَر
	صَغير	←	أَصْغَر
	طَويل	←	أَطْوَل
	قَصير	←	أَقْصَر

لكِن، ماذا نَفعَل في حالة أنّ الصِفة لَها حَرف مُضَعَّف مِثل جَديد أو قَليل أو لَذيذ حَيثُ الحَرف الأخير مُتَكرِّر؟ فَيَصير الحَرف المُضَعَّف حَرفاً مُشَدَّداً على سَبيل المِثال:

١٠	جَديد	سَيّارَتي أَجَدُّ مِن سَيّارَتِك.	*newer than*	not أَجْدَد
١١	قَليل	عَدَدُ سُكّانِ الإسكَندَريّةِ أَقَلُّ مِن عَدَدِ سُكّانِ القاهِرة.	*less than*	not أَقْلَل
١٢	لَذيذ	النَقانِقُ أَلَذُّ مِن الهَطْ ضَغ.	*more delicious than*	not أَلْذَذ

لِمُراجَعةِ اسمِ التَفضيل، اقرأ الجُزء الخامِس من الدَرس الحادي عشر.

تمرين ١٧

اشتقّ (derive) اسم تفضيل مِن الصِفة بَينَ القَوسين.

مِثال: بِناية «سيرز» (طَويل) مِن بِنايةِ «إمبايَرسَتيت». أطْوَل ______

١- ما (صَغير) وِلاية في الوِلاياتِ المُتّحِدةِ الأمريكيّة؟ ______

٢- هذِهِ (لَذيذ) حَلوى أكلتُها حَتّى الآن. ______

٣- تَظُنُّ رانية أنَّ زَوجَة سامي (جَميل) فَتاة في البَلدة. ______

٤- عَدَدُ دَفاتِري (قَليل) مِن عَدَد دَفاتِرِك. ______

٥- يَسكُن أحمَد في (جَديد) شَقّة في البِناية. ______

٤- مُراجَعة الفِعْل المُعتَلّ

لَقَد قَدَّمنا في الجُزء الثالِث من الدَرس الثالِث عشر والجُزء السابع من الدَرس السابع عشر نَوعَين من الأفعالِ المُعتَلّة الّتي يَتألّف جَذرُها من حَرف عِلّة أي الألف أو الواو أو الياء. وَقَد رأينا ثلاثة أنواع من هذِه الأفعال ألا وهي:

أ- **المِثال**: الفِعل الّذي حَرفُه الأوّل هو حَرف عِلّة كَما نَرى في مِثال ١٣:

١٣ وَضَعَ وَجَدَ وَسِعَ وَصَلَ

ب- **الأجوَف**: الفِعل الّذي حَرفُه الثاني هو حَرف عِلّة، انظُر إلى مِثال ١٤:

١٤ قالَ فازَ زارَ نامَ

ج- **الناقِص**: الفِعل الّذي حَرفُه الثالِث هو حَرف عِلّة كَما نَرى في مِثال ١٥:

١٥ مَشى جرى بَقِيَ نَسِيَ

دَعنا الآن أن نَنظُر إلى الفِعل المِثال الّذي يُعرَف بالإنكليزيَة بـ (assimilated) لِسَبَب وَجيه (good reason) ألا وهو حَرفُه الأوّل يَتحَوّل من حَرف عِلّة إلَى حَرف التاء المُشدَّدة في الوَزَن الثامِن. هيّا نَتأمّل هذه العَمَليّة في الأفعال أَخَذ و وَسِع و وَصَلَ.

	الجَذر		الوَزَن النَظَريّ		اِفْتَعَلَ	المعنى
	الفِعل المِثال في وَزَن افتَعَلَ					
١٦	أَخذ	←	اِئتَخذَ	←	اِتّخذَ	*to take*
	وَسِع	←	اِوتَسَعَ	←	اِتَّسَعَ	*to accommodate*
	وَصَل	←	اِوتَصَل	←	اِتَّصَل	*to contact*

خُلاصةُ الفِعلِ المُعتَلّ

لِكُلّ فِعل من الأفعالِ المُعتّلة خَصائص مُشتَرَكة:

١- في المُضارِع، يَتحَوّل حَرفُ العِلّة إلى مُقابِله من الحَرَكات في صيغةِ المَجزوم:

	مرفوع		مجزوم	
١٧	يَقول	←	يَقُلْ	و ← ُ
	يَجري	←	يَجرِ	ي ← ِ

٢- يُحذَف حَرفُ العِلّة في الأمر:

	الماضي		المُضارِع		الأمر
١٨	وَصَلَ	←	يَصِلُ	←	صِلْ
١٩	مَشى	←	يَمشي	←	اِمشِ
٢٠	قال	←	يَقولُ	←	قُلْ

٣- يَسقُط حَرفُ العِلّةِ الأخير لاسمِ الفاعِل في حالةِ النكِرة بَينما في حالةِ المَعرِفة يَظَلّ حَرفُ العِلة ظاهِراً.

			اسمُ الفاعِل			
	الفِعل		النكِرة		المَعرِفة	المَعنى
٢١	بَقِيَ	←	باقٍ	←	الباقي	*to remain*
٢٢	جَرى	←	جارٍ	←	الجاري	*to run*
٢٣	مَشى	←	ماشٍ	←	الماشي	*to walk*
٢٤	نَسِيَ	←	ناسٍ	←	الناسي	*to forget*

تمرين ١٨

اِستِخدام لَمْ + المُضارِع المَجزوم: اِنفِ (negate) هذه الجُمَل مُستَخدِماً لَمْ وَفقاً لِلمَعلومات أعلاه:

١- بَقيتُ في المَكتَبة أكثَرَ مِن ساعتَين.

٢- مَشى رياض إلى المَدرَسة.

٣- فَهِمَتْ سَلمى الدَرس كُلَّه.

٤- نَسيتُ أنْ أكتُب رِسالة لِصَديقي.

٥- سَكنوا في الدارِ البَيضاء.

تمرين ١٩

آ- **أجِبْ عن هذِهِ الأسئلة حَسَبَ نَصِّ الاستِماع.**

١- أينَ شاهَد رِياض مُباراةَ كُرةِ القَدَم؟

٢- لِماذا لَم يَكُنْ سُهَيل سَعيداً في نِهايةِ المُباراة؟

٣- مَن حَضَّرَ الحَلوى؟

ب- **أكتُبْ «خَطَأ» أو «صَواب» بِجانبِ كُلِّ جُملَة وصَحِّحِ الجُمَلَ الخَطأ.**

٤- حَضَّرَ سُهَيل الشاي والحِمَّص.

٥- اِستَمتَعَ رِياض وأصدِقاؤه بالمُباراة.

٦- لَم يَكُنْ والِدا سُهَيل في البَيت في وَقتِ المُباراة.

ت- **اختَرِ التَكْمِلةَ المُناسِبة حَسَب نَصِّ الاِستِماع.**

٧- في وَقتِ المُباراة كانَ هُناكَ ________ أشْخاص في بَيت سُهَيل.

☐ أربعة ☐ خَمسة ☐ سِتّة ☐ سَبعة

٨- أكَلَ الأصدِقاءُ الحِمَّص مع ________ .

☐ الشاي ☐ الحَلوى ☐ أم سُهَيل ☐ الفُلَيفُلة

٩- لَم يَكُنِ الأصدِقاء سُعَداء في نِهايةِ المُباراة لأنّ ________ لَم يَفُزْ.

☐ صَديقَهُم سُهَيل ☐ فَريقَهُم

☐ والِدَ سُهَيل ☐ رِياض

١٠- شاهَدَ الأصدِقاء ________ المُباراة على التِلفاز.

☐ كُلَّ ☐ بَعْضَ ☐ جُزءاً مِن ☐ مُعْظَم

١١- شاهَد رِياض المُباراة في ________ .

☐ دارِهِ ☐ بَيتِ صَديقِه

☐ المَلعَب ☐ المَدرَسة

١٢- شَرِبَ الأصدِقاءُ الشاي ________ أنْ أكَلوا الحِمَّص.

☐ قَبْلَ ☐ بَعْدَ ☐ مع ☐ عِندَ

المُفْرَدات

استمِع إلى المُفْرَدة بالعَرَبيّة ثم أعِد نُطْقَها مرّتين.

never, not at all	أبَداً (adv.)
to hold, to contain	اتَّسَعَ (يَتَّسِعُ) اتِّساع (v.)
to contact	اِتَّصَلَ (يَتَّصِلُ) اِتِّصال (بِـ) (v.)
to agree (with someone)	اِتَّفَقَ (يَتَّفِقُ) اِتِّفاق (مَعَ) (v.)
pear	إجّاص (n., m.)
red	أحمَر ج حُمْر (adj.)
to notify, to inform	أخْبَرَ (يُخْبِرُ) إخْبار (v.)
blue	أزرَق ج زُرْق (adj.)
to use, to utilize, to employ	استَخدَمَ (يَستَخدِمُ) استِخدام (v.)
yellow	أصْفَر ج صُفْر (adj.)
eggplant	باذِنجان (n., m.)
green peas	بازِلاء (n., f.)
okra	بامْية (n., f.)
slowly	بِبُطءٍ (adv.)
seed, kernel	بِذرة ج بُذور (n., f.)
watermelon	بِطّيخ (n., m.)
cow, cattle	بَقَرة ج أبْقار / بَقَر (n., f.)
to remain, to stay	بَقِيَ (يَبْقى) بَقاء (v.)
tomato	بَنَدورة (طَماطِم في مصر) (n., f.)
white	بَيضاء ج بيض (n./adj., f.)

spice, condiment, seasoning . . . . (n., m.) تابِل ج تَوابِل

approximately, about, nearly, roughly . . . . (adv.) تَقريباً

berry . . . . (n., m.) توت

garlic . . . . (n., m.) ثوم

to run, to flow, to hurry, to rush, to happen, to occur . . . . (v.) جَرى (يَجري) جَري

horse . . . . (n., m.) حِصان ج أَحْصِنة

party . . . . (n., f.) حَفْلة ج حَفَلات

lettuce . . . . (n., m.) خَسّ

especially, particularly . . . . (adv.) خُصوصاً

corn . . . . (n., f.) ذُرة

perhaps, probably. . . . . (adv.) رُبَّما

basket . . . . (n., f.) سَلّة ج سِلال

a kind of toasted thin bread . . . . (n., m.) سَميط

to explain, to expound, to illustrate . . . . (v.) شَرَحَ (يَشرَحُ) شَرْح

sandwich . . . . (n., f.) شَطيرة ج شَطائِر

to grill, to broil . . . . (v.) شَوى (يَشوي) شَي

to laugh . . . . (v.) ضَحِكَ (يَضْحَكُ) ضِحْك

public . . . . (adj.) عامّ

stick, rod, cane . . . . (n., f.) عَصا ج عُصِيّ

it seems; it appears . . . . على ما يَبْدو (أنّ)

grape . . . . (n., m.) عِنَب

non-, un-, other than, different from. . . . . (n., m.) غَيْر

to win . . . . (v.) فازَ (يفوزُ) فَوز

green beans . . . . (n., f.) فاصولية

team, company, band, troupe. . . . . (n., f.) فَريق ج فِرَق

to think, to reflect, to ponder. . . . . (v.) فَكَّرَ (يُفَكِّرُ) تَفْكير
(not to believe)

green (bell) pepper . . . . (n., f.) فُلَيْفُلة

to understand, to comprehend, ... (v.) فَهِمَ (يَفْهَمُ) فَهْم
to realize

peanuts . . . . (n., m.) فول (سوداني)

rule, principle, basis, foundation, base . . . (n., f.) قاعِدة ج قَواعِد

cauliflower . . . . (n., m.) قَرنَبيط

like, as . . . . (prep.) كَـ

sufficient . . . . (active participle) كافٍ (الكافي)

ball, sphere . . . . (n., f.) كُرة ج كُرات

basketball . . . . كُرةُ السَلّة

table tennis . . . . كُرةُ الطاولة

volleyball . . . . الكُرةُ الطائرة

football/soccer . . . . كُرةُ القَدَم

water polo. . . . . كُرةُ الماء

tennis . . . . كُرةُ المَضرِب

zucchini . . . . (n., m.) كوسا

kernel, seed . . . . (n., m.) لُبّ ج لُبوب

delicious, delightful, tasty . . . . (adj., m.) لَذيذ

to play . . . . (v.) لَعِبَ (يَلعَبُ) لُعْب

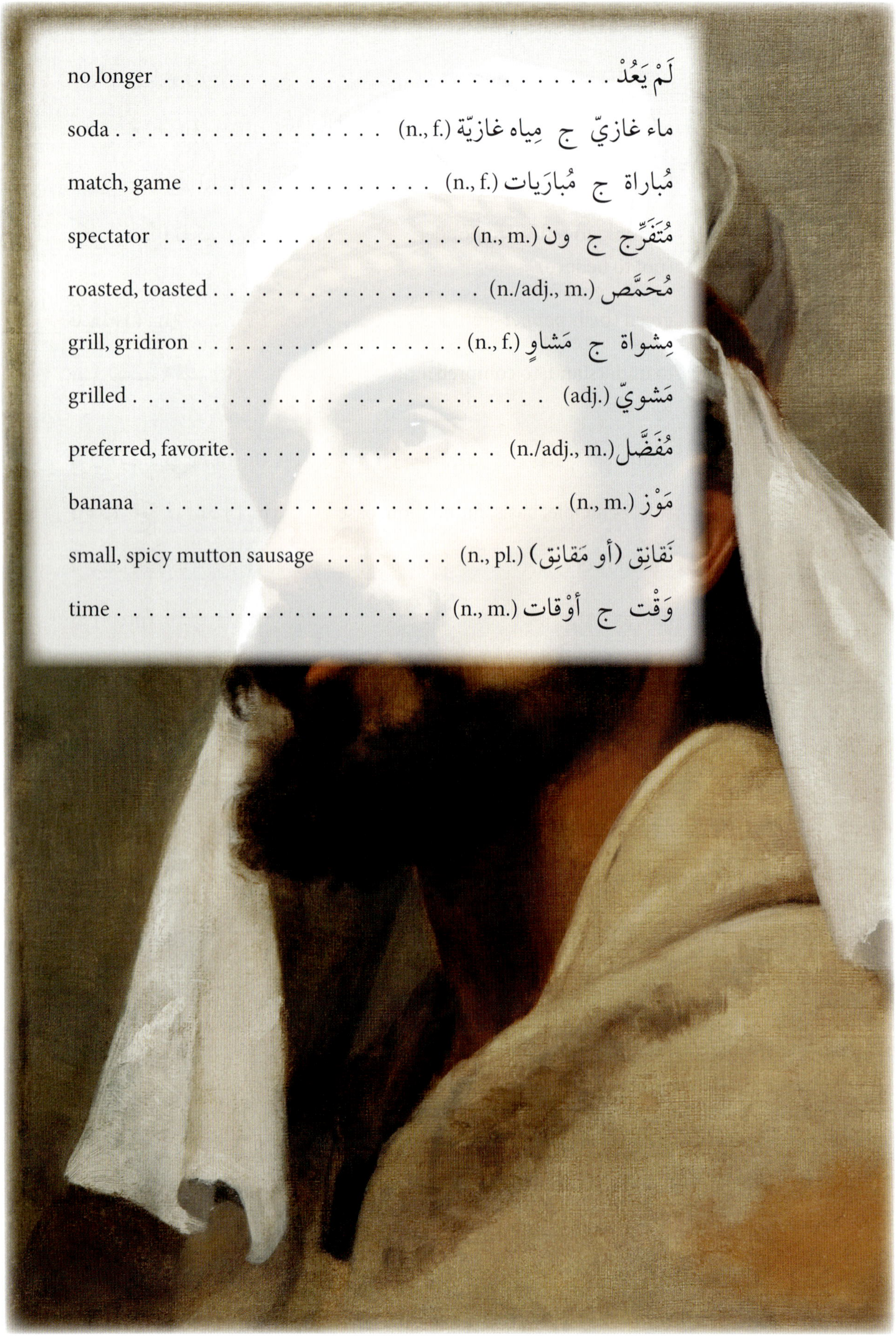

لَمْ يَعُدْ	no longer
ماء غازيّ ج مِياه غازيّة (n., f.)	soda
مُباراة ج مُبارَيات (n., f.)	match, game
مُتَفَرِّج ج ون (n., m.)	spectator
مُحَمَّص (n./adj., m.)	roasted, toasted
مِشْواة ج مَشاوٍ (n., f.)	grill, gridiron
مَشويّ (adj.)	grilled
مُفَضَّل (n./adj., m.)	preferred, favorite
مَوْز (n., m.)	banana
نَقانِق (أو مَقانِق) (n., pl.)	small, spicy mutton sausage
وَقْت ج أوْقات (n., m.)	time

عرض فانتازيا في موسم طانطان في المغرب

الدرس الحادي والعشرون

أهدافُ الدَرس

- وَصْفُ البِلاد والدُوَل وعَدَدِ السُكّان والمُنتَجات
- وَصْفُ الجِهاتِ الأربع والمَعالِم الجُغرافية
- تَعَلُّم كِلا وكِلتا
- التَعبير عن الاِستِثناء بِاستِخدام إلاّ وغَير

رُكنُ المُفْرَداتِ الجَديدة

أطَلَّ (يُطِلُّ) إطلال (على)	*to overlook*
اِعْتبرَ (يعْتَبِرُ) اِعْتِبار	*to consider*
أنْتجَ (يُنْتِجُ) إنْتاج	*to produce*
تَألَّف (مِن)	*to consist (of)*
جِهاز ج أجْهِزة	*device*
حَدَّ / يَحُدُّ / حَدّ	*to border*
شَكَّلَ (يُشَكِّلُ) تَشْكيل	*to form*
صَبَّ (يَصُبُّ) صَبّ	*to flow into; to pour*
صَنَعَ (يَصْنَعُ) صِناعة	*to make*
مَنْفَذ	*outlet*
نَبَعَ (يَنْبَعُ) نَبْع	*to spring from, to flow from*
نِفْط	*oil, petroleum*

المُفرَدات الجَديدة في صُوَر عديدة

جَبَل ج جِبال

زَرَعَ (يَزْرَعُ) زِراعة

سِلْسِلة ج سَلاسِل

ساحِل ج سَواحِل

سَهْل ج سُهول

نَسيج ج أنْسِجة

وَسَط ج أوساط

عَلَم ج أعلام

تمرين ١

وافِق بين كُلّ كَلِمة ومُضادِتها واكتُب الكَلِمَتين في الوَسَط.

١-	واسِع		فَقير
٢-	كَبير		صَبَّ
٣-	طَويل		تَحْتَ
٤-	غَنيّ		ضَيِّق
٥-	بَعيد		جَميل
٦-	كَثير		قَصير
٧-	نَبَعَ		صَغير
٨-	فَوق		قَريب
			قَليل

تمرين ٢

وافِق بين كُلّ كَلِمة وما يُناسِبُها واكتُب الكَلِمَتَين في الوَسَط.

١-	عَلَم		بَحر
٢-	بَلَد		ميناء
٣-	جَزيرة		شِعار
٤-	سَفينة		زِراعة
٥-	صِناعة		رِياضة
٦-	نِفْط		قُطْر
			غاز

تمرين ٣

اختَر الكَلِمَةَ الّتي لا تُناسِب باقي الكَلِمات في كُلّ مَجْموعة وبيِّن السَبَب.

١-	مُحيط	بَحر	وَطَن	بُحَيرة	نَهر
٢-	صِناعة	ساحِل	جَبَل	صَحراء	سَهْل
٣-	قُطْن	تَبغ	قَمْح	خُضار	نَسَمة
٤-	ذُرة	شَمال	شَرْق	غَرْب	جَنوب
٥-	خَليج	سُكّان	ميناء	بَحر	سَفينة

العَرَض: اعرض للطلاّب خريطة مدينتك كي تقدّم لَهُم بعض المفردات الرئيسة من هذا الدرس، مثل:

يقع، يطلّ، يحدّ، شمال، جنوب، شرق، غرب

صِف لَهم بعضَ المناطق في مدينتك مستخدماً المصطلحات المشتركة بين معظم بلاد العالم، مثل:

«هذه مدينتنا وهي تطلّ على نهر كذا الذي يمر بكذا ولايات ويصب في بحيرة كذا. يبلغ عدد سكان مدينتنا كذا وهي ثاني أكبر مدينة في ولايتنا من حيث المساحة.»

النشاط الأول: اعرض للطلاّب خريطة واطلُب منهم وصفها مستخدمين الكلمات المناسبة من هذا الدرس، على سبيل المثال:

«أين تقع هذه الولاية؟ أي مدن تطلّ على بحيرة كذا؟ كم ولاية تحد ولايتنا؟»

النشاط الثاني: اعرض للطلاّب تمرين تركيب الجمل الموجود في أسفل هذه الصفحة واستخدمه مع خريطة كي يساعد الطلاّب في إنتاج جمل وصفية سليمة متعلقة ببعض المدن والبلاد العربية. لاحظ أن هناك طرق متعددة كي تُركَّب جملاً من كلمات الجدول. يُستحسن أن ينتج الطلاّب جملةً ويشير إلى المكان المقصود على الخريطة في نفس الوقت.

التطبيق: في مجموعات من اثنين:
احزر المكان: أعطِ كلّ مجموعة خريطة لمدينة أو ولاية أو بلد. اطلُب من كلّ مجموعة إنتاج وصف مكان معين في الخريطة يشبه أسلوب النصوص في هذا الدرس. وبعد حوالي عشر دقائق من كتابة وصفهم، اطلُب من كلّ مجموعة قراءة وصفها من غير أن تذكر اسم المنطقة الموصوفة وعلى باقي الطلاّب حزْر اسم المنطقة الموصوفة. اعرض للصفّ خريطة العالم كي تساعدهم في الحزر.

تمرين ٤

أكمِلِ الجُمَل بِالاختِيارِ المُناسِبِ.

١- كوبا ________ تَقَع في البَحرِ الكاريبي.

☐ مَنفَذ ☐ جَزيرة ☐ مُحيط ☐ ميناء

٢- ________ الوِلاياتُ المُتَّحِدةُ الأمرِيكيّة مِن ٥٠ وِلاية.

☐ تُطِلّ ☐ تَقَعُ ☐ تُشكِّل ☐ تَتألَّفُ

٣- زُرْتُ بِلادَ شَمالِ إفريقية ________ تونِس.

☐ إلاّ ☐ إلى ☐ بِـ ☐ لِذلِكَ

٤- يوجَدُ مَصارِف ________ في مَدينةِ نيويورك.

☐ ضَيِّقة ☐ خَصيبة ☐ عَديدة ☐ شَرقيّة

٥- كَم ________ في العَلَمِ الأمرِيكيّ؟

☐ نَجمةً ☐ جَزيرةً ☐ وادِياً ☐ قُطْراً

٦- ماذا ________ كَندا مِن الشَمال؟

☐ يوجَدُ ☐ يَقَعُ ☐ يَتألَّفُ ☐ يَحُدُّ

٧- الجُبن مِن ________ الحَليب.

☐ صِناعاتِ ☐ مُنتَجاتِ ☐ أجهِزةِ ☐ مِساحاتِ

٨- هُناكَ ________ كَثيرة في الدُكّان.

☐ رُكّاب ☐ سُكّان ☐ حُدود ☐ بَضائِع

	سورية		البَحرِ	العَرَبيّ
يَقَعُ / تَقَعُ	تونِس	في	المُحيط	النيل
يَحُدُّ / تَحُدُّ	الكُوَيت	على	الجَنوبِ	فِلَسطين
يُطِلُّ / تُطِلُّ	القاهِرة	مِن	الخَليج	شِبهِ الجَزيرةِ العَربيَّة
	الرِياض		نَهرِ	المُتَوَسِّط
	المَغرِب		وَسَطِ	الأطلَسيّ

جُغرافِيّة الوَطَن العَربيّ والوِلايات المُتَّحِدة الأمريكيّة

خَريطة الوَطَن العَرَبيّ والعالَم

يَقَعُ الوَطَنُ العَرَبِيُّ في قارّتَينِ هُما آسيا وإفريقية. تَقَع تِسعة أقطار عَرَبيّة في إفريقية واثنا عَشَر قُطْراً في آسيا. يَتألَّفُ الوَطَنُ العربيّ مِن خَمسة أقاليم جُغرافيَّة هي بِلادُ الشام وما بَينَ النَهرَين (العِراق) وشِبْهُ الجَزيرةِ العَرَبيّة ووادي النيل وشَمال إفريقية.

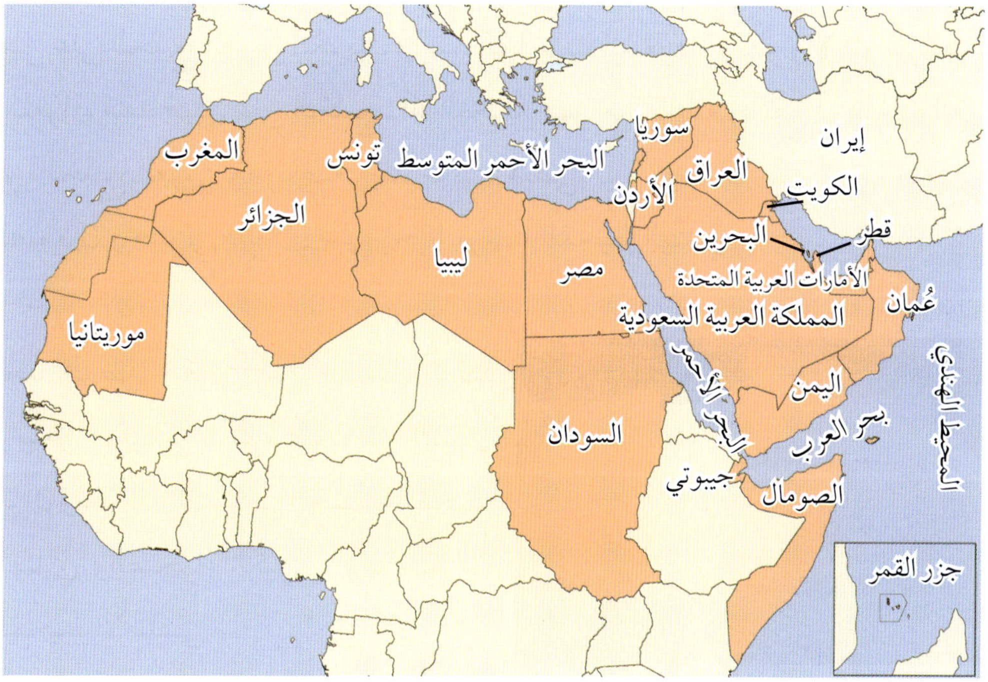

خَريطةُ الوَطَن العَربيّ

حُوضِ البَحر المُتَوَسِّط

تُطِلّ بَعضُ الأقطارِ العربيّة على البَحرِ الأبْيَضِ المُتَوَسِّط مِثل سوريا ولُبنان وفِلَسطين ومِصر وليبيا وتونس والجزائِر والمَغرِب.

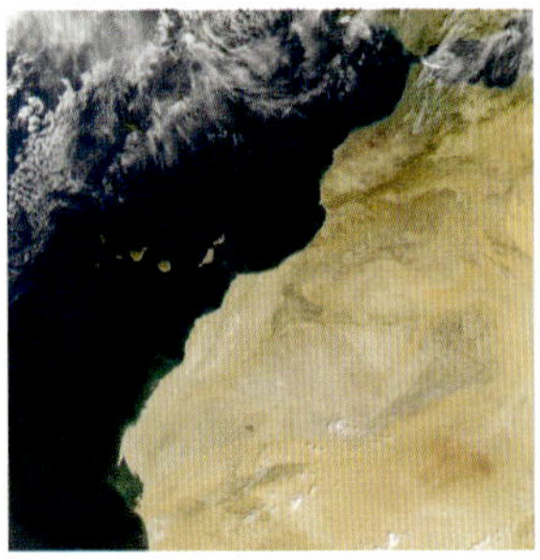
المَغرِبُ وموريتانيا

يُطِلُّ المَغرِبُ وموريتانيا على المُحيطِ الأطلَسيّ.

دُوَل البَحر الأحمَر

وتُطِلّ خَمسة بُلْدان على البَحرِ الأحمَر هي مِصر والسودان واليَمَن والمَملَكةُ العربيّةُ السُعوديّة والأردُنّ. لكِنَّ الأردُنّ لَهُ مَنفَذ ضَيِّق فَقَط على البَحرِ الأحمَر هو ميناءُ العَقَبة.

شِبْهُ الجِزيرةِ العَرَبيّةِ

يُطِلّ على الخَليج العربيِّ الكويت والمَملَكةُ العربيّةُ السُعوديّة وقَطَر والإماراتُ العربيّة، ولِلعِراق مَنفَذ ضَيِّق على الخَليج. أمّا البَحرين فهو جَزيرة صَغيرة تَقَع في الجُزءِ الغَربيّ مِن الخَليجِ العَربيّ وهو أصْغَر بَلَد عَربيّ. ويُطِلّ اليَمَن وعُمان على بَحرِ العَرَب. أمّا الصومال وجيبوتي فَيُطِلّان على بَحرِ العَرب والمُحيطِ الهِنْديّ.

شَمالُ إفريقية

يَحُدُّ الوَطَنَ العَربيّ مِن الشَمال تُركيّا والبَحرُ الأبْيَضُ المُتَوَسِّط، ومِن الشَرق إيران وبَحرُ العَرَب، ومِن الجَنوب المُحيطُ الهِنديّ والصَحراءُ الكُبرى، ومِن الغَرب المُحيطُ الأطلَسيّ.

الوِلايات المُتَّحِدة الأمريكيّة

تَقَعُ الوِلاياتُ المُتَّحِدةُ الأمريكيّة في أمريكا الشَماليّة إلاّ وِلاية هاوائي. يَحُدُها مِن الشَرق المُحيطُ الأطْلَسيّ، ومِن الغَرب المُحيطُ الهادي، ومِن الشَمال كَندا، ومِن الجَنوب المِكسيك وخَليجُ المِكسيك.

خَريطةُ الولاياتِ المتحدةِ الأمريكيّة

أمّا وِلاية ألاسكا فَتَقَع شَمال غَرب كَندا، ووِلاية هَوائي في وَسَطِ المُحيطِ الهادي. أصغَر وِلاية أمريكيّة مِن حيثُ المِساحة هي «رود آيلاند» في شَرقِ الوِلاياتِ المُتَّحِدة على المُحيطِ الأطلَسيّ، وأكبَرُها ألاسكا، لكِنَّها أقَلُّ الوِلايات بِعَدَدِ السُكّان.

سوريا

تَقَع سوريا في شَمالِ الوَطَنِ العَربيّ. يَحُدُّها مِن الشَمال تُركِيّا ومِن الشَرق العِراق ومِن الجَنوب الأردُنّ ومِن الجَنوب الغَربيّ لُبنان وفِلَسطين ومِن الغَرب البَحرُ الأبْيَضُ المُتوَسِّط.

خريطةُ الجُمهوريةُ العربيةُ السوريّة

عاصِمة سوريا هي دِمَشق وتَقَع في جَنوبِها الغَربيّ وهي أكبَر مُدُنِها وأقدَم مَدينة في العالَمِ سُكِنَت دونَ انقِطاع.

ثاني أكبَر مَدينة هي حَلَب وتَقَع في الشَمال. هُناكَ صِناعات عَديدة في كِلتا المَدينتَين وبالقُرب مِنهُما. تَقَع مَدينتا حِمْص وحماة بَينَ حَلَب ودِمَشق. اللاذِقيّة ميناء سوريا الأوَّل، وطَرطوس ميناء آخَر على الساحِلِ السوريّ. أمّا بانياس فهي ميناء نِفطيّ. تَقَعُ السُوَيداء في جَنوب سوريا والقامِشلي في شَمالِها الشَرقيّ. أمّا مَدينة دَيرِ الزَوْر فتَقَع على نَهرِ الفُراتِ الّذي يَنْبُع مِن تُركِيّا ويمُرّ بِسوريا ثُمَّ بِالعِراق.

مِساحَة سوريا ١٨٥١٠٠ كيلومِتراً مُربَّعاً (٧١٤٦٧ ميلاً مُربَّعاً) وعَدَد سُكّانِها ٢٣ مِليون نَسَمة تَقريباً. يوجَد في سوريا زِراعَةُ الحُبوب والزيتون والفَواكِه والخُضَر والقُطْن والتَبْغ. هُناكَ أيْضاً صِناعاتُ النَسيج والأجهِزَةِ الكَهرَبائِيَّة والنِفْط وتجميعُ السيارات ومُنتَجاتُ الحَليب وغير ذلِك.

مِساحات كَبيرة مِن أراضي سوريا صَحْراء أو شِبه صَحْراء كَباديةِ الشام، لكِنْ هُناكَ أيْضاً سُهول خَصيبة جِدّاً مِثل حَوران جَنوبيّ دِمَشق، وسَهْلُ الغاب قُربَ الساحِلِ السوريّ، وسُهولُ الجزيرة في شَمال شَرقيّ سوريا.

بِالإضافةِ إلى نَهرِ الفُرات هُناكَ نَهرُ العاصي الّذي يَنبُع مِن لُبنان ويَجري شَمالاً إلى حِمص وحَماة ثُمَّ يَصُبّ في البَحرِ المُتَوَسِّط. هُناكَ نَهرُ الخابورِ الَّذي يَنبُع مِن تُركِيّا ويَسير جَنوباً لِيَصُبّ في نَهرِ الفُرات. أمّا نَهر بَرَدى فَهو نَهر صَغير يَروي السُهول قُرب دِمَشق.

شِعار سوريا

شِعار سوريا هو طائر العُقاب وفي وَسَط العَلَم نَجمَتان خَضراوان، والكَلِماتُ المَكتوبة على الشِعارِ هي «الجُمهوريةُ العَربيّةُ السورية».

يوجَد جِبال عالية في سوريا كَجَبَلِ الشَيْخ في جَنوب غَرب دِمَشق الَّذي يصل ارتِفاعُه إلى ٢٨١٤ مِتراً (٩٢٣٢ قَدَماً) وهو جُزء مِن سِلسِلة جِبال لُبنانَ الشَرقيّة ويُعْتَبر أعلى جَبَل فيها. هُناكَ جِبالُ العَلَويّين على طولِ الساحَلِ السوريّ، وجَبَلُ العَرَب في الجَنوب.

عَلَم الجمهورية العربية السورية
(أحمَر وأبْيَض وأسود ونَجمتان خَضراوان)

وِلاية أوهايو

تَقَع وِلاية أوهايو في الجُزءِ الشَرقيّ مِن الوِلاياتِ المُتَّحِدة، وتُعْتَبر أيْضاً واحِدة مِن وِلاياتِ الغَربِ الأوسَط. يَحُدُّها مِن الشَمال بُحَيرة إيري، ومِن الشَمالِ الغَربيّ وِلاية ميشِغَن، ومِن الغَرب وِلاية إندِيانا، ومِن الجَنوب وِلاية كِنتكي، ومِن الجَنوبِ الشَرقيّ وِلاية فِرجينيا الغَربيّة (وِسْت فِرجينيا)، ومِن الشَرق وِلاية بِنْسِلفانيا.

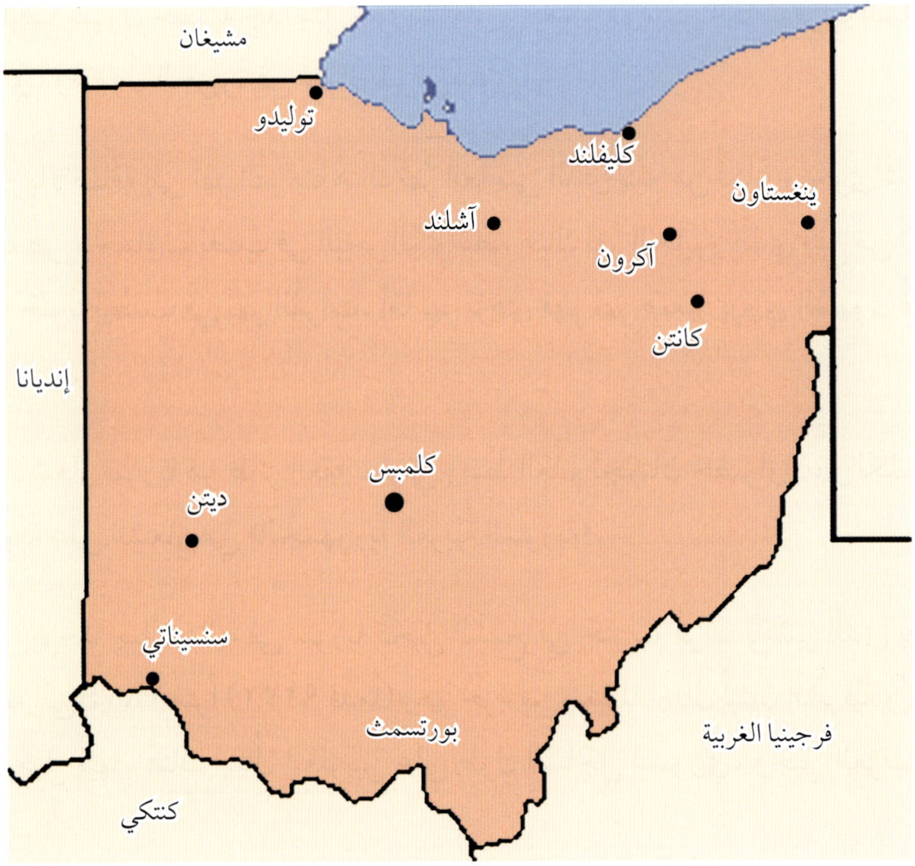

خَريطة وِلاية أوهايو

عاصِمة أوهايو هي مَدينة كَلَمبَس وتَقَع في وَسَط أوهايو. أكبَر مُدُن أوهايو هي كليفلَند وتَقَع في شَمال شَرقِ الوِلاية وتُطِلّ على بُحَيْرة إيري. ورُبَّما تَكون كَلَمبَس أكبَر مَدينة فيها. تُعْتَبَر سِنسِناتي مِن أجمَل مُدُن أوهايو وهي تَقَع في الجَنوبِ الغَربيّ مِن الوِلاية. أمّا توليدو فَتَقَع في شَمال غَرب أوهايو على الحُدود بَينَ وِلايتَي أوهايو وميشِغَن، وهي مَدينة صِناعيّة. وهُناكَ آكرَن وكانتَن في شَمال شَرق أوهايو وكِلتاهُما مَدينتان صِناعِيَّتان كَذلكِ.

مِساحة أوهايو ١٠٦٧٦٥ كيلومِتراً مُرَبَّعاً (٤١٢٢٢ ميلاً مُرَبَّعاً) وعَدَد سُكّانِها ١١ مِليون نَسَمة تَقريباً. أوهايو وِلاية صِناعِيّة تأتي في إنتاجِها الصِناعِيّ بَعدَ وِلايَتي نيويورك وكاليفورنيا، وهي زِراعِيَّة كَذلِكَ وتُنتِجُ الذُرَة والقَمح ومُنتَجاتِ الحَليب والأبقار.

شِعار وِلاية أوهايو

لِأوهايو ميناءان هامّان على بُحَيْرَة إيري هُما كليفلَند وتوليدو. وتُعْتَبَر سِنسِناتي ميناء هامّاً أيْضاً على نَهر أوهايو الّذي يُشَكِّلُ الحُدودَ الجَنوبِيَّة ونِصفَ الحُدودِ الشَرقيّة لِلوِلاية.

مُعظَم أوهايو سُهول خَضْراء ولا يوجَد فيها جِبال إلاّ في الجَنوبِ الشَرقيّ على الحُدود مع فِرجينيا الغَربيّة. هُناكَ بُحَيْرات عَديدة وعِدّة أنهار صَغيرة. أمّا نَهر أوهايو فَلا يَنْبُع مِن أوهايو بَل يَبْدَأ عِند مَدينة بِتسبرِغ في وِلاية بِنسِلفانيا ويَصُبّ في نَهر الميسيسيبي عِند بَلدة كايرو في وِلاية إلينوي. طولُهُ ١٥٧٩ كيلو مِتراً وتَسير فيهِ سُفُنُ الرُكّاب والبَضائِع.

تمرين ٥

أجِب عَن هذه الأسئِلة حَسَبَ نَصّ القِراءة.

١- ما القُطْر العَرَبيُّ الَّذي تَحُدُّهُ مصر مِن الشَرق والجَزائِر مِن الغَرب؟
٢- أيّ قُطْر يَقَع في شَمالِ الوَطَنِ العَرَبيّ؟
٣- ما البَحْرُ الَّذي يُطِلُّ الأردُنّ عَليه؟
٤- ماذا يَحُدُّ الوِلاياتِ المُتَّحِدة مِن الغَرب؟
٥- أيّ بَلَد غير عَرَبيّ لَهُ حُدود مع سوريا؟
٦- ما بَعض مُنتَجات سوريا؟
٧- كَم وِلاية تَحُدّ وِلاية أوهايو؟
٨- هَل الإنتاجُ الصِناعِيّ في أوهايو كَبير؟ اشْرَحْ ذلِك.

تمرين ٦

أكتُبْ «خَطَأ» أو «صَواب» بِجانب كُلّ جُملَة وصَحِّحِ الجُمَلَ الخَطَأ.

١- تُطِلُّ البَحْرَين على الخَليج العَرَبيّ.

٢- أكبَرُ الوِلاياتِ الأمريكيّة بِالمِساحَة هي تِكساس.

٣- يَنْبُع نَهرُ العاصي مِن تُركِيّا ويَصُبّ في الخَليجِ العَرَبيّ.

٤- كانتَن ميناء هامّ على بُحَيْرة إيري.

تمرين ٧

اكتُبْ أسئِلة مُناسِبة لِهذِهِ الإجابات.

١- ثَلاثة أقطار عَرَبيّة تُطِلّ على هذا البَحر.

٢- هُما تُركِيّا وإيران.

٣- خَليجُ المِكسيك والمِكسيك.

٤- هو مَدينة بانياس.

٥- أحَدَ عَشَرَ مليون نَسَمة.

تمرين ٨

اِختَر التَكمِلَةَ المُناسِبة حَسَب نَصِّ القِراءة.

١- تَقَع __________ أقطار عَرَبيّة في إفريقية.

☐ ٩ ☐ ١٢ ☐ ٢٠ ☐ ٢٢

٢- يُطِلُّ الأردُنّ على __________ .

☐ البَحرِ المُتَوَسِّط ☐ البَحرِ الأحْمَر

☐ الخَليج العَرَبيّ ☐ بَحرِ العَرَب

٣- __________ أصغَر قُطر عَرَبيّ.

☐ عُمان ☐ قَطَر ☐ البَحرَين ☐ لُبنان

٤- تَقَع وِلاية ألاسكا في__________.

☐ المُحيطِ الهادي ☐ المُحيطِ الأطلَسيّ

☐ أمريكا الشَماليّة ☐ كَندا

٥- تُعْتبَر__________ أصغَر وِلاية أمريكيّة مِن حَيثُ عَدَدِ السُكّان.

☐ رود آيلاند ☐ ديلاوير ☐ ألاسكا ☐ هَوائي

٦- أقدَم مَدينة في العالَم سُكِنَتْ دونَ انقِطاع هي __________ .

☐ دِمَشق ☐ حَلَب ☐ القاهِرة ☐ بَغداد

٧- __________ مِن المُنتَجات السورية.

☐ النِفط ☐ التَبْغ ☐ القُطْن ☐ كُلُّ ما سَبَق

٨- تَقَع جِبالُ العَلَوِيّين __________ سورية.

☐ في جَنوب ☐ على ساحِل ☐ في شَرق ☐ في وَسَط

٩- يَحُدّ أوهايو مِن الشَمال __________ .

☐ كَنَدا ☐ ميشِغَن ☐ أيوا ☐ بِنسلفانيا

١٠- يُشَكِّل نَهر أوهايو __________ .

☐ أكبَر أنهارِ الوِلاية ☐ الحُدودَ الجَنوبيّةَ الشَرقيّة والجنوبيّة

☐ حُدودَ الوِلاية ☐ ميناء هامّاً

١١- __________ مِن أجمَل مُدُن أوهايو.

☐ سِنسِناتي ☐ كَلَمبَس ☐ كليفلَند ☐ توليدو

١٢- لا يوجَد __________ في وَسَط وشَمال أوهايو.

☐ صِناعات ☐ جِبال ☐ سُهول ☐ مَوانِئ

درّاجات في مَدينة دِمشق

تمرين ٩

أعِدْ تَرتيب الكَلِمات في كُلّ مَجموعة لِتُشَكِّل جُمَلاً مُفيدة.

١- ساحِلِ - على - تَقَعُ - مِلبورن - الجَنوبيّ - أستراليا
٢- العَرَبيّ - ضَيِّقٌ - على - مَنفَذٌ - الخَليج - لِلعِراقِ
٣- الوَطَنِ - مِنَ - واحِدَةٌ - الأقاليمِ - الشامِ - العَرَبِيِّ - في - بِلادُ - الجُغرافيةِ
٤- النِفطَ - الزِراعيّةَ - تُنتِجُ - والمَنتوجاتِ - الجَزائِرُ

تمرين ١٠

١- **الكِتابة**: اقرأ النَصَّ التالي ثُمَّ اكتُب على الخَريطةِ المَوجودةِ فوقَهُ اسمَ البَلَدِ الَّذي يَصِفُهُ النَصُّ وأسماءَ مُدُنِهِ وأنهارِه وجِبالِه وصَحرائِه والأقطارَ الَّتي تَحُدُّه. بَيِّنْ بَعضَ الصِناعات والزِراعات حَسَبَ مَكانِها.

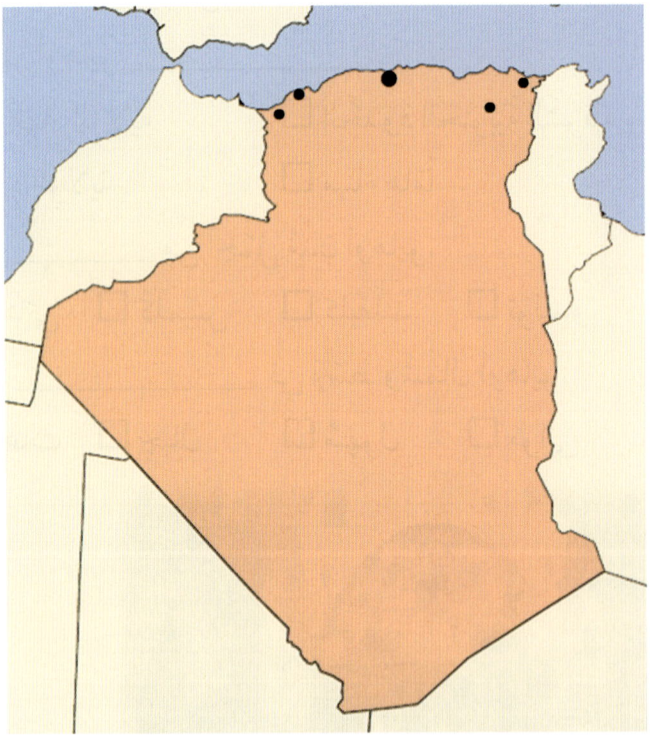

يَحُدُّ القُطرَ الجَزائِريّ مِن الشَمال البَحرُ الأبْيَضُ المُتَوَسِّط ومِن الغَرب المَغرِب ومِن الجَنوبِ الغَربيّ موريتانيا ومالي، ومِن الجَنوبِ

الشَرقيّ النيجَر، وتَحُدُّه مِن الشَرق ليبيا وتونِس. عاصِمةُ الجَزائِر هي مَدينةُ الجَزائِر وتَقَع في شَمالِ البِلاد على ساحِلِ البَحرِ المُتَوسِّط، وهي ميناء هامّ وفيها صِناعةُ النِفط والسَيّارات. ومِن أهمِّ المُدُنِ الأخرى وَهران وتَقَع على الساحِل في غَربيِّ الجَزائِر، وتَقَع تِلِمسان في الشَمالِ الغَربيّ مِن البِلاد لكِنَّها لَيسَتْ على الساحِل. أمّا مَدينة عَنّابة فتَقَع في الشَمالِ الشَرقيّ على ساحِلِ البَحر، وقَسَنطينة في الشَمالِ الشَرقي أيْضاً، لكِنَّها إلى الجَنوبِ الغَربيّ مِن عَنّابة.

تَقع جِبالُ الأطْلَس على طولِ الساحِلِ إلى الجَنوب مِنه قَليلاً، ويَقع بَينَ هذِهِ الجِبال والبَحرِ المُتَوسِّط سُهول خَصيبة تُستَخدَم لِلزِراعة. مُعظَمُ الأراضي جَنوب جِبالِ الأطلَس صَحْراويّة.

عَدَد سُكّانِ الجَزائِر ٣٣ مليون نَسَمَة تَقريباً. يَعمَل نِصْفُ السُكّان في الزِراعة ويُنتِجونَ العِنَب والبُرتُقال والحُبوب والفَواكِه. تُنتِجُ الجَزائِر أيْضاً النِفط والغاز. ويوجَد إلى جانِبِ الزِراعة صِناعةُ السَيّارات بِالإضافةِ إلى صِناعات أخرى.

أجِب عَن هذِهِ الأسئِلة حَسَبَ نَصِّ تَمرين ١٠.

٢- كَم عَدَدَ سُكّانِ الجزائر؟

٣- اكتُب اسمَ صِناعَة مِن الصِناعاتِ الهامّة في الجَزائِر.

٤- ماذا يوجَد جَنوبَ جِبالِ الأطلَس؟

تمرين ١١

الكِتابة: اكتب وصفاً لِمَدينتِك أو وِلايتِك أو بَلَدِك مِثلَ الوَصفِ في تَمرين ١٠ وفي وَصفِ سوريا. بَيِّنْ اسمَ البَلَد ومَكانَه مِن حَيثُ البِلادُ الأخرى والمدُن والأنهار والبُحَيرات والزراعة والصِناعة والسُكّان.

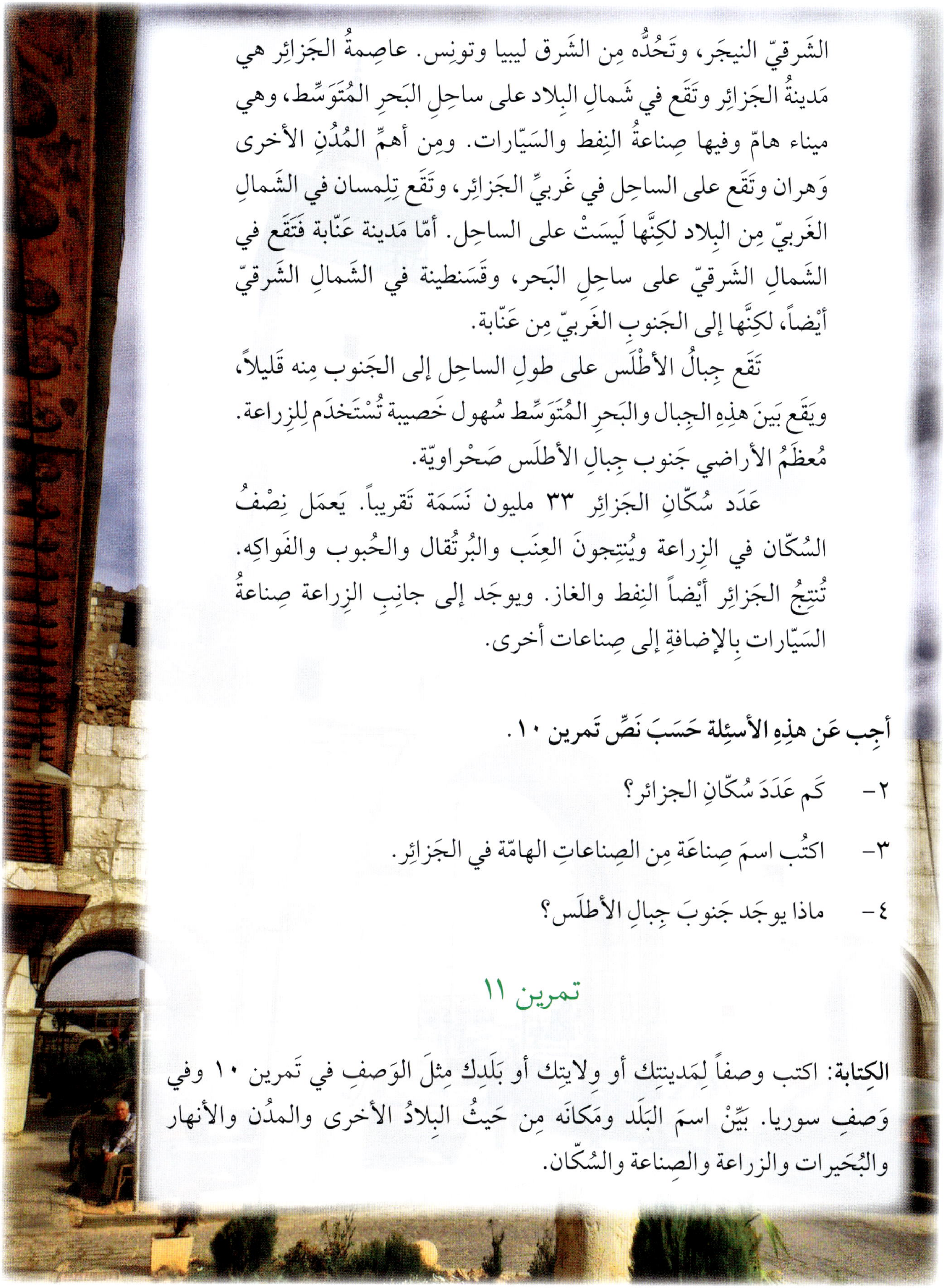

دمشق القديمة - باب شرقي

تمرين ١٢

الكِتابة: صِفِ القُطرَ العِراقيّ حَسَبَ المَعلوماتِ المَوجودة على الخَريطة. استَخدِمِ النَصّ في التَمرين ١٠ والنَصّينِ عَن سوريا وأوهايو كأمثِلة.

تمرين ١٣

المُحادَثة: اسأل زَميلك:

١- صِفْ لي مَدينَتَك.

٢- أيْنَ تَقَع سِلْسِلة جِبال روكي وهل تُريد(ين) زيارتَها؟

٣- ما الأجْمَل في رأيك، الساحِل الأمريكيّ الغَرْبيّ أم الشَرْقيّ ولِماذا؟

٤- أيْنَ تُنْتَجُ السيّارات في أمريكا؟

٥- أيّ وِلاية تَقَع في وَسَط أمْريكا ؟

تمرين ١٤

تَمرينُ المُشاهَدة: شاهِدوا الدَرْسَ الحادي والعشرين على الشابِكة.

١- ما صِفات سوقِ الحَميدية؟ ______________________

____

____

٢- لِماذا يُوجَد ثُقوب في سَقْفِ السوق؟ ______________________

____

____

٣- ما المدينَتانِ اللتان تَقَعان على الساحِلِ السوريّ؟ ______________________

____

____

٤- إذا زُرت سوريا أيها الطالب العزيز، أيّ مُدُن تُريد/ ين أن تَزور/ ي ولِماذا؟

____

____

٥- ضَع دائرة حَولَ المُدُنِ الّتي زارَها سامِر:

حمص اللاذقية حماة دير الزور بانياس طرطوس حلب

تمرين ١٥

المُحادَثة: الأسواقُ العَربيّة: اِحكِ قصة لِزَميلك في الصَفّ عّما تَعرِف عن السوق العَرَبيّة وقارِنها بالأسواق في مَسقَط رأسِك (المَكان حَيثُ تَرَبَّيت فيه). ما هي التَشابُهات والاختِلافات بينَهُما. هل في مَدينَتِك سوق تَبيع الخُضر الناضِج أو الفَواكه الناضِجة وماذا تَشتَري منها عادةً. ماذا يُعجبك في سوق الحَمَدية؟ وماذا تُريد أن تَشتَري منها لِنفسِك أو لأصدِقائك لو تَسَوّقت فيها؟

العَرض: صِف لِلطلاّب الأماكن التي زرتها مستخدماً الجهات الأربع على سبيل المثال:

«لقد سافرت إلى الساحل الغربي لأمريكا وسبحت في المحيط الهادي. أفضّل الساحل الغربي عن الساحل الشرقي لأنّ شواطئ الساحل الغربي أجمل وأمواج البحر أعلى. ليس هناك محيط في شمال أمريكا، ولكن يوجد في شمال شرقي البلد بحيرات كبيرة وفي جنوب شرق أمريكا يوجد خليج المكسيك.»

الممارسة: اسأل الطلاّب أين يسكنون من حيث غرفة الصف أو في الولاية، مثلاً:

«كيف نصل إلى بيتك من غرفة صفنا؟»
«أين بيتك في المدينة؟»

١- الجِهات الأربَع

تَدخُل الجِهاتُ الأربع على الجُمَل العَرَبيّة بِصفةِ الظَرف أو الجار والمَجرور، كَما تَرى في هذا الباب.

آ- الظُروف

حين نَصِف المَوقِع الجَغرافيّ، فإنّ الاتجاه المُستخدَم يأتي في حالة النَصب كَما تَرى في المِثال ١:

١	تَقعُ الإسكَندَريّةُ شَمالَ القاهِرةِ.

إنَّ الجِهاتَ الأربع هي أسماء بالعَرَبيّة، لِذا فإنّها تَتكَوّن من مُضاف ومُضاف إليه. لِهذا السَبَب كَلِمةَ القاهِرةِ مَجرورة بالكَسرة في المِثال ١ أعلاه لأَنَّها مُضاف إليه.

ويُبَيِّن لَنا المِثال ١ أنّ مَدينةَ الإسكَندَريّة تَقع إلى شَمالِ القاهِرة ونَستَطيع أن نَرى هذا المَفهوم بالطَريقةِ الآتية:

الإسكَندَريّة ❍

القاهِرة ❍

ب-   الجِهات الأربَع: الجار والمَجرور

حين نَذكُر الجِهاتَ الأربع في شَرح مَواقِع جَغرافيّة، فأنّ العَلاقة المَكانية (spatial relationship) تَختَلِف. اِقرأ المِثال ٢ أدناه وتأمّل الخَريطة المُلوّنة الّتي تَحته.

٢	تَقَعُ الإسكَندريّةُ في شَمالِ مِصر.
	تَقَعُ الإسكَندريّةُ في شَماليِّ مِصر.

يَدُلُ المِثال ٢ عَلى كُلِّ المِنطقةِ الشَمالية في مِصر وليس فَقَط أنّ الإسكندرية تَقع شَمالَ القاهِرة. نَرى هذِه العَلاقة المَكانية في الخَريطة أدناه:

نُلاحظ في المِثال ٢ أعلاه، أنّ الكَلِمة شَماليّ اسم نِسبة.

تمرين ١٦

المُحادَثة: إجرِ مُقابَلةً مع زميل من زُملائك واسأله عن الدَولة الّتي أقام فيها أو زارَها في حياتِه. يُستَحسَن أن يُحاوِل اِستِخدام الجِهات الأربع والجِهات البَينيّة (أي شَمال غَربيّ وجَنوب شَرقيّ إلخ.) في شَرحِه. وعلى الطالِب الّذي يُجيب عن هذِه الأسئلة أن يَرسُم خَريطة لهذا المَكان. وعِند اِنتِهاء رَسم الخَريطة، قارِن بَينها والواقِع.

وَقَعَ	اِعْتبَرَ	حَدّ	أَنْتَجَ	صَنَعَ	سِلْسِلة	وَسَط	عاصِمة
أَعْجَبَ	اِسْتَمْتَعَ بِـ	اِسْتَطاع	حُدود	شَرْق	غَرْب	شَمال	جَنوب

٢- الاسم: كِلا وكِلتا "both of"

الكَلِمتان كِلا (لِلمُذكَّر) وكِلتا (لِلمُؤنَّث) هُما اسمان يَدُلّان على المُثَنّى (أي اِثنان من شَيء). وتُشَكِّل الكَلِمتان إضافة مع الاسم الّذي يَليهُما أي أنّهُما مُضافان وأيضاً مَبنيان أي لا يُعرِبان (they do not change form) مَهما كان مَحلّهما في الجُملة.

٣	كِلا الكِتابَينِ كُتِبَ بِالعَرَبيَّة.
٤	كِلتا السَيّارتَينِ أتَتْ مِن ديترويت.

مُلاحَظة: نَعتَبِر كِلا وكِلتا اِسماً مُفرَداً رَغم دلالتِهما على المُثنّى.

٥	**مُذكَّر**	قَرأتُ كِلا الكِتابَين.	**مَنصوب**
٦	**مُؤنَّث**	زُرْنا كِلتا المَدينتَين.	
٧	**مُذكَّر**	كَتَبْتُ إلى كِلا الطالِبَين.	**مَجرور**
٨	**مُؤنَّث**	أعْرِفُ طُلّاباً مِن كِلتا الجامِعتَين.	

الضَمائر المُتَّصِلة: حين نُضيف إلى كِلا أو كِلتا الضَمير المُتّصِل هُما فَأنّهُما يُعرَبان. ونَستَطيع أن نَرى هذا في حالة الرَفع (الفاعِل في المِثال ٩) حالة النَصب (المَفعول بِهِ في المِثال ١٠) أو حالة الجَرّ (المَجرور في المِثال ١١).

٩	جاء الطالِبان كِلاهُما.	**حالة الرَفع**
	جاءت الطالِبتان كِلتاهُما.	
١٠	قَرأتُ الكِتابَينِ كِلَيْهِما.	**حالةُ النَصب**
١١	اِسْتَمتَعنا بِالزيارتَين كِلتَيْهِما.	**حالةُ الجَرّ**

العَرض: اقرأ قصة لِلطلّاب قد كتبتها تذكر فيها أمثلة كثيرة من المستثنى «سكنت في أمريكا طول حياتي إلّا سنتين حينما سكنت في سوريا. وطول الفترة التي قضيتها في الشام لم أتكلّم غير العربية مع أصدقائي العرب. وكل يوم من أيام الأسبوع ذهبت إلى الجامعة ما عدا يوم الجمعة الذي ذهبت فيه إلى سوق الحميدية وأعجبتني كل المحلات التجارية الموجودة هناك إلّا واحداً.»

الممارسة: اطرح على الطلّاب أسئلة استيعاب حول القصة التي كتبتها أو اطرح أسئلة عليهم تتطلب استخدام أداة من أدوات الاستثناء، مثلاً:

«هل قرأت كل كتابك هذا؟»
«هل تقرأ الجريدة كل يوم؟»
«هل زرت كل الولايات في الولايات المتحدة؟»
«هل تأتي إلى هذا الصف كل يوم؟»

التطبيق: في مجموعات من اثنين. حضّر ورقة عليها أسئلة تشابه الأسئلة أعلاه أو في تمرين ١٦ واطلب من المجموعات إيجاد الأجوبة من زملائهم. اطلب منهم الإفادة بما علموا من أصدقائهم واجعلهم جمع رصيد نتائجهم على السبورة.

تمرين ١٧

التَحويل: حَوِّلِ الجُمَل الآتية إلى اللُغةِ العَربيّة مُستَخدِماً الشَكلِ الصَحيح من كِلا أو كِلتا.

1. Arabic and Hebrew are Semitic (ساميّ) languages, and both of them are written from right to left.
2. Both his sisters study medicine at this university.
3. I read both his letters.
4. There is a telephone in both houses.

٣- المُستَثنى بِاستِخدام ما عَدا وإلاّ وغَيْر

لَقد تَعَلّمنا في الدُروس السابِقة الاِستِثناء باستِخدام أدواتِ المُستَثنى ما عَدا وإلاّ وغَيْر.

آ- **أداة الاِستِثناء ما عَدا**

إنّ الاسم الّذي يَلي أداة الاِستثناء ما عَدا في حالة النَصب (راجِع اِستِخدام ما عَدا في الدَرس السابع عشر).

١٢	أتى جَميعُ الطُلاّبِ ما عَدا واحِداً.

ب- **أداة الاِستِثناء إلاّ**

لا تُؤثِّر أداةُ إلاّ على الجُملة ما عَدا الحالتَين الآتيتَين:

١- في الجُملة المَنفيّة (negative sentence) كَما نَرى في المِثال ١٣.

٢- المُستَثنى مِنه غَير مَذكور كَما نَرى في المِثال ١٤.

١٣	ما وَصَلَ إلاّ أحْمَدُ.	مَرفوع
١٤	لا تُحِبُّ أختي إلاّ الحِمَّصَ.	مَنصوب
١٥	لا يُطِلُّ الأردُنُّ إلاّ على البَحرِ الأحْمَر.	مَجرور

إنّ المُستَثنى مِنه أحْمَدُ في المِثال ١٣ أعلاه مَرفوع لأنه فاعِل الجُملة، وفي المِثال ١٤، الحِمَّصَ المَفعول بِه لِذا هُو مَنصوب بالفَتحة. أمّا بِالنِسبة إلى المِثال ١٥، فَالبَحرِ مَجرور بِحَرف الجَرّ على.

في الجُملةِ العَرَبية، تَنصُب أداةُ المُستَثنى المُستَثنى مِنه الّذي يَليها مُباشَرةً في الجُملة، كَما تَرى في الأمثِلة الآتية:

١٦	وَصَلَ الطُلاّبُ إلاّ خالِداً.	حالةُ النصب
١٧	نَظَّفَ الرَجُلُ كُلَّ السَيّاراتِ إلاّ سَيّارَتَك.	
١٨	كَتَبْتُ إلى كُلِّ أَصْدِقائي إلاّ واحِداً مِنهُم.	

ج- أداة الإستِثناء غَيْر

بِما أنّ كَلِمة غَيْر اسم، فَهو يُشَكِّل إضافةً مع المُستَثنى منه الّذي يَليه في الجُملة. أمّا بِالنِسبة إلى الإعراب، فَفي الجُمَل غير المَنفية (انظُر إلى مِثال ١٩) تأتي في حالةِ النَصب وتُوافِق إعراب أداةِ المُستَثنى إعرابَ المُستَثنى منه في الجُمَلِ المَنفية (انظُر إلى الأمثِلة ٢٠-٢٢).

١٩	وَصَلَ الطُلاّبُ غَيرَ خالِدٍ (= إلاّ خالِداً).	مَنصوب علامته الفَتحة	جُملة عادية
٢٠	ما وَصَلَ طُلاّبٌ غَيْرُ خالِدٍ.	في مَحَلّ رَفع فاعِل	جُمَل مَنفيّة
٢١	لا تَعرِفُ أُمّي غَيْرَ العَرَبيّةِ.	في مَحَلّ نَصب مَفعول به	
٢٢	ما كَتَبْتُ لِغَيرِ خالِدٍ.	مَجرور بَعد حَرف الجَرّ لِـ	

تمرين ١٨

المُحادَثة: اِستِخدام المُستَثنى: مَن في صَفّك:

1. has traveled to every continent except Antarctica (قارّة القُطْبِ الجَنوبيّ)
2. has seen all but one of Johnny Depp's movies
3. has read all but the last lesson of this book
4. has watched nothing but reality television (البَرامِج الواقِعيّة)
5. has visited a country that borders Saudi Arabia
6. was born in a state that borders Ohio
7. has lived on a peninsula
8. has visited both the East and West Coasts of America
9. has swum in both the Atlantic and Pacific Oceans
10. has walked in a desert

تمرين ١٩

١- اسْتَمِعْ إِلى النَصّ ثُمَّ اكتُبْ على الخَريطَة اسمَ البَلَدِ الَّذي يَصِفُهُ النَصّ وأسماء مُدُنِهِ وجِبالِه وسُهولِهِ والبِلادَ الَّتي تَحُدُّه مِن كُلّ جانِب.

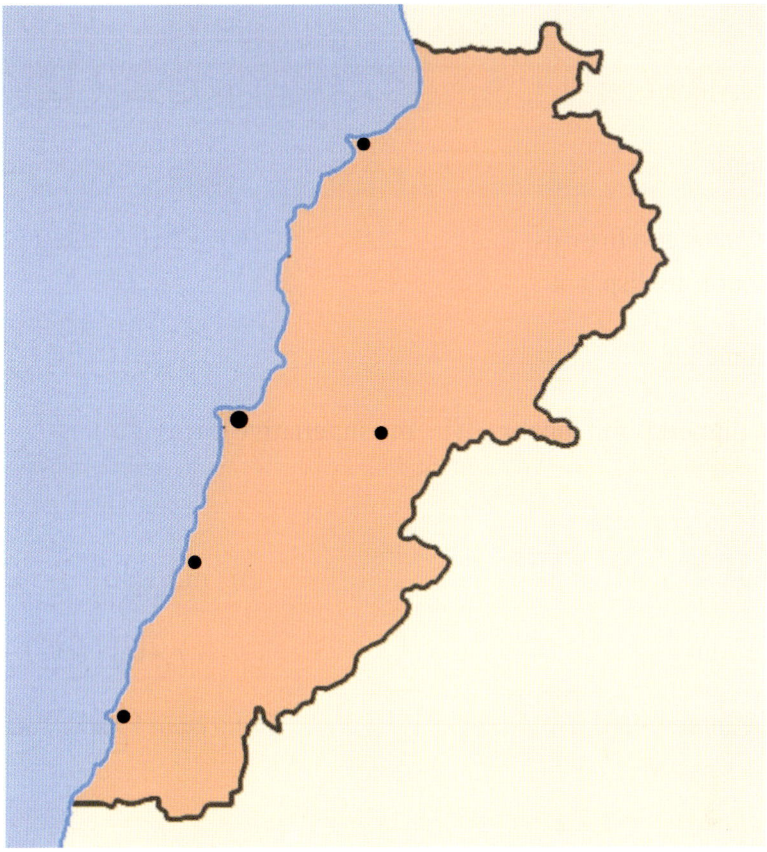

أجِب عَن الأسْئِلَة الآتية.

٢- لِماذا تُعْتَبَر عاصِمَة هذا البَلَد العاصِمَةَ التِجارِيَّة لِلشَرقِ الأوسَط؟

٣- ما المُنتَجاتُ الزِراعِيَّة في هذا البَلَد؟

٤- آلسُهول (أ+السُهولُ) أكثَر في هذا القُطر أمِ الجِبال؟

المُفْرَدات

استمِع إلى المُفْرَدة بالعَرَبيّة ثم أعِد نُطْقَها مرّتين.

during	أثْناء
Asia	آسيا (n., f.)
to overlook (s.t.)	أطَلَّ (يُطِلُّ) إطْلال (v.)
Atlantic	أطلَسيّ (adj.)
to discharge a firearm, to shoot; to dispatch	أطْلَقَ (يُطْلِق) إطْلاق (v.)
to consider	اِعتبَرَ (يعتبِرُ) اِعتِبار (v.)
top, highest point, upper	أعْلى ج أعالٍ (n., m., superlative form)
Africa	إفريقية (n., f.)
region	إقليم ج أقاليم (n., m.)
to produce	أنتجَ (يُنتِجُ) إنتاج (v.)
to be interrupted, to be severed	اِنقَطَعَ (يَنقَطِعُ) اِنقِطاع (v.)
Iran	إيران
semiarid desert	بادِية ج بَوادٍ (n., f.)
merchandise, goods	بِضاعة ج بَضائِع (n., f.)
ice cream	بوظة (n., f.)
to consist of, to comprise	تَألّفَ (يَتألّفُ) تَألُّف (v.)
traditional	تَقْليديّ (adjective)
date (fruit)	تَمْر ج تُمور (n., m.)
hole	ثَقْب ج ثُقوب (n., m.)
mountain	جَبَل ج جِبال (n., m.)

to test, to try (≠ to attempt). . . . . (v.) جَرَّبَ (يُجَرِّبُ) تَجْرِبة

island . . . . (n., f.) جَزيرة ج جُزُر

geography . . . . (n., m.) جغرافية

south . . . . (n., m.) جَنوب

device, apparatus, appliance . . . . (n., m.) جِهاز ج أجهِزة

to border, to demarcate, to limit . . . . (v.) حَدَّ (يَحُدُّ) حَدّ

border, edge, boundary, borderline . . . . (n., m.) حَدّ ج حُدود

shoe . . . . (n., m.) حِذاء ج أحْذية

map . . . . (n., f.) خَريطة ج خَرائِط

fertile . . . . (adj.) خَصيب

gulf, bay . . . . (n., m.) خَليج ج خُلجان

passenger, rider . . . . (n., m.) راكِب ج رُكّاب

trip, journey, flight . . . . (n., f.) رِحْلة ج رَحَلات

bullets; lead (n., m.) رَصاص

to irrigate, to water . . . . (v.) رَوى (يَروي) رَيّ

to plant, to cultivate. . . . . (v.) زَرَعَ (يَزرَعُ) زَرْع، زِراعة

coast, shore . . . . (n., m.) ساحِل ج سَواحِل

ceiling . . . . (n., m.) سَقْف ج سُقوف

range, series, chain . . . . (n., f.) سِلسِلة ج سَلاسِل

plain. . . . . (n., m.) سَهل ج سُهول

semi-, quasi; similarity . . . . (n., m.) شِبْه ج أشباه

emblem, sign, slogan . . . . . . (n., m.) شِعار ج شِعارات، أشعِرة

داخِل بَيت تَقليديّ في دِمشق

to form, to constitute . . . . (v.) شَكَّلَ (يُشَكِّلُ) تَشكيل

to flow into . . . . (v.) صَبَّ (يصُبُّ) صَبّ

desert . . . . (n., f.) صَحْراء ج صَحاري

to manufacture, to make . . . . (v.) صَنَعَ (يَصنَعُ) صِناعة

characteristic . . . .(n., f.) صِفة ج صِفات

narrow, tight . . . . (adj.) ضَيِّق

capital city . . . . (n., f.) عاصِمة ج عَواصِم

high, elevated . . . . (adj.) عالٍ (العالي)

several, multiple . . . . (adj.) عَديد

throughout, all the way . . . . على طُول

flag, banner . . . . (n., m.) عَلَم ج أعْلام

pistachio . . . . (n., m.) فُسْتُق

continent . . . . (n., f.) قارّة ج قارّات

country . . . . (n., m.) قُطْر ج أقْطار
(almost exclusively used for Arab countries)

cotton . . . . (n., m.) قُطْن

wheat . . . . (n., m.) قَمْح

both . . . . (n.) كِلا

what . . . . (adverbial particle) ما

ocean . . . . (n., m.) مُحيط ج مُحيطات

square . . . . (adj.) مُرَبَّع

area . . . . (n., f.) مِساحة ج مِساحات

made (of /from) . . . . (passive participle) مَصْنوع (مِن)

covered (with) . . . . (passive participle) مُغَطّى (بِـ)

المِكسيك (n., f.) .... Mexico

مُنتَج ج مُنتَجات (n., m.) .... product

مَنْفَذ ج مَنافِذ (n., m.) .... outlet

نَبَعَ (يَنبُعُ) نَبْع (v.) .... to spring, to originate, to flow

نَحْو ج أنْحاء (n., m.) .... section, manner, mode, fashion

نَسيج (n., m.) .... textile, tissue, fabric

نِفْط (n., m.) .... petroleum, crude oil

الهادي (adj.) .... Pacific

وَسَط ج أوساط (n., m.) .... middle, central

مَدينة دِمشق

الدرس الثاني والعشرون

أهدافُ الدَرس

- وَصْف بَرامَج تِلفازيّة وإذاعيّة
- اِستِخدام على + أنْ
- اِستِخدام يُمْكِن
- التَقديم لِـ لَم يَعُدْ
- مُراجَعةُ الاسم المَوصول العامّ ما
- تَقديم الحَرف أنْ بعد ظَرفَي الزَمان بَعْدَ وقَبْلَ
- تَقديم الاسم بِضْع

رُكنُ المُفْرَداتِ الجَديدة

إذاعة ج إذاعات	*broadcasting station*
اِسْتَمَعَ (يَستَمِعُ) اِسْتِماع (إلى)	*to listen (to)*
اِشْتَرَكَ (يَشْتَرِكُ) اِشْتِراك (في)	*to participate (in)*
أمْكَنَ (يُمْكِنُ) إمْكان	*to be possible*
حَزَرَ (يَحْزِرُ) حَزْر	*to guess*
حَسَّنَ (يُحَسِّنُ) تَحْسين	*to improve (s.t.)*
خِلالَ	*during, through*
شَخْص ج أشْخاص	*person*
طَبْعاً (مِن طَبيعة)	*of course; naturally*
ظَهَرَ (يَظْهَرُ) ظُهور	*to appear*
عادَ (يَعودُ) عَوْد	رَجَعَ (يَرجِعُ) رُجوع
ماتَ (يَموتُ) مَوْت	*to die*

free of charge	مَجّاني
for the sake of	مِن أجْل (+ مَصدَر)
via (by means of)	مِن خِلالِ
system	نِظام ج أنْظِمة
including	بِما في ذلِكَ

المُفرداتُ الجَديدةُ في صُوَر عَديدة

اِسْتَمَعَ (يَسْتَمِع) اِسْتِماع

غَنّى (يُغَنّي) غِناء

رَقَصَ (يَرْقُص) رَقْص

طِفْل ج أطْفال

الفَضاء

قَمَر ج أقْمار

مُتَزَوِّج ج مُتَزَوِّجون

مُمَثِّل ج مُمَثِّلون

تمرين ١

اختَرَ الكَلِمةَ الّتي لا تُناسِب باقي الكَلِمات في كُلِّ مَجْموعة وبَيِّنِ السَبَب.

١-	بَرنامَج	مُسلسَل	أخبار	لُغة
٢-	بَثّ	مَجّاني	قَناة	مَوجة
٣-	عَودة	موسيقا	أغنية	مُغنّية
٤-	حَيَوان	طَبيعة	تِجارة	أشجار
٥-	مَوْجة	إذاعة	مَحطّة	طِفل

تمرين ٢

وافِق بَين كَلِمات مِنَ العَمودِ الأيْمَن وكَلِمات مِنَ العَمودِ الأيْسَر واكتُب الكَلِمَتَين في الوَسَط.

١-	إذاعة		مُمتاز
٢-	قناة		سوق
٣-	إعلانات		أكثر
٤-	تُوُفِّيَ		بَثّ
٥-	مُغَنٍّ		مَوجة
٦-	جَيِّد		عاميّة
٧-	فَصيحة		أغنية
٨-	مُعظَم		تِجارة
			ماتَ

تمرين ٣

اختَر التكْمِلةَ المُناسِبة حَسَب نَصِّ القِراءة.

١- أشاهِد مُسَلسَلي المُفَضَّل على ____________ سِتة.

☐ المَحَطّة ☐ القَناة ☐ اللاسِلكي ☐ المَوجَة

٢- تُريد أختي أنْ تَعمل ____________ بَعد تَخَرُّجِها.

☐ فَصيحة ☐ عاميّة ☐ أُغنية ☐ مُذيعة

٣- شاهَدتُ ____________ على التِلفاز مع المُغَنّية مَيّادة حِنّاوي.

☐ مُقابَلة ☐ موسيقا ☐ مُمتازة ☐ مُسَلسَلاً

٤- ____________ إلى الأغاني مِن مُسَجِّلتي.

☐ أستَمِع ☐ أشاهِد ☐ أفهَم ☐ أُحسِّن

٥- أختي الكَبيرة ____________ مِن رَجُل جَزائريّ.

☐ مُغَنّية ☐ مُمَثِّلة ☐ مُتَزَوِّجة ☐ موسيقيّة

الإذاعة والتِلفاز

في الوِلايات المُتَّحِدة والوَطَن العربيّ

مِن يَومِيّات عَدنان مارتيني

مُنذُ أنْ أتَيتُ إلى الولاياتِ المُتَّحِدة لَمْ أعُدْ أشاهِدُ التِلفاز كَما كُنتُ أشاهِدُه في حَلَب، رُبَّما لأنَّني الآن مَشغول بِدِراسَتي ولَيْسَ عِندي الوَقت لِمُشاهَدةِ البَرامِج والمُسَلسَلاتِ الكَثيرة. لكِنَّني أشاهِدُ الأخبار كُلّ يَوم صَباحاً قَبل أنْ أذهَب إلى الجامِعة ومَساءً بَعد عَودَتي مِنها. وأشاهِد كَذلِكَ بَعضَ المُسَلسَلات أحياناً.

الأخبار

أشاهِد غالِباً بَرنامَج «صَباحُ الخَيْرِ يا أمريكا» على القناة سِتّة في الساعةِ السابِعة صَباحاً مِن مَحَطّة «إي بي سي». نَشْرَةُ الأخبار في هذِه المَحطَّة مُدَّتُها نِصف ساعة لكِنَّها سَريعة. يَقرأُ المُذيع أو المُذيعةُ الخَبَرَ في بِضع دَقائِق ثُمَّ تَظهَرُ الإعلاناتُ التِجاريّة. وهذِه الإعلانات تَظهَر في أيِّ وَقت خِلالَ المُسَلسَلات والأفلام والبَرامِج، وهذا شَيء لا يُعجِبُني.

في المَساء أشاهِدُ الأخبار أوَّلاً على القَناة ٣٤ مِن مَحَطّة «پي بي إس»، ونَشْرَةُ الأخبار في هذِه المَحطّة طَويلة وفيها أخبار مِن أمريكا والعالَم وكَذلِكَ مُقابَلات مع أشْخاص عَديدين. تَبُثّ هذِه المَحطّة بَرامِج عِلمِيّة مُمتازة عَن الحَيَوانات والطَبيعة، وهِي مَحَطّة عامَّة ولَيْسَتْ تِجاريّة. حين يكون عِندي وَقت أُفَضِّل أنْ أشاهِد هذِهِ البَرامِج.

مُقابَلة

في الساعةِ السادِسة والنِصف أشاهِدُ الأخبار على إحدى القَنَواتِ الَّتي تَبُثّ عليها المَحطّاتُ التِجاريَّة «إن بي سي» و«سي بي إس». أشاهِد أحياناً بَعضَ المُسَلسَلات مِثلَ «ستينجَر ثينجز» و«جيم أوف ثرونز»، أي «صَراع العُروش» و«هاوس أوف كاردز»،

العَرَض: هذه فرصة ذهبية كي تعرض على الطلاّب لأوّل مرّة في حياتهم دقيقة من برنامج أخبار عربي أصلي (من الشابكة أو التلفاز أو الراديو) أو من أغنيتك المفضّلة. ليس عليك أن تجعل البرنامج درساً كاملاً، بل يكفي أن يشاهده الطلاّب أو يستمعوا إليه للتذوّق ثمّ اطرح عليهم سؤالاً بسيطاً مثل:

«ماذا فهمتم من البرنامج/ الأغنية؟»

«هل كان هناك كلمة أو كلمات معروفة في النص؟»

قد تودُّ أن تكتب ما يقول لك الطلاّب من أفكارهم أو مفاهيمهم أو حتى كلماتهم على السبورة مثل نشاط استثارة الأفكار. وإذا كان هناك كلمة مقدمة من الطلاّب ولم تظهر في المقطع، اكتب علامة استفهام بجانبها وقل: **«دعنا نستمع مرة ثانية إلى النص لنتأكد من وجود هذه الكلمة أو عدم وجودها.»**

مع وجود العديد من الكلمات والأفكار والمفاهيم على السبورة، حاول أن توجّه الطلاّب إلى فكرة المقطع الرئيسة. يمكنك أن تسهّل هذه العملية عليهم بتصنيف الكلمات المكتوبة على السبورة في فئات منطقية معقولة.

قد تودّ أن تسأل الطلاّب عن آراءهم في الموسيقا العربية/ الشرقية. اعرض عليهم الموسيقا العربية الكلاسيكية والعصرية ودعهم يقارنون بين النوعين.

أي «بَيت من وَرَق». يُعجِبُني أيْضاً بَرنامَجي «عِشرين على عِشرين» و«سِتّونَ دَقيقة».

يوجَد في أمريكا نِظامان لِلبَثِّ التِلفزيونيّ واحِد لاسِلكيّ وهو مَجّانيّ والآخَر سِلكيّ (ويُسَمّى كَيبل هُنا) ويُمْكِن أنْ تَحصُل عليهِ مُقابِل اشتِراك شَهريّ. يَحْصُلُ الناس من النِظامِ اللاسِلكيّ على المَحطّاتِ الكَبيرةِ الثَلاث: «سي بي إس» و«أي بي سي» و«إن بي سي» بِالإضافةِ إلى «پي بي إس» (المَحَطّةِ العامّة) وكَذلِكَ مَحطّتَي «فوكس» و«سي إن إن».

أمّا النِظامُ السِلكيّ فَفيهِ عَشَراتُ القَنَوات لِلأفلامِ السينَمائيّة والأطفال والتاريخ والعُلوم والموسيقا وبَيعِ البَضائعِ التِجاريّة وغَيْر ذلِكَ كَثير. شاهدتُ مَرّة قَناة «ديسكفري» وأعجَبَتْني جِداً بِسَبَبِ البَرامِجِ العِلميَّةِ الَّتي تَبُثُّها يَومِيّاً.

حين أقرأ دُروسي مَساءً في الشَقَّة أحِبّ أنْ أسْتَمِع إلى الإذاعة وهُناكَ عَدَد كَبير مِن المَحطّات. أستَمِع عادةً إلى ما يُعجِبُني مِن الأغاني والموسيقا مِن مَحطّات على المَوجة «إف إم» لكِنْ هُناكَ أيْضاً مَحطّات كَثيرة على المَوجَةِ المُتَوسِّطة. إذاعَتي المُفَضَّلة هي الإذاعةُ العامّة «إن پي آر» لأنَّ فيها أخباراً وبَرامِج مُمتازة. في الشُهورِ الأولى حين أتَيْتُ إلى الوِلاياتِ المُتَّحِدة كُنتُ أستَمِع إلَيها عِدّة ساعات كُلَّ يوم وساعَدَتني كَثيراً في تَحسين لُغَتي الإنكليزيّة.

أمّا مِن أجلِ الأغاني والموسيقا فأستَمِع إلى عِدّة مَحطّات. تُعجِبُني الموسيقا الحَديثة وأغاني «ستيفي وَندَر» و«مادونا» و«غلوريا إستِفان» وغيرِهِم. لكِنْ عِندي أيْضاً أغانٍ لِمُغَنين عَرَب مِثل فَيروز وصَباح فَخري ووَديع الصافي وراغِب علامة ومُحَمّد عَبدُه. أحصُل على هذِه الأغاني من بَرنامَج «سبوتيفاي».

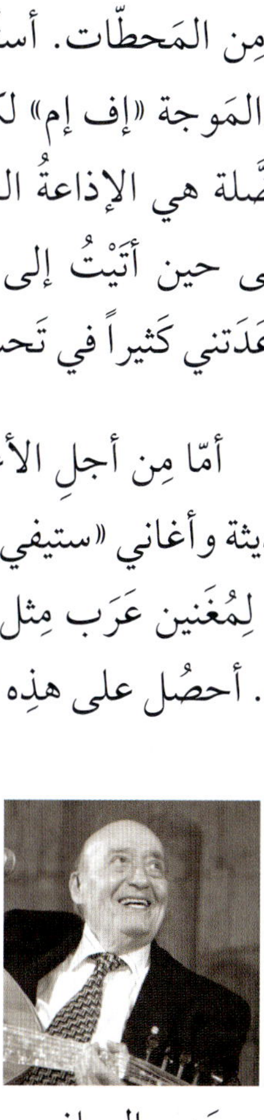
وَديع الصافي

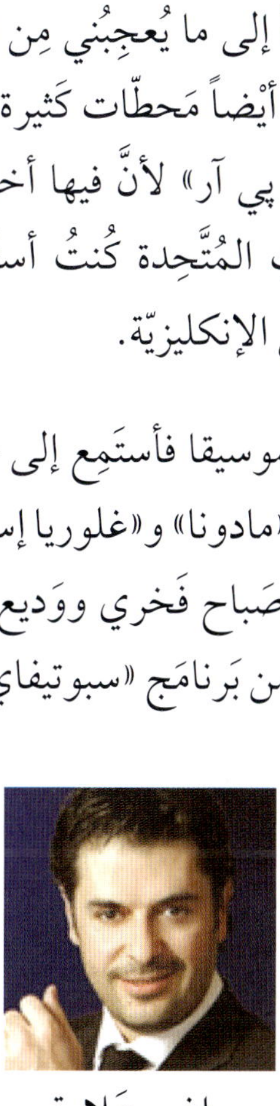
راغِب عَلامة

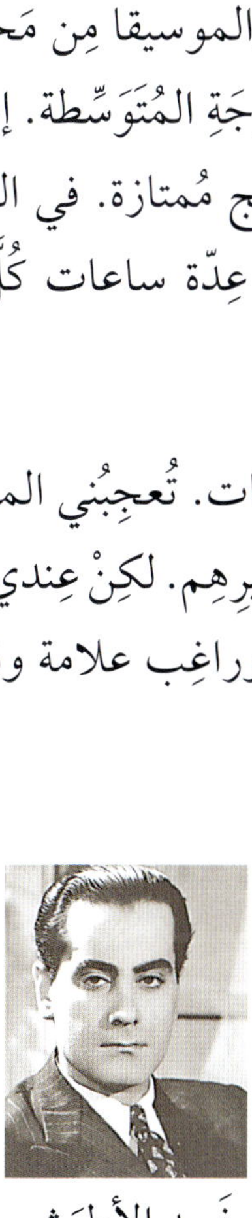
فَريد الأطرَش

«هل أعجبتكم الموسيقا العربية؟ ماذا أعجبتكم أكثر الموسيقا الكلاسيكية أم العصرية؟ ما الاختلافات أو التشابهات التي لاحظتها بين النوعين؟»

تثير انتباه الطلاّب الفواصل الإعلانية التلفزيونية العربية الأصلية. اعرض على الطلاّب فاصلاً إعلانياً أو اثنين ثمّ اسألهم:
«كيف تختلف الإعلانات العربية عن الإعلانات الأمريكية في رأيكم؟ ما هي التشابهات بين النوعين إن وُجِدَت؟»

من يوميّات مايكل براون

صِرتُ الآن أفهَم كَثيراً مِمّا أسمَع في الإذاعة والتِلفاز. أشاهِدُ التِلفاز ساعة أو ساعتَينِ كُلّ يَوم مَساءً ويُساعِدُني هذا كَثيراً في تَحسين لُغَتي العربيّة، الفَصيحة والعامِيّة. هُناكَ بَرامِج بالعَرَبيّةِ الفَصيحة كَالأخبار والمُقابَلات والبَرامِج العِلميّة وغَيرِها. أمّا المُسَلسَلاتُ الإذاعيّة والتِلفزيونيّة فَمُعظَمُها بِالعامِيَّة، وأنا أريد تَحسينَهُما كِلتَيْهِما.

في شَهر رَمَضان بَثَّ التِلفزيون المِصريّ بَرنامَجاً غِنائيّاً أحَبَّه مُعظَمُ المِصريّين اسمُه «فَوازير رَمَضان»، وعَلِمتُ أنَّهُ يُبَثّ أيْضاً في أقطار عَرَبيّة أُخرى. قَدَّمَتْ هذا البَرنامَج اليَوميّ مُمَثِّلة ومُغَنِيّة اسمُها «نيللي»، كانَت تَرقُص وتُغَنّي أُغنية تَصِف فيها شَيئاً وكان على مُشاهِدي البَرنامَج أنْ يَحزِروا هذا الشَيء. لكِنّي لَم أحْزِرْ أيّ شَيء وَصَفَته.

مُعظَمُ المِصريّين يُحِبّون أمَّ كُلثوم ويَسمَعونَها كُلّ يَوم. كانَت أمُّ كُلثوم مُغَنّيَة مَشهورة جِدّاً في مِصر وفي كُلِّ الوَطَنِ العَرَبيّ. بَدَأت الغِناء في العِشرينات وغَنَّتْ دونَ انقِطاع في مِصر وفي عَدَد مِن الأقطارِ العَرَبيّة حَتّى تُوُفِيَت في عام ١٩٧٥.

عبد الحليم حافظ

أمُّ كُلثوم

ومن المُغَنّينَ المَشهورينَ الَّذين ماتوا ولا يَزالُ الناس يَسمَعون أغانيهِم ويُحِبّونَها مُحَمَّد عَبدُ الوَهّاب وأمُّ كُلثوم وفَريدُ الأطْرَش وعَبدُ الحَليم حافِظ وفايزة أحمَد وغَيرُهُم.

العَرض: دع الطلاّب يستمعون إلى أغنية عربية أو أغنيتين أو يشاهدون دقيقة أو دقيقتين من برنامج تلفزيوني عربي.

النشاط: اسأل الطلاّب:
«ماذا حدث هنا؟»
«ما الموضوع الرئيس؟»

التطبيق: نشاط جماعي: اطلب من الطلاّب أن يجدوا من في الصفّ:
«شاهد برامج عربية من قبل؟»
«يعرف أغنية عربية وما هي؟»
«شاهد فيلما عربيا وما اسم الفيلم؟»
«استمع إلى فيروز/ أم كلثوم/ عبد الحليم حافظ؟»

اطلُب من الطلاّب أن يفيدوا الآخرين بما علموا من تذوّق الموسيقا العربية أو البرامج العربية ثمّ ناقشهم في أمور الأفلام والبرامج التلفزيونية والمطربين العرب أو غيرهم.

طَبعاً هُناكَ عَدَد كَبير من المُغَنّينَ الأحياء، ومن أشهَرِهِم اليَوم وَردَة الجَزائِرية ومَيّادة حِنّاوي وعَمْرو دياب ونانسي عجرم. الأولى أتَتْ إلى القاهِرة من الجَزائر في السِتّينات، والثانية من سوريا، والثالث من مِصر، أما الرابعة والأخيرة فهي لبنانيّة.

ميّادة حِنّاوي

وردة الجزائرية

عمرو دياب

نانسي عجرم

هُناكَ طَبعاً مُغَنّون ومُغَنيّات في الأقطارِ العَربيّةِ الأخرى. مُغَنيَتي المُفَضَّلَة من غَيرِ المِصريّات هي فَيروز. لا تُسمَع أغانيها في مِصر كَثيراً لكِنَّها مَوجودة في السوق. بَدَأتْ فَيروز الغِناء في سوريا (١٩٥٢) ولبنان (١٩٥٧) في خَمسيناتِ القَرنِ العِشرين وهي لاتَزال تُغَنّي إلى الآن. صَوت فَيروز جَميل جِدّاً ويُحِبُّهُ اللُبنانيّون والسوريّون خُصوصاً. كانَت مُتَزَوّجة من عاصي الرَحباني الَّذي كان موسيقِيّا مُمْتازاً ، ولَها ابن منهُ اِسمُه زِياد الرَحباني وهو موسيقيّ ومُغَنٍّ أيْضاً. غَنَّتْ فَيروز في مُعظَمِ الأقطارِ العَربيّة وفي أوروبا وأوستراليا والوِلاياتِ المُتَّحِدة حَيثُ كانَت أوَّل مُغَنِيّة عَربيّة تُغَنّي في قاعَة «كارنغي» في نيويورك وكانَ ذلِكَ في ٢٩ أيلول ١٩٧٢.

فَيْروز

بَرامِج إذاعة وتلفزيون

من الجرائِدِ العربية

قَمَرٌ صِناعيٌّ

هُناكَ مَحطّة إذاعة أو أكثَر، ومَحَطّة تِلفزيون أو أكثَر في كُلّ قُطْر عَربيّ. يوجَدُ اليوم أيْضاً مَحطّات فَضائيّة، أيْ بَرامِج تِلفزيونيّة من عِدّة أقطار عَربيّة تُبَثّ من خِلالِ القَمَرِ الصِناعيِّ العربيّ «عَرَبسات »وغيرِه من الأقمار كَنايل سات.

	الفضائية المغربية		تلفزيون
١٢,١٥	نور الإيمان، صلاة الجمعة، الأخبار	١٠,٠٠	صور وموسيقا
١,٣٠	السلسلة العربية التاريخية «ميراث السنين»	٣,٣٠	برنامج أجنبي
٢,٣٠	النشرة الجوية	٤,٠٠	لبنان هذا النهار
٣,٠٠	«مرايا» برنامج عن المرأة	٤,٣٠	رسوم متحركة
٣,٣٠	الفلم العربي «القانون واللعبة»	٥,٠٠	ستاديوم
٥,٣٠	الأخبار الدولية	٥,٣٠	رياضة من حول العالم
٥,٥٥	ألعاب القوى من مدينة كولونيا	٦,٠٠	الأرض الطيبة
٨,٣٠	الجريدة المتلفزة الرئيسية	٦,٣٠	برنامج عربي
٩,١٠	ركن المفتي	٧,٣٠	أخبار لبنان والعالم هذا المساء
٩,٣٥	السهرة السينمائية العربية «لعبة الانتقام»	٨,٠٠	برنامج أجنبي
١١,٠٠	منوعات غنائية	٨,٣٠	فيلم أجنبي
١١,١٠	الأخبار الأخيرة	١٠,٠٠	أوتوغراف
١١,٣٠	حفلات أقيمت بالمغرب	١١,٠٠	خليك بالبيت
١,٢٠	ما تيسر من الذكر الحكيم	١٢,٠٠	أخبار آخر السهرة
١,٣٠	ختام البرامج		

يُمكِنُك أنْ تَقرَأ بَرامِجَ الإذاعة والتِلفزيون في مُعظَمِ الجَرائِد العربيّة، بِما في ذلِكَ بَرامِجُ المَحطّاتِ الفَضائِيّة. في ما يَلي بَعض هذِهِ البَرامِج من جَرائِد عَربيّة. اقرأها وحاوِل أنْ تَعرِف من أيّ قُطر عَربيّ كُلّ من هذِه البَرامِج، وهل هي بَرامِج إذاعية أو تِلفزيونيّة.

القناة الأولى	
٧,٠٠	صباح الخير يا مصر والقرآن الكَريم
١٠,١٣	سينما الأطفال
١١,٠٧	نشرة الأخبار
١١,٢٧	مجلة المرأة
١٢,٢٠	إذاعة خارجية
١,٣٠	مسلسل سر الأرض
١,٤٩	اللقاء الأسبوعي للشيخ الشعراوي
٢,٣٥	مع النجوم
٢,٤٦	فلم الزهور الفاتنة
٤,٥٨	لقاء الأجيال
٥,٢٨	صندوق الدنيا
٦,٠٠	الأخبار وحدث في مثل هذا اليوم
٦,٣٠	رسالة مهرجان القراءة للجميع
٧,٣٠	مسلسل من الذي لا ينساك
٨,٣٠	حديث الروح
٩,٠٠	الأخبار
٩,٥٣	فكّر ثواني واكسب دقائق
١١,٣٦	حلقتان من مسلسل الفرسان
١٢,٠٠	آخر الأنباء
١,١٠	مسلسل ألف ليلة وليلة
١,٤٢	فوازير أم العريف
٢,٠٨	ابتسامة آخر الليل
٢,٣٣	القرآن الكريم

برامج الإذاعة	
٥,٢٧	الافتتاح
٦,١٥	الأخبار الأولى
٦,٤٥	معكم على الهواء
١١,٣٠	مسابقة الأغاني المحلية
١,٠٠	قصص من العالم
١,٣٠	الشرطة في خدمة الشعب
٢,١٥	الأخبار الثالثة
٣,٠٠	برنامج قصة في تمثيلية
٤,١٥	المجلة الاقتصادية
٥,٠٠	المسلسل اليومي
٥,٣٠	صوت القوات المسلحة
٦,٠٠	في رحاب اللغة
٨,٠٠	حكاية شاعر
١٠,٠٠	سوريَّة اليوم
١٢,٠٠	الشعر والليل موعدنا
١٢,٣٠	معالم من الوطن العربي الكبير
١,١٥	الأخبار السابعة
١,٣٠	شخصيات روائية
٢,١٥	آخر المشوار

تمرين ٤

أجِب عن هذه الأسئِلة حَسَبَ نَصِّ القِراءة.

١- ما الَّذي ساعد عَدنان على تَحسين لُغَتِهِ الإنكليزيّة؟

٢- أين شاهَد عَدنان بَرامِج عن الحَيَوانات؟

٣- اكتُب اسمَ أحدِ البَرامِجِ التلفزيونيّة في رَمَضان بِمصر.

٤- مَن المُغَنّي المَشهور من المُغَنّينَ الأحياء في مِصر؟

٥- كَم نَشرة أخبار يَبُثُّ التلفزيون المِصريّ؟

٦- في أيّ وَقت تَبدأ بَرامِجُ الإذاعةِ السوريّة ومَتى تَنتَهي؟

٧- ما اسم بَرنامَج المرأة في التلفزيون المَغرِبيّ؟

٨- ما الكَلِمةُ المُستَعمَلَة في المَغرِب بَدَلاً مِن «مُسَلسَل»؟

٩- مَتى يُمكِن أنْ تَسمَعَ الموسيقا والأغاني في تلفزيون لُبنان؟

١٠- ما البَرنامَجُ الَّذي يُبَثّ مِن مِصر في الساعةِ السادِسَة مَساءً؟ اشرحْه كَما تَفهَمُه بِالعَربيّة أو الإنكليزيّة.

اكتُب اسم الشَخص أو الشيءِ الَّذي تَصِفُهُ الجُمَلَ الآتية:

١١- هي مِن الجَزائِر.

١٢- يُشاهِدُهُ عَدنان مِن مَحَطّة «إن بي سي».

١٣- هي بِالعاميَّةِ المِصريّة.

١٤- يُحِبُّها اللُبنانيّون والسوريّون.

اكتُبْ «خطَأ» أو «صَواب» بِجانِب كُلِّ جُملَةٍ وصَحِّح الجُمَلَ الخَطأ.

١٥- كانَ عَدنان يُشاهِدُ التِلفزيون في حَلَب أكثَر مِن أمريكا.

١٦- لا تُعجِب عَدنان الإعلاناتُ التِجاريّة.

١٧- على مُشاهِدي بَرنامَج «فَوازير رَمَضان» أنْ يُغَنّوا مع المُغَنّية.

١٨- تُوفِيَت فايزة أحمَد عامَ ١٩٧٥.

١٩- يُبَثّ مُسَلسَل «ألف لَيلة ولَيلة» مِن التِلفزيون المَغرِبيّ.

٢٠- «ابتسامة آخِرِ اللَيل» هي آخِر فِقرة في التلفزيون المِصريّ.

تمرين ٥

عَرِّف العِبارات التالية حَسَبَ نَصِّ القِراءة:

١- التِلفازُ السِلكيّ
٢- اللُغَةُ العَربيّةُ الفَصيحة
٣- فَوازير رَمَضان
٤- زِياد الرَحباني
٥- مَعالِم من الوَطَنِ العربيّ الكَبير
٦- رِياضة مِن حَولِ العالَم

تمرين ٦

المُحادَثة: اسأل زَميلك في الصَفّ ما هو بَرنامَجُهُ المُفَضَّل التلفزيونيّ أو الإذاعيّ.

اِحكِ لِزَميلك في الصَفّ:

* لِماذا يُعجِبك هذا البَرنامَج أكثَر من غَيرِه
* مَن بَطَلُ البَرنامَج وما شَخصيّتُه
* مَتى تُشاهِد البَرنامَج أو تَستمع إليه ومع مَن
* مُنذُ مَتى بَدأت تَتَفرّج على بَرنامَجك المُفَضّل

حاوِل أن تَستَخدِمَ الكَلِماتِ المَوجودة في المُرَبّعات أدناه.

وعِند اِنتِهاء النَشاط، اِحكِ لِزُملائك في الصَفّ ما عَلِمت منه عن بَرنامَجِه المُفَضَّل.

اِعْتبَر	وَصَفَ	يَبْدو	يَظْهَر	اِسْتَمْتَعَ بِـ	اِشْتَرَكَ	اِسْتَمَعَ (إلى)	مَوجة
يُمْكِنُني	طَبْعاً	على أنْ	مُسَلْسَل	أسْتَطيعُ أنْ	يُعْجِبُني	شَخص ج أشْخاص	إذاعة

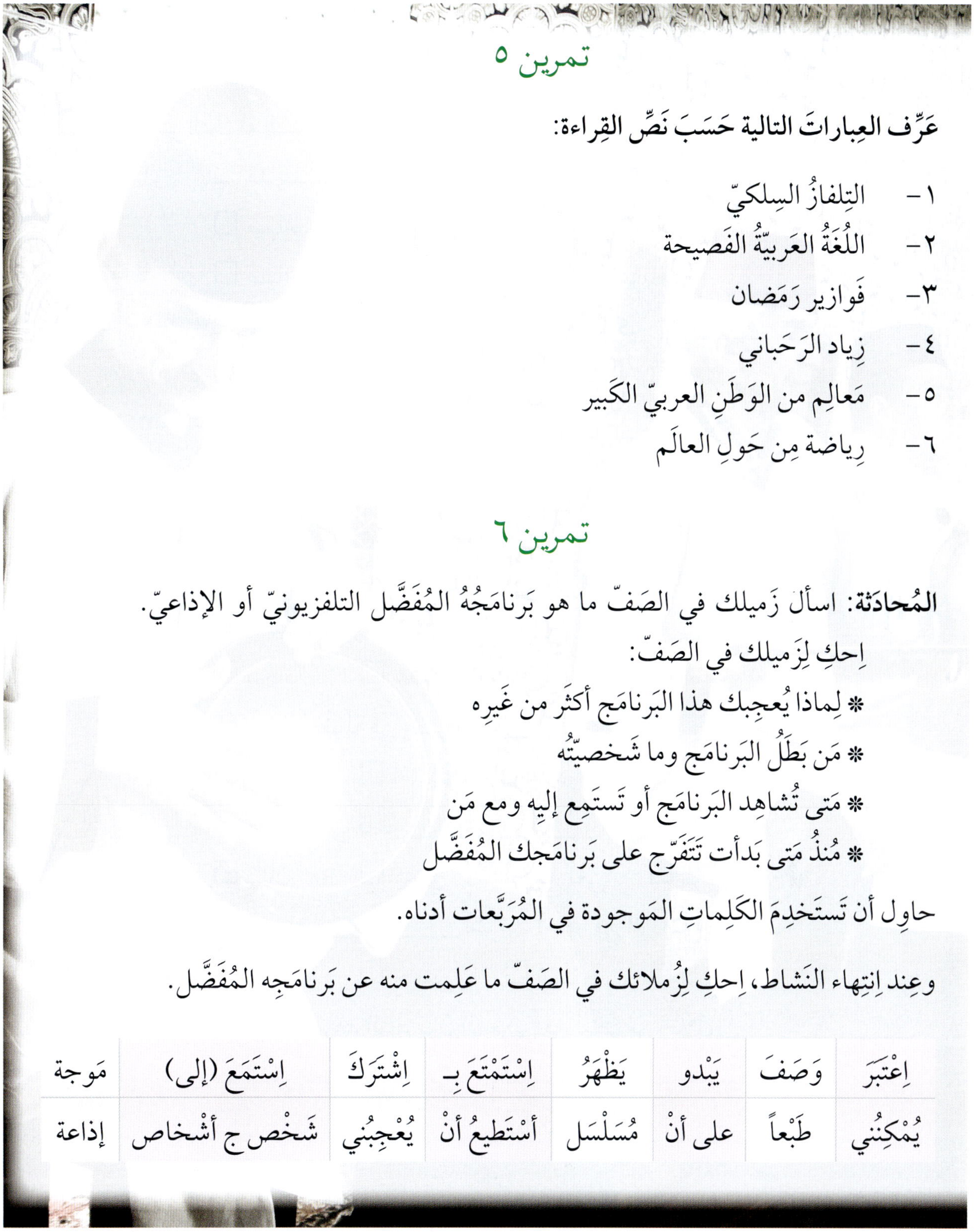

الموسيقا المَغرِبيّة التَقليديّة

تمرين ٧

اختَر التكمِلةَ المُناسِبة حَسَبَ نَصِّ القِراءة.

١- يُشاهِد عَدنان الأخبار ______________ .

☐ صَباحاً ☐ مَساءً

☐ صَباحاً وظُهراً ☐ صَباحاً ومَساءً

٢- نَشرةُ الأخبار في المَحطّاتِ التِجاريّةِ الأمريكيّة ______________ .

☐ طَويلة ☐ سَريعة ☐ جَميلة ☐ قَصيرة

٣- تَظهَرُ الإعلاناتُ التِجاريّة ______________ الأخبار في أمريكا.

☐ دونَ ☐ قَبْلَ ☐ بَعْدَ ☐ خِلالَ

٤- مَحَطّة «بي بي إس» ______________ .

☐ طَويلة ☐ تِجاريّة ☐ عامّة ☐ عِلميّة

٥- نِظامُ البَثِّ التلفزيونيّ اللاسلكيّ ______________ .

☐ مَجّانيّ ☐ عِلميّ ☐ عَديد ☐ عاميّ

٦- المُغَنّيةُ المُفضّلة في مِصر هي ______________ .

☐ فَيروز ☐ أمّ كُلثوم ☐ مادونا ☐ فايزة أحمد

٧- غَنَّت فَيروز في قاعة ______________ .

☐ لُبْنان ☐ كِنِدي ☐ كارنِغي ☐ الرَحباني

٨- هُناكَ ______________ نَشرات أخبار في الإذاعةِ السوريَّة.

☐ أربع ☐ خَمس ☐ سِتّ ☐ سَبع

٩- يُمكِن أنْ يُشاهَدَ التلفزيون المَغربيّ في لُبنان مِن خِلالِ ______________ .

☐ القَمَرِ الصِناعيّ العَرَبيّ ☐ مَحَطّة تلفزيونيّة مَغربيّة

☐ الإذاعةِ المَغربيّة ☐ البَثّ التلفزيونيّ المِصريّ

العود

تمرين ٨

صَنِّف كَلِمات مِن النَصوص الرئيسة تَحتَ الفِئات الآتية:

١	مَحطّات تلفزيون	٢	مُسَلسَلات	٣	برامِج	٤	إذاعة	٥	مُغَنّون ومُغَنيات	٦	لُغة

تمرين ٩

أعِدْ تَرتيبَ الكَلِمات في كُلّ مَجموعة لِتُشَكِّل جُمَلاً مُفيدة.

١- مِن – إلى – المُفَضَّلة – الشابكة – أغانيَّ – أستَمِعُ

٢- دِمَشقَ – صَباحاً – إذاعةُ – الخامِسة – بَثَّها – تَبدَأ – الساعةِ – في

٣- مُذيعةً – إذاعةِ – أختُ – في – حَلَب – تَعمَلُ – صَديقي

تمرين ١٠

أعِدْ تَرتيبَ الجُمَل لِتُشَكِّل فِقرة مُفيدة دونَ تغيير مَكانِ الجُملةِ الأولى.

١- أوَّلُ شَيء أفعَلُه صَباحاً هو الذَهاب إلى الحَمّام.

٢- بَعد مُشاهَدة مُسَلسَلي المُفَضَّل أنام نِصف ساعة فَقَط.

٣- في الساعةِ الثامِنة صَباحاً أذهَب إلى عَمَلي.

٤- في المَساء أشاهِد أنا وزَوجي فيلماً مِن التِلفاز أو مِن الإذاعة.

٥- بَعدَ ذلِكَ أجلِس أمامَ التِلفاز وأشاهِدُ الأخبار أثناءَ تَناوُلِ الفَطور.

٦- حين أعود إلى البَيت بَعدَ الظُهر أشاهِد مُسَلسَلي المُفَضَّل.

٧- خِلالَ العَمَل استَمِع إلى الإذاعة.

تمرين ١١

تَمرينُ المُشاهَدة: شاهِدوا الدَرْسَ الدرسَ الثاني والعشرين على الشابِكة.

١- مَن مِن المُطرِبينَ العَرَب الّذين يَسْتَمِع إليهم الناس في مِصر؟ ________

____

____

٢- املأ الفراغات في الحوار التالي:

مايكل: من هو ________ العَرَبيّ ________ أو ________ العَرَبيّة ________ ستيف؟

ستيف: أنا أحِبّ فَيروز جداً و________ إلَيها كُلّ يَوم في الصَباح وأحِبّ أيضاً ماجِدة الرومي.

مايكل: وأنت سامر؟

سامر: طبعاً ________ فَيروز وأحِبّ ________ إلى عَبد الحَليم حافِظ.

مايكل: وأنت عدنان؟

عدنان: طبعاً فَيروز ________ ________ ________ ________ ________ وَديع الصافي ومُحمّد عَبدُه وصَباح فَخري وراغِب علامة وعَمرو دياب فأنا عِندي ________ لَهُم.

سامر: وأنت مايكل من هو ________ العَرَبيّ ________ أو ________ العَرَبيّة ________؟

مايكل: أنا بِصراحة ________ ________ ________ فَيروز كثيراً وأحِبّ أن ________ عَمرو دياب وراغِب علامة.

ستيف: ومَن هو ________ الغَربيّ ________ عَدنان؟

٣- ماذا يَفعَلُ عدنان ليُحَسِّنَ لُغَتَهُ الإنكليزيّة؟ ________________

____

٤- لِلمُحادَثة: مِن المَشهَد المَرئيّ:

في بِدايةِ المَشهَد نَرى مايكل وصَديقَهُ سامِر يَزوران بَعضَ الأماكِنِ السياحيّة في دِمَشق بِما فيها سوقُ الحَميديّة وقَهوةُ النوفرة والجامِعُ الأُمَويّ. ما هي الأماكِن في سوريا أرَدتَ أن تَزورها لَو كُنت في مَطرَح مايكَل ولِماذا؟ وإذا زُرت سوق الحَميديّة، ما هي الأشياء التي تودُّ شِراءَها ولِماذا؟

١- التَعبير عن الضَرورة بِاستِخدام على + أنْ "have to"

في نُصوص هذا الدَرس، قَدّمنا التَعبير على + أنْ الّذي هُو من الطُرُق العَديدة بالعَربيّة كي نُعَبِّر عن الضَرورة. يَبدأ هذا التَعبير بِحَرفِ الجَرّ على، ومع أنّ الفِعل يَجِب يَسبُق التَعبير نَظَريّاً (theoretically)، فأنّه مَحذوف (omitted) في الواقِع.

حين نَستَخدِم على + أنْ، يأتي اسم أو ضَمير مُتَصِّل أو شبه جُملة بعد حَرفِ الجَرّ على. هيّا نَنظُر إلى مِثال مأخوذ من النَصّ الرئيس:

١	على مُشاهِدي البَرنامَج أنْ يَحزِروا هذا الشَيء.	*The program's viewers have to guess what it is.*

في المِثال ١ أعلاه، تأتي الإضافة مُشاهِدي البَرنامَج بَعد حَرف الجَرّ على. فاعِلُ الجُملة مُشاهِدي البَرنامَج في حالة الجَرّ لأنّه مَجرور بِالجار على. وكَما تَعلَم، أنّ الحَرف أنْ يُقدِّم الأفعال بِالعَرَبيّة وفي هذِه الجُملة يُقَدِّم الفِعل يَحزِروا الّذي يأتي في المُضارِع المَنصوب (راجِع الباب الأوّل في الدرس الثامِن عشر).

حين يَلي حَرف الجَرّ على ضَمير مُتَّصِل فَتَتَحَوّل الألَف في على إلى ياء. وإذا أخَذنا الجُملة من المِثال ١ لِيُبَيِّن هذه العَمَليّة وَاستَبدَلنا (substituted) الفاعِل بِضَمير مُتَّصِل، فَسَيكون لَدَينا النَتيجة الآتية:

٢	عليهِم أنْ يَحزِروا هذا الشَيء.	*They have to guess what it is.*

العَرض: اعرض على الطلاّب بعض الأشياء التي عليك وعليهم الفعل مثلاً:
«عليّ أن أحضر إلى الصفّ قبلكم.»
«عليّ أن أحضّر للصفّ كلّ يوم!»
«على الطلاّب أن يقرأوا الدرس قبل أن يأتوا إلى الصف»
«عليكم أن تأتوا إلى الدرس في الساعة كذا.»
«على كلّ طالب أن يكتب يومياته بالعربية.»
«علينا ألاّ ننسى عيد ميلاد فلان.»

النشاط: اسأل الطلاّب هذه الأسئلة أو مثلها:
«ماذا عليك أن تفعل في عطلة نهاية الأسبوع هذه؟»
«ماذا عليك أن تفعلي بعد أن تستيقظي من النوم؟»
«ماذا عليك ألا تفعلي بعد التخرج؟»
«ماذا على الرئيس أن يفعل لينجح؟»
«ماذا على المطرب أن يفعل ليصبح مشهوراً؟»

التطبيق: في مجموعات من اثنين أو ثلاثة: اطلب من كل مجموعة أن يسألوا بعضهم بعضاً سؤالاً أو سؤالين من الأسئلة أعلاه أو مثلها ثمّ اطلّب منهم أن يفيدوا الآخرين بما علموا من المعلومات.

نستطيع أن نستبدِلَ أنْ المَصدَريّة بِمَصدر، كَما نَرى في المِثال ٣ أدناه:

٣	علَيْهِم حَزْرُ هذا الشَيء.	*They must guess the thing.*

مُلاحَظة: إذا أَرَدت اِستِخدام المَاضي مع على + أن، فَلَيسَ علَيك إلاّ زيادة كانَ أمام على. انظُر إلى المِثال ٤ أدناه:

٤	كانَ علَينا أنْ نَحزِرَ هذا الشَيء.	*We had to guess what it was.*

مُلاحَظة: إذا أَرَدت أن تَتَكَلَّم في صيغة المُتَكَلِّم مُستَخدِماً على، أي (أنا + على) فَعلَيك أن تَزيد شَدّة على الياء، مَثَلاً:

٥	كانَ علَيَّ أنْ أحزِرَ هذا الشَيء.	*I had to guess what it was.*

تمرين ١٢

التَحويل من الإنكليزيّة إلى العَرَبيّة: اِستخدِم التَعبير على + أن في تَحويلِ الفِقرةِ الآتية:

What do we have to do today? I have to have a cup of coffee after I get up in the morning! Likewise, my father has to read the paper while he eats breakfast. After that, he has to go to work, and I have to go to school. I had to do my homework last night before I went to sleep, but I didn't finish it, so now I have to do it before I get to school. I have to get to school early today to talk to Sāmī about our soccer game tonight. We have to get to the field at 7:00 p.m. for our big game. After the game, Sāmī told me that he has to watch his favorite TV program, so I might watch it with him . . . , but I don't have to.

٢- التَعبير عن الاِحتِمال بِاستِخدام الفِعْل أَمْكَنَ "to be possible"

إلَيك طَريق من الطُرُق نَستَطيع بِواسِطتِه أن نُعَبِّر عن الاِحتِمال وهو بِاستِخدام الفِعل أَمْكَن الّذي يَتَصَرّف مِثل الفِعل المَعروف أَعْجَب من حَيثُ الضَمير المُتَّصِل. إنّ الفَرق بَين الفِعلَين هو أنّ الضَمير المُتّصِل لِلفِعل أَعْجَب هو مَفعول بِه بَينما الضَمير المُتَّصِل لِلفِعل أَمْكَنَ فاعِل كَما نَرى في المِثال ٦ أدناه:

٦	هَلْ يُمكِنُكَ مُساعَدَتي؟	*Are you capable of helping me?*

قَد يَكون المَفعول بِه لِلفِعل أَمْكَنَ مَصدراً، كَما رأَينا في المِثال ٦ أعلاه، أو مِثل كُلّ الأفعالِ العَرَبيّة نَستَطيع اِستِبدالَه بِـ أَنْ المَصدَريّة كَما يُوجَد في المِثال ٧:

٧	هَلْ يُمكِنُكَ أَنْ تُساعِدَني؟	*Is it possible for you to help me?*

الفاعِل في المِثالَين ٦ و٧ هو الضَمير المُتَّصِل ـك، لكِن يُمكِنُه أن يَكون اسماً كَذلِكَ كَما نَرى في المِثال ٨ أدناه:

٨	هَلْ يُمكِنُ أَحمَدُ أنْ يُساعِدَني؟	*Can Ahmed help me?*

هُناكَ بَعضُ الأفعال بِاللُغةِ العَرَبيّةِ الّتي قَد يَكون لَها مَفعول بِه مع ضَمير مُتّصِل (المِثال ٧) أو اسم (المِثال ٨) والفِعل ساعَدَ هو فِعل آخَر من أفعال هذا النَوع. والضَمائر الّتي تَلحَقُ الأفعال هي نَفس الضَمائر الّتي تَلحَقُ الأسماء ماعَدا المُتَكَلِّم المُفرَد.

نَستطيع أن نَرى الفَرق في الهِجاء والاِستِخدام لِلضَمير المُتَّصِل في المُتَكَلِّم المُفرَد في المِثالَين ٦ و٧ أعلاه. في المِثال ٦، حَرف الياء قد لَحِق بِالمَصدَر مُساعَدة ونَتيجة هذه العَمليّة هي الكَلِمة المُرَكَّبة مُساعَدَتي أي (my help). أمّا في المِثال ٧، فقَد لَحِق المَفعول بِه ني بِالفِعل تُساعِدُ وأنتَج تُساعِدُني أي (you help me).

مُلاحَظة: إنّ النون الّتي تَفصِل الفِعل عن الياء نُسَمّيها نون الوِقاية وهي زائدة أي لَيس لَها وَظيفة نَحوية.

العَرض: استعمل الفعل أمكن كثيراً في جمل أو قصة ثمّ اجعل حواراً مع طالب أو طالبين واسأله أسئلة مثل:
«يا مايكل، هل يمكنك أن تأخذني معك بالسيّارة إلى المدينة؟»
«لا يمكنني أن أحمل هذه الطاولة وحدي.»
«يمكن أن تكتبوا صفحة واحدة ليوم غد.»

النشاط: اسأل الطلاّب ماذا يمكنهم أن يفعلوا أو لا يفعلوا مثلاً:
«هل يمكنك أن تتكلم بالـ(لغة ما)؟»
«هل يمكنك أن تغني جيداً؟»
«هل يمكنك العزف على آلة موسيقية؟»
«هل يمكنك أن تسوقي سيّارتك إلى الحفلة الموسيقية؟»
«هل يمكنك أن تعطيني مِليون دولار؟»
«كيف يمكنك أن تحصل على درجة عالية في هذا الصف؟»

التطبيق: نشاط جماعي: افعل تمرين ١٢.

العَرض: اكتب قصة قصيرة تستعمل فيها التعبير لم يعد كثيراً، مثل الآتي:

«لم أعد أحب مشاهدة التلفاز لأن البرامج المعروضة فيه لم تعد تعجبني أبداً. ألم يعد هناك مسلسلات شيقة على التلفاز. ولهذا السبب أنا لم أعد أجلس أمام التلفاز ساعة بعد ساعة في انتظار برنامج جيد.»

الممارسة: اسأل الطلاّب أسئلة تتطلب التعبير لم يعد في أجوبتهم، كالآتي:
«هل تلعب بألعاب الأطفال؟»
«هل تدرس في المدرسة الابتدائية؟»
«هل تشاهد برنامج افتح يا سمسم؟»
«هل تركب درّاجتك إلى كل مكان؟»

التطبيق: في مجموعات من اثنين أو ثلاثة: وزّع على الطلاّب ورقة مكتوب عليها أسئلة مثل الأسئلة أعلاه واطلُب منهم أن يحاولوا استخدام التعبير لم يعد في أجوبتهم.

الخُلاصة

١- ضَمير المَتكَلِّم المُفرَد الّذي يَلحَق الاسم هو ي (مِثل بَيتي)

٢- ضَمير المُتكَلِّم المُفرَد الّذي يَلحق الفِعل هو ني (مِثل شاهَدَني)

		الضَميرُ المُتَّصِل		المَفعول بِهِ	
٩	أنا	←	ي	←	ني

٣- اِستِخدام لَمْ يَعُدْ “no longer”

نَستَخدِم الفِعل عادَ / يَعودُ (to return) في هذا التَعبير لكِن حين يَدخُل حَرف النَفي لَمْ عليهِ فَيَصير المَعنى (no longer) كَما نَرى في المِثال ١٠ أدناه.

١٠	لَمْ يَعُدْ أحمَدُ يَسكُنُ هُنا.	*Ahmed no longer lives here.*

لاحِظ أنّ الفِعل في التَعبير لَمْ يَعُدْ في المُضارِع المَجزوم والفِعل يَسكُن الّذي يَليه في الجُملة كَذلِك في المُضارِع. وهذا يَعنى أنّ الفِعل الّذي يَلي التَعبير لَمْ يَعُدْ دائماً في المُضارِع ولَهُما نَفس الفاعِل. إذا غَيَّرنا الفاعِل من التَذكير إلى التأنيث فَسَنرى أنّ الفِعلَين صارا مُؤنَّثين، كَما يُوجَد في المِثال ١١ أدناه:

١١	لَمْ تَعُدْ سَلمى تَسكُنُ هُنا.	*Salmā no longer lives here.*

تمرين ١٣

المُحادَثة: مَن مِن زُملائك في الصَفّ:

1. no longer watches a lot of TV
2. no longer likes to watch *The Simpsons*
3. no longer listens to American music, but prefers to listen to Arabic music
4. no longer has time to play sports, but has to study
5. is able to watch Arabic programs on TV
6. is able to cook Arabic food
7. is able to listen to an Arabic broadcasting station

أخبِر الجَميع بِما عَلِمت من المَعلومات بعد اِنتِهاء النَشاط.

٤- مُراجَعة الاسم المَوصول العامّ ما

عُموماً يَدُل الاسمُ المَوصولُ العامّ على الأسماء غير العاقِلة أي (non-rational). ومن هذِه الناحية، يُشبِه الطَريقة الّتي تُستخدَم فيها الكَلِمة (what) بِالإنكليزيّة:

١٢	آكُلُ ما أريد.	*I eat what I want.*

في المِثال ١٢ أعلاه، الاسمُ المَوصولُ العامّ ما يَحلّ مَحَلَّ الاسمِ المَوصولِ الخاصّ الّذي يَعني الشيء الّذي (راجِع الباب ٤ في الدرس التاسع عشر). الجَدير بِالذِكرِ أنَّ حُروف الجَرّ قد تَلحَق بِالاسم المَوصول ما، إلَيكم بَعض الأمثِلة من هذا النَوع:

	مِن + ما = مِمّا	
١٣	لَمْ يُعجِبْني شَيءٌ مِمّا سَمِعتُ.	*I didn't like any of what I heard.*

في المِثال ١٣، مِمّا كَلِمة مُرَكَّبة من حَرف الجَرّ مِن والاسم المَوصول ما.

	عَن + ما = عَمّا	
١٤	لا أعرِفُ عَمّا يَتكَلّمونَ.	*I don't know what they are talking about.*

في المِثال ١٤، الكَلِمة المُرَكَّبة عَمّا مُكَوّنة من حَرفِ الجَرّ عن والاسم المَوصول ما.

	بِـ + ما = بِما	
١٥	يَمكِنُكَ أنْ تَأتيَ إلى هُنا بِما عَلَيْكَ مِن مَلابِس.	*You could come here in whatever clothes you are wearing.*

تمرين ١٤

حَوِّل إلى العربية ما يلي بِاسْتِعمالِ ما.

1. Write down in Arabic what you heard on the news.
2. I like what I see (what I see pleases me).
3. She is happy with what she has.
4. You may purchase these Arabic books with whatever money you have on you.

٥- الحَرف أنْ بَعد ظَرف الزَمان

بِالإنكليزيّة، نَستطيع أن نَستَخدِم جُملة كامِلة بعَد ظَرف الزَمان أو المَكان:

١٦	We had dinner after we had gone to the movies.

في اللُغة العَربيّة، الحَرف أنْ مُستَخدَم كي يَفصِل الفِعل عن بَعدَ وقَبلَ.

١٧	تناوَلنا العَشاءَ بَعدَ أنْ ذَهَبْنا إلى السينَما.	We ate supper after going to the movies.

يُمكِن أن نَستَخدِمَ الفِعل أو المَصدَر بعد ظَرفي الزَمان قَبلَ وبَعدَ، فَبِإمكانِنا اِستِخدام المَصدَر. دَعنا نَنظُر إلى نَفس الجُملة الّتي ظَهَرَت في المِثال ١٧ لكِن هذِه المَرّة يأتي المَصدر بَعد ظَرف الزَمان.

١٨	تَناوَلنا العَشاءَ بَعدَ ذَهابِنا إلى السينَما.	We ate supper after going to the movies.

بَعد ظَرفِ الزَمان قَبلَ نَستَخدِمُ الفِعل المُضارِع فَقَط لا غير، وبَعد ظرف الزَمان بَعدَ نَستَخدِمُ الفِعل المُضارِع أو الماضي. تأمّل المِثال الآتي:

١٩	بَدأتُ دِراسةَ اللُغةِ العَربيّةِ قَبْلَ أنْ أُسافِرَ إلى مِصر.	I began studying Arabic before I traveled to Egypt.

العَرض: من الصعب على الطالب الأمريكي ألا يستخدم فعلاً ماضياً بعد قبل أن. من المفيد أن تستعمل كثيراً من أنشطة الترجمة كي تثبت هذه الفكرة في أذهانهم وتسهّل عليهم إدماجها في كلامهم.

الممارسة: اكتب بعض الجمل بالإنكليزية واطلب من الطلاّب ترجمتها سوياً في نشاط جماعي في الصف. يستحسن أن تستخدم فعلاً ماضياً قبل الكلمة (before) في كل جملة إنكليزية وعليهم أن يترجموها مستخدمين الفعل المضارع بعد قبل أن بالعربية، مثل الجمل الآتية:

1. Before I went to Syria, I had studied in Egypt.
2. Before I started reading, I was watching TV.
3. Before I went to sleep, I had eaten dinner.
4. Before I spoke to my mother on the phone, I had spoken to my father.
5. Before I drank coffee, I had read the newspaper.

الخُلاصة

١- لابُدّ من اِستِخدام فِعل مُضارِع بَعد ظَرف الزَمان قَبلَ، بَينما نَستَطيع اِستِخدام فِعل ماضٍ أو مُضارِع بعَد ظَرف الزَمان بَعدَ.

٢- نَستَخدِم أنْ كَي نَفصِل الظَرف عن الفِعل، وإذا أتى اسم بَعد ظَرف الزَمان، فَلا نَستَخدِم أنْ إطلاقاً.

تمرين ١٥

املأ الفراغ: اِختَر ظَرفَ الزمانِ المُناسِب وَفقاً لِلسياق.

قَبْلَ	قَبْلَ أنْ	بَعْدَ	بَعْدَ أنْ

١- عُدْتُ إلى البيت __________ تكلمتُ مع أصدِقائي.
٢- لا يُمْكِن مَها أنْ تُسافِر إلى مِصر إلاّ __________ تَحْصُلَ على تأشيرة.
٣- شاهَد مُصطَفى المُسَلسَل __________ ينام.
٤- لَمْ يخرُجْ أحَد مِن الحَفلة إلاّ __________ نهايتها.
٥- يَشرَبُ العَرَب عادة فِنجان قَهوة __________ الأكل.
٦- رَكِبتُ الحافلة __________ انتظَرتُها طَويلاً.
٧- يقولُ الأطِباء لا تأكُل __________ السِباحة.

تمرين ١٦

المُحادَثة: مَن مِن زُملائك في الصَفّ:

1. read before they went to sleep last night
2. usually reads before they go to sleep
3. works out before they go to school
4. works out after they return home
5. listens to music before class.
6. listens to music after class.

أخبِر الجَميع بِما عِلمت من المَعلومات بعد اِنتِهاء النَشاط.

٦- الاسم بِضْع "a few"

غالِباً ما نَستَخدِم بِضع حين نَتكَلّم عن الأعداد ما بَين ٣ إلى ١٠، وفي الواقِع، إنّ الأعداد بَين ٣-١٠ والاسم بِضع لَهُما خاصيّة (characteristic) مُشترَكة ألا وهي حُكم العَدَد المُفرَد أي يُخالِف المَعدود دائماً. نَستَخدِم بِضع مع المؤنَّث وبِضعة مع المُذَكَّر. لاحِظ أنّ المَعدود بَعد بِضع نَكِرة غَير مَعرِفة.

٢٠	عِندي بِضْعُ صَديقات في الدارِ البَيضاء.	صَديقة مُفرَد مُؤنَّث لِذا نَستخدِم بِضْع
٢١	قَرَأتُ بِضْعَةَ كُتُبٍ عن تاريخ أوروبا.	كِتاب مُفرَد مُذَكَّر لِذا نَستخدِم بِضعة

تمرين ١٧

حَوِّل ما يلي إلى العَرَبيّة بِاسْتِعمالِ بِضْعة أو بِضْع .

1. I read a few newspapers on the plane.
2. I spent a few weeks in Beirut.
3. My friend bought a few books on the Arab world when she was in Syria.
4. I stayed in the hotel for a few days.

تمرين ١٨

اكتُبْ «خَطأ» أو «صَواب» بِجانِبِ كُلِّ جُملَة وصَحِّح الجُمَلَ الخَطأ.

١- السَيِّدةُ الّتي تَتكلّم على الشَريطِ المُسجَّل مُتَزَوِّجة.

٢- مُسَلسَل «الجَوارِح» مِن دَولةِ الإمارات.

أجِب عَن هذه الأسئلةِ حَسَبَ النَصِّ المُسَجَّل.

٣- لِماذا يُعجِب هذِه السَيِّدة مُسَلسَلُ الجَوارِح؟

٤- أينَ تُشاهِدُ السَيِّدةُ البَرامِجَ التونِسيّة والمَغربيّة؟

اَختَر التكملةَ المُناسِبة حَسَبَ النَصّ المُسَجَّل.

٥- صُوِّرَ مُسَلسَلُ «الجَوارِح» في ________.

☐ الصَحراء ☐ سوريَّة ☐ المَغرِب

٦- مَوعِد مُسَلسَلِ «الجَوارِح» ________ .

☐ التاسِعة صَباحاً ☐ التاسِعة مَساءً ☐ الحادية عَشرَة

٧- لُغة مُسَلسَلِ «الجَوارِح» ________ .

☐ العامِيّةُ السوريَّة ☐ العامِيّةُ المِصريّة ☐ العَربيةُ الفَصيحة

٨- تُشاهِدُ السَيِّدةُ المُسَلسَلاتِ العامِيَّة مِن تلفزيون ________ .

☐ تونِس ☐ المَغرِب ☐ دِمَشق وعَمّان

أكمِلِ الجُمَلَ الآتية مِن النَصِ المُسَجَّل.

٩- يَبُثُّ التلفزيون هذِه الأيّام مُسَلسَلاً ________.

١٠- هُناكَ طَبعاً مُسَلسَلات أُخرى لكِنّها لَيْسَتْ تاريخِيّة ________.

المُفْرَدات

استمِع إلى المُفْرَدة بالعَرَبيّة ثم أعِد نُطْقَها مرّتين.

for the sake of, because of	أجْل (مِن أجْلِ)
broadcasting station	إذاعَة ج ات (n. f.)
to listen	اِسْتَمَعَ (يَسْتَمِعُ) اِسْتِماع (v.)
to enroll in, to subscribe to	اِشْتَرَكَ (يَشْتَرِكُ) اِشْتِراك (v.)
song	أُغْنية ج أغانٍ (n., f.)
to be possible	أمْكَنَ (يُمكِنُ) إمْكان (v.)
to broadcast	بَثَّ (يَبُثُّ) بَثّ (v.)
a few	بِضْع (n.)
to guess	حَزَرَ (يحْزِرُ) حَزْر (v.)
to improve, to make better	حَسَّنَ (يحَسِّنُ) تَحْسين (v.)
a living person	حَيّ ج أحْياء (n., m.)
during, through	خِلال (prep.)
to dance	رَقَصَ (يرقُصُ) رَقْص (v.)
wire	سِلْك ج أسْلاك (n., m.)
to hear	سَمِعَ (يَسْمَع) سَمْع (v.)
tape	شَريط ج أشْرِطة (n., m.)
person	شَخْص ج أشْخاص (n., m.)
honestly, candidly	صَراحةً (بِصَراحةٍ) (n., f.)
of course	طَبْعاً (adv.)
nature	طَبيعة (n., f.)
child	طِفْل ج أطْفال (n., m.)

to appear, to become visible . . . . (v.) ظَهَرَ (يَظهَرُ) ظُهور

to go back, to return . . . . (v.) عادَ (يعودُ) عَوْد

colloquial, vulgar, dialectal . . . . (adj.) عاميّ

to sing . . . . (v.) غَنّى (يُغَنّي) غِناء

riddle . . . . (n., f.) فَزّورة ج فَوازير (عامية مِصرية)

pure, good, clear, standard,. . . . . (adj.) فَصيح
or literary, Arabic

space . . . . (n., m.) فَضاء

moon, satellite . . . . (n. m.) قَمَر ج أقْمار

channel . . . . (n., f.) قَناة ج قَنَوات

cable. . . . . (n., m.) كيبِل

what . . . . (relative pronoun) ما

to die . . . . (v.) ماتَ (يموتُ) مَوْت

married man . . . . (n., m.) مُتَزَوِّج ج ون

free of charge . . . . (adj.) مَجّانيّ

announcer . . . . (n., m.) مُذيع ج ون

series, serial . . . . (n., m.) مُسَلسَل ج مُسَلسَلات

entertainer . . . . (n., m.) مُطْرِب ج مُطْرِبون

singer . . . . (n., m.) مُغَنٍّ ج ون

interview . . . . (n. f.) مُقابَلة ج ات

excellent. . . . . (adj.) مُمْتاز ج ون

actor, representative . . . . (n., m.) مُمَثِّل ج ون

by means of, via. . . . . مِن خِلالِ

wave. . . . . (n., f.) مَوْجة ج ات

نَشْرة ج نَشَرات (.n., f) .... bulletin, report

نِظام ج أَنْظِمة (.n., m) .... system

رَقص الطوارق التَقليديّ في ليبيا

الدرس الثالث والعشرون

أهدافُ الدَرس

- وَصْفُ المِهنة والوَظيفة
- وَصْفُ الأنْشِطةِ المُتعَلِّقة بالسَفَر
- التَقديم لِلحَرف الفاء
- تَعَلُّم وَظيفة الحَرف قَدْ
- التَقديم لِلبَدَل the permutative

رُكنُ المُفْرَداتِ الجَديدة

اِرْتَفَعَ (يَرْتَفِعُ) اِرْتِفاع	*to rise*
أَصَرَّ (يُصِرُّ) إصرار	*to insist*
اِعْتَقَدَ (يَعْتَقِدُ) اِعْتِقاد (أنَّ)	*to think (that)*
اِنْتَظَرَ (يَنْتَظِرُ) اِنْتِظار	*to wait*
تَعَرَّف (يَتَعَرَّفُ) تَعَرُّف (على)	*to become acquainted (with)*
تَعَوَّدَ (يَتَعَوَّدُ) تَعَوُّد (على)	*to be accustomed (to)*
حَضَرَ (يَحْضُرُ) حُضور	*to attend*
خارِج	*outside; abroad*
عَبَرَ (يَعبُرُ) عُبور	*to cross (a street)*
غادَرَ (يُغادِرُ) مُغادَرة	*to leave*
مُواصَلات	*means of transportation*

المُفرداتُ الجَديدةُ في صُوَر عَديدة

ضَحِكَ (يَضْحَكُ) ضِحْك

دَفَعَ (يَدْفَعُ) دَفْع

عَكْس

صَحَفيّ ج ون

مُزْدَحِم (بِـ)

مُلَوَّث

هَدية ج هَدايا

مَصْنَع ج مَصانِع

تمرين ١

واقِق بين كَلِمات العَمودِ الأيْمَن وكلِمات العَمودِ الأيْسَر واكتُب الكَلِمَتين في الوَسَط.

١-	صَحيفة		رياضة
٢-	شَريط		أسرة
٣-	لاعِب		نادِل
٤-	تأشيرة دُخول		اِسْتَضاف
٥-	عائِلة		مَصرِف
٦-	مَطعَم		جَريدة
٧-	نُقود		مَنزِل
٨-	دار		مُسَجِّلة
			جَواز سَفَر

تمرين ٢

اخترَ الكَلِمةَ الّتي لا تُناسِب باقي الكَلِمات في كُلِّ مَجْموعة وبَيِّن السَبَب.

١- صَحَفِيّ	مَجلّة	عاصِمة	جَريدة
٢- مَصرِف	عائلة	أسرة	أقرِباء
٣- مُواصلات	قِطار	طائِرة	حَلوى
٤- نامَ	تَجَوَّلَ	سافَرَ	مَشى

عَدنان في مَدينة دِنْـفر

في عُطلة فَصلِ الرَبيع سافَرَ عَدنان مارتيني بِالطائِرة مِن مَدينة كَلمبَس في أوهايو حَيثُ يَدرُس عِلمَ الحاسوب في جامِعة وِلاية أوهايو إلى مَدينة دِنْـفر عاصِمة وِلاية كولورادو. نَزَل في دِنْـفر في مَنزِل عائِلة أمريكيّة هي عائِلةُ السَيِّد والسَيِّدة آلَن. تَسْتَضيف عائِلة آلَن الطُلّابَ الأجانِب خِلالَ العُطلات لِمُدّة أسبوع أو أسبوعَين.

مَنزِل عائِلة آلَن

أوهايو وكولورادو على خَريطةِ الوِلاياتِ المُتَّحِدة

يَعمَلُ السَيِّد تشارلز آلَن صَحَفِيّاً ويَكتُب لِمَجلّة في دِنْـفر ولِصُحُف ومَجلاّت أُخرى في الوِلاياتِ المُتَّحِدة، وتَعمَل زَوجَتُه آليس مُحاسِبةً في مَصرِف. تشارلز وآليس لَهُما اِبن وابنة. الابن، واسمُه پول، طالِب في جامِعة كولورادو في بولدَر حَيثُ يَدرُس العُلومَ السِياسِيّة وهُو لاعِب كُرة قَدَم أيضاً. أمّا ابنَتُهُما هِذَر فَهي تَدرُس التِجارة في جامِعة كاليفورنيا في سانتا كروز وتَعمَل أيضاً نادلةً في مَطعَم هُناكَ ثَلاث ساعات كُلَّ يَوم.

العَرض: اعرِض على الطلاّب صوراً يظهر فيها أشخاص من مهن مختلفة ثم علّق عليها. وننصحك باستخدام التعبير **يعمل أخي معلّماً.** بدلاً من **يعمل أخي كمعلّم.**

النشاط: اسأل الطلاّب أين يشتغل أفراد عائلتهم أو أصدقائهم. تأكّد من استيعاب الآخرين ما قال المجيب بطرح بعض الأسئلة عليهم مثل:
أ- «**يا مارك، هل لك أخ أو أخت؟**»
ط- «**نعم لي أخت.**»
أ- «**هل تعمل أختك؟**»
ط- «**نعم. تعمل أختي مدرسة.**»
أ- «**أي مدرسة تعمل فيها وكم سنة عملت هناك؟**»
ط- «**تعمل في مدرسة كذا الابتدائية وتعمل هناك منذ خمس سنوات.**»
أ- «**يا ليسا، هل لمارك أخ أو أخت؟**»
ليسا- «**نعم، له أخت وهي تعمل مدرسة في مدرسة كذا الابتدائية وتعمل هناك منذ خمس سنوات.**»

التطبيق: دع الطلاّب يتكلّمون عن عملهم أو عن عمل أصدقائهم أو عمل أفراد عائلتهم. يستحسن أن يقلد الطالب أسلوب نص القراءة في هذا الدرس.

پول آلن لاعِبُ كُرةِ قَدَم

السَّيِّدُ تشارلز آلن صَحَفيّ

السَّيِّدة آلَن مُحاسِبة

هِذَر آلَن نادِلة

زار عَدنان وَسَطَ المَدينة وعَدَداً مِن البُيوتِ القَديمة هُناك. وفي يَومِ السَبت حَضر مع عائِلة آلَن مُباراة كُرة قَدَم في مَلعَبِ المَدينةِ الَّذي يُسمّيهِ أهلُها «المَلعَبَ العالي» لأَنَّهُ يَرتَفِع ميلاً عَن سَطْحِ البَحر.

في اليَومِ التالي ذَهَبوا بِالسَيّارة إلى جِبال «الروكي» وتَناوَلوا طَعامَ الغَداء في مَطعَم قَديم في الجِبال وقَد أعجَبَهُ ذلِكَ جِدّاً. في طَريقِ العَودَة مَرّوا بِمَصنَع بيرَة «كورز» وهو مَصْنَع كَبير يَعمَل فيهِ مِئاتُ العُمّال.

لَقَد اسْتَمتَع عَدنان بِهذِه الزِيارة اسْتِمتاعاً كَبيراً، وفي نِهايَتِها شَكَرَ السَيِّد والسَيِّدة آلَن على كَرَمِهِما واسْتِضافَتِهِما لَهُ. قَدَّم لَهُما هَديَّة وهي قُرص مُدمَج مُسَجَّل عَلَيْهِ موسيقا وأغانٍ عَرَبيّة. وقَدَّم كَذلِكَ مِفرَشاً جَميلاً لِطاوِلَةِ الطَعام مَصنوعاً في دَمَشق. عاد عَدنان إلى كَلَمبَس كَما أتى مِنها بِالطائِرة.

تمرين ٣

أكمِلِ الجُمَلَ الآتية مِن نَصِّ القِراءة.

١- سافَر عَدنان إلى دِنْفر بِـ ____________.

٢- تَعمَلُ هِذَر ____________.

٣- تَستَضيف عائِلةُ السَيِّد آلَن الطُلاّب ____________.

٤- شاهَد عَدنان في جِبالِ الروكي مَصنَع ____________.

٥- يُسَمّي الناس في دِنْفر مَلعَبَ المَدينة «المَلعَبَ العالي» لأنَّهُ ____________.

العَرضُ: اعرض على الطلاّب صوراً تظهر فيها عدّة وسائل مواصلات وعلّق عليها مِثل الآتي:

«سافر بالطائرة إلى بغداد وغادرت الطائرة المطار في موعدها. نزل في فندق صغير ونظيف.
اشتريت تذكرة قطار بالدرجة الأولى. وصل القطار إلى المحطة مساء.
كانت الحافلة مزدحمة بالناس ولم أجد مقعداً أجلس فيه.
ساقت سيّارتها إلى الجامعة يومياً.
ركبت درّاجتي إلى المكتبة.»

النشاط: اسأل الطلاّب من منهم قد سافر إلى ولاية أخرى أو بلد آخر.
«من سافر إلى ولاية/ دولة أخرى غير هذه؟»
«كيف سافرت؟»
«كم ساعة بقيت في المحطّة/ المطار؟»
«بكم كانت تذكرة الـ. . . »
«متى وصلت إلى ذلك المكان؟»
«هل كان أحد في استقبالك هناك؟»

التطبيق: في مجموعات من اثنين: اطلب من الطلاّب أن يتكلموا عن رحلة أو سفرة قد قاموا بها إلى مكان آخر مستخدمين أسئلة تشبه الأسئلة الواردة أعلاه. وعند نهاية النشاط، اطلب منهم أن يفيدوا بما علموا من زملائهم في الصف واستكشف في أجوبتهم ما يساعدهم في زيادة أفكارهم عن السفر.

أكتُبْ «خَطَأ» أو «صَواب» بِجانب كُلّ جُملَة وصَحّحِ الجُمَلَ الخَطَأ.

٦- مَدينة دِنْـفَر عالية.

٧- يوجَد خَمسة أشخاص في عائِلة آلَن.

٨- يَدرُس پول آلَن التِجارة في جامِعة كولورادو.

٩- قَدَّم عَدنان هَديّة لِلسَيِّد والسَيِّدَة آلَن.

أجِب عَن هٰذِه الأسئلة حَسَبَ نَصّ القِراءة.

١٠- مَن يَعمَل مُحاسِباً؟

١١- ماذا يَعمَلُ السَيِّد آلَن؟

١٢- ماذا فَعَل عَدنان يَومَ السَبت؟

١٣- أينَ صُنِعَ مِفرَشُ الطاوِلة؟

تمرين ٤

وافِق بيَن كَلِمات العَمود الأيْمَن وكَلِمات العَمود الأيْسَر واكتُب الكَلِمَتَين في الوَسَط.

١-	جُنَيه		أسرة
٢-	مَقعَد		أُجرة
٣-	قَرية		انتَظَرَ
٤-	اعتَقَدَ		كُرسيّ
٥-	مِثلُ		عَكْس
٦-	قَريب		ظَنَّ
٧-	مُلَوَّث		وَصَلَ
٨-	غادَرَ		بَلدة
٩-	سَيّارة		نَقِيّ
			لَيرة

تمرين ٥

أعِدْ ترتيب الكَلِمات في كُلّ مَجموعة لِتُشكِّل جُمَلاً مُفيدة.

١- الأجانِبَ - آلَن - الطُلاّبَ - عائلةُ - تَستَضيفُ

٢- جُنيهاً - القِطار - عَشَرَ - تَذكِرَة - بِأرْبَعَة - اشتَرَيتُ

٣- مُزدَحِمةٌ - القاهِرةِ - مُلَوَّث - شَوارِعُ - وهَواؤُها - بِالناسِ

٤- العيدِ - لالينيا - في - المِنيا - مَدينةَ - زارَتْ

العَرَض: احكِ للطلاب قصة مثيرة حدثت معك في إحدى رحلاتك في الخارج أو احكِ عن رحلة لالينيا (إلى اليسار).

النشاط: اطرح على الطلاّب سؤالاً عامّاً عن رحلة طالب في الصف. **«هل حدث معك شيء شيّق في سفرتك إلى (مكان ما)؟»**

التطبيق: في مجموعات من اثنين أو على انفراد. اطلب من الطلاّب أن يكتبوا قصة قصيرة عن رحلة شيقة قاموا بها. حاول أن تساعد الطلاّب الذين تواجههم صعوبات.

لالينيا تَزور المِنيا

لالينيا غولدزبري طالِبة أمريكيّة تَدرُسُ اللُغَةَ العَرَبيّة في جامِعة وِلاية أوهايو، وقَد ذَهَبَتْ إلى الجامِعةِ الأمريكيّة في القاهِرة لِمُدَّة سَنَة دِراسيّة لِدِراسةِ العَرَبيّة هُناك. في العُطلات زارَتْ لالينيا أماكِن عَديدَة في مِصر وخارِجِها. هذا ما كَتَبَتْهُ إلى أستاذِها عَن رِحلَتِها إلى المِنيا.

في اليَومِ الأوَّل مِن عيد الفِطْر رَكِبتُ سَيّارة أجرة مِن حَيّ العَجوزة إلى مَحَطَّةِ الجيزة لِلقِطارات ودَفَعْتُ لِلسائق ثَلاثة جُنَيهات أجْرَةَ السَيّارة. كانَت المَحَطّة مُزدَحِمة بِالناس، رُبَّما بِسَبَبِ العيد. أعتَقِد أنَّ مَحَطّة رَمسيس كانَت مُزدَحِمة أيْضاً، لكِنَّني لَمْ أذهَبْ إليها في ذلِكَ اليَوم. اشتَرَيتُ تَذكِرة بِالدَرَجَةِ الثانية بِأرْبَعة عَشَر جُنَيهاً، وتَدافَعتُ مع مِئاتِ الرُكّاب لِلحُصول على مَقعَد مع أنَّ لي مَقعَداً مَحجوزاً. أظُنّ أنَّ الناس تَعَوَّدوا على التَدافُع في المُواصَلاتِ العامّة.

مَرَّ القِطار بِقُرى عَديدَة ووَصَلتُ المِنيا بَعد ثَلاث ساعات ونِصف حَيثُ كان أخو صَديقي في استِقبالي في المَحَطّة. رَكِبتُ معهُ سَيّارَتَهُ الَّتي ساقَها في شَوارِعِ البَلَدَة لأتَعَرَّفَ عليها. المِنيا بَلدَة لَيْسَت كَبيرة ولا أعرِف عَدَد سُكّانِها تَماماً. كان فيها الكَثير مِن الأشجارِ الخَضراء وكانَ الهَواء نَقيّاً غَيرَ مُلَوَّث والشَوارِع هادئة بِعَكْسِ القاهِرة، حَتّى أنّني شاهَدْتُ عَدَداً كَبيراً مِن النُجوم في السَماء في اللَيل.

مَرَرنا بِشارِعٍ يُسَمّى الكورنَيش تَقَع على أحَد جانِبَيه حَديقة عامّة واسِعة كان فيها عَدَد كَبير مِن الناس بَعضُهُم يَمشي وبَعضُهُم يَلعَب ويَتَنَزّه. قالَ لي أخو صَديقي إنَّ الحَديقة لا يوجَد فيها هذا العَدَد مِن الناس عادةً، لكنَّها كانَت مُزدَحِمة في ذلِكَ اليَوم بِسَبَبِ العيد. عَبَرنا إلى الجانِبِ الآخَر مِن نَهرِ النيل حَيثُ توجَد مَزارِعُ المَوز، وشاهَدْنا أنواعاً مُختَلِفة مِن الناس مُعظَمُهُم مِن الفَلاّحين.

بَقِيتُ مع أسرة صَديقي ثَلاثة أيّام وهي أيّامُ العيد. كُلّ شَيء في المَنزِل كان يَدُلّ على العيد، الحَلوى الَّتي تُسَمّى «كَعْكَ العيدِ» وبَرامِجُ الإذاعة والتِلفاز الخاصّة والزيارات إلى بُيوتِ الأصدِقاء والأقرِباء.

في نِهايَة عُطلةِ العيدِ رَجَعتُ إلى القاهِرة. كان مَوعِدُ القِطار في الساعةِ السادِسة صباحاً وأخَذَني الأب إلى المَحَطَّة بِسَيّارتِه وانتَظَرَني هُناكَ حَتّى غادَرَ القِطارُ المَحَطّة.

جَلَستُ في القِطار إلى جانِبِ شابّ، وقَد قَدَّم لي حَلوى وهي كَعكُ العيد فَرَفَضتُ، لكِنَّهُ أصَرّ فأخَذتُ واحِدة. ثُمَّ مَرَّ بائعُ الشاي فَسَألَني إنْ كُنتُ أريد كأس شاي فَقُلتُ لا. بَعدَ قَليل سَألَني إنْ كُنتُ مِن القاهِرة أم مِن المِنيا، فَضَحِكتُ بَيني وبَين نَفسي مِن هذا السؤال السَخيف لأنّهُ لا شَكلي ولا كَلامي يَدُلاّن على أنّي مِصريّة، لكِنَّني كُنتُ سَعيدة أنَّهُ ظَنّ أنّي مِصريَّة. قالَ لي هذا الشابّ إنَّهُ مِن أسوان وتَكَلَّمنا عَن الدِراسة، وسَرّهُ كَثيراً أنّي كُنتُ أدرُسُ العَربيّة. كان يَقرأ كِتاباً خِلالَ الرِحلَة وأصَرّ أنْ يُقَدِّمَهُ لي كَهَديّة. كانَ الكِتاب عَن الخَليفَة عليّ. لَقَد اسْتَمتَعتُ بِهذِه الرِحلة أيّما اسْتِمتاع وقَد أزورُ المِنيا ثانيةً.

تمرين ٦

أكمِلِ الجُمَلَ الآتية مِن نَصِّ القِراءةِ الثاني.

١- كَتَبَتْ لالينيا إلى أستاذِها عَن ______________.

٢- تَسكُن لالينيا في حَيّ ______________.

٣- كانتَ المَحطّة ______________ بِسَبَبِ العيد.

٤- تَقَع مَزارِعُ المَوز ______________.

٥- تَستَغرِقُ الطَريق مِن القاهِرةِ إلى المِنيا ______________.

٦- كانَ الشابّ في القِطارِ يَقرَأ كِتاباً عِن ______________.

تمرين ٧

أكتُبْ «خَطَأ» أو «صَواب» بِجانب كُلّ جُملَة وصَحِّحِ الجُمَلَ الخَطَأ.

١- تَدافَعَ الناس لِلحُصول على مَقعَد في القِطار لأنَّ المقاعِد قَليلة.

٢- لالينيا طالِبة مِصريّة.

٣- استَقبَلَ لالينيا في المَحَطّة أخو صَديقِها.

٤- جَلَسَتْ لالينيا في طَريقِ العَودَة إلى جانِب سَيِّدة مِصريّة.

٥- حَصَلَتْ لالينيا على هَدِيَّة مِن عائِلة صَديقِها.

٦- هَواءُ القاهِرة مُلَوَّث.

تمرين ٨

المُحادَثة: اِحكِ مع زميلك في الصَفّ عن الفَرق بَين أيّامِ العيد وأيّامِ العَمَل. قَد تُساعِدك المواضيع الآتية:

١- **الطَعام**: ما هو الطَعامُ الخاصّ بِالعيد، ومَن يحَضِّرُه في بَيتك؟ كَيف الحَرَكة في السوق والمَطاعِم أيامَ العيد، وهل هي أكثَر اِزدِحاماً أم أقَلّ؟

٢- **المَواصَلات**: أي نَوع من السَفَر يُعجِبك أكثَر، السَفَر بِالطائِرة أم بِالسيّارة أم بِالقِطار ولَماذا؟ في أيّام العيد هل تَدفَع أكثَر لِتَذكرة أم أقَلّ ولِماذا؟ هل الشَوارِع في مَدينتك أكثَر اِزدحاماً أم أقَلّ ولَماذا؟

٣- **الناس**: هل يُريد أهلُ مَدينتك أن يُساعِدوا الآخرين أكثرَ أيّامَ العيد وهل يُعطون هَدايا لِلأشخاص الّذين يَعرِفونَهُم فَقَط أم يَتبرَّعون (donate) أيضاً؟ وماذا تَفعل أنت؟

وبَعد أن تَنتَهي من هذا النَشاط، قارِن بَين تَجارِبك وتَجارِب لالينيا أيّامَ العيد في مِصر. وفي نَشاط جَماعي، تَتكلّم مع زملائك في الصَفّ عن تَجارِبك في أيّامِ العيد في مَدينتك وفي الخارِج.

تمرين ٩

أعِدْ تَرتيبَ الجُمَل لِتُشكِّل فِقرة مُفيدة:

حَدائق المَنارة في المَغرِب

١- أرادَ بْرِت آدمز أنْ يَزورَ المَغرِب.
كانَتِ الرِحلةُ طَويلةً واستَغرَقَت ١٥ ساعةً تَقريباً.
رَكِبَ برِتْ سَيّارةَ أجرةٍ مِن المَطارِ إلى الفُندُق.
اتَّصَلَ بِأمِّهِ بِالهاتِفِ مِن الفُندُقِ وأخبَرَها بِوصولِه إلى المَغرب.
ثانياً اشتَرى تَذكِرةَ طائِرةٍ على الخُطوطِ المَلكيّةِ المَغربيّة.
في يَومِ السَفَرِ أخَذَتْهُ أمُّهُ إلى المَطارِ بِسَيّارتِها.
وحَصَلَ في الفُندُقِ على غُرفةٍ بِسَريرٍ واحِدٍ مع حَمّامٍ بِداخِلِها.
أوّلاً كانَ علَيهِ أنْ يَحصُلَ على تأشيرةِ دُخول.
فَقَد وَصَلَ إلى مَطارِ الدارِ البَيضاء في اليَومِ التالي.
لِذلِكَ أرسَلَ جَوازَ سَفَرِهِ إلى السِفارةِ المَغربيّةِ بِواشِنطَن.

تمرين ١٠

صَنِّف كَلِمات مِن هذا الدَرس تَحتَ الفِئات الآتية:

١	عيد	٢	بيئة	٣	مواصَلات	٤	زِراعة

تمرين ١١

تَمرينُ المُشاهَدة: شاهِدوا الدرسَ الثالث والعشرين على الشابِكة.

١- ما رأي عَدنان في أمريكا؟ ______________________________

____

٢- كَيْفَ ساعَدَ هِشام صَديقه عَدنان في التَعَوُّد على الحياة في أمريكا؟ ______________

____

____

٣- لِماذا أحَبَّ مايكل زيارته إلى الشام؟ ______________________________

____

____

٤- ما هو الاخْتِلاف بَيْنَ فِكْرة ستيف الّتي جاء بِها إلى سوريا وفِكرتِه الآن؟ ________

____

____

تمرين ١٢

المُحادَثة: رَجَع سامِر من السَفَر إلى الشام، وقال: ((اِشتقتلِك اِكتير يا شام)). اِحكِ عن شُعورك حين تُسافِر إلى الخارِج أو تَسكُن في الغُربة. ما هي الأشياءُ الّتي تَحِنّ إليها حين تكون بَعيداً عن الأهل والأصدِقاء؟ بَعضُ المَواضيعِ الّتي قد تُساعِدك في الحَديث هي:

* الأهل والأصدِقاء
* الطَعام
* الثَقافة
* الأماكِن كَالبَيت والوَطَن

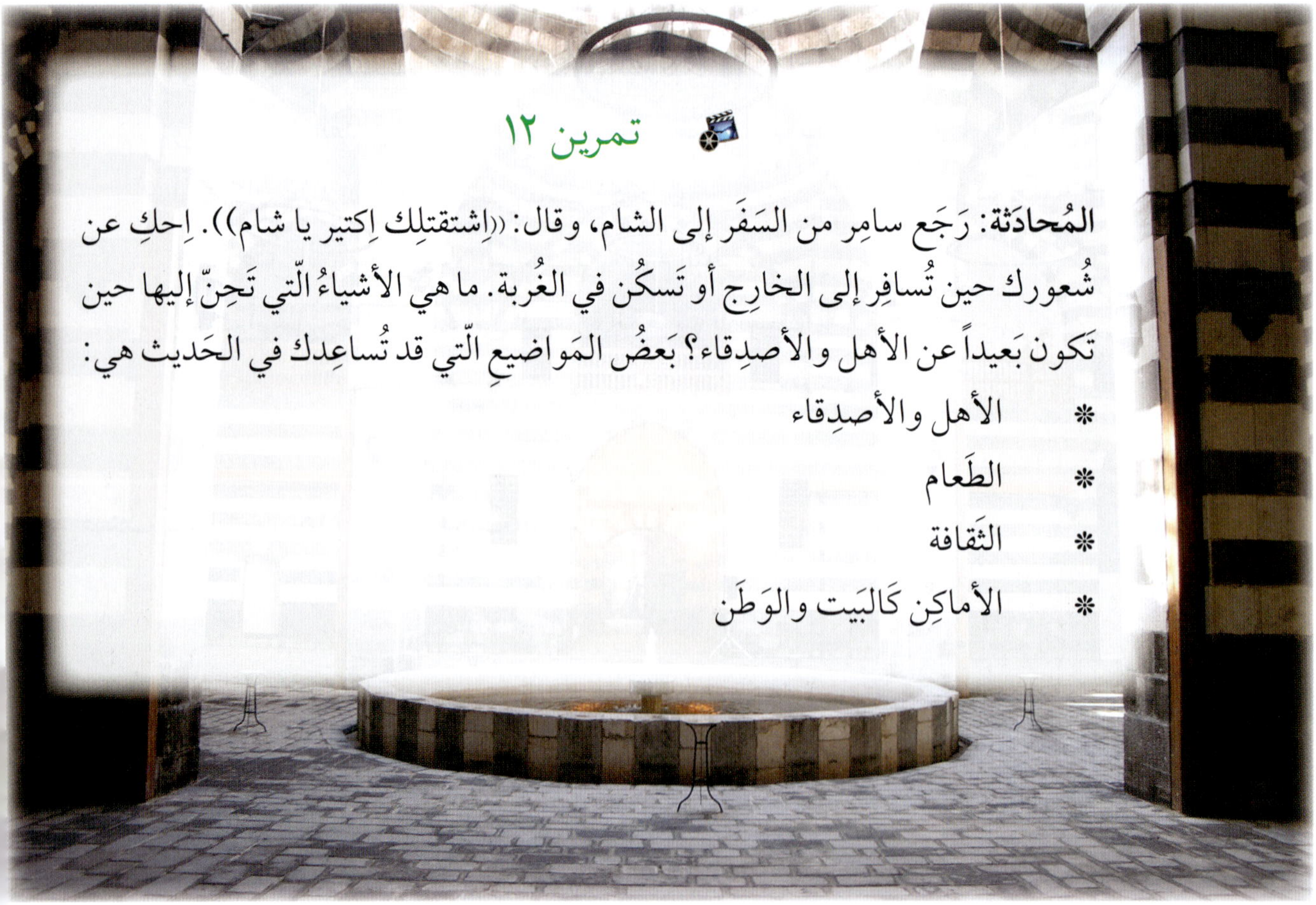

خان أسعد باشا في دِمشق

١- إستِخدام الحَرف الفاء

الفاء حَرف عَطَف (conjunction) في الجُملةِ العَرَبيّة ويَكتَسِب مَعناه من سياقِها في الجُملة. وكَما هو الحال في باقي الحُروفِ المُكوَّنة من حَرف واحِد (مِثل الواو والباء والكاف واللام)، أنّه يَلحَق بِالكَلِمة الّتي تليه.

آ- الفاء المُلحَقة بالاسم

الفاء لَها مَعنَيان حين تَلحَق بالاسم:

١- يَدُلّ على عَمَليّة تَدريجيّة، كَما نَرى في المِثال ١:

١	يَوماً فَيَوماً	*day by day*
	شَيئاً فَشَيْئاً	*bit by bit*

٢- يَصِفّ تَرتيب الحَدَث أو المَكان، كَما نَرى في المِثال ٢ أدناه:

٢	سافَرَ عَدنان فَسامِر.	*Adnān traveled and then Sāmir.*
	مَرَرْنا بِحَلَبَ فَحماةَ فَحِمصَ فَدِمَشق.	*We passed through Aleppo, Hama, Homs, and then Damascus.*

ب- الفاء المُلحَقة بالفِعْل

لا نَستَطيع أن نَذكُر كُلّ مَعاني الحَرف الفاء هُنا لأنّها كَثيرة جِداً، فَسَنكتَفي بِذِكر مَعانيها الرئيسة. في هذا الدَرس، وَرَدَ الحَرف فاء أربع مَرّات في جُملتَين مُتتاليتَين، ومن حَيثُ أسلوب الكِتابة بِالعَرَبيّة، هذا مَقبول لِلغاية. تأمّل المِثال ٣ أدناه:

٣	قَدَّمَ لي حَلوى وهي كَعكُ العيدِ فَرَفَضتُ، لكِنَّهُ أصَرَّ فَأخَذتُ واحِدة. ثُمَّ مَرَّ بائِعُ الشاي فَسَألَني إنْ كُنتُ أريدُ كأسَ شاي فَقُلتُ لا.

اِستِخدامُ الفاء في حَديثِنا اليَوميّ: من بَين معاني الحَرف الفاء هو (so) بالإنكليزيّة. على سَبيل المِثال، حين نَستَحضِر أفكارنا أو نَستَرجِع مَعلومة، نَستَطيع القَول: فاااااااا (faaaaaaaaa) بِمَعنى (soooooo). فَعِندَما نَرجع من مُقاطَعة حَديث، نَستأنِفه مُستَخدِمين هذا الحَرف. ومن أجل إدماج هذا الحَرف في كَلامِنا اليَومي، نَستَطيع أن نَستَنِد إلى الطَريقة الّتي نَستَخدِم (so) فيها بِالإنكليزيّة.

العَرض: استعمل موادّ أصليّة أو معدلّة أو مبتكرة تظهر فيها استعمالات الحرف قد المختلفة، بما فيها الحروف التي تلحق بها (اللام والواو والفاء). اشرح لهم معانيها بالعربية مثل الآتي:

«قد أسافر إلى مصر بمعنى من الممكن أن أسافر إلى مصر.
وقد سافرت إلى مصر بمعنى بالإنكليزية:»

I (had) traveled to Egypt.

اشرح للطلاّب أنّ وظيفة لقد هي لتقديم فكرة بينما وقد وفقد يربطان أفكار جديدة بما سبقهما واستخدامهما يشبه استخدام حرفي الواو والفاء في الجملة لكن حين نزيد عليهما الحرف قد علينا أيضاً أن نزيد (have) أو (had) بالترجمة.

٢- وَظيفة الحَرف قَدْ

هُناكَ وَظيفتان رئيستان لِلحَرف قَد وكِلتاهُما يَعتَمِد على زَمَن الفِعل الّذي يَليه يَعني فِعل ماضٍ أو مُضارِع:

آ- قَدْ + الفِعْل الماضي

يَدُلّ الحَرف قَد على فِعل تام ويُشبِه (has) أو (have) بِالإنكليزيّة:

٤	أرجو أنْ يَكونَ الكِتابُ قَدْ أعجَبَك.	*I hope the book has pleased you.* **Idiomatically:** *I hope you liked the book.*

في الحَقيقة، لَيسَ لِلحَرف قَدْ مقابِل بِالإنكليزيّة، ومع ذلِك، فإنّ بَعضَ الكَلِمات قد تُستعمَل لِيَدُلّ على نَفس الدَلالة (مِثل، have أو had أو indeed). وحين تَشمَل جُملة عَرَبيّة فِعلَين ماضيَين فإنّ الحَرف قَدْ يَدُلّ على أنّ الفِعل الّذي يَليه قَد حَدث أوّلاً، أي أنّ الفِعل الأوّل قَد سَبَق الفِعل الثاني:

٥	وَصَلتُ إلى الصَفِّ في التاسِعةِ والرُبع وكانَ الدَرسُ قَدْ بَدَأ.	*I arrived in the classroom at 9:15 and the lesson had already started.*

إنّ دَلالة الحَرف قَدْ في المِثال ٥ أعلاه، لَيست وَظيفته الوَحيدة في حالة إنّه يَظهَر في جُملة فيها فِعلان ماضيان، إنّما يُبيّن المِثال ٦ أنّه قَد يُستَعمَل لِتوكيد الفِعل الثاني:

٦	تَناوَلتُ الغَداءَ في مَطعَمٍ قَديمٍ وقَد أعجَبَني.	*I had lunch in an old restaurant and I indeed enjoyed it.*

يُوضِح لَنا المِثال ٦ أنّ في بَعض الجُمل الّتي تَشمل فعلَين ماضيَين، نَستَعمِل الحَرف قَدْ لِلتَوكيد، لكِنه لا يَدُلّ على تَرتيب الحَدَث، أي إنّه لا يَدُلّ على ما حَدَثَ أوّلاً أو ثانياً.

وهُناك بَعض الحُروف (أي اللام والواو والفاء) الّتي تَلحَق بِه ولِكُلّ منها مَعنى خاصّ:

	اللام + قَدْ	
٧	لَقَد دَرَسَ العَربيَّةَ في المَغرِب.	*He has studied Arabic in Morocco.*

	الواو + قَدْ	
٨	شاهَدتُ فيلماً مُمتازاً وقد نَسِيتُ اسمَهُ الآن.	*I saw an excellent movie, and/but I have forgotten its title now.*

	الفاء + قَدْ	
٩	لَمْ أشتَرِ كِتابَ غَسّان كَنَفاني فَقَد قَرَأتُهُ مِن قَبل.	*I didn't buy Kanafani's book because I had read it before.*

ب- قَدْ + الفِعل المُضارِع

يَدُلّ الحَرف قَدْ + الفِعل المُضارِع على التَوقُّع، أو بِكَلام آخَر مُمكِن. إنّه لا يؤثر على الفِعل الّذي يَليه:

	قَدْ + المُضارِع	
١٠	قَدْ أسافِرُ إلى عَمّانَ غَداً.	*I might travel to Amman tomorrow.*
١١	قَدْ يَنزِل المَطَرُ اليَومَ.	*It might rain today.*

الخُلاصة

الحَرف قَدْ + الفِعل الماضي

* يَدُلّ الحَرف قَدْ + الفِعل الماضي على حَدَث تامّ كامِل لا يَنقُصه شيء وأيضاً يَدُلّ على التوكيد.

* في جُملة فيها فِعلان ماضيان، الحَرف قَدْ يَدُل إمّا على تَرتيب الحَدَث، أي إنّ الفِعل الّذي يَلي قَدْ حَدَث قَبلَ الفِعل الآخَر، أو على التوكيد.

الحَرف قَدْ + الفِعل المُضارِع

* يَدُلّ الحَرف قَدْ + الفِعل المُضارِع على التَوَقُّع أو الاحتِمال أو الإمكانية.

العَرض: اعرِض على الطلّاب صوراً يظهر فيها أشخاص أو أماكن قد تُستعمَل كالبَدَل:
«هذه صورة لهشام صديقي المفضل.
هذا هو عدنان، طالب سوريّ يدرس في أمريكا.
هذا هو الأمين العام للأمم المتحدة أنطونيو غوتيراس.
هذه هالة بستاني زميلة سحر حلاق.»

النشاط: اكتب بعض الأسماء على السبورة حتّى ترى إذا استطاع الطلّاب الأتيان بالبدل لها.

إبراهام لينكون (رئيس أمريكا السادس عشر)
الصفوف التي أخذها الآن (التاريخ والكيمياء)
برنامجي المفضل (أصدقاء)
روسيا (أكبر دولة في العالم من حيث المساحة)
شيكسبير (أشهر كاتب في التاريخ)

التطبيق: في مجموعات من اثنين: حضر ورقة مكتوب عليها بعض الأسماء التي لها بدل واضح، واطلُب منهم أن يكتبوه في جملة شاملة كاملة. وبعد حوالي دقيقتين، اطلب من طالب أن يكتب جملة مجموعته على السبورة ثمّ، راجع الجمل معاً من حيث القواعد وأسلوب الكتابة.

تمرين ١٣

التَحويل: حَوِّل هذِه الجُمَل إلى العَرَبيّة مُستَخدِماً الحَرف قَدْ وَفقاً لِلمَعلومات أعلاه:

1. They (m., pl.) may travel to Damascus by plane.
2. I saw her house and I really liked it.
3. When we got to our friends' house, they had already had dinner.
4. I arrived at her house after the party had started.
5. I have indeed watched all of the Harry Potter movies.

٣- البَدَل Substitution or the Permutative

البَدَل هو اِسم أو شِبه جُملة يَحِلّ مَحَلّ الاسم الّذي يَسبُقه مُباشَرةً. ويُمكِنه أن يَكون بَديلاً كامِلاً لِلاسم المَقصود (مِثل: المَدينة المُنَوَّرة = المَدينة، أو التُفّاحة الكَبيرة = نيويورك). هيّا نَتأمّل بَعضَ الأَمثِلةِ المأخوذة من دَرسِنا:

١٢	سافَرَ عَدنان إلى مَدينةِ دِنفَر عاصِمةِ وِلايةِ كولورادو.	*Adnān traveled to the city of Denver, the capital of Colorado.*

في المِثال ١٢، التَعبير عاصِمةِ ولايةِ كولورادو يَحِلّ مَحَلّ مَدينةِ دَنفِر. وكَما تَرى، إذا حَذفنا الكَلِمَتَين مَدينة دَنفِر، فَمَعنى الجُملة يَبقى كَما هو لأن البَدَل يُفيد نَفس مَعنى المُبدَل مِنه. لاحِظ أنّ البَدَل لَه نَفس إعراب المُبدَل مِنه (قارِن مَدينةِ = مَجرور بالكَسرة وعاصِمةِ = مَجرور بالكَسرة)

إلَيك مِثال يَدخُل عليه البَدَل حين يَكونُ المُبدَل مِنه مَمنوعاً من الصَرف. تَذَكّر بِأنّ المَمنوع من الصَرف يُعرَب بِالفَتحة في حالتَي النَصب والجَرّ (راجِع باب ٢، الدرس الخامس عشر).

١٣	سافَرَ رامي إلى عَمّانَ عاصِمةِ الأردُن.	*Adnān traveled to Amman, the capital of Jordan.*

بِاعتِبار أنّ عَمّانَ مَمنوعة من الصَرف، فإنّها لا تُعرَب بِالكَسرة رَغم أنّها في حالة الجَرّ وجارُّها إلى، بَل تُعرَب بِالفَتحة بَينَما نَرى أنّ البَدَل يُعرَب بِالكَسرة وهذا مَحَلّها من الإعراب الصَحيح.

تمرين ١٤

اكتُب خطاً تَحتَ البَدَل في الجُمَل الآتية واشكُل أواخِر كَلِماتِه:

١- دَفَعتُ لِلسائِقِ ثَلاثةَ جُنَيهاتٍ أجرة السَيّارة.

٢- زُرنا القاهِرةَ أكبَر مُدُنِ إفريقيا.

٣- وَصَلنا صَباحاً إلى الرِباط عاصِمة المَغرِب.

٤- سَكَنَتْ لَيلى في «بيز ووتر» حَيّ العَرَبِ في لَندَن.

باب توما في دِمشق (١٨٩٠-١٩٠٠)

٤- مُراجَعة الإضافة

يُسمّى أوَّل اسمِ الإضافة المُضاف، ولا يُمكِنه أنْ . . .

١- يُعَرَّف بِلام التَعريف = الـ.

٢- يُنَوَّن أي يأخُذ التنوين.

٣- يَنتَهي بِنون الجَماعة = مُعَلِّمونَ يَعني نَحذُف نون الجَماعة في الإضافة مِثل:

١٤	مُعَلِّمون	+	المَدرسة	=	مُعَلِّمو المَدرسةِ	*teachers of the school*

لَقَد وَرَدَت الجُملة الآتية في آخِر نَصِّ القِراءة في هذا الدَرس:

١٥	أَرَدتُ أنا وصَديقتايَ آن ورينا أن نَزورَ سوريا.	*My two friends (f.) Anne and Rina wanted to visit Syria.*

إنّ الاسم صَديقتايَ مؤلَّف من الاسم المُثّنى صَديقتان + ي، وهذا يُساوي إضافة بِالعَرَبيّة. وبِما أنّ الاسم صَديقاتان هو المُضاف، فَتَسقُط نون الجَماعة منه.

١٦	صَديقتان	+	ي	=	صَديقتايَ	*my two friends (f.)*
	والِدان	+	ي	=	والِدايَ	*my two parents*

٥- وَظيفة حَرف الشَرْط إنْ

يُشبِه حَرفُ الشَرط إنْ الكَلِمة (if) بِالإنكليزيّة ويُقدِّم لَنا شَرطاً قَد يَحصُل—يَعني لَيس شَرطاً اِفتِراضياً مِثل لَوْ، بَل شيء قَد يَحدُث في الواقِع. تُقدِّم لَنا إنْ الشَرطيّة جُملة نُسَمّيها الجُملة الشَرطيّة وهي مُؤَلَّفة من جُملتَين ألا وهُما: ١_جُملة الشَرط و ٢_ جواب الشَرط. في كِلتا الجُملتَين فِعل وهذان الفِعلان قَد يأتيان في الجُملة بالماضي أو المُضارِع أو الماضي والمُضارِع معاً في نَفسِ الجُملة الشَرطيّة.

اقرأ الأمثِلة الآتية وتأمّلْها:

١٧	إنْ تَزُرْ حَلَبَ تُعجِبْك.	If you visit Aleppo, you'll like it.
١٨	إنْ زُرتَ حَلَبَ أعجَبَتْك.	
١٩	إنْ تَزُرْ حَلَبَ أعْجَبَتْك.	
٢٠	إنْ زُرتَ حَلَبَ تُعجِبْك (أو تُعجِبُك).	

كَما تَرى، عِندَنا أربعة خيارات نَستَطيع اِستِعمالَها. ولِكُلّ مِنها حُكم مُعَيَّن يَختَلِف عَن غَيرِه. هيّا نَنظُر إلَيها بِدِقّة:

* حين يأتي الفِعل بَعد أداةِ الشَرط إنْ مُباشَرةً، لابُدّ من أن يُجزَم أي يأتي في حالة الجَزم، كَما هو الحال في المِثالَين ١٧ و١٩ أعلاه.
* حين يأتي فِعل مُضارع في جواب الشَرط، كَما وَرَد في المِثال ٢٠، فإنّه يُمكِن أن يأتي في حالتَي الرَفع أو الجَزم.

إنّ العِبارة الشائعة إنْ شاء الله (God willing) خَير مِثال على اِستِخدام أداةِ الشَرط إنْ، وفي الحَقيقة، هي شَكل من أشكال المِثال ٢٠ أعلاه.

وفي حالة عَدم وُجود جواب الشَرط، فإنّ جُملةَ الشَرط تَشمل فِعلاً ماضياً، كَما رأينا في النَصّ الرئيس في هذا الدَرس.

٢١	سألَني إنْ كُنتُ أريدُ كأسَ شاي.	*He asked me if I wanted a glass of tea.*

تمرين ١٥

المُحادَثة فيها قَدْ أو إنْ: مَن مِن زُملائك في الصَفّ:

1. might travel to Syria this summer
2. might study abroad this summer
3. might work in Washington, the capital of America
4. would swim in the Red Sea, if they traveled to Egypt
5. would learn to play guitar, if they had time
6. would wake up earlier, if they were able

تمرين ١٦

أجِب عَن الأسئِلة حَسَب نَصِّ الاستِماع.

١- إلى أيّ بَلَد سَتكونُ الرِحلة؟

٢- كَم يَوماً سَتَبقى الصَديقات في القاهِرة؟

٣- هَل سَتُسافِرُ المُتكَلِّمة مع صَديقاتِها؟ لِماذا؟

أكتُبْ «خَطَأ» أو «صَواب» بِجانب كُلّ جُملَة وصَحِّحِ الجُمَلَ الخَطأ.

٤- مَسجِد مُحَمَّد عليّ في الإسكَندَريّة.

٥- مُدَّةُ الرِحلة إلى الإسكَندَريّة ثَلاثَة أيّام.

٦- سَيكونُ السَفَر إلى الأقصر بِالحافِلة.

٧- لَن تُسافِرَ الفَتاة مع صَديقاتِها لأنَّها تَعرِف مِصر.

أكمِلِ الجُمَل بِالاختيارِ المُناسِب حَسَب نَصِّ الاستِماع.

٨- سَتَزورُ الصَديقات في القاهِرة ______________.

☐ المَكتبات الكُبرى ☐ المُتحَف المِصريّ ☐ البَحرَ المُتوَسِّط

٩- الأهرامات مَوجودة ______________.

☐ قُربَ القاهِرة ☐ في الأقْصُر ☐ في جَنوب مِصر

١٠- سَتأخُذُ الصَديقات رِحلة ______________.

☐ خاصّة ☐ عامّة ☐ جامِعيّة

١١- لَيسَ عِندَ الفَتاة ______________.

☐ وَقت ☐ هُويّة ☐ صَديقات

١٢- الآثارُ الفِرعَونيّة مَوجودَة ______________.

☐ في الطَريق إلى الأقْصُر ☐ في الإسكَندَريّة

☐ في مَسجِد مُحَمَّد عليّ

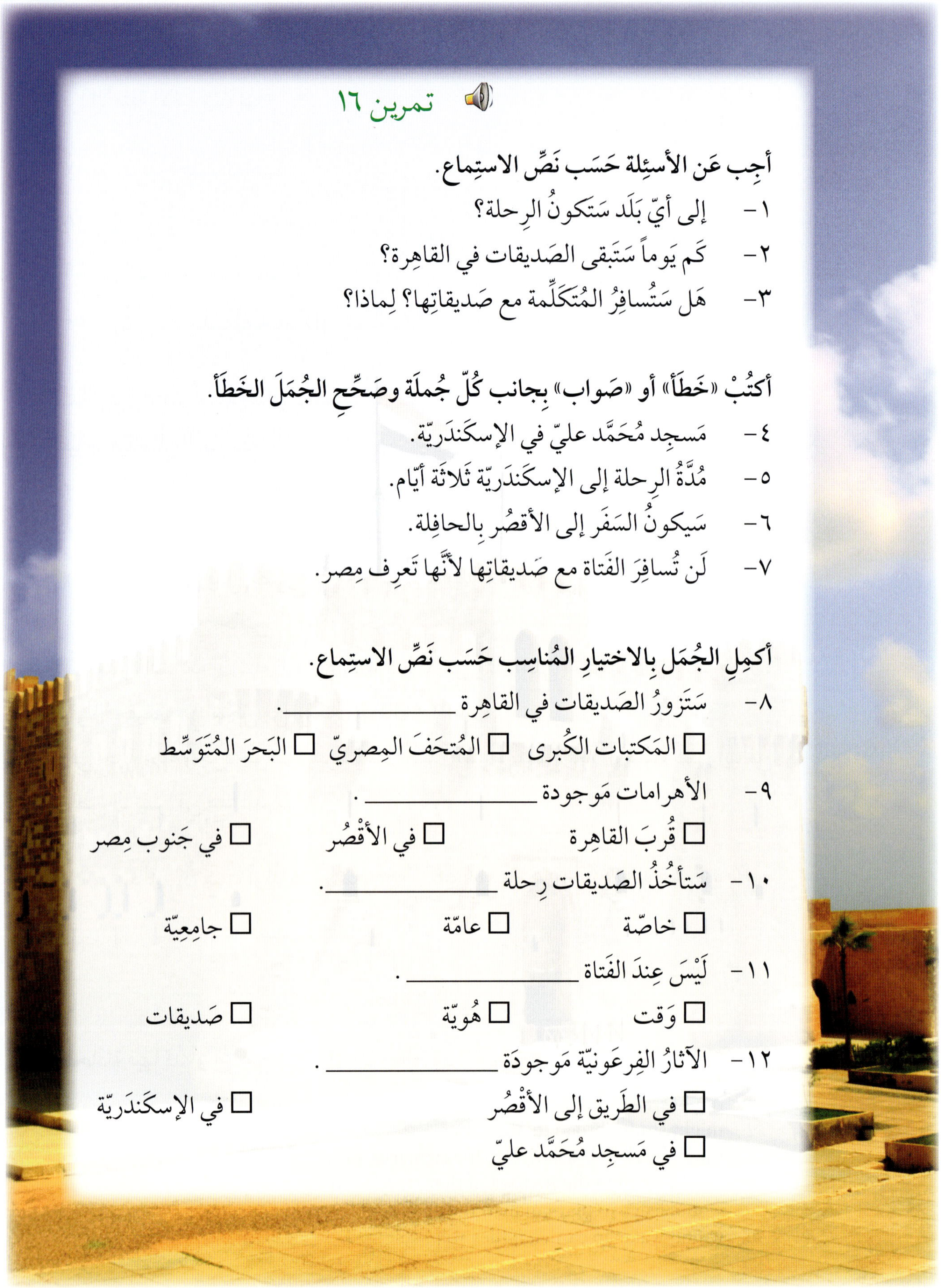

قلعة قايتباي في الإسكندرية

المُفْرَدات

استمِع إلى المُفْرَدة بالعَرَبيّة ثم أعِد نُطْقَها مرّتين.

اِخْتَلَفَ (يَخْتَلِفُ) اِخْتِلاف (عَن) (v.)	to differ (from)
اِرتَفَعَ (يرتَفِعُ) اِرتِفاع (v.)	to rise, to be higher
اِستَضافَ (يستَضيفُ) استِضافة (v.)	to host
اِشْتاقَ (يَشْتاقُ) اِشْتِياق (لـ/ إلى) (v.)	to long (for), to yearn
أصَرَّ (يُصِرُّ) إصْرار (v.)	to insist
اِعتَقَدَ (يَعتَقِدُ) اِعتِقاد (v.)	to believe
اِقْتَرَبَ (يَقْتَرِبُ) اِقْتِراب (مِن) (v.)	to draw near, get close (to)
إنْ (particle)	if
اِنتَظَرَ (يَنْتَظِرُ) اِنتِظار (v.)	to wait
أيَّما (n.)	immensely, greatly (intensifies the following noun)
بَسيط ج بُسطاء (adj.)	simple
تأشيرة دُخول (n., f.)	visa
تَدافَعَ (يَتَدافَعُ) تَدافُع (v.)	to push, shove one another
تَعَرَّفَ (يَتعَرَّفُ) تَعَرُّف (على) (v.)	to be acquainted with
تَعَوَّدَ (يَتَعَوَّدُ) تَعَوُّد (على) (v.)	to be accustomed to
تَنَزَّهَ (يَتَنَزَّهُ) تَنَزُّه (v.)	to stroll; to have a good time; to go on a picnic
جَواز (سَفَر) (n., m.)	passport
حَضَرَ (يحْضُرُ) حُضور (v.)	to attend, to be present
خارِج (n.)	outside
خَفَّفَ (يُخَفِّفُ) تَخْفيف (عَن) (v.)	to diminish the difficulty of

خَليفة ج خُلَفاء (n., m.)	caliph, successor
دَرَجة ج دَرَجات (n., f.)	class, step, level, degree
دَفَعَ (يَدْفَعُ) دَفْع (v.)	to pay
رِحْلة ج رِحلات (n., f.)	trip, journey, flight
ساقَ (يَسوقُ) سِياقة (v.)	to drive
سَخيف ج سُخَفاء (n./adj.)	silly, absurd, foolish
سَرَّ (يَسُرُّ) سُرور (v.)	to please, to be glad
سَطْح ج سُطوح (n., m.)	surface, level
سِياسيّ (adj.)	political
شَيِّق (adj.)	interesting, thrilling
صَحَفِيّ ج ون (n., m.)	journalist
صَحيفة ج صُحُف (n., f.)	newspaper
ضَحِكَ (يَضْحَكُ) ضِحْك (v.)	to laugh
عَبَرَ (يَعبُرُ) عُبور (v.)	to cross
عَكْس (n.)	opposite, reverse, contrary
غادَرَ (يُغادِرُ) مُغادَرة (v.)	to leave
فَلاّح ج ون (n., m.)	peasant, farmworker
قَد (particle)	no meaning, denotes completed action, emphasis, or possibility
قَريب ج أقارِب (n., m.)	a relative
قَلْب ج قُلوب (n., m.)	heart
كَـ (prep.)	as, like
كَرَم (n., m.)	hospitality, generosity
كَلام (n., m.)	speech, speaking

player . . . . (n., m.) لاعِب ج ون

a variation of *qad* . . . . (particle) لَقَد

society, community . . . . (n., m.) مُجْتَمَع ج مُجْتَمَعات

accountant . . . . (n., m.) مُحاسِب ج ون

crowded . . . . (adj.) مُزدَحِم

farm . . . . (n., f.) مَزْرَعة ج مَزارِع

recorded . . . . (n./adj.) مُسَجَّل

factory, plant . . . . (n., m.) مَصْنَع ج مَصانِع

tablecloth . . . . (n., m.) مَفرَش ج مَفارِش

seat, bench, armchair . . . . (n., m.) مَقْعَد ج مَقاعِد

enjoyable . . . . (active participle) مُمْتِع

polluted . . . . (adj.) مُلَوَّث

house, residence . . . . (n., m.) مَنزِل ج مَنازِل

view, panorama . . . . (n., m.) مَنْظَر ج مَناظِر

means of transportation . . . . (n., f.) مُواصَلة ج مُواصَلات

waiter. . . . . (n., m.) نادِل ج نُدُل

mint, peppermint . . . . (n., m.) نَعناع

pure . . . . (adj.) نَقيّ

quiet, serene . . . . (adj.) هادِئ

present, gift . . . . (n., f.) هَدِيّة ج هَدايا

بهارات في السوق

الدرس الرابع والعشرون

أهدافُ الدَرس

- مُراجَعة أفرادِ العائلة وعلاقتهم
- وَصْفُ المِهنة
- اِستِخدام اللَقَبَين أبو وأُمّ
- مُراجَعة اِسمِ التَفضيل
- التَعبير عن السَبَب مُستَخدِماً لـِ وكَي
- مُراجَعةُ المَصْدَر

رُكنُ المُفْرَداتِ الجَديدة

اِخْتارَ (يَخْتارُ) اِختِيار	*to choose*
اِسْتَوْرَدَ (يَسْتَوْرِدُ) اِسْتيراد	*to import*
اِعْتَنى (يَعْتَني) اِعْتِناء (بِـ)	*to care for*
أقامَ (يُقيم) إقامة	*to reside*
بَدا (يَبدو) بُدُوّ	*to appear*
تَقاعَدَ (يَتَقاعَدُ) تَقاعُد	*to retire*
رَدَّ (يرِدُّ) رَدّ	*to respond*
سَجَّلَ (يُسَجِّلُ) تَسْجيل	*to register*
صَدَرَ (يَصدُرُ) صُدور	*to issue*
مُلاحَظة ج مُلاحَظات	*note; observation*
مِهْنة ج مِهَن	*occupation; profession*
مُؤَلَّف (مِن)	*comprised of*
نَفْس ج أنْفُس	*same*

تمرين ١

وافِق بين كَلِمات العَمودِ الأيْمَن وكَلِمات العَمودِ الأيْسَر واكتُب الكَلِمَتَين في الوَسَط.

١-	كُبرى		نَهار
٢-	اِلْتَقَطَ		بَحر
٣-	يَمين		بَنات
٤-	سَفينة		صُغرى
٥-	مَحَلٌّ تَجاري		يَسار
٦-	بَنون		واسِع
٧-	لَيْل		صَوَّرَ
			دُكّان

تمرين ٢

أعِدْ تَرتيبَ الكَلِمات في كُلّ مَجموعة لِتُشَكِّل جُمَلاً مُفيدة.

١- لِلبَنين - في - مَروانُ - بَحَلَب - ثانويَّةٍ - يَدرُسُ - مَدرسَةٍ

٢- لِبَيعِ - السَيّاراتِ - أبي - غِيارِ - عِندَ - واسِعٌ - عَدنان - قِطَعِ - مَحَلٌّ

٣- كَيْ - عَدنان - بِعائِلَتِها - عَمَلِها - تَقاعَدَتِ - تَعتَنيَ - أُمُّ - عَن

٤- مارتيني - ومُحاسِبٌ - في - ياسِر - عُمّالٍ - ثَلاثَةُ - وبائِعان - يَعمَلُ - مَحَلّ

العَرض: قد تُفيدك شجرة عائلتك وصورهم في جعل سياق صالح لتقديم المفردات الجديدة الواردة في هذا الدرس. ركّز على العلاقات الأسروية الجديدة المقدّمة فيه.

«هذه صورة عمّي الّذي يسكن في تكساس حيث يعمل محاسبا في مصرف. وهذه عمّتي زوجته (بدل) وهي ربة بيت وقد درست في جامعة تكساس حيث حصلت على إجازة جامعية الباكلوريوس في التجارة. وهذه خالتي الممثلة المشهورة وهي مثّلت في عدّة أفلام معروفة.»

حاول أن تكرّر مفاهيم القواعد ونقاطها الواردة في الدروس السابقة لتثبتها في ذهن الطالب.

الممارسة: اطرح على الطلاّب أسئلة عامة عن عائلة الطلاّب مثل:

((هل لك خال أو خالة؟ أين تسكن خالتك وماذا تعمل؟))

تأكّد من استيعاب الطلاّب الاستماعي بطرح أسئلة عليهم عمّا فهموا من أجوبة زملائهم.

التَطبيق: اطلُب من الطلاّب إحضار بعض الصور لعائلتهم. ثمّ اطلُب منهم وصف صورهم لزملائهم في الصف وشجّع المستمع أن يسأل أسئلة للمتكلّم. وبعد دقيقتين أو ثلاث، اطلُب منهم أن يبدّلوا أدوارهم.

النشاط الثاني: اطلُب من طالب أن يتطوّع في وصف صوره إلى زملائه.

تمرين ٣

اخترَ الكَلِمةَ الّتي لا تُناسِب باقي الكَلِمات في كُلّ مَجْموعة وبَيِّن السَبَب.

١-	استيراد	صورة	التَقَطَ	ظَهَرَ
٢-	عام	سَنة	عَمّ	عُمُر
٣-	رِسالة	طِبّ	تِجارة	عِلْمُ الحاسوب
٤-	بِضاعة	دُكّان	مُدَرِّس	مَحَلّ تِجاري
٥-	كَيْ	أَيُّ	لِذلِكَ	لِـ
٦-	جَواز سَفَر	عامِل	مُحاسِب	مُوَظَّف

تمرين ٤

أعِدْ ترتيبَ الجُمَل لِتُشَكِّل فِقرة مُفيدة. لا تُغَيِّر مَكانَ الجُمْلةِ الأولى.

١- دَرَسَتْ هالة الصيدَلة في جامِعَة دِمِشق. * pharmacy, pharmacology

اشتَريا داراً كَبيرة في دِمشق مُؤَلَّفة مِن ثَلاثة طوابِق.

تَعَرَّفَتْ في المُستَشفى على زَوجِها مازِن الّذي كان يَعمَل طَبيباً. * hospital

أمّا الطابَقُ الثاني فَسَكنوا فيه.

وتَخَرَّجَتْ مِنَ الجامِعة في العام ٢٠٠٢.

حين صار أولادُهُما في سِنِّ المَدرَسة انتَقَلا إلى دِمشق.

بَعدَ تَخَرُّجِها عَمِلَت صَيدلانِيّةً في مَشفى في مَدينةِ الكُوَيت. * pharmacist

والطابَقُ الأوّل صار عِيادَةً لمازِن.

صار لِهالة ومازِن بِنتان ووَلَدان.

في الطابَقِ الأرضِيّ مَحَلّ تِجاريّ واسِع فَتَحَتْهُ هالة صَيْدَلِيّة. * pharmacy

أُسرة عَدنان مارتيني

القِصّة

هذِهِ صورة أُسرة عَدنان مارتيني. لَقَد أرسَل أبو عَدنان صورةَ العائِلة مَعَ رسالة إلى ابنِهِ عَدنان الَّذي يَدرُس عِلمَ الحاسوب في جامِعة ولاية أوهايو في الولاياتِ المتحدةِ الأمريكيّة. يَظهَر في الصورة أبو عَدنان في أسفَلِ الصورة إلى اليسار وتَظهَر أمّ عَدنان جالِسةً إلى يَسارِه. تَظهَر في أعلى الصورة إلى اليَمين أخت عَدنان أماني، وعُمُرُها إحدى وعِشرون سَنة وهي في كُلّيّة الصيدلة. أمّا أختُها الصُغرى أمينة فَهي لَيسَت في الصورة لأنَّها كانَت في دار جَدّتِها حينَ التُقِطَت الصورة. أمينة في الصَفِّ العاشِر وعُمُرُها خَمس عَشْرَة سَنة وهي تَذهَب إلى المَدرسةِ الثانَويّةِ الجَديدة لِلإناث في مَدينة حَلَب في سوريا. يَقِف مَروان بَين أُختِه وأخيه رامي. مروان طالِب في الصَفِّ الثاني عَشَر العِلمِيّ في المَدرسةِ الثانَويّةِ لِلبَنين وعُمرُهُ سَبعة عَشَر عاماً.

ياسِر مارتيني وزوجته

أبوعَدنان، واسمُه ياسِر مارتيني، تاجِر في الخامِسة والخَمسين من عُمرِه. لَهُ مَحَلّ تِجاريّ في حَلَب فَتَحَهُ مُنذُ خَمسة وعشرين عاماً يَبيع فيهِ قِطَع غِيار لِبَعضِ السيّاراتِ الألمانيّة كَفولكسفاكن وأوبِل. مَحَلّ أبي عَدنان واسِع وهو مُؤَلَّف مِن دُكّان لبَيع قِطَعِ الغِيار ومَكتَب لَهُ وآخَر لِلمُحاسِب، وهُناكَ مَخزَن كَبير لِتَخزينِ البِضاعة. يَعمل عِندَهُ في المَحَلّ مُحاسِب واحِد وبائعان وثَلاثة عُمّال لِنَقلِ البِضاعة مِن المَحَلّ وإليه. يستَورِدُ السَيِّد ياسِر مارتيني بِضاعتَه مِن ألمانيا وتَصِلُه إلى حَلَب بالشاحِنات غالِباً وأحياناً بالبَحْر عَن طريق ميناءِ اللاذِقيّة، لكنَّها تَتَأَخَّر عادةً بِهذِه الطَريق. لِذلِكَ فَهو يُسافِر إلى ميونيخ وكولون وفرانكفورت ليشتريَ البِضاعة بِنَفسِه مِن ألمانيا.

الجمهورية العربية السورية
RÉPUBLIQUE ARABE SYRIENNE

وزارة الداخلية
MINISTÈRE DE L'INTÉRIEUR

إدارة الهجرة والجوازات
DÉPARTEMENT DE L'IMMIGRATION & DES PASSEPORTS

صدر بمدينة: حلب: Fait à: Alep

في اليوم: السادس من شهر نيسان ٢٠٠٧
Le 6 avril ٢٠٠٧

وينتهي مفعوله بتاريخ ٥ نيسان ٢٠١٣
Et expire le 5 avril ٢٠١٣

رقم التسجيل ٣٦١٧٣٥٤٢

الاسم والشهرة: ياسِر مارتيني
اسم الأب: عَبد الغَني
اسم الأم: رُقَيَّة
مكان الإقامة الحالي: حلب
تاريخ ومكان الولادة: حلب ١٥ آب ١٩٥٥
المِهنة: تاجِر
الشعر: أسوَد
الطول: ١٧١ سنتيمتر
اللون: أسمَر
العينان: بُنيتان
التوقيع: ياسر مارتيني

صَفحَتان من جَواز سَفَر السيِّد ياسِر مارتيني

أمّ عَدنان، واسمُها سامية كَحّال، عُمرُها خَمسون عاماً. هي رَبَّة بَيت الآن ولا تَعمَل، لكِنَّها كانَت مُدَرِّسَة لُغة فَرَنسيّة في إحدى مَدارِسِ الإناثِ الثانوِيّة في حَلَب. تَقاعَدَتْ السَيِّدة سامية كَحّال عَن العَمَل مُنذُ ثَماني سَنوات كَي تَعتَني بوالِدَتِها المَريضة وبمَنزِلِها وزَوجِها وأولادِها. فَكانت تَعمَل في المنزِل في النَهار وتَزور صديقاتَها مَساءً وفي اللَيل تَبقى مَعَ عائِلَتِها.

سافَرَتْ أمّ عَدنان خارِج سوريا مَرَّة واحِدة مَعَ زَوجِها إلى ألمانيا مُنذُ سَنَتَين ومَرَّة أخرى إلى الوِلاياتِ المُتّحدة لِزيارة ابنِها عَدنان، لكِنَّها سافَرَتْ وَحدَها ومَعَ زَوجِها عِدّة مَرّات إلى دِمشق واللاذِقيّة وكَذلِك إلى لُبنان والأردُنّ.

سامية كَحّال

كَتَب أبو عَدنان الرِسالةَ التالية إلى ابنِهِ عَدنان في أمريكا وأرسَلَ لَهُ مَعَها صورةَ العائِلة. يُخبِر أبو عَدنان ابنَه في الرِسالة أنَّ والدِتَهُ سَتزورُهُ في الولاياتِ المُتحدة في الصيفِ المُقبِل وأنَّهُ لَن يَستَطيع أنْ يَكون مَعَها في هذِه الزِيارة.

رِسالة ياسِر مارتيني إلى ابنِه عَدنان

حلب في ٢٢ أيار ٢٠٠٨

ابني الحبيب عدنان، السلامُ عليكَ ورحمةُ اللّه.

أرجو أن تصلكَ رسالتي هذه وأنتَ في أحسن حال. كلُّنا بخير والحمد للّه. كتبتُ لكَ رسالة في الشهر الماضي وما وصلني منكَ ردٌّ عليها. أما وصلتكَ رسالتي؟ آخر رسالة منكَ كان تاريخها ٧ كانون الثاني. أرجو أن تكتبَ لنا دون تأخير.

أكتب هذه الرسالة لأخبركَ أن والدتكَ تريد أن تسافر إليكَ في شهر آب. لن أستطيع أن أسافر معها هذه المرّة لأني مشغول جداً. يجب أن أسافر إلى ألمانيا في آب المقبل من أجل استيراد بضاعة لمحلي.

اشتريتُ تذكرة طائرة لوالدتكَ على الخطوط الجوية الهولندية. تغادر طائرتها مطار دمشق في يوم الخميس ١٤ آب وتصل إلى شيكاغو في اليوم نفسه. أرجو أن تستقبلها في المطار لأنها كما تعلم لا تتكلم الإنكليزية ولا تعرف أحداً على الطائرة.

والآن إليكَ أخبار الأسرة. أخوكَ أيمن كلّمنا بالهاتف من دمشق وهو بخير ويرسل لكَ سلامه. أخوكَ رامي لا يزال يدرس في الجامعة ويعمل سائقاً في شركة البرادات، وهو سعيد بذلكَ. خالكَ أحمد انتقل في الشهر الماضي وعائلته إلى دمشق حيث سيعمل مدرساً للفيزياء في إحدى المدارس الثانوية. تقاعد عمكَ زهير من عمله في وزارة التربية، وهو يقول إن حياة المتقاعد تعجبه كثيراً. جدتكَ أم ياسر ترسل لكَ سلامها وتشكركَ على الهدية التي أرسلتها لها. أكتب لنا عن أخباركَ وإلى اللقاء.

والدكَ

تمرين ٥

المُحادثة :تفعيلُ المُفرَدات:

أحضِر بَعضَ الصُوَر لأُسرَتك إلى الصَفّ كَي تَصِفَها لِزُملائك، ثُمَّ في مَجموعات من اِثنَين، حاوِل أن تَستَخدِم كُلَّ الكَلِمات الوارِدة في المُربَّعات أدناه في وَصفِها مع زَميلك:

يَظهَر	مُؤلَّف مِن	إلى يَمين	أقام	أعْلى	أخَذ	أكْبَر مِن
يَبدو	كي / لِـ	إلى يَسار	تَقاعَدَ عن	أسْفل	اِلْتَقَط	أصْغَر مِن

تَذَوَّق الثَقافة العَربيّة

مُلاحَظة ثقافية حَولَ الدِراسة في سوريا. . . حينَ يَصِلُ الطالِب إلى الصفِّ الحادي عَشَر يَختارُ الفَرعَ العِلميّ أو الفَرعَ الأدبِيّ ويَبقى فيهِ سَنَتَين.

الفَرْعَ العِلمِيّ

في الفرعِ العِلمِيّ يَدْرُسُ الرياضيّات والكيمياء والفيزياء وعِلمَ الأَحْياء والجيولوجيا.

أمّا في الفَرعِ الأدبِيّ فَيدرُس لُغَتين أجنَبِيَّتَين والأدَب والشِعْرَ العَرَبيّ والفَلسَفة والتاريخ والجُغرافيا وعِلم الاجتِماع.

الفَرع الأدبيّ

التمرين ٦

محادثة: إسأل زَميلك في الصَفّ:

1. has a passport
2. has traveled abroad
3. has lived abroad
4. has relatives abroad
5. knows where Aleppo is
6. has written a letter in Arabic
7. can read Arabic handwriting

أخبِر زُملائك في الصَفّ بِما عِلمت من مُحادَثاتك معَهُم مُستَخدِماً أكبَر قَدَر من التَفاصيل وحاوِل أن تَتَفَنَّن (be creative) في كَلامك.

تمرين ٧

آ- **أجب عن الأسئلةِ التالية حَسَبَ نَصِّ القِراءة:**

١- في أيّ صَف أمينة؟

٢- ما اسْم أخت عَدنان الصُغرى؟

٣- أينَ يَقِف مَروان في الصورة؟

٤- مِن أين يَستَوْرِد ياسِر مارتيني بِضاعَتَهُ؟

٥- كَمْ مُوَظَّفاً يَشتَغِل في مَحَلّ أبي عَدنان؟

٦- لماذا يُسافِر أبو عَدنان إلى ألمانيا؟

٧- ماذا كانَت تَعمَل أمّ عَدنان؟

٨- مَتى تَقاعَدَت عن العَمَل ولِماذا؟

٩- مَتى كَتَب عَدنان آخِر رِسالة إلى أسرَتِه؟

١٠- مَن أمّ ياسِر؟

قلعة الحصن في سوريا

ب - أكتُبْ «خَطَأ» أو «صَواب» بِجانب كُلّ جُملَة وصَحِّحِ الجُمَلَ الخَطَأ.

١١- تَذهَب أمينة إلى مَدرَسة ثانويَّة لِلبَنين.

١٢- يَدرُس رامي عِلمَ الحاسوب في أمريكا.

١٣- مَروان أصْغَر إخوَة عَدنان وهو في السابِعة عَشْرَة مِن عُمرِه.

١٤- تَصِل بِضاعَةُ السَيِّد مارتيني إلى ميناءِ اللاذِقيّة دائماً.

١٥- لَمْ تَزُرْ أمّ عَدنان أمريكا.

١٦- خال عَدنان مُتَقاعِد الآن.

ج - اختَر التكمِلةَ المُناسِبة حَسَبَ النَصّ.

١٧- ياسِرمارتيني لَهُ . . .

☐ مَحَلّ تِجاريّ ☐ سَيّارة ألمانية

☐ سَيّارة فولكسفاكن ☐ مَحَلّ في ألمانيا

١٨- يَستَوْرِد ياسِر مارتيني بِضاعَتَه مِن . . .

☐ حَلَب ☐ الشاحِنات

☐ البَحْر ☐ ألمانيا

١٩- مَحَلّ أبي عَدنان مَوجود في . . .

☐ دِمَشق ☐ حَلَب

☐ اللاذِقيّة ☐ ألمانيا

٢٠- أوبِل اسم . . .

☐ سَيّارة ألمانية ☐ مَحَلّ ياسِر مارتيني

☐ قِطَع غِيارِ السَيّاراتِ ☐ مَخْزَن سَيّارات

٢١- يَستَورِد أبو عَدنان بِضاعَتَهُ غالِباً عَن طَريقِ . . .

☐ البَحْر ☐ الشاحِنات

☐ الجَوّ ☐ القِطارات

٢٢- أمّ عَدنان . . . الآن.

☐ مُدَرِّسة لُغَة فَرَنسيّة ☐ رَبَّة بَيت

☐ جَدّة ☐ مُوظَّفة

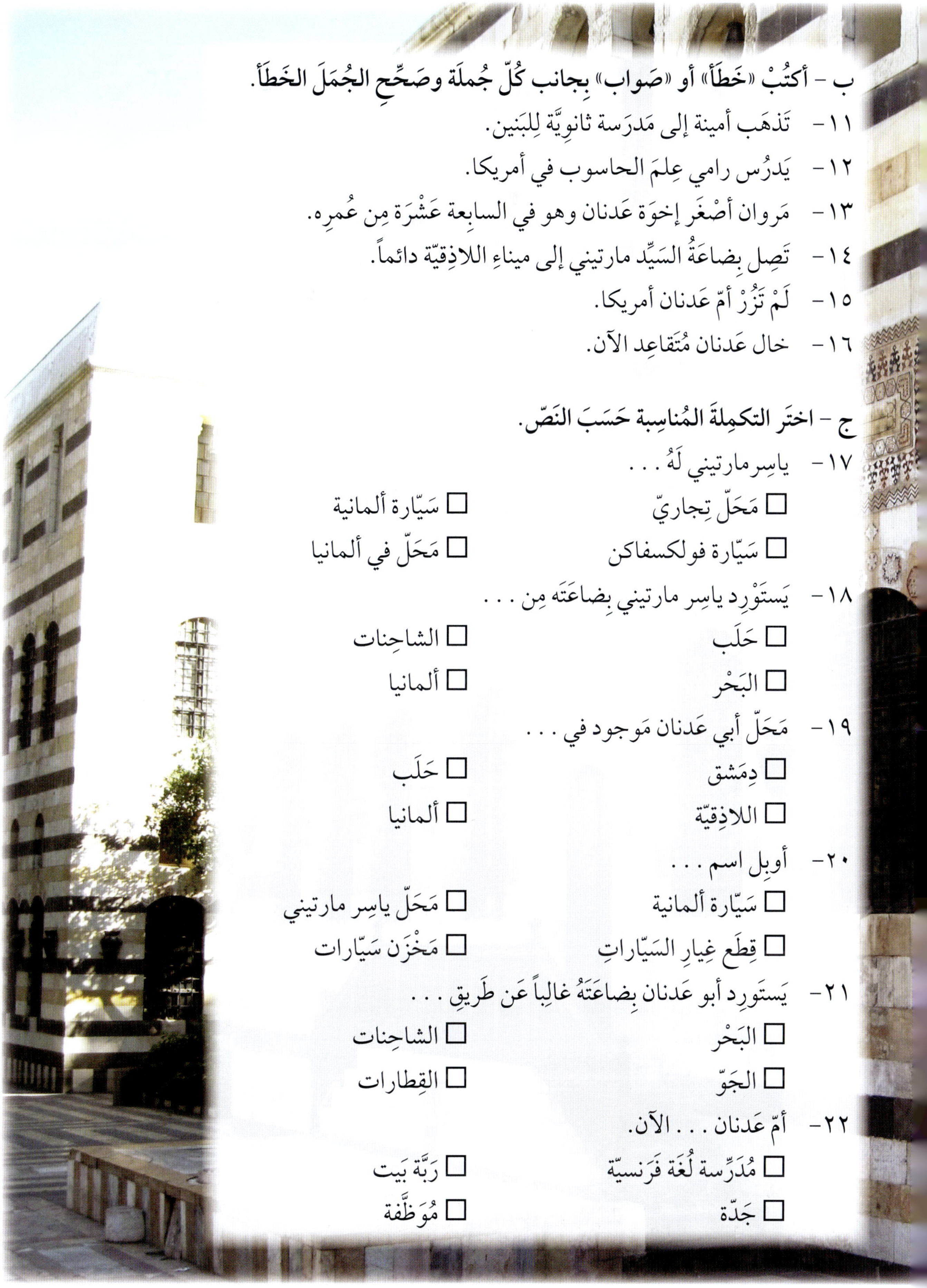

داخِل قَصر العَظم في مَدينة دِمشق

٢٣- أحمَد هو . . . عَدنان.

☐ خال ☐ عَمّ

☐ جَدّ ☐ أخو

٢٤- سَتُسافِر أمّ عَدنان إلى أمريكا على الخُطوطِ الجَوِيّة . . .

☐ السوريّة ☐ الألمانيّة

☐ الهولنديّة ☐ الأردنيّة

تمرين ٨

اكْتُبْ في كلّ عَمود (column) كَلِمات مِن النَصّ تُناسِبُ الكلِمات في السَطر الأوّل.

١	جَواز سَفَر	٢	عائِلة	٣	تِجارة	٤	مَدارِس	٥	مِهَن	٦	بِلاد

مَدينة اللاذقية في سوريا

تمرين ٩

الكِتابة: تَصوَّر أنَّ هذه الصورةَ تُمَثِّلُ اجتماع أساتذة وطُلابٍ مِن قِسْمِ اللُغةِ العَربية. أعطِ لِكلّ شَخص في الصورة اسماً مِن عِندك ثمَّ اكتُب وَصْفاً كالوَصفِ المَوجود في الفِقرةِ الأولى مِن الدَرس مُستَخدِماً أفعالاً وكَلِمات مِثل:

يَظهَر	يَجلِس	أعلى	خَلفَ	إلى جانِب	إلى يَمين
يَبدو	يَقِف	أسفَل	أمامَ	يُشير	إلى يَسار

العَرض: قدّم للطُلاّب بعض الأمثلة لاسم التفضيل المؤنَّث الّتي قد تعرّضوا لها سابقاً:

اللغة العربية الفُصْحى
درجة الحرارة الصُغْرى/ العُظمى
مصر العُليا والسُفلى

ثمّ راجِع مع الطُلاّب بعض الصفات واشرح لهم طريقة اشتقاق اسم التفضيل منها. قارن صور الأشخاص والجوامد، كما ترى في الأمثلة أدناه.

مدينة شيكاغو أكبر من مدينة توليدو.
دمشق أقدم مدينة في العالم.
النيل أطول نهر في العالم.

الممارسة: اسأل الطُلاّب أسئلة مثل:

«ما اسم أكبر مدينة سكنت فيها؟»
«ما اسم أحسن فيلم شاهدته؟»
«ما ثاني أطول نهر في العالم؟»
«هل الفيل أسرع من الحصان أم العكس؟»
«ما أعلى جبل في العالم؟»

تَذَوّق الثقافة العَرَبيّة

الألقاب العَرَبيّة: كَما هو الحال في لُغات كَثيرة، هُناك عِدّة طُرُق نُنادي فيها الأشخاص. وكَما تَعلَم، نَستَطيع نِداء الرَجُل بالألقاب الآتية: أخ وسَيِّد وأستاذ ودكتور. أمّا بالنِسبة إلى المَرأة، فَنُناديها: أخت وآنِسة وسيِّدة وسِت وأستاذة ودكتورة. بالإضافة إلى ذلِك، في دُوَل عَديدة في الوَطن العَرَبيّ، يَستَخدِم أهلُها لَقبَي أبو وأُمّ وبَعده اسم الابن الكَبير وهذا من عادات العَرَب وتَقاليدِهم. على سَبيل المِثال، حين نُنادي رَجُلاً أبو سَليم بَدلاً من اسمِه الأوّل فهو يَدُلّ على الاحتِرام لَهُ أو أنّ المَوقَف رَسميّ، ومن المُعتاد أن يُعرَف شَخصاً ما فَقط بلَقَبه (مَثَلاً أبو سامِر أو أُمّ هِشام). لَيسَ كُلّ المُجتَمَعات العَرَبيّة تَعتبِر الألقاب مِثل هذِهِ شَيئاً إيجابيّاً. في المَراكِز الحَضَريّة في مِصر، مَثَلاً، لَقَبي أبو وأُم مُقتَصِرة على الطَبَقة العامِلة.

تمرين ١٠

تَمرينُ المُشاهَدة: شاهِدوا الدَرْسَ الرابع والعشرين على الشابِكة.

١- ماذا يَعمَل أبو عَدنان؟ ________________________________

____

____

٢- لِماذا تقاعَدَت أمّ عَدنان عن العَمَل؟ ________________________

____

____

٣- مَتى ستَزور والدة عَدنان أمريكا؟ ____________________________

____

____

٤- لِماذا لا يستَطيعُ والِدُ عدنان أن يأتي إلى أمريكا مع زوجتِه؟ __________

____

____

تَذَوَّق الثَقافة العَربيّة

في المَشهَد المَرئيّ على الشابِكة، سَمِعنا عَدنان يَرُدّ على سُؤال سامِر عن حالة أفراد عائلتِه قائلاً:

((كُلُّهُم بِخَير ويُسلِّمون علَيكُم كَثيراً.))

نَستَطيع أن نَرُدّ على أي سُؤال عن حالة شَخص بِمِثل هذا القَول، على سَبيل المِثال:

- كَيف حال فُلان الفُلانيّ؟
- فُلان الفُلانيّ بِخَير ويسَلِّم عليك.

تمرين ١١

المُحادَثة:

في المَشهَد المَرئيّ، نَرى الشباب يَتحَدَّثون ويُدَردِشون ويَشرَبون الأركيلة في مقهى. ما التَشابُهات والاختِلافات بين الخُروج مع الأصدِقاء في الوَطَنِ العَرَبيّ وفي أمريكا. إلى أين تَذهَب مع أصدِقاءك وعَما تَتَحَدَّث وماذا تَفعَل معهُم عادةً؟ هل جَرّبت الأركيلة وما رأيك فيها؟ هل في أمريكا عادة مُقابِلة للأرجيلة وما هي؟

١- مُراجَعة اسم التَفضيل

كَما تَعلَم، اِسمَ التَفضيل بِالعَرَبيّة وَزَنُه أفْعَل ونَستَخدِم أفْعَل + مِن حين نُقارِن بَين شَيئَين (مِثل: أنا أطْوَل من عَدنان). لاحِظ أنّ اسمَ التَفضيل مؤلَّف من اسمَين أي المُضاف والمُضاف إليه وهُما يُشَكِّلان الإضافة (مِثل: أطْوَلُ رَجُل) أو قَد نُعَرِّفُه (مِثل: أخي الأكْبَر أو إخوتي الأكابِر أو أختي الكُبْرى أو أخَواتي الكُبْرَيات)، كَما هو وارِد في الجَدوَل أدناه:

اسم التفضيل				
الصِفة	المُذَكَّر	الجَمع المُذَكَّر	المُؤنَّث	الجَمع المُؤنَّث
كَبير	أكْبَر	أكابِر	كُبرى	كُبرَيات
صَغير	أصْغَر	أصاغِر	صُغرى	صُغرَيات
عالٍ	أعلى	أعالي	عُليا	-----
سافِل	أسْفَل	أسافِل	سُفلى	سُفلَيات
يَمين	أيمَن	-----	يُمنى	يُمنَيات
يَسار	أيْسَر	-----	يُسرى	يُسْرَيات

مُلاحَظة: تذَكَّر أنّ وَزنَ الصِفة يَتَغَيَّر حَسَبَ الإفراد والتَثنية والجمع والتَذكير والتأنيث، على سَبيل المِثال:

المُفرَد	المُثنّى	الجمع	المُؤنَّث	المُثنّى المُؤنَّث	الجمع المُؤنَّث
كَبير	كَبيران	كِبار	كَبيرة	كَبيرتان	كَبيرات

إنَّ التَفضيل بِالعَرَبيّة اسم ولِهذا نُسَمّيه اسمُ التَفضيل وعادةً يأتي في صيغةِ التَذكير، لكِن أحياناً يأتي في صيغةِ التأنيث أيضاً كَما رأينا في النَصّ الرئيس في هذا الدَرس:

١	أخْتُ عَدنان الصُغرى	*Adnān's youngest sister*

يُبَيِّن لَنا المِثال ١ أعلاه اسمَ التَفضيلِ المُؤنَّث الّذي وَزنُه فُعْلى، وتَستَطيع أن تَرى أوزان اسمِ التَفضيلِ الأخرى في الجَدوَل في الصَفحة السابقة.

٢- حَرفا لِـ وكَي "in order to"

حَرفا لِـ وكَي من مَجموعة أحرُف تَدُلّ على التَعليل (reason) وتَستَطيع أن تَستَخدِمُهُما على انفِراد (لِـ أو كَي كَما تَرى في المِثال ٢) أو معاً (لِكَي كَما تَرى في المِثال ٣).

مُلاحَظة: لَيسَ هُناكَ أي فَرق في المَعنى بَينَ الحَرفَين.

٢	حَضَرَتْ أمُّ عَدنان إلى أمريكا كَيْ تزورَ ابنَها.	*Umm Adnān came to America in order to visit her son.*
٣	حَضَرَتْ أمُّ عَدنان إلى أمريكا لِكَيْ تزورَ ابنَها.	*Umm Adnān came to America in order to visit her son.*

تمرين ١٢

المُحادَثة: اسأل زَميلك في الصَفِّ الأسئلةَ الآتية وحاوِل اِستِخدام لِـ أو كَي في أجوِبتِك:

1. why he/she chooses to study at this university/college/school
2. why he/she chooses to study Arabic
3. why he/she has a car/bike
4. why he/she does/doesn't have a job
5. why he/she will/will not stay home this weekend
6. why he/she will/will not do his/her homework tonight
7. why he/she wants to graduate.

مُلاحَظة: تَذَكَّر أنَّنا رأينا أحرُف أخرى تَنصِبُ الفِعلَ الّذي يليُها مِثل لَنْ (الّذي يَنفي الفِعل المُضارِع ويَدُلّ على المُستَقبَل) وأنْ (الّذي يَلي بعضَ الأفعال مِثل أراد وأَحَبَّ - انظُر إلى المِثالَين ٤ و٥). وكَما تَتَذَكَّر أنَّ المُضارِعَ المَنصوب علامتُه فَتحة على آخِر حَرفِ الفِعل (مَثلاً: لَنْ يَكْتُبَ) أو (الطُلّاب لَنْ يَكتُبوا) حَيث تَسقُط نون الجَماعة من الفِعل (المِثال ٦).

٤	أُحِبُّ أنْ أتكَلَّمَ العَرَبيّة.	*I like speaking Arabic.*
٥	أُريدُ أنْ أتَكَلَّمَ العَرَبيّة.	*I want to speak Arabic.*
٦	إنَّ الطُلّاب لَنْ يَكْتُبوا الرِسالة.	*Indeed, the students won't write the letter.*

تمرين ١٣

املأ الفَراغ: اكْتُب الإعراب الصَحيح في المُضارِع لِلفِعل الّذي بَين القَوسَين. لاحِظ أنّ الفِعل الّذي بَين القَوسَين في الماضي. شَكِّل كُلّ أحرُفِ الفِعل.

مِثال: أظُنّ أنَّني لَنْ (زار) أَزورَ فلوريدا هذا الشِتاء.

١- يُريد هِشام وأماني أنْ (سَكَنَ) ________ في مَدينة كبيرة.

٢- أظُن أنَّ أصدقائي لَنْ (أتى) ________ إلى الصَفِّ اليَوم.

٣- هَل تُحِب أنْ (شَرِبَ) ________ الشاي مَعَ السُكَّر؟

٤- حَضَرْتُ إلى هذِه الجامِعة كَيْ (دَرَسَ) ________ العَرَبيّة.

٥- مَنْ يُريد أنْ (اِعتنى) ________ بِقِطَّتي حين أسافِر؟

٦- ذَهَبْنا إلى مَطعَم عَرَبيّ لِـ (أَكَلَ) ________ الفَلافِل.

قد يسألك الطُلّاب لماذا يأتي الفعل منصوبا بعد الأحرف لـ وكي وحتّى. إنّ العلماء العرب يقولون إن بعد هذه الأحرف كلّها يأتي الحرف أنْ نظرياً، مثل:

حتّى أنْ، لـأن، كي أنْ

العَرَض: حضّر قصة قصيرة ترد فيها أمثلة كثيرة لهذين الحرفين، على سبيل المثال:

«حضرت هالة الدرس لتتعلّم العلوم السياسية وكانت تأتي إلى الصفّ مبكّرةً كي تجلس في الصف الأمامي حيث صوت الأستاذ أوضح. ظنّت هالة أنّ دراسة العلوم السياسية أحسن طريقة لتحصل على عمل ممتاز ووافق أبوها على هذا الرأي.»

النشاط الأوّل: بعد أن قرأت على الطلّاب قصتك القصيرة، اسألهم أسئلة تبدأها أداة الاستفهام لماذا كي يجعل الطالب يجيب مستخدماً لـ أو كي أو حتّى كما ترى في الأمثلة:

«لماذا درست هالة العلوم السياسة؟ لماذا حضرت الصفّ مبكرة؟»

«لماذا جلست في الصف الأمامي؟»

النشاط الثاني: اسأل الطلّاب أسئلة فيها لماذا:

«لماذا تدرس في هذه الكلّيّة؟

هل تحبّ مشاهدة الأخبار؟ (لماذا؟)»

«هل تستمع إلى الإذاعة؟ (لماذا؟)»

«هل تظنّين أنّ هذا الفيلم جيّد؟»

التطبيق: في مجموعات من اثنين: حضّر للطُلّاب حوالي خمسة أسئلة تطلب من المجيب استخدام الأحرف لـ وكي وحتّى في أجوبتهم أو يمكنك أن تستخدم تمرين ١١ إلى اليمين.

٣- مُراجَعة المَصدَر

مُلاحَظة: بالنِسبة إلى أوزانِ الفِعل المَزيد. في باب ٣ في الدرس العاشِر، قَدَّمنا لَكُم أشكال المَصدَر المُختَلِفة. وقَد عَلِمنا أنّ لِكُلّ وَزنِ الفِعل المَزيد مَصدَر مُختَلِف وجَدير بالذِكرِ أنّ الوَزنَ الوَحيدَ الّذي لَه أكثَر من مَصدَرَين هو الوَزنُ الأوّل ولِباقي الأوزان (أي من الوَزنِ الثاني إلى العاشِر) مَصدَر واحِد أو مَصدَرَين (راجِع باب ١ في الدَرس السادِس عشر حَيثُ يوجَد جَدوَل أوزانِ الفِعل المَزيد).

وَرَدَت في هذا الدَرس، بَعض حالاتِ المَصدَر المُستَخدِمة مع حَرفِ الجَرّ لـ الّذي يَجُرُّ المَصدَر، كَما نَرى في المِثال ٧ أدناه:

٧	لِبَيْع قِطَع الغِيار	*for selling spare parts*
	لِتَخزينِ البِضاعة	*for storing the merchandise*

يأتي المَصدَر كَاسم في الجُملة العَرَبيّة، فَإنّه قد يَلعَب دَور فاعِل الجُملة (كَما نَرى في المِثال ٨) والمَفعول بِه (كَما نَرى في المِثال ٩).

٨	تُعجِبُني دِراسةُ الأدَب.	*Studying literature pleases me.*
٩	أريدُ بَيْعَ سَيّارَتي القديمة.	*I want to sell my old car.*

اختَر قِصة قصيرة أو فِقرة تظهر فيها مصادر كثيرة. أعتقد أن القصة حتى لو كانت صعبة قليلاً على الطُلّاب، لن يفهموا فحواها فحسب، بل النقاط القواعدية التي تودّ التركيز عليها أيضاً بشرط أنّ القصة مألوفة لهم. على سبيل المثال، قصة ربّ الخواتم مفيدة وصالحة لهذا الغرض بسبب كثرة المصادر الواردة فيها.

التطبيق: في مجموعات من اثنين: وزّع على الطُلّاب الفقرة المحضّرة أو القصة القصيرة واطلُب منهم أن يستخرجوا المصدر ويفيدوا بمعناه ووزنه. أعطِ الطُلّاب حوالي سبع دقائق أوعشر كي ينتهوا من النشاط ثمّ راجعها معهم.

تمرين ١٤

اِستِخراجُ المَصدَر واشتِقاقُ جَذرِه: ١_ اكتُب خَطاً تحتَ المَصدَر و٢_ اكتُب حالتَه من الإعراب فَوقَه (مَثَلاً: الفاعِل أو المَفعول بِه) و٣_ اكتُب جَذرَ المَصدَر في الفَراغ الّذي بِجانب الجُملة كَما تَرى في المِثال. لاحَظ أنّ لِبَعض الأجوِبة أكثَر من مَصدَر.

مِثال: ذَهَبَت الزَوجَة إلى عَمَلِها بَعد تَحضيرِ الفَطور. عمل، حضر

١- يُريد أحمَد بَيْع سَيّارته القَديمة لِيَشتَري سَيّارة جَديدة. ____________

٢- لَم أرَ أختي مُنذُ كِتابة هذِه الكَلِمات. ____________

٣- أعرِفُ اللُغةَ الألماينة لكِنْ لا يُمكِنُني التكلُّم بِها. ______________

٤- سَوفَ أعمَل في شَرِكة تِجاريّة بَعد تَخَرُّجي. ______________

٥- اسْتِضافَتُكُم في بَيتي تَسُرّني جِدّاً. ______________

٦- يُعجِبُني التَنَزُّهُ على شاطِئِ البَحر. ______________

تمرين ١٥

أجِب عن السؤالَين حَسَبَ نصِّ الاستماع:

١- أين تَسكُنُ الفَتاة ووالِداها ؟

٢- مَنْ يَعمَل ويَسكُن في الدارِ البَيْضاء ؟

قَصر العَظم في مَدينة دِمشق

أكتُبْ «خطَأً» أو «صَواب» بِجانب كُلّ جُملَة وصَحِّحِ الجُمَلَ الخطَأ.

٣- تَدرُسُ الفَتاةُ الهَنْدَسةَ الكَهْرَبائية.

٤- لِلفَتاة أخ يَدرُس في أمريكا.

أكمِل الجُمَل بِالاخْتيارِ المُناسِب حَسَبَ نَصِّ الاستِماع.

٥- سَتَصِل أسرة نِزار إلى فيلادلفيا على طائرة ______________.

☐ سورية ☐ مَغربية ☐ أمِريكية

٦- اشترى الوالِد ______________ سَفَر.

☐ تَذكِرة ☐ تَذكِرَتَي ☐ ثلاث تَذاكِر

أكمِلْ الجُمَلَ التاليّة حَسَبَ نَصِّ الاستِماع.

٧- تُريدُ الفَتاة أنْ تَرى ______________

٨- سَتبقى الفَتاة ووالِداها في الدارِ البَيضاء مُدّة ______________.

المُفْرَدات

استمِع إلى المُفْرَدة بالعَرَبيّة ثُمَّ أعِد نُطْقَها مرّتين.

to choose . . . . (v.) اِخْتارَ (يَخْتارُ) اِخْتِيار

last, latest . . . . (adj.) آخِر

department . . . . (n., f.) إدارة ج إدارات

to import . . . . (v.) اِسْتَوْرَدَ (يَسْتَوْرِدُ) اِسْتيراد

bottom, lowest point, . . (n., m., superlative form) أَسْفَل ج أسافِل
lower

to resemble . . . . (v.) أَشْبَهَ (يُشْبِهُ) شَبه

to take care of, to tend . . . . (v.) (بـِ) اِعْتَنى (يَعْتَني) اِعتِناء

top, ... (n., m., superlative form) أَعْلى ج أعالٍ
highest point, upper

to reside in . . . . (v.) أقام (يُقيم) إقامة

to pick up; to take (a picture) . . . . . . (v.) اِلْتَقَطَ (يَلْتَقِطُ) اِلْتِقاط

female . . . . (n., f.) أُنْثى ج إناث

salesperson . . . . (n., m.) بائِع ج بائعون

to appear, to seem . . . . (v.) بَدا (يَبدو) بُدُوٌّ

brown . . . . (adj.) بُنّيّ

merchant, businessman . . . . (n., m.) تاجِر ج تُجّار

to be late . . . . (v.) تَأَخَّرَ (يَتَأَخَّرُ) تَأَخُّر

to retire (from work) . . . . (v.) (عن) تَقاعَدَ (يَتَقاعَدُ) تَقاعُد

signature . . . . (n., m.) تَوْقيع

grandfather . . . . (n., m.) جَدّ ج جُدود

geology . . . . (n., f.) جيولوجيا

maternal uncle . . . . (n., m.) خال ج أخْوال

to store . . . . (v.) خَزَّنَ (يُخَزِّنُ) تَخْزين

guide . . . . (n., m.) دَليل ج أدِلاّء

to refer to, to review . . . . (v.) راجَعَ (يُراجِعُ) مُراجعَة

to respond, to answer. . . . . (v.) رَدَّ (يَرُدُّ) رَدّ

to register, to record . . . . (v.) سَجَّلَ (يُسَجِّلُ) تَسْجيل

tourist . . . . (adj.) سياحيّ

hair . . . . (n., m.) شَعْر ج شُعور / أشْعار

poetry, poem . . . . (n., m.) شِعْر ج أشْعار

last name, surname. . . . . (n., f.) شُهْرة

to issue . . . . (v.) صَدَرَ (يَصْدُرُ) صُدور

youngest, smallest . . . . صُغرى superlative of صَغيرة,

pharmacist . . . . (n., f.) صَيدلانِيّة

pharmacy . . . . (n., f.) صَيْدَليّة

height . . . . (n., m.) طول

paternal uncle. . . . . (n., m.) عَمّ ج أعْمام

age. . . . . (n., m.) عُمُر ج أعْمار

eye. . . . . (n., f) عَيْن ج عُيون

spare (part), change . . . . (n., m) غِيار ج غيارات

branch, subdivision. . . . . (n., m.) فَرْع ج فُروع

to talk to, to speak with. . . . . (v.) كَلَّمَ (يُكَلِّمُ)

expresses completed action . . . . (particle) لَقَد
with a perfect tense verb

retired person. . . . . (n., m.) مُتَقاعِد ج مُتَقاعِدون

store, shop; place, location . . . . (n., m.) مَحَلّ ج مَحَلات

store, warehouse . . . . (n., m.) مَخْزَن ج مَخازِن

teacher . . . . (n., m.) مُدَرِّس ج مُدَرِّسون

sick, ill, patient . . . . (adj., m) مَريض ج مَرْضى

hospital . . . . (n., m.) مُسْتَشْفى

passive participle . . . . مَفعول

note, observation . . . . (n., f.) مُلاحَظة ج مُلاحظات

occupation, profession . . . . (n., f.) مِهْنة ج مِهَن

consisting of, comprising. . . . . . (passive participle) مُؤَلَّف (مِن)

same. . . . . (n., f.) (. . .الـ) نَفْس ج أَنْفُس

ministry, department . . . . (n., f.) وِزارة ج وِزارات
in an administration

جامِع الزَيتونة في مَدينة تونس عام ١٨٩٩

نواعير حماة

Appendix A

Arabic Alphabet and Diacritical Marks

حروف الهجاء العربية
وعلامات التشكيل

الرمز	أشكال الحرف في مواضع الكلمة			اسم الحرف	الحرف
Symbol	Final	Medial	Initial	Name	Letter
ā	ـا	ـا	ا	ألف	ا
b	ـب	ـبـ	بـ	باء	ب
t	ـت	ـتـ	تـ	تاء	ت
ṯ	ـث	ـثـ	ثـ	ثاء	ث
j	ـج	ـجـ	جـ	جيم	ج
ḥ	ـح	ـحـ	حـ	حاء	ح
ḳ	ـخ	ـخـ	خـ	خاء	خ
d	ـد	ـد	د	دال	د
ḏ	ـذ	ـذ	ذ	ذال	ذ
r	ـر	ـر	ر	راء	ر
z	ـز	ـز	ز	زاي	ز
s	ـس	ـسـ	سـ	سين	س

š	ـش	ـشـ	شـ	شين	ش
ṣ	ـص	ـصـ	صـ	صاد	ص
ḍ	ـض	ـضـ	ضـ	ضاد	ض
ṭ	ـط	ـطـ	طـ	طاء	ط
ẕ	ـظ	ـظـ	ظـ	ظاء	ظ
ʿ	ـع	ـعـ	عـ	عين	ع
ġ	ـغ	ـغـ	غـ	غين	غ
f	ـف	ـفـ	فـ	فاء	ف
q	ـق	ـقـ	قـ	قاف	ق
k	ـك	ـكـ	كـ	كاف	ك
l	ـل	ـلـ	لـ	لام	ل
m	ـم	ـمـ	مـ	ميم	م
n	ـن	ـنـ	نـ	نون	ن
h	ـه	ـهـ	هـ	هاء	ه
w/ū	ـو	ـو	و	واو	و
y/ī	ـي	ـيـ	يـ	ياء	ي
ā	ـى			أَلِف مَقصورة	ى
t	ـة			تاء مربوطة	ة

ʾ	ـأ ـؤ ـئ	ـأ ـؤ ـئـ	أ إ	هَمزة	ء
a	*fatḥa*			فَتحة	َ
u	*ḍamma*			ضَمّة	ُ
i	*kasra*			كَسرة	ِ
-an	*tanwīn*			تَنوين بالفَتح	ً
-un	*tanwīn*			تَنوين بالضَمّ	ٌ
-in	*tanwīn*			تَنوين بالكَسْر	ٍ
sakūn signifies the absence of a short vowel				سُكون	ْ
šadda indicates a doubled consonant				شَدّة	ّ
madda denotes a *hamza* and a long *alif*				مَدّة	آ

Appendix B

A Key to the Arabic Sound System and the Transliteration System Used in the Textbook

الحرف Arabic Letter	الرمز Roman Symbol	Example/Description
ا	*ā*	*a* as in *far* and *bad*
ب	*b*	*b* as in *bet*
ت	*t*	*t* as in *two*
ث	*ṯ*	*th* as in *three*
ج	*j*	*j* as in *judge*
ح	*ḥ*	*h*-like sound produced with constriction
خ	*ḳ*	*ch* as in Scottish *loch* or German *Bach*
د	*d*	*d* as in *dip*
ذ	*ḏ*	*th* as in *then*
ر	*r*	*r* as in Spanish *perro* (trilled *r*)
ز	*z*	*z* as in *zip*
س	*s*	*s* as in *sad*
ش	*š*	*sh* as in *show*
ص	*ṣ*	*s* as in *sod*
ض	*ḍ*	*d* as in *dark*
ط	*ṭ*	*t* as in *tar*

ظ	*ẓ*	*th* as in *thine*
ع	ʿ	a fricative sound produced in the throat
غ	*ġ*	roughly similar to the German *r*; a gargling sound
ف	*f*	*f* as in *fit*
ق	*q*	roughly similar to the *c* in *cot*, but further back
ك	*k*	*k* as in *kit*
ل	*l*	*l* as in *leak*
م	*m*	*m* as in *mint*
ن	*n*	*n* as in *nil*
ه	*h*	*h* as in *hat*
و	*ū*	*oo* as in *pool*
و	*w*	*w* as in *wet*
ي	*ī*	*ee* as in *feel*
ي	*y*	*y* as in *yet*
ى	*ā*	*a* as in *dad* (a form of *alif* in the final position)
ة	*t*	see the discussion on *tāʾ marbūṭa* in Unit 3 (Workbook)
ء	ʾ	glottal stop; the stop before *a* in *above*
َ	*a*	roughly similar to *u* as in *but*
ُ	*u*	*u* as in *pull*
ِ	*i*	*i* as in *bill*

Appendix C

Verb Conjugations

This appendix contains a representative sample of verb conjugation paradigms. At the top of each table, الماضي (past) with المضارع (present) are listed next to each other followed by the pattern of the verb and its roman numeral, the المصدر (verbal noun), اسم الفاعل (active participle), and اسم المفعول (passive participle). Each table has separate pronouns in the right-hand column followed by the conjugations of المضارع: المرفوع والمنصوب والمجزوم (indicative, subjunctive, jussive) in that order, and الأمر (imperative). All are in the active voice. The conjugations are classified according to person: first, second, and third. Only one conjugation for the second-person dual masculine and feminine (أنتما) is provided. Feminine pronouns follow masculine pronouns.

ظَنَّ (يَظُنُّ) (فَعَل I) (ظَنٌّ – ظانّ – مَظنون)

to think, to presume

Imperative	Jussive	Subjunctive	Indicative	Past	Pronoun
الأمر	المضارع المجزوم	المضارع المنصوب	المضارع المرفوع	الماضي	الضمير
	أَظُنَّ	أَظُنَّ	أَظُنُّ	ظَنَنْتُ	أنا
	نَظُنَّ	نَظُنَّ	نَظُنُّ	ظَنَنّا	نَحنُ
ظُنَّ	تَظُنَّ	تَظُنَّ	تَظُنُّ	ظَنَنْتَ	أنتَ
ظُنّي	تَظُنّي	تَظُنّي	تَظُنّينَ	ظَنَنْتِ	أنتِ
ظُنّا	تَظُنّا	تَظُنّا	تَظُنّانِ	ظَنَنْتُما	أنتما
ظُنّوا	تَظُنّوا	تَظُنّوا	تَظُنّونَ	ظَنَنْتُم	أنتُم
اِظْنُنَّ	تَظْنُنَّ	تَظْنُنَّ	تَظْنُنَّ	ظَنَنْتُنَّ	أنتُنَّ
	يَظُنَّ	يَظُنَّ	يَظُنُّ	ظَنَّ	هُوَ
	تَظُنَّ	تَظُنَّ	تَظُنُّ	ظَنَّتْ	هِيَ
	يَظُنّا	يَظُنّا	يَظُنّانِ	ظَنّا	هُما
	تَظُنّا	تَظُنّا	تَظُنّانِ	ظَنَّتا	هُما
	يَظُنّوا	يَظُنّوا	يَظُنّونَ	ظَنّوا	هُم
	يَظْنُنَّ	يَظْنُنَّ	يَظْنُنَّ	ظَنَنَّ	هُنَّ

تكلَّمَ (يَتَكَلَّمُ) (تفعّل V) (تَكَلُّم – مُتَكَلِّم – مَتَكَلَّم)

to talk, to speak

Imperative	Jussive	Subjunctive	Indicative	Past	Pronoun
الأمر	المضارع المجزوم	المضارع المنصوب	المضارع المرفوع	الماضي	الضمير
	أَتكلَّمْ	أَتكلَّمَ	أَتَكَلَّمُ	تكلَّمْتُ	أنا
	نتكلَّمْ	نتكلَّمَ	نتكلَّمُ	تكلَّمْنا	نَحنُ
تكلَّمْ	تتكلَّمْ	تتكلَّمَ	تتكلَّمُ	تكلَّمْتَ	أنتَ
تكلَّمي	تتكلَّمي	تتكلَّمي	تتكلَّمينَ	تكلَّمْتِ	أنتِ
تكلَّما	تتكلَّما	تتكلَّما	تتكلَّمانِ	تكلَّمْتُما	أنتما
تكلَّموا	تتكلَّموا	تتكلَّموا	تتكلَّمونَ	تكلَّمْتُم	أنتُم
تكلَّمْنَ	تتكلَّمْنَ	تتكلَّمْنَ	تتكلَّمْنَ	تكلَّمْتُنَّ	أنتُنَّ
	يتكلَّمْ	يتكلَّمَ	يتكلَّمُ	تكلَّمَ	هُوَ
	تتكلَّمْ	تتكلَّمَ	تتكلَّمُ	تكلَّمَتْ	هِيَ
	يتكلَّما	يتكلَّما	يتكلَّمانِ	تكلَّما	هُما
	تتكلَّما	تتكلَّما	تتكلَّمانِ	تكلَّمَتا	هُما
	يتكلَّموا	يتكلَّموا	يتكلَّمونَ	تكلَّموا	هُم
	يتكلَّمْنَ	يتكلَّمْنَ	يتكلَّمْنَ	تكلَّمْنَ	هُنَّ

كانَ (يَكونُ) (فَعَل I) (كَوْنٌ – كائِن – مَكون)

to be

Imperative	Jussive	Subjunctive	Indicative	Past	Pronoun
الأمر	المضارع المجزوم	المضارع المنصوب	المضارع المرفوع	الماضي	الضمير
	أكُنْ	أكونَ	أكونُ	كُنْتُ	أنا
	نكُنْ	نكونَ	نكونُ	كُنّا	نَحنُ
كُنْ	تكُنْ	تكونَ	تكونُ	كُنْتَ	أنتَ
كوني	تكوني	تكوني	تكونينَ	كُنْتِ	أنتِ
كونا	تكونا	تكونا	تكونانِ	كُنْتُما	أنتما
كونوا	تكونوا	تكونوا	تكونونَ	كُنتُم	أنتُم
كُنَّ	تكُنَّ	تكُنَّ	تكُنَّ	كُنْتُنَّ	أنْتُنَّ
	يَكُنْ	يَكونَ	يَكونُ	كانَ	هُوَ
	تكُنْ	تكونَ	تكونُ	كانَتْ	هِيَ
	يَكونا	يَكونا	يَكونانِ	كانا	هُما
	تكونا	تكونا	تكونانِ	كانتا	هُما
	يَكونوا	يَكونوا	يَكونونَ	كانوا	هُم
	يَكُنَّ	يَكُنَّ	يَكُنَّ	كُنَّ	هُنَّ

أعطى (يُعْطي) (أَفْعَل IV) (إعْطاء – مُعْطٍ – مُعْطىً)

to give

Imperative	Jussive	Subjunctive	Indicative	Past	Pronoun
الأمر	المضارع المجزوم	المضارع المنصوب	المضارع المرفوع	الماضي	الضمير
	أُعْطِ	أُعْطِيَ	أُعْطي	أَعْطَيْتُ	أنا
	نُعْطِ	نُعْطِيَ	نُعْطي	أَعْطَيْنا	نَحنُ
أعْطِ	تُعْطِ	تُعْطِيَ	تُعْطي	أَعْطَيْتَ	أنتَ
أعْطي	تُعْطي	تُعْطي	تُعْطينَ	أَعْطَيْتِ	أنتِ
أعْطِيا	تُعْطِيا	تُعْطِيا	تُعْطِيانِ	أَعْطَيْتُما	أنتما
أعْطوا	تُعْطوا	تُعْطوا	تُعْطونَ	أَعْطَيْتُمْ	أنتُم
أعْطينَ	تُعْطينَ	تُعْطينَ	تُعْطينَ	أَعْطَيْتُنَّ	أنتُنَّ
	يُعْطِ	يُعْطِيَ	يُعْطي	أَعْطى	هُوَ
	تُعْطِ	تُعْطِيَ	تُعْطي	أَعْطَتْ	هِيَ
	يُعْطِيا	يُعْطِيا	يُعْطِيانِ	أَعْطَيا	هُما
	تُعْطِيا	تُعْطِيا	تُعْطِيانِ	أَعْطَتا	هُما
	يُعْطوا	يُعْطوا	يُعْطونَ	أَعْطَوْا	هُم
	يُعْطينَ	يُعْطينَ	يُعْطينَ	أَعْطَيْنَ	هُنَّ

أَحَبَّ (يُحِبُّ) (أَفْعَل IV) (حُبٌّ – مُحِبٌّ – مُحَبٌّ)

to like, to love

Imperative	Jussive	Subjunctive	Indicative	Past	Pronoun
الأمر	المضارع المجزوم	المضارع المنصوب	المضارع المرفوع	الماضي	الضمير
	أُحِبَّ	أُحِبَّ	أُحِبُّ	أَحبَبْتُ	أنا
	نُحِبَّ	نُحِبَّ	نُحِبُّ	أَحْبَبْنَا	نَحنُ
أَحْبِبْ	تُحِبَّ	تُحِبَّ	تُحِبُّ	أَحْبَبْتَ	أنتَ
أَحِبّي	تُحِبّي	تُحِبّي	تُحِبّينَ	أَحْبَبْتِ	أنتِ
أَحِبّا	تُحِبّا	تُحِبّا	تُحِبّانِ	أَحْبَبْتُما	أنتما
أَحِبّوا	تُحِبّوا	تُحِبّوا	تُحِبّونَ	أَحْبَبْتُمْ	أنتُم
أَحْبِبْنَ	تُحْبِبْنَ	تُحْبِبْنَ	تُحْبِبْنَ	أَحْبَبْتُنَّ	أنتُنَّ
	يُحِبَّ	يُحِبَّ	يُحِبُّ	أَحَبَّ	هُوَ
	تُحِبَّ	تُحِبَّ	تُحِبُّ	أَحَبَّتْ	هِيَ
	يُحِبّا	يُحِبّا	يُحِبّانِ	أَحَبّا	هُما
	تُحِبّا	تُحِبّا	تُحِبّانِ	أَحَبَّتا	هُما
	يُحِبّوا	يُحِبّوا	يُحِبّونَ	أَحَبّوا	هُم
	يُحْبِبْنَ	يُحْبِبْنَ	يُحْبِبْنَ	أَحْبَبْنَ	هُنَّ

أرادَ (يُريدُ) (أفْعَل IV) (إرادة – مُريد – مُراد)

to want

Imperative	Jussive	Subjunctive	Indicative	Past	Pronoun
الأمر	المضارع المجزوم	المضارع المنصوب	المضارع المرفوع	الماضي	الضمير
	أُرِدْ	أُريدَ	أُريدُ	أَرَدْتُ	أنا
	نُرِدْ	نُريدَ	نُريدُ	أَرَدْنا	نَحنُ
أرِدْ	تُرِدْ	تُريدَ	تُريدُ	أَرَدْتَ	أنتَ
أريدي	تُريدي	تُريدي	تُريدينَ	أَرَدْتِ	أنتِ
أريدا	تُريدا	تُريدا	تُريدانِ	أَرَدْتُما	أنتما
أريدوا	تُريدوا	تُريدوا	تُريدونَ	أَرَدْتُمْ	أنتُم
أرِدْنَ	تُرِدْنَ	تُرِدْنَ	تُرِدْنَ	أَرَدْتُنَّ	أنتُنَّ
	يُرِدْ	يُريدَ	يُريدُ	أَرادَ	هُوَ
	تُرِدْ	تُريدَ	تُريدُ	أَرادَتْ	هِيَ
	يُريدا	يُريدا	يُريدانِ	أَرادَا	هُما
	تُريدا	تُريدا	تُريدانِ	أَرادَتا	هُما
	يُريدوا	يُريدوا	يُريدونَ	أَرادوا	هُم
	يُرِدْنَ	يُرِدْنَ	يُرِدْنَ	أَرَدْنَ	هُنَّ

عَنى (يَعْني) (فَعَل I) (عَني – عانٍ – مَعْنيّ)

to mean

Imperative	Jussive	Subjunctive	Indicative	Past	Pronoun
الأمر	المضارع المجزوم	المضارع المنصوب	المضارع المرفوع	الماضي	الضمير
	أَعْنِ	أَعْنِيَ	أَعْني	عَنَيْتُ	أنا
	نَعْنِ	نَعْنِيَ	نَعْني	عَنَيْنا	نَحنُ
اِعْنِ	تَعْنِ	تَعْنِيَ	تَعْني	عَنَيْتَ	أنتَ
اِعْني	تَعْني	تَعْني	تَعْنينَ	عَنَيْتِ	أنتِ
اِعْنِيا	تَعْنِيا	تَعْنِيا	تَعْنِيانِ	عَنَيْتُما	أنتما
اِعْنوا	تَعْنوا	تَعْنوا	تَعْنونَ	عَنَيْتُمْ	أنتُم
اِعْنينَ	تَعْنينَ	تَعْنينَ	تَعْنينَ	عَنَيْتُنَّ	أنتُنَّ
	يَعْنِ	يَعْنِيَ	يَعْني	عَنى	هُوَ
	تَعْنِ	تَعْنِيَ	تَعْني	عَنَتْ	هِيَ
	يَعْنِيا	يَعْنِيا	يَعْنِيانِ	عَنَيا	هُما
	تَعْنِيا	تَعْنِيا	تَعْنِيانِ	عَنَتا	هُما
	يَعْنوا	يَعْنوا	يَعْنونَ	عَنَوْا	هُم
	يَعْنينَ	يَعْنينَ	يَعْنينَ	عَنَيْنَ	هُنَّ

اِشْتَرى (يَشْتَري) (اِفْتَعَل VIII) (اِشتِراء – مُشْتَرٍ – مُشْتَرى)

to buy

Imperative	Jussive	Subjunctive	Indicative	Past	Pronoun
الأمر	المضارع المجزوم	المضارع المنصوب	المضارع المرفوع	الماضي	الضمير
	أَشْتَرِ	أَشْتَرِيَ	أَشْتَري	اِشْتَرَيْتُ	أنا
	نَشْتَرِ	نَشْتَرِيَ	نَشْتَري	اِشْتَرَيْنا	نَحنُ
اِشْتَرِ	تَشْتَرِ	تَشْتَرِيَ	تَشْتَري	اِشْتَرَيْتَ	أنتَ
اِشْتَري	تَشْتَري	تَشْتَري	تَشْتَرينَ	اِشْتَرَيْتِ	أنتِ
اِشْتَرِيا	تَشْتَرِيا	تَشْتَرِيا	تَشْتَرِيانِ	اِشْتَرَيْتُما	أنتما
اِشْتَروا	تَشْتَروا	تَشْتَروا	تَشْتَرونَ	اِشْتَرَيْتُم	أنتُم
اِشْتَرينَ	تَشْتَرينَ	تَشْتَرينَ	تَشْتَرينَ	اِشْتَرَيْتُنَّ	أنتُنَّ
	يَشْتَرِ	يَشْتَرِيَ	يَشْتَري	اِشْتَرى	هُوَ
	تَشْتَرِ	تَشْتَرِيَ	تَشْتَري	اِشْتَرَتْ	هِيَ
	يَشْتَرِيا	يَشْتَرِيا	يَشْتَرِيانِ	اِشْتَرَيا	هُما
	تَشْتَرِيا	تَشْتَرِيا	تَشْتَرِيانِ	اِشْتَرَتا	هُما
	يَشْتَروا	يَشْتَروا	يَشْتَرونَ	اِشْتَرَوا	هُم
	يَشْتَرينَ	يَشْتَرينَ	يَشْتَرينَ	اِشْتَرَيْنَ	هُنَّ

وَصَلَ (يَصِلُ) (فَعَل I) (وُصول – واصِل – مَوْصول)

to arrive

Imperative	Jussive	Subjunctive	Indicative	Past	Pronoun
الأمر	المضارع المجزوم	المضارع المنصوب	المضارع المرفوع	الماضي	الضمير
	أَصِلْ	أَصِلَ	أَصِلُ	وَصَلْتُ	أنا
	نَصِلْ	نَصِلَ	نَصِلُ	وَصَلْنا	نَحنُ
صِلْ	تَصِلْ	تَصِلَ	تَصِلُ	وَصَلْتَ	أنتَ
صِلي	تَصِلي	تَصِلي	تَصِلينَ	وَصَلْتِ	أنتِ
صِلا	تَصِلا	تَصِلا	تَصِلان	وَصَلْتُما	أنتما
صِلوا	تَصِلوا	تَصِلوا	تَصِلونَ	وَصَلْتُم	أنتُم
صِلْنَ	تَصِلْنَ	تَصِلْنَ	تَصِلْنَ	وَصَلْتُنَّ	أنتُنَّ
	يَصِلْ	يَصِلَ	يَصِلُ	وَصَلَ	هُوَ
	تَصِلْ	تَصِلَ	تَصِلُ	وَصَلَتْ	هِيَ
	يَصِلا	يَصِلا	يَصِلانِ	وَصَلا	هُما
	تَصِلا	تَصِلا	تَصِلانِ	وَصَلَتا	هُما
	يَصِلوا	يَصِلوا	يَصِلونَ	وَصَلوا	هُم
	يَصِلْنَ	يَصِلْنَ	يَصِلْنَ	وَصَلْنَ	هُنَّ

اِتَّصَلَ (يَتَّصِلُ) (اِفْتَعَل VIII) (اِتِّصال - مَتَّصِل - مُتَّصَل)

to contact, to connect

Imperative	Jussive	Subjunctive	Indicative	Past	Pronoun
الأمر	المضارع المجزوم	المضارع المنصوب	المضارع المرفوع	الماضي	الضمير
	أَتَّصِلْ	أَتَّصِلَ	أَتَّصِلُ	اِتَّصَلْتُ	أنا
	نَتَّصِلْ	نَتَّصِلَ	نَتَّصِلُ	اِتَّصَلْنا	نَحنُ
اِتَّصِلْ	تَتَّصِلْ	تَتَّصِلَ	تَتَّصِلُ	اِتَّصَلْتَ	أنتَ
اِتَّصِلي	تَتَّصِلي	تَتَّصِلي	تَتَّصِلينَ	اِتَّصَلْتِ	أنتِ
اِتَّصِلا	تَتَّصِلا	تَتَّصِلا	تَتَّصِلانِ	اِتَّصَلْتُما	أنتما
اِتَّصِلوا	تَتَّصِلوا	تَتَّصِلوا	تَتَّصِلونَ	اِتَّصَلْتُم	أنتُم
اِتَّصِلْنَ	تَتَّصِلْنَ	تَتَّصِلْنَ	تَتَّصِلْنَ	اِتَّصَلْتُنَّ	أنتُنَّ
	يَتَّصِلْ	يَتَّصِلَ	يَتَّصِلُ	اِتَّصَلَ	هُوَ
	تَتَّصِلْ	تَتَّصِلَ	تَتَّصِلُ	اِتَّصَلَتْ	هِيَ
	يَتَّصِلا	يَتَّصِلا	يَتَّصِلانِ	اِتَّصَلا	هُما
	تَتَّصِلا	تَتَّصِلا	تَتَّصِلانِ	اِتَّصَلَتا	هُما
	يَتَّصِلوا	يَتَّصِلوا	يَتَّصِلونَ	اِتَّصَلوا	هُم
	يَتَّصِلْنَ	يَتَّصِلْنَ	يَتَّصِلْنَ	اِتَّصَلْنَ	هُنَّ

عَلَّق (يُعَلِّقُ) (فَعَّل II) (تَعْليق – مُعَلِّق – مُعَلَّق)

to hang

Imperative	Jussive	Subjunctive	Indicative	Past	Pronoun
الأمر	المضارع المجزوم	المضارع المنصوب	المضارع المرفوع	الماضي	الضمير
	أُعَلِّقْ	أُعَلِّقَ	أُعَلِّقُ	عَلَّقْتُ	أنا
	نُعَلِّقْ	نُعَلِّقَ	نُعَلِّقُ	عَلَّقْنا	نَحنُ
عَلِّقْ	تُعَلِّقْ	تُعَلِّقَ	تُعَلِّقُ	عَلَّقْتَ	أنتَ
عَلِّقي	تُعَلِّقي	تُعَلِّقي	تُعَلِّقينَ	عَلَّقْتِ	أنتِ
عَلِّقا	تُعَلِّقا	تُعَلِّقا	تُعَلِّقانِ	عَلَّقْتُما	أنتما
عَلِّقوا	تُعَلِّقوا	تُعَلِّقوا	تُعَلِّقونَ	عَلَّقْتُمْ	أنتُم
عَلِّقْنَ	تُعَلِّقْنَ	تُعَلِّقْنَ	تُعَلِّقْنَ	عَلَّقْتُنَّ	أنتُنَّ
	يُعَلِّقْ	يُعَلِّقَ	يُعَلِّقُ	عَلَّقَ	هُوَ
	تُعَلِّقْ	تُعَلِّقَ	تُعَلِّقُ	عَلَّقَتْ	هِيَ
	يُعَلِّقا	يُعَلِّقا	يُعَلِّقانِ	عَلَّقا	هُما
	تُعَلِّقا	تُعَلِّقا	تُعَلِّقانِ	عَلَّقَتا	هُما
	يُعَلِّقوا	يُعَلِّقوا	يُعَلِّقونَ	عَلَّقوا	هُم
	يُعَلِّقْنَ	يُعَلِّقْنَ	يُعَلِّقْنَ	عَلَّقْنَ	هُنَّ

اِنْتَقَلَ (يَنْتَقِلُ) (اِفْتَعَل VIII) (اِنْتِقال – مُنْتَقِل – مُنْتَقَل)

to move, to relocate

Imperative	Jussive	Subjunctive	Indicative	Past	Pronoun
الأمر	المضارع المجزوم	المضارع المنصوب	المضارع المرفوع	الماضي	الضمير
	أَنْتَقِلْ	أَنْتَقِلَ	أَنْتَقِلُ	اِنْتَقَلْتُ	أنا
	نَنْتَقِلْ	نَنْتَقِلَ	نَنْتَقِلُ	اِنْتَقَلْنا	نَحنُ
اِنْتَقِلْ	تَنْتَقِلْ	تَنْتَقِلَ	تَنْتَقِلُ	اِنْتَقَلْتَ	أنتَ
اِنْتَقِلي	تَنْتَقِلي	تَنْتَقِلي	تَنْتَقِلينَ	اِنْتَقَلْتِ	أنتِ
اِنْتَقِلا	تَنْتَقِلا	تَنْتَقِلا	تَنْتَقِلانِ	اِنْتَقَلْتُما	أنتما
اِنْتَقِلوا	تَنْتَقِلوا	تَنْتَقِلوا	تَنْتَقِلونَ	اِنْتَقَلْتُمْ	أنتُم
اِنْتَقِلْنَ	تَنْتَقِلْنَ	تَنْتَقِلْنَ	تَنْتَقِلْنَ	اِنْتَقَلْتُنَّ	أنتُنَّ
	يَنْتَقِلْ	يَنْتَقِلَ	يَنْتَقِلُ	اِنْتَقَلَ	هُوَ
	تَنْتَقِلْ	تَنْتَقِلَ	تَنْتَقِلُ	اِنْتَقَلَتْ	هِيَ
	يَنْتَقِلا	يَنْتَقِلا	يَنْتَقِلانِ	اِنْتَقَلا	هُما
	تَنْتَقِلا	تَنْتَقِلا	تَنْتَقِلانِ	اِنْتَقَلَتا	هُما
	يَنْتَقِلوا	يَنْتَقِلوا	يَنْتَقِلونَ	اِنْتَقَلوا	هُم
	يَنْتَقِلْنَ	يَنْتَقِلْنَ	يَنْتَقِلْنَ	اِنْتَقَلْنَ	هُنَّ

اِسْتَخْدمَ (يَسْتَخْدِمُ) (اِسْتَفْعَلَ X) (اِسْتِخْدام – مُسْتَخْدِم – مُسْتَخْدَم)

to use

Imperative	Jussive	Subjunctive	Indicative	Past	Pronoun
الأمر	المضارع المجزوم	المضارع المنصوب	المضارع المرفوع	الماضي	الضمير
	أَسْتَخْدِمْ	أَسْتَخْدِمَ	أَسْتَخْدِمُ	اِسْتَخْدَمْتُ	أنا
	نَسْتَخْدِمْ	نَسْتَخْدِمَ	نَسْتَخْدِمُ	اِسْتَخْدَمْنا	نَحنُ
اِسْتَخْدِمْ	تَسْتَخْدِمْ	تَسْتَخْدِمَ	تَسْتَخْدِمُ	اِسْتَخْدَمْتَ	أنتَ
اِسْتَخْدِمي	تَسْتَخْدِمي	تَسْتَخْدِمي	تَسْتَخْدِمينَ	اِسْتَخْدَمْتِ	أنتِ
اِسْتَخْدِما	تَسْتَخْدِما	تَسْتَخْدِما	تَسْتَخْدِمانِ	اِسْتَخْدَمْتُما	أنتما
اِسْتَخْدِموا	تَسْتَخْدِموا	تَسْتَخْدِموا	تَسْتَخْدِمونَ	اِسْتَخْدَمْتُمْ	أنتُم
اِسْتَخْدِمْنَ	تَسْتَخْدِمْنَ	تَسْتَخْدِمْنَ	تَسْتَخْدِمْنَ	اِسْتَخْدَمْتُنَّ	أنتُنَّ
	يَسْتَخْدِمْ	يَسْتَخْدِمَ	يَسْتَخْدِمُ	اِسْتَخْدَمَ	هُوَ
	تَسْتَخْدِمْ	تَسْتَخْدِمَ	تَسْتَخْدِمُ	اِسْتَخْدَمَتْ	هِيَ
	يَسْتَخْدِما	يَسْتَخْدِما	يَسْتَخْدِمانِ	اِسْتَخْدَما	هُما
	تَسْتَخْدِما	تَسْتَخْدِما	تَسْتَخْدِمانِ	اِسْتَخْدَمَتا	هُما
	يَسْتَخْدِموا	يَسْتَخْدِموا	يَسْتَخْدِمونَ	اِسْتَخْدَموا	هُم
	يَسْتَخْدِمْنَ	يَسْتَخْدِمْنَ	يَسْتَخْدِمْنَ	اِسْتَخْدَمْنَ	هُنَّ

Appendix D

Texts of Postcards and Letters from Lessons 19 and 24

١ - بِطاقةُ مايكِل براون إلى أُستاذَتِه

الإسْكَندَريّة ١٩/ ٩/ ٢٠٠٨ أُسْتاذَتي الكَريمة زَيْنَب. سَلامٌ مِنَ الإسكَندَريّة. وَصَلتُ وأصْدقائي بَعْدَ ظُهْرِ اليَوم وأكَلْنا في مَطْعَمٍ جَيِّدٍ ومَشَيْنا عَلى الكورنَيْش وَسَبَحنا في البَحر. أكتُبُ لَكِ مِنَ الفُندُق قَبْلَ أنْ أنامَ. أرجو لَكِ عُطلَةً سَعيدة. مايكِل	الأستاذة زَيْنَب طَه مَرْكِزُ دِراسةِ اللُغَة العَرَبيَّة الجامِعةُ الأمريكيَّةُ بِالقاهِرة القاهِرة جُمهوريَّةُ مِصْرَ العَرَبيَّة

٢- بِطاقةُ عَدنان مارتيني إلى أسرَته:

أورلاندو ٨/ ٩/ ٠٨ أعزّائي الغالين، السلامُ عَلَيكُم أكتُبُ لَكُم مِن أورلاندو. وَصَلتُ إلى هُنا مُنْذُ ثَلاثَةِ أيّام لِزيارَةِ ديزني وُرلد. أنزِلُ هُنا في فُندُق رامادا. ديزني مَدينَةُ مَلاهٍ عَظيمة شاهَدْتُ فيها إبكَتْ سِنتَر وأعجبَني كَثيراً. تَناوَلْتُ طَعاماً مَغربيّاً في المَطعَم المُراكِشيِّ وتَكَلَّمتُ العَرَبيَّةَ مَعَهُم. استَمْتَعْتُ بِهذِهِ الرِحْلة. عَدنان	السيِّد ياسِر مارتيني المُحْتَرَم ١١٥ شارِع البُحتُري، طابَق ٣ حَلَب، الجَمْهوريّة العَرَبيّة السوريّة

٣- رِسالَةُ عَدنان إلى صَديقِهِ مازِن (الدرس ١٩):

كَلَمبَس في ٢١ أيلول ٢٠٠٨
أخي العَزيز مازِن، سَلامٌ حارٌ لَكَ مِن كَلَمبَس.

كَيفَ حالُكَ يا أخي؟ لم تَصِلْني مِنكَ أيّةُ رِسالةٍ مُنذُ مُدّةٍ طويلةٍ كَتَبتُ لَكَ رِسالةً في شَهرِ آذار الماضي ولَم يَصِلْني منكَ أيُّ شَيء، لِذلِكَ ظَنَنْتُ أنَّكَ انتقَلتَ مِن عُنوانِكَ القَديم في حَلَب. عَلِمتُ مِن مَروان بَعدَ ذلِكَ أنَّكَ انْتَقَلْتَ إلى جامِعَةِ دِمَشق، وَهُوَ الّذي أعْطاني عُنْوانَكَ الجَديد. هَل يُعجِبُكَ السَكَنُ و الدِراسَةُ في دِمَشقَ؟
أنا كَما تَعْلَم أدرُسُ عِلمَ الحاسوبِ في جامِعَةِ وِلايَةِ أوهايو. بَعدَ أيّام سَيَبدَأُ العامُ الدِراسِيُّ الجَديد، وهذِهِ هِيَ سَنَتي الثانِيَةُ هُنا. أنا سَعيدٌ في كَلَمبَس وأسْتَمْتِعُ بِالسَكَنِ فيها وبِالدِراسَةِ كَذلِك.
في الأسابيعِ الثلاثةِ الماضِيَةِ زُرتُ مَدينَةَ نيويورك وأتلانتك سيتي وشلّالاتِ نَياغرا في كَنَدا وكذلِكَ «ديزني ورلد» وهِيَ مَدينَةُ مَلاهٍ كَبيرةٌ جِدّاً في مَدينةِ أورلاندو في فلوريدا. اِستَمتَعتُ بِهذِهِ الزِياراتِ كَثيراً. أرجو أنْ أزورَ وِلايَةَ كاليفونيا في السَنَةِ المُقبِلَةِ إنْ شاءَ الله، و«لاس فيغاس» أيْضاً.
أرجو أنْ تَكتُبَ لي عَنكَ وعَن دِراسَتِك. لَكَ مِنّي أطيَبُ السَلامِ وإلى لِقاءٍ قَريبٍ في حَلَب.

أخوكَ المُخلِص
عَدنان

٤- رِسالةُ ياسِر مارتيني إلى ابنِهِ عَدنان (الدرس ٢٤):

حلَب في ٢٢ أيّار ٢٠٠٨

ابني الحَبيب عَدنان، السلامُ علَيكَ ورَحمَةُ الله.

أرجو أنْ تَصِلَكَ رِسالَتي هذِهِ وأنتَ في أحسَنِ حال. كُلُّنا بِخَير والحَمْدُ لله. كَتَبتُ لَكَ رِسالةً في الشَهرِ الماضي وما وَصَلَني مِنكَ رَدٌّ علَيْها. أما وَصَلَتْكَ رِسالَتي؟ آخِرُ رِسالةٍ مِنكَ كانَ تاريخُها ٧ كانونَ الثاني. أرجو أنْ تَكتُبَ لَنا دونَ تأخير.

أكتبُ لَكَ هذِهِ الرِسالةَ لأُخبِرَكَ أنّ والدَتَكَ تُريدُ أنْ تُسافِرَ إلَيكَ في شَهرِ آب. لَن أستَطيعَ أنْ أسافِرَ مَعَها هذِهِ المرّة لأنّي مَشغولٌ جِدّاً. يَجِبُ أنْ أسافِرَ إلى ألمانيا في آبَ المُقبِلِ مِن أجلِ استيراد بِضاعَةٍ لِمَحلّي.

اشتَرَيتُ تَذكِرةَ طائِرةٍ لِوالِدَتِكَ عَلى الخُطوطِ الجَوِيَّةِ الهولَنْديّة. تُغادِرُ طائِرتُها مَطارَ دِمَشقَ في يَومِ الخَميس ١٤ آب وتَصِلُ إلى شيكاغو في اليَومِ نَفسِه. أرجو أنْ تَستَقبِلَها في المَطارِ لأنَّها كَما تَعلَم لا تَتَكَلَّمُ الإنكليزيّةَ ولا تَعرِفُ أحَداً عَلى الطائِرة.

والآنَ إليكَ أخبارَ الأُسْرَة. أخوكَ أيْمَن كَلَّمَنا بِالهاتِفِ مِن دِمَشقَ وهُوَ بِخَيْرٍ ويُرسِلُ لَكَ سَلامُه. أخوكَ رامي لا يَزالُ يَدْرُسُ في الجامِعةِ ويَعمَلُ سائِقاً في شَرِكةِ البَرّادات، وهُوَ سَعيدٌ بِذلِك. خالُكَ أحْمَد انتَقَلَ في الشَهرِ الماضي وعائِلَتُه إلى دِمَشقَ حَيْثُ سَيَعمَلُ مُدَرِّساً لِلفيزياءِ في إحدى المدارس الثانَويّة. تَقاعَدَ عَمُّكَ زُهَيْر مِن عَمَلِهِ في وِزارةِ التَربية، وهُوَ يَقولُ إنَّ حَياةَ المُتَقاعِدِ تُعجِبُهُ كَثيراً. جَدَّتُكَ أُمّ ياسِر تُرسِلُ لَكَ سَلامَها وتَشكُرُكَ على الهَدِيَّةِ الّتي أرسَلتَها لَها. اكتُبْ لَنا عَن أخبارِكَ وإلى اللِقاء.

والِدُك

Cumulative Vocabulary

أ

a question particle to form yes/no questions [3] .... أَ
father [5] .... (n., m.) أب ج آباء
August [11] .... (n., m.) آب
to return [19] .... (v.) آبَ (يَؤوبُ) إياب
elementary [5] .... (adj.) ابْتِدائيّ
never, not at all [20] .... (adv.) أبَداً
son [5] (n., m.) ابْنٌ ج أبْناء
a 14th-century Arab historian and sociologist [3] .... (proper noun) ابْنُ خَلْدون
daughter [5] .... (n., f.) ابْنَة ج بَنات
Abu Dhabi (*abū ẓabī*) [4] .... (n., f.) أبو ظَبي
white [19] .... (n., m.) أبيَض ج بيض
to come [11] .... (v.) أتى (يَأتي) إتيان (إلى)
to hold, to contain [20] .... (v.) اتَّسَعَ (يَتَّسِعُ) اتِّساع
to contact [20] .... (v.) اِتَّصَلَ (يَتَّصِلُ) اتِّصال (بِـ)
to agree (with someone) [20] .... (v.) اِتَّفَقَ (يَتَّفِقُ) اِتِّفاق (مَعَ)
furniture [18] .... (n., m.) أثاث
ruin, antiquity, artifact, relic [19] .... (n., m.) أثَر ج آثار
during [21] .... أثْناء
two [3] .... (n., m.) اِثنان
Monday [11] .... (n., m.) الإثْنَين
to respond, to answer [19] .... (v.) أجابَ (يُجيبُ) إجابة
pear [20] .... (n., m.) إجّاص
social gathering [16] .... (n., m.) اِجْتِماع ج اِجْتِماعات
to lease, to let [18] .... أجَّر (يؤجِّر) تأجير
rent, wage, fare [18] .... (n., f.) أُجْرة ج أُجور
for the sake of, because of [22] .... أجْل (مِن أجْلِ)
foreigner [17] .... (n., m.) أَجْنَبيّ ج أَجانِب
foreign [17] .... (adj.) أجْنَبيّ / أجْنَبيّة

to meet, to gather [18] .... اِجْتَمَعَ (يَجْتَمِع) اِجْتِماع (.v)
to like [7] .... أَحَبَّ (يُحِبُّ) حُبّ، مَحَبّة (.v)
to celebrate [15] .... اِحْتَفَلَ (يَحْتَفِلُ) اِحْتِفال (.v)
one [9] .... أَحَد ج آحاد (.n., m)
Sunday [11] .... الأَحَد (.n., m)
statistics [9] .... إِحْصاء (.n., m)
to bring [8] .... أَحْضَرَ (يُحْضِرُ) إِحْضار (.v)
red [20] .... أَحمَر ج حُمْر (.adj)
biology [4] .... أَحْياء (.f., pl)
sometimes [7] .... أحياناً (.adv)
brother [5] .... أَخ ج إخوة (.n., m)
to notify, inform [20] .... أَخْبَرَ (يُخْبِرُ) إِخْبار (.v)
sister [5] .... أُخْت ج أَخَوات (.n., f)
to select [24] .... اِخْتارَ (يَخْتارُ) اِخْتِيار (.v)
to differ (from) [23] .... اِخْتَلَفَ (يَخْتَلِفُ) اِخْتِلاف (عَن) (.v)
to take [17] .... أَخَذَ (يَأْخُذُ) أَخْذ (.v)
other [18] .... آخَر ج آخَرون (.n., m)
last, latest [24] .... آخِر (.adj)
green [12] .... أَخْضَر ج خُضْر (.adj., m)
department [24] .... إدارة ج إدارات (.n., f)
literature [2] .... أَدَب ج آداب (.n., m)
proper noun (man's name) [2] .... أديب (.n., m)
then, therefore [19] .... إذاً
March [11] .... آذار (.n., m)
broadcasting station [22] .... إذاعَة ج ات (.n., f)
to want [7] .... أرادَ (يُريدَ) إرادة (.v)
Wednesday [11] .... الأَرْبعاء (.n., m)
four [3] .... أَرْبَعة (.n., f)
to rise, to be higher [23] .... اِرتَفَعَ (يرتَفِعُ) اِرتِفاع (.v)
Jordan [4] .... الأُرْدُنّ (.n., f)
rice [8] .... أُرُزّ (.n., m)
to send [17] .... أَرْسَلَ (يُرسِلُ) إِرْسال (.v)

ground, land [2] . . . . (n., f.) أرْض ج أراضٍ
Arizona [4] . . . . (n., f.) أريزونا
couch [18] . . . . (n., f.) أريكة ج أرائِك
blue [20] . . . . (adj.) أزرَق ج زُرْق
week [11] . . . . (n., m.) أُسْبوع ج أسابيع
professor, teacher [1] . . . . (n., m.) أسْتاذ ج أساتِذة
to rent, to hire [18] . . . . (v.) استأجَرَ (يَستأجِرُ) استِئجار
to bathe, to take a bath or shower [13] . . . . (v.) اسْتَحَمَّ (يَستَحِمُّ) استِحْمام
to use, to utilize, to employ [16] . . . . (v.) استَخدَمَ (يَستَخدِمُ) اِستِخدام
to become a martyr [16] . . . . (passive v.) أُسْتُشْهِدَ (يُستَشْهَدُ) اِسْتِشهاد
to host [23] . . . . (v.) اِستَضافَ (يستَضيفُ) استِضافة
to be able [6] . . . . (v.) اِسْتَطاعَ (يَسْتَطيعُ) اِسْتِطاعة
information [6] . . . . (n., pl.) اِسْتِعلامات
to spend time [29] . . . . (v.) اِسْتَغْرَقَ (يَسْتَغْرِقُ) اِسْتِغْراق
to receive (s.o.) [17] . . . . (v.) اسْتَقبَلَ (يَسْتَقبِلُ) اسْتِقبال
independence [15] . . . . (n., m.) اِسْتِقلال
to enjoy [19] . . . . (v.) استَمتَعَ (يَستَمتِعُ) استِمتاع بِـ
to listen [22] . . . . (v.) اِسْتَمَعَ (يَسْتَمِعُ) اِسْتِماع
to import [24] . . . . (v.) اِسْتَوْرَدَ (يَسْتَوْرِدُ) اِسْتيراد
to wake up [9] . . . . (v.) اِسْتَيْقَظَ (يَسْتَيْقِظُ) اِسْتيقاظ
extended family [10,14] . . . . (n., f.) أُسْرة ج أُسَر
to establish, to found [16] . . . . (v.) أسَّسَ (يُؤَسِّسُ) تأسيس
sorry [6,12] . . . . (n., m.) آسِف / (n., f.) آسِفة
bottom, lowest point, lower [24] . . . . (n., m., superlative) أسْفَل ج أسافِل
Islam [15] . . . . (n., m.) إسلام
name (n., m.) اِسم ج أسْماء
black [16] . . . . (n., m.) أسْوَد ج سود
Asia [21] . . . . (n., f.) آسيا
to resemble [24] . . . . (v.) أشْبَهَ (يُشْبِهُ) شَبَه
to long (for), to yearn [23] . . . . (v.) (لِـ/ إلى) اِشْتاقَ (يَشْتاقُ) اِشْتِياق
to buy [7, 11] . . . . (v.) اِشتَرى (يَشتري) شِراء
to enroll in, to subscribe to [22] . . . . (v.) اِشْتَرَكَ (يَشْتَرِكُ) اِشْتِراك

to become [14] .... أَصْبحَ (يُصْبِح) (.v)

to insist [23] .... أَصَرَّ (يُصِرُّ) إِصْرار (.v)

yellow [20] .... أَصْفَر ج صُفْر (.adj)

to overlook (s.t.) [21] .... أَطَلَّ (يُطِلُّ) إِطْلال (.v)

Atlantic [21] .... أطلَسيّ (.adj)

to discharge a firearm, to shoot; to dispatch [21] .... أَطْلَقَ (يُطْلِق) إِطْلاق (.v)

to consider [21] .... اِعتَبَرَ (يَعتَبِرُ) اِعتِبار (.v)

to believe [17] .... اِعتَقَدَ (يَعتَقِدُ) اِعتِقاد (.v)

to take care of, to tend [24] .... اِعْتَنى (يَعْتَني) اِعتِناء (بِـ) (.v)

to please [18] .... أَعْجَبَ يُعْجِبُ (.v)

to give [7] .... أعطى (يُعطي) أَعْطِ (.v) (imperative) إِعْطاء (verbal n.)

top, highest point, upper [21] .... أَعْلى ج أعالٍ (n., m., superlative)

advertisement [18] .... إِعْلان ج إِعْلانات (.n., m)

most knowledgeable [6] .... أعلَم (n., superlative)

to be assassinated [16] .... أُغْتيلَ (يُغتالُ) اِغتِيال (passive v.)

song [22] .... أُغنِية ج أغانٍ (.n., f)

Africa [21] .... إفريقية (.n., f)

to reside in [24] .... أقام (يُقيم) إقامة (.v)

to draw near, to get close (to) [23] .... اِقْتَرَبَ (يَقْتَرِبُ) اِقْتِراب (مِن) (.v)

region [21] .... إقليم ج أقاليم (.n., m)

to eat [8] .... أَكَلَ (يأكُلُ) أَكْل (.v)

certainly, surely [11] .... أكيد (exclamation)

Pakistan [10] .... الباكِسْتان (.n., f)

good-bye .... إلى اللقاء

until [19] .... إلى أنْ

except, minus [9] .... إلاّ (particle)

now [3] .... الآن (n., m)

device, gadget, machine, apparatus [19] .... آلة ج آلات (.n., f)

to meet, to converge, to encounter [19] .... التَقى (يَلتَقي) التِقاء (.v)

to take, to make (a picture) [19] .... التَقَطَ (يَلتَقِطُ) التِقاط (.v)

inflammation, infection [17] .... الْتِهاب ج اِلتِهابات (.n., m)

who, that [19] .... الَّتي (.n., f)

who, that [19]	الَّذي (n., m.)
the name of the letter *alif*	أَلِف (n., f.)
thousand [9]	أَلْف ج آلاف (n., m.)
God [3]	الله (n., m.)
God knows [6]	اللهُ أَعْلَم
pain [17]	أَلَم ج آلآم (n., m.)
to hurt [17]	آلَمَ (يُؤلِمُ) (v.)
Germany [10]	ألمانيا (n., f.)
German [10]	ألمانيّ (adj.)
or (particle used in questions) [3]	أَمْ (conjunction)
mother [5]	أُمّ ج أُمَّهات (n., f.)
as for, but, yet, however [17]	أمّا (particle)
United Arab Emirates [4]	الإمارات (n., f.)
in front of [18]	أمامَ (prep.)
to examine, to test [19]	اِمتَحَنَ (يَمتَحِنُ) امتِحان (v.)
woman [3]	اِمرأة ج نِساء (n., f.)
yesterday [11]	أَمْس (adv.)
to be possible [22]	أَمْكَنَ (يُمكِنُ) إمْكان (v.)
prince [16]	أمير ج أُمَراء (n., m.)
librarian [6]	أمينُ/ أمينةُ مَكتَبةٍ (n., m./f.)
that (after verbs similar to "to think") [11]	أَنَّ (particle)
that (after the verb "to say") [11]	إِنَّ (particle)
to (infinitive) [18]	أَنْ (particle)
if [23]	إنْ (particle)
hopefully (*lit.* "God willing") [11]	إنْ شاءَ الله (set phrase)
I	أنا (pron.)
you	أَنْتَ (pron., m. sg.)
you	أَنْتِ (pron., f. sg.)
to produce [21]	أنتَجَ (يُنتِجُ) إنتاج (v.)
to elect [16]	اِنْتَخَبَ (يَنتَخِبُ) اِنتِخاب (v.)
to wait [14]	اِنتَظَرَ (يَنْتَظِرُ) انتِظار (v.)
to move, to relocate [13]	اِنتَقَلَ (يَنتَقِلُ) اِنْتِقال (v.)

you (pron., m. pl.) أَنْتُمْ

you (pron., f./m. pl.) أَنْتُما

you (pron., f. pl.) أَنْتُنَّ

to end [8, 9] . . . . (v.) (مِن) اِنْتِهاء (يَنْتَهي) اِنْتَهى

female [24] . . . . (n., f.) إناث ج أُنْثى

Andalusia, Muslim Spain [16] . . . . (n., f.) الأَنْدَلُس

Indiana [4] . . . . (n., f.) إنديانا

to be interrupted, to be severed [21]. . . . . (v.) اِنقِطاع (يَنقَطِعُ) اِنقَطَعَ

English [5] . . . . (adj., m.) إنْكليزيّ

English (language) [3]. . . . . (adj., f.) الإنكليزية

hello, welcome (response to a greeting) . . . . (n., m.) أَهْلاً

or (used with statements) [3]. . . . . (conjunction) أو

Europe [18]. . . . . (n., f.) أوروبا

first [5] . . . . (n., m.) أوائِل ج أوَّل

those [2] . . . . (pl., demonstrative) أولائك

which [7] . . . . (n., f.) أيَّةُ / (n., m.) أيّ

May [11]. . . . . (n., m.) أيّار

rent [18] . . . . (n., m.) إيجارات ج إيجار

Iran [21] . . . . (n., f.) إيران

too, also [1]. . . . . (adv.) أَيْضاً

September [11] . . . . (n., m.) أَيْلول

immensely, greatly (intensifies the following noun) [23]. . . . . (n.) أيّما

where (question particle) أَيْنَ

ب

on, in, by, with, for [1] . . . . (prep.) بـ

name of the letter *bā* . . . . (n., f.) باء

door (n., m.) باب

semi-arid desert [21] . . . . (n., f.) بَوادٍ ج بادِية

eggplant [20]. . . . . (n., m.) باذِنجان

cold [12] . . . . (adj., m.) بارِد

yesterday [11] . . . . (n., f.) **البارِحة**

green peas [20] .... (n., f.) بازِلاء
to sell [7] .... (v.) باعَ (يَبيعُ) بَيْع
early [19] .... (adverbial) باكِراً
Pakistan [10] .... (n., f.) **الباكِسْتان**
okra [20] .... (n., f.) بامْية
salesperson [24] .... (n., m.) بائِع ج بائعون
slowly [20] .... بِبُطء
to broadcast [22] .... (v.) بَثَّ (يَبُثُّ) بَثّ
in need of [13] .... بِحاجةٍ (إلى)
sea [12] .... (n, m.) بَحْر ج بِحار
lake [12] .... (n., f.) بُحَيْرة ج بُحَيْرات
fine, well .... بِخَيْر
to appear, to seem [24] .... (v.) بَدا (يَبدو) بُدُوٌّ
to begin [9] .... (v.) بَدَأ (يَبْدأ) بِداية، بَدْء
beginning [17] .... (n., f.) بِداية ج بِدايات
seed, kernel [20] .... (n., f.) بِذرة ج بُذور
refrigerator (Syria) [18] .... (n., m.) بَرّاد ج بَرّادات
orange [8] .... (n., m.) بُرتُقال
program [6] .... (n., m.) بَرْنامِج ج بَرامِج
mail, post [19] .... (n., m.) بَريد
only (Syrian colloquial) [17] .... بَسّ
because of [17] .... بِسَبَب
simple [23] .... (adj.) بَسيط ج بُسطاء
onion [14] .... (n., m.) بَصَل
merchandise, goods [21] .... (n., f.) بِضاعة ج بَضائِع
a few [22] .... (n.) بِضْع
card [3] .... (n., f.) بِطاقة ج بِطاقات
watermelon [20] .... (n., m.) بِطّيخ
after [9] .... (prep.) بَعْدَ
some [11] .... (n., m.) بَعْضُ
each other [17] .... (n., m.) بَعْضُهُم بَعضاً

far [11] .... (adv.) بَعيد
grocer [18] .... (n., m.) بَقّال ج بَقّالون
cow, cattle [20] .... (n., f.) بَقَرة ج أبْقار / بَقَر
to remain, to stay [19] .... (v.) بَقِيَ (يَبْقى) بَقاء
rather, but [4] .... (particle) بَلْ
country [15] .... (n., m.) بَلَد ج بِلاد
small town [3] .... (n., f.) بَلْدة ج بَلْدات
local, popular [18] .... (adj.) بَلَديّ
including [22] .... (phrase) بِما في ذلِك
to build, to construct [19] .... (v.) بَنى (يَبني) بِناء
building [4] .... (n., f.) بِناية ج بِنايات
girl [5] (n., f.) بِنْت ج بَنات
tomato [20] .... (n., f.) بَنَدورة (طَماطِم في مصر)
Bangladesh [10] .... (n., f.) **بَنْغلاديش**
bank (colloquial) [18] .... بَنْك ج بُنوك
brown [24] .... (adj.) بُنّيّ
gate [17] .... (n., f.) بَوّابة ج بَوّابات
ice cream [21] .... (n., f.) بوظة
house, home [2] .... (n., m.) بَيْت ج بُيوت
egg [8] (n., m.) بَيْض
white [20] .... (n./adj., f.) بَيضاء ج بيض

ت

spice, condiment, seasoning [20] .... (n., m.) تابِل ج تَوابِل
merchant, businessman [24] .... (n., m.) تاجِر ج تُجّار
to be late [18] .... (v.) تَأخَّرَ (يَتَأخَّرُ) تَأخُّر
history [16] .... (n., m.) تاريخ ج تَواريخ
ninth [5] .... (adj.) تاسِع
visa [23] .... (n., f.) تأشيرة دُخول
to consist of, to comprise [21] .... (v.) تَألَّفَ (يَتَألَّفُ) تَألُّف + مِن
insurance [18] .... (n., m.) تأمين ج تأمينات
those [2] .... (dual, nom.; *rare*) تانِكَ

salad made with finely chopped parsley, cracked wheat,
tomatoes, lemon juice, and olive oil [13] .... (n., f.) تَبّولة

trade, business, commerce [2] .... (n., f.) تِجارة

to wander about, to tour [19] .... (v.) تَجَوَّلَ (يَتجَوَّلُ) تَجَوُّل

to graduate [15] .... (v.) تَخَرَّجَ (يتخرَّجُ) تَخَرُّج

to push, to shove one another [23] .... (v.) تَدافَعَ (يَتَدافَعُ) تَدافُع

ticket [19] .... (n., f.) تَذكِرة ج تَذاكِر

education, upbringing [15] .... (n., f.) تَرْبية

nine [3] .... (n., f.) تِسْعة

October [11] .... (n., m.) تِشرين الأوَّل

November [11] .... (n., m.) تِشرين الثاني

come here! [8] .... (imperative) تَعال

to be acquainted with [11] .... (v.) تَعَرَّفَ (يَتَعرَّفُ) تَعَرُّف (على) (v.)

to learn [1] .... (v.) تَعَلَّمَ (يَتَعَلَّمُ) تَعَلُّم

instruction, education [15] .... (n., m.) تَعليم

to be accustomed to [23] .... (v.) تَعَوَّدَ (يَتَعَوَّدُ) تَعَوُّد (على)

apple [8] .... (n., m.) تُفّاح

differential equations [5] .... (n., m.) تَفاضُل

if you please [7] .... (imperative) تَفَضَّلْ/ تَفَضَّلي

to retire (from work) [24] .... (v.) تَقاعَدَ (يَتَقاعَدُ) تَقاعُد (عن)

approximately, about, nearly, roughly [20] .... (adv.) تَقريباً

traditional [21] .... (adj.) تَقْليديّ

calendar [11] .... (n., m.) تَقويم ج تَقاويم

my pleasure, with pleasure, gladly, at your service (colloquial) [16] .... تكرَم عَيْنك

to speak [6] .... (v.) تَكَلَّمَ (يَتَكَلَّمُ) تَكَلُّم

television .... (n., m.) تِلْفاز

that [2] .... (n., f. sg.) تلك

telephone (colloquial) [18] .... (n., m.) تَليفون ج تَليفونات

exactly (adv.) تماماً

statue [19] .... (n., m.) تِمثال ج تَماثيل

dates [21] .... (n., m.) تَمر ج تُمور

July [11] .... (n., m.) تَمّوز

discrimination [16] . . . . (verbal n., m.) تَمييز
to eat, to take, to reach for sth. [8] . . . . (v.) تَناوَلَ (يَتَناوَلُ) تَناوُل
to stroll, to have a good time, to go on a picnic [23] . . . . (v.) تَنَزَّهَ (يَتَنَزَّهُ) تَنَزُّه
tanwīn (diacritical mark signaling indefiniteness) . . . . (n., m.) تَنوين
berry [20] . . . . (n., m.) توت
to pass away [16] . . . . (passive v.) تُوُفِّيَ (يُتَوَفّى) وَفاة
signature [24] . . . . (n., m.) تَوْقيع
those [2] . . . . (dual, acc., gen.; *rare*) تَيْنِك

ث

third [5] . . . . (adj.) ثالِث
eighth [5] . . . . (adj.) ثامِن
second [5] . . . . (n., m.) ثانٍ (الثاني)
secondary [10] . . . . (adj.) ثانَوِيّ
hole [21] . . . . (n., m.) ثُقْب ج ثُقوب
three [3] . . . . (n., f.) ثَلاثة
Tuesday[11] . . . . (n., m.) الثُلاثاء
refrigerator (Egypt) [18] . . . . (n., f.) ثَلاّجة ج ثَلاّجات
a third [9] . . . . (n., m.) ثُلْث ج أَثْلاث
snow [12] . . . . (n., m.) ثَلْج ج ثُلوج
then, and again [13] . . . . (conjunction) ثُمَّ
eight [3] . . . . (n., f.) ثَمانِية
revolution [15] . . . . (n., f.) ثَوْرة ج ثَورات
garlic [20] . . . . (n., m.) ثوم

ج

sitting [17] . . . . (n., m.) جالِس ج جالِسون
mosque [16] . . . . (n., m.) جامِع ج جَوامِع
university [1] . . . . (f.) جامِعَة ج جامِعات
side [1] . . . . (n., m.) جانِب
to come [11] . . . . (v.) جاء (يَجيءُ) مَجيء
prize, award [16] . . . . (n., f.) جائِزة ج جَوائِز

algebra [16]. . . . . (n., m.) جَبْر

mountain [21]. . . . . (n., m.) جَبَل ج جِبال

name of a town in Syria [3] . . . . (n., f.) جَبْلة

cheese [8] . . . . (n., m.) جُبْن ج أجْبان

grandfather [24] . . . . (n., m.) جَدّ ج جُدود

wall [1]. . . . . (n., m.) جِدار ج جُدْران

new [1]. . . . . (adj.) جَديد

to run, to flow; to hurry, to rush; to happen, to occur [20] . . . . (v.) جَرى (يَجري) جَري

to test, to try (≠ to attempt) [21] . . . . (v.) جَرَّبَ (يُجَرِّبُ) تَجْرِبة

to be wounded, to be hurt [16]. (passive v.) جُرِحَ (يُجرَحُ) جَرح

newspaper . . . . (n., f.) جَريدة ج جرائد

part [18] . . . . (n., m.) جُزْء ج أجْزاء

island [21] . . . . (n., f.) جَزيرة ج جُزُر

abundant [6]. . . . . جَزيلاً

geography [21] . . . . (n., m.) جغرافية

dishwasher [18]. . . . . (n., f.) جَلاّية ج جَلاّيات

to sit [8] . . . . (v.) (imperative) جَلَسَ (يَجلِسُ) جُلوس (اِجلِسْ)

Islamic month (*Jumādī al-āḳira*) [11] . . . . (n., f.) جُمادى الآخِرة

Islamic month (*Jumādī al-'ūlā*) [11] . . . . (n., f.) جُمادى الأولى

Friday [11] . . . . (n., m.) الجُمعة

camel [19]. . . . . (n., m.) جَمَل ج جِمال

republic [16]. . . . . (n., f.) جُمهوريّة ج جُمهوريّات

beautiful, good looking [10] . . . . (adj.) جَميل ج (ون)

south [21]. . . . . (n., m.) جَنوب

[Egyptian] pound [18]. . . . . (n., m.) جُنيه ج جُنَيْهات

device, apparatus, appliance [21] . . . . (n., m.) جِهاز ج أجهزة

to prepare [13] . . . . (v.) جَهَّزَ (يُجَهِّزُ) تَجْهيز

passport [23]. . . . . (n., m.) جَواز (سَفَر)

good [6] . . . . (adj.) جَيِّد

well [6] . . . . (adv.) جَيِّداً

army [16] . . . . (n., m.) جَيْش ج جُيوش

geology [24] . . . . (n., f.) جيولوجيا

ح

hot [12] .... (adj., m.) حارّ
to fight [16] .... (v.) حارَبَ (يُحارِبُ) حَرْب / مُحارَبة
calculator .... (n., f.) حاسِبة ج حاسِبات
computer .... (n., m.) حاسوب ج حَواسيب
ready, all set (polite expression) [8] .... (participle) حاضِر
bus, tram [13] .... (n., f.) حافِلة ج حافِلات
grain, cereal [8] .... (n., m.) حَبّ ج حُبوب
pill [17] .... (n., f.) حَبّة ج حَبّات
till, until [11] .... (particle) حَتّى
pilgrimage [15] .... (n., m.) حَجّ
to border, to demarcate, to limit [21] .... (v.) حَدَّ (يَحُدُّ) حَدّ
border, edge, boundary, borderline [21] .... (n., m.) حَدّ ج حُدود
conversation [9] .... (n., m.) حَديث ج أحاديث
modern [9, 10] .... (adj.) حَديث
park, garden [18] .... (n., f.) حَديقة ج حَدائِق
shoe [21] .... (n., m.) حِذاء ج أحْذية
heat [12] .... (n., f.) حَرارة
war [16] .... (n., f.) حَرْب ج حُروب
campus; sacred possession [26] .... (n., m.) حَرَم ج أحْرام
liberty, freedom [19] .... (n., f.) حُرِّيّة ج حُرِّيّات
silk [23] .... (n., m.) حَرير
to guess [22] .... (v.) حَزَرَ (يحْزِرُ) حَزْر
June [11] .... (n., m.) حَزيران
account [16] .... (n., m.) حِساب ج حِسابات
to improve, to make better [22] .... (v.) حَسَّنَ (يحَسِّنُ) تَحْسين
good [23] .... (adj.) حَسَن
very well, okay (a response denoting agreement) [8] .... (adv.) حَسَناً
horse [20] .... (n., m.) حِصان ج أحْصِنة
to obtain, to get, to acquire [16] .... (v.) حَصَلَ (يَحصُلُ) حُصول + على
to attend, to be present [23] .... (v.) حَضَرَ (يحْضُرُ) حُضور

to prepare [8] .... (v.) حَضَّرَ (يُحَضِّرُ) تَحضير

party [20] .... (n., f.) حَفْلة ج حَفَلات

right, law [2] .... (n., m.) حَقٌّ ج حُقوقٌ

bag; briefcase [4] .... (n., f.) حَقيبة ج حقائب

to tell a story; to talk [16] .... (v.) حَكَى (يَحْكي) حِكاية

government [17] .... (n., f.) حُكومة ج حُكومات

Aleppo [1] .... (n., f.) حَلَب

to shave [13] .... (v.) حَلَقَ (يَحْلِقُ) حَلْق

dessert, sweets [15] .... (n., f.) حَلْوى ج حَلوَيات

ornament, jewelry [23] .... (n., m.) حَلي ج حُليّ

milk [8] .... (n., m.) حَليب

bathroom [13] .... (n., f.) حَمّام ج حمّامات

dip prepared from chickpeas, sesame seed paste, lemon juice [9] .... (n., m.) حِمَّص

to carry [17] .... (v.) حَمَلَ (يَحْمِلُ) حَمْل

[bath] tub [18] .... (n., m.) حَوْض ج أَحْواض

around [23] .... (adj.) حَوْلَ

neighborhood, borough [14] .... (n., m.) حَيّ ج أَحْياء

a living person [22] .... (n., m.) حَيّ ج أَحْياء

where, when [6] .... (adv.) حَيْثُ

when [11] .... (adv.) حينَ

animal [19] .... (n., m.) حَيَوان ج حَيَوانات

خ

servant [18] .... (n., m.) خادِم ج خَدَم

outside [23] .... (n.) خارِج

special, particular (to) [15] .... (adj.) خاصّ (بِـ)

maternal uncle [24] .... (n., m.) خال ج أَخْوال

fifth [5] .... (adj.) خامِس

news story [13] .... (n., m.) خَبَر ج أَخْبار

bread [8] .... (n., m.) خُبْز

baker [18] .... (n., m.) خَبّاز ج خَبّازون

to stamp, to seal [23] .... (v.) خَتَمَ (يَخْتِمُ) خَتْم

to go out, to exit [16] .... خَرَجَ (يَخرُجُ) خُروج (v.)
map [21] .... خَريطة ج خَرائِط (n., f.)
autumn [12] .... خَريف (n., m.)
closet, cupboard [4] .... خِزانة ج خَزائِن / خِزانات (n., f.)
to store [24] .... خَزَّنَ (يُخَزِّنُ) تَخْزين (v.)
lettuce [20] .... خَسّ (n., m.)
wood, lumber, timber [18] .... خَشَب ج أخْشاب (n., m.)
especially, particularly [20] .... خُصوصاً (adv.)
fertile [21] .... خَصيب (adj.)
vegetables [13] .... خُضرة ج خُضَر (n., f.)
green [12] .... خَضْراء ج خُضْر (adj., f.)
vegetables; greens [8] .... خَضْراوات (n., f.)
greengrocer [18] .... خُضَريّ ج خُضَريّون (n., m.)
orator, preacher, speaker [16] .... خَطيب ج خُطَباء (n., m.)
to diminish the difficulty of [23] .... خَفَّفَ (يُخَفِّفُ) تَخْفيف (عَن) (v.)
light (in weight) [8] .... خَفيف (adj.)
during, through [22] .... خِلال
to disrobe, to take off [23] .... خَلَعَ (يَخلَعُ) خَلْع (v.)
behind [18] .... خَلْفَ (prep.)
to allow (s.o. to do sth.) (Syrian colloquial) [14] .... خَلّي + attached pron.
gulf, bay [21] .... خَليج ج خُلجان (n., m.)
caliph, successor [23] .... خَليفة ج خُلَفاء (n., m.)
five [3] .... خَمْسة (n., f.)
Thursday [11] .... الخَميس (n., m.)
pig, swine [8] .... خِنزير ج خَنازير (n., m.)
horse [20] .... خَيْل (n., m.)

د

house [10] .... دار ج دور (n., f.)
warm [12] .... دافِئ (adj., m.)
always [19] .... دائماً (adverbial)
chicken [8] .... دَجاج (n., m.)

to enter [16] . . . . (v.) دَخَلَ (يَدخُلُ) دُخول

to smoke [19] . . . . (v.) دَخَّن (يُدَخِّنُ) تَدْخين

bicycle (n., f.) دَرّاجة ج دَرّاجات

study [10] . . . . (n., f.) دِراسة ج دِراسات

of school, academic [5] . . . . (adj.) دِراسِيّ

degree (temperature), step [12] . . . . (درجة حرارة) (n., f.) دَرَجة ج دَرَجات

study [4] . . . . (v.) دَرَسَ (يَدرُسُ) دِراسة / دَرْس

lesson [11] . . . . (n., m.) دَرْس ج دُروس

defense [16] . . . . (n., m.) دِفاع ج دِفاعات

notebook . . . . (n., m.) دَفْتَر ج دَفاتِر

to pay [16] . . . . (v.) دَفَعَ (يَدْفَعُ) دَفْع

defense [16] . . . . (n., m.) دِفاع ج دِفاعات

minute [9] . . . . (n., f.) دَقيقَة ج دَقائِق

shop, store [18] . . . . (n., f.) دُكّان ج دَكاكين

to indicate, to point out [23] . . . . (v.) دَلّ (يَدُلُّ) دَلالة

guide [24] . . . . (n., m.) دَليل ج أدِلّاء

international [9] . . . . (n., m.) دُوَلِيّ

without [8] . . . . (prep.) دونَ

cock, rooster [15] . . . . (n., m.) ديك ج دِيَكة

turkey [15] . . . . (n., m.) ديك حَبَش

dinar (currency in Algeria, Bahrain, Iraq, Kuwait) [18] . . . . (n., m.) دينار ج دَنانير

ذ

corn [20] . . . . (n., f.) ذُرة

chin (when used with "to shave," it signifies shaving one's beard) [13] (n., f.) ذَقْن ج ذُقون

that [2] . . . . (n., m. sg.) ذلِكَ

to go [7, 10] . . . . (v.) ذَهَبَ (يَذْهَبُ) ذَهاب (إلى)

with, of, owner of [15] . . . . (n., m.) ذو ج ذَوو

Islamic month (d̲ū al-ḥijja) [11] . . . . (n., m.) ذو الحِجّة

Islamic month (d̲ū al-Qiʻda) [11] . . . . (n., m.) ذو القِعدة

ر

to see [17] .... رَأى (يَرى) رُؤية (v.)

fourth [5] .... رابِع (adj.)

to refer to, to review [24] .... راجَعَ (يُراجِعُ) مُراجعَة (v.)

ذهب (Syrian colloquial) [19] .... راح (يروح) + ع (v.)

head [15] .... رأس ج رُؤوس (n., m.)

passenger, rider [21] .... راكِب ج رُكّاب (n., m.)

wonderful; awesome [11] .... رائع (active participle)

housewife [17] .... رَبَّةُ بَيْت ج رَبّات بُيوت (n., f.)

quarter [9] .... رُبْع ج أرْباع (n., m.)

perhaps, probably [20] .... رُبَّما (adv.)

spring [12] .... رَبيع (n., m.)

Islamic month (*Rabīʿal-āḳir*) [11] .... رَبيع الآخِر (n., m.)

Islamic month (*Rabīʿal-ʿawwal*) [11] .... رَبيع الأوَّل (n., m.)

to organize [13] .... رَتَّبَ (يُرَتِّبُ) تَرْتيب (v.)

to hope [19] .... رَجا (يَرجو) رَجاء (v.)

Islamic month (*Rajab*) [11] .... رَجَب (n., m.)

to return, to go back [13] .... رَجَعَ (يَرْجِعُ) رُجوع (v.)

man [3] .... رَجُل ج رِجال (n., m.)

future marker (= "will" in Syrian colloquial) [17] .... رَح

trip, journey, flight [21] .... رِحْلة ج رِحلات (n., f.)

cheap, inexpensive [23] .... رَخيص (adj.)

to respond, to answer [24] .... رَدَّ (يَرُدُّ) رَدّ (v.)

letter, message [13] .... رِسالة ج رَسائِل (n., f.)

bullets; lead [21] .... رَصاص (n., m.)

to reject [16] .... رَفَضَ (يَرفُضُ) رَفْض (v.)

to dance [22] .... رَقَصَ (يرقُصُ) رَقْص (v.)

number [3] .... رَقْم ج أرْقام (n., m.)

to ride, to mount [19] .... رَكِبَ (يَركَبُ) رُكوب (v.)

Islamic month (*Ramaḍān*) [11] .... رَمَضان (n., m.)

to irrigate, to water [21] .... رَوى (يَروي) رَيّ (v.)

Roman [23] . . . . (adj.) رومانيّ
Riyadh (capital of Saudi Arabia) . . . . (n., f.) الرياض
sport [2] . . . . (n., f.) رِياضَة ج رِياضات
of sports; athletic [2] . . . . (adj.) رياضِيّ
mathematics, calculus [1] . . . . (n., f.) رياضِيّات
leader, president [16]. . . . . (n., m.) رَئيس ج رُؤَساء
wind [12] . . . . (n., f.) ريح ج رِياح

ز

to visit [6, 11] . . . . (v.) زارَ (يَزورُ) زِيارة
plus [3] . . . . (n., m.) زائِد
butter [8] . . . . (n., f.) زُبْدة
to plant, to cultivate [21] . . . . (v.) زَرَعَ (يَزرَعُ) زَرْع، زِراعة
wild thyme [8] . . . . (n., m.) زَعتَر
leader (popular) [16]. . . . . (n., m.) زَعيم ج زُعَماء
alley, narrow street [23]. . . . . (n., m.) زُقاق ج أزِقّة
colleague, coworker [17] . . . . (n., m.) زَميل ج زُمَلاء
flower [12] . . . . (n., f.) زَهْرة ج زَهْرات / أزْهار
husband [5] . . . . (n., m.) زَوْج ج أزْواج
wife [5]. . . . . (n., f.) زَوْجَة ج زَوْجات
olive [8] . . . . (n., m.) زَيْتون
to adorn, to decorate [15] . . . . (v.) زَيَّنَ (يُزَيِّنُ) تزيين

س

shall, will [11] (future particle) سَـ
seventh [5] . . . . (adj.) سابِع
square, courtyard [15] . . . . (n., f.) ساحة ج ساحات
coast, shore [21] . . . . (n., m.) ساحِل ج سَواحِل
sixth [5] . . . . (adj.) سادِس
unsweetened (coffee) [19] . . . . (adj., f.) سادة
to move, to walk, to travel, to march, to flow [19] . . . . (v.) سارَ (يَسيرُ) سَيْر

brilliant, shining [12] . . . . (adj., m.) ساطِع
to ask [6] . . . . (v.) سأَلَ (يسأَلُ) سؤال
mail carrier [17] . . . . (n., m.) ساعٍ ج سُعاة (ساعي بَريد)
to help, to assist [8, 17] . . . . (v.) ساعَدَ (يُساعِدُ) مُساعَدة
o'clock, hour [9] . . . . (n., f.) ساعَة ج ساعات
to travel [19] . . . . (v.) سافَرَ (يُسافِرُ) سَفَر
to drive [23] . . . . (v.) ساقَ (يَسوقُ) سِياقة
safe, secure, healthy [17] . . . . (n., m.) سالِم ج سالِمون
to equal [3] . . . . (v.) ساوى (يُساوي) مُساواة
to do (Syrian colloquial) [14] . . . . (v.) ساوى (يساوي)
driver, chauffeur [10] . . . . (n., m.) سائِق ج سائقون
reason, cause [17] . . . . (n., m.) سَبَب ج أَسْباب
Saturday [11] . . . . (n., m.) السَبْت
to swim [12] . . . . (v.) سَبَحَ (يَسْبَحُ) سِباحة
seven [3] . . . . (n., f.) سَبْعة
six [3] (n., f.) سِتّة
to register, to record [24] . . . . (v.) سَجَّلَ (يُسَجِّلُ) تَسْجيل
prisoner [23] . . . . (n., m.) سَجين ج سُجناء
water heater [18] . . . . (m. sg.) سَخّان لِلماء
silly, absurd, foolish [23] . . . . (n./adj.) سَخيف ج سُخَفاء
to please, to be glad [23] . . . . (v.) سَرَّ (يَسُرُّ) سُرور
bed [4] . . . . (n., m.) سَرير ج أَسِرّة
surface, level [23] . . . . (n., m.) سَطْح ج سُطوح
Saudi Arabia . . . . (n., f.) السُعودية
happy, pleased, joyful [19] . . . . (n., m.) سَعيد ج سُعَداء
embassy [23] . . . . (n., f.) سِفارة ج سِفارات
to fall [12] . . . . (v.) سَقَطَ (يَسْقُطُ) سُقوط
ceiling [21] . . . . (n., m.) سَقْف ج سُقوف
sugar [8] . . . . (n., m.) سُكَّر
to live, to reside [3] . . . . (v.) سَكَنَ (يَسْكُنُ) سَكَن
(student) living, residence, dormitory [3]. . . . . (verbal n., m.) سَكَنُ (الطُلاّب)
basket [20] . . . . (n., f.) سَلّة ج سِلال

سِلسِلة ج سَلاسِل (n., f.) .... range, series, chain [21]

سَلَطة ج سَلَطات (n., f.) .... salad [8]

سِلْك ج أسْلاك (كيبل) (n., m.) .... wire, cable [22]

سَلَّمَ (يُسَلِّمُ) تَسْليم (v.) .... to save, to protect [15]

سَماء ج سَماوات (n., f.) .... sky [12]

سَمِعَ (يَسْمَع) سَمْع (v.) .... to hear [22]

سَميط (n., m.) .... a kind of toasted thin bread [20]

سِنٌّ ج أسْنان (n., f.) .... tooth [13]

سِنّ (n., m.) .... age of a person [15]

سَنة ج سَنَوات / سُنون (n., f.) .... year [6, 11]

سَهل ج سُهول (n., m.) .... plain [21]

سُؤال ج أسئِلة (n., m.) .... question, query [19]

سَوْفَ (future particle) .... shall, will [11]

سوق ج أسْواق (n., f.) .... market [10]

سياحيّ (adj.) .... tourist [24]

سَيّارة ج سَيّارات (n.,m.) .... car [23]

سِياسيّ (adj.) .... political [23]

ش

شاءَ (يَشاءُ) مَشيئة (v.) .... want, will [3]

شابّ ج شَباب (n., m.) .... young man [16]

شاحِنة ج شاحِنات (n., f.) .... truck [18]

شارِع ج شَوارِع (n., m.) .... street [3]

شاطِئ ج شَواطِئ (n., m.) .... beach [12]

شاعِر ج شُعَراء (n., m.) .... poet [16]

شاغِر (adj.) .... empty [23]

الشام (n., f.) .... Syria, Damascus, Greater Syria [17]

شاهَدَ (يُشاهِدُ) مُشاهَدة (v.) .... to see, to watch, to witness [13]

شاي (n., m.) .... tea [8]

شُباط (n., m.) .... February [11]

شِبْه ج أشباه (n., m.) .... semi-, quasi; similarity [21]

winter [12] .... شتاء (n., m.)
tree [12] .... شَجَرة ج شَجَرات / أشْجار (n., f.)
person [22] .... شَخْص ج أشْخاص (n., m.)
personality, character [16] .... شَخصِيّة ج شَخصِيّات (n., f.)
drink, beverage, sherbet [17] .... شَراب ج أشْرِبة، شَرابات (n., m.)
to drink [8] .... شَرِبَ (يَشرَبُ) شُرْب (v.)
to explain, to expound, to illustrate [20] .... شَرَحَ (يَشرَحُ) شَرْح (v.)
bed sheet [11] .... شَرْشَف ج شَراشِف (n., m.)
company [18] .... شَرِكة ج شَرِكات (n., f.)
tape [22] .... شَريط ج أشْرِطة (n., m.)
sandwich [20] .... شَطيرة ج شَطائِر (n., f.)
emblem, sign, slogan [21] .... شِعار ج شِعارات، أشعِرة (n., m.)
Islamic month (*ŝa'bān*) [11] .... شَعبان (n., m.)
hair [24] .... شَعْر ج شُعور / أشْعار (n., m.)
poetry, poem, knowledge [24] .... شِعْر ج أشْعار (n., m.)
apartment [3] .... شَقّة ج شُقَق (n,. f.)
thank you [3] .... شُكْراً
to form, to constitute [21] .... شَكَّلَ (يُشَكِّلُ) تَشكيل (v.)
waterfall [19] .... شَلاّل ج شَلاّلات (n., m.)
north [19] .... شَمال (n., m.)
sun [12] .... شَمْس ج شُموس (n., f.)
of the sun; solar [1] .... شَمْسِيّ (adj.)
month [11] .... شَهْر ج أشْهُر / شُهور (n., m.)
last name, surname [24] .... شُهْرة (n., f.)
appetizing [8] .... شَهي (adj.)
what (Syrian colloquial) [14] .... شو (interrogative particle)
to grill, to broil [20] .... شَوى (يَشوي) شَي (v.)
Islamic month (*ŝawwāl*) [11] .... شَوّال (n., m.)
thing, object [1] .... شَيء ج أشْياء (n., m.)
interesting, thrilling [23] .... شَيِّق (adj.)

ص

soap [13] . . . . (n., m.) صابون
to become [15] . . . . (v.) صارَ (يَصيرُ) صَيْر، صَيْرورة، مَصير
pure, clear, not cloudy [12] . . . . (adj., f.) صافِية (adj., m.) صافٍ
to fast [15] . . . . (v.) صامَ (يَصومُ) صَوْم
to flow into [21] . . . . (v.) صَبَّ (يصُبُّ) صَبّ
morning [8] . . . . (n., m.) صَباح
journalism [14] . . . . (n., f.) صِحافة
desert [21] . . . . (n., f.) صَحْراء ج صَحاري
journalist [23] . . . . (n., m.) صَحَفِيّ ج ون
plate [13] . . . . (n., m.) صَحْن ج صُحون
health [9, 18] . . . . (n., f.) صِحّة
bon appétit (Syrian colloquial) [19] . . . . صَحّة وهَنا
clear, fine (of weather) [12] . . . . (adj., m.) صَحْوٌ
newspaper [23] . . . . (n., f.) صَحيفة ج صُحُف
to issue [24] . . . . (v.) صَدَرَ (يَصْدُرُ) صُدور
friend [1] . . . . (n., m.) صَديق ج أصْدِقاء
honestly, candidly [22] . . . . (n., f.) صَراحةً (بِصَراحة)
youngest, smallest [24] . . . . صُغرى superlative of صَغيرة,
small; young [4] . . . . (adj., m.) صَغير
class [1] . . . . (n., m.) صَفّ ج صُفوف
zero [3] . . . . (n., m.) صِفْر ج أصْفار
Islamic month (*ṣafar*) [11] . . . . (n., m.) صَفَر
characteristic [21] . . . . (n., f.) صِفة ج صِفات
to pray; to bless [15] . . . . (v.) صَلّى (يُصَلّي)
industry [19] . . . . (n., f.) صِناعة ج صِناعات
to manufacture, to make [15] . . . . (v.) صَنَعَ (يَصنَعُ) صِناعة
to make a picture, to portray, to illustrate [19] . . . . (v.) صَوَّرَ (يُصَوِّرُ) تَصوير
picture . . . . (n., f.) صورة ج صُوَر
pharmacology [6] . . . . (n., f.) صَيْدَلَة
pharmacist [24] . . . . (n., f.) صَيدلانيّة

pharmacy [24] . . . . (n., f.) صَيْدَلِيّة
summer [11] . . . . (n., m.) صَيْف

ض

ranking officer [16] . . . . (n., m.) ضابِط ج ضُبّاط
to laugh [20] . . . . (v.) ضَحِكَ (يَضْحَكُ) ضِحْك
opposite, anti-, adversary, opponent [17] . . . . (n., m.) ضِدٌّ ج أَضْداد
molar tooth [17] . . . . (n., m.) ضِرْس ج أَضْراس، ضُروس
guest [11] . . . . (n., m.) ضَيْف ج ضُيوف
narrow, tight [21] . . . . (adj.) ضَيِّق

ط

floor, storey, flat [6, 18] . . . . طابَق ج طَوابق
male student [1] . . . . (n., m.) طالِب ج طُلاّب
female student [1] . . . . (n., f.) طالِبة ج طالِبات
table . . . . (n., f.) طاوِلة ج طاوِلات
airplane [11] . . . . (n., f.) طائِرة ج طائِرات
medicine [2] . . . . (n., m.) طِبّ
of course [22] . . . . (adv.) طَبْعاً
nature [22] . . . . (n., f.) طَبيعة
physician, doctor [17] . . . . (n., m.) طَبيب ج أَطِبّاء
way, road [12] . . . . (n., f.) طَريق ج طُرُق، طُرُقات
food [15] . . . . (n., m.) طَعام ج أَطْعِمة
taste, flavor [23] . . . . (n., m.) طَعْم ج طُعوم
patty made from ground beans and spices fried in oil (Egypt) [8] . . . . (n., f.) طَعْمِيّة
child [5] . . . . (n., m.) طِفْل ج أَطْفال
weather [12] . . . . (n., m.) طَقْس ج طُقوس
to request; to order (i.e., in a restaurant) [16] . . . . (v.) طَلَبَ (يَطْلُب) طَلَب
height [24] . . . . (n., m.) طول
Toulon (a town in southern France) [16] . . . . (n., f.) طولون
tall [10] . . . . (n., m.) طَويل ج طِوال

good [17] .... طَيِّب ج طَيِّبون (n., m.)
bird [23] .... طَيْر ج طُيور (n., m.)

ظ

to think, to believe [11] .... ظَنَّ (يَظُنُّ) (v.)
to appear, to become visible [22] .... ظَهَرَ (يَظهَرُ) ظُهور (v.)
noon [8] .... ظُهْر (n., m.)

ع

to return [6, 13] .... عادَ (يَعودُ) عَوْدة (v.)
usually [7] .... عادَةً (adv.)
tenth [5] .... عاشِر (adj.)
capital city [21] .... عاصِمة ج عَواصِم (n., f.)
high, elevated [21] .... عالٍ (العالي) (adj.)
world [13] .... عالَم ج عَوالِم (n., m.)
scholar, scientist [16] .... عالِم ج عُلَماء (n., m.)
sociologist [16] .... عالِم اجْتِماع (n., m.)
year [17] .... عام ج أعْوام (n., m.)
public [20] .... عامّ (adj.)
worker, laborer [12] .... عامِل ج عُمّال (n., m.)
colloquial, vulgar, dialectal [22] .... عاميّ (adj.)
colloquial [14] .... عاميّة (active participle)
nuclear family [5] .... عائِلَة ج عائِلات (n., f.)
phrase [15] .... عِبارة ج عِبارات (n., f.)
to cross [23] .... عَبَرَ (يَعبُرُ) عُبور (v.)
crowded (Syrian colloquial) [17] .... عَجْقة (n., f.)
number (quantity) [19] .... عَدَد ج أعْداد (n., m.)
lentils [14] .... عَدَس (n., m.)
a number of, several [2] .... عِدَّةُ (n., f.)
several, multiple [21] .... عَديد (adj.)
Arab .... عَرَبيّ (adj.)
Arabic (language) [3] .... العَرَبيّة (n., f.)

show, demonstration, performance [19] .... عَرْض ج عُروض (n., m.)
to know [3] .... عَرَفَ (يَعرِفُ) مَعْرِفة (v.)
to introduce someone to someone else [16] .... عَرَّفَ (يُعَرِّف) تَعريف (على) (v.)
dear, esteemed, beloved [19] .... عزيز ج أعِزّاء (n., m.)
honey [8] .... عَسَل (n., m.)
dinner [8و 13] .... عَشاء ج أعْشِية (n., m.)
ten [3] .... عَشَرة (n., f.)
stick, rod, cane [20] .... عَصا ج عُصِيّ (n., f.)
juice [8] .... عَصير (n., m.)
to be off from work [15] .... عَطَّلَ (يُعَطِّلُ) تَعْطيل (v.)
break; vacation [13] .... عُطْلة ج عُطلات (n., f.)
weekend [14] .... عُطْلة نِهاية الأسْبوع (n., f.)
great, important, imposing [19] .... عَظيم ج عُظَماء (adj./n., m.)
you're welcome [1] .... عَفْواً (adv.)
group of ten [6] .... عَقْد ج عُقود (n., m.)
cord used to hold a male's headdress in place [10] .... عِقال ج عُقُل (n., m.)
group of ten; decade [6] .... عَقْد ج عُقود (n., m.)
opposite, reverse, contrary [23] .... عَكْس (n., m.)
on [1] .... عَلى (prep.)
in general, generally [18] .... على العُموم
throughout, all the way [21] .... على طُول
it seemed; it appeared [20] .... على ما يَبْدو (أنّ)
relation [9] .... عَلاقة ج عَلاقات (n., f.)
to hang [18] .... عَلَّقَ (يُعَلِّقُ) تَعْليق (v.)
flag, banner [21] .... عَلَم ج أعْلام (n., m.)
to know [17] .... عَلِمَ (يَعْلَمُ) عِلْم (v.)
science, discipline [2] .... عِلْم ج عُلوم (n., m.)
sociology [16] .... عِلْم اجْتِماع (n., m.)
of science, scientific [2] .... عِلميّ (adj.)
knowledgeable [6] .... عَليم (adj.)
paternal uncle [24] .... عَمّ ج أعْمام (n., m.)
mayor [14] .... عُمْدَة ج عُمَد (n., m.)

عُمُر ج أعْمار (n., m.)	age [1]
عَمِلَ (يَعْمَلُ) عَمَل (v.)	to work [10]
عَنى (يَعْني) (v.)	to mean [9]
عِنَب (n., m.)	grape [20]
عِنْدَ (prep.)	at (expressing possession)
عُنصُر ج عَناصِر (n., m.)	race, element [16]
عُنصُريّ (adj.)	racial [16]
عُنوان ج عَناوين (n., m.)	address [3]
عِيادة ج عِيادات (n., f.)	doctor's practice, clinic [18]
عيد ج أعْياد (n., m.)	celebration, festivity, feast day, day, holiday, *eid* [14]
عيدُ الأضْحى (n., m.)	Feast of Immolation/sacrifice (after *Haj*), Greater Bairam [15]
عيدُ الشُكْرِ (n., m.)	Thanksgiving [15]
عيد العُمّال (n., m.)	Labor Day [12]
عيدُ الفِصْح (n., m.)	Easter [15]
عيدُ الفِطْرِ (n., m.)	feast of breaking the Ramadan fast [15]
عيدُ الميلاد (n., m.)	Christmas [15]
عَيش (n., m.)	bread (Egypt) [18]
عَيْن ج عُيون (n., f.)	eye [24]

غ

غادَرَ (يُغادِرُ) مُغادَرة (v.)	to leave [23]
غاز ج غازات (n., m.)	[butane] gas [18]
غالٍ (n., m.)	expensive, dear [19]
غالِباً (adv.)	often, mostly, generally [19]
غائِم (adj., m.)	cloudy; overcast [12]
غُتْرة ج غُتَر/ غُترات (n., f.)	a male's headdress [10]
غَداً (adv.)	tomorrow [11]
غَداء ج أغْدِية (n., m.)	lunch [13]
غَرْب (n., m.)	west [19]
غُرْفَة ج غُرَف (n., f.)	room [1]
غُروب (n., m.)	sunset [17]
غَسّالة ج غَسّالات (n., f.)	washing machine [18]

to wash [13] .... (v.) غَسَلَ (يَغْسِلُ) غَسْل

rich, wealthy [17] .... (n., m.) غَنيّ ج أغنِياء

to sing [22] .... (v.) غَنّى (يُغَنّي) غِناء

spare part; change [24] .... (n., m) غِيار ج غيارات

non-, un-, other than, different from [7, 20] .... (n., m.) غَير

to change sth. [13] .... (v.) غَيَّرَ (يُغَيِّرُ) تَغيير

rain cloud [12] .... (n., f.) غَيْمة ج غُيوم

ف

and, then, so [17] .... (coordinating particle) فَـ

deluxe, fancy, excellent, luxurious [18] .... (adj.) فاخِر

to win [20] .... (v.) فازَ (يفوزُ) فَوز

green beans [20] .... (n., f.) فاصولية

benefit, use, advantage [17] .... (n., f.) فائدة ج فَوائِد

girl, young woman [10] .... (n., f.) فَتاة ج فَتَيات

dawn, daybreak [15] .... (n., m.) فَجْر

brush [13] .... (n., f.) فُرْشاة ج فَراشٍ

lit. "a happy opportunity," *meaning* "good to meet you" [9] .... فُرْصَة سَعيدة

branch, subdivision [24] .... (n., m.) فَرْع ج فُروع

pharaoh [19] .... (n., m.) فِرعَون ج فَراعِنة

band, company, troupe [19] .... (n., f.) فِرقة ج فِرَق، أفْرِقة

French (language) [3] .... (n., f.) الفَرَنْسِيَّة

team, company, band, troupe [20] .... (n., f.) فَريق ج أفرقة

riddle [22] .... (n., f.) فَزّورة ج فَوازير

pistachio [21] .... (n., m.) فُسْتُق

Classical Arabic (*lit.*: "most eloquent") [14] .... (superlative) فُصْحى

(academic) term, season [5] .... (n., m.) فَصْل ج فُصول

pure, good, clear, standard, or literary Arabic [22] .... (adj.) فَصيح

space [22] .... (n., m.) فَضاء

silver [23] .... (n., f.) فِضّة

to prefer [14] .... (v.) فَضَّلَ (يُفَضِّل) تَفْضيل

breakfast [8] .... (n., m.) فَطور

pie [15] .... (n., f.) فَطيرة ج فَطائِر

to do [7] .... (v.) فَعَلَ (يَفعَلُ) فِعْل

only; no more than [5] .... (particle) فَقَطْ

poor [17] .... (n., m.) فَقير ج فُقَراء

to think, to reflect, to ponder (not to believe) [20] .... (v.) فَكَّرَ (يُفَكِّرُ) تَفْكير

idea [14] .... (n., f.) فِكْرة ج أفْكار

peasant, farmworker [23] .... (n., m.) فَلاّح ج ون

philosophy [16] .... (n., f.) فَلْسَفة ج فَلسَفات

patty made from ground beans and spices fried in oil (Syria) [8] . . (n., m.) فُلفُل ج فَلافِل

green (bell) pepper [20] .... (n., f.) فُلَيفُلة

cup [8] .... (n., m.) فِنْجان ج فَناجين

hotel [11] .... (n., m.) فُنْدُق ج فَنادِق

to understand, to comprehend, to realize [20] .... (v.) فَهِمَ (يَفْهَمُ) فَهْم

fava beans [8] .... (n., m.) فول

peanuts [20] .... (n., m.) فول (سوداني)

physics [5] .... (n., f.) فيزياء

philosopher [16] .... (n., m.) فَيْلَسوف ج فَلاسِفة

ق

to meet [11] .... (v.) قابَلَ (يُقابِلُ) مُقابَلة

to drive [23] .... (v.) قاد (يَقودُ) قِيادة

boat [19] .... (n., m.) قارِب ج قَوارِب

continent [21] .... (n., f.) قارّة ج قارّات

rule, principle, basis, foundation, base [20] .... (n., f.) قاعِدة ج قَواعِد

to say [11] .... (v.) قالَ (يَقولُ) قَوْل

to do, to perform [16] .... (v.) قامَ (يَقومُ) قِيام

to gamble [19] .... (v.) قامَرَ (يُقامِرُ) مُقامَرة، قِمار

law [16] .... (n., m.) قانون ج قَوانين

Cairo (capital of Egypt) .... (n., f.) القاهِرة

leader (military) [16] .... (n., m.) قائد ج قُوّاد / قادة

before [11] .... (adv.) قَبْلَ

[no meaning; denotes completed action, emphasis, or possibility] [23] ..... (particle) قَد

Jerusalem .... (n., f.) القُدْس

foot [23] .... (n., f.) قَدَم ج أقْدام

to serve, to provide [19] .... (v.) قَدَّمَ (يُقَدِّمُ) تَقديم

old, ancient [10] .... (adj.) قَديم ج قُدَماء

to read [7] .... (v.) قَرَأَ (يَقرَأُ) قِراءة

nearby, close [7] .... (adv.) قُرْب

pumpkin [15] .... (n., m.) قَرْع

cauliflower [20] .... (n., m.) قَرنَبيط

close, near [11] .... (adv.) قَريب

a relative [23] .... (n., m.) قَريب ج أقارِب

village [16] .... (n., f.) قَرية ج قُرى

priest [16] .... (n., m.) قِسّيس ج قَساوِسة

story [23] .... (n., f.) قِصَّة ج قِصَص

short [10] .... (n., m.) قَصير ج قِصار

to spend time [13] .... (v.) قَضى (يَقضي) قَضاء

train [14] .... (n., m.) قِطار ج قِطارات

country (almost exclusively used for Arab countries) [21] .... (n., m.) قُطْر ج أقْطار

piece [8] .... (n., f.) قِطْعة ج قِطَع

cotton [21] .... (n., m.) قُطْن

heart [23] .... (n., m.) قَلْب ج قُلوب

to worry [17] .... (v.) قَلِقَ (يَقْلَق) قَلَق

pencil, pen .... (n., m.) قَلَم ج أقلام

little [6] .... (adj.) قَليل

a little [6] .... (adv.) قَليلاً

wheat [21] .... (n., m.) قَمْح

moon, satellite [22] .... (n., m.) قَمَر ج أقْمار

of the moon, lunar [1] .... (adj.) قَمَريّ

shirt [11] .... (n., m.) قَميص ج قُمْصان

channel [22] .... (n., f.) قَناة ج قَنَوات

coffee [8] .... (n., f.) قَهْوة

arch [14] .... (n., m.) قَوْس ج أقْواس

powerful, strong [10] .... (adj.) قَويّ ج أقوِياء

ك

like, as [20] .... (prep.) كَـ
writer, scribe [16] .... (n., m.) كاتِب ج كُتّاب / كَتَبة
glass [8] .... (n., f.) كَأس ج كُؤوس
sufficient [20] .... (active participle) كافٍ (الكافي)
to be (was, were) [11] .... (v.) كانَ (يَكونُ) كَوْن
December [11] .... (n., m.) كانون الأوَّل
January [11] .... (n., m.) كانون الثاني
kebab, minced meat on a skewer with parsley and onion [9] .... (n., m.) كَباب
big, large; old (in age) [10]............................. (n., m.) كَبير ج كِبار
big [5] .... (adj.) كَبير
book .... (n., m.) كِتاب ج كُتُب
writing [13] .... (n., f.) كِتابة
to write [7] .... (v.) كَتَبَ (يَكْتُبُ) كِتابة
much, a great deal [13] .... (n., m.) كَثير ج كَثيرون / كِثار
a great deal [8] .... (adverbial) كَثيراً
also, as well [19] .... كَذلِكَ
hospitality, generosity [23].. (n., m.) كَرَم
ball, sphere [20] .... (n., f.) كُرة ج كُرات
basketball [20] .... كُرةُ السَلّة
table tennis [20] .... كُرةُ الطاولة
volleyball [20].. الكُرةُ الطائرة
football/soccer [20].. كُرةُ القَدَم
water polo [20] .... كُرةُ الماء
tennis [20] .... كُرةُ المَضرِب
chair .... (n., m.) كُرْسيّ ج كَراسٍ
for the sake of (Syrian colloquial) [16].. كرمال
generous [16] .... (adj.) كَريم ج كُرَماء
headdress [10] .... (n., f.) **كوفِيّة ج كوفيّات**
every, all, the whole [9, 12] .... (n.) كُلّ
both [21] .... (n.) كِلا

speech, speaking [23] . . . . (n., m.) كَلام

to cost [23] . . . . (v.) كَلَّفَ (يُكَلِّفُ) تَكْليف

to talk to, to speak with [24] . . . . (v.) كَلَّمَ (يُكَلِّمُ)

word [3] . . . . (n., f.) كَلِمَة ج كَلِمات

college [2] . . . . (n., f.) كُلِّيَّة ج كُلِّيّات

how many/much [3] . . . . (interrogative particle) كَمْ

as [17] . . . . (particle) كَما

أيضاً (Syrian colloquial) [14] . . . . كَمان

electricity [17] . . . . (n., f.) كَهْرَباء

zucchini [20] . . . . (n., m.) كوسا

headdress [10] . . . . (n., f.) كوفِيّة ج كوفيّات

cable [22] . . . . (n., m.) كيبل

kilometer [19] . . . . (n., m.) كيلومِتر ج كيلومِترات

chemistry [5] . . . . (n., f.) كيمياء

ل

to, for, by [6] . . . . (prep.) لِـ

in order to [7] . . . . (part.) لِـ + يَفْعَل

no . . . . (negative particle) لا

Don't worry about it (said when s.o. thanks you for sth.) [6] . . . . لا شُكْرَ على واجِب

necessary [16] . . . . (active participle) لازِم

player [23] . . . . (n., m.) لاعِب ج ون

because [13] . . . . (particle) لأَنَّ

kernel, seed [20] . . . . (n., m.) لُبّ ج لُبوب

to wear [10] . . . . (v.) لَبِسَ (يَلبَسُ) لُبْس

yogurt [13] . . . . (n., m.) لَبَن

lightly salted, partially dehydrated yogurt with olive oil [14] . . . . (n., f.) لَبنة

meat [8] . . . . (n., m.) لَحم ج لُحوم

عِنْدَ [19] . . . . (prep.) لَدى

for this reason, therefore [14] . . . . (demonstrative) لِذلِكَ

delicious, delightful, tasty [20] . . . . (adj., m.) لَذيذ

nice [5] . . . . (adj.) لَطيف

to play [20] . . . . لَعِبَ (يَلعَبُ) لَعْب (v.)
game, play, ride [19] . . . . لُعبة ج لُعبات، ألعاب (n., f.)
language [2] . . . . لُغَة ج لُغات (n., f.)
of language, linguistic [2] . . . . لُغَويّ (adj.)
[expresses completed action with a perfect tense verb] [24] . . . . لَقَد (particle)
but [1] . . . . لكِنْ (particle, weak version)
but [1] . . . . لكِنَّ (particle, strong version)
not (particle used to negate past-tense verbs) [17] . . . . لَمْ (particle)
no longer [20] . . . . لَمْ يَعُدْ
why [13] . . . . لِماذا (particle)
negates future (= will not) [19] . . . . لَنْ + المضارع المنصوب
blackboard . . . . لَوح ج أَلْواح (n., m.)
if you would; please [1] . . . . لَو سَمَحْت
color [12] . . . . لَوْن ج أَلْوان (n., m.)
[Syrian] pound; lira [18] . . . . لَيْرة ج لَيْرات (n., f.)
not [1] . . . . لَيسَ (particle)
لِماذا (Syrian colloquial) [14] . . . . لَيْش
night [12] . . . . لَيْل (n., m.)
(a) night [17] . . . . لَيْلة ج لَيالٍ (n., f.)

م

meter [18] . . . . م (مِتْر) ج أمْتار (n., m.)
what (question particle used in front of nouns) [3] . . . . ما
[particle used to negate past-tense verbs] [10] . . . . ما (particle)
except [17] . . . . ما عَدا (particle)
water [8] . . . . ماء ج مِياه (n., m.)
soda [20] . . . . ماء غازيّ ج مِياه غازيّة (n., f.)
to die [22] . . . . ماتَ (يموتُ) مَوْت (v.)
school subject, course [4] . . . . مادّة ج مَوادّ (n., f.)
what (used with verbs) [3] . . . . ماذا
what's your opinion? [8] . . . . ما رأيُك
previous, last, past [17] . . . . ماضٍ (الماضي) (adj.)

rainy [12] .... (adj., m.) ماطِر
objection [11] .... (active participle) مانِع
match, game [20] .... (n., f.) مُباراة ج مُبارَيات
blessed [15].................................. (n., m.) مُبارَك
one coming early [13] .... (n., m.) مُبَكِّر ج مُبَكِّرون
building, construction [19] .... (n., m.) مَبنى ج مَبانٍ
one coming late [13] .... (n., m.) مُتأخِّر ج مُتَأخِّرون
when [8].................................. (question particle) مَتى
united [9] .... (adj., m.) مُتَّحِد
museum [19] .... (n., m.) مُتحَف ج مَتاحِف
enthusiastic [11] .... (active participle) مُتَحَمِّس
metro [18] .... (n., m.) مِترو
married [3].................................. (n., m) مُتزَوِّج ج مُتزَوِّجون
spectator [20] .... (n., m.) مُتَفَرِّج ج ون
retired person [24] .... (n., m.) مُتَقاعِد ج مُتَقاعِدون
intermediate [15] .... (adj., m.) مُتَوَسِّط
something similar, like, such as [19].................................. (n., m.) مِثْلُ ج أمْثال
free of charge [22].................................. (adj.) مَجّانيّ
society, community [23] .... (n., m.) مُجْتَمَع ج مُجْتَمَعات
magazine [7].................................. (n., f.) مَجَلَّة ج مَجَلّات
kitchen sink [18].................................. (n., m.) مَجْلى ج مَجالٍ
accountant [23].................................. (n., m.) مُحاسِب ج ون
accounting [9].................................. (n., f.) مُحاسَبة
lawyer, attorney-at-law, counsel [16] .... (n., m.) مُحام ج مُحامون
loving [19] .... (n., m.) مُحِبّ ج مُحِبّون
engine, motor [10] .... (n., f.) مُحَرِّك ج مَحَرِّكات
Islamic month (*muḥarram*) [11] .... (n., m.) مُحَرَّم
station [14].................................. (n., f.) مَحَطّة ج مَحَطّات
place; store [1, 7].................................. (n., m.) مَحَلّ
roasted, toasted [20] .... (n./adj.) مُحَمَّص
ocean [21].................................. (n., m.) مُحيط ج مُحيطات
laboratory [2] .... (n., m.) مَخْبَر ج مَخابِر

bakery [18] .... مَخْبَز ج مَخابِز (n., m.)
laboratory [2] .... مُخْتَبَر ج مُخْتَبَرات (n., m.)
store, warehouse [24] .... مَخْزَن ج مَخازِن (n., m.)
[floor] plan, map [18] .... مُخَطَّط ج مُخَطَّطات (n., m.)
sincere, faithful (sincerely yours) [19] .... مُخلِص ج مُخلِصون (n., m.)
period, duration [19] .... مُدّة ج مُدَد (n., f.)
teacher [24] .... مُدَرِّس ج مُدَرِّسون (n., m.)
school [17] .... مَدْرَسة ج مَدارِس (n., f.)
stewed [13] .... مُدَمَّس (adj.)
boss; director [6] .... مُدير ج مُدَراء (n., m.)
city, town .... مَدينة ج مُدُن (n., f.)
announcer [22] .... مُذيع ج ون (n., m.)
to pass, to go by [19] .... مَرَّ (يَمُرُّ) مُرور (v.)
mirror [18] .... مِرْآة ج مَرايا (n., f.)
square [21] .... مُرَبَّع (adj.)
jam, preserve [8] .... مُرَبّى ج مُرَبَّيات (n., m.)
elevated [18] .... مُرْتَفِع (active participle)
toilet [18] .... مِرْحاض ج مَراحيض (n., m.)
center [23] .... مَرْكَز ج مَراكِز (n., m.)
comfortable [18] .... مُريح (adj.)
sick, ill, patient [24] .... مَريض ج مَرْضى (n., m)
once, one occurrence [13] .... مَرّة ج مَرّات (n., f.)
crowded [14] .... مُزْدَحِم (adj.)
farm [23] .... مَزْرَعة ج مَزارِع (n., f.)
abloom [12] .... مُزْهِر (adj.)
area [21] .... مِساحة ج مِساحات (n., f.)
help, assistance [6] .... مُساعَدة (verbal n.)
evening [8] .... مَساء (n., m.)
swimming pool [2] .... مَسْبَح ج مَسابِح (n., m.)
hospital [24] .... مُسْتَشْفى (n., m.)
mosque [19] .... مَسجد ج مَساجِد (n., m.)
recorded [23] .... مُسَجَّل (adj./n.)

مُسَجِّلة ج مُسَجِّلات (n., f.) ... recorder [23]
مَسرَح ج مَسارِح (n., m.) ... theater, stage [19]
مُسَلسَل ج مُسَلسَلات (n., m.) ... show, (television) series [13]
مُسْلِم ج مُسْلِمون (n., m.) ... Muslim, one of the Islamic faith [15]
مَسْلوق (passive particle) ... boiled [8]
المَسيح (n., m.) ... Christ [15]
مَشى (يَمْشي) مَشي (v.) ... walk [11]
مُشاهَدة (verbal n.) ... watching [13]
مُشْتاق ج مُشْتاقون (n., m.) ... one who is longing, yearning [19]
مَشْغول ج مَشْغولون (n., m.) ... busy [13]
مُشَكَّل (passive participle) ... mixed, assorted [16]
مُشْمِس (adj.) ... sunny [12]
مَشْهور ج (ون)، مَشاهير (participle) ... famous, well-known [14]
مِشواة ج مَشاوٍ (n., f.) ... grill, gridiron [20]
مَشويّ (adj.) ... grilled [20]
مِصْباح ج مَصابيح (n., m.) ... lamp [18]
مِصْر (n., f.) ... Egypt
مَصْرِف ج مَصارِف (n., m.) ... bank [18]
مِصعَد ج مَصاعِد (n., m.) ... elevator, lift [19]
مَصْنَع ج مَصانِع (n., m.) ... factory, plant [23]
مَصْنوع (مِن) (passive participle) ... made (of/from) [21]
مَطار ج مَطارات (n., m.) ... airport [11]
مَطْبَخ ج مَطابِخ (n., m.) ... kitchen [8]
مَطَر ج أمْطار (n., m.) ... rain [12]
مُطْرِب ج مُطْرِبون (n., m.) ... entertainer [22]
مَطْعَم ج مَطاعِم (n., m.) ... restaurant [8]
مُطِلٌّ (verbal n.) ... overlooking [18]
مَعَ (prep.) ... with [1]
مَعاً (adv.) ... together [13]
مَعَ أنَّ ... though, although [19]
مُعايَدة ج مُعايَدات (n., f.) ... greeting [17]
مُعْتَدِل (adj.) ... moderate [12]

paste [13] .... (n., m.) مَعْجون ج مَعاجين

most [12] .... (n.) مُعْظَم

you're right [14] .... مَعك حَقّ

pasta, macaroni [14] .... (n., f.) مَعْكَرونة

teacher [15] .... (active participle) مُعَلِّم ج مُعَلِّمون

information [15] .... (n., f.) مَعلومة ج مَعلومات

meaning [3] .... (n., m.) مَعْنى ج مَعانٍ / المعاني

sunset [15] .... (n., m.) مَغْرِب

Morocco .... (n., f.) المَغْرِب

washbasin, bathroom sink [18] .... (n., f.) مَغْسَلة ج مَغاسِل

covered (with) [21] .... (passive participle) مُغَطّيً (بِـ)

singer [22] .... (n., m.) مُغَنٍ ج ون

key .... (n., m.) مِفْتاح ج مَفاتيح

tablecloth [23] .... (n., m.) مِفْرَش ج مَفارِش

vocabulary item [7] .... (n., m.) مُفْرَدة ج مُفْرَدات

preferred, favorite [20] .... (n./adj., m.) مُفَضَّل

effectiveness, validity [24] .... (passive participle) مَفعول

opposite, across from [18] .... (adv.) مُقابِل

interview [22] .... (n., f.) مُقابَلة ج ات

coming, next, following [19] .... (n., m.) مُقبِل ج مُقبِلون

introduction [16] .... (n., f.) مُقَدِّمة ج مُقَدِّمات

cafeteria [8] .... (n., m.) مَقْصَف ج مَقاصِف

seat, bench, armchair [23] .... (n., m.) مَقْعَد ج مَقاعِد

fried [8, 13] .... (adj.) مَقليّ

place, location [16] .... (n., m.) مَكان ج أَمْكِنة

office [2] .... (n., m.) مَكْتَب ج مَكاتِب

library, bookstore, bookcase [2] .... (n., f.) مَكْتَبة ج مَكْتَبات

written [17] .... (n., m.) مَكْتوب

Mexico [21] .... (n., f.) المِكسيك

note, observation [24] .... (n., f.) مُلاحَظة ج مُلاحظات

clothes [18] .... (n., m.) مَلبَس ج مَلابِس

playground, sports field [2] .... (n., m.) مَلْعَب ج مَلاعِب

مَلِك ج مُلوك (n., m.)	king [16]
مَلِكة ج مَلِكات (n., f.)	queen [23]
مَلْهىً ج مَلاهٍ (n., m.)	place of entertainment [14]
مُلَوَّث (adj.)	polluted [23]
مِليون (n., m.)	million [19]
مُمْتاز ج ون (adj.)	excellent [14]
مُمْتِع (active participle)	enjoyable [23]
مُمَثِّل ج ون (n., m.)	actor, representative [22]
مَمْلَكة ج مَمالِك (n., f.)	kingdom [23]
مَنْ (question particle and relative noun)	who [5]
مِن (prep.)	from, of
مِن أجلِ	for the sake of [22]
مِن خِلالِ	via; by means of [22]
مِن فَضْلِك	please [6, 7]
مُناسَبة ج مُناسَبات (n., f.)	occasion [15]
مُنتَج ج مُنتَجات (n., m.)	product [21]
مِنْحة ج مِنَح (n., f.)	scholarship, grant, gift [17]
مُنْذُ (prep.)	since, for [19]
مَنزِل ج مَنازِل (n., m.)	house, residence [23]
مِنْطَقة ج مَناطِق (n., f.)	region [15]
مَنْظَر ج مَناظِر (n., m.)	view, panorama [23]
مَنْفَذ ج مَنافِذ (n., m.)	outlet [21]
منيح ج امْناح (adj.)	جَيِّد (Syrian colloquial) [16]
مُهَنْدِس ج مُهَندِسون (n., m.)	engineer [14]
مِهْنة ج مِهَن (n., f.)	occupation, profession [24]
مُواصَلة ج مُواصَلات (n., f.)	means of transportation [23]
مُوافِق (active participle)	agree [6, 8]
مُوافَقة (verbal n.)	agreement, approval [6]
مَوْجود (n., m.)	found, existing, present [1]
مَوْجة ج ات (n., f.)	wave [22]
مُؤَرِّخ ج مُؤَرِّخون (n., m.)	historian [16]
مَوْز (n., m.)	banana [20]

worker; employee [6] .... (n., m.) مُوَظَّف (ج) مُوَظَّفون
time, appointment [9] .... (n., m.) مَوْعِد ج مَواعيد
[cooking] range [18] .... (n., m.) مَوْقِد ج مَواقِد
[bus] stop, parking lot [18] .... (n., m.) مَوْقِف ج مَواقِف
birthday, birthplace [15] .... (n., m.) مَوْلِد
consisting of, comprising [24] .... (passive participle) مُؤَلَّف (مِن)
hundred [6] .... (n., f.) مِئة ج مِئات
square, field, arena [19] .... (n., m.) مَيدان ج مَيادين
birth, birthday [15] .... (n., m.) ميلاد ج مَواليد
port [19] .... (n., m.) ميناء ج مَوانِئ

ن

waiter [23] .... (n., m.) نادِل ج نُدُل
window .... (n., f.) نافِذة ج نَوافّذ
minus [3] .... (n., m.) ناقِص
to fall asleep; to sleep [9] .... (v.) نامَ (يَنامُ) نَوْم
plant [23] .... (n., m.) نَبات ج نَباتات
to spring, to originate, to flow [21] .... (v.) نَبَعَ (يَنْبُعُ) نَبْع
prophet [15] .... (n., m.) نَبيّ ج أنْبياء
section, manner, mode, fashion [21] .... (n., m.) نَحْو ج أنْحاء
to stay (in a place) [11] .... (v.) نَزَلَ (يَنْزِلُ) نُزول
relative adjective .... (n., f.) نِسْبة
person (used in population counts) [19] .... (n., f.) نَسَمة ج نَسَمات
to forget [13] .... (v.) نَسِيَ (يَنسى) نِسْيان
textile, tissue, fabric [21] .... (n., m.) نَسيج
bulletin, report [22] .... (n., f.) نَشْرة ج نَشَرات
half [9] .... (n., m.) نِصْف ج أنْصاف
to clean [13] .... (v.) نَظَّفَ (يُنَظِّفُ) تَنظيف
eyeglasses .... (n., f.) نَظّارة ج نَظّارات
system [22] .... (n., m.) نِظام ج أنْظِمة
clean [14] .... (adj., m.) نَظيف
yes .... نَعَم

mint, peppermint [23] . . . . (n., m.) نَعناع
same [24] . . . . (n., f.) (. . .الـ) نَفْس ج أَنْفُس
petroleum, crude oil [21] . . . . (n., m.) نِفْط
to be sent into exile, to be expelled [16] . . . . (passive v.) نُفِيَ (يُنْفى) نَفْيٌ
to move sth. somewhere; to transport [23] . . . . (v.) نَقَلَ (يَنْقُلُ) نَقل
small, spicy mutton sausage [20] . . . . (n., f. pl.) نَقانِق (أو مَقانِق)
pure [23] . . . . (adj.) نَقيّ
daytime [12] . . . . (n., m.) نَهار
end [14] . . . . (n., f.) نِهاية ج نِهايات
to get up [13] . . . . (v.) نَهَضَ (يَنهَضُ) نُهوض
kind, sort [15,17] . . . . (n., m.) نَوْع ج أَنْواع
sleeping [11] . . . . (verbal n.) نَوْم
April [11] . . . . (n., m.) نيسان

هـ

these [2] . . . . (dual, f., nom.) هاتانِ
phone . . . . (n., m.) هاتِف ج هَواتِف
these [2] . . . . (dual, f., acc., gen.) هاتَيْنِ
Pacific [21] . . . . (adj.) الهادي
quiet, serene [23] . . . . (adj.) هادِئ
important, significant [19] . . . . (n./adj.) هامٌّ ج هامّون
present, gift [23] . . . . (n., f.) هَدِيّة ج هَدايا
this . . . . (n., m.) هذا
these [2] . . . . (dual, m., nom.) هذانِ
these [2] . . . . (dual, m., acc., gen.) هذَيْنِ
this . . . . (n., f.) هذِه
pyramid [19] . . . . (n., m.) هَرَم ج أهرام / أهرامات
(question particle for yes-no questions) [3] . . . . هَلْ
now (Syrian colloquial) [18] . . . . هَلَّق أو هَللأ
they . . . . (pron., m., pl.) هُم
they . . . . (pron., m., dual) هُما
they . . . . (pron., f., pl.) هُنَّ

here [9] .... (demonstrative) هُنا
there, there is/are [1] .... (demonstrative) هُناكَ
Pacific [21] .... (adj.) الهادي
to congratulate, to felicitate (on the occasion of) [15] .... (v.) هَنَّأ (يُهَنِّئُ) تَهنئة
India [10] .... (n., f.) الهِنْد
engineering [2] .... (n., f.) هَنْدَسَة
he .... (pron.) هُوَ
air [23] .... (n., m.) هَواء
these (human plural) [2] .... (m., pl.) هؤُلاءِ
identity [3] .... (n., f.) هُويّة ج هُويّات
she .... (pron.) هِيَ

و

and [1] .... (conjunction) وَ
one [3] .... (n., m.) واحِد
spacious, large [18] .... (adj.) واسِع
father, parent [19] .... (n., m.) والِد ج والِدون
by God, I swear, really (used to add emphasis) [13] .... وَاللّه
to find [17] .... (v.) وَجَدَ (يَجِدُ) وُجود
there is/are, to exist [18] .... (passive of وَجَدَ) وُجِدَ (يوجَدُ)
face [13] .... (n., m.) وَجْه ج وُجوه
alone, by himself [9] .... (adv.) وَحْدَهُ
sole, only [5] .... (n., m.) وَحيد ج وَحيدون
paper .... (n., f.) وَرَقَة ج أوْراق
ministry, department in an administration [24] .... (n., f.) وِزارة ج وِزارات
minister [16] .... (n., m.) وَزير ج وُزَراء
pillow [11] .... (n., f.) وِسادة ج وَسائِد
middle, central [21] .... (n., m.) وَسَط ج أوساط
middle [4] .... (adj., f.) وُسْطى
handsome [10] .... (adj., m.) وَسيم ج (ون)
scarf, sash [23] .... (n., m) وِشاح ج أوشِحة، وَشائح
to arrive, to reach a destination [11] .... (v.) وَصَلَ (يَصِلُ) وُصول

to put [18]. . . . . (v.) وَضَعَ (يَضَعُ) وَضْع

homeland . . . . (n., m.) وَطَن ج أوطان

time [20]. . . . . (n., m.) وَقْت ج أوْقات

to be located; to fall down [18]. . . . . (v.) وَقَعَ (يَقَعُ) وُقوع / وَقْع

state . . . . (n., f.) وِلاية ج وِلايات

the United States of America [6, 9]. . . . . (n., f.) الوِلاياتُ المُتَّحِدةُ الأمريكيّة

boy [5] . . . . (n., m.) وَلَد ج أَوْلاد

to be born (passive) [15] . . . . (v.) وُلِدَ (يولَدُ) وُلود

ي

[vocative particle used to call the attention of the addressee] [3] . . . . يا

Japan [10] . . . . (n., f.) اليابان

Japanese (language) [3] . . . . (n., f.) اليابانِيَّة

hand [13] . . . . (n., f.) يَد ج أَيْدٍ

left [18]. . . . . (n., m.) يَسار

you (m. sg.) are able [6]. . . . . (v.) يُمْكِنُكَ

right [18] . . . . (n., m.) يَمين

there is; there are [18] . . . . (v. pass.) يُوجَد

day [11] . . . . (n., m.) يَوْم ج أيّام

today [11] . . . . (adv.) اليَوْم

diary, daily journal [11]. . . . . (n., f.) يَوْمِيّة ج يومِيّات

Index

A

Adnan in Denver.. 535

Adnan in New York, Florida 422

Adnan Martini's Daily Journal 270

Adnan Martini's Family 558

Adverbials of Time 154

Adverbs of Place 403

Adverbs of Time and Place 433

American and Arab Personalities 334

Arab and American Radio and TV............510

Arab Family..211

Arab, Islamic, and American Festivities ..309

Arabic Last Names 87

Attached Pronouns Suffixed to Verbs 140

B

Broken Plurals...161

C

Calendars in the Arab World 239

Cardinal Numbers 11 and 12 116

Cardinal Numbers 1–10 50

Cardinal Numbers 20-90 117

Cardinal Numbers 13–19 116

Cardinal Numbers 20-90 117

Cardinal Numbers 11-999 115

Case.. 208

Cases of the Noun 136

Cases of the Nouns in the إضافة Structure 31

Colloquial Arabic 37

Comparative and Superlative 231

Conjugation 113

Conjugations of لَيسَ 13

Content Questions 45

Contrasting: The Particles لكِنْ and لكِنَّ 9

Converting Temperature Scales 261

D

Defective Verb صار 326

Defective Verbs Revisited 469

Defective Verbs with Nominal Sentences 237

Definite and Indefinite Nouns 18

Definite and Indefinite Relative Clauses . 441

Definite إضافة 446

Definiteness of an إضافة Structure 32

Definiteness 210

Demonstratives: Gender Agreement 7

Describing Activities in All Time Frames 223

Describing Background 65

Describing Daily Activities 151

Describing Family Members 81

Describing School Subjects 82

Dictionary Use 48

Diptotes (Partially Inflected Nouns) 319

Doubly Transitive Verbs 133

E

Eliciting Information 54

Enumerating: The Coordinating Particle و.. 6

Expressing Admiration Using ما شاء الله 55

Expressing Degree 110

Expressing Lack of Knowledge أعلم الله..... 109

Expressing Likes and Dislikes 153

Expressing Necessity 521

Expressing Possession with مع and لِـ 138

Expressing Possibility 524

Expressing Reason 296

Expressing Regret or Apology Using آسِف 108

F

Favorite Sports and Foods 455

Food and Drink 159

Forming Dual Nouns 68

Forming the Imperative 131

G

Gender 207

Geographical Directions 496

Geography of the Arab World and US 483

Giving an Oath 283

More on Arabic Names 142

N

Negating Future Time 435

Negating Imperative Verbs 277

Negating the Past Tense Verb 202

Negating the Present-Tense Verb using لا...49

Negating with لَيسَ....................................... 12

Negation... 112

Nisba Revisited 29

Nominal Sentences 10

Noun-Adjective Agreement Revisited 206

Number (Singular, Dual, Plural) 206

Number-Noun Agreement 69

Numbers 1–10 with Nouns 71

Numbers: Hundreds and Thousands 187

O

Objects of Prepositions 89

Objects of Verbs 88

H

Hala Boustani's Daily Activities 269

I

إضافة Construction 34

Identifying Objects: هذا and ذلِكَ............... 35

Inside the Numbers 119

إضافة Structure Revisited 163

J

Journal of an Arab Student in America .. 220

L

Lalainya Visits al-Minya 538

Language Accuracy 397

Lulwa al-Qatami 194

M

Making Polite Requests with من فضلك and Using تفضَّل 29

Mass and Count Nouns 186

Michael's Apartment 388

Michael in Cairo and Alexandria 420

Michael Brown's Daily Journal 291, 457

Review of the Verbal Noun 570
Reviewing the Relative "What" 525
Revisiting the إضافة Structure 236
Role of Demonstratives 298

S

School Surroundings and Facilities 25, 29
School Surroundings 3
Secrets of Arabic: Forms of the Verb 340
Secrets of the Language: Prefixes Suffixes.113
Seeking and Providing Information 44
Some Journals of Michael Brown 512
Sound Feminine Plurals 161
Sound Masculine Plurals 160
Suppressing Initial Sound of the Article ..325

T

Telling Time Formally 171
Telling Time Informally 184
Tens 20-90, masculine feminine nouns 118
Terms of Address 104
Ordinal Numbers Revisited 348
Ordinal Numbers 91

P

Partitive Nouns 259,276
Past Continuous 465
Plurals of Non-Rational Nouns 160
Plurals of Nouns 160
Prepositions 4
Pronouns of Separation 93
Pronunciation the Attached Pronoun هُ...133

Q

Question Words 45

R

Radio and Television Programs 514
Referent Pronouns in Relative Structures 442
Relative pronouns (that, what): 440
Relative Pronouns (who) 437
Requesting and Declining Things Politely 149
Review of Prepositions 445

The Permutative 546

The Preposition بـ 242

The Question Particle كَم 55

The Relative Noun Revisited 300

The Role of the Emphatic قَد 544

The Strong Version لكِنَّ 9

The Subject and Deputy Subject 323

The Two Particles لـ وكَي 568

The Weak Version لكِنْ 10

U

Understanding Color Forms 467

Use of كِلا 498

Use of لكِنْ and لكِنَّ 14

Using بِضع 527

Using لَم يَعُد 524

Using a particle to indicate reason 280

Using لـ after "to Say" 297

Using قبل and بعد 224

Using Exception 499

The Accusative Case 137

The Arabic Verb 48

The Comparative Revisited 567

The Conditional 548

The Definite Article: Assimilating and Non-Assimilating Sounds 15

The Five Nouns 315

The Four Seasons and Weather 253

The Genitive Case 137

The Gerund; the Verbal Noun 204

The إضافة Structure 30

The Imperative.....................................130, 158

The Nominative Case 136

The Number 100 119

The Numbers one and two (1, 2) 69

The Numbers three through ten (3–10) .. 70

The Particle أن with Adverbs of Time 526

The Particle يا 55

The Passive Voice 321

The Past Tense Verb الفعل الماضي 200

Using Prepositions 401

Using the Comparative 468

Using the Conditional 294

Using the Conjunction فَـ 543

Using the Subjunctive 396

Using قالَ إنَّ 230

Using ظَنَّ إنَّ 225

Using أي 128

V

Verb Patterns and the Root System 342

Verb Position in Arabic Sentences 281

Verb Stem and Root 48

Verbs with Doubled Consonants 227

W

Weak Verbs 278

What People Eat in the Morning 150

Word Order and Gender Agreement 29

Writing Letters and Cards 432

Y

Yes/No Questions 45

فِهْرِس عربيّ

أ

أداةُ الاِستِثناء إلاّ ٤٩٩

أداةُ الاِستِثناء غَير ٥٩٩

أداةُ الاِستِثناء ما عَدا ٤٩٩

إدغام حَرفِ الجَرّ والاسمِ المَوصول ٤٤١

أدوات الاستفهام ٤٥

الإذاعَة والتلفاز ٥١٠

استخدام أيّ ١٢٩

استِخدام ما شاء الله ٥٥

استخدام ما معنى ؟ ٥٤

اِستِخدامُ اسمِ التفضيل الّذي لَه حَرف مُضَعَّف ... ٤٧٨

اِستِخدامُ الحَرف الفاء ٥٢٣

اِسْتِخْدام الحَرْف أنّ ٢٢٦

اِسْتِخْدام حَرْفِ الجَرّ لِ بَعْدَ الفِعْل قال ٢٩٧

اِسْتِخْدام حَرْفِ الشَّرْط أمّا ... فَـ ٢٩٤

اِستِخدام حُروف الجَرّ ٤٠١

استخدام ظَنَّ أنَّ ٢٢٥

اِسْتِخْدام قالَ إنَّ ٢٣٠

اِسْتِخْدام قَبْلَ وبَعْدَ ٢٢٤

اِستِخدام كان + المُضارِع المَرفوع ٤٦٥

اِسْتِخْدام لأنَّ ٢٨٠

اِسْتِخْدام لِذلِكَ ٢٩٧

استخدام لكن ولكنَّ ١٤٠٩

استخدام واو القَسَم ٢٨٣

أُسرَة عَدنان مارتيني ٥٥

الاسم (مُعرّف ونكِرة) ١٨

اِسْم التَفْضيل ٢٣١

الـ التعريف والحروف الشمسية والقمرية ١٥

الاسم المجرور ٨٩

الاسمُ الموصوفُ النَكِرة ٤٤١

اسم النسبة ٢٩

الاسم بِضْع ٥٢٧

الاِسم كِلا / كِلتا ٤٩٨

أسماء الإشارة والتذكير والتأنيث ٧

الأسْماءُ الخَمْسة ٣١٥

الأسماء العربية ١٤٢

الأسماء الموصولة الخاصة ٤٣٨

الأسْماءُ المَوصولة الّذي والّتي ٣٤٧

الأسماء الموصولة العامة ما ومَن ٤٤١

الإضافة .... ٣٠، ٤٤٦

الأعداد الأصلية ١١-٩٩٩ .... ١١٥

الأعداد الأصلية ١٣-١٩ .... ١١٧

الأعداد الأصلية ٢٠-٩٠ .... ١١٦

الأعداد الأصلية من ١ إلى ١٠ .... ٧٠

الأعداد الترتيبية ٩١

الأعداد من ١ إلى ١٠ .... ٥٠

أعْياد أمريكيّة ٣١١

أعياد عَرَبيّة وإسلاميّة ومَسيحيّة وأمريكيّة ٣٠٩

الأفعال المُتعدّية لمفعولين ١٣٣

الألقاب العَرَبيّة .... ١٠٤، ٥٦٥

الأنشطة اليومية ١٥١

أوزان الفِعل المَزيد ٣٤٠-٣٤٢

أوزانُ الفِعلِ المَزيد ومعانيها ٣٤٢

أين مكتب المُدير؟ ١٠٢

أنْ ٨٦-٨٧

ب

البَحث عن الكَلِمة في القاموس ٣٤٣

البَدَل ٥٤٦

بَرامِج إذاعة وتلفزيون ٥١٤

بَعْض / كُلّ / مُعْظَم ٢٥٩

ت

تَحديد جَذر الكَلِمة ٣٤٣

تَحديد وَزن الكَلِمة ٣٤٣

تَحْويل دَرَجةِ الحَرارة ٢٦١

ترتيب الكلمات في الجملة والتذكير والتأنيث ٢٩

تَرْكيب الجُمْلة العَرَبيّة: الفِعْل ٢٨١

تركيب العدد ١١٩

تصريف الفعل المضارِع .... ٤٩، ١١٣

تطابق الأسماء مع العدد ٦٩

التَعبير عن الاِحتِمال بِاستِخدامِ الفِعل أمْكَنَ ٥٢٣

التعبير عن الأسف ١٠٨

التَعبير عن الضَرورة بِاستِخدام على ... أنْ ٥٢١

التعبير عن درجة المعرفة (كثيراً، قليلاً) ١١٠

التعبير عن عدم المعرفة ١٠٩

تعريف الأسماء بأسماء الإشارة ٣٦

التعريف والتنكير في الإضافة ٣٢

تقسيم الساعة ١٧٣

التَقْويم الغَرْبيّ ٢٤١

التَقْويم الهِجْريّ ٢٤٠

التَقويم في العالَم العَرَبيّ ٢٣٩

ج

الجَرّ ١٣٧

جرائد ومجلات عربية ١٢٧

جُغرافِيَّةُ الوَطَنِ العَرَبيّ وأمريكا ٤٨٣
جَمْع تكسير ١٦١
جَمْع مُذَكَّر سالِم ١٦٠
جَمع مُؤنَّث سالِم ١٦١
الجملة الإسمية ١٠
الجِهات الأربع ٤٩٦
الجِهات الأربَع: الجار والمَجرور ٤٩٧

ح

حالات الاسم ١٣٦
حالات الأسماء في الإضافة ٣٢
الحالةُ الإعْرابيّة ٢٠٨
حَرْف الجَرّ البَاء ٢٤٢
حرف العطف و ٦
الحَرف أنْ بَعد ظَرف الزَمان ٥٢٦
حَرف نَفي المُستقبَل لَنْ ٤٣٥
حَرفا لِـ وكَي ٥٦٨
حروف الجر ٤
حُروف الجَرّ في فِئَتَين ٤٠٢
الحصول على المعلومات وتقديمها ٤٤

خ

الخُضَر ٤٥٨
الخليج ١٩٩
طلب ورفض مهذّبان ١٤٩
رسالة ياسر مارتيني إلى ابنِهِ عَدنان ٥٦٠
الرَفْع ١٣٦
رِياضات وأطعِمة مُفَضَّلة ٤٥٥

ز

زَيُّ الرَّجُل الخليجي وبعض البلاد الأخرى ٢٠٠
زِياد يقرأ جريدة ١٥١

س

الساعة بلغة بسيطة ١٨٤
سَحَر في جامِعةِ حَلَب ١٧٧
سُعاد ريماوي ٣١٢
سَلامة اللُغة ٣٩٧
سوريا ٤٨٦

ش

شَخْصِيّات أمريكيّة وعَرَبيّة ٣٣٤

ض

ضمائر الفَصل ٩٣
الضَمائر المُتَّصِلة بالأفعال ١٤٠
الضَميرُ العائد ٤٤٢

ط

طالِبَتان في جامِعَة حَلَب ٦٥
الطعام والشراب ١٥٩
طلب مُهذّب ١٣٠
غرفة مكتبي ٢٦

ظ

ظرف الزمان ١٥٤

ظَرف المَكان ٤٠٣

ظَرفًا الزَمان والمَكان ٤٣٣

الظُروف ٤٩٦

ع

العائلة العربية ١٩٨

عائلة مازن نجّار ٨١

العائلة والأسرة ٢١٢

العدد ١٠٠ .... ١١٩

العددان ١ و٢ .... ٦٩

عَدَم اِستِخدامِ الضَميرِ العائد ٤٤٣

عدم نُطق الهمزة في الـ التعريف ١٨٦

عَدنان في مَدينة دِنْفر ٥٣٥

عَدنان مارتيني في نيويورك وكَندا وفلوريدا ٤٢٢

عُطلة نِهاية الأسبوع في البِلاد العَرَبيّة ٢٢٢

العُقود ٢٠-٩٠ .... ١١٨

عيدان إسلاميّان ٣١٠

عيدان مَسيحِيّان ٣١٠

غ

الغائب ١١٥

الفعل وجذر الكلمة ٤٨

الفَواكِه ٤٥٩

ف

الفاء السابقة للاسم ٥٤٣

الفاء السابقة للِفعل ٥٤٣

الفاعِل ونائِبُ الفاعِل ٣٢٣

الفِعل أَعْجَبَ ٣٩٨

فعل الأمر وتصريفه ١٣٠

الفِعلُ الماضي الأجوَف ٣٢٢

الفِعلُ الماضي الناقِص ٣٢٢

الفِعْل الماضي ٢٠١

الفِعْل المَبْني لِلمَجهول ٣٢١

الفِعلُ المَبني لِلمَجهول: الفِعلُ الماضي ٣٢١

الفِعلُ المَبني لِلمَجهول: الفِعلُ المُضارِع ٣٢٢

الفِعلُ المُجَرَّد ٣٤٠

الفِعلُ المَزيد ٣٤٠

الفِعل المشدَّد ٣٢٧

الفِعل المضارع الأجوَف ٣٢٣

الفِعلُ المُضارِع المِثال ٣٢٣

الفِعلُ المُضارِع الناقِص ٣٢٣

الفِعْلُ المُعْتَلّ ٢٧٨

الفِعلُ الناقِص صارَ ٣٢٦

مايكل براون في القاهِرَةِ والإسكَندَريَّة ٤٢٠

ق

قَدْ + الفِعل الماضي ٥٤٤
قَدْ + الفِعل المُضارِع ٥٤٥
قِراءةُ الساعة........ ١٧١
قراءة المئات والآلاف ١٨٧
قراءة المئات والآلاف ١٨٧

ك

كانَ وأخَواتُها ٢٣٧
كِتابةُ الرسالة والبِطاقة البَريديّة ٤٣٢
كَلِمات مِثْل بَعْض ٢٧٦

ل

لالينيا تَزور المِنيا ٥٣٨
اللُغة في الخَليج ٢٠٠
اللَهجات العامية ٣٧
لُؤلُؤَة القَطامي فَتاة عَرَبِيَّة مِن قَطَر ١٩٤
اللَون ٤٦٨
اللَون في المفرد والمثنى والجمع ٤٦٧

م

ما تحبّ وما لا نحبّ ١٥٣
ماذا تَفعَل هالَة بُستاني كُلَّ يَوْم؟ ٢٦٩
مايكِل براون في القاهِرَة........ ١٧٨
المفرد والمثنى والجمع ٢٠٦
المَفعولُ بِهِ ٨٨
المُتكلِّم ١١٤
المُثَنّى ٦٨
مَحَلّ اِسْم الإشارة في الجُمْلة العَرَبيّة ٢٩٨
المُخاطَب........ ١١٤
مُخَطَّط شَقَّة مايكِل ٣٨٨
المدرسة ٣
المدرسة ومرافقها ٢٥
المرأة العربية ١٩٨
مُراجَعة اسم التَفضيل ٥٦٧
مُراجَعة اِسْم النِّسْبة مِئَويّ ٣٠٠
مُراجَعةُ الاِسمِ المَوصولِ العامّ ما ٥٢٥
مُراجَعةُ الإضافة ٢٣٦
مُراجَعةُ العَدَدِ التَرتيبيّ ٣٤٧
مُراجَعةُ الفِعلِ المُعتَلّ........ ٤٦٩
مُراجَعة المَصدَر ٥٧٠
مُراجَعة حُروفِ الجَرّ........ ٤٤٥
المصدَر........ ٢٠٤
المُضاف والمُضاف إليه ١٦٣
مُطابَقةِ الصِّفة لِلمَوْصوف ٢٠٦
جمع الاسم غير العاقل (الأشياء) ٧٣
المعدود وغير المعدود ١٨٦

مُلاحَظة ثقافية حَولَ الدِراسة في سوريا ٥٦١
المُلكية بالحرفين (مَعَ ولـِ) ١٣٩
المَمْنوع مِن الصَرف ٣١٩
من أسرار العربية: السوابق واللواحق ١١٣
مِن الأسْماء الخَمْسة الخاصّة ٢٥٣
مَن يقرأ هذه الجرائد والمجلات ١٢٨
مِن يَوميّات عَدنان مارتيني ٤٥٦
مِن يَومِيّات عَدنان مارتيني ٥١٠
من يوميّات مايكل براون .... ٤٥٧، ٥١٢

ن

نسبة الأُسَر ٨٧
النَصب ١٣٧
نُطق الضمير المُتّصِل ـه ١٣٣
نَفي الفِعْل الماضي ٢٠٢
نفي الفعل المضارع ٤٩
نفي المضارع ١١٢
النفي بـ لَيسَ ١٢
نَفي فَعْل الأمْر ٢٧٧
النكِرة والمعرفة ٢٠٩

و

الوَجبة الصباحية ١٥٠
وَصْفُ الأنْشِطة في الماضي والمُضارِع والمُستَقْبَل ... ٢٢٣
وصف المواد الدراسية ٨٢
وَظيفةُ الحَرف قَدْ ٥٤٤
وَظيفة حَرفِ الشَرْط إنْ ٥٤٨
الوِلاياتُ المُتَّحِدةُ الأمريكيّة ٤٨٥
وِلاية أوهايو ٤٨٨

ي

يا ٥٥
يَوْميّات طالِب عَرَبيّ في أمريكا ٢٢٠
يَومِيّات عَدنان مارتيني .... ٢٩٢، ٢٧٠
يَومِيّات مايْكِل بْراوْن ٢٩١

Illustration Credits

audio icon by Clker-Free-Vector-Images/Pixabay.com/ CC0 Public Domain

video icon by Frag from KDE-look.org/Wikimedia Commons/GNU LGPLv3

textured background (as on pages 10, 12, 16, 18, and elsewhere throughout book) by Andrey Zeigarnik/Flickr/CC BY 2.0

lesson opener banners:

lesson 1 (blue floral, altered to green) pgs. 2–3 © Azat1976/Shutterstock; corner tile (altered to green) pgs. 2–3 Xavier Allard/Flickr/CC BY 2.0; lesson 2 (red and purple pattern) pgs. 24–25 Atif Gulzar/Wikimedia Commons/CC by 3.0; gold burst corner tile pgs. 24–25 Phillip Maiwald/ Wikimedia Commons/CC by 3.0; lesson 3 (vector Islamic pattern) pgs. 42–43 © Azat1976/ Shutterstock; four-square blue corner tile pgs. 42–43 © aniana/Shutterstock; lesson 4 (orange honeycomb) pgs. 64–65 pxhere/CC0; red & gold corner tile pgs. 64–65 natassa64/pixabay/CC0; lesson 5 (blue pattern) pgs. 80–81 © Marchenko Oleksandr/Shutterstock; corner tile (altered to blue) pgs. 80–81 Xavier Allard/Flickr/CC BY 2.0; lesson 6 (blue checkers) pgs. 100–101 Benjamin Sperandio/Flickr/CC BY-SA 2.0; purple corner tile pgs. 100–101 Paul Thompson/Flickr/CC BY-SA 2.0; lesson 7 (Indo-Persian red) pgs. 124–25 Albert Racinet/Rawpixel/CC0 1.0; lesson 8 (green floral/orange star) pgs. 146–47 © Kutlayev Dmitry/Shutterstock; blue & yellow corner tile pgs. 146–47 Masrur Ashraf/Flickr/CC BY-ND 2.0; lesson 9 (cream phoenix) pgs. 170–71 Chris/Flickr/ CC BY-SA 2.0; white star down corner tile pgs. 170–71 Mikołaj Pasiński/Flickr/CC BY 2.0; lesson 10 (elegant H blue) pgs. 192–93 © Azat1976/Shutterstock; diamond star corner tile pgs. 192–93 © Anna Poguliaeva/Shutterstock; lesson 11 (white star down) pgs. 216–17 Mikołaj Pasiński/ Flickr/CC BY 2.0; teapot corner tile pgs. 216–17 Ashley Van Haeften/Flickr/CC BY 2.0; lesson 12 (vector Islamic pattern) pgs. 250–51 © Azat1976/Shutterstock; four-square blue corner tile pgs. 250–51 © aniana/Shutterstock; lesson 13 (red/gold/Moroccan detail) pgs. 266–67 Benjamin Esham/Flickr/CC BY-SA 2.0; gold pendant corner tile pgs. 266–67 Guillén Pérez/Flickr/CC BY-ND 2.0; lesson 14 (orange & green/crooked star) pgs. 288–89 MCAD Library/Flickr/CC BY 2.0; architectural columns corner tile pgs. 288–89 Jashy/Wikimedia Commons/CC BY-SA 3.0; lesson

15 (book design/blue) pgs. 306–7 Walters Art Museum Illuminated Manuscripts/Flickr/Public Domain; Ramadan Kareem calligraphy corner tile pgs. 306–7 فنافن الإعلامية/Flickr/CC BY-ND 2.0; lesson 16 (columns/arches/screen) pgs. 330–31 Joelle Nebbe-Mornod/Flickr/CC BY 2.0; lesson 17 (woven star tiles) pgs. 354–55 Jose Manuel 12394/Wikimedia Commons/Public Domain; lesson 18 (brown/white woven screen "CHOUFANI wrought iron & interior") pgs. 384–85 Design/Flickr/CC BY-ND 2.0; orange sunburst corner tile pgs. 384–85 Kris/Flickr/CC BY 2.0; lesson 19 (ivory banner [mosque dome] & corner mosaic tile) pgs. 416–17 dynamosquito/Flickr/CC BY-SA 2.0; lesson 20 (green tile pattern) pgs. 452–53 pxhere/CC0; anchor/quatrefoil corner tile pgs. 452–53 Sailko/Wikimedia Commons/CC BY-SA 3.0; lesson 21 (orange/blue circles) pgs. 478–79 Deanora/Shutterstock; star corner tile pgs. 478–79 Jean-Pierre Dalbéra/Wikimedia Commons/CC BY 2.0; lesson 22 (black/gold interlace) pgs. 506–7 Leonardo Aguiar/Flickr/CC BY 2.0; gold with blue spiral circle corner tile pgs. 506–7 Mathias Apitz/Flickr/CC BY-ND 2.0; lesson 23 (orange/blue/black [black paddle] Alhambra tile) pgs. 532–33 Darla دارلا Hueske/Flickr/CC BY-ND 2.0; orange sunburst corner tile pgs. 532–33 Kris/Flickr/CC BY 2.0; lesson 24 (marble floor; altered) pgs. 554–55 Fulvio Spada/Flickr/CC BY-SA 2.0; orange sunburst corner tile pgs. 554–55 Kris/Flickr/CC BY 2.0

other banners:

(green floral/orange star) pgs. 4–5, 14–15, 34–35, 40–41, 52–53, 56–57, 70–71, 76–77, 82–83, 96–97, 200–201, 236–37, 274–75, 304–5, 310–11, 324–25, 332–33, 362–63, 406–7, 414–15, 428–29, 434–35, 460–61, 486–87, 520–21, 534–35 © Kutlayev Dmitry/Shutterstock; (blue floral) pgs. 6–7, 38–39, 44–45, 72–73, 86–87, 104–5 (altered to green), 140–41, 160–61 (altered to green), 162–63, 166–67 (altered to green), 176–77, 190–91, 194–95, 246–47, 264–65 (altered to green), 298–99, 326–27, 352–53, 376–77, 380–81 (altered to green), 390–91 (altered to green), 398–99, 462–63, 540–41, 558–59 © Azat1976/Shutterstock; (neon green & brown star) pgs. 8–9, 26–27, 50–51, 128–29, 152–53, 214–15, 240–41, 270–71, 502–3 © New Line/Shutterstock; (orange & green/crooked star) pgs. 10–11, 36–37, 58–59, 66–67, 106–7, 112–13, 130–31, 178–79, 212–13, 222–23, 244–45, 248–49, 260–61, 284–85, 294–95, 314–15, 338–39, 342–43, 360–61, 392–93,

426–27, 456–57, 490–91, 518–19, 524–25, 546–47, 572–73 MCAD Library/Flickr/CC BY 2.0; (red and purple pattern) pgs. 12–13, 120–21, 378–79, 492–93, 512–13, 566–67 Atif Gulzar/ Wikimedia Commons/CC by 3.0; (green tile pattern) pgs. 16–17, 20–21, 90–91, 108–9, 272–73, 370–71, 388–89, 404–5, 410–11, 516–17 pxhere/CC0; (elegant H blue) pgs. 18–19, 30–31, 54–55, 78–79, 84–85, 122–23, 136–37, 180–81, 196–97, 308–9, 328–29, 350–51, 358–59, 436–37, 476–77, 496–97, 514–15, 538–39, 556–57 © Azat1976/Shutterstock; (white star down) pgs. 22–23 Mikołaj Pasiński/Flickr/CC BY 2.0; (red/gold/Moroccan detail) pgs. 28–29, 32–33, 46–47, 88–89, 118–19, 164–65, 172–73, 218–19, 228–29, 344–45, 394–95, 468–69, 526–27, 542–43 Benjamin Esham/ Flickr/CC BY-SA 2.0; (blue with white star) pgs. 48–49, 68–69, 114–15, 142–43, 186–87, 202–3, 226–27, 242–43, 276–77, 290–91, 320–21, 340–41, 366–67, 422–23, 448–49, 472–73, 550–51, 560–61 © Azat1976/Shutterstock; (aqua bottle) pgs. 60–61, 134–35, 296–97, 312–13, 424–25, 544–45, 562–63 pxhere/CC0; (orange honeycomb) pgs. 62–63, 74–75, 126–27, 158–59, 168–69, 188–89, 206–7, 230–31, 268–69, 336–37, 372–73, 412–13, 430–31, 446–47, 488–89, 504–5, 570–71 pxhere/CC0; (orange flower) pgs. 92–93, 102–3, 126–27, 138–39, 148–49, 198–99, 286–87, 302–3, 322–23, 368–69, 396–97, 458–59, 498–99, 522–23 Paul Thompson/Flickr/CC BY-SA 2.0; (purple flower) pgs. 110–11, 156–57, 184–85, 204–5, 208–9, 224–25, 232–33, 262–63, 278–79, 282–83, 316–17, 346–47, 374–75, 400–401, 418–19, 438–39, 466–67, 480–81, 508–9, 528–29, 548–49, 564–65 Paul Thompson/Flickr/CC BY-SA 2.0; (vector Islamic pattern) pgs. 144–45, 174–75, 210–11, 234–35, 256–57, 318–19, 432–33, 470–71, 482–83, 510–11, 552–53 © Azat1976/Shutterstock; (blue pattern) pgs. 154–55, 402–3, 440–41, 454–55, 500–501, 536–37 © Marchenko Oleksandr/ Shutterstock; (blue modeled) pgs. 182–83, 220–21, 238–39, 252–53, 300–301, 348–49, 356–57, 420–21, 464–65, 484–85, 530–31, 568–69 Paul Thompson/Flickr/CC BY-SA 2.0; (Hafiz tomb blue) pgs. 116–17, 258–59, 292–93, 334–35, 382–83, 386–87, 442–43, 574–75 Pentocelo/Flickr/CC BY 3.0; (green Moroccan tiles) pgs. 94–95, 98–99, 132–33, 150–51, 280–81, 364–65, 408–9, 444–45, 450–51, 474–75, 494–95 Mikołaj Pasiński/Flickr/CC BY 2.0

illustrations:

map of dialects xxviii Rafy/Wikimedia Commons/CC BY-3.0; entrance to school 2 © Rabbee alhaj

Othman; the word "morning" calligraphy 3 Hussein Alazaat/Flickr/CC BY 2.0; classroom interior 3 © Allen Clark; Hala Bustani 4 © Fotoluminate LLC/Shutterstock; penguins (between) 4, 403 Christopher Michel/Flickr/CC BY 2.0; flowers in front of man 4, 403 ProFlowers/Flickr/CC BY 2.0; basketball in net 4, 403 slgckgc/Flickr/CC BY 2.0; bouquet behind man 4, 403 ProFlowers/Flickr/CC BY 2.0; pencil on book 4, 403 Simon Carr/Flickr/CC BY-SA 2.0; pencil beside book 4, 403 Quinn Dombrowski/Flickr/CC BY-SA 2.0; toy stormtrooper limbo 4, 403 JD Hancock/Flickr/CC BY 2.0; pole vaulter 4, 403 Jacey O Samsel/Flickr/CC BY 2.0; classroom 5 krebsmaus07/Flickr/CC BY 2.0; things in a backpack 7 loran/Flickr/CC BY-ND 2.0; backpack 8 Mobile Edge Laptop Cases/Flickr/CC BY-SA 2.0; computer 8 Karla Vanessa Redor/Flickr/ C BY 2.0; picture with frame 8 Glen Dahlman/Flickr/CC BY-SA 2.0; book 8 PHGCOM/Wikimedia Commons/Public Domain; papyrus paper 8 Abu `Ubayd al-Qasim b. Sallam al-Harawi/Wikimedia Commons/CC0; phone 8 Zach Vega/Wikimedia Commons/CC BY-SA-3.0; bicycle 8 /pxhere/CC0; pencil 8 © Vitaly Zorkin/Shutterstock; desk 8 © Svetlana Happyland/Shutterstock; whiteboard 8 © Iasha/Shutterstock; teacher 10 © Zurijeta/Shutterstock; Rana 10 © SnowWhiteimages/Shutterstock; Sandy 10 © arek_malang/Shutterstock; art "eye of a mosque" 11 dynamosquito/Flickr/CC BY-SA 2.0; teacher with book 12 © ESB Professional/Shutterstock; teacher in library 12 © Zurijeta/Shutterstock; student reading on bench 12 © arek_malang/Shutterstock; dancers 13 Heather/Flickr/CC BY-NC 2.0; house interior courtyard (background) 17 © Allen Clark; teacher with students 18 © Zurijeta/Shutterstock; interior of classroom 19 © Allen Clark; school entrance (background) 20 © Allen Clark; Bin Yousef School (background) 22 Jean & Nathalie/Flickr/CC BY 2.0; Hassan II Mosque 23 © Juanamari Gonzalez/Shutterstock; Ali bin Yousef School 24 © Jennifer Stone/Shutterstock; student in class 25 © Robert Kneschke/Shutterstock; College of Medicine 25 Osm Agha/Wikimedia Commons/Public Domain; College of Information Technology 25 Wikimedia Commons/CC BY-SA-3.0; briefcase 26 © tinka's/Shutterstock; math teacher 26 © nikkytok/Shutterstock; student ID 26 © Robert Kneschke/Shutterstock; teacher ID 27 © ZouZou/Shutterstock; student union, University of Jordan 27 Tarawneh/Wikimedia Commons/CC BY-SA-3.0; University of Damascus 28 Syrian Eng/Wikimedia Commons/CC BY-SA-3.0; courtyard, Damascus University 29 Bryn Pinzgauer/Wikimedia Commons/CC BY 2.0;

Aleppo University Business School 30 Majd Mohabek/Wikimedia Commons/CC BY-2.0; Al-Azam Palace in Damascus 33 Bassel Khabbaz/Wikimedia Commons/CC BY-SA-4.0; woman with old car 36 © Everett Collection/Shutterstock; computer 36 Karla Vanessa Redor/Flickr/CC BY 2.0; female student 36 © Pressmaster/Shutterstock; Abraham Lincoln 36 Alexander Gardner/Wikimedia Commons/Public Domain; car 36 © Rawpixel.com/Shutterstock; house 36 David Sawyer/Flickr/CC BY-SA 2.0; bicycle 36 /pxhere/CC0; paper 36 David Swart/Flickr/CC BY 2.0; book bag 36 Mobile Edge Laptop Cases/Flickr/CC BY-SA 2.0; glasses 36 © Evgeny Karandaev/Shutterstock; phone 36 Zach Vega/Wikimedia Commons/CC BY-SA-3.0; pointing finger 36 OpenClipart-Vectors/pixabay/CC0; café, Damascus (background) 37 Omar/Wikimedia Commons/CC BY-2.0; "wrong" icon 38 © 3D-Man.eu/Shutterstock; "right" icon 38 © CoraMax/Shutterstock; Cairo University (background) 39 Faris Knight/Wikimedia Commons/CC BY-SA-4.0; medical manuscript 41 Rogers Fund, 1913, Metropolitan Museum of Art/Wikimedia Commons/Public Domain; cameraman filming interview 42 Chatham House/Wikimedia Commons/CC BY 2.0; camera interview 44 © withGod/Shutterstock; Jableh City 44 فادي شاهين/Wikimedia Commons/Public Domain; Port of Jableh 44 فادي شاهين/Wikimedia Commons/Public Domain; Roman theater in Jableh 44 LorisRomito/Wikimedia Commons/CC BY-SA-3.0; two women on phone 50 Garry Knight/Flickr/CC BY 2.0; family checking in 51 Holidayextras/Flickr/CC BY 2.0; photo id 52 © Fotoluminate LLC/Shutterstock; two young women studying languages 53 The LEAF Project/Flickr/CC0 1.0; vendor in Jerusalem 56 James Emery/Flickr/CC BY 2.0; coffee vendor 56 James Emery/Flickr/CC BY 2.0; house courtyard Al Azam 57 Wisal Ahdab/Wikimedia Commons/CC BY-SA-3.0; classroom 58 © Allen Clark; phone 58 ADMC/pixabay/CC0; car 58 © Rawpixel.com/Shutterstock; apartments Abu Dhabi 58 © Robert Wright/Flickr; photo id 52 © Fotoluminate LLC/Shutterstock; Al Azam Palace 58 Neil and Kathy Carey/Flickr/CC BY-SA 2.0; Al-Pasha Hotel (background) 59 James Filipi/Flickr/CC BY-SA 2.0; courtyard with fountain and trees (background) 61 Mohammad Aljandali/Flickr/CC BY-SA-4.0 lamps in market (background) 63 selfthy/Flickr/CC BY 2.0; Old Aleppo street 64 OmarHafez/Wikimedia Commons/CC BY-SA-3.0; two female students 65 © Fotoluminate LLC/Shutterstock; bed 66 frankieleon/Flickr/CC BY 2.0; two beds 66 Design Folly/Flickr/CC BY-SA 2.0; flatiron building 66 Jeffrey Zeldman/Flickr/CC BY 2.0; two buildings 66 Engin_Akyurt/pixabay/CC0; Aleppo Castle (background) 66 Alaaalyaseen/Wikimedia Commons/CC BY-SA-3.0; Christian quarter, Aleppo (background) 72 Dirk D./Wikimedia Commons/CC BY-SA-3.0; Aleppo fortress at night 74 © Francisco Javier Gil/Shutterstock; pencil 75 Andrew Taylor/Flickr/CC BY 2.0; book bag 75 Mobile Edge Laptop Cases/Flickr/CC BY-SA 2.0; chairs 75 David Clark/PublicDomainPictures.net/CC0; watch 75 James Cape/Flickr/CC BY-SA 2.0; houses 75 Mattinbgn/Wikimedia Commons/CC BY-SA-3.0,2.5,2.0,1.0; students 75 © Allen Clark; computer 75 500photos.com/Pexels/CC0; keys 75 Onderwijsgek/Wikimedia Commons/CC BY-SA-3.0; female student 75 © Fotoluminate LLC/Shutterstock; glasses 75 © Evgeny Karandaev/Shutterstock; cars 75 Ben/Flickr/CC BY-SA 2.0; Aleppo market 76 OmarHafez/Wikimedia Commons/CC BY-SA-3.0; City of Aleppo 78 Anas Al Rifai/Wikimedia Commons/CC BY-SA-3.0; Aleppo Castle 79 paolo mutti/Flickr/CC BY-ND 2.0; family picture 80 © Monkey Business Images/Shutterstock; man 81 © Monkey Business Images/Shutterstock; woman 81 © Monkey Business Images/Shutterstock; girl 81 © Monkey Business Images/Shutterstock; boy 81 © Monkey Business Images/Shutterstock; Nadia talking on phone 82 © Rehan Qureshi/Shutterstock; Adnan college student 82 © Di Studio/Shutterstock; engineering 83 Dinesh Cyanam/Flickr/CC BY 2.0; biology 83 Dunk/Flickr/CC BY 2.0; chemistry set 83 zhouxuan12345678/Flickr/CC BY-SA 2.0; Aleppo Citadel (background) 85 (Ergo)/Wikimedia Commons/CC BY-2.0; drawings of boy, dad, grandfather 87 freepik.com; book cover 88 Afek91/Wikimedia Commons/CC0; names on a magazine cover 88 Aziz J.Hayat/Flickr/CC BY 2.0; photographer's name article 88 Aziz J.Hayat/Flickr/CC BY 2.0; coffee (background) 93 /pxhere/CC0; Iftar buffet 95 (background) traveljunction/Flickr/CC BY-SA 2.0; olive vendor (background) 97 yeowatzup/Flickr/CC BY 2.0; hanging lantern (background) 99 Beshr Abdulhadi/Flickr/CC BY 2.0; road signs 100 Andrew Nash/Flickr/CC BY-SA 2.0; Balbak temple 102 Paul Saad/Wikimedia Commons/CC BY-SA-4.0; college student asking question 104 © aslysun/Shutterstock; businessmen talking 104 © Maksym Poriechkin/Shutterstock; Egyptian telegram 105 Government of Egypt/Wikimedia Commons/Public Domain; man and two women speaking 105 U.S. Embassy Jerusalem/Flickr/CC BY-SA 2.0; classroom 105 U.S. Army Corps of Engineers Europe District/Flickr/CC BY 2.0; speaker introducing Hussein at podium 106 Magharebia/Flickr/CC BY 2.0; one man 109 Aziz J.Hayat/ Flickr/CC BY 2.0; one woman 109 © Alena Getman/Flickr; two men 109 Jaguar MENA/Flickr/ CC BY 2.0; two women 109 Tribes of the World/Flickr/CC BY-SA 2.0; men 109 Arian Zwegers/ Flickr/CC BY 2.0; women 109 © Alena Getman/Flickr; conversation on park benches 109 Sharon Mollerus/Flickr/CC BY 2.0; three women talking 110 U.S. Embassy Jerusalem/Flickr/CC BY-SA 2.0; lamp 111 (background) Maxim/Flickr/CC BY-SA 2.0; pharmacist 112 Rhoda Baer/ Wikimedia Commons/Public Domain; Moroccan buildings (background)122 /pxhere/CC0; buildings 123 pxhere/CC0; Iraq street with newsstand 124 Chatham House/Wikimedia Commons/CC BY-2.0; reading newspapers 125 Tarek/Flickr/CC BY-ND 2.0; man writing 125 Quinn Dombrowski/Flickr/CC BY-SA 2.0; magazine cover 125 Flickr/Public Domain; newspapers 125, 127 Steven Damron/Flickr/CC BY 2.0; Egyptian newspaper al-Ahram 127 Ahram/Wikimedia Commons/Public Doman; Asharq al-Awsat newspaper 127 AdamAppel/ Wikimedia Commons/CC BY-SA 4.0; al-Hayat newspaper 127 Wikimedia Commons/Public Domain; al-Dustour newspaper 127 Jordan Press and Publishing Company/Wikipedia Commons/Public Domain; Arabs reading newspapers 128 Tribes of the World/Flickr/CC BY-SA 2.0; man reading newspaper (color) 128 Carolyn Coles/Flickr/CC BY 2.0; Al-Rafid magazine 128 Abdulla Al Muhairi/Flickr/CC BY 2.0; man reading with smile 128 fiat.luxury/Flickr/CC BY-ND 2.0; man and woman with laptop 129 Vancouver Film School/Flickr/CC BY 2.0; man buying newspaper 129 Ben Mason/Flickr/CC BY 2.0; man giving pen to woman 130 © VP Photo Studio/Shutterstock; men on street looking at newspapers 133 Adam Jones/Flickr/CC BY-SA 2.0; Palestinian market (background) 143 Moataz1997/Wikimedia Commons/CC BY-SA-4.0; newspaper press (background) 144 Aljazirah2014/Wikimedia Commons/CC BY-SA-3.0; tea 146 Ali علي from Riyadh من الرياض/Flickr/CC BY 2.0; coffee cup 147 Alpha/Flickr/CC BY-SA 2.0; butter 147 Ali علي from Riyadh من الرياض/Flickr/CC BY 2.0; apple 147 Joe King/Flickr/CC BY 2.0; orange 147 The Ewan/Flickr/CC BY-SA 2.0; Bedouins eating 147 krebsmaus07/Flickr/CC BY 2.0; woman drinking 147 © diplomedia/Shutterstock; love hearts 147 Kaydee H/Flickr/CC BY-SA 2.0; tea 147 Ali علي from Riyadh من الرياض/Flickr/CC BY 2.0; eggs 147 Amy Ross/Flickr/ CC BY-ND 2.0; bread 147 mike feist/Flickr/CC BY-SA 2.0; cheese 147 Skånska Matupplevelser/

Flickr/CC BY-ND 2.0; milk 147 Nick Piggott/Flickr/CC BY 2.0; waiter taking woman's order 149 © CandyBox Images/Shutterstock; waiter taking man's order (cropped)149 Nik Wheeler/Saudi Aramco World/SAWDIA; cereal and milk 150 Steven Wilke/Flickr/CC BY-ND 2.0; glass of water 150 Ryan Hyde/Flickr/CC BY-SA 2.0; college student (Michael Brown) 150 © Phase4Studios/Shutterstock; college student (Cathy White) 150 © Rido/Shutterstock; Hala Bustani 150 © Fotoluminate LLC/Shutterstock; honey 150 © Billion Photos/Shutterstock; men in market 151 Enric Fradera/Flickr/CC BY-ND 2.0; Michael Brown with a book 151 © Phase4Studios/Shutterstock; table of food, Morocco (background) 152 © Allen Clark; spices (background) 158–59 /pxhere/CC0; toy stormtrooper handing present 160 Pascal/Flickr/CC0 1.0; sheesh taook (menu) 164 Ron Dollete/Flickr/CC BY-ND 2.0; hummus (menu) 164 Ali علي from Riyadh من الرياض/Flickr/CC BY 2.0; chicken sandwich (menu) 164 /pxhere/CC0; Coca-Cola 164 Evan Blaser/Flickr/CC BY 2.0; fatoosh (menu) 164 D@LY3D/Flickr/CC BY 2.0; kabaab (menu) 164 PersianDutchNetwork/Wikimedia Commons/CC BY-SA-3.0; olives 165 Gwili/Wikimedia Commons/CC BY-SA-3.0,2.5,2.0,1.0; market display Aleppo (background) 168 paolo mutti/Flickr/CC BY-ND 2.0; Aleppo Souq 169 Beshr Abdulhadi/Flickr/CC BY 2.0; Moroccan water clock 170 Michal Osmenda/Wikimedia Commons/CC BY-SA-2.0; Big Ben 171 Alberto/Flickr/CC BY-SA 2.0; two female students talking 172 U.S. Embassy Tel Aviv/Flickr/CC BY-ND 2.0; clock (10:15) 173 Cristian Bortes/Flickr/CC BY 2.0; clock (2:20) 173 Kees Wielemaker/Flickr/CC BY-ND 2.0; clock (10:30) 173 Jordi Marsol/Flickr/CC BY 2.0; digital alarm clock (11:25) 173 © MIMV LLC; al-Jazari's elephant clock, manuscript 173 Al-Jazari/Wikimedia Commons/Public Domain; Cairo radio 174 Dan Lundberg/Flickr/CC BY-SA 2.0; Syrian TV antennas 174 Hani Zaitoun/Wikimedia Commons/CC BY-SA-3.0; public clock (3:20) 174 Herzi Pinki/Wikimedia Commons/CC BY-SA-4.0; public clock (5:05) 174 oatsy40/Flickr/CC BY 2.0; public clock (4:15) 174 Mark Morgan/Flickr/CC BY 2.0; public clock (8:30) 174 fsse8info/Flickr/CC BY-SA 2.0; public clock (7:05) example 174 Sandstein (public domain)/Wikimedia Commons/Public Domain; public clock (12:10) example 174 © EMJAY SMITH/Shutterstock; public clock (10:35) 175 oatsy40/Flickr/CC BY 2.0; public clock (9:55) 175 oatsy40/Flickr/CC BY 2.0; public clock (1:45) 175 Elliott Brown/Flickr/CC BY 2.0; wall clock (9:40) 175 Mike Sansone/Flickr/CC BY 2.0;

Luxor obelisk 175 David Monniaux/Wikimedia Commons/CC BY-SA-1.0; clock till and after example 175 Pixabay/pexels/CC0; nine clocks 176 pixabay/CC0; Sahar and Hala 177 © Fotoluminate LLC/Shutterstock; accounting 177 Ken Teegardin/Flickr/CC BY-SA 2.0; statistics 177 Lukas/pexels/CC0; international relations 177 © EM Karuna/Shutterstock; American University, Cairo 178 Stephenieloren/Wikimedia Commons/CC BY-SA-3.0; astrolabe (background) 181 Poulpy/Wikimedia Commons/CC BY-SA 3.0; Al-Jazari's candle clock 188 Farruk ibn Abd al-Latif (CB)/Wikimedia Commons/Public Domain; Al-Jazari's castle clock 191 Wikimedia Commons/Public Domain; Burj Khalifa 192 pxhere/CC0; boy walking 193 David McDermott/Flickr/CC BY 2.0; worker making copper 193 Christine Olson/Flickr/CC BY-ND 2.0; driver 193 Jordan Davis/Flickr/CC BY-SA 2.0; Hala Bustani 193 © Fotoluminate LLC/ Shutterstock; friends (two women) 193 Gareth Williams/Flickr/CC BY 2.0; tall and short (basketball player) 193 Valerie Everett/Flickr/CC BY-SA 2.0; weight lifter 193 Vitaliy Saveliev/ Виталий Савельев/Wikimedia Commons/CC-BY-SA 3.0; big house in Doha 194 Lars Plougmann/Flickr/CC BY-SA 2.0; the city of Doha 194 Francisco Anzola/Flickr/CC BY 2.0; bedroom in Doha 194 TravelingOtter/Flickr/CC BY-SA 2.0; the University of Qatar 194 Hamran/ Wikimedia Commons/CC-BY-SA 3.0; old car 195 Craig Howell/Flickr/CC BY 2.0; Porsche 195 lacomj/Flickr/CC BY-SA 2.0; car engine 195 © Jeremy/Flickr; student at University of Qatar (Hussein) 195 Sky2105/Wikimedia Commons/CC BY-SA-3.0; buildings in Doha (background) 197 Francisco Anzola/Flickr/CC BY 2.0; map of Arab countries 199 by William L. Nelson; Yasser Arafat 200 Saar Yaacov, GPO/Wikimedia Commons/ CC BY-SA-3.0; Fahad bin Abdullah Al Saud 200 Wikimedia Commons/CC BY-SA 4.0; Monterey, California (background) 203 /pxhere/CC0; Qur'an 207 Itchyklikfinger/Flickr/CC BY-SA 2.0; Islamic arch (background) 212 Luca/Flickr/CC BY 2.0; Islamic minaret 215 Jude Lee/Flickr/CC BY 2.0; astrolabe 216 MnM 11 NA 1/Rama/ Wikimedia Commons/CC BY-SA-3.0-FR; calendar strip 216 Wellcome Collection/Wikimedia Commons/CC BY-4.0; calendar strip (red background) 216 Wellcome Collection/Wikimedia Commons/CC BY-4.0; calendar 217 © Jupiterimages Corporation; Burj Al-Arab 217 Joi Ito/ Flickr/CC BY 2.0; walking 217 Evan Long/Flickr/CC BY-NC 2.0; sleeping 217 peasap/Flickr/CC BY 2.0; shirt 217 FLATSEVEN/Flickr/CC BY-SA 2.0; astrolabe (background) 219 Evan Bench/

Flickr/CC BY 2.0; Dubai airport 220 VanLap Hoàng/Flickr/CC BY 2.0; airplane 220 Glyn Lowe/Flickr/CC BY 2.0; Columbus International Airport 221 Sam Howzit/Flickr/CC BY 2.0; Mirror Lake, Ohio State University 221 marada/Flickr/CC BY-ND 2.0; deboarding Cairo airport 221 Dennis Jarvis/Flickr/CC BY-SA 2.0; chemistry lab 225 Kurt Barnett/Wikimedia Commons/CC BY-SA-3.0; Omayyad Mosque (background) 229 OmarHafez/Wikimedia Commons/CC BY-SA-3.0; drinking tea 230 Paul Stocker/Flickr/CC BY 2.0; family pictures (younger, older) 233 Harsha K R/Flickr/CC BY-SA 2.0; old man 234 © ZouZou/Shutterstock; young man 234 © ProStockStudio/Shutterstock; tortoise and hare 234 © Antonio Jorge Nunes/Shutterstock; woman (short hair) 234 © VAndreas/Shutterstock; woman (long hair) 234 © Valua Vitaly/Shutterstock; race car 234 © MriMan/Shutterstock; Volkswagon car 234 Karen Arnold/PublicDomainPictures.net/CC0; Eiffel Tower 234 © Giancarlo Liguori/Shutterstock; burj Khalifa 234 © Ilona Ignatova/Shutterstock; textiles (background) 235 Sam Howzit/Wikimedia Commons/CC BY-2.0; Old Cairo (background) 241 Tarek/Flickr/CC BY-ND 2.0; astrolabe (background) 243 Groume/Flickr/CC BY-SA 2.0; souq in Aleppo 245 reibai/Flickr/CC BY 2.0; Arabic sundial 249 Chadica/Wikimedia Commons/CC BY-2.0; seasons 250 Adam Lebaigue/Wikimedia Commons/CC BY-SA-4.0; day/night 251 © Jupiterimages Corporation; sunny 251 Joseph/Flickr/CC BY-SA 2.0; thermometer 251 Bernard Gagnon/Wikimedia Commons/CC-BY-SA 3.0, 2.5, 2.0, 1.0; flower 251 Mohamed Malik/Flickr/CC BY 2.0; cloud 251 Erik Wilde/Flickr/CC BY-SA 2.0; the sun 251 NASA Goddard Photo and Video/Flickr/CC BY 2.0; rain 251 George Hodan/PublicDomainPictures.net/CC0; tree 251 Tambako the Jaguar/Flickr/CC BY-ND 2.0; blue sky 251 Tom Woodward/Flickr/CC BY-SA 2.0; overcast skies 251 © zozma*/Flickr; house in summer (background) 252 www.twin-loc.fr/Flickr/CC BY 2.0; rainy 253 /pxhere/CC0; beach 253 Don Graham/Flickr/CC BY-SA 2.0; falling leaves 253 Rory/Flickr/CC BY 2.0; falling snow 253 Rob Shenk/Flickr/CC BY-SA 2.0; symbols for sun, rain, snow, clouds 254 © Jupiterimages Corporation; lightning cloud (background) 254 © Anthony Quintano/Flickr; Moroccan beach (background) 259 Maxim Massalitin/Wikimedia Commons/CC BY-SA-2.0; Nejmeh Square, Beirut (background) 260 Heinz Hövel/Wikimedia Commons/CC BY-SA-3.0; Annaba, Algeria (background) 262 Dan Sloan/Wikimedia Commons/CC BY-SA-2.0; four seasons, mosiac 265 Dennis Jarvis/Wikimedia Commons/CC BY-SA-2.0;

downtown Beirut 266 Alain Abou-Atmeh/pexels/CC0; toothbrush and toothpaste 267 Thegreenj/ Wikimedia Commons/CC BY-SA-3.0; brushing teeth 267 /pxhere/CC0; baby bathing 267 Lars Plougmann/Flickr/CC BY-SA 2.0; waking up 267 Loren Kerns/Flickr/CC BY 2.0; watching TV 267 © Paul Townsend/Flickr; Hala Bustani 269 © Fotoluminate LLC/Shutterstock; washing hands 269 Sarah Laval/Flickr/CC BY 2.0; fixing breakfast 269 Mike Moss/Flickr/CC BY-ND 2.0; fava bean 269 Eaeeae/Wikimedia Commons/CC BY-3.0; bus in Damascus 269 High Contrast/ Wikimedia Commons/CC BY-3.0-DE; beef kebab 269 AAB_BAA/Flickr/CC BY 2.0; olives 270 Rene Schwietzke/Flickr/CC BY 2.0; Syria TV logo 270 Wikimedia Commons/CC BY-SA-3.0; shaving 270 Hendrik Dacquin/Flickr/CC BY 2.0; restaurant in Damascus 271 Jan Smith/Flickr/ CC BY 2.0; Jordanian market (background) 272 Pir6mon/Wikimedia Commons/CC BY-SA-3.0,2.5,2.0,1.0; Lebanese restaurant (background) 274 Hector Abouid/Flickr/CC BY 2.0; inside Arab restaurant (background) 281 Joi Ito/Flickr/CC BY 2.0; Wadi Rum valley, Jordan (background) 286–87 Raya Sharbain/Wikimedia Commons/CC BY-SA-4.0; inside restaurant 288 Hani Arif/Flickr/CC BY 2.0; visiting family 289 © Iakov Filimonov/Shutterstock; Union Pacific train 289 Jerry Huddleston/Flickr/CC BY 2.0; Cairo train station 289 Andrew A. Shenouda/ Flickr/CC BY 2.0; Gamal Abd El Nassar 289 Wikimedia Commons/Public Domain; engineer 289 Seattle Municipal Archives/Flickr/CC BY 2.0; journalism 289 Magharebia/Wikimedia Commons/ CC BY-2.0; al-Mohandisein in Cairo 290 Arria Belli/Wikimedia Commons/CC BY-SA-2.0; face from food label 291 © Jupiterimages Corporation; koshari 291 Amy Ross/Flickr/CC BY-ND 2.0; map of Egypt 292 by William L. Nelson; Al-Minya train station 292 Faris knight/Wikimedia Commons/CC BY-SA-4.0,3.0,2.5,2.0,1.0; Cedar Point 292 Jeremy Thompson/Flickr/CC BY 2.0; Nile River in al-Minya 293 مصطفي ابوبكر/Wikimedia Commons/CC BY-SA-3.0; the Egyptian Museum 295 Mohamedsamir1994/Wikimedia Commons/CC BY-SA-4.0; fishing boat Tripoli, Lebanon 301 Cazz/Flickr/CC BY 2.0; alleys in Old Damascus 302 Amer Jazaerli/Flickr/CC BY 2.0; bike in Qanawat, Damascus 304 reibai/Flickr/CC BY 2.0; market in Damascus 305 Hani Zaitoun/Wikimedia Commons/CC BY-SA-3.0; mosque in Kuwait, Ramadan 306 guillaumepaumier.com/Wikimedia Commons/CC BY-3.0; breaking the fast, Ramadan in Egypt 308, 370 (cropped) Mustafa Shorbaji/Wikimedia Commons/CC BY-SA-4.0; Egyptian flag 309

Open Clip Art/Wikimedia Commons/Public Domain; Moroccan flag 309 Denelson83, Zscout370/Wikimedia Commons/Public Domain; flag of Yemen 309 Wikimedia Commons/Public Domain; Tunisian flag 309 Orange Tuesday/Wikimedia Commons/Public Domain; Algerian flag 309 Skopp/Wikimedia Commons/Public Domain; Syrian flag 309 FDRMRZUSA/Wikimedia Commons/CC BY-SA-3.0; Iraqi flag 309 Wikimedia Commons/Public Domain; Omani flag 309 FDRMRZUSA/Wikimedia Commons/Public Domain; Lebanese flag 309 FDRMRZUSA/Wikimedia Commons/Public Domain; Christmas tree 311 Tom Ipri/Flickr/CC BY-SA 2.0; Resurrection of Christ (Raphael, São Paolo Museum of Art) 311 Wikimedia Commons/Public Domain; Thanksgiving 311 Sharon Mollerus/Flickr/CC BY 2.0; Fourth of July 311 Joe Ravi/Wikimedia Commons/CC BY-SA-3.0; Labor Day stamp 311 U.S. Postal Service/Wikimedia Commons/Public Domain; Martin Luther King Jr. 311 Phil Stanziola, New York World-Telegram & Sun/Library of Congress/Wikimedia Commons/Public Domain; Suad Rimawi (Iraqi young woman) 312 © pathdoc/Shutterstock; lamps on carpet 320 Sharaf/Flickr/CC BY-ND 2.0; henna on hand (background) 325 peter klashorst/Wikimedia Commons/CC BY-2.0; lamps in trees, Cairo (background) 326 Annemee Siersma/Flickr/CC BY-ND 2.0; Sayyida Zanib Street during Ramadan (background) 329 Heba Otefy/Wikimedia Commons/CC BY-SA-4.0; Ibn Khaldoun 330 Reda Kerbouche/Wikimedia Commons/CC BY-SA-4.0; Gamal Abd el-Nasser 330 Essam Azouz/Wikimedia Commons/CC BY-SA-4.0; Martin Luther King Jr. 330 Wikimedia Commons/Public Domain; Martin Luther King Jr. 330 Dick DeMarsico/New York World-Telegram & Sun/Library of Congress/Wikimedia Commons/Public Domain; The Carpet Merchant (background) (Jean-Léon Gérôme, Minneapolis Institute of Art, The William Hood Dunwoody Fund) 333 Wikimedia Commons/Public Domain; George Washington (Gilbert Stuart, Clark Art Institute) 334 Wikimedia Commons/Public Domain; Abraham Lincoln 334 photo by Anthony Berger/Library of Congress/Wikimedia Commons/Public Domain; maps of Algeria, Syria, Egypt, Spain/Portugal 335–36 by William L. Nelson; Martin Luther King Jr. (cropped) 335 Dick DeMarsico/New York World-Telegram & Sun/Library of Congress/Wikimedia Commons/Public Domain; abd al-qādir al-mazini 335 Miscellaneous Items in High Demand, PPOC, Library of Congress/Public Domain; Yousef al-Adma 335 موقع التاريخ السوري/Wikimedia Commons/CC

BY-SA-3.0; Nasser 335 Stevan Kragujević/Wikimedia Commons/CC BY-SA-3.0; Ibn Khaldoun 336 Tunisian Community Center/Wikimedia Commons/CC BY-SA-3.0; Arab School (John Frederick Lewis, Metropolitan Museum of Art) 339 Wikimedia Commons/Public Domain; excerpt from Hans Wehr dictionary 341 Allen Clark; women making carpets (background) 343 Library of Congress/Wikimedia Commons/Public Domain; Muiz Street in Cairo 344 Hossametsh20/Wikimedia Commons/CC BY-SA-4.0; Roman ruins in Jordan (background) 349 Mahmood Salam/Flickr/CC BY 2.0; Old Cairo street 350 (background) masterplaan/Flickr/CC BY 2.0; arches (background) 353 Michael Cohen/Flickr/CC BY 2.0; candles 354 12:00⊠/Flickr/CC BY-SA 2.0; Ramadan lamps 354 /pxhere/CC0; feast meal Morocco 354 Murcotipton/Wikimedia Commons/CC BY-SA-4.0; coffee for feast 354 Ali علي from Riyadh من الرياض/Flickr/CC BY 2.0; Eid card 356 Ali علي from Riyadh من الرياض/Flickr/CC BY 2.0; food for Eid al-Fitr 357 Khammal92/ Wikimedia Commons/CC BY-SA-4.0; woman holding tray 357 Sarah Altamimi/Flickr/CC BY 2.0; blue Eid card 357 Sumaya Al-Hasan/Flickr/CC BY-SA 2.0; Eid greeting card blue 358 فنافن الإعلامية/Flickr/CC BY-ND 2.0; dentist 358 Irina Patrascu Gheorghita/Flickr/CC BY 2.0; man and woman greeting 358 © Netfalls Remy Musser/Shutterstock; dental clinic interior 358 Laumedia/ Wikimedia Commons/CC BY-SA-4.0; Eid greeting card yellow 358 فنافن الإعلامية/Flickr/CC BY-ND 2.0; woman at airport 359 airbus777/Flickr/CC BY-NC-ND 2.0; Adnan's face 364 Hamed Saber/Flickr/CC-BY 2.0; Arab man's face 360, 364 Tony Alter/Flickr/CC BY 2.0; Arab student male 360, 364 Taston/Flickr/CC BY-ND 2.0; Arab student's face male 360, 364 Quinn Dombrowski/Flickr/CC BY-SA 2.0; Arab student's face female 360, 364 tommerton2010/Flickr/ CC BY 2.0; mail courier 360 Elvert Barnes/Flickr/CC BY-SA 2.0; greeting card 362 /pxhere/CC0; map of Arab countries 364 by William L. Nelson; Adnan 364 Hamed Saber/Flickr/CC BY 2.0; breaking the fast (cropped) 370 Mustafa Shorbaji/Wikimedia Commons/CC BY-SA-4.0; interior al-Aqsa mosque 372 معتز توفيق اغبارية/Wikimedia Commons/CC BY-SA-4.0; Jerusalem during Ramadan 373 Zivya/Wikimedia Commons/CC BY-SA-3.0; painting of girls dressing for Eid 377 Etienne Dinet/Wikimedia Commons/Public Domain; night scene after breaking the fast 379 Lambert Heller/Flickr/CC BY 2.0; Ramadan meal 380 Hamed Saber/Flickr/CC BY 2.0; streets decorated 383 Przemyslaw "Blueshade" Idzkiewicz/Wikimedia Commons/CC BY-SA-2.5; Cairo at night 384 Guillén Pérez/Flickr/CC BY-ND 2.0; Cairo in the evening 384 Frank Schulenburg/Flickr/CC BY-SA-3.0; Cairo Opera House 384 Gian Cornachini/Flickr/CC BY 2.0; Cairo and the Nile 384 Maher Najm/Flickr/CC BY 2.0; mirror 385 Jurii/Wikimedia Commons/CC BY-3.0; bathtub 385 Jennifer C./Flickr/CC BY 2.0; toilet 385 www.trek.today/Flickr/CC BY 2.0; sink 385 Jennifer C./Flickr/CC BY 2.0; refrigerator 385 Consumer Reports/Wikimedia Commons/CC BY-SA-4.0; stove 385 M. Minderhoud/Wikimedia Commons/CC BY-SA-3.0; bookcase 385 Dietmar Rabich/Wikimedia Commons/CC BY-SA-4.0; lamp 385 russellstreet/Flickr/CC BY-SA 2.0; Albrecht-Michael-Jacob Jacobs, The Street of the Sultan Mosque in Cairo 387 Ahmet Asar/Flickr/CC BY-SA 2.0; Michael Brown's apartment 388 © ma3d/Shutterstock; living room 389 jinkazamah/Flickr/CC BY 2.0; bedroom 389 jinkazamah/Flickr/CC BY 2.0; bathroom 389 Triumph Mountain Properties/Flickr/CC BY-ND 2.0; kitchen 389 jinkazamah/Flickr/CC BY 2.0; pickup truck 389 dave_7/Flickr/CC BY 2.0; Michael's apartment building 390 Francesco Gasparetti/Wikimedia Commons/CC BY-2.0; Michael's house map 390 Courtesy of Scribble Maps; Victor Pierre Huguet, interior scene (making coffee) 393, 414 © Ahmet Asar/Flickr; storyboard 394–95 © Falara/Shutterstock; apartment for rent ad 396 M.Al-Baker/Flickr/CC BY-ND 2.0; pencil on book 4, 403 Simon Carr/Flickr/CC BY-SA 2.0; flowers in front of man 4, 403 ProFlowers/Flickr/CC BY 2.0; bouquet behind man 4, 403 ProFlowers/Flickr/CC BY 2.0; basketball in net 4, 403 slgckgc/Flickr/CC BY 2.0; pencil beside book 4, 403 Quinn Dombrowski/Flickr/CC BY-SA 2.0; toy stormtrooper limbo 4, 403 JD Hancock/Flickr/CC BY 2.0; toy stormtrooper limbo 4, 403 JD Hancock/Flickr/CC BY 2.0; pole vaulter 4, 403 Jacey O Samsel/Flickr/CC BY 2.0; penguins (between) 4, 403 Christopher Michel/Flickr/CC BY 2.0; Alberto Pasini, A Ferry on the Nile (cropped, background) 405 © Ahmet Asar/Flickr; alley (background) 406 Jorge Láscar/Flickr/CC BY 2.0; apartment model 18 407 © ma3d/Shutterstock; building in Jerusalem (background) 408 /pxhere/CC0; Google Earth image 409 Courtesy of Google Maps; alley in Yemen (background) 410 Rod Waddington/Flickr/CC BY-SA 2.0; alley in Dubai (background) 413 Mathias Apitz/Flickr/CC BY-ND 2.0; Victor Pierre Huguet, interior scene (making coffee) 393, 414 © Ahmet Asar/Flickr; 17th-century Al-Suhymi house in Cairo 415 Dr. EOMR/Wikimedia Commons/CC BY-SA 4.0; pyramids 416 Jeaaann/Wikimedia Commons;

Sphinx 416, 426 Roderick Eime/Flickr/CC BY-ND 2.0; fortress, Alexandria 416 Taver/Flickr/CC BY-ND 2.0; downtown Alexandria 416 Aleksandar Cocek/Flickr/CC BY-SA 2.0; citadel, Alexandria 416 Osama Awny/Wikimedia Commons/CC BY-SA-4.0; bike rider 417 Comrade King/Flickr/CC BY 2.0; questions 417 Derek Bridges/Flickr/CC BY 2.0; taking a picture 417 Bruce Aldridge/Flickr/CC BY-SA 2.0; taking a test 417 Alberto G./Flickr/CC BY 2.0; animals 417 Rachel Kramer/Flickr/CC BY 2.0; closet 417 Wjablow/Wikimedia Commons/CC BY-SA-3.0; ticket 417 Sludge G/Flickr/CC BY-SA 2.0; builders building 417 Scott Lewis/Flickr/CC BY 2.0; pyramids 420 Ricardo Liberato/Wikimedia Commons/CC BY-SA-2.0; camels 420 Sara Yasser Soliman/ Wikimedia Commons/CC BY-SA-3.0; Alexandria port 421 D-Stanley/Wikimedia Commons/CC BY-2.0; corniche, Alexandria (in amber light) 421 Amr56/Wikimedia Commons/CC BY-SA-4.0; postal stamp (Alexandria) 421 Jacquesverlaeken/Wikimedia Commons/Public Domain; satellite view of river & delta 422 pxhere/CC0 1.0 Public Domain; Egyptian museum 422 James Byrum/ Flickr/CC BY-SA-2.0; Times Square 423 Andrés Nieto Porras/Flickr/CC BY-SA 2.0; Niagara Falls 423 FHG Photo/Flickr/CC BY 2.0; boats under Niagara 424 Andrew Eland/Flickr/CC BY-SA 2.0; Statue of Liberty 424 Sue Waters/Flickr/CC BY-SA 2.0; Atlantic City 424 Marco Verch/Flickr/CC BY 2.0; U.S. postal stamp 424 Bureau of Engraving and Printing. Designed by James Barkley/ Wikimedia Commons/Public Domain; Disney World 425 SteamFan/Wikimedia Commons/CC BY-2.5; Sphinx (cropped, background) 426 Roderick Eime/Wikimedia Commons/CC BY-ND 2.0; Qasr al-Nil Bridge 428 Mohamed Samir yousef/Wikimedia Commons/CC BY-SA-3.0; Al-Azhar park 430 Yasser Nazmi/Wikimedia Commons/CC BY-SA 3.0; Egyptian postcard 433 Travelers in the Middle East Archive (TIMEA)/Wikimedia Commons/CC BY-SA-2.5; postal stamp 433 Wikimedia Commons/Public Domain; Alexandria castle 437 © Shaima nabil/Wikimedia Commons/CC BY-SA-3.0; market of instruments (background) 444 Noha Fawzy Elsayed/ Wikimedia Commons/CC BY-SA-4.0; map of Syria/Lebanon/Israel/Jordan 447 by William L. Nelson; Alexandria sea boats (background) 447 Ahmedherz/Wikimedia Commons/CC BY-SA-4.0; Talat Harb 448-49 Mohamed Samir yousef/Wikimedia Commons/CC BY-SA-3.0; El-Mutazah Palace (background) 450 Mina.maher.aziz/Wikimedia Commons/CC BY-SA-3.0; pyramids 451 Walkerssk/pixabay/CC0; King Abdullah Sports City Stadium 452 Manaf228/

Wikimedia Commons; baseball 452 Vegasjon/Wikimedia Commons/CC BY-SA-4.0; running 454 Dru Bloomfield/Flickr/CC BY 2.0; spectators 454 দেবর্ষির্ রায়/Flickr/CC BY-SA 2.0; winning 454 The White House/Wikimedia Commons/Public Domain; team 454 Marc Wengler/Wikimedia Commons/CC BY-SA-2.0-DE; table tennis 455 Janine/Flickr/CC BY-ND 2.0; baseball 455 Paul Horner/Flickr/CC BY-SA 2.0; basketball 455 Massimo Finizio/Wikimedia Commons/CC BY-SA-2.0-IT; Arabic sausage 456 © شيف نونا/Flickr; park grill 456 Infrogmation of New Orleans/Wikimedia Commons/CC BY-SA-2.0; volleyball 456 Martin Charette/Flickr/CC BY 2.0; soccer 456 Markbarnes/Wikimedia Commons/CC BY-2.5; American football 456 John Martinez Pavliga/Flickr/CC BY 2.0; simit 457 Wikimedia Commons/CC BY-SA-3.0; logo of al-Ahly soccer team 457 Momen50000/Wikimedia Commons; walking on a street in Cairo 457 Ahmed Hussien/Wikimedia Commons/CC BY-SA-3.0; bike racing 458 Rob Annis/Flickr/CC BY 2.0; horse racing 458 Tsutomu Takasu/Flickr/CC BY 2.0; water polo 458 Charles Luk/Flickr/CC BY-ND 2.0; tennis 458 Marianne Bevis/Flickr/CC BY-ND 2.0; okra 458 yuki tanaka/Flickr/CC BY-SA 2.0; lettuce 458 Yorvik/Wikimedia Commons/Public Domain; peas 458 liz west/Flickr/CC BY 2.0; fasolia 458 Dimitris Siskopoulos/Flickr/CC BY 2.0; hot pepper 458 Koshy Koshy/Flickr/CC BY 2.0; zucchini 458 cristina.sanvito/Flickr/CC BY 2.0; eggplant 458 albastrica mititica/Flickr/CC BY 2.0; green pepper 458 Mike Mozart/Flickr/CC BY 2.0; apple 459 Apple and Pear Australia Ltd/Flickr/CC BY 2.0; oranges 459 Frédérique Voisin-Demery/Flickr/CC BY 2.0; grapes 459 agerpoint/Flickr/CC BY 2.0; bananas 459 jster91/Flickr/CC BY 2.0; berries 459 Paul Downey/Flickr/CC BY 2.0; watermelon 459 Purple Slog/Flickr/CC BY 2.0; mango 459 gomagoti/Flickr/CC BY-SA 2.0; pear 459 Apple and Pear Australia Ltd/Flickr/CC BY 2.0; palm trees with woman 461 EladeManu/Flickr/CC BY 2.0; food from Marrakesh 463 EladeManu/Flickr/CC BY 2.0; colors (background, ceramics) Morocco 469 Khalid Albaih/Flickr/CC BY 2.0; soccer (background) 473 Chensiyuan/Wikimedia Commons/CC BY-SA-4.0; Portrait of a Bedouin, Berthe Worms, São Paolo Museum of Art (background) 476 Ahmet Asar/Flickr; fantasia at festival in Morocco 477 Maxim Massalitin/Wikimedia Commons/CC BY-SA-2.0; globe and book 478 Rémi Mathis/Flickr/CC BY-SA 2.0; desert plains 480 llee_wu/Flickr/CC BY-ND 2.0; coast 480 Tom Hilton/Flickr/CC BY 2.0; chain 480 Peter Shanks/Flickr/CC BY 2.0; agriculture 480 Dennis Jarvis/Wikimedia

Commons/CC BY-SA-2.0; mountains 480 Gorgo/Wikimedia Commons/Public Domain; American flag 480 HARRIS.news/Wikimedia Commons/CC BY-SA-3.0; archery target 480 renatomitra/Flickr/CC BY-SA 2.0; fabric 480 Snaps880/Flickr/CC BY-SA-3.0; map of world 483 by William L. Nelson; map of Arab world 483 by William L. Nelson; map of Mediterranean Basin 484 NASA/Wikimedia Commons/Public Domain; map of Morocco 484 NASA; map of Red Sea 484 NASA/Wikimedia Commons/Public Domain; map of the Arab Pensinsula 484 NASA/Wikimedia Commons/Public Domain; map of North Africa 484 NASA/Wikimedia Commons/Public Domain; map of United States 485 by William L. Nelson; map of Syria 486 by William L. Nelson; seal of Syria 487 Tonyjeff, based on national symbol, with the help of AnonMoos/Wikimedia Commons/Public Domain; flag of Syria 487 FDRMRZUSA/Wikimedia Commons/Public Domain; map of Ohio 488 by William L. Nelson; seal of Ohio 489 State of Ohio/Ohio General Assembly/Wikimedia Commons/Public Domain; bicycles and buildings 491 twiga_swala/Flickr/CC BY-SA 2.0; map of Algeria 492 by William L. Nelson; East Gate, Damascus (background) 493 علي الصمادي/Wikimedia Commons/CC BY-SA-3.0; map of Iraq 494 by William L. Nelson; cardinal directions 496 Brosen~Commonswiki/Wikimedia Commons/CC BY-2.5; map of Egypt 497 NordNordWest/Wikmedia Commons/CC BY-SA 3.0; map of Lebanon 501 by William L. Nelson; house interior courtyard 503 Martin Talbot/Flickr/CC BY 2.0; Damascus 505 Abdulsalam Haykal/Wikimedia Commons/CC BY-2.0; Fairouz 506 Wissam Chidiak/Wikimedia Commons/CC BY-SA-3.0; Abd al-Halem Hafiz 506 maoed/Wikimedia Commons/Public Domain; Umm Kulthum 506 Wikimedia Commons/Public Domain; background scrapbook Umm Kulthum 506 Passantadnan/Wikimedia Commons/CC BY-SA-4.0; listening 508 Yuliya Libkina/Flickr/CC BY 2.0; actor 508 Ahmed Zayer/Wikimedia Commons/CC0; marriage 508 Flashback Tunisie/Flickr/CC BY-ND 2.0; the moon 508 Sean X Liu/Flickr/CC BY-SA 2.0; space 508 NASA/JPL-Caltech/Harvard-Smithsonian CfA; child 508 Izzeddeen Al Karajeh/Flickr/CC BY 2.0; dance 508 U.S. Embassy Tel Aviv/Flickr/CC BY-SA 2.0; singer 508 Wikimedia Commons/Public Domain; interview 510 © IxMaster/Shutterstock; news 510 U.S. Department of State/Wikimedia Commons/Public Domain; Yaser al-Azma 511 Wikimedia Commons/CC0; Farid al-Atrash 511 Cyrus243/Wikimedia Commons/CC BY-SA-3.0; Wadih el Safi 511 Wikimedia

Commons/Public Domain; Umm Kulthum 512 Tribes of the World/Flickr/CC BY-SA 2.0; Abd al-Halem Hafiz 512 Wikimedia Commons/Public Domain; Mayada El Hennawy 513 Magharebia/ Wikimedia Commons/CC BY-2.0; Amru Diab 513 Kareem Nour/Wikimedia Commons/CC BY-SA-3.0; Nancy Ajram 513 7asson77ll980/Wikimedia Commons/CC BY-SA-3.0; Wardah al-Jazairia 513 FTOUKI/Wikimedia Commons/CC BY-SA 4.0; Farouz 513 Essam Azouz/ Wikimedia Commons/CC BY-SA 4.0; satellite 514 NOAA satellites/Flickr/Public Domain; Moroccan musicians (background) 517 Hernán Piñera/Flickr/CC BY-SA 2.0; oud (background) 518 Rosier/Flickr/CC BY-SA-3.0; musical instruments (background) 520 Deror avi/Wikimedia Commons/CC BY-SA-3.0; folkdance (background) 528–29 Osama Awny/Wikimedia Commons/ CC BY-SA-4.0; traditional Tuareg dance 531 Bashar Shglila/Wikimedia Commons/CC BY-SA-4.0; Corniche benches, Cairo 532 Gary Denham/Flickr/CC BY-ND 2.0; sunset by Corniche, Cairo 532 AforRebel1/Wikimedia Commons/CC BY-SA-4.0; present 534 Droid Gingerbread/Flickr/CC BY 2.0; pollution 534 Mujaddara/Wikimedia Commons/CC BY-SA-3.0; Arab journalist 534 محمد بوحتة/Wikimedia Commons/CC BY-SA-4.0; paying 534 Jimmy Baikovicius/Flickr/CC BY-SA 2.0; laughing 534 Vegan Feast Catering/Flickr/CC BY 2.0; factory 534 mrhayata/Flickr/CC BY-SA 2.0; magnets 534 © Jupiterimages Corporation; crowded 534 © Evan Cunningham/Flickr; house in Denver 535 Jeffrey Beall/Flickr/CC BY-SA 2.0; map of Midwestern states 535 by William L. Nelson; journalist 536 Nikolas Becker/Wikimedia Commons/CC BY-SA-3.0; football player 536 Sgt. Tyler J. Bolken/Wikimedia Commons/Public Domain; waitress 536 Petr Kratochvil/ PublicDomainPictures.net/CC0; accountant 536 /pxhere/CC0; map of Egypt 538 by William L. Nelson; Moroccan house 541 photophilde/Flickr/CC BY-SA 2.0; As'ad Pasha caravansary, Damascus (background) 542 Dan/Flickr/CC BY-SA 2.0; Straight Street, Damascus (background) 547 Library of Congress/Detroit Photographic Company/Wikimedia Commons/Public Domain; Alexandria, Egypt (background) 550 Hossam-eldin-mostafa/Wikimedia Commons/CC BY-SA-3.0; spices 553 James Filipi/Flickr/CC BY-SA 2.0;

Aleppo 554 UNESCO/Lucia Bruni/Wikimedia Commons/CC by-2.0; Aleppo 554 Seyr-U Zafer/ Wikimedia Commons/CC by-2.0; Aleppo inside the Great Mosque 554 yeowatzup/Wikimedia Commons/CC by-2.0; Baron Hotel at night 554 Jon Martin/Wikimedia Commons/CC by-2.0;

Saint Elijah Maronite Cathedral, Aleppo 554 Marti McFly/Wikimedia Commons/CC by-2.0; Aleppo, Queik River 554 Rokos Frangos/Wikimedia Commons/CC by-2.0; Aleppo at night 554 Richard Renwick/Wikimedia Commons/CC by-2.0; family photo 558 © Mahdi Alosh; dad and mom's picture 558 © Mahdi Alosh; man's ID photo 559 © Mahdi Alosh; mom's picture 559 © Mahdi Alosh; chemistry jars 561 Tweenk/Wikimedia Commons/CC BY-3.0; School of Athens (cropped), Raphael 561 Vatican Museums/Wikimedia Commons/Public Domain; Krak des Chevaliers 562 Jerzy Strzelecki/Wikimedia Commons/CC BY-SA-3.0; Alatham Palace (background) 563 Dickelbers/Wikimedia Commons/CC BY-SA-3.0; Latakia, Syria 564 Victor.ibrahiem/Wikimedia Commons/CC BY-SA-3.0; geography lesson 565 © Jupiterimages Corporation; window of Alatham 571 Saleh.photography/Wikimedia Commons/CC BY-SA-3.0; mosque in Tunisia 574 Photoglob AG, Zürich/Library of Congress/Wikimedia Commons/Public Domain; waterwheel, Syria 575 Sheam k/Wikimedia Commons/CC BY-SA-3.0